WERWOLF!

PERRY BIDDISCOMBE

Werwolf!
The History of the National
Socialist Guerrilla Movement,
1944–1946

UNIVERSITY OF TORONTO PRESS
Toronto Buffalo

© University of Toronto Press Incorporated 1998
Toronto Buffalo
Printed in Canada

ISBN 0-8020-0862-3 (cloth)

Printed on acid-free paper

Canadian Cataloguing in Publication Data

Biddiscombe, Alexander Perry, 1959–
    Werwolf! : the history of the National Socialist
    Guerrilla Movement, 1944–1946

    Includes bibliographical references and index.
    ISBN 0-8020-0862-3

    1. Unternehmen Werwolf.   2. World War, 1939–1945 – Germany.
    3. Germany – History – 1933–1945.   I. Title.

    D757.B54 1998   940.53l38l0943   C97-931453-4

This book has been published with the help of a grant from the Humanities and Social
Sciences Federation of Canada, using funds provided by the Social Sciences and
Humanities Research Council of Canada.

University of Toronto Press acknowledges the financial assistance to its publishing
program of the Canada Council for the Arts and the Ontario Arts Council.

Contents

Acknowledgments

First of all, I want to express my deepest appreciation to my PhD supervisor, Professor D.C. Watt. On many occasions, when the path seemed lost, Professor Watt kept me on course and provided a sense of direction for my work. I also found inspiration in his excellent scholarship, and I hope that this work fully meets the high standards that he has always set for himself and his students. Thanks also to Professors Richard Overy and Zara Steiner, who read the dissertation from which this text is descended, and presided over my viva in 1991. Their help and advice are also appreciated.

I would also like to thank the many librarians and archivists who helped me over the decade from 1985 to 1995, particularly Dr Wolfe, Mr Reese, and Mrs Marks, at the U.S. National Archives; Mme Hepp at the Service Historique de l'Armée de Terre; Dr Werner at the Bundesarchiv; and Dr Ringsdorf at the Bundesmilitärarchiv. Professor Nish, of the London School of Economics, kindly pointed me towards the Bramstedt Collection in the Robbins Library, while Professor Erickson, of the University of Edinburgh, helped me with sources related to the Eastern Front. A PhD student previously under my co-supervision here at the University of Victoria, Chris Madsen, helpfully volunteered several pieces of information on the Werwolf that he came across in the course of his research on the demobilization of the German Navy in 1945–6. My compliments also to the Interlibrary Loans staffs at the University of New Brunswick and the University of Victoria for their extensive efforts to gather much essential material for me.

A number of people provided me with their reminiscences, either in interviews or by letter, and to these people I am especially grateful. Everyone who helped me out in this way is listed in the bibliography.

My thanks are due also to the German Historical Institute, London, and to the

Central Research Fund of the University of London, which provided the generous funding for research trips to Germany and France.

I am also grateful for the work done by Mrs Margaret Pirie, of Fredericton, NB, who diligently typed her way through reams of material and word-processed an early version of the text. Thanks also to Mrs June Bull and Mrs Kathy Mariam at the University of Victoria, both of whom worked on my extensive rewrites of various chapters.

Thanks as well to Rob Ferguson, at the University of Toronto Press, who gave me a hearing at a major publishing house and helped to guide my efforts through to the point of completion.

Finally, I want to express my gratitude and love to my family, particularly my son, Alex; my mother; and my grandmother. Most of all, I want to thank my wife, Sharon, who has used her expertise as a librarian to help me in the preparation of my bibliography and has patiently supported me through a long and sometimes trying exercise. I could have done nothing without her.

February 1997
Victoria, BC

Foreign Terms and Abbreviations

Abwehr	lit. 'defence'; German Military Intelligence
AFP	Agence France-Presse
Allgemeine-SS	General-SS
'Antifa'	Anti-Fascist Committee
BdM	Federation of German Girls (Bund deutscher Mädel), female branch of the HJ
BdS	Security Police Commanders (Befehlshaber des Sicherheitsdienst)
Bürgermeister	mayor
CAD	Civil Affairs Division
CIC	American Army Counter-Intelligence Corps
DAF	German Labour Front (Deutsche Arbeitsfront)
Deuxième Bureau	French Intelligence
Edelweiss Piraten	dissident youth gangs
EPD	German Unification Pary (Einigungspartei Deutschlands)
FAK	German Front Intelligence (Front Aufklarung)
FFI	French Forces of the Interior (Forces Françaises l'Intérieur), armed wing of the French Resistance
FHO	Foreign Armies East (Fremde Heere Ost), German High Command Intelligence on the Eastern Front
Flüsterpropaganda	whisper propaganda
franc-tireur	sniper in civilian clothes
Gau (pl. *Gaue*)	Nazi Party administrative region
Gauleiter	Nazi regional chief
Gauleitung	regional Nazi Party leadership staff
Gebirgsjäger	German mountain troops
Gestapo	Secret State Police during the Third Reich (Geheimstaatspolizei); part of the RSHA

G-2	American military designation for Counter-Intelligence
G-5	American military designation for Civil Affairs/Military Government
HJ	Hitler Youth (Hitler Jugend)
HSSPF	Higher SS and Police Leader (Höhere SS- und Polizeiführer)
Kleinkrieg	lit. 'war of small detachments'; guerrilla war
KPD	German Communist Party (Kommunistische Partei Deutschlands)
Kreisleiter	Nazi area chief; subordinate to a *Gauleiter*
Kreisleitung	area-level Nazi Party leadership staff
Kripo	Criminal Police (Kriminalpolizei), part of the RSHA
KTI	Criminal Technical Institute (Kriminaltechnisches Institut)
Landsturm	Prussian Minutemen
Luftwaffe	German Air Force, 1935–45
maquis	bush bands
maquisards	bush fighters
MG	Military Government
NAPO	National Political Training Institute (Nationalpolitische Erziehung-sanstalt)
NKVD	Soviet Ministry of Internal Security (Narodnyi Kommissariat Vnutrennikh Del)
NSDAP	National Socialist German Workers' Party (Nationalsozialistische Deutsche Arbeiterpartei)
NSF	National Socialist Leadership Corps (Nationalsozialistische Führung), in the Wehrmacht
NSFO	National Socialist Leaderships Corps officer (NS-Führungs-offizier)
NSV	National Socialist People's Welfare Organization (National-sozialistische Volkswohlfahrt)
Oberbürgermeister	Lord Mayor
OKH	German Army High Command (Oberkommando des Heeres)
OKW	Wehrmacht High Command (Oberkommando der Wehrmacht)
Ortsgruppenleiter	local Nazi chieftain; subordinate to a *Kreisleiter*
OZNA	Yugoslav Secret Police (Odeljenje za zastitu naroda)
Panzer	tank
Panzerfaust	one-shot bazooka used in the later years of the Second World War
Pimpfe	preliminary stage of the HJ, for boys aged ten to fourteen
Reichsdeutsche	Germans living within the bounds of the Reich in 1938
Reichsführer-SS	Himmler's title as SS chief
RSHA	Reich Security Main Office (Reichssicherheitshauptamt)
SA	Storm Troopers (Sturmabteilung)

SD	SS Security Service (Sicherheitsdienst); part of the RSHA
SHAEF	Supreme Headquarters, Allied Expeditionary Force
SS	Guard Corps (Schutzstaffel), Nazi élite movement
SVP	South Tyrolean People's Party (Südtirol Volkspartei)
Vehme	medieval vigilante courts, and twentieth-century death squads
Volksdeutsch	ethnic Germans living outside Germany
Volkssturm	lit. 'people's storm'; German mass militia, 1944–5
Wandervogel	German youth movement in late nineteenth and early twentieth centuries
Waffen-SS	Combat-SS
Wehrkreis (pl. *Wehrkreise*)	Home Military District
Wehrmacht	German Armed Forces during the Third Reich
Werwolf	lit. 'werewolf'; National Socialist guerrilla and resistance movement, 1944–5. The term also applies to semi-mythical seventeenth-century guerrilla bands, and to post–First World War 'Free Corps' and parapolitical groups. Hermann Löns and Peter von Heydebreck spelled the term 'Wehrwolf,' thus incorporating the word for 'defence' (*wehr*), and this form was used occasionally in the mid-1940s.
Wolfsangel	lit. 'Wolf's curve'; a Werwolf symbol
'Zeppelin'	SD organization for guerrilla war and espionage in Russia

American infantrymen of the 35th Division sweep Saareguemines, in eastern France, for snipers. SS *francs-tireurs* were active in Saareguemines for weeks after its capture in December 1944.

Field Marshal Montgomery and his liaison officers, April 1945. Several days after this photo was taken, Majors Peter Earle (front row, second from right) and John Poston (back row, second from right) were ambushed by HJ minutemen. Earle was wounded and Poston was killed.

The remains of a hotel and radio tower destroyed in a guerrilla attack on Mount Brocken in the Harz, 30 April 1945. The Harz was menaced by Werewolves and other desperadoes for several months after its occupation. (William Vandivert, *Life*)

Five civilian snipers captured by soldiers of the American 42nd Infantry Division after they were found hiding in cellars in Würzburg, 4 April 1945.

A Toothless Wonder

An Allied view of Werwolf radio. From *The Age* (Melbourne), 18 April 1945

A display of Werwolf equipment captured by the 233rd CIC detachment and stored in the basement of CIC headquarters at Idar-Oberstein.

Two American anti-aircraft machine-gunners posted outside the Palatine town of Bad Kreuznach, 22 March 1945. During this period, Bad Kreuznach, a key communications centre, was affected by a heavy spate of civilian sniping.

An American halftrack moves past a dead German soldier near Rheinhards, 2 April, while rounding up bypassed SS forces in the Taunus. SS units in this region had been ordered by Hitler to form Werwolf Battle Groups and harass the Americans.

THE WEREWOLVES

"Of course it's rather hard to do the goose-step like this."

An Allied view of Hitler and Himmler as Werewolves. From *Punch*, 11 April 1945

A fire of suspicious origin, possibly set by Werewolves, rages in a U.S. 4th Armoured Division fuel dump, 17 September 1945.

Suspected Werewolves being brought in for questioning by U.S. XII Corps soldiers in Lower Bavaria.

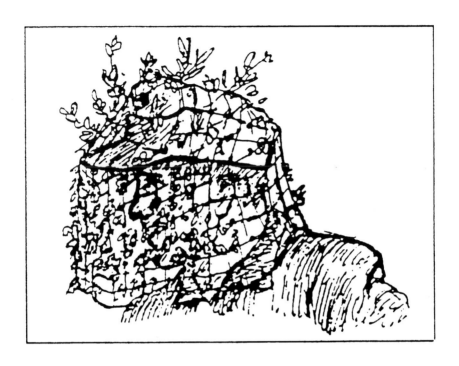

Werwolf camouflage. From *Werwolf: Winke für Jagdeinheiten,* the Werwolf guerrilla training manual

The bodies of German guerrillas killed by soldiers of the U.S. 89th Infantry Division. Note the civilian clothes.

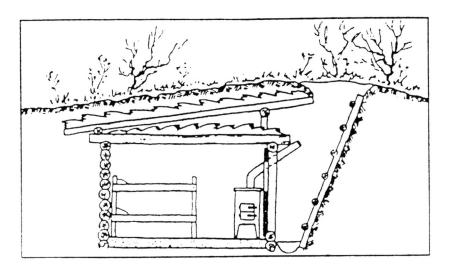

Cross-sectional view of a Werwolf bunker. From *Werwolf: Winke für Jagdeinheiten*

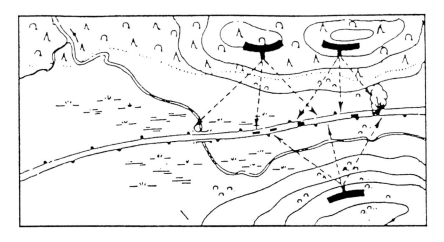

Training diagram for a Werwolf ambush. From *Werwolf: Winke für Jagdeinheiten*

Above and opposite: Captured Werewolf Richard Jarczyk facing execution by an American firing squad. From *Picture Post*, 12 May 1945

Die Bedienung der Panzerfaust Zeichnung: Transozean

An instructional diagram from the Nazi Party newspaper *Völkischer Beobachter* (17 February 1945), showing civilians how to fire a Panzerfaust.

USA.-Soldateska drangsaliert deutsche Kinder

Mjölnir

Roosevelt stellte Gangster, Kidnapper, Zuchthäusler in die Armee ein —

A Nazi view: German children in the occupied territories show resolution in the face
of American 'gangsters, kidnappers, and convicts.' From *Völkischer Beobachter,*
19 January 1945

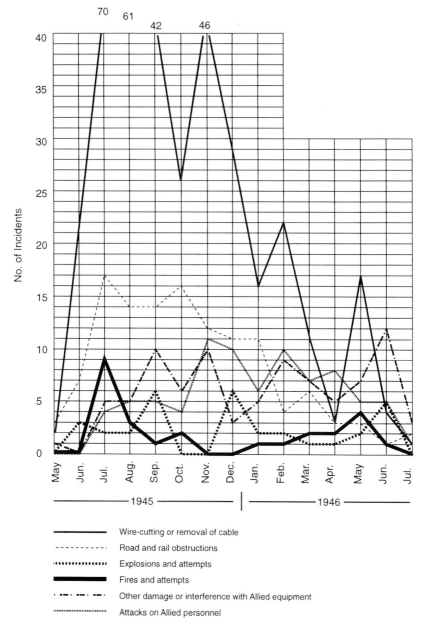

Incidents of sabotage and suspected sabotage in the British Zone of Occupation, 1945–6. From the Central Commission Germany (British Element) 'Intelligence Review' no. 12, September 1946

A Werwolf stencil, 'the sign of the dark men,' at the entrance to a railway station in Bremen. Such insignia were meant to intimidate Germans. From *Life*, 28 May 1945

Vyhláška

Zakazuji s okamžitou platností jakékoliv srocování a páchání násilností.

Po 20. hodině nesmí se nikdo zdržovati na ulicích mimo úředních orgánů a vojáků.

Neuposlechnutí trestá se smrtí.

Ústí nad Labem, dne 31. července 1945.

Josef Vondra
předseda MNV.

Tiskárna bři Krausově, národní správa, Ústí n.L.

Leaflet circulated in Aussig following the explosions and riots in July 1945. Signed by National Committee chairman Josef Vondra, it reads: 'I forbid any assembly of people and use of violence. After 20.00 hours, no one is allowed in the streets except official functionaries or soldiers. This order is in force immediately and transgression is punishable by death.'

WERWOLF!

Introduction

The orthodox opinion on Nazi partisan warfare is that it was non-existent, or a myth produced by a last-minute propaganda campaign launched by Joseph Goebbels. One historian goes so far as to claim that Germany 'did not produce a single saboteur, far less a resistance movement,' and another that 'Werwolf guerrillas never fired a shot.'[1] Many of those writing about Nazi Germany do not bother to pass such judgments, obviously because they believe the resistance movement, the Werwolf, merits not even a mention. A corollary of this belief is the perception that the German populace was obedient, subdued, and totally apathetic during the transitional stage, or so-called Zero Hour, when the Third Reich crumbled and control of Germany passed to the victorious powers of the Grand Alliance.[2] This impression was formed during the occupation period and continues to be widely accepted today. Undeniably, it is a partial truth, but not the entire truth, if only because the total breakdown and atomization of the Reich makes such generalizations oversimplified. Recent developments in 'everyday history' – our understanding of the social and political conditions that exist at local levels – have already undercut the idea of a 'master narrative' for the war or a 'master theme' for the Nazi period. This work of dismantling the 'master theme' should now be extended to include 'Zero Hour.'

In truth, there was an active Nazi resistance campaign during the transitional period. This type of activity was fairly widespread in geographic terms, although it was a scattered and sporadic struggle that varied in intensity, by region, and failed to jolt the advancing Allied and Soviet armies. In some areas, the campaign caught fire, in other areas it did not; similarly, among some social classes and age groups the campaign had an appeal, among others it did not. Perhaps it is true that, in the final analysis, the Werwolf was one of the 'dead ends' of history, although it is also true that it was a cul-de-sac that shaped the terrain around it: Allied occupation policy, and even strategy, was determined negatively by the Werwolf threat. As well, the lack of success of the Nazi resistance should not deny it recognition as much the same kind of phenomenon as that experienced in occupied Europe from 1940 to 1945, if on a slightly smaller scale. Even the most celebrated anti-Nazi groups did not succeed in seriously undermining the presence of the occupying power until Allied and Soviet troops had already pushed back the frontiers of the Axis 'New Order.' It should also be noted that Nazi guerrillas, unlike the other European resistance movements, lacked the impression of mass involvement that inevitably came with final triumph, when scores of opportunistic recruits sought at the last minute to align themselves with the winning side.

The fact that the Werwolf did not appear to enjoy the enthusiastic support of the German people is not surprising; however, neither does it render the movement insignificant. Guerrilla and underground movements have seldom enjoyed the backing of a majority of the populations around them, even in countries occupied by foreign armies. Typically, such movements have been regarded as dangerous jabs at authority which often result in heavy reprisals against persons either not involved in the armed opposition or involved only against their will. Strong evidence suggests, for instance, that the legendary French *francs-tireurs* of 1870–1 were, in reality, frequently refused food by their countrymen; that they were threatened or arrested by French peasants; and that, in some areas, the Prussians were warmly greeted.[3] That does not mean that there were no genuine *francs-tireurs* in 1870–1, or that they did not play an important role. It simply means that such forces often operated in a hostile environment. Usually, widespread support for resistance movements has emerged only when it appears they might succeed in actually displacing existing authority, or if they seem balanced on the edge of military victory. In this regard, the Werwolf was particularly overshadowed by the hugely inflated anti-German resistance forces of 1944–5, and it was tainted with the prejudice of an overly romanticized view of the popular nature of resistance warfare that developed in conjunction with the success of the pro-Allied movements. In addition, some of the occupiers suspected that German civilians were not really as opposed to the Werwolf as they pretended.

There is also no evidence that German 'national character' was unsuited for partisan warfare, as is sometimes claimed. In truth, Germany has a long tradition of irregular warfare, including various 'peasant revolts,' guerrilla unrest during the Thirty Years War (especially the action of legendary Werewolves in Lower Saxony), the 'people's rising' of the Landsturm in 1813, and the savageries of the 'Free Corps' of the period 1918–23. During the nineteenth century the Landsturm was maintained as a vague kind of final call-up, and even during the 'Fulfilment' era of the 1920s rudimentary plans were made for a guerrilla defence of borderland regions under the banner of a 'Field Ranger Corps.' Interestingly, one of the paramilitary groups active during this period, Lieutenant Peter von Heydebreck's Volunteer Ranger Band, eventually evolved into a semi-political outfit called the Wehrwolf, which was an attempt to reanimate the spirit of the seventeenth-century guerrillas celebrated by Hermann Löns in his book of the same name.[4] Vigilantism also has a long history in Germany, dating especially to the 'secret courts,' or Vehme, of the late Middle Ages. The neo-romantics of the 'Free Corps' and the early National Socialist German Workers' Party (NSDAP) were impressed by this tradition, bearing, as it did, features that recurred continually in Nazi ideology: violence, ritualism, archaic formalism, the arbitrary exercise of power. There was some contention in 1945 that Werewolves and Vehme terrorists were 'incompatible with the principles of chivalrous fighting traditional with the German Army and people,'[5] but this narrow concept of honour was ephemeral compared with customs and habits that were more deeply rooted.

The claim that guerrilla warfare was culturally inappropriate for Germans has a lot to do with hackneyed conceptions of 'Prussianism,' and not much to do with the actual situation in 1944–5. It is true that the Prussian autocracy of the seventeenth and eighteenth centuries was unsympathetic to forms of military mobilization motivated by popular enthusiasm rather than discipline; it is also true that the unification of Germany in the nineteenth century was achieved by this same class of autocrats and did not involve popular uprisings or partisan warfare. As a result, Germany lacked a guerrilla tradition comparable with that of some countries in Mediterranean Europe. On the other hand, the rise of German nationalism inspired military reformers in the early nineteenth century to create the first mass armies in which the soldiery was motivated by patriotism rather than fear, and this in turn allowed for the development of skirmishing tactics that had been impossible for the tightly controlled line formations of an earlier period. As the military art developed in Germany over the course of the next century, influenced by the 'cauldron battles' of the 1860s and 1870s, the 'elastic defence' and infiltration tactics of 1917–18, and the innovations forced by the restrictions of the Versailles Treaty, a recognition of the importance of mobility, individual initiative, and flexibility became key attributes that the German military sought to inculcate in its officers. Such men were hardly the rigid Prussian automatons of popular legend – witness, for instance, the achievements of Paul von Lettow-Vorbeck's German East African raiders during the later years of the First World War.[6] Although the Prussian military tradition emphasized partisan warfare as an *adjunct* to regular operations – a point which will come up again in the course of this text – there was an open field for the employment of such tactics.

A careful examination of surviving evidence shows that, contrary to conventional wisdom, there was in 1944–5 a string of guerrilla attacks aimed at both the enemy powers and the German 'collaborators' who worked with the occupiers in maintaining civil government. The number of such incidents probably peaked in the spring of 1945, when bridges were destroyed by saboteurs, Allied and Soviet soldiers murdered and their vehicles ambushed, public buildings mined or bombed, and underground leaflets widely used to threaten domestic opponents of the defeated Nazi regime. Even after conditions settled into the unhappy postwar routine established by the occupying powers, minor sabotage continued, particularly such acts as the cutting of telephone lines; the erection of roadblocks and 'decapitation wires'; vandalism against military vehicles; and attacks upon occupation troops, mainly sniping and bodily assaults. In a number of instances, bombing and arson attacks were carried out upon such targets as Military Government facilities, denazification courts, and Communist meeting-halls. There is a marked difference, of course, between isolated incidents and a genuine trend, and one of the purposes of this work is to present sufficient evidence (albeit much of it anecdotal) to suggest the latter.

Most of this resistance took the form of sporadic, small-scale actions on the part of bypassed troops, militant individuals, or tiny gangs. In this regard, it had much in common with the violent practices of the earlier Nazi 'Time of Struggle,' the pre-1933 period, when spasmodic threats or acts of violence were undertaken on local Nazi initiative rather than as cogs in a larger and more impersonal terror machine. In retrospect, of course, the reality of such scattered resistance in a country which had been home to a radical and pervasive totalitarian movement makes much more intuitive sense than the claim that Nazi resistance was totally lacking. Nazi fanaticism, in fact, did not totally disappear in a puff of smoke. On the other hand, Werwolf actions were typically vicious, fanatical, sporadic, and on a small scale, so small in fact that the enemy rarely directed much attention towards them.

Because such activities were so savage and eminently pointless, they have formed no basis for a postwar myth, unlike the relatively minor harassments of the Landsturm during 1813 or the sabotage attacks in the Ruhr in 1923. References to the Werwolf in postwar German literature are frequent and reveal a considerable degree of traumatization by authors remembering the final months of the war. According to Roderick Watt, this feeling may be attributable to memories of the distrust and mutual suspicion that the Nazi regime had encouraged among Germans.[7] There are at present a few Germans who regard the Werwolf as an inspirational theme for neo-Nazi violence, being encouraged in this by 'old' Nazis and by republished versions of the 1945 Werwolf combat manual, but such opinions flourish only among a minute radical fringe.[8] In general, the Werwolf made Germans uncomfortable at the time it was active, and the term and concept continue to elicit negative feelings.

Foreigners sometimes regard the movement with more sympathy than do Germans, reinterpreting it through a lens of chic anti-Americanism, and seeing it as a European reaction against alien influences. This kind of romantic revision forms the subtext to Danish director Lars von Trier's 1991 film noir *Europa* (released in 1992 in North America as *Zentropa*). Von Trier implies that the Werwolf was a sinister organization, but says little about the movement's Nazi character; instead, there is an implicit moral equivalency established between the resisters and the American occupiers, and one of the film's main Werwolf protagonists is depicted as a confused and misguided patriot. In Russia, where there is at present a buoyant market for copies of *Mein Kampf*, the Werwolf has become an important theme for right-wingers. In 1994, several dozen 'mystical fascists' based in the city of Yaroslavl, north of Moscow, formed a 'Werewolf Legion.' For two years these youths terrorized 'Jews, communists and democrats,' desecrated churches, and planned attacks against movie theatres showing Steven Spielberg's *Schindler's List.* A similar group, the 'Society of Wolves,' was formed in St Petersburg by a maverick Marxist–Leninist ideologist named Bezverkhy.[9]

While the Werwolf is not – for the most part – fondly remembered in Germany, the movement never assumed quite as negative a cast in Germany's borderland territories, such as the Sudetenland, Silesia, and the South Tyrol. There was a disproportionally large number of Werwolf incidents in these areas, and, in the South Tyrol, where the local Germanic population was not deported, violent neo-Nazi resistance continued into the 1960s. In these areas, the Werwolf could portray itself as a self-defence force, seeking to protect the attachment of ethnic Germans to their traditional regions. A concentration on the home region, or *Heimat*, had always been one of the primary building-blocks of German nationalism, and the Werwolf was able to exploit this very powerful feeling.

Before the collapse of the Third Reich, the dying Nazi regime attempted to provide structures of organization and direction for the resistance movement, but this effort was split up among various SS, party, and government agencies. The basic Werwolf diversionary groups were under the purview of the SS-Police establishment, which also maintained a loose suzerainty over an autonomous Hitler Youth (HJ) partisan program. The party, meanwhile, was entrusted with political aspects of the Werwolf movement, which eventually resulted in the dissemination of nihilistic neo-Nazi doctrines that sprang from Goebbels's fertile imagination and were spread mainly by means of radio propaganda. No aspect of the movement was intended primarily to influence events after the final capitulation of the Reich, although a few subsections did make last-minute plans for survival, usually without great effect.

Considering the breadth of such involvement by the main institutions of the Nazi state, it might be argued that, although the Werwolf failed to lay a strong basis for *organized* resistance, this failure was not attributable to lack of effort. In fact, the Werwolf movement constituted one of the last major military and political initiatives of the Third Reich, and in light of the stress and tension caused by the approaching conclusion of a lost war, it most vividly revealed the true nature of the Nazi regime. Seen in these terms, two points are immediately obvious: first, that the Nazi Reich was hardly a unified totalitarian state, but rather was a feudal patchwork of rival fiefs and bureaucratic principalities, each usually in conflict with the others; and, second, that the Nazi regime had slid a great deal in terms of mass support since the movement's golden days in the mid-1930s. Considered as a referendum on the New Order, the Werwolf revealed a regime which (by 1944) was isolated and out of touch.

The Werwolf was also an intrinsic element of a larger Nazi 'Terror,' which began in July 1944 and was analagous to the Jacobin 'Terror' of 1793–4 or the Bolshevik 'Terror' of 1918. In all these cases, the enemy was at the gates; internal foes and 'defeatists' had to be crushed; and, since the authority of the state was imperilled, much of the intimidation was an extrajudicial 'terror from below.' Once again, this suggests something very important about the nature of the regime: since support for the Nazi regime was badly eroded (or gone) by the spring of 1945, the Werwolf was a means of trying to add to its coercive powers (at a time it badly needed to do so), while, at the same time, not detracting from its legitimacy. In one sense, the NSDAP was spontaneously moving back to a position of opposition even before it had been displaced. Thus the Werwolf transcended the murky boundary lines among being a vigilante movement aimed at saving an existing order, a reactionary movement aimed at restoring a lapsed order, and a revolutionary movement aimed at creating a new order.[10]

These various themes are more fully developed in chapters 1 to 4 of this book, which focus mainly upon the organizational, ideological, and social character of the Werwolf movement. Chapter 5 describes the various natural strongholds to which German guerrillas were drawn, and chapter 6 discusses the particular opportunities and challenges faced by Nazi partisans in Germany's peripheral borderlands. Chapter 7 examines the profound impact that the Werwolf had upon both Western Allied and Soviet occupation policy.

What is being attempted here, in the final analysis, is to disinter the story of the Werwolf, to gauge the limits of the movement's success, to measure its negative influence, and to explain its ultimate failure. The goal is not an aggressive revisionism, but rather a neutral stocktaking of forgotten people and incidents. The hope is that such an account will be read in conjunction with the existing literature to create a more balanced view.

1

Gothic Guerrillas: The Bureau 'Prützmann' and the SS-Werwolf

By 1944, with military crises unfolding in both the East and the West, Germany was forced by its own weakness to fall back upon a strategy in which guerrilla warfare played a major role. This is a repeated theme in German history, and the country's leaders had previously pursued such a course both during the period of Napoleonic domination, from 1807 to 1813, and during the unhappy years of the early Weimar Republic. It is crucial to note, however, that in the previous 140 years a certain sense of guerrilla warfare had developed in Germany, and that this view both accommodated the prejudices of German culture and fit the generally autocratic nature of the Prussian/German state. In short, the modern German understanding of partisan warfare was limited by the fear that disaster would arise from any wholesale subjugation of the prerogatives of the state to the desires of the mobilized masses. Thus, the German partisans of 1813 were 'conservative' in the sense that they fought for the status quo and were authorized by the Prussian ruling caste,[1] and this pattern was repeated by the paramilitaries of the 1918–23 period. Clausewitz, writing in the wake of 1813, failed to see partisan warfare as a means of inciting radical social change or as a war-winning strategy. In his influential writings, he interpreted guerrilla fighting simply as a defensive rising of 'armed peasantry,' undertaken once the homeland was invaded, but organized as a diversionary adjunct to regular operations. In fact, he claimed that, without direction by special military detachments, the local inhabitants would usually lack the confidence and initiative to take up arms.[2] Although the revolutionary undertones of National Socialism would eventually influence the guerrilla-warfare campaign of 1944–5, the initial preparations were shaped by this Clausewitzian view of partisan operations as a diversionary sideshow.

Thus, the original strategy in 1944–5 was not to win the war by guerrilla operations, but merely to stem the tide, delaying the enemy long enough to allow for a political settlement favourable to Germany. On the basis of captured enemy civil-affairs directives, and the publicity surrounding the 'Morgenthau Plan,' the Nazi regime knew that the Western Powers intended a Draconian occupation of the entire country.[3] To Hitler and company, however, the break-up of the enemy coalition seemed to shimmer clearly on the horizon, and they hoped that, in the midst of such an eventuality, the Western Allies would moderate their demands. The Nazi regime was also engaged in the Clausewitzian aim of wearing down its opponents so that the preconditions for the imposition of a harsh peace – namely, 'unconditional surrender' – would become prohibitively costly.

These strategies were elementally flawed. They failed to take into account the universal opprobrium that the Nazi regime had brought upon itself, which provided the necessary mortar to cover cracks in the enemy alliance, and which also served to make 'unconditional surrender' non-negotiable. Such plans also neglected to take into account basic internal weaknesses. One of the main problems, for instance, was the lack of a popular basis for the New Order, even in old Nazi heartlands such as East Prussia and Franconia. In addition, 'the Hitler myth' was dead, and the regime was edging towards becoming a dictatorship based almost entirely upon terror rather than upon popular consent.[4] Nazi promises of a just peace were still accepted at face value by only a few blinded devotees of the movement. Most Germans had lost faith in the party, and although they were too physically and morally exhausted to turn against it, they were also too tired – and too disabused of notions of glory – to burn their homes, or snipe at the enemy, or valiantly enrol in the ranks of the mass militia.[5] Even in the East, this factor applied, although there was a greater natural basis for guerrilla warfare on that front. Gradually, as the final collapse loomed increasingly near, the Werwolf became something akin to a means of revenge which the fanatics pitted against their own people as well as against the enemy.

Another problem was the behind-the-scenes disorganization associated with almost every aspect of the Nazi state. This administrative chaos has been variously regarded either as an unintentional result of Hitler's sloppy management style and his inchoate doctrines, or as a deliberate Hitlerian tactic meant to incite factionalism, and thus increase the Führer's ascendant power and prestige (the former explanation, incidentally, seems more likely). The most precise formulation of this anarchic situation is Peter Hüttenberger's model of a tripartite 'pact,' which, he argues, dated from 1933 and mediated relations among the three 'pillars of power' in the Third Reich: the National Socialist Party (including the state bureaucracy that it penetrated, fragmented, and increasingly dominated); the Wehrmacht; and Big Business. The German Labour Front (DAF) and the Reich Food Estate remained in inferior positions throughout the period, although, after the mid-1930s, another subordinate player, the 'Guard Corps (SS)/Security Service (SD)/Gestapo complex,' increasingly came into its own, re-creating the system as a quadripartite 'polycracy.'[6] While these were the major fault lines, innumerable cracks and fissures extended into each of these 'pillars of power,' reproducing in miniature the 'polycratic' nature of the overall system. Separate offices, sub-bureaux, regions, and individuals were continually pitted one against another in an ongoing struggle for domination and control of plunder.

As a result of this institutionalized disorder, loyalty in the Third Reich was transformed into a sort of medieval fealty, and the raging confusion encouraged Nazi leaders to construct personal bases of power by reserving from the common pool whatever resources they had managed to acquire. Thus the Nazi system of administration was factionalized rather than totalitarian, and the concept of a monolithic commonwealth existed only in propaganda. It was, in short, hardly the kind of 'folkish community' of which German romantics had long dreamt, and which would perhaps have provided a suitable base for guerrilla warfare.[7] Moreover, feudal anarchy actually increased as the war reached a crisis stage, and as violent charges and recriminations tended to fly with even greater abandon between the chief Nazi satraps. Naturally, this atmosphere characterized the guerrilla program, which was perhaps the last initiative of the fading Reich worth a bureaucratic battle. 'The inner chaos,' as a British intelligence report noted, 'was never better exemplified than in the Werewolf movement.'[8]

The Organization of the SS-Werwolf

Discussions about the need for a Nazi guerrilla organization actually began among German intelligence officers in 1943, and tended to centre around a number of immediate precedents from German history. By the spring of 1944, such deliberations had aroused the interest of the head of the SS-Main Office, Gottlob Berger, himself an officer with guerrilla experience from the 1920s. We know that, during this period, the 1813 Landsturm decree was unearthed and circulated; that evaluations of an interwar guerrilla agency, the 'Field Ranger Service,' were withdrawn from the military archives in Potsdam and put in the hands of interested readers; and that relevant passages from Clausewitz's *On War* were examined in detail.[9] As noted above, all these sources of inspiration implied a traditional Prussian-style guerrilla movement that would cooperate with the regular Army in a policy of diversion and delay, although certain SS leaders were also inspired by several of the more expansive underground movements that proliferated during the Second World War. In fact, a special top-secret SS unit was formed in order to study these movements in detail, and specialists from this unit were sent to observe the Warsaw Rising in 1944, apparently in conjunction with the Abwehr and the Warsaw Gestapo. The Polish Home Army was considered a revolutionary movement par excellence.[10]

The actual SS guerrilla organization was formed in September 1944,[11] and its organizational structure was perhaps influenced by a memorandum submitted by SS-General Richard Hildebrandt, a senior SS-Police official on the Eastern Front. The Hildebrandt memo, dated 19 September, sketched out an organization almost identical to that which soon took form. (Ironically, Hildebrandt later got mixed up with the circle around armaments minister Albert Speer, which devoted itself to bringing the war to an early conclusion and preventing guerrilla warfare.)[12]

The designation for this set-up was 'Werwolf,' a term borrowed either directly or indirectly from Hermann Löns, whose book *Der Wehrwolf*, a romantic saga about seventeenth-century guerrillas on the Lüneberg Heath, had given the term a common currency. Although *Der Wehrwolf* had been published in 1910, and Löns himself was long gone – killed in France during the initial weeks of the First World War – its influence remained. Löns wrote in much the same vein as his contemporaries Rudyard Kipling, Jack London, and Knut Hamsun, telling adventure stories that emphasized the struggle for survival, the raw appeal of nature, and the power of the land. Certainly, his vision of a close-knit peasant community, more united by race than divided by class, struck a chord in the modern German consciousness, as did as his sympathy for vigilantism and his 'fear of encirclement.' *Der Wehrwolf* was, as Walter Linden notes, the basic book of the folkish movement, and its sales were rivalled only by Hitler's *Mein Kampf*, surpassing half a million copies by 1939 and 800,000 by 1945.

Beyond the Löns iconography, the term 'Werwolf' was probably also supposed to suggest the terrors of lycanthropy – blood-lust by individuals who appeared ordinary during daylight hours and moved undetected through civil society. Such an interpretation fit well into the Gothic aesthetics of the SS, as did the association with wolves, a favourite symbol for Hitler and a mythological metaphor for chaos and *Götterdämmerung*. In a recent apologia for Löns, Roderick Watt argues that the lycanthropy connotation was exclusive, and that Löns's *Der Wehrwolf* was not a source of inspiration for the partisans of 1944–5. Watt's evidence is orthographic: he clearly shows that the Nazi regime favoured the spelling 'Werwolf' – suggesting lycanthropes – over the Lönsian 'Wehrwolf,' and to this detail he attaches much weight. However, considering the wide familiarity of Germans with Lön's novel, this thesis is hard to swallow, particularly since sources in 1944–5 – the *Deutsche Allgemeine Zeitung* for one – specifically referred to Löns's 'peasant chronicle,' although they changed the spelling in order to meet the demands of the new orthodoxy. What seems more likely is that the Nazis were attempting to prevent an association between their guerrillas and the interwar movement led by Peter von Heydebreck, which had used the Löns spelling. The Bund Wehrwolf of the 1920s had been an early competitor to the NSDAP, and its leadership had embodied the archetypical 'Free Corps,' buccaneer mentality that Hitler despised. Interestingly, von Heydebreck himself had eventually wound up in the SA, like many of his freebooting comrades, but he was killed in the 'Blood Purge' of June 1934. It was probably this story, rather than anything associated with Löns's book, that the Nazis did not wish to recall.[13]

In any case, the 'Werwolf' name was used as early as October 1944,[14] although it is uncertain who originally fostered its adoption. Otto Skorzeny later claimed that the name was originally suggested by Party Secretary Martin Bormann, and it is true that Löns's *Der Wehrwolf* was republished in great numbers during the fall of 1944 under the purview of the party chancellery. On the other hand, a former staff member of Werwolf central headquarters noted that the designation was selected by the chief of the organization, Hans Prützmann. Arno Rose suggests that the name may have been chosen by Gottlob Berger, who was a great fan of Löns's. Whatever the case, there was some opposition to the name, from both inside and outside the organization. It was generally felt that the term 'Werwolf' was unmilitary in spirit and suggested bands of armed civilians who would be subject to summary execution if captured by the enemy.[15]

One of the most basic problems with the new movement was that it was not put under the purview of the military, upon which suspicions of treason had fallen. Rather, it was placed under the control of the SS, and even within this sphere it was *not* associated with the Waffen-SS, which was the combat wing of Himmler's empire. Moreover, the Werwolf was independent of the SS security service, the SD, as well as of the SD's parent agency, the Reich Security Main Office (RSHA), an arrangement which naturally created a coolness between the new movement and the intelligence community. It seems, in fact, that the main RSHA chiefs, SS-Generals Ernst Kaltenbrunner and Walter Schellenberg, set out from the beginning to disable the main body of the movement, which remained outside their control. Instead, the Werwolf was placed under the direction of Himmler's own regional police inspectors, the Higher SS and Police Leaders (HSSPF). Quite obviously, Himmler was accustomed to ensuring that his will would be done within the Reich by using the police as his main lever of control, and in 1944–5 he could not adjust his thinking to any other pattern.[16] Employment of the HSSPF also suggests that the Werwolf, from the very beginning, was considered an instrument of terror.

Another of the most delimiting features of the new movement, evident from the Hildebrandt memorandum onward, was that it was never seen as anything more than a mere diversionary organization meant to function in Germany's borderlands, at least not until the last dark days of the war. Any intimation that the armed forces might fail to protect the frontiers of the Reich smacked of 'defeatism,' at least in the Nazi view. This led the SS guerrillas to proceed on the assumption that their group was limited to the few areas already occupied or immediately threatened by the enemy. This confusion of morale with common sense meant that no preparations were made for resistance in the interior until well into 1945.[17]

Conceived within this narrow mandate, SS partisans, were regarded, in a strict Clausewitzian sense, as a means of harassing enemy lines of communication, particularly rail lines. Nazi leaders hoped that Allied and Soviet troops would have to divert forces to the rear in order to deal with such problems. Werewolves were also charged with committing impromptu acts of political and economic sabotage; killing collaborators; spreading propaganda; infiltrating enemy Military Government offices; collecting intelligence on enemy means of supply and transportation routes; and encouraging the population in boycotts and passive resistance (although, during the last days of the war, the guerrillas became less trusting of the population and warned them to keep to themselves).[18] *Völkischer Beobachter*, the official newspaper of the NSDAP, compared Nazi guerrilla warfare to the harassment of Allied convoys by U-boat wolf-packs, with hunter groups tracking down wayward three-ton heavy-goods vehicles unescorted by tanks, in the same way that submarines picked off straggling merchant ships unescorted by destroyers.[19] Captured documents show that the Werwolf was also regarded as the core of future guerrilla bands and local resistance movements, since it was expected that Wehrmacht stragglers and disaffected Nazi civilians in the enemy rear would naturally coalesce around such a nucleus.[20]

These duties were to be carried out by 'groups,' or small cells of four to six men, which in turn were organized into 'sectors' (alternatively called 'platoons'), consisting of six to ten cells; six to eight 'sectors' formed a 'section.' Cell members were equipped with small arms, hand-grenades, bazookas, and an array of Nipolit and Donarit plastic explosives, often contained in a kit resembling a lunch-box. Each Werwolf member was supposed to carry fifteen to twenty pounds of explosive material, plus foot-mines and unexploded American incendiary sticks, of which the Germans had collected a total stock of approximately 250,000. American and British weapons were obtained through parachute drops in Holland, by which the Allies had hoped to equip Dutch patriots, but which actually fell into the hands of the SS.[21] Werewolves were also issued military uniforms, but were given free latitude to dress in civilian clothes in 'emergency cases.'[22]

Werwolf groups were provided with hidden ammunition caches, and, in at least one instance, it was later discovered that a Werewolf had assumed the guise of a forest ranger in order to keep watch over secret stocks of sabotage material hidden in the woods.[23] Various agencies of the German government and military also did some detailed studies about the use of natural caves as large-scale secret supply dumps.[24] Left behind enemy lines, Werwolf groups were based in hidden bunkers, or galleries, which the Germans called 'strong points.' These bunkers were intended as living-quarters and command posts, and the importance accorded to them made Werwolf groups immobile, territorially based units, much like the initial Soviet partisan detachments of 1941, or the Chinese Communist territorial guerrilla platoons that fought the Japanese. In the southern and central Rhineland, most galleries consisted of camouflaged caves, unused mine shafts, air-raid shelters, or derelict factories, but, farther north, the dense woods of the Reichswald afforded an opportunity for the construction of custom-made bunkers. About thirty such installations were dug by Ruhr miners on loan from the Hibernia mining concern, apparently under the purview of the director of 'West Wall Construction.' The main means of communication with German lines was by wireless transmitter or line-crossers, although there was also a nebulous plan to link the galleries by means of an underground telephone net in the Rhineland operated by post-office technicians.[25]

To oversee the Werwolf, Himmler on 19 September appointed a 'personal representative' who was given the title General Inspector for Special Abwehr. Unfortunately for the Nazis, the SS-Police official assigned to this post was General Hans Prützmann, a charter member of the SS aristocracy whose undeniable wit and intelligence were more than offset by his vast conceit and notable lack of attention to business. During the early stages of the Werwolf, Prützmann emerges in the historical record as a blustery figure who bragged that his organization would bring about 'a radical improvement in Germany's military situation,' and who delighted in showing off secret sabotage equipment to impressionable associates and acquaintances.[26]

A native of East Prussia, Prützmann, a handsome man, had celebrated his forty-third birthday shortly before his posting. Like several other senior SS leaders, his most notable physical characteristic was a facial scar suffered during a sword duel. He also had a background similar to those of SS contemporaries such as Himmler and Heydrich. These men belonged to a generation barely too young to have fought in the Great War, but not too young to have joined the postwar Free Corps, which provided their conduit into right-radical politics.

Prützmann joined the SS in 1930, and rose rapidly. He was already an SS-Lieutenant-General by 1935, when Himmler himself attended Prützmann's wedding in East Prussia. In March 1937 he was stationed as HSSPF in Hamburg, then transferred to the same post in Königsberg, and thence on to a dual posting as HSSPF of both Ukraine and southern Russia. During two and a half years of savage 'security work' in the East, Prützmann accumulated a nearly unrivalled knowledge of guerrilla warfare, and he was one of the figures who dickered with the Ukrainian Partisan Army to bring it into alliance with Germany. In a more general sense, he was responsible for the attempt to conduct a 'scorched earth' retreat from Ukraine, and, in the Nazi view, guerrilla warfare was closely related to such extreme tactics. This experience, plus his background in East Prussia, stood Prützmann in good stead to serve as the SS partisan chief, particularly since Werwolf units were first deployed on the Eastern Front.[27] By the fall of 1944, German evacuation of the USSR meant that Prützmann's old posts as an HSSPF in that country had become redundant and, in October, after he had been reassigned to the Werwolf, the SS personnel office requested permission to announce that Prützmann had been relieved of his former duties.[28] It should also be noted that, during this entire period, Prützmann formally retained his post as HSSPF in Königsberg, although he was replaced by an acting HSSPF from 1941 to 1944.[29]

The construction of the SS guerrilla inspectorate began with the formation of a central staff, Bureau 'Prützmann,' which was first based at Petz, near Berlin, and later transferred to Rheinsburg, Frederick the Great's one-time residence, northwest of the German capital. There was no danger of Prützmann and company being tied to a home base, however, since the ostentatious General Inspector soon equipped himself with a private train on which he could travel throughout Germany. At various sidings, special telephone cables were installed, setting up direct lines to different parts of the country.

Prützmann's staff of 200 was organized like that of a military corps and was led by SS-Colonel Karl Tschiersky, former head of the Eastern Desk at SD (Foreign Intelligence). As part of his job at the SD, Tschiersky had run Operation 'Zeppelin,' a large-scale attempt to infiltrate anti-Soviet guerrillas into the rear of the Red Army. This task was quite obviously valuable preparation for tackling a project like the Werwolf. While with the SD, however, Tschiersky had run afoul of the infamous SS commando chief Otto Skorzeny, a growing presence in the SD, and the personal animosity between Tschiersky and Skorzeny thereafter became part of the generally frosty relations between the Werwolf and the RSHA. Tschiersky was replaced in the spring of 1945 by SS-Brigadier Opländer, an official on the staff of HSSPF Karl Frank in Bohemia–Moravia, whose services Prützmann had specifically requested.

The main staff members of the Bureau 'Prützmann' were SA-Brigadier Sie-bel, in charge of training and technical administration (Inspectorate 'I'); SS-Colonel D'Alquen, the commander of the Waffen-SS Propaganda Company (the '"Kurt Eggers" Standard') and a media specialist who had run Operation 'Scorpion,' the diffusion of 'Russian Liberation' propaganda on the Eastern Front; SS-Colonel Kotthaus, in charge of personnel matters; and Frau Maisch, who led a female component of the Werwolf. In the spring of 1945, a regular military officer, Lieutenant-General Juppe, was also named as Prützmann's 'deputy,' an appointment that reflected the increasingly close relations between the Werwolf and the Army.[30] Needless to say, the dominant role played by veterans of the Eastern Front suggests that the SS-Werwolf was focused mainly in an eastward direction.

Regionally, the Werwolf was organized according to the boundaries of the Wehrmacht's home defence regions (*Wehrkreise*) and, within these districts, it was controlled by the Higher SS and Police Leaders, who locally represented Himmler in his capacity as Chief of German Police. Under a system first devised for the borderland HSSPF, and then extended to the remainder of the Reich, each HSSPF was ordered by Himmler to appoint a special representative to control the local recruitment, training, and deployment of Nazi guerrillas. Thus was devised the position of 'Werwolf Commissioner,' later designated 'Commander of Special Abwehr.' Prützmann preferred that Army officers serve in these local posts, since he wished to build his essentially civilian organiza-tion around a military core.[31] Associated bodies, such as the party, the (HJ), and the SA, were also supposed to appoint their own regional Werwolf commission-ers to maintain contact with the SS movement, although it is unlikely that all these officials were ever actually appointed.[32]

Because the Werwolf movement was based upon the HSSPF command struc-ture, its organizational character was shaped by the role of the HSSPF within the dual chain of command that existed within the SS. The office of the HSSPF had originally been created during the late 1930s as a means of breaking the monopoly of command channels established by the senior headquarters of the various offices within Himmler's SS-Police empire, particularly the Waffen-SS and the Security Police. The highly centralized chain of command within these subunits had led to a stifling parochialism that made local cooperation between two or more branches of the overall SS organization difficult to achieve. Thus, Himmler introduced the HSSPF as a means of preventing the constituent parts of his empire from falling apart, and he particularly used the channel as a means of bypassing the SS central offices, especially the RSHA, in order to carry out 'special tasks.'[33]

Because the HSSPF had a measure of authority over local offices of the regular police, the RSHA, and the Waffen-SS, such officials had the ability (at least in theory) to draw together the resources regarded by Himmler as necessary for the success of his partisan units. Moreover, many of the HSSPF had personal experience in the occupied Eastern territories, and, like Prützmann, they were supposed to have accumulated a specialized knowledge of partisan warfare. The important thing to note, however, is that the original *raison d'être* of the HSSPF was the regional centralization of all the branches of the overall organization, as opposed to centralized direction in Berlin of individual SS and police agencies. This pattern of horizontal rather than vertical organization was naturally bequeathed to the Werwolf. Prützmann was formally attached to the SS-Main Office,[34] but otherwise was directly subordinate to Himmler, meaning that the Bureau 'Prützmann' was the only intermediate command channel between Himmler and the HSSPF (in their capacity as regional Werwolf organizers).

This system of regionalization had definite advantages. For instance, it allowed for a degree of local improvisation foreign to our standard conception of 'totalitarianism,' and it was suitable for a period when the geographic unity of the Reich was collapsing under the strain of Anglo-American air attacks. On the other hand, the system's great weakness was that HSSPF officials, by their very nature, were isolated from regular command channels, and therefore stood upon a weak bureaucratic foundation. Because they lacked their own resources of men and material, they were effective only when called upon by the Reichsführer to perform a 'special task': only in this event did the flow of business switch from the routine channels to the special channel running from Himmler via the HSSPF to the local RSHA commanders, the Security Police Commanders (BdS). When 'special tasks' extended over a considerable period, as was the case for the Werwolf, the RSHA and other SS agencies could raise substantial roadblocks to protracted demands on their resources. Thus, the HSSPF was essentially an outsider, often at conflict with the RSHA, the Waffen-SS, and the party,[35] and this problem was transferred directly to the Werwolf organization, superimposed upon the HSSPF system of command.

The Eastern Front

For better or worse, this system was first applied in the German borderland regions and then it gradually spread inward. On the Eastern Front, Werwolf units were first launched during the fall of 1944 in Prützmann's old fief of East Prussia, which was also an early testing-ground for the mass militia, or Volkssturm. The first secret supply caches were laid at the same time, stocked with weapons and three months' worth of food. One of the original Werwolf detachments was a nine–member 'Special Unit' under the command of a Sergeant

Bioksdorf, which was recruited during October from a section of the 'Hermann Goering' Division that had been posted to guard Goering's country estate on the Rominten Heath. Supplied with explosives, radio transmitters, and ten carrier pigeons, this group had a mandate to reconnoitre Soviet movements and organize German stragglers and civilians for partisan warfare. They managed to transmit ten messages back to German lines and tried to blow up two bridges before they were rolled up by the Red Army in mid-November 1944.[36]

Prützmann had a special relationship with the East Prussian Werwolf. Because the acting HSSPF in Königsberg fell ill about the time that Werwolf was launched, the Werwolf chief returned to take over personally as HSSPF. In fact, Prützmann continued to serve in this capacity for the rest of the war,[37] which gave East Prussia a distinctive status within the overall movement. Prützmann's idea of basing Werwolf groups in camouflaged underground bunkers seems to have been predicated upon the suitability of such structures in the deep East Prussian forests.[38]

In areas to the south and west of East Prussia, there were problems in calling the Werwolf into being. In Posen and Pomerania, the establishment of Werwolf groups was restricted to regions with a local German ethnic majority, although the genuinely German parts of Pomerania were some of the most Nazified areas of the entire Reich. In the General Government (Poland), orders to activate the Werwolf were disseminated to SS-Police offices in the autumn of 1944, although not much of an organization was in place before the Russians advanced. A few small detachments of Volksdeutsche and Polish or Ukrainian collaborators were fielded, but with few positive results.

Efforts in Silesia (Wehrkreis VIII) were much more profitable, and this ethnic 'peninsula' eventually became the area on the Eastern Front where the Werwolf was the most active. One of the major factors behind this relative success was that the military authority in Silesia, Army Group 'Centre,' under the fanatic Field-Marshal Ferdinand Schörner, was strongly in favour of the movement and took measures to facilitate its establishment and operations. Moreover, in January, a local Front Intelligence (FAK) unit under Captain Kirn was ordered by Himmler to train Silesian Werwolf groups and to help in the establishment of weapons, food, and medical dumps, all of which was done. Polish estimates suggest that at least a thousand Werewolves were fielded in Lower Silesia.[39]

Overall, preparation of special supply caches and stay-behind groups had begun in November 1944, and by 1945 Werwolf units were deployed, at least sporadically, along the most easterly extensions of the Eastern Front. During the same period, the Soviets noted that a considerable number of stay-behind saboteurs were overrun by the rapid advances resulting from the Winter Offensive in Poland and eastern Germany.[40] Both sides fought savagely: east of Nielkoppe, members of a ten-man Werwolf group were hopelessly surrounded by a Soviet Ministry of Internal Security (NKVD) patrol, but they still tried to shoot their way out of their gallery, losing seven of their number in the process. In eastern Austria, a Werwolf detachment reconnoitring a Russian armoured column near Bruck an der Leitha was sighted by the enemy. The Soviet response was to locate the spotters in their foxholes and then run over the depressions with their tank treads. Off to the west, in the Vienna Woods, members of a Werwolf rearguard – in uniform – were butchered, and their bodies mutilated, after they were overrun by the Russians.[41]

After March 1945, considerable efforts were made to divert the Soviets away from the impending assault upon Berlin, and, even during the final advance upon the capital, numerous German guerrilla detachments permitted themselves to be overrun. 'They hid in basements and in ruins,' noted Marshall Chuikov, 'and [they] allowed the forward units of our advancing forces to pass, and sometimes the rearward units as well, and then opened fire, with the object of sowing panic in the rear and slowing down or paralysing action along the front line.'[42] Near Pankow, two drunken Werewolves fired at the backs of Soviet troops, and in Steglitz Werwolf snipers fired on Red Army rear echelons, necessitating a Soviet operation to clean out an apartment block.[43] An American war correspondent, reporting from the inner city on 27–8 April, noted that there was plenty of sniping behind Russian lines, and that civilians lived in abject terror, knowing that 'the least suspicion of sniping means death.'[44] One Werwolf group fought to the last cartridge in Halensee; another slipped out of the capital, but was caught and wiped out by Russian forces along the Elbe.[45]

Even after the capital fell, Werwolf arsonists and snipers continued to remain active. 'Red' Berlin had never been a Nazi stronghold, so the guerrillas attempted to keep Berliners 'loyal' by maintaining a hostile divide between the occupation forces and the population of the capital. They torched Soviet food stores and buildings bedecked in white flags and, using explosives cached in April 1945, also managed to blow up a Russian car park and a printing plant working for the Red Army. Well after the capitulation of the city on 2 May, Soviet troops continued to drop at the hands of Nazi snipers. Among the casualties were three unidentified Red Army soldiers whose bodies were discovered on the grounds of the Botanical Gardens on 15 May; a Soviet officer shot from ruins along the Berlinstrasse on 17 May; and two Soviet railway guards attacked near Potsdam on the night of 22–3 July (one killed and one wounded). There is even some suspicion that the death on 16 June of Berlin's city commandant, General N.E. Berzarin, came as a result of an ambush in Charlottenburg.[46]

Postwar skirmishing continued in other areas of eastern Germany as well, and Soviet and Polish Communist sources report that Werewolves remained active throughout 1945–6. Although some of these claims were undoubtedly exaggerated in order to provide an excuse for anti-German raids in areas of the Reich annexed by Poland, there is some independent evidence that German partisans were active. Radio intercepts, for instance, show that some 200 Werewolves remained behind the Soviet front in East Prussia after the end of the war and, according to an eyewitness account, German partisans in the forests of eastern Pomerania succeeded in rescuing German civilians from deportation to the USSR.[47]

The Western Front

Although operations in the West never equalled the intensity evident in the eastern German provinces, the western marches were not forgotten. In September, Prützmann and his adjutant toured Wehrkreis VI, comprising Westphalia and the northern Rhineland, and they instructed the local HSSPF, SS-General Karl Gutenberger, to form a *Wehrkreis* guerrilla organization. Similar arrangements were soon made with the other Rhenish HSSPF, Jürgen Stroop and Otto Hofmann, who controlled, respectively, Wehrkreis XII (the Eifel, the Palatinate, the Saar, southwestern Hesse, and Lorraine) and Wehrkreis V (Baden, Württemberg, and Alsace). Each HSSPF was told to assemble a small staff to control the new organization, and to appoint a 'Werwolf Commissioner' (respectively, SS-Colonel Raddatz, SS-Captain Gunther, and SS-Lieutenant Müller). Three Waffen-SS officers were also dispatched in order to select volunteers for 'Battalion West.' Two months later, the HSSPF of Wehrkreis X, Graf von Bassewitz, was also authorized to organize Werwolf formations in the extreme northwest corner of the Reich, which was one of the Nazi heartlands north of the Main.[48]

Initial Werwolf infiltration teams in the West were deployed in Alsace and Lorraine at the end of 1944. The first was a detachment sent to investigate conditions in the newly occupied city of Metz, all four members of which disappeared; the second was a three-man unit committed in the Weissenburg area in order to determine the feasibility of organizing a local resistance movement. One member of the Weissenburg team clawed his way back to German lines in December 1944, where he delivered a highly informative report, but he was subsequently sent back out on a similar operation in advance of the German 'North Wind' Offensive, and from this mission he did not return. In general, the SS was hesitant about preparing the Alsatians and Lorrains for guerrilla warfare because of the fear that any weapons made available would be turned against the Germans themselves.[49]

The first units with their own underground galleries were arrayed in late January and February 1945, mainly in the Reichswald, the Eifel, the Saar, the Palatinate, and Baden. Deployment was accomplished by allowing the teams to be deliberately overrun, although a small number of guerrillas were also air-dropped into the Allied rear.[50] Such initial efforts, however, did not produce much effect. One major problem was that the cultural character of the northern Rhineland made it the worst single spot in Germany to start a partisan war. In general, the population was possessed by anti-Prussian sentiments and had a cosmopolitan disdain for any form of rabid nationalism. The presence of a strongly Catholic majority – with an intense degree of confessional cohesion – had also prevented the NSDAP from developing much support in the area. In the last free elections in the fall of 1932, support for the Catholic Centre Party had held up better in the Rhineland than in any other area of Germany, and the electoral district of Cologne–Aachen was one of only two regions in which the Nazis failed to take at least 20 per cent of the vote.[51] In addition to these factors, the inhabitants of the big cities, such as Cologne, knew that the presence of the enemy in their towns meant the end of their targeting by Allied bombers, and for this deliverance they were happy to pay the price of foreign military occupation.[52] There were a few Nazi strongholds in the Rhineland, such as Koblenz, and there were some genuine Nazis, a number of whom traced their activism to the post–First World War resistance movement against Allied occupation and separatism.[53] As a rule, however, the fanatics had debouched for the east bank of the Rhine well before the arrival of the Allies. Left behind was a population that was lukewarm, at best, in its support of the Hitler regime, and was unalterably opposed to any manifestations of guerrilla warfare.[54]

In this kind of atmosphere, the partisans themselves were so demoralized that, when Werwolf galleries were overrun by the Allies, the guerrillas meekly surrendered. Most of the captives were only too willing to denounce fellow Werewolves still in the field, and they pliantly led American Army Counter-Intelligence Corps (CIC) officers to remaining 'strong points.' Other Werewolves fled into the surrounding countryside with the intention of drifting back into civilian life. Only in one case was a Werwolf gallery actually defended against American intruders, and in this instance two of the occupants were killed attempting to break out, while a third was captured. At Monschau, German parachutists were reported by local civilians and were 'turned in to [American] tactical units.'[55]

If there were any small successes in this region, they came in the Palatinate and the Saarland, the only areas on the west bank of the Rhine that had shown much enthusiasm for the NSDAP during the age when Germans had still been allowed to express independent political opinions. These areas had less of a

Catholic majority than districts to the north, and even the local Catholic population had the dubious distinction of being the most 'Nazified' Catholics in western Germany. Inhabitants of the southern Rhineland, farmers in particular, had long traditions of rural populism that had been successfully subsumed by the NSDAP, and they were also possessed by fears of French domination and annexationism – the French had occupied the Palatinate from 1918 to 1930 and had run the Saar as an economic protectorate, under loose League of Nations oversight, until 1935.[56] Thus, there was a conceivable base for Werwolf efforts,[57] and it is no surprise that unsettling 'incidents' occurred occasionally. At Saarlautern, innocuous-looking German civilians booby-trapped the billets of an American chemical mortar company and, at Neunkirchen, a bomb mounted on the springs of an American jeep blew up on the morning of 3 April, badly injuring two men.[58] At Bad Kreuznach, Werwolf cells managed to cajole the population into a fighting mood and, according to Supreme Headquarters, Allied Expeditionary Force (SHAEF), 'a considerable number of troops had to be diverted to eliminate sniping activity.' Several weeks later, in mid-April, a Werwolf organization was uncovered and the CIC made seventeen arrests.[59] This town was one of the few areas where the SS-Werwolf played an important role in the fighting, not only as a result of the diversionary effect of its operations, but also because Bad Kreuznach was a key road junction, where the Americans required good order so that they could push armoured units through to the Rhine and cut off the attempted withdrawal of the German Seventh and First armies.

Although the SS-Werwolf was subsequently extended into the inner *Wehrkreise*, it was never as well organized as it had been in the original borderland regions, mainly because Prützmann dallied on such organizational matters in order to spare the thought of Allied or Soviet penetrations into the German heartland. In Weimar, for instance, the commando chief Skorzeny inspected the local Werwolf in March 1945 and found it suffering from a variety of ills: some of the partisans had been conscripted; arms and ammunition were in short supply; no provision had been made for contacting higher echelons by radio; and the guerrillas had only a vague conception of their assignment.[60] In many areas, local party and police officials supposed to form the core of the organization often found themselves opposed to it in both practice and principle. In Vienna and Augsburg, the local *Gauleiter* refused to cooperate with the Werwolf; in Peine, the Kreisleitung cancelled a local Werwolf action by the HJ; in Leipzig, the police president ordered the criminal police to spy on the movement and report back to him.[61] In Austria, Allied intelligence officers later concluded that 'those charged with [Werwolf] activities did little more than talk, and tried, for the sake of their own safety, to give the impression that the orders were being obeyed.'[62] Bureaucracies are infamous for fumbling when they do their best; imagine what happens when they deliberately do their worst.

Despite these impediments, the Werwolf had a wider popular base in central Germany than in the Rhineland, which was noticeable as the Allies reached such areas as Lower Saxony, Hesse, and Württemberg, where the population as a whole was more hostile than in areas farther west. It is true that the Ruhr, with its Catholic, urban, and working-class character, was a poor bet to support Nazi resistance, and that the HSSPF West made few preparations for the region, aside from a vague intention to raise recruits by means of leafletting.[63] Elsewhere, however, areas east of the Rhine typically had Evangelical majorities, which meant the near-absence of the type of Catholic confessional loyalties that had watered down the resistance impulse in the Rhineland. As suggested by pre-1933 voting statistics, the NSDAP had established powerful strongholds in a stretch of moorlands running across Lower Saxony from the Dutch border to Altmark, and branching north to Schleswig–Holstein. These districts were inhabited by middling farmers who had traditionally supported agrarian protest movements and had been brought to their knees by the interwar agricultural crisis. Such homogeneous farmers' communities, where there was a limited understanding of the capitalist ethos and a lack of class tensions in the absence of large estates, were natural stamping-grounds for National Socialism. Even as early as 1928, the Nazis had made inroads in areas where legitimate nationalist-conservatism was weak, and where they were able to attract local notables to their banners. In addition, Naziism had a strong following in the Prussian 'new' states (i.e., those acquired after 1866), and in the old 'middle states,' such as Thuringia, where the party had been successful in transforming anti-Prussian particularist tendencies into a raw form of anti-modernism.[64] The particular geographic configuration of Allied bombing and the ground advance had done little to erode potential surliness. The population of the countryside and small cities of central Germany had escaped some of the murderous bombing and heavy fighting that had done so much to break the spirit of their compatriots living to the west. Allied non-fraternization and requisitioning policies encouraged further bad feeling, and German civilians, as a British observer noted, began 'scowling a hostility we have not seen before.'

Certainly, this change in tone was immediately felt by the advancing Americans. The U.S. Ninth Army reported that 'anti-Allied feeling is more marked in central Germany than in the Ruhr and Rhineland,' and that Lippe and Schaumburg–Lippe 'were more thoroughly Nazified than any other [provinces] that the Army had occupied ... It was almost impossible to find suitable personnel for the various governmental functions at the city, county, and provincial level.' In the Höxter district, Military Government officers noted 'that Nazism has penetrated ... much more than in the Rhineland ... The attitude is often sullen and uncooperative.' The historian of the 18th Infantry Division saw Hanover town as the dividing line in terms of sentiment – 'Along the Rhine, the white flags were plentiful and people quite freely expressed themselves against the Nazi regime, although it was always difficult to judge the sincerity of these sentiments. East of Hanover, however, the change was marked. White flags were scarce and more people in conversation identified themselves with the Nazi regime.'[65]

Even here, where the population was unfriendly, there was little appetite for guerrilla warfare,[66] and the party had long abused its support, even among elements that had originally boosted it, especially because of its hostility towards religion, its control policies in agriculture, its corruption, and its failure to protect the skies above Germany. Ian Kershaw is right in contending, however, that these negative factors were nearly balanced, at least among the peasantry and the middle classes, by an increasing sense of integration.[67] Certainly, the number of Werwolf 'incidents' began to escalate. In early April, an American military surgeon was bushwhacked after he left camp in order to help German civilians near Haltern, in Westphalia. U.S. troops investigating the incident later found the physician's driver shot dead, while both the doctor and the jeep seemed to have disappeared into the ether. In the countryside north of Magdeburg, an artillery liaison pilot and his driver were killed by machine-gun and bazooka fire as their jeep drove along a road in a rear area. On the Elbe, a trooper from the U.S. 161st Field Artillery Battalion was captured by Germans, who took his name, rank, and serial number, and then shot him in the leg; in Bavaria, an American soldier was similarly kidnapped by two civilian Werewolves, who applied lit cigarettes to his face in an attempt to make him reveal American troop dispositions.[68]

Werewolves in central Germany also made inventive use of booby-traps; American jeeps, for instance, were occasionally blown up by bombs placed under their chassis.[69] Werewolves also laid land-mines and strung 'decapitation wires,' which were neck-level bands of cord stretched tightly across thoroughfares likely to be traversed by Allied motorcycles or light vehicles. On the Miehlen–Bettendorf route, in the Taunus, two riders in an American truck were injured on 1 April when the vehicle struck a wire and detonated two charges on the road shoulder, and mines planted by young civilians were similarly found on railways, highways, and bridges in Frankfurt.[70] Such tactics were also in evidence at Dannenberg, a long-time Nazi bastion near the Elbe River. Allied truck drivers in this area found that roads behind the lines were strewn with mines, even roads that were marked as clear. One teamster noted: 'I was driving my jeep with a trailer loaded with ammunition, following another jeep by about 150 yards when I saw the jeep hit a mine. The explosion killed Private First Class Ed Wolicki and injured another Company B driver. In the same area I was lucky enough to notice a wire strung across the road. It was strong enough to decapitate a person. Those weren't the only cases like that for we found others. In this instance, we had previously driven over the same road a few hours earlier without finding any trouble.' Several weeks later, a number of Werewolves were captured in this same vicinity.[71] In the western suburbs of Bremen, newly arrived British troops caught several parties of civilians laying mines, and one of these desperate Werewolves foolhardily engaged a British armoured car with a pistol, only to be mowed down by the vehicle's Besa.[72]

Another favourite Werwolf tactic was to interfere with enemy communication lines by blowing up bridges. At Laubach, in Hesse, and Vlotho, in Westphalia, bridges behind Allied lines were demolished, and at Münden, north of Kassel, several young guerrillas were arrested, while skulking around a bridge, in possession of a notched pistol and a supply of explosives. In Düsseldorf, a saboteur cut the moorings of a coal barge in the early-morning hours of 27 April, whereafter the vessel was carried swiftly down the Rhine by the spring freshet and smashed into an American pontoon span, causing extensive damage.[73]

Particular mention must be made of two regions in the interior that were distinguished by Herculean efforts, especially by Prützmann's personal intervention in overriding the prerogative of the local HSSPF to choose their own Werwolf commanders. In both these areas, Prützmann chose his own officials, who took orders directly from him rather than from the regional HSSPF.

One of these cases was Wehrkreis XIII, Franconia, which in the Nazi view required an extra measure of guerrilla activity to befit its reputation as the spiritual centre of National Socialism. Middle and Upper Franconia were populated by Evangelical majorities that had formed some of the NSDAP's earliest and strongest bases of support, particularly because the party had been wily enough to exploit regional antagonisms against the Catholic political establishment in Bavaria. Even in 1945, National Socialism retained a vigorous local following; SHAEF's Civil Affairs/Military Government branch (G-5) reported that the population of Nuremberg was 'openly pro-Nazi.' The case of Lower Franconia was more problematic: this area was inhabited by a heavily Catholic majority who had long been loyal to the cause of Catholic Bavarian particularism and, at best, were late converts to National Socialism. However, even here, party membership sky-rocketed in the years 1933–5, so that, by the latter year, the region had the highest per-capita proportion of 'March converts' in the entire Reich.[74]

With such favourable factors in mind, the Franconian HSSPF, Benno Martin, was ordered in February 1945 to appoint a 'Werwolf Commissioner,' but Martin stood true to the Nazi code of unwarranted optimism – believing the Allies would never reach his *Wehrkreis* – and therefore delayed the posting until early April. Although a local SS-Police official was finally appointed, Prützmann immediately intervened and replaced the local choice with Dr Hans Weibgen, a fanatic Nazi answerable directly to the Bureau 'Prützmann.' Weibgen quickly imported some of his own people into the embattled region, including two SS officers from Berlin, who were supposed to prepare the Nuremberg Gestapo for 'the coming Freedom Movement.'[75]

Not surprisingly, the major cities along the Main River were protected with fanatic tenacity, by both soldiers and civilians, and *Völkischer Beobachter* bragged that here 'in the Frankish heartland of Europe,' German defensive efforts were 'especially tough and unwavering.' At Aschaffenburg, in Lower Franconia, the local *Kreisleiter* formed the entire population into Battle Groups, pledging 'unlimited hatred for the cursed enemy.' Children appeared at rooftops and second-storey windows in order to snipe and toss grenades at U.S. infantrymen, which forced the Americans to call in heavy armour and fighter-bombers in order to pummel Nazi strongholds. Commanders of the U.S. Seventh Army gave orders for the community to be 'annihilated,' and the defenders surrendered only after a week of heavy fighting. Veterans of the 45th Infantry Division, which had been bloodied in Sicily, Italy, and Alsace, grimly reported that the combat at Aschaffenburg was the most brutal yet encountered.[76]

Similar opposition met the advancing Americans forty miles to the southeast, at Würzburg, which had already been largely destroyed in a horrific fire-bombing in 1944. When U.S. forces kicked their way into the city, Werewolves and Volkssturm men retreated into subterranean tunnels and resurfaced in the rear of American forces, attacking them from behind. After two days of heavy combat, Würzburg fell to troops of the U.S. Seventh Army on 5 April, and surviving Wehrmacht units fled the city. However, the fanatic *Oberbürgermeister*, who had lost his son in the battle, refused to capitulate, and called upon local civilians to maintain resistance. A day later the final civilian-resistance nests in Steinberg and the Bismarck Woods were blasted into oblivion by American fighter-bombers and artillery, and the American conquest of the city was complete. There was no formal surrender because all the defenders were either killed or captured in battle.[77]

The same sequence again repeated itself in Middle Franconia, particularly at Nuremberg, home of the infamous NSDAP rallies. The local Gestapo was trained for guerrilla warfare, although such preparations were admittedly hampered by the frequency of enemy air attacks, a shortage of weapons, and increased cuts in electrical current. The local *Wehrkreis* commander, Weisenberger, was favourably inclined towards the Werwolf, and reportedly allowed

large stocks of equipment to be withdrawn from military armouries. The Gauleitung also levied civilian men and women in a so-called people's call-up, and
Nurembergers were told, in true Werwolf fashion, that 'if we have no weapons,
then we will bound upon the Americans and bite their throats ... '[78]

The bitter struggle subsequently fought in the city fully matched its billing.
As American units smashed their way into the inner city on 19 April, they met
intense civilian resistance grouped around stalwart troops of the SS 17th Infantry Division. Boys of fourteen desperately sniped or tossed hand-grenades at the
invaders, and a few civilians without weapons lunged at the enemy with pick
handles and axes. Because civilian snipers hid in spider holes, and then fired at
the backs of the advancing Americans, rear areas had to be continually combed
and then combed, again. Despite all such efforts, however, the core of the Franconian capital fell on the morning of 20 April – Hitler's fifty-sixth birthday –
after a savage four-day battle. Almost all the senior civil and NSDAP officials
in the city had committed suicide.[79]

A second area of particular concentration for the Werwolf was the Alpine
region of Tyrol–Voralberg, particularly after March 1945, when Hitler reportedly ordered Prützmann to prepare the Werwolf for a long fight and, if neces-
sary, to retreat into the Austrian Alps in order to join the SS for a last stand.[80]
The 'Werwolf Commissioner' in the area (Wehrkreis XVIII) was Captain
Anton Mair, but the Tyrol–Voralberg was independently controlled by SS-
Major Kurreck, who, like Tschiersky, had been transferred to Werwolf from
Operation 'Zeppelin.' Kurreck was appointed in late 1944, and although
attached to the staff of Gauleiter Hofer, he was responsible directly to the
Bureau 'Prützmann.' Mair also reported directly to Prützmann after his HSSPF,
SS-General Rösener, showed signs in April 1945 of wanting to abandon the
Werwolf project.[81]

Although Tyrol–Voralberg was the heart of the so-called Alpine Redoubt, the
northern and northeastern approaches to the area – namely, Wehrkreise XVII
(Northern Austria) and VII (Southern Bavaria) – received lesser attention. Preparations in the former were begun in January 1945, under HSSPF Schimana and
Werwolf Commissioner Fahrion,[82] and in the latter only in late March 1945,
under HSSPF von Eberstein and Werwolf Commissioner Wagner. These
extremely tardy preparations on the northern edge of the redoubt suggest that
the Nazis were surprised by the rate of the Allied thrust into central Germany,
and because of this delay neither von Eberstein nor Wagner had much hope for
the success of the organization in the Bavarian Alps. In fact, the period of time
from Wagner's appointment (13 April) until the day when he fled from office in
the face of the American advance (28 April) was a mere two weeks.

After appointing Wagner, von Eberstein – a moderate who was well liked in

Munich – had hoped to have rid himself of the whole distasteful Werwolf matter. However, he was disconcerted to find that he would not be allowed to fade away in true soldierly fashion, thus avoiding the scrutiny of the advancing Allied forces. Because of American drives that had nearly sundered the Reich in two by mid-April, most central Reich offices were being split into autonomous northern and southern sections, and the unenthusiastic von Eberstein, on the strength of his reputation as a 'veteran Nazi fighter,' found himself chosen as plenipotentiary for the entire southern component of the SS-Werwolf. When SA-Brigadier Karl Siebel arrived with news of this unwanted promotion on 20 April, von Eberstein was aghast and refused to accept the order unless it was put into written form, something which Siebel could not immediately produce. By the time that Siebel got back to von Eberstein, who by now had been chased out of Munich and set up headquarters in a town on the Sternbergersee, his name had been withdrawn for the appointment. In fact, von Eberstein had also been replaced as HSSPF for southern Bavaria, effective 20 April 1945, and his place was taken by a more fanatical Nazi. Siebel himself assumed the post of Alpine plenipotentiary for the Werwolf, and in view of the obvious recalcitrance of the southern Bavarians, the fanatical Weibgen was given a wider sphere of responsibility as Franconian 'Werwolf Commissioner,' taking further areas of Bavaria under his control.[83]

Organizational Problems

Before fully considering these final days, however, the narrative must first return to the more general problems contributing to this ultimate collapse – problems which lay, at least part, in the inadequacy of the Werwolf's bureaucratic foundation. A Wehrmacht document noted, for instance, that 'the Werwolf has no provisionment organization nor will one be built ...,'[84] so it was clear that the organization was totally dependent in such matters upon the Army, the Waffen-SS, and such RSHA sabotage groups as Skorzeny's 'SS Ranger Units' and FAK formations. Supplies were also drawn from the Nazi welfare agency, the National Socialist People's Welfare Organization (NSV). Transportation was supposedly provided by the HSSPF's own 'K-Staff,' or Motor Pool.[85]

Obviously, this system depended essentially upon the goodwill of quartermasters among the agencies involved, and it therefore quickly broke down. By the final year of the war, the various German armed forces faced such severe shortages that they were unlikely to pass on supplies willingly to a nebulous partisan organization. Skorzeny's SS 'Ranger Units,' for instance, were struggling to bring about their own activation, and at this formative stage were hardly likely to offer enthusiastic support to their rival. Skorzeny told his Supply Officer that Prützmann's representatives could be given 10 to 20 per cent of SS 'Ranger' stocks, but in no circumstances would their own interests be jeopardized to maintain an adequate flow of supply to the Werwolf. All difficulties were supposed to be reported to Skorzeny's headquarters at Friedenthal, and eventually complaints arrived from each SS 'Ranger' unit regarding 'exorbitant demands' by Werwolf organizers. Skorzeny categorically refused each such request.[86]

The regional HSSPF frequently complained about lack of supplies, even in the critical Alpine Redoubt, although a concerted effort was made to send weapons, food, and treasure into this region, all of which were subsequently hidden in secret caches and caves.[87] Allied intelligence reports noted that Werwolf supplies were 'in many areas completely inadequate,' and that, if the SS partisans had hoped to operate effectively, they would have been forced to depend largely on supplies salvaged from abandoned Wehrmacht ordnance depots or stolen from the enemy.[88] Prützmann's only limited success in this field was attained by following Skorzeny's advice to get supplies directly from local munitions plants. This method at least ran on a first-come-first-served basis,[89] and thereby eliminated the severe difficulties of long-distance transportation.[90] There is also some evidence that the Army and the Armaments Ministry sometimes attempted to hinder the delivery of supplies to the Werwolf,[91] presumably in an effort to defang the organization, although it is not clear how much this obstructionist manoeuvre was actually responsible for shortages.

The recruitment and training system was a similar jumble, euphemistically described as the 'snowball system' because the movement was supposed to grow as it gained momentum.[92] Because the Werwolf lacked exclusive rights to any specific pool of personnel, it once again ended up with the leftovers sent to it by other agencies. Originally, this recruitment hodgepodge consisted of five basic mustering channels:

1 / The Waffen-SS: 'Recruiting Commissions' of the SS-Main Office toured local offices of the HJ, the SA, and various other party agencies, from which volunteers were obtained and then examined by a 'Mustering Commission.' Party chiefs in the borderland *Gaue* were also instructed to provide a list of recommended volunteers to the local HSSPF, the recruits thereafter being called-up through Waffen-SS 'Recruiting Offices.' As well, some Waffen-SS divisions apparently set up special 'Demobilization Centres,' where SS volunteers were equipped with phoney demobilization papers and civilian clothes, then secretly posted to underground service against the enemy occupation forces. Literally thousands of these men were rounded up by the

Americans in mid-April 1945 (one of whom told his captors that he had no desire to be a Werwolf). Many of the sergeants and junior officers of the Werwolf were also seconded from the Waffen-SS, as were all of the organization's medics.[93]

The problem with this system was that there was no incentive to send first-rate people to the Werwolf; thus the Waffen-SS naturally kept the best young men for its own units, while the *Gauleiter* also reserved suitable recruits for the party's own system of local defence – namely, the Volkssturm.[94] A notable example of this problem involved a fierce skirmish in the spring of 1945 between the Waffen-SS and the Werwolf, fought entirely over recruitment. Werwolf officers in Wehrkreis XII apparently convinced officials in the local SS recruiting office in Wiesbaden that the Werwolf had been given exclusive rights to several classes of HJ trained at a local camp, and to the 1927 class of the local Reich Labour Service, most of whom would have normally gone to the Waffen-SS. With 2,000 to 3,000 young recruits at stake, this was a considerable acheivement for the local Werwolf. However, this news soon reached the ears of the Waffen-SS overlord, SS-General Berger, who swiftly radioed the local HSSPF, Stroop, and forbade him to hand over any of 'his boys' to the Werwolf.[95]

2 / The Army: In the autumn of 1944, a number of men were released by the Army for partisan training, and a limited number of soldiers were also provided by the divisions and corps in the borderland districts, and by the Army weapons schools. The most valuable military recruits were those with technical qualifications, such as radio operators, although most Army personnel attached to the Werwolf had only recently been inducted, and were passed on to Werwolf training schools immediately after basic training.[96]

3 / The RSHA: This medium of recruitment ran through the regional Security Police Commanders (BdS), who controlled local offices of the Gestapo, the SD, and the Criminal Police (Kripo), and who were subordinate to the HSSPF under the 'special tasks' chain of command running downward from Himmler. The first BdS appeal for Werwolf recruits was issued at Düsseldorf in mid-September 1944, and called for 'old party members' willing to undergo a demolitions course, and thereafter cause damage in the enemy rear. Unlike the other two recruitment channels, this one had considerable success, mainly because the kind of Gestapo and SD men thus attracted to the Werwolf banner were often so hopelessly compromised that the idea of surrender was unbearable: the Werwolf thus became something of an alternative means of suicide. The SD, in particular, found its offices in eastern

Germany drained by BdS recruitment campaigns for the Werwolf and other last-minute defence measures. Once recruited, such elements frequently tended to organize themselves as a group apart from recruits who had been stampeded into the organization, and they apparently regarded themselves as the cream of the Werwolf crop.[97]

4 / Refugees from the Russian-occupied East: This body of recruits lay among the large numbers of evacuees from Soviet-occupied zones, a group solicited with a request for 'volunteers for special employment in the interior of the country.' It is not clear what medium was used to select and approach these eastern refugees, although it is known that the NSV was instructed to give all possible aid to recruitment efforts. It is also known that an SS officer attached to the Bureau 'Prützmann' toured Bohemia–Moravia in March 1945, encouraging the recruitment of evacuees from Silesia and the Riesengebirge.[98] At least one such Werwolf unit, composed of Silesian women thirsting for revenge, was deployed with bazookas in the Battle of Berlin.[99]

5 / Priests and former priests: Nazi leaders hoped prelates would be willing to fight the Soviets on the basis of religious principle as well as ideological fervour. This brainwave was suggested by Himmler himself, who 'felt [that] a number of former Catholic clerics could perhaps be disguised as clergy behind the Russian lines; surely they would still understand their priestly business.' At the party chancellery, officials even suggested founding 'a new Catholic order with the objective of saving Christianity before Bolshevism' – a kind of twentieth-century revival of the Teutonic Knights. It was also felt that if the Vatican failed to give sanction, there were independent Catholic groups that would work together with the Reich, even without the licence of Rome.

Not surprisingly, the Soviets, Poles, and Czechs subsequently arrested scores of German priests and other religious leaders on the charge that they organized resistance. In most cases these claims were simply a pretext to harass a prominent segment of the intelligentsia, which, by its very nature, was anti-Communist. On the other hand, there were some instances where genuine evidence seemed to implicate clerical activists – the proverbial wolves in sheep's clothing. In Bohemia, the returning Czech authorities found several monasteries hiding Werwolf and Volkssturm supply caches, and the monks were allegedly involved in resistance activities. A CIC unit at Marienbad confirmed that weapons, explosives, Nazi propaganda material, and radio-transmitting equipment were all uncovered at the Tepl Monastery, near Pilsen.[100]

It must also be noted that the HJ also controlled its own semi-autonomous wing of the organization, which in turn had its own system of recruitment, about which more will said in chapter 2.

This scatter-shot method of recruitment generally did not produce good results. The number of recruits, in the first place, was simply insufficient and, until the last month of the war, total membership in the organization probably never exceeded 5,000 or 6,000 guerrillas.[101] In fact, Prützmann and Siebel both complained vigorously about the lack of partisan trainees, particularly those who were already skilled radio operators or scouts, and SS recruiters were occasionally heard to tell Army officers that the enlistment of volunteers was extremely difficult.[102] Recruiters, therefore, resorted to such expediencies as conscription, particularly of older recruits,[103] and the tricking of would-be volunteers by providing a purposefully vague or fallacious description of the activities that Werewolves would be called upon to perform.[104] These practices naturally led to problems when the conscripts and deluded volunteers found out what was really expected of them, such as penetrating enemy lines in civilian clothes, or accepting ampoules of poison to swallow in case of impending capture. Many of the recruits subsequently deserted or refused to undergo training, and Himmler reacted by threatening drop-outs with a concentration-camp sentence.[105]

Recruits, both willing and unwilling, were trained by Wehrmacht, Waffen-SS, and SS 'Ranger' officers, usually veterans of anti-partisan warfare in the East, although a largely abortive effort was also made to recruit interwar 'Field Rangers' as instructors. Instruction was conducted at HJ and Waffen-SS schools, and Skorzeny was also forced to share his SS 'Ranger' training camps at Friedenthal, Neustrelitz, Kileschnowitz, and Kloster Tiefenthal. The entire program was coordinated with the chief of SS-Anti-Partisan Units, and SS-Major Erhardt, on this staff, was frequently in liaison with the Bureau 'Prütz-mann' and with the Training Section of the Army High Command (OKH).

The courses given under this regime were based on translations of Soviet guerrilla training manuals, although in January 1945 a comprehensive German manual was printed under the title *Werwolf: Winke für Jagdeinheiten* (Werwolf: Tips for Ranger Units). Courses were given in sabotage, Morse, wireless transmission, terrain reconnaissance, and assassination techniques, plus all the usual regimens of drill, athletics, and speed marching. At the Werwolf camp outside Passau, field exercises involved firing live ammunition at Werwolf recruits. Female agents were specially trained to act as spies while serving as clerks and secretaries in Military Government offices. Each recruit was deprived of ID papers, not only to prevent identification by the Allies in case of capture, but also to deprive him or her of individuality, and thus to accentuate total surrender to the aims of the organization. In place of his or her own name and life history, the recruit received a new identity, complete with Waffen-SS pay book and dog tags.[106] Each new pupil was also required to sign a pledge:

1. I bind myself to take part in the operations of the Werwolf.
2. I acknowledge that any surrender whatsoever of the explosive materials to the American authorities will be punished by death.
3. After the retreat of the German front I am to be accountable for the boxes which have been left behind.
4. Mention of the course which has taken place will be considered treason and punished accordingly.
5. A cowardly reluctance during the period of occupation will likewise be punished.

Reichsführer – SS   Höhere SS und
Heinrich Himmler   Polizei Führer West
                                     [Signature of the enrollee]

It is interesting to note that this pledge, unlike the military oath to Hitler, was not directed towards an individual but to the organization itself, and to the principle of national resistance.[107]

Despite the fact that training was tough, it was also very short, ranging anywhere from five days to five weeks. Considering all the topics covered, even the longest of these courses was extremely crammed. The Western Allies decided, upon the basis of preliminary contact with the Werwolf, that guerrilla training had been 'hurried and superficial,' although the Soviets saw matters from a different perspective. They had long been subjected to the deployment of waves of half-trained Ukrainian, Baltic, and Belorussian agents in their rear areas, and they suggested that the training of German sabotage teams actually improved during the last year of the war (although the overall number of saboteurs decreased).[108] Whatever the merits of this comparison, Prützmann believed that training was not as complete as it could have been, and on several occasions he complained to Skorzeny that the instruction given by SS 'Ranger' officers was insufficient in detail. The commando chief replied that, given time limits and the pressure on SS 'Ranger' personnel for other duties, more complete courses were impossible to provide.[109]

It should also be noted that the SS 'Rangers' usually taught only Werwolf group leaders, and that the instruction received by the rank and file was probably even less thorough. FAK officers who visited a Werwolf unit near Stettin in March 1945, for instance, noted that there was a significant lack of trained instructors, and that, as a result, extra strain was put upon officers leading Werwolf groups behind Soviet lines. At the Sudeten town of Kaaden, a flak defence guard half-finished a training course for a band of young girls before she even realized, to her horror, that she was training a Werwolf unit.[110]

Since these myriad difficulties in training – not to mention recruitment and supply – were, at least in part, caused by the Werwolf's lack of a firm bureaucratic base, it soon became obvious that the organization could not properly establish itself without the patronage of a well-grounded military or paramilitary agency that could hold its own amid a desperate struggle for resources. Himmler, with his eye for bureaucratic detail, seems to have grasped this underlying factor, and during a meeting of SS security chiefs in November 1944 he actually offered control of the Werwolf to Skorzeny, a proposition that would have kept the Werwolf firmly within the SS orbit. Prützmann, who was present, reportedly lowered his head and uncomfortably shuffled his papers, but Skorzeny refused the assignment respectfully, saying he already had more than enough work to fill his time.[111] It is apparent that Skorzeny thought that the Werwolf was an inefficient and unnecessary duplication of his own SS 'Ranger' program,[112] into which he had invested much time and effort, and it is possible that he also believed that the latter would eventually replace the Werwolf, being converted into a full-scale guerrilla organization.

While Skorzeny did not take control of the Werwolf, he did negotiate a number of agreements with Prützmann that ensured FAK participation in the deployment of Werwolf groups. FAK units were told to provide the Werwolf with training officers and give limited access to FAK supplies, particularly on the Eastern Front, for which they were reciprocally given partial operational control of Werwolf activity.[113] Similar agreements were negotiated between Prützmann and the military High Command on the Eastern Front.

Werwolf Terrorism

With operational control of the Werwolf slipping through his fingers, Prützmann gradually turned to more eclectic pursuits, such as the possibility of mass-murder by poison. This idea was actually an updated version of the ancient trick of poisoning the wells, always the centre-piece of any 'scorched earth' campaign. The RSHA had already begun the production of poisons for food and alcohol in the fall of 1944, and in October a conference on the matter was held at an SS-Police research centre in Berlin called the 'Criminal Technical Institute' (KTI). Prützmann apparently took an immediate interest in the matter, particularly since the KTI was already a source of suicide ampoules for the use of Werewolves themselves. In fact, before long the entire project was turned over to the purview of Department IVb of the Bureau 'Prützmann,' along with large quantities of poisons. By early 1945, tests on the injection of lethal doses of methyl into alcohol had been carried out – this had already been decided upon during the October conference as the best means of poisoning liquor – and further tests on more exotic chemicals were under way.[114]

Knowledge of such poisoning methods was widely disseminated among potential Nazi resisters, and special squads were dispatched along both the Western and the Eastern fronts, the task of which was to poison liquor and food likely to be consumed by Allied and Soviet troops.[115] Unfortunately, this was probably the most successful of all Werwolf programs, at least in terms of a body count, and its effect lingered well into the postwar period. The Surgeon General of U.S. forces in Europe reported that, from February to July 1945, 188 soldiers were killed by methyl alcohol in liquor, and as late as 1946 two U.S. soldiers in Ludwigsburg died from consuming schnapps so loaded with harmful ingredients that the authorities considered its sale 'an organized form of sabotage.' In response, the American Command ordered U.S. forces in southern Germany not to use captured German foodstuffs, even if they outran their supply units. Losses among Soviet troops in Eastern Europe were probably even higher than those among the Western Allies, and Red Army headquarters in Austria issued a warning to Russian troops in the summer of 1945, noting that 'many fatal casualties' had resulted from consumption of toxic spirits left behind by 'the Hitlerite scoundrels.'[116]

Meanwhile, the Germans also somehow discovered that SHAEF had authorized the possible use of non-lethal gases against Werwolf detachments or other German forces holding out after the cessation of 'organized resistance.' Naturally, this discovery gave a boost to Nazi Jacobins, such as Goebbels, who were looking for an opportunity to make use of Germany's own stocks of poison gas.[117] Thus, in the last weeks of the war, the Armaments Ministry came under pressure to transfer such substances to the Werwolf and other guerrilla groups. In a postwar interview, Albert Speer apparently told British interrogators that Werwolf officials were forwarded from his agency to the Wehrmacht Ordnance Department, which supplied the deadly material. There is no evidence that these stocks were actually used by the Werwolf or any other military group, although advancing Allied forces did discover underground caches of poison gas and other chemical-warfare substances, as well as secret pilot plants seemingly designed to begin the further production of such material after enemy occupation. I.G. Farben had produced these stocks of poison gas, as well as a highly flammable liquid called 'N-Stoff,' which burst into flames upon contact and emitted noxious fumes.[118]

The Werwolf was also involved with such seamy activities as assassinations and intimidations by threat of violence. In October 1944, Himmler enacted a decree that forbade unevacuated civil officials in enemy territory from performing 'any service to the enemy,' although the provision of essential administrative and welfare services for the remaining population was permitted. This decree was soon supplemented by secret orders to the HSSPF West, Karl Gutenberger, authorizing 'our organization behind the American Front to execute death sentences upon traitors.' Nazi hierarchs subsequently began singling out officials in the occupied territories who incurred their displeasure and were made the object of Vehme assassination teams, and it was rumoured that all *Bürgermeister* in the Rhineland were slated for elimination. Some of these conspiracies failed to come to fruition. For instance, Werwolf 'hit' teams were sent to stalk the German-Jewish police president of Cologne, Karl Winkler, and the *Bürgermeister* of Goebbels's home town of Rheydt, but in neither of these cases did the Vehme detachments get within range of their targets. At Landau, in the Palatinate, a band of youths threatened the police chief with death, but the French arrested six teenage terrorists before any trouble could occur.[119]

On the other hand, there were a number of instances in late March and April 1945 where civil officials in Allied- and Soviet-occupied territory were liquidated by Werwolf assassins. In Westphalia, American-appointed mayors at Krankenhagen and Kirchlengern were killed by Werwolf murderers, and in the Russian-occupied outskirts of Berlin, policemen who had failed to stop the hoisting of white flags were similarly laid low.[120] The single most important Vehme mission, Operation 'Carnival,' was undertaken against Franz Oppenhoff, *Oberbürgermeister* of the ancient imperial capital of Aachen. This assignment was originally given to the SS 'Rangers,' but they referred it back to the Werwolf on the grounds that it was a domestic Reich matter, and thus beyond their purview. Prützmann subsequently ordered the HSSPF West to assemble a special detachment, and Gutenberger, in turn, picked a former SS 'Ranger' volunteer, Lieutenant Herbert Wenzel, who put together his own small team. This unit was dropped by parachute into the Maastricht panhandle of The Netherlands on the night of 20 March, after which they crossed the German frontier, in the process killing a Dutch border guard. Five days later, several members of the unit approached Oppenhoff's home and, disguised as downed German airmen, sought out the hapless mayor and shot him through the head.[121] The ironic side to this story is that Oppenhoff himself had frequently been criticized by the Allies for giving Nazis jobs in his administration, and only under direct pressure from one of President Roosevelt's envoys did he reform the civic government in early March 1945.[122]

The effect of outrages like the Oppenhoff killing was immediately noticeable. Even in Aachen, it had been difficult to find a suitable candidate brave enough to accept the mayoralty, and after the *Oberbürgermeister*'s killing, the task became even harder, both in Rhenish towns that had been occupied for some time and in newly occupied communities in central Germany. Some people who had accepted appointments heard about the Werwolf and were too frightened to ever show up for work.[123] Moreover, in Nazi-held territory, civic officials who were preparing for the Allied advance also became alarmed about Werwolf activities; in Stuttgart, Oberbürgermeister Strölin wrote to the local HSSPF, Hofmann, claiming that a continuation of city government was provided for in Himmler's 1944 directive, and that clear guidelines were needed regarding the propriety of performing administrative tasks in occupied areas. It was bad enough, Strölin noted, that civic officials might bear the brunt of Allied reprisals against the 'Freedom Movement,' without these same officials being the target of the movement itself. In fact, Strölin feared that he himself was already being stalked.[124]

Officials like Strölin had good reason for worry,[125] particularly since, even in Nazi-held territory, the Werwolf functioned as a strong-arm unit for advocates of Hitler's 'scorched earth' resistance. The direct and indirect connivance of the collapsing regime in such activity thus gave the Werewolves an aspect not unlike that of 'death squads' later characteristic of right-wing terrorism in Latin America. Werewolves were instructed that 'traitors' were fair game even in areas not yet occupied by the enemy,[126] with the rationalization that such elements would in future hinder the construction of a resistance movement. Thus, in certain regions the 'Werwolf' theme became a virtual licence for the extrajudicial suppression of dissidents by the party (about which more will be said in chapter 4).

This expanded role for the Werwolf resulted directly from the disastrous collapse of morale and the obvious lack of any capacity for further national resistance, obvious even among the middle and lower strata of the NSDAP that formed the usual bulwark of the regime. It also formed the logical culmination of the overall SS drive against 'traitors,' a campaign that had burned hot since the 20 July putsch attempt. A tendency towards authoritarian vigilantism, even within party ranks, became evident in August 1944, when Bormann suspended the proceedings of party courts in favour of summary judgments by competent political leaders.[127] Thereafter, the legalized arbitrariness of the Nazi system quickly degenerated into an open, extrajudicial capriciousness – the terror from below. Drum-head courts-martial accelerated within the military, and, as the front slipped backward into German territory, the differences between civil and military justice all but disappeared. On 13 February 1945, the Justice Ministry authorized 'Summary Courts in Areas of the Reich Threatened by the Enemy,' and an HJ memorandum later in the month recommended that wavering officials be shot – even, if necessary, by their subordinates. Bormann found this latter document so essential – given the state of morale – that he circulated it among his *Gauleiter*.[128] Finally came extralegal 'Flag Orders,' which stipulated that anyone flying a white flag was subject to immediate execution.[129] National Socialism, as Sebastian Haffner notes, had turned upon the Germans themselves as its final victim: if the population would not faithfully participate in a true 'people's war,' then it would be punished in a final flurry of destruction.[130]

The more zealous members of the Werwolf naturally thrived within such a climate, and beginning in March 1945 they were found freely smearing town walls with such fearsome sayings as 'Beware traitor, the Werwolf watches' and 'Whoever deserts the Führer will be hanged as a traitor.' Red Werwolf runes began to appear on the doors of would-be collaborators.[131] Moreover, Vehme units went on a killing spree, executing deserters, political unreliables, and mayors or civil servants who had the gall to prepare for the continuation of civil life with a modicum of destruction. All were shot or hanged, and their bodies tagged with Werwolf warning notes. Werewolves under the HSSPF West were suspected of complicity in the assassination of a senior German officer, General Diether Korst, and the Frisian Werwolf was rumoured to have stalked the police chief of Bremen, Major-General Schroers (although he was never attacked). On 28 March, the *Bürgermeister* of the eastern Ruhr town of Meschede was assassinated, even though Meschede was still behind German lines and was not overrun until two weeks later. Werwolf Radio later announced that the mayor had been killed by the Werwolf. Werewolves were especially active in Augsburg during the last few days before the city fell to the Americans: on 26 April, a Werwolf sniper fired a shot at the co-leader of the German Freedom Movement of Augsburg, grazing him in the temple, and two days later a Werwolf squad – made up of stragglers from the 407th Infantry Division – summarily executed a 'defeatist.'[132]

In western Germany, priests were special targets because of the suspicion that many of them would preach a doctrine of Christian conciliation with the Allies, and because of the recognition that, once the Nazi administration was evacuated or destroyed, the Church would be left as the only institution capable of mediating between the victors and the vanquished population. 'There will be,' said Goebbels, 'a good field of activity for our terror groups here.'[133] Not surprisingly, several priests were attacked, and some who were not were warned to maintain a hostile posture towards 'the murderers of our wives and children.'[134]

Finally, the frenzy began to feed even upon the party itself (a fate which seems a rather common affliction of revolutionary movements throughout history). Werewolves tracked down party officials who had fled their posts in the face of danger, which was hardly a rare occurrence in 1944–5. Near Lüneburg, where a party leader was caught attempting to sneak away from the village of Kirchhorst, the official in question was executed on the spot by Werewolves from his own staff.[135] Werewolves also loomed behind local NSDAP leaders who considered minimizing the destructiveness of the collapse. At Ingelheim, the Volkssturm commander, a 'veteran Nazi fighter' named Berndes, was lynched by party vigilantes after he had attempted to hinder the defence efforts of 'unresponsible elements, in particular the young.' A placard was affixed to his body, saying, 'So dies anyone who betrays the Fatherland.'[136] No less a figure than Franz Hofer, the political chief of the Alpine Redoubt, was threatened with Werwolf retaliation after he called publicly for the cancellation of defence measures for Innsbruck.[137] Similarly, in south Germany, the *Kreisleiter* of Donauwörth, Philipp Meyer, had to go to ground after he discovered he was being stalked by two Werwolf officers sent from Hesse. He, too, had supported efforts to minimize chaos at the time of collapse, much to the detriment of defence efforts.[138] Major party dissidents, such as the armaments minister, Albert Speer, and the *Gauleiter* of Hamburg, Karl Kaufmann, were forced to build personal-guard units as a defence against Nazi terrorists. 'The Wehrwolf's activities,' the British were later told by Speer, 'were directed against people like him more than against the Americans.'[139]

Nazi terrorists were also needed to augment the Wehrmacht, which stubbornly baulked at carrying out Hitler's infamous 'scorched earth' decrees. On 19 March, the *Gauleiter* were given partial responsibility for the destruction of industrial enterprises and elements of the infrastructure of possible use to the enemy, thus unbounding the raw anti-industrialism so long dormant within National Socialism. Like a twentieth-century Ned Ludd, Prützmann dutifully visited German industrialists to discuss the uncomfortable possibility of placing saboteurs within factories to make sure that they were destroyed before the arrival of the Allies or the Soviets.[140] Volkssturm and Werwolf 'Demolition Troops' were trained and deployed, and these saboteurs occasionally became involved in mêlées with outraged workers who angrily defended the nation's industries and its economic infrastructure. In the Lichtenburg borough of Berlin, for instance, a Werwolf 'Demolition Group' showed up at the district waterworks with a bomb, but they were chased off by one-time trade-unionists organized by a local pastor.[141]

The first area so affected was Upper Silesia, where the Gauleitung and the SS had prepared their own demolition plans long before Hitler's March 1945 decree. When the 1945 Winter Offensive began, Werwolf groups spread throughout the province, equipped with a mandate from the *Gauleiter* to destroy factories, mines, and bridges. However, two factors minimized the destruction. First, the Soviets advanced so quickly that there was little time for demolitions or dismantling. Second, Silesian German workers, not certain that the Soviets and Poles would deport them, worked hard to prevent the destruction of the material basis for their own future prosperity. When Werwolf demolition crews showed up, they were often confronted by 'spontaneous workers' militias' that forcibly prevented the destruction of machines, workshops, or mines.[142]

Such fights were also common in the Ruhr, where the HSSPF West appointed an SS-major to control special Werwolf 'Demolition Groups.' This officer soon discovered, however, that the local *Gauleiter*, Florian, was opposed to blowing up anything, and that the Gauleitung was supported by Speer, who handed out machine-guns to plant and mine managers so that they could protect their installations. Armed miners defended the 'Zollverein' pit near Essen against 'Demolition Troops,' and when the Americans reached Erkenschwick they encountered 'a minor civil war' involving 'two underground movements, one pro and one anti-Nazi.' In this case an attempt to blow up the 'Hermann Goering Works' was derailed by anti-Nazi mine workers, and when the local *Ortsgruppenleiter* showed up at a nearby mine, accompanied by a Nazi demolition squad, he was confronted by armed labourers and white-collar managers. 'First you destroy our mine, then you leave,' shouted the pit boss. In the ensuing flurry of gunfire, the *Ortsgruppenleiter* was killed. American authorities in this area subsequently rounded up twenty-five civilians who had been trained in a Nazi sabotage school, as well as uncovering hidden stores of munitions.[143]

Special 'Demolition Troops' also had a mandate to destroy facilities *after* they had fallen into enemy hands, and some installations that were not destroyed prior to the enemy advance were readied for demolition by stay-behind agents. At Trier, for instance, the electricity-generating station was prepared for destruction by stay-behind saboteurs, although the explosives were discovered by American troops before they could be detonated.[144] At Krefeld, a suspected Nazi demolitions agent was apprehended by the CIC after a fire at the Siempelkamp Machine Works. Siempelkamp was the first important arms producer captured by the Allies, and the fire destroyed various construction sketches, formulas, and intricate machine parts that were the functional heart of the plant.[145] At Eschweiler, near Aachen, fourteen managers and foremen in the local coal mines were arrested after the discovery of a plot to minimize production and spread demoralizing rumours among the workforce. Allied Civil Affairs Division (CAD) investigations in February 1945 showed that sabotage plans were in place before the German retreat from the area, specifically calling for the removal of parts from the ventilation system and power plant, so that the mines would be debilitated but still capable of production in case German forces ever returned.[146]

The Werwolf was also involved in the mining of buildings likely to be used as billets or headquarters by the enemy, and which could subsequently be detonated by time-delay fuses or by saboteurs. Such tactics were used by the Wehrmacht with great success in Lorraine, where they caused numerous casualties among soldiers of the U.S. Third Army,[147] and the Werwolf soon learned the trick. In the Rhineland, Werewolves blew up an American command post in Mutzenach on 28 March 1945, killing the mayor of the village in the process. Several weeks later they also destroyed a schoolhouse in Neuss, but this attempt fell wide of the mark because American troops using the building as a billet abandoned it shortly before the explosion. At Tidofeld, near Norden, Werewolves on 9 May blew up two military barracks that were being used by surrendered German troops. A Wehrmacht deserter told Canadian Field Security that a local Werwolf unit was angry because Norden had fallen to the Allies without a fight, and large caches of German munitions were passing into enemy hands with no attempt to destroy them. In Bremen, a police station mined shortly before the arrival of the British blew up on the morning of 4 June 1945, killing five Americans and thirty-nine Germans, and injuring a much larger number of people. This blast was especially severe because the initial explosion detonated a huge depot of arms and munitions stored in the building.[148]

On the Eastern Front, a Soviet intelligence report suggested that the Germans had plans to blow up various structures in the Soviet rear fifteen to twenty days *after* they were overrun by the Red Army.[149] In March 1945, Werwolf demolition experts, seconded from the KTI in Berlin, were involved in a complex plan to blow up Hermann Goering's palatial East German estate, Karinhall, under the feet of Soviet troops. The plan was for stay-behind agents to blast the estate into rubble while Soviet soldiers frolicked and relaxed amid the luxury, and it was abandoned only because of technical constraints, such as the difficulty in hiding enough explosives in the cellar of the huge mansion.[150]

Not content with physical destruction, the drowning regime also arranged the ruination of the nation's cultural treasures, thus matching destruction of the material basis of the Reich with an effort to destroy the nation's heritage. During March and April 1945, the *Gauleiter* of Berlin, Saxony, Saxony–Anhalt, Thuringia, and Upper Danube were all instructed to blow up caches of artwork that had been previously stored in their *Gaue* in order to protect such material from bombing. In the German capital, youthful Werewolves overran an art depot established by the Berlin Museum in the Friedrichshain flak tower, which was held by German forces until the night of 2–3 May. Housed in this sanctuary were precious cultural treasures that had already survived the ravages of time, and which continued to remain intact while innumerable Allied bombs rained down upon the city. Unfortunately, these artefacts did not survive the Werwolf:

teenage fanatics wired the depot, detonated the charges, and thus destroyed a large part of the cache. A second and even more destructive raid in mid-May laid waste to the contents of three entire floors of the tower, including the Berlin Museum's National Gallery; its Painting Gallery; various collections of antiques and sculptures; plus holdings of the Egyptian, Märkische, Crafts, and Ethnological museums. This spree of unbridled vandalism cost the Berlin Museum more than *all* the combined damage incurred through enemy bombing or ground warfare, and included the loss of 800 Greek terracotta pieces, 300 ancient vases, 441 sculptures, 2,800 antique glasses, plus thousands of diverse *objets d'art*.[151]

A similar bombing took place after the end of the war at a former NSDAP administrative building in Munich, which was being used by the Americans as a depot for recovered art. Although this building was guarded, there was ready access for saboteurs via a network of tunnels which had external access to the cellars below the structure. In addition to material damage, a German workman was blown to bits in this explosion.[152]

In the final analysis, however, such terrorism produced fear and confusion, but it could not induce the spirit of national resistance that had failed to emanate spontaneously from the natural wellsprings of German feeling. In fact, Werwolf intimidation only increased public hatred of an already discredited regime: assassination of civic officials, for instance, caused not only fear, but also resentment – 'The Ludendorffs lose our wars,' said liberal satirist Erich Kästner, 'while the Erzbergers lose their lives.' Even Ernst Jünger, the voice of the 'Front Generation,' considered such acts as a sign of increasing anarchy, and an observer from the Harz Mountains saw it as a step towards civil war.[153] In a few instances, diversionist groups were forcibly disbanded or run out of town by local officials, and German civilians sometimes led occupation troops straight to Werwolf supply caches. In at least one case, in the Soviet Zone, civilians were allowed to raid a dump in return for their help in uncovering it for the authorities. In the Rhineland, one of the cooks attached to the Hibernia firm compliantly led American CIC agents to several of the underground galleries excavated by the company. At Singen, near the Swiss border, two dozen Werwolf partisans were denounced by their countrymen and were quickly put under lock and key by the French authorities. In the Harz, American officers recruited German estate-owners, along with their foresters, to sally out into the woods, make contacts with Werwolf elements, and convince them to surrender.[154]

Occasionally, Germans themselves reacted towards Werewolves violently. At Oberaudorf, in the heart of the Alpine Redoubt, a local Werwolf leader was killed by members of a neighbourhood 'Antifa,' and in early May, the Americans also discovered the remains of a Werwolf who had been murdered and left lying in his subterranean bunker in the Rhineland. Several similar incidents – lynchings of Werewolves by indignant mobs – were reported from Berlin.[155] At Düsseldorf, where SS-Police officers made some desperate last-minute preparations for 'scorched earth' actions and Werwolf operations, an 'Antifa' briefly overthrew the city's police president on 16 April, but the conspirators were then themselves toppled and killed by loyalist Nazi police and Gauleitung officials, even as the Americans marched into the city.[156]

Final Disintegration

Despite the efforts of the Werwolf to enforce the spirit of resistance in everyone else, the organization's own morale was disastrous, and steadily became worse as the moment of final collapse drew nearer.[157] Prützmann himself led the way: by the spring of 1945 his vanity had disappeared and his mood wavered wildly between an overexpressive confidence and desperate drunken nights in which he contemplated suicide.[158] As well, he seemed increasingly interested in collaborating with the Reich's foes rather than in wholeheartedly resisting enemy occupation. Not only was Prützmann associated with Himmler's last-minute attempts to negotiate with the Western Powers, but he also established his own independent effort to achieve a general armistice with the British and Americans.[159] In so doing, he attempted to remove the Werwolf's *raison d'être* in western Germany and reorient it solely towards the East.

This story began in mid-March 1945 and played itself out in Prützmann's old fief of Hamburg, where the Werwolf chief had once served as HSSPF. Prützmann presumably had good contacts in the area, and during this period he resumed close relations with Gauleiter Karl Kaufmann, a veteran party leader who had soured on the war, especially after the Hamburg fire-bombing in 1943, and had since decided in favour of capitulation to Germany's Western enemies.[160] Prützmann hinted that he shared Kaufmann's dour appraisal of the overall strategic situation. Three weeks later, the Werwolf chief arrived in Hamburg with important news: Himmler, he said, had agreed to cancel the Werwolf's guerrilla operations in western Germany, converting it into an agency with which to spread the idea of accommodation with the West. From this point onward, said Prützmann, the Werwolf would work for an armistice with the Western Powers and for the continued defence of Reich frontiers in the East. The final aim would be an anti-Bolshevik union of Europe designed to protect its 'age-old cultural values.'[161]

What are we to make of this bold initiative? Several salient facts do suggest that such an alteration of the Werwolf was at least under consideration at the most senior levels of the SS. First of all, a draft SS plan from 3 April 1945, per-

haps prepared by SS-Colonel Franke-Grieksch of the RSHA, discussed a drastic restructuring of the 'Freedom Movement,' which was now described as a
rally 'of front soldiers true to their oath to the Führer.' Although this document
continued to refer to Hitler and Himmler in reverential terms, it denounced a
'treacherous party bureaucracy' that had promoted 'an un-German and biased
Führerprinzip in domestic policy and a hollow, shady power politics in foreign
affairs.' The correct path was provided, not by communism, or by capitalism, or
by parliamentary democracy, or by regional particularisms, but by a reformed
Nazi administration based upon the rule of the law and the authority of a bicam-
eral assembly, and also through the agency of an egalitarian socio-economic
policy. External relations were to be guided by participation in a European con-
federation based upon respect for the rights of 'all European peoples to shape a
distinctive existence, and to maintain an independent conception of public
order, customs and political organization.' As well, Germany would seek a 'true
brotherhood' with the other Nordic nations of Europe, the final aim of which
was the voluntary formation of a Pan-German Reich. Both of these goals comprised the final culmination of a trend that had developed in SS policy and
propaganda after 1940, as the Waffen-SS assumed a more Pan-German and
European character. Obviously, the movement aimed at 'the liberation
of the German people from the yoke of foreign oppression and occupation,'
but nothing was said about violent resistance – only that 'men of the German Freedom Movement battle hopelessness, despondency, lack of purpose and
betrayal,' all in order to create a just peace and ensure the strength necessary
for reconstruction.[162]

Second, Himmler in late April told the head of the Luftwaffe's special-
services squadron that his main intent was to achieve a 'special peace' with
the Western Powers and to subsequently form an anti-Communist 'Free Corps'
in Mecklenburg and Holstein. The model at the back of Himmler's mind was the
1813 War of Liberation. It is perhaps important to note that the Reichsführer's
main intended emissary for his 'special peace' initiative, the Swedish humani-
tarian Count Folke Bernadotte, had demanded cancellation of the Werwolf if he
were to carry an armistice proposal to Eisenhower.[163]

And, third, Himmler spoke on several occasions concerning his doubts about
the Werwolf, as well as his concerns over the plan to organize a Werwolf
redoubt in the Alps. As early as February, he had made disparaging comments
about guerrilla warfare, saying that, 'for Germans, this partisan dirt is as suitable as a cow for laying eggs.'[164] Himmler told Schellenberg in mid-April that
he would 'try to think of some way to finish this business,' and several weeks
later, when requested to issue instructions on deploying Waffen-SS units in possible last stands or Werwolf operations, he seemed paralysed by indecision.[165]

On 1 May, within hours of Hitler's death, Himmler denounced his former master, telling the famous flyer, Hanna Reitsch, that the Führer had been mad to want the fight to continue – 'It should have been stopped long ago.'[166]

Given all these facts, however, clear and unambiguous documentary evidence also shows that the Werwolf was still fully functional in western Germany throughout April 1945. Certainly, some regional Werwolf chiefs knew that their leaders were attempting to dicker with the enemy, but any tentative plans to cancel operations in the West were never implemented. In fact, even as late as May 1945, sabotage agents were still being sent across the Elbe with orders to blow up railway tracks and Allied airfields. Moreover, during the period in which Prützmann was casting himself as an angel of peace in Hamburg, he showed up in Düsseldorf in a belligerent mood, berating the HSSPF West about 'lack of progress' in the Rhineland, and pushing to sack the local 'Werwolf Commissioner,' SS-Colonel Raddatz.[167] Thus, the plan to alter the Werwolf was, at most, nebulous and provisional – more of a trial balloon than a solid decision.

Prützmann's tendency to push this vague intention as a firmly established fact reveals, in truth, an intense desire to ingratiate himself with the rebellious party element at Hamburg, perhaps in the hope of getting one foot into the camp of the dissidents, while leaving the other in the camp of the die-hard resisters. In any case, the local HJ-Werwolf chief was soon won over to this new purpose, and the city's military garrison also seemed to frown upon underground resistance activity. However, the overall 'Werwolf Commissioner' in Hamburg, SS-Colonel Knoll, was a Nazi fanatic who remained loyally bound to the cause of last-ditch resistance.[168]

After Prützmann made his startling announcement about the Werwolf's supposed new course, Kaufmann announced his own plan to act independently in ensuring that the population of northwest Germany was not butchered in a useless attempt to defend the area. Although Prützmann worried about the danger of openly expressing such views, he admitted thorough agreement with the proposal, and by the end of the month he had answered the *Gauleiter*'s call to help in arranging a truce on the Northwest Front. At the time of Hitler's death, both men were attempting to contact the Danish Resistance in the hope of using it as an intermediary through which to negotiate with the British.[169] Prützmann's last message to his Werwolf followers instructed that 'unnecessary losses' be avoided, particularly among young Werewolves.[170]

By the beginning of May, the point of ultimate disintegration was rapidly approaching, and the overlords of the Werwolf began their final run for cover. Both Himmler and Prützmann headed north to Flensburg, in order to be in the vicinity of Grand Admiral Dönitz, the new centre of power in the dissolving

Reich. But Dönitz cared little for the pretensions of either of these men, and he thought so poorly of the Werwolf that, during a radio address on 5 May, he cancelled its activities in western Germany. More will be said about Dönitz and the military in chapter 3, but for now it will suffice to note that the new Reich president refused the services of Himmler as a security and intelligence chief, since he had absolutely no desire to discredit himself by association with this heinous figure. Himmler, in turn, glumly retreated to consider the few remaining portals to an impossibly bleak future. Some of his adjutants encouraged him to give himself up and formally disband the SS, thereby preventing the possibility of Werwolf opposition to either Dönitz or the Allies. Himmler declined to wrap up officially either the SS or the Werwolf, but neither was there talk of any further fighting. As one deputy noted, 'save yourselves' became the watchword, and the recommended method was to submerge within the Wehrmacht: Himmler himself went to ground on 6 May disguised as a sergeant in the 'Secret Field Police.' Weapons belonging to Himmler's entourage were cached near Leck with the help of a local forest ranger. The SS chief then wandered northern Germany for several weeks incognito and, when captured by the British on 23 May, bit one of the poison ampoules that had been so widely distributed within the Werwolf organization. He died within several minutes.[171]

Concurrently, half a dozen of Himmler's key aides, members of the SS-Main Office involved in planning underground warfare, were captured by the British during a number of round-ups in Schleswig–Holstein, particularly a sweep of Arenholz on 17 May.[172] One of these figures was none other than Hans Prützmann. During the last days before the capitulation, Prützmann styled himself as 'liaison officer' between Himmler and Dönitz, even though Dönitz had not the least desire to liaise with Himmler, and the position was thus entirely superfluous. Prützmann also gave up effective leadership of the Werwolf or, in the spirit of his Hamburg dalliances, no longer regarded the organization as an active entity. 'I spoke to Prützmann on several occasions,' said a fellow SS officer, 'at Plön as well as later at Flensburg, and I gained the impression that he was trying to find a niche for himself and beyond that had nothing more to do with the "Werewolf" organization.'[173]

On 5 May, Prützmann witnessed Himmler's maudlin farewell speech, and then toyed with the idea of escaping in a U-boat or an airplane. In actuality, however, the popinjay was soon captured by the British and immediately sent to a detention camp. He initially tried to convince British interrogators that in November 1944 he had been replaced by SA-Brigadier Siebel as 'General Inspector for Special Abwehr,' but, when this lie failed to lead the British astray, he visited the latrine and, like Himmler, departed the world by means of a cyanide ampoule.[174]

While Prützmann had originally headed north to Schleswig–Holstein, his headquarters staff, under the command of Siebel, had retreated south, towards the Alpine Redoubt, and Opländer was seen during late April in Prague, loitering around and awaiting further instructions. However, not only did the Bureau travel in a different geographical direction than its chief, it was also on a different path philosophically, most notably in the sense that these officers remained much more devoted than Prützmann to the idea of last-ditch resistance and diversionary activity. In fact, while on the way to the redoubt, Prützmann's aides developed a bold strategy for postwar Werwolf operations. The main intent, remarkably similar to the later formulations of Brazilian urban-guerrilla leader Carlos Marighela, was to harass the occupation forces, cause reprisals, and thereby create a mutual hatred between the population and the occupation troops. It was foreseen that such a program would eventually create the conditions for a political revival of National Socialism and also lay the groundwork for a rebellion in case of major armed conflict between East and West.[175]

In truth, however, the Bureau's fate was somewhat less grandiose than these plans suggested. After reaching Maishöfen, the headquarters staff was formed into a seventy-five-man Werwolf task force, and this unit was subsequently instructed to destroy a V-2 facility near Garmisch–Partenkirchen that had been captured by the Americans. The formation was shot up and dispersed by American forces while on its way to carry out this ill-fated mission. Three Werewolves were killed, and seven were wounded.[176]

The regional sections of the Werwolf collapsed in a number of ways. Many of the HSSPF emulated their leader by negotiating surrender, while several others went to ground incognito. The HSSPF Posen, SS–Lieutenant-General Reinefarth, was arrested on Hitler's orders when he led an unauthorized breakout of 1,500 Volkssturm men, troops, and Werewolves from the besieged 'fortress' of Küstrin.[177] Meanwhile, a number of local organizations unofficially dissolved or were formally terminated. A particularly notable example was the abolition of the Styrian Werwolf by Gauleiter Ueberreither on 4 May, which shows that such disintegration sometimes occurred even in areas about to fall to the Red Army.[178] South of Berlin, a twelve-man Werwolf group at Luckenwalde disintegrated when its leader fled westward, and only a pair of demoralized survivors remained on hand to be swept up by the NKVD several months later.[179]

Postwar Activities

In a few cases, some of the most fanatic Werwolf chiefs made preliminary plans for postwar activity. The basic strategy was to lay low and intact until conditions for sabotage and guerrilla warfare improved. American authorities, for instance, obtained the minutes of a secret meeting of Werwolf 'Subgroup VIIa, Section 4e,' where it was decided that local Werwolf agents should pose as anti-Nazis and otherwise make every conceivable effort to win the confidence of Allied Military Government and security officers. We must maintain, said the record, 'iron discipline within our own radius and absolute execution of given commands.'[180] In southeastern Bavaria, Werwolf cells under the command of a Gestapo officer named Huber received very similar instructions. Their plan was to remain inert for approximately six weeks, but to incite resentment of the occupation forces by spreading stories of rape by black soldiers. The next stage was to begin a large-scale sabotage campaign and to assassinate collaborators. All cessation orders from the Dönitz government were to be ignored on the assumption that they would be issued only to fool the Allies.[181]

A few cells sputtered into the postwar period and independently engaged in harassment operations. SHAEF's deputy commander, Air Marshal Tedder, noted in late May 1945 that the Werwolf had not caused much trouble since the war, although 'here and there we have found small groups of three or four men or teenage boys who seek to make life difficult for us.' An Allied intelligence report in June 1945 noted that, since the capitulation, 'isolated cases of wire cutting, sniping and arson' had been traced to Werwolf members.[182] In Fulda, the Werwolf terrorized a local secretary of the Communist Party,[183] and, in the southeast Bavarian town of Freyung, a local Werwolf cell was suspected of complicity in a long series of incidents, including the blockage of roads, wire-cutting, assaults on American troops, and the spread of subversive propaganda.[184] In the hills around Stuttgart, a few Werwolf bazooka teams reportedly held out for a month after the war, but the Allies reacted harshly, shooting guerrillas on sight.[185] At Nuremberg, former Waffen-SS trooper Alfred Zitzmann led his Werwolf group in the bombing of a denazification court, and it is possible that this same unit was also responsible for a number of other bombings.[186]

In various areas, there was evidence of Werwolf sloganeering and pamphleteering, and in several cases 'collaborators' were threatened or attacked. In the autumn of 1945 American authorities certainly identified such intimidation as 'a serious threat to Military Government and its appointed representatives.'[187] In August 1945, a Berlin banker and the police chief of Zehlendorf were both killed in suspected Werwolf 'hits'; in the Rhineland, a *Bürgermeister* was injured when his motorcycle struck a 'decapitation wire' on 18 June 1945; and, in Bavaria, several political assassinations were reported during the first year after the end of the war.[188] For several years after 1945, Nazi troublemakers continued to snip wires, vandalize Allied military vehicles, and burn Military Government facilities, the point of which, as noted by the U.S. Seventh Army, was to 'decrease the duration of the occupation by harassing resistance action.'[189] Occasionally, Allied enlisted men and officers were attacked, and when Field Marshal Montgomery's airplane crashed on 22 August 1945, slightly injuring the British Zone chief, there was some suspicion of sabotage. In the northwest German town of Aurich, long a Nazi stronghold, a British security officer was attacked by an assassin sent from Oldenburg, who had a specific mandate to kill him. In the American Zone, the boss of the university denazification purge, Edward Hartshorne, was ambushed on the Autobahn in what Peter Merkyl rightly calls 'a fehme-style assassination.' Hartshorne's sudden removal in August 1946 probably had a detrimental effect on the reform of German higher education.[190]

For their part, the Allies incarcerated large numbers of Werewolves in the two years following the German capitulation, and Allied courts were still delivering death sentences as late as 1948.[191] In the first month after the capitulation, as the number of arrests began to escalate, 2,000 suspected Nazi subversives were apprehended in the northern Ruhr alone, and by 1946 the Americans and British together held 80,000 political prisoners, largely in order to emasculate the Nazi resistance movement.[192] Overall, however, the Americans and British concluded, even in the summer of 1945, that, as a nationwide network, the original Werwolf was irrevocably destroyed, and that it no longer posed a threat to the occupation.[193] The fire beneath the ashes was not completely dead, but neither was it any longer capable of setting Germany alight. On the other hand, an epidemic of individual acts of terrorism was harder to suppress than a national conspiracy because the former offered no signs of linkages that could be detected by and serve as leads for Allied investigators.

The Soviets and their East European allies were not so sanguine about the Werwolf, and they continued to worry about the organization well into the 1950s.[194] They believed that the organization's leaders had made plans to continue terrorist and diversionist activities into the postwar period,[195] and there is a considerable body of evidence suggesting that certain Werewolves in Eastern Europe attempted to keep their groups intact. For instance, a Werwolf unit near Bütow, in Pomerania, continued to function against the Soviets until the fall of 1945, when it staged a break-out and slashed its way to the western zones of Germany.[196] Austrian Nazis interrogated by the British reported that, even despite the Styrian *Gauleiter*'s cessation order on 4 May, some groups intended to keep working against the Red Army, and NKVD records show that a sixteen-man Werwolf detachment was active in the woods near Löben until it was overrun by a Russian patrol on 30 May 1945.[197] In August 1945, several targets (including a power transformer and a Communist Party meeting-hall) were bombed in the Vienna suburb of Florisdorf, apparently the work of Werwolf fanatics.[198]

In the Soviet Zone of Germany, Werwolf leaflets still circulated as late as 1946, some of which openly encouraged attacks upon Red Army troops. As for Werwolf cells, 'the practical activity of such groups,' said a Soviet report, 'has been expressed through the perpetration of acts of terror and diversion.' On the night of 12 August 1945, saboteurs in the Thuringian town of Mulhausen succeeded in setting fire to a goods train, and in 1946 a grenade attack against the Soviet Central Zone administration building in Berlin injured fifteen 'collaborators.' Town mayors 'collaborating' with the occupiers were also attacked and beaten, particularly in Mecklenburg. At Senftenberg, Nazi guerrillas attacked Soviet outposts and derailed a train. Gradually, however, as the Soviet vice tightened, Werwolf operations declined in number and effectiveness. The NKVD succeeded in 'turning' many captured activists, thereby uncovering more of the network, and numerous Werwolf cells and individual cadres were rounded up by the occupying power. In Saxony alone, forty-two Werwolf groups were uncovered and 'liquidated' in the course of 1946. The count of captured Werewolves, which already stood at more than 600 in June 1945, jumped to 3,336 by October 1946. Nearly 240,000 'sympathizers' and other suspected 'subversives' were herded into a gruesome prison-camp system, and more than a third of these unfortunates died in captivity.[199]

The main goal of surviving Werwolf groups was to play a role in any forthcoming Allied advance against the Soviets, and in Poland and Czechoslovakia they hoped to use such an opportunity to restore German sovereignty. Their basic *raison d'être*, said an NKVD assessment, 'is to participate on the side of the Anglo-Americans in preparation for a supposed war against the Soviet Union, which the Nazi underground regards as inevitable.' Werwolf units in Silesia certainly functioned on this basis, and hope for Allied help in restoring the old frontiers was a primary element in their postwar propaganda.[200] In southern Moravia, five Werewolves captured by the Czechs at Znaim told their captors that they were waiting for American air-drops of arms and equipment. They expected to aid the advancing American forces by guerrilla activity, and then by subsequent service as a police agency after the Americans had arrived.[201]

As in western Germany, some surviving groups were also instructed to disguise members as anti-Nazis – plans were afoot for this sort of activity well before the end of the war – and, in Poland, Werewolves were encouraged to patch up relations with the Poles, at least superficially:

Local Germans [said a captured directive] should curry favour with Polish nationals in order to avoid deportation, and should meanwhile exploit opportunities to reorganize organizations of German life. German experts, engineers, technicians, etc., should attempt to derive Polish citizenship from their positions in Polish factories and work-places, and they should gain the confidence of Poles in order to conduct espionage and sabotage. For this purpose, special instructions will prepare for a current underground intelligence organization. In future, relevant instructions will come from the Central in Dresden ... Through Germans already in the organization, contacts will be established, for the time being social, with Poles of communist convictions who presently fill gov-ernment positions.

Not surprisingly, the Poles, Czechs, and Soviets were suspicious even of Ger-mans who claimed to have been hostile to the Nazi regime, and, in the Soviet Zone, the Russian security forces methodically dismantled local 'Antifas' on the claim that they had been infiltrated by Nazis.[202]

In actual fact, Werwolf ranks in Germany and Austria were quickly thinned by aggressive Soviet counter-insurgency operations. By the time that the British assumed control of Styria in August 1945, they found that the Russians had largely smashed the Werwolf and that its leaders had been evacuated into the massive labyrinth of the Soviet security establishment, never to be seen again.[203] In some areas there were denunciations and consequent liquidations: eight alleged Werewolves fingered at Scheibner Kirchensteig, in Austria, were shot on 19 May 1945 on the initiative of the local Soviet commandant. An NKVD regi-ment stationed in Saxony–Anhalt reported that resistance activity in that prov-ince had almost disappeared by the spring of 1946 owing to the break up of original Werwolf cells.[204] In 1947, a Werwolf plot to blow up the Red Army war memorial in central Vienna was foiled before the bombers could set their charges, mainly because an informant snitched to the occupation authorities.[205]

The Werwolf probably survived more completely in ethnic German areas of Poland and Czechoslovakia because the initial array of Soviet security forces had been insufficient, particularly in Poland, where NKVD detachments often found themselves outgunned by large Polish counter-revolutionary bands.[206] Moreover, in the first few months after the war, the tentative new regimes in Poland and Czechoslovakia lacked sufficient security muscle for a showdown. This problem was partially resolved in the summer and fall of 1945, when both the Poles and Czechs rallied to launch major raids against the Werwolf, and they succeeded in wiping out much of the core of the movement,[207] although some cells did stagger on into 1946–7. However, the Soviets and their allies probably also had a longer-range concern: what if German intelligence officers captured by the Western Powers should trade their knowledge of Werwolf nets in the East in return for preferential treatment and advantages? Could these cells then be revived under hostile Allied control? In other words, were the eastern Werewolves entirely deluded in expecting eventual Western support?

The Western Allies were still providing the Soviets with tidbits of information on the Werwolf as late as 1946,[208] but it seems likely that, as the Cold War began, this inclination to share information ended completely. Subsequently, Soviet security concerns may have been partially valid, since Western intelligence agencies began to view Werwolf organizations in the East less like enemies and more like potential assets. NKVD documents suggest that, as early as 1946, the Western Allies dispatched agents into the Soviet Zone, not only for reconnaissance, but also to terrorize Russian troops and pro-Soviet collaborators, much of which was done under the banner of the 'Edelweiss Piraten.' A British intelligence digest from 1947 confirms that, by this date, the British were so convinced of a fundamental breech between themselves and the Russians that they were actively considering whether or not to exploit an anti-Soviet resistance leader who had offered his services (although in the final analysis the individual in question was offered to the Americans).[209] E.H. Cookridge claims that the Americans, when faced with similar opportunities, were more than happy to employ such resources. According to Cookridge, German intelligence officers who surrendered to the Americans in 1945 knew a considerable amount about the eastern Werwolf, and they were able to make use of this information once they were encouraged to form anti-Soviet intelligence networks under American patronage. During the late 1940s, a small number of these officers were actually dispatched into Saxony with the hope of reviving dormant Werwolf cells and other underground networks dating from 1945. Generally, these missions were very dangerous, because of the stringency of Soviet control measures, and such activities usually ended in disaster.[210] It is still notable, however, that Soviet security concerns were not entirely misplaced.

Despite the fact that the Werwolf functioned sporadically in the postwar period, perhaps a final assessment of the organization should not be based upon this eventual breakdown. Given its mandate, the Werwolf was never intended to operate in a post-capitulation environment. Considered solely in light of its assigned task of harassing the enemy rear while the Wehrmacht was still in the field, the Werwolf achieved mixed results. It is true that enemy lines of communication were occasionally sabotaged, and that the Soviets and Western Allies were occasionally forced to draw men from the front in order to deal with disruptions in the rear. The Red Army, in particular, had to allocate considerable numbers of men for guard duty wherever worthwhile industrial or military targets were captured intact, and they were also forced to form ten- to twenty-man 'Search Units' for the purpose of hunting down German guerrillas.[211] On the other hand, the Werwolf never succeeded in Prützmann's aim of promoting a so-called radical improvement in Germany's military fortunes, and it might rightly be argued that much of the disruption in the rear of the invading armies was actually caused by military straggler bands having little or no connection with the Prützmann agency. In actuality, most of the SS groups were quickly liquidated, or they dissolved as a result of centrifugal forces within the units themselves.

It is thus impossible not to conclude that the Werwolf was poorly organized, that it suffered from a terminal case of bureaucratization, and that most of the limited successes in German guerrilla warfare were gained despite the organization rather than because of it. The most basic mistakes were the absence of an extensive mandate; a misguided anticipation of civilian sympathy; the stasis encouraged by tying Werewolves to immobile underground galleries;[212] the lack of a competent leader; and the fact that no major organization elected to take the Werwolf under its wing and provide a secure availability of supplies and qualified personnel. This last problem was the worst, because it left the Werwolf unprepared to survive amid the Darwinian battle for resources that had arisen by 1944–5. In retrospect, it appears that Himmler placed the organization under a command channel in which he had an opportunity for personal interventions, but that, unlike Churchill, with his Commandos, or John Kennedy, with his Green Berets, the Reichsführer failed to pay the special attention required to ensure the full-fledged success of such a group. In fact, he was plagued by severe second doubts about the entire project. In a war-weary nation short of resources, time, and manpower – and subject to physical disintegration from the effects of falling bombs and invading enemy armies – such problems were insurmountable.

But could it have been otherwise? The nature of the Hitler dictatorship drove it towards bureaucratic confusion, while, at the same time, a people dragged through six years of debilitating effort could hardly have been expected to support further destruction, particularly not self-destruction. In any case, such elaborate advance efforts to prepare for guerrilla fighting not only were doomed by the condition of the German Reich and its people, but were perhaps ill-conceived in the first place. The British had experienced considerable difficulties with the same matter in 1940, and in the cases of Yugoslavia and the Soviet Union, standing plans for guerrilla activity in the rear of an invading army had made little impact on the actual course of partisan warfare. An apt example in the German context was the geographic configuration of guerrilla activity within the collapsing Reich: although the Werwolf was better prepared for partisan warfare in the Rhineland, it was the area between the Rhine and the Elbe that became more of a problem for Western Allied forces. The primary reasons were that Werwolf groups and bands of stragglers were able to exploit suitable terrain features, and the populace tended to be more hostile than in areas farther west – and these factors were much more important than organizational preparations.

Aside from putting arms caches and supply dumps in place, it might be argued that a retreating power can do little to encourage a kind of activity that must, by its very nature, emanate from popular sources (although it can be organized subsequently). Sabotage leaders, writes one authority, 'are less chiefs in the military sense than they are chiefs of popular tribes. They must be men who have arisen from the people ... By gaining distinction among their fellows, they gain the individual confidence of their followers.'[213] This is not to argue that guerrilla activity cannot be encouraged, Special Operations Executive style, but it must be concluded that elaborate bureaucracies intended to 'seed' partisan warfare are of limited value.

2

A Nursery Tale:
The Hitler Youth and the Werwolf

Aside from the SS organizational core, by far the most integral portion of the Werwolf was the Hitler Youth (HJ), the source of most of the human material for the movement. Some Werwolf cells were composed entirely of teenage fanatics, and almost all units had at least several HJ members. The team that assassinated the *Oberbürgermeister* of Aachen comprised a sixteen-year-old HJ activist, a young woman from the female component of the HJ (the Federation of German Girls – BdM), an SS 'Ranger' officer, an SS NCO, plus two scouts with experience in the Border Patrol. The dynamism and vitality of youth were seen as essential to the success of Operation 'Carnival,' and to the well-being of the guerrilla movement as a whole. As an American Counter-Intelligence Corps (CIC) agent noted, 'only teenagers had the fanaticism and the lingering belief in victory necessary in order to throw themselves into *Werwolf* work.'[1]

The Militarization of the Hitler Youth

The HJ was originally formed in 1922, and during the 1930s it mushroomed into a mass movement, membership having become compulsory just before the war. From the beginning, it represented the side of the German Youth Movement with a militaristic character, although it is also retained a certain sense of romantic egalitarianism derived from such predecessors as the Wandervogel, which diluted its predilection towards authoritarianism. Although there was a strict *Führer*, or 'leader,' principle imposed upon the organization, there was also a degree of bonhomie between leaders and followers, and this relationship was later extended to such formations as the SS 'Hitler Youth' Division. None the less, the basic nature of the movement was military, or, more accurately, premilitary. By the mid-1930s, the Army and SS had begun to provide trainers for HJ exercises, and special courses were run by veterans of the Great War. By 1938, more than a million boys were enrolled in target-shooting programs. Such premilitary training intensified after the outbreak of the war, and in the spring of 1942 a series of special facilities, called 'Defence Training Camps,' were organized in order to provide instruction in basic infantry tactics for *all* male teenagers. At the same time, HJ members began to perform a number of police or semi-military jobs: HJ boys and BdM girls acted as night watchmen, couriers, guides for refugees, air-raid wardens, mailmen, fire-fighters, Red Cross volunteers, and, eventually, beginning in January 1943, flak gunners. Release of HJ personnel for this final function was key because it comprised the initial subjection of adolescent boys to enemy fire, although the regime could well argue (and did) that all German civilians had already been exposed to peril because of the Allied bombing campaign. None the less, there was already some doubt about whether half-uniformed 'flak helpers' were actually soldiers protected by the Geneva Convention, or whether they were just *francs-tireurs*.

If undertaking anti-aircraft defence did not mark the opening salvo in a 'children's crusade,' the next step in this direction certainly did: after several months of talks between the SS and the HJ leadership, orders were issued in June 1943 for the raising of SS Division 'Hitler Youth,' which was quite obviously meant to serve as a test case for the combat deployment of HJ boys. Recruits were drawn from the 'Defence Training Camps,' mostly seventeen- and eighteen-year-olds, although it was not uncommon to find younger boys also enrolled.[2]

Commensurate with its expanding military functions, the HJ also began to throw its weight around at home. According to a former member, the HJ had by 1944–5 effectively risen to power *over* the party at local levels, and HJ officers freely threatened bureaucrats with death should they show any signs of cowardice. When the Palatinate was threatened with American occupation in February 1945, 'there was in evidence a strong trend among leaders of the HJ ... to assume more domineering attitudes.' One observer noted that 'there was disagreement with army officers about jobs on which HJ boys were used, and with *Kreisleiter* of the Party. HJ leaders insisted on more influence and important positions and, in some cases, gained control of the *Volkssturm*.' Similarly, in Franconia, a local HJ chief was bold enough to 'seize' a thousand metal supply containers from the Army, and to 'loot' a local supply depot at Amberg, so that the HJ could undertake its own guerrilla-style operations. In southern Bavaria, at Landsberg, the local HJ leadership organized a 'placarding action' on the night of 19–20 April, whereby teams of boys were dispatched to plaster the town with posters encouraging die-hard resistance, but a nervous and uninformed *Ortsgruppenleiter* mistakenly shot one of the boys under the cover of darkness.[3]

The Hitler Youth Guerrilla Program

With the decision to launch a levy *en masse* in the autumn of 1944, the HJ finally began to metamorphose into the fanatic *ralliement* that had always been envisioned, suitable either for action against foreign enemies or for domestic terrorism. Leaders of the HJ desperately wanted to follow the path of the SS Division 'Hitler Youth' and convert the entire movement into a combat organization. In August 1944, Chief of Staff Helmut Möckel suggested the training of 100,000 boys for 'self-defence squads' that could fight slackers at home or enemy guerrillas along the fringes of the Reich, and in the autumn HJ irregulars were armed with infantry weapons to guard field-works crews against French partisans. Even before the creation of the Volkssturm, the HJ headquarters staff – the 'Reich Youth Leadership' – had already made plans for building 'Herbert Norkus' battle units, so named for a HJ 'martyr' killed in a street-fight in 1932. However, the call-up of the new mass militia provided convenient cover for these levies, with the only problem being that the Volkssturm did not make fast-enough use of the 300,000 teenagers offered by the HJ. A particular disappoint-ment was that fifteen- , sixteen- , and seventeen-year-olds were reserved for the so-called third wave of the Volkssturm, which was called up only as a last-gasp effort in the spring of 1945. Even in the fall of 1944, however, it was feared that the spirit of the Volkssturm would be undercut by the first waves of elderly recruits, so that the HJ foresaw its own boys being 'corrupted' through contact with the older men. Thus, it was announced on 30 October that HJ troops of the age group born in 1928 would be formed into distinctive units under HJ leaders, which meant that HJ combat units subsequently functioned only very loosely under Volkssturm cover. This applied particularly to the infamous tank-destroyer formations which sprang up in every corner of the unoccupied Reich, and which were so unconventional in their style and tactics that they loosely fell under the Werwolf label.[4] (More will be said of these units in chapter 3.) HJ reconnaissance parties also skirted the boundaries of guerrilla warfare; in north-ern Germany, British troops captured armed bands of HJ skulking behind their lines, marked only by Volkssturm brassards.

Aside from the Volkssturm, the other main interest of the Reich Youth Lead-ership was in organizing outright guerrilla and reconnaissance units to function in Allied-occupied territory. As early as the summer of 1944, a number of HJ officials in western Germany were withdrawn from their regular duties in order to undergo special training, and a number of HJ boys were also prepared for line-crossing operations, especially by Front Intelligence (FAK) units. One fifteen-year-old captured by the Allies told of attending a sabotage camp near the Dutch border, where, from July to September 1944, 400 HJ teenagers were pushed through a training course by German and Flemish SS instructors. According to the Higher SS and Police Leader (HSSPF) Rhein–Westmark, Jürgen Stroop, a directive was later issued by the Reich Youth Leadership ordering the *entire* HJ to be trained for guerrilla warfare, and this claim was partially supported by the local HJ chief for Koblenz, Schneider, who asserted that all boys born in 1929–30 were slated for such a purpose. This alleged directive was issued *circa* November 1944. On the other hand, there is evidence suggesting that, at least in practice, recruits were drawn only from among 'the most fanatical and wildest boys of the HJ,' and that the program was strictly limited to the western bank of the Rhine. Whatever the case, a number of HJ leaders along the Rhine seemed very enthusiastic – their home regions were already under direct threat of enemy occupation – and one of them, HJ-Brigadier Kloos, from Usingen, in Hesse, was chosen in early October 1944 to lead the entire HJ guerrilla program.

All this independent initiative probably came as an unwelcome surprise to the Bureau 'Prützmann,' which was itself eyeing HJ personnel as one of the mainstays for the SS-Werwolf program. By the end of 1944, there was obviously a need to coordinate operations between the SS and the HJ, thereby preventing overlapping and unnecessary duplication of effort. As a result, a conference of senior SS and HJ leaders was held around the turn of 1945 at Potsdam, including both Prützmann and Kloos, and it was decided that Kloos's staff should be attached to the Bureau 'Prützmann' and henceforth function as a subordinate arm of the Werwolf. Kloos's organization subsequently arrived at Rheinsberg, where they were suitably disguised as a recruitment staff for the SS Division 'Hitler Youth,' and Kloos himself assumed the title of 'Reich Youth Leadership HJ Commissioner.' Kloos also paid visits to the western HSSPF, informing them loosely about his work, and the HSSPF were told that, in future, 'Hitler Youth groups or individuals [were] to be organized under the tactical direction of SS and Police Commanders.' On 25 January, HSSPF in the East were also informed of these new arrangements. Throughout the Reich, 'Werwolf Commissioners' were appointed to coordinate HJ operations. It was also around this same time that the code-word 'Werwolf' was first applied to the HJ guerrilla program; this was a natural fit since Löns's work had been extremely popular among German youth since the days of the Wandervogel.

However, despite this resolution of command channels, the HJ continued to act effectively as master in its own house. The HJ maintained its own recruitment network and a separate system of training schools, each of which was little known to organizers in the SS-Werwolf. Not surprisingly, Werwolf officers complained bitterly about the lack of cooperation between the two wings of the movement, and one HSSPF was even led to assume that the SS effort to annex the HJ program had failed. On the other side of the fence, HJ-Werwolf leaders continued to believe that the entire program was run solely by the Reich Youth Leadership, and that Werwolf groups were to be built entirely from boys of the HJ.[5]

HJ recruitment for Werwolf activities was subject to loose inspection by 'special agents' answerable to the HSSPF, but otherwise it had little to do with recruitment channels fostered by the main body of the movement. Basically, regional offices of the HJ contacted leaders at the local level and ordered them to select anywhere from six to twelve candidates for Werwolf training. These youths were picked for their political reliability and intelligence, and were specifically *not* supposed to be prominent members of the HJ. Members of the BdM were also chosen, based on their suitability for training as radio operators. Other girls worked as typists and clerks in the Werwolf. Only a limited number of local leaders were involved in the movement: in HJ Territory 'Nordmark' (i.e., Frisia/Schleswig–Holstein), there were twenty local chiefs, but only five were chosen to organize Werwolf operations, and each of these consequently became responsible for four HJ districts. Along the Rhine, where the recruitment effort was most intense, special recruitment pamphlets were prepared by a HJ office in Wiesbaden, which got priority access to paper and printing supplies.

After recruitment, children chosen for service attended brief preparatory courses at the 'Defence Training Camps' or at other institutions connected with the HJ. All training matters were organized and coordinated by a special battalion called 'Albert Leo Schlageter,' which was under the purview of Kloos's office at the Bureau 'Prützmann.' Two boys captured by the Americans described being recruited from a HJ Sports Instructors' School in March 1945, along with a number of other HJ volunteers. From the sports school they travelled to a Werwolf training camp called 'ABS Rhoda Rhön,' where they were taught to conduct underground propaganda and carry out minor sabotage. Special emphasis was put on tricks such as cutting telephone lines, and then temporarily resealing the breaks in order to prevent immediate detection of the sabotage. Other courses were more intensely military: at a HJ camp in the Palatinate, at Waldmohr, SS NCOs taught orienteering to fifteen- and sixteen-year-old recruits, and they ran the boys through one-week courses familiarizing them with Mauser rifles, machine-guns, bazookas, and hand-grenades. Groups of twenty-five teenagers received plenty of ammunition for training (at a time when there was a dire shortage in the Wehrmacht), and they were intensively worked by four NCOs per group, an instruction ratio of almost one to six. The graduates of these courses were then either provided as cadres to the SS-Werwolf – especially HJ radio operators, who were highly qualified – or deployed as wholly HJ-Werwolf groups. In at least one case, at Eningen, near Reutlingen, the staff and students of an entire HJ training camp were transformed, in February 1945, into a unit called the Württemberg Close Combat Battalion 'Wehrwolf,' whose members were clothed in old Afrika Korps uniforms. For the masses of children outside the special training camps, and for those stranded behind enemy lines, leaflets were prepared giving detailed instructions on how to perform sabotage or string decapitation wires – 'Take anything from the enemy you can. His front lines depend on what rear areas can send him. So the more you take away from him, the more you will be doing for your country.'[6]

By the end of 1944, boys launched into action either by special training or by HJ propaganda began to make sporadic appearances behind enemy lines. Some of the first such agents were taken prisoner in eastern Belgium during the height of the Ardennes Offensive. Captured HJ guerrillas told the Americans that either they were recruited informally – one twelve-year-old described instructions issued by a retreating SS-sergeant in September 1944, ordering him to collect weapons and commit sabotage – or they were specifically sent across the lines by the Malmedy HJ chief, Walter Dennis. Some of these boys cached weapons, sabotaged U.S. communication lines and vehicles, and held clandestine meetings. In one case, a HJ agent from Bütgenbach succeeded in informing Dennis about American artillery positions and specific numbers of U.S. troops and equipment.[7] Similar teams were active during the German counteroffensive in Alsace, where they collected intelligence, switched road signs, snipped wires, and spread tacks along the main thoroughfare in Saverne. The Americans regarded such gangs as 'a security threat of considerable proportions,' particularly HJ reconnaissance teams trained by FAK units.[8]

Once American forces sliced deep into the Rhineland, the numbers of HJ-Werewolves behind Allied lines escalated from dozens into hundreds. Two HJ scouts were picked up on 23 February attempting to spy on troop movements along the Gangelt–Geilenkirchen road; another two were arrested by the 104th Infantry Division; ten HJ line-crossers were overrun by the 7th Armoured Division; five BdM radio agents were captured by the CIC in Krefeld; fifteen HJ guerrillas were rounded up near Bonn between 18 and 22 March, all of them equipped with sabotage kits – and the list went on. In one instance, a member of the Pimpfe, the preliminary stage of the Hitler Youth, managed to kill an American infantryman. 'We had stopped to re-form,' remembered a witness, 'when a small boy, 9 or 10 years old, asked a soldier for some chocolate. He was a cute looking youngster and from force of habit the soldier put his hands in his pockets to see if he had any. Then the cute little boy drew a pistol from his clothes and shot the man in the abdomen. He couldn't miss, he was so close.'[9]

Many such boys were members of special units formed by the leaders of the Rhenish HJ, such as Kirsch of Bonn and Schneider of Koblenz, who had themselves succeeded in reaching the east bank of the Rhine, and by March 1945 had begun to organize river-crossing operations. Such Werewolves crossed the Rhine in rubber boats and terrorized Cologne, where they may have been responsible for a number of knife attacks against U.S. soldiers. A Wehrmacht officer familiar with Schneider's headquarters in Montabaur, at the fringe of the Westerwald, estimated that he (Schneider) had gathered almost a hundred young volunteers from Koblenz, who were clothed in Army-cadet uniforms and 'were very keen.' These boys specialized in pouring sugar into the gas tanks of Allied vehicles, although, by mid-March, Schneider had also obtained explosives from the Army and was planning sabotage on a grander scale.

After the Allies smashed their way across the Rhine, they overran the bases of operation for such raids, and in the process they encountered considerable clusters of Werwolf guerrillas. In a range of hills east of Bonn, American troops overran a HJ guerrilla band led directly by Kirsch; at Diez, in the Lahn Valley, they arrested 5 heavily armed partisans who admitted being part of a larger group of 200 HJ saboteurs; and, at Bensheim, 3 HJ Werewolves were apprehended on 31 March, and they also revealed that they were members of a local group of 250 boys, each of whom had sworn to kill American soldiers. A further 10 boys were captured near Bensheim on 15 April, and they admitted that their final instructions from the HJ leadership were to lay in wait, pending receipt of further orders for sabotage. They were also told 'to remain good National Socialists and never accept another doctrine whatever the Americans should try to make them believe.'[10]

By the end of April, Allied forces had also overrun the central interior, where HJ organizers were less prepared for partisan warfare, but none the less made desperate, haphazard efforts to encourage such unrest. One half-formed detachment was uncovered in late April at Alsfeld, in Hesse, where seven boys captured by the CIC confessed to plotting attacks against American communication lines, mainly in order to capture weapons and transport. All seven youths wore Nazi badges under the lapels of their jackets, and they admitted coterminous membership in the HJ and the Werwolf.[11] At Magdeburg, a 'considerable number' of such partisans were killed when they sniped at U.S. troops, and, near Leipzig, HJ groups commanded by SS officers infiltrated American lines and occasionally approached U.S. troops with weapons hidden under their shirts. One American rear-echelon column was ambushed by teenagers who hid behind a wall and hurled hand-grenades at American soldiers. In Saxony–Anhalt, a group of adolescent guerrillas overran a car park full of captured German vehicles, where they spent a night engaged in a spree of malicious vandalism.[12] Along American supply lines near Hanover, a young boy was killed (along with all the members of his team) when he approached an American tank with an explosive charge that detonated prematurely. At Dinslaken, in the Ruhr, and at Memmingen, in Swabia, young schoolboys shot U.S. soldiers, and in the rear of the U.S. Ninth Army, a ten-year-old girl killed two Americans. At Calbe, yet another HJ guerrilla fired a round at a U.S. officer, but he missed and was killed in a hail of return fire, an incident that the CIC said 'had a salutary effect upon the population ...' Near Oldenburg, soldiers of the British 7th Armoured Division caught a number of HJ-Werewolves unloading bazookas from a wagon hidden behind a haystack. In the rear of the Ninth Army, a fourteen-year-old boy blew up a mid-town bridge in decidedly professional fashion, and, in the occupation sector of the U.S. 94th Infantry Division, HJ mined their local headquarters in Düsseldorf, which was occupied by U.S. forces after the fall of the city. In this latter case, disaster was averted only when an informer told CIC agents about the hidden explosives.[13]

A special trouble spot was the Altmark, a wooded region adjacent to the Elbe that also served as a haunt for Wehrmacht stragglers. According to a U.S. journalist who passed through the district in late April 1945, it was 'one of the hottest [areas] yet overrun for activity of the Jugend and the so-called Werewolves,' and members from a number of small bands had been apprehended. Typically these boys were aged from eleven to sixteen, although they were led by adult men. A HJ cell in Stendel did its best to cause trouble until being rolled up by the CIC, and, in Tangermünde, young Werewolves fired upon advancing U.S. infantry, which in turn prompted the Americans to shell the buildings and towers housing these snipers.[14]

There is evidence that the Red Army also ploughed into similar obstacles during its stop-and-start advance through Germany's eastern provinces. As in the West, HJ teams were employed by the Germans for reconnaissance, and, on the Oder Front, two boys won the Iron Cross for recovering important documents from behind Soviet lines.[15] Sabotage units were also deployed: on the night of 4 February, one such team ventured behind Russian lines around the besieged city of Elbing, where they succeeded in blowing up a Soviet tank. A month later, a similar squad was overrun by the Soviet security forces (NKVD) in the forested hills west of Litwald. All three boys were captured in civilian clothes, although they were armed with pistols, and they confessed that their mission was 'to carry out diversionist/terrorist acts against the Red Army.'

The single most successful operation along the Eastern Front, much celebrated in Nazi propaganda, was a Hitler Youth attack against Red Army billets in the Upper Silesian industrial town of Hindenburg. According to a German account, a HJ 'Battle Group' formed up shortly after the Russian conquest of the city, and they pledged themselves to avenge Soviet plunderings. Arming themselves with guns and demolition charges, the HJ Werewolves surrounded the Hindenburg Colonial School, where sixty Red Army troopers were making merry. After reconnaissance by two scouts, the HJ overran Soviet outposts and tanks guarding the school, and they then tossed their bombs through the doors and windows of the facility. The multiple blasts caused the structure to collapse, and buried most of the Russians.[16]

Regional Variants

Little is known about the local organizational efforts behind this last-minute sabotage campaign, so four examples will have to suffice in illustrating the regional particularities of the movement. In Inspectorate 'West,' the western-most subdivision of HJ administrative territory, the head of the guerrilla program was HJ-Major-General Gustav Memminger, the chief of the Press and Propaganda Branch of the Reich Youth Leadership, and a close friend of Joseph Goebbels's. In February 1945, Memminger supervised the preparation of recruitment propaganda and, late in the month, he ordered HJ chiefs in the Rhineland to establish resistance nests and supply depots, and to undertake sabotage against Allied forces. The special Reich Youth Leadership representative, Kloos, was also personally involved in efforts to establish a special Werwolf training school near Bonn. For practical purposes, efforts were concentrated in the Saar and the Palatinate, particularly once the military situation west of the Rhine began to deteriorate.

It is important to note, however, that the focus of Memminger's program gradually began to shift away from leaving boys behind Allied lines towards evacuating all available manpower to the eastern bank of the Rhine, where the intention was to set up raiding units or to submit the boys 'for intensive training to form the core of the force ... for a last-ditch stand to turn the tide of the war under the *Führer*.' This amended plan of action was communicated to the Rhenish HJ leaders during a meeting convened by SS-Lieutenant-Colonel Max Keller, head of HJ Territory 'Westmark' (and 'Werwolf Commissioner' for Gauleiter Josef Burckel). From this point onward, the main mission of the Rhenish HJ was to form boys into Werwolf 'March Groups' and get them safely across the Rhine. Many of the 20,000 youths rounded up for construction work in the Rhineland hid in order to avoid such evacuations, even though HJ leaders had permission to summarily execute all malingerers, and the number actually withdrawn across the river was only a fraction of the levy raised to build defence works. However, one group of 3,000 boys retreated from the southern

Rhineland to the Odenwald, and was last seen running for Thuringia, still only a step ahead of the Americans.[17]

The single most important HJ-Werwolf project in the Rhineland was 'Blocking Group "Elector Balduin,"' which was the brainchild of a Rhenish HJ officer named Rolf Karbach. 'Balduin' functioned under the operational purview of Wehrkreis XII, and had two responsibilities: defence of ground not yet overrun by the Allies, and the deployment of 'Werwolf groups' to harass Allied lines of communication. 'Balduin' guerrilla detachments operated mainly in the Hunsrück and the Eifel, sometimes with the support of local forest rangers. One of Karbach's ideas had been to exploit the tunnel system which lay underneath much of the Rhineland, and his guerrillas made effective use of this network. According to Jürgen Stroop, special successes were recorded in the Hunsrück, where a munitions plant was destroyed, and an Allied fuel dump was set on fire. As well, stretches of railway track near the Hunsrück–Höhenstrasse were blown up. None of these events, however, is substantiated by Allied records.

Whatever its successes, none of the 'Balduin' group's exploits seem to have reflected any credit on Karbach. His gung-ho sense of radicalism burned so brightly that it left everybody around him in a shadow. Even Jürgen Stroop, who had dutifully murdered thousands of Jews in the East on grounds of Nazi idealism, considered Karbach not fully sane. Therefore, even though the 'Balduin' operation had the personal blessing of Himmler, numerous roadblocks were thrown up in Karbach's path: the local *Gauleiter* advised local government and forestry officials not to cooperate; Berger would not give Karbach permission for the recruitment of HJ who were otherwise bound for the Waffen-SS; and Stroop conspired with the local Wehrkreis commander, General Osterkamp, in order to have the whole project shelved. Before long, Karbach was banished from the Rhineland and shuffled off to a new post with the HJ central directorate,[18] an ironic commentary on the nature of administrative success in the Third Reich.

Preparations were even more haphazard in HJ Territory 'Nordmark,' where the Werwolf was organized by HJ-Brigadier Hans Colling. Under the codeword 'Stieglitz,' Colling began recruiting personnel in March 1945, and he also established a training camp at Schönberg in Schleswig, which was commanded by HJ-Captain Haukohl. By late April, district detachments had been formed and, in at least one case, a supply truck had arrived from the south, carrying explosives. On order of the territorial leadership, these explosives were hurriedly buried and the hiding-places were mapped. It is possible that some of this material was used against the British, and there is no doubt that a number of Werewolves retreated to the Segeburg Forest, where they helped to organize a miniature redoubt. Colling himself ran loose until October 1945, when his hiding-place in the Lüneberg Heath was raided by British Field Security and he was taken prisoner, complete with poison ampoules and secret Werwolf plans sewn into the lining of his jacket. In the accompanying mêlée, a British officer was wounded and one of Colling's companions was killed. In many other cases, however, the movement simply collapsed; the HJ chief in Eutin, for one, later recalled gathering together his dozen-man Werwolf unit on the eve of the British arrival, whereupon he urged them to disband and return home. Werwolf activities, he counselled, 'would only recoil upon the civilian population.'[19]

A similar pattern of last-minute confusion also characterized conditions in the HJ territory headquartered at Brandenburg, in the rear of the Eastern Front. By early April, it had finally dawned on party officials that the Soviets were likely to soon charge across the Oder, and that east–central Germany was thus fated to serve as a battleground. During this period, a conference of thirty HJ officials was held in Brandenburg, and it was arranged to set up HJ-Werwolf teams under the leadership of a mysterious individual identified in NKVD documents as 'F.' Special attention was directed towards maintaining the conspiratorial nature of the movement. Although there were only several weeks in which to conduct unhindered organization, some progress was made: one local leader later remembered gathering more than 150 adolescent Werewolves under his command. As usual, supply stores were laid, weapons were distributed, and measures were taken to link the regional groups with a radio-communications junction in Brandenburg.

Some of these bands disintegrated in an inglorious panic, such as at Beltsig, where the local HJ chieftain abandoned his group and fled for safety to the Elbe, in turn rendering his unit toothless and ineffective.[20] On the other hand, at Rathenow, a unit of thirty HJ-Werewolves was ruthlessly effective in knocking out T-34 tanks with their bazookas. At a time when the rest of the German Twelfth Army had been chased to the Elbe and was preparing to surrender, these Werewolves, along with a handful of stragglers and young officers, were still hanging on, animated by the hope that the British would switch sides and come to rescue them. For a week in early May, they owed their lives only to the restraint of a Soviet Guards Division camped east of the town, which waited for them to retreat or surrender without immediately bringing them under artillery fire. A small party of German officers from the west visited Rathenow, *circa* 5–6 May, although they were treated with suspicion by the Spartans. The guerrillas were informed that the British were not ready to launch an anti-Soviet crusade, but, while they were dejected at hearing this news, they now resolved to be the last soldiers anywhere to offer armed resistance to the Soviet colossus. They were subsequently cut off and wiped out long after most the Twelfth Army had sullenly trooped into prisoner-of-war cages.[21]

The Psychology of HJ Guerrillas

One of the key questions concerning the HJ-Werwolf was that of morale, because, of all the institutions of the Third Reich, the HJ was believed to be most likely to display the fanatical spirit necessary for guerrilla warfare. The Nazis and the Allies alike subscribed to this assumption. Certainly, there was no lack of initiative at the top. Since 1940, the leader of the HJ had been Arthur Axmann, a thirty-two-year-old careerist who had already literally sacrificed his right arm for the Reich (in a fire-fight on the Russian Front in 1941). In the spring of 1945, Axmann made repeated calls for die-hard efforts, saying that German children would never capitulate, and he bragged of Werwolf activities behind the Western Front. 'Youth,' he declared, 'has become the soul of our national resistance.' Axmann himself stayed in besieged Berlin in order personally to lead HJ 'Battle Groups,' and he was one of the last people to see Hitler alive.

A similar sense of verve was displayed by Axmann's chief of staff, Helmut Möckel, who died in a motor accident on 27 February 1945 while on a tour of southwest Germany, recruiting volunteers for the Werwolf. Möckel's last words included instructions for prospective Werewolves, and the physician who attended Möckel's passing was warned that he and his family would be shot if he divulged anything of what he had heard. Reports from Switzerland subsequently suggested Möckel's death was faked, and that he had really escaped to Spain in order to conduct clandestine operations from abroad, but there is no evidence to suggest that this was true.

An equally important figure was the HJ's chief ideologist, Gottfried Griesmayr, who was in charge of HJ indoctrination and dreamed of spearheading a neo-Nazi movement, rising phoenix-like from the ashes and wholeheartedly committed to the 'pure teachings of the Führer.' It was Griesmayr who prepared the HJ memorandum suggesting that 'weaklings' should be shot, even by their subordinates if necessary, and it will be recalled that this idea had been accepted quickly by Martin Bormann. Nazi rabble-rousers, in the spring of 1945, were also pushing for the publication of Griesmayr's radical tome, *The Folkish Ideal*, although, given the fact that the undertaking was still in the planning stage as late as mid-March, it seems unlikely that the book was ever produced.[22]

However, while no one would doubt the ruthless tenacity of figures in the senior HJ leadership, there was considerable evidence of more mixed feelings at lower echelons. This was rather unexpected, given the near-total monopoly of control over young minds exercised by the regime since 1933–4, but it was none the less obvious. Seemingly, the influence of parents, priests, and unindoctrinated teachers never broke down as completely as had been anticipated. At

München–Gladbach, the CIC was surprised to learn that the leader of a twelve-man Werwolf anti-tank unit had ignored his orders because his mother had forbidden him to attack American armour![23]

In the final weeks, even the Reich Youth Leadership was forced to acknowledge these annoyingly persistent family attachments. Axmann, on 20 April, admitted, 'I understand the great anxiety of our mothers ... I can assure them I am fully aware of the great and heavy responsibility I have shouldered.' Hitler, too, he said, was a concerned parent in the most general sense. 'In each German boy, and in each German girl, the *Führer* sees his own son and his own daughter ... The hearts of our German youth belong to him.'[24] Perhaps he even failed to recognize the subconscious desires of the Nazi leadership, which demanded the spilling of young blood as an atonement for the alleged 'failings' of its own people.

One might well wonder how the Nazis hoped to motivate young fighters, given the desperate straits in which Germany found itself. The basic device was the same technique that had been employed for twenty years: to offer violent posturing as a solution to problems, and risk taking as a recipe for success, all within an idealized framework of high purpose and self-abnegation. In fact, a HJ-Werwolf order dating from early March 1945 and originating with the district leadership in the Moselle area cynically instructed guerrilla trainers to 'implant in young minds a heroic romantic psychosis' as a means of providing motivation. Several themes were layered upon this basic foundation. Obviously, HJ-Werewolves were told that their actions were patriotic: a sabotage pamphlet captured by the Allies near Brenzhausen ended with the exhortation 'Everything that hurts the enemy will benefit our soldiers.' Similarly, an appeal to Lower Saxon Werewolves exhorted children to have faith in German victory, and to stay defeat until the Wehrmacht could get its footing and recover its ability to clear the enemy from German soil. And, in truth, some young people believed in victory until a frightfully late date. To buttress patriotism, propagandists inspired fear: kids in a 'Defence Training Camp' in Austria were told that the enemy intended to sterilize every male German from the age of fifteen. Nazi ideologists also appealed to the pride of youth, suggesting that their moment had finally come, and that they could bring about a momentous reversal in the fortunes of war that older generations had failed to achieve. Including girls in this pitch also implied that a gender previously pushed into the shadows would now get a chance to prove its worth in the most direct sort of way. And, finally, HJ propagandists reminded teenagers of the need for revenge. Axmann, in late March 1945, asserted the need to 'avenge the shame brought upon our homes, our mothers and our sisters by a blindly raging enemy.'[25] Needless to say, this appeal had a special impact upon teenagers from the evacuated eastern provinces.

The dynamics of German society were little understood or appreciated by the occupying powers. 'The military command had a war to win,' remembered a CIC officer (who was also a German émigré), and they coldly regarded the psychological states of HJ saboteurs 'as uninteresting peripheral matters.' Their usual answer to problems with the HJ was to execute troublemakers or subject them to lengthy prison sentences, and American Military Police and CIC personnel were known to beat up their juvenile captives in order to extract information and destroy the remnants of Werwolf groups. Suspected young Werewolves under fourteen years of age were sometimes seen behind the wire of ad hoc American internment camps along the Rhine, often clad only in pyjamas or underwear, because they had been arrested at night. There they stood, in the rain and cold, day and night, ankle-deep in the mud of unsheltered compounds. Matters were even worse behind Russian lines, where the NKVD made common use of torture, and thousands of teenage captives were destined to grow up in Soviet labour camps, often under the dubious wing of 'veteran party comrades' who were imprisoned in the same compounds. Members of the 'Volkssturm–Hitler Youth' were often summarily executed. Some kids who were spared were recruited by the NKVD and, when released, were forced to go among their friends and act as *agents provocateurs*.

However, there were a few sensitive souls who realized that the real way to improve the minds of German youth was to repair the German family. Boys captured by the Western Allies frequently broke into tears and begged to be reunited with their parents – an option that previously had seemed most uninviting to such rebellious spirits – and Allied security officers sometimes recommended clemency on these grounds, although the disposition of such cases was usually out of their hands.[26] One British military court made a practice of calling forth the parents of adolescent guerrillas to ask why they had not kept their sons in order. In one case, the forthright answer was that Hitler had destroyed the basis of parental authority. In this instance, the court restored such authority by fiat, enjoining the parents of several boys to take whatever measures were necessary to guarantee good behaviour. 'The parents were overjoyed,' said one observer, 'and I saw a gleam in one mother's eye as she marched her erring offspring out of Court.' French military courts also tried to induce a renewed sense of parental responsibility, and in at least one case a tribunal fined a German father 5,000 marks when his sixteen-year-old son was caught in possession of a pistol.[27]

Among the boys and girls themselves, there was often a happy re-emergence of common sense, which bubbled to the surface even through the thickest muck of ideology and thought control. In one case, two sixteen-year-old boys told the Allies that an attempt had been made to recruit them as Werewolves while they attended a HJ leadership school in the Harz Mountains. They were made to sign documents that they had not read, then told that they were novice Werewolves and had a day to consider becoming full-fledged guerrillas. Since these boys refused this generous offer, as reason rightly dictated, they were sent to a political reformatory at Ballenstedt, near Quedlinburg, where they were thrown together with 600 similar recalcitrants. Even yet, however, HJ officers had not given up on these supposed slackers. While at Ballenstedt, they were trained in guerrilla tactics and ordered to recruit boys for ad hoc resistance units once they were behind Allied lines. Our two informants wisely ran away when the Americans approached.[28]

There were other, similar cases. One three-man unit actually slipped through American lines with orders to attack targets of opportunity, but, once across the lines, they almost immediately headed for home, on the way throwing their equipment into a manure pit. This was an act with an unmistakable symbolic resonance. The CIC finally caught up with these young men and interrogated them, although they did not arrest them – 'The boys did not appear to be thoroughly indoctrinated with Naziism, nor did they seem interested in carrying out the mission the Germans had assigned them.' At Tübingen, a HJ-Werwolf group – showing no desire to fight or to 'scorch the earth' – refused an assignment to destroy a local water reservoir and actually chased away members of an Army demolitions team preparing to blow up a bridge over the Neckar River. At Sulzbach, a HJ leader terrorized the village by plastering it with threatening signs and slogans, but once an impressive column of American tanks rolled through the town, he meekly gave up on his plans for guerrilla activity and was interned as a POW. Other boys were also shattered by the sound and fury of the enemy's passage. At Pleismar, near Leipzig, a formation of eighty adolescent Werewolves attacked an American armoured column, but once the tanks returned fire and three boys were killed, the remainder of the guerrillas broke and ran, many of them crying hysterically.[29]

It was also impossible for HJ boys not to notice that the great majority of German society was opposed to the Werwolf, which had a demoralizing effect even upon young fanatics. In a number of cases, Germans themselves took steps to ensure that HJ Werewolves brought no harm to their towns or to German property. At the village of Pech, in the Rhineland, the regional Volkssturm commander chased a HJ-Werwolf leader out of the area and 'warned the village people not to let any strangers come into town anymore'; at Brettheim, near Crailsheim, a HJ anti-tank unit was forcibly demobilized by local civilians (for which three of these concerned citizens were hanged by an SS Summary Court); in Halle, an elderly woman disarmed two sixteen-year-old Werewolves, stripped them of their uniforms and clad them in bathrobes, and then buried their bazookas in her backyard; in the Sudetenland, at Komotau, local police broke up a HJ band led by two drunken SS soldiers.[30] There was a fear among HJ leaders that German civilians would ruthlessly denounce Werewolves unless the partisans escaped suspicion by posing as refugees, and, as a result, the HJ was usually forced to send its guerrillas outside their home regions.[31]

Of course, even despite these impediments, there was a functioning core of desperate individuals who gave the Werwolf some real bite. A number of HJ Werewolves taken prisoner near Aachen were so fanatical that the guards could not open the doors to their cells without having the boys rush out and fall upon their captors. They had to be fed by sliding victuals through a narrow crack in the door. At Limfort, a fifteen-year-old was caught snipping American wires; he admitted that his mission was to 'hurt American supply lines,' and he proved a totally recalcitrant Nazi, telling his captors that he wished all German boys would copy his actions. At Magdeburg, one U.S. tank commander considered HJ troops 'German Boy Scouts,' and, after giving them 'a kick in the pants,' sent them home. Many of these boys, however, rejected this reprieve and were subsequently killed after they had returned to battle. In the Harz, a German refugee hiding in the woods witnessed the deployment in mid-April 1945 of a troop of sixteen- and seventeen-year-old Werewolves, who had been sent into the forest to track down escaped Russian prisoners-of-war. According to her account, the boys brought to their task all of 'the carefree brutality engendered by their youth and upbringing.'

The psychological profile of a teenager captured near Bonn suggested that in this case – which was typical – Werwolf warfare was a kind of extended rebellion against the boy's parents. Unlike many of his fellow Werewolves, this lad did not cry or whimper when interrogated, although he did coolly explain his situation. His father was off to war – he did not know where – and, although only fifteen, he had already freed himself of his mother's care and influence. His progress through the ranks of the HJ had been slow, so he desperately wanted to prove himself, although he also admitted that he had not the slightest idea about who really provided his orders or controlled his movements as a guerrilla. However, even this erstwhile fanatic was partially broken by his CIC interrogators: after being repeatedly told how senseless his sabotage activities had been, he was no longer sure that he had done the right thing, and he wished to see his mother again for the first time in years. 'Everything that he believed in suddenly lost its worth,' noted his interrogator. 'There remained only the family, which could at least offer sure support until he could reorientate himself.'

A similar story involved a seventeen-year-old BdM chieftain from Monschau who was arrested in January 1945 because she had helped organize a clique, the

'Heimat-True,' which occupied itself by assembling outside Military Government headquarters and poking fun at American soldiers. This girl's diary, which was seized, made for interesting reading, as its author had given vent to all the opinions typical of a teenage Nazi fanatic: Americans were cowards who were winning the war only through material superiority; 'Wonder Weapons' could yet save the Third Reich; collaborators were sickening. Her club, she said, resolutely refused such American enticements as cigarettes and continued to fight 'for the ideals of our irreplacable Führer.' In this case, too, however, the subject was rapidly disillusioned by the counter-arguments of her captors, and within several months of her arrest she consented to record a radio address, appealing for members of Hitler Youth not to attack Allied forces. In March 1945 she was returned to her parents in Monschau, whom she had earlier defied.[32]

While the institution of the family was frequently lauded as a final hope for the 'lost boys' of the HJ, we ought not to over-romanticize its importance or influence. Psychological assessments of young Germans suggested that, in this authoritarian and patriarchal society, attachment to the HJ sometimes served as an escape from a harsh and frustrating home life. Hitler himself had set the necessary tone in *Mein Kampf*, where he called for youth to be domineering and aggressive – 'the free, splendid beast of prey must once again flash from its eyes.'[33] Postwar interviewers of German children found that, when the subjects were asked to imagine war, they often fantasized about conditions where their parents were dead or absent. Moreover, they frequently spoke of taking up arms themselves, and adolescents – at an age when the peer group had become very important – sometimes speculated about forming bands under such conditions.[34]

Proponents of die-hard resistance tended to fall into three groups, defined by such criteria as personality type, age, and social origin. First, there were the corps of HJ leaders, bourgeois egoists who were not ideological in any meaningful sense, but enjoyed wielding power and were personally ambitious. This group was especially associated with the increased militarization of the HJ after 1939, which many rank-and-file members of the movement hated. By the last years of the war, many of these leaders were also deeply resented by subleaders who were a decade younger; this rejection, in turn, developed into an obvious cooling of feelings about the Nazi regime itself. Several teenage dissidents told the Americans in 1944 that only 'the paid leaders' were still enthusiastic about the HJ. 'These chaps have never before had such an easy life, with their own cars, a steady job and assured promotions.' Such perquisites were apparently worth a fight.

A second group comprised misguided idealists whose sense of self was built around the National Socialist state. Alexander Mitscherlich has drawn a fascinating portrait of the child made 'fatherless' by war or, more generally, by the pressures of modern industrial society. Such a child found a substitute in the great totalitarian leader and in the myths promoted by this figure. He or she was able to release inner aggression because his or her Führer rarely called for moderation or self-control: the child was simply released, and with this process came a contingent feeling of indestructibility, as individuality merged into a mass identity.

A third category consisted of intelligent boys of humble origin who had benefited through Nazi social measures and the partial collapse of class barriers. An officer of the U.S. First Army who encountered such adolescents near Paderborn described them as 'little city toughs – dead-end kids.' 'They are better than the average run of German soldiers,' he noted, 'and still are enthusiastic over Nazi ideas.' Arthur Axmann, in a blunt speech on 26 March 1945, reminded youth that only by saving the existing system 'would they ensure the ability to advance socially.' Eric Hoffer has rightly noted that the 'free poor' – people who are poverty-stricken but have a chance for social mobility – have traditionally comprised fodder for fanatical movements because they value equality and fraternity more than they do individual freedom.

Allied authorities noted hopefully, however, that neither the 'dead-enders' nor the true believers seemed irredeemably bad. 'They are frank about their past convictions,' said a British report; 'the collapse came as a more sudden shock to them and their disappointment is greater than that of the others. It is amongst them, apart from the staunchly religious, that one finds the greatest willingness to believe in the revelations of the horror camps and Nazi baseness and dishonesty. However, their reaction is not as in the cases of the religious ones hatred, but grief.'[35] Mitscherlich argues that identification with the Führer, no matter how intense it once seemed, was actually superficial, because the ersatz father-figure never provided the intense give-and-take of a genuine father–child relationship. The final product was a generation of 'nobody's children,' who lived with little sense of history and were, by their very nature, creatures of the moment. They were psychologically capable of quickly jettisoning any commitment to Hitler or to the precepts of National Socialism, although this process was accompanied by a considerable degree of disorientation. 'When the pressure to obey was suddenly removed,' says Mitscherlich, 'the individual no longer understood himself.'

Postwar Activities

In various areas, such half-demoralized radicals attempted to continue the fight, even after the final German surrender. Swiss journalists reported in late May

1945 that Nazi youths were still ambushing Allied troops, stringing decapitation wires, and mining stretches of highway, all of which had caused casualties
among the occupation forces. At Bamberg, two HJ boys blew up an abandoned
German ammunition train on 25 May, and they admitted previously receiving
instructions to start as many fires as possible, particularly in order to impede
Allied rail traffic. In Stuttgart, HJ-Werewolves painted threats on the walls of
the city and held secret meetings, and two HJ members in Innsbruck were
engaged in the same kind of activity. At the Franconian town of Ansbach, HJ
boys led by a twenty-one-year-old self-styled 'Führer,' Kurt Hoesch, conducted
illegal propaganda, cached explosives, and terrorized women who consorted
with American soldiers. The ring-leaders in this group had been trained in
special sabotage schools during the last days before the German capitulation.
A similar band was rounded up in Bremen after it had terrorized German 'collaborators' by attacking their homes. At Karlsruhe, four ex-leaders of the HJ
'Marine Section' were arrested after holding illegal meetings and maintaining
contacts with other HJ staff members. At Minden, one of the main trouble spots
in the British Zone, young HJ-Werewolves emerged on the rooftops at night,
whence they disturbed the sleep of British soldiers by howling. In response, the
British occupiers typically fired off a barrage from their Sten guns and pistols in
order to clear the roofs.[36]

One of the most interesting such cases was in Munich, where there was a
considerable volume of reports about Werwolf activity in the first months after
the end of the war.[37] Some of these difficulties were caused by twenty HJ-
Werewolves whose circle was penetrated in November 1945 by an Office of
Strategic Services (OSS) undercover agent. Described as 'snot-nosed brats,'
none of these boys had fought, except possibly in the Volkssturm, and they were
so incompetent that they failed to notice their new companion wearing an
American ID bracelet, or smoking American cigarettes. None the less, the band
had done, or was planning to do, harm to U.S. forces, including ambushing
American troops and bombing a Military Police (MP) post, and there was thus a
need to deal quickly with this incipient threat. After attending several of the
group's meetings at an underground barn near the Deutsches Theater, the OSS
agent passed on a list of a dozen names to the local provost marshal, and a contingent of heavily armed MPs raided the housing complex where the boys lived.
After a number of apartments were searched, the Werewolves were captured
and the scene was invaded by forlorn mothers and grandmothers, each insisting
that her lad was really a good boy and could not possibly be mixed up in this
Werwolf nastiness.[38]

By the fall of 1945, American authorities regarded remnants of the HJ as
'one of the greatest potential threats to security in both the American and Allied

Zones of Occupation.' One intelligence summary described a rising tendency for teenagers to 'show contempt for the rules and regulations laid down by military authority':

In some cases [continued the report] this may be nothing more serious than a flippant reply, a display of arrogance, a derisive shout at a passer-by, or the writing of anonymous notes in which military personnel are threatened. In other instances resistance is more overt in nature: missiles are hurled at passing vehicles; lone members of the military are attacked; German girls who associate with the occupying troops are physically punished; government equipment and fuel are stolen. In a limited number of instances juvenile resistance has taken a very serious turn. American soldiers have been murdered; communication wires have been cut; wire or cable has been strung across the highway in the hope of killing or maiming the occupants of the vehicle; and secret meetings are held for the purpose of planning subversive activity. To be sure, most of the more flagrant violations show a certain degree of adult leadership and instigation, but the very fact that there exists among German youth the will to execute such plans is sufficient to warrant serious consideration.[39]

Similar groups existed in the Soviet Zone. At Wismar, two HJ cadres gathered weapons and planned attacks against the Red Army, at least until they were arrested by the NKVD in March 1946. These boys had garnered some success in recruiting former Wehrmacht soldiers for their band. At Zödenick, in Brandenburg, members of the HJ were organized by an adult woman, who rented eight apartments as hide-outs, and then prepared her young charges for a program of sabotage and assassination. A Soviet patrol arrested the leader and several other members of this group in early July 1945. In Saxony, a number of nine-man cells originally organized by the HJ regional office in Merseburg survived well into 1946. 'Our aim,' admitted a captured HJ-Werewolf, 'was to attack lone cars and soldiers of the Red Army, and to steal arms and alcoholic beverages. [As well, we wanted] to recruit new members to the Werwolf organization in order to strengthen it and to wage active combat against the occupation army.' These forces spread Werwolf propaganda, and were suspected of launching sporadic terror actions, such as a New Year's Day sniping attack against a Red Army guard company in Merseburg, which wounded one man.[40]

The Axmann Plan

None of this activity was very surprising, nor was it different from the post-capitulation operations sporadically undertaken by groups from the SS wing of the Werwolf. What was radically different about the fate of the HJ-Werwolf was that the movement's *leadership* made detailed preparations for survival in a fully occupied Germany, and that they attempted to carry out aspects of this plan. There was no real parallel for this in the Bureau 'Prützmann' or in the other control mechanisms associated with the SS-Werwolf.

Among the senior Nazi leadership, only Arthur Axmann spared the time and bother to prepare a detailed scheme for the period when most – or all – of Germany would be occupied. This 'Axmann Plan' took shape in March and April 1945, when, as a preliminary step, the headquarters of the Reich Youth Leadership was shifted from Berlin to the site of a HJ élite training school at Bad Tölz, in the Bavarian Alps. Plans were also made to preserve the 'essence of the nation' by moving 35,000 HJ leaders to the inaccessible hill country of southern Germany and Bohemia, whence they could maintain cohesion and harass the occupation forces. Axmann foresaw an imminent war between the Western Powers and the Soviet Union, so for him the trick of survival was to stick together until the HJ could join the Western Allies in a final campaign against the hordes from the East. Senior couriers were sent out to the four corners of the Reich – Erich Schröder to the north, Ernst Overbeck to the west, Hans Winter to the southeast, Gottfried Griesmayr to Austria and Bohemia – and these couriers carried orders for local HJ leaders to retreat southwards. Cadres were told that they need not show up with arms and equipment, since a half-year's supplies were to be provided by the Wehrmacht. If evacuation proved impossible, HJ organizers were told to go to ground and await the development of a favourable climate for underground work.[41] Griesmayr, for one, followed this plan in Bohemia, where he sent armed HJ boys into the woods and personally took charge of their 'spiritual education.' On 5 May, he and a number of other HJ and SS leaders gathered at the town of Prachatitz, where they founded a rejuvenated NSDAP based upon a new ten-point program.[42]

In truth, an unknown number of HJ guerrillas actually reached the southern mountains, where they were directed to carry out partisan warfare and prepare for the outbreak of a new conflict.[43] Some officials were very enthusiastic: the Upper Bavarian HJ chief, HJ-Major-General Panzer, 'had quite unrealistic illusions as to the effect of partisan activities against the advancing Allies.' Tyrolean HJ leaders trusted in their ability to carry out guerrilla warfare because of their experience in underground operations prior to 1938, and some of the evacuees from the north were caught up in this enthusiasm, despite the terrible odds pitted against them. 'No power on earth would succeed in destroying our community, the fellowship of the corps of Hitler Youth Leaders,' as one BdM chief remembered it. 'I sought salvation in the idea that now a new period of illegal activity would begin, although no one knew what its political purpose would be. So we adjusted ourselves to the idea of fighting on ... I cannot remember a single one of us lamenting the disaster which had overtaken us. This was due less to our heroism than to our blindness about the finality of the disaster.' At Siegsdorf, in the Bavarian Alps, a local HJ officer contented himself with the idea that the Americans would leave behind only 60,000 occupation troops, and that these would be feeble, second-grade men. 'We can always produce 60,000 Hitler Youth. That's only one each. And then, in one night ... it's all done.' When a local Volkssturm NCO sounded a sceptical note and declared himself *not* to be a Werwolf, the answer was: 'It's not the same for you. You're old!'[44]

Training for this last-minute levy was carried out at a number of mountain huts: near Benediktbeuern, for example, a school for HJ special forces was set up as early as February 1945 in the 'Tutzingerhütte.' This camp was under the supervision of the SS and was manned by NCOs from Mountain Regiment 98, stationed at Garmisch. Near the end of the war, one of the trainers at the camp, Sergeant Max Reutemann, was made responsible for organizing the Benediktbeuern Werwolf, along with a local forest ranger and HJ-Colonel Müller from Bad Tölz. This detachment subsequently exploited the food and weapons earlier laid away for the personnel of the training camp. At the time of the collapse, the faculty and students of the HJ élite school at Bad Tölz also fled into the mountains in order to form a 250-man guerrilla unit, and they, too, benefited from supplies that had earlier been cached.[45] HJ-Colonel Johannes List launched an identical undertaking at the hut 'Zur Schönen Aussicht,' near Salzburg, and SS personnel were involved in yet another, similar project at mountain cabins near Tanzstatt, in Carinthia. At Bad Reichenhall, a special school trained signals personnel withdrawn from the threatened districts in the Sudetenland and Upper Silesia.[46]

Along the Eastern Front in Austria, HJ-Lieutenant-General Hans Lauterbacher organized a special HJ Battle Group, dubbed 'Werwolf,' which comprised two fanatical battalions manned at the senior echelons by Army and Waffen-SS officers. This unit performed well in conventional fighting in Vienna and it then protected the Sixth SS Panzer Army until it was withdrawn from combat on 17 April and marched westwards.[47] In addition, special HJ 'Ranger Commandos' were drawn from the Battle Group and sent behind Russian lines. Despite fuel shortages inhibiting the deployment of such bands, the Germans were still able to launch a considerable guerrilla war in eastern Austria, where Werwolf units terrorized 'collaborators' and laid mines. They even had some successes in drawing Soviet troops away from hard-pressed Wehrmacht forces. One sixty-five-man detachment infiltrated Soviet lines by crawling through the canals and storm drains of the Austrian capital, and then breaking out to the Vienna Woods, where they were joined by a small band of bypassed Vlassovites and, in concert with them, were able to launch a campaign of bloody mayhem. On 13 April, they attacked an assemblage of Soviet troops and armour at Kitzendorf, destroying three tanks and several armoured cars; on 18 April, they overran a horse-drawn supply column in hand-to-hand fighting near the Hängendenstein, in the process replenishing their supplies; on the following night, they made an unsuccessful attempt to blow up a rail viaduct at Eichgraben, although they managed to damage the same railway east of Press-bawm, where they also demolished a small bridge; on the same day, they destroyed a railway station at Rekawinkel, which was being used as a billet by Russian *pionnier* troops; on 21 April, they ambushed a Soviet supply column near Klausenleopoldsdorf, destroying three trucks; several nights later, they threw grenades and fired at some Soviet wagons, and then attacked an enemy bivouac in the Kaumberger Forest; and, on May Day, they surprised celebrating Soviets by blowing up a fuel-supply depot at Hainfeld, an act which also involved shooting up the guard detachment. By this time, however, the formation had been reduced to a handful of boys who spent most of their time desperately dodging Soviet anti-partisan units. They returned to German lines on 5 May, nearly a month after they had left, only to be told that evening that Dönitz was prohibiting any future escapades of a similar nature. None the less, Dönitz accepted Prützmann's nomination of the expedition's leader, sixteen-year-old Alfred Borth, for the Knight's Cross, although the war ended before Borth could receive his award.[48]

Smaller units were also fielded in the western Alps, where they were armed by the Waffen-SS and the HSSPF,[49] and along the northern approaches to the mountains it was not unusual for American armour to encounter such bands. These youthful fanatics terrorized their own civilians with Werwolf leaflets, and there were reports of children playing 'dead' near roadways as American infantrymen trudged along, only to rise again once the Americans were passed and then fire at them from the rear. 'The world of those children of the Hitler Youth was coming to an end [remembered one American officer]. Soon there would be nothing left ... Denied the opportunity to be real soldiers, to wear a proper uniform and fight as soldiers in a formal unit, those kids were determined to show us that they knew how to sacrifice themselves. There was one boy who we took prisoner. His rocket had hit my tank but had not exploded. I was livid that this snotty brat should endanger my life and I was out of that tank cuffing him about the head and shouting. When I let go of him he fell to the grass crying and saying something ... What that child was saying was that he should have died for the *Führer*.'[50] Such incidents sometimes led to nasty consequences: at Wellenhof, in Voralberg, a HJ evacuee from Berlin was murdered, and his remains thrown into a stream bed after he had killed several French troops with a Panzerfaust; while at Scharding, in Upper Austria, HJ captives were executed by the Americans, and their bodies dumped into the Inn River.[51]

In other cases, fanatics retreated deep into the mountains and held out: the training huts near Benediktbeuern were manned by HJ and SS men for months *after* the capitulation, and Sergeant Reutemann enthusiastically made plans to attack local civilians cooperating with the Americans. Forest Ranger Höfner, meanwhile, kept the hut inhabitants informed about events in the populated valleys. These cabins were abandoned only in July 1945, when the Americans launched raids into the surrounding mountains. In Austria, eighteen-year-old Walter Kuhn, the son of the erstwhile 'American Bund' leader, Fritz Kuhn, was captured by the CIC on 2 July, when he wandered out of the hills. He had been selected to lead one of the HJ groups in the mountains. Ironically, when he was picked up, Kuhn was wearing a sweater in the colours of his former high school in New York City. Similarly, Johannes List was also captured in the summer of 1945, when he descended from his mountain hideaway to visit his wife. CIC reports described List as one of the most dangerous of all HJ-Werwolf leaders.[52]

While Axmann's followers were desperately fighting a rearguard action in the Alps, the HJ chief himself – as we know – remained in the Reich capital in order to direct defence efforts. After Hitler's death, however, Axmann infiltrated the Soviet ring around the city, and he then fled to hide-outs in Bohemia and southern Germany, where he remained for seven months and kept in contact with his followers. During this period of illegal activity, Axmann was also on the move, touring around occupied Germany in order to coordinate his underground movement. In fact, when the Americans finally caught up with him, Axmann was arrested at a roadblock, attempting to cross between the Soviet and U.S. zones.[53]

The real mark of genius in the Axmann Plan was its provision for a continuing and self-replenishing source of funds for Werwolf activity. First of all, Axmann appointed his principal deputy, HJ-Major-General Franke of Dresden, as the leader of the politico-military wing of the Alpine Werwolf. Franke was given 50,000 marks in order to establish cover by opening a publishing firm for children's literature, and, with this money in pocket, he eventually relocated to Marburg. More important, however, Axmann also transferred a much larger sum, more than 1.5 million marks, to his economic adviser, Willi Heidemann, an ex-schoolteacher and brigadier in the HJ. Heidemann, too, was dispatched to the Alps, in this case as the head of an independent economic section of the HJ-Werwolf. He quickly emerged as a Nazi version of Oliver North, in the sense that he was responsible for financing a project through a sensitive and critical period, when regular funds were lacking. In order to achieve this, Heidemann was given orders to minimize contacts with active Werewolves, but to build a legal business enterprise in close association with the American Military Government. At the time of the final capitulation, the Reich paymaster handed an extra 10 million marks to a HJ official named Dreblow, who in turn passed much of this money on to Heidemann. When Dreblow died in October 1945, control of this secret stash was assumed by another HJ official, Werner Kowalski. Both Dreblow and Kowalski were employees of Heidemann during the immediate postwar period.

With money and clear directives in hand, Heidemann based himself in Bad Tölz, and in late April made a sound investment by buying Tessmann and Sons, a transportation company with offices throughout Germany. One of Tessmann's managers, a member of the Allgemeine-SS named Leebens, was apparently bitter about the loss of the company's head offices in Dresden at the time of the February 1945 phosphorous bombings, and he was happy to sell the business to Heidemann for the fire-sale price of 10,000 marks, contingent upon the stipulation that he himself remain a partner in the firm. Tessmann and Sons subsequently became the basis of Heidemann's operations, since its nature as a transport company improved Werwolf communications, and its dealings in food and coal gave it close contacts with General Patton's lax Military Government in Bavaria. One American officer, a Captain Goodloe, was even involved in some of Heidemann's business dealings. Simultaneously, of course, Heidemann retained liaison with Franke, and he provided a flow of funds for desperadoes throughout southern Germany. During the summer of 1945, he also proved himself an adept businessman, and, by the end of the year, he had bought six additional companies and expanded throughout the American and British zones, and into Austria. Moreover, an extensive network of contacts was built up among some of the most important names in German business, such as the Krupp family, who used their influence to smooth the way for Heidemann's expansion into the Ruhr. Fear of the Deuxième Bureau, notably, kept Heidemann out of the French Zone.

Meanwhile, leaders of the HJ-Werwolf in the British Zone had also begun to reorganize in a spontaneous fashion. The key figure was the head of the HJ-Personnel Bureau, Willi Lohel, who had been stranded in Oldenburg at the end of the war and was one of the main figures ordered to go to ground and await further instructions. By July 1945, however, Lohel felt he could no longer remain inactive, and on his own initiative he began to re-establish contact with his former comrades, and also drew up a bombastic twelve-point program for 'the future of German youth.' The main emphasis of Lohel's contacts were mutual aid, collection of intelligence, the organized forgery of identification documents, and the gradual establishment of a neo-Nazi political movement. Similar goals were held by two other important figures in the British Zone, HJ-

Lieutenant-Generals Kurt Badäus and Ernst Overbeck and, during the fall of 1945, these two men, together with Lohel, presided over the gradual consolidation of a movement of like-minded HJ leaders. Called the 'Society of the Just,' this nebulous conspiracy was mainly political in nature, and its economic wing, unlike its parallel in the American Zone, was underdeveloped. Lacking any last-minute injections of party funds that would have enabled the purchase of a major concern such as Tessmann and Sons, Lohel and company wasted their time with amateurish plans to support subversive activity through bee-keeping, selling hand-made crafts, and running a travelling puppet show.

The most practical figures of the northern movement, such as Badäus, realized that the success of their group was contingent upon the establishment of a close association with the Heidemann combine and the southern leadership corps. To some extent, this was achieved: Gustav Memminger, leader of the Rhenish HJ-Werwolf, was appointed as liaison between the northern and southern movements, and officers such as Overbeck were able to re-establish direct contact with Axmann. In fact, Axmann visited the British Zone in early November 1945, meeting with Overbeck, Memminger, Winter, and other HJ leaders in Lübeck. However, what the British Zone chieftains really wanted was financing, and this they never received. Heidemann was extremely reluctant to part with any of his precious resources, and he rudely stood up Badäus at an introductory meeting between the two men in Kassel. He made quite clear, through his representatives in the north, that he could not undertake commitments to finance the British Zone conspiracy 'until such time as he felt that he had achieved a sufficient degree of success to cover himself and his associates, and to ensure the financial stability of his business.' Lohel tried to slide around this roadblock by going straight to Kowalski, whom he knew to be in charge of party funds dispersed at the end of the war. However, Kowalski, who was employed by Heidemann, gave the same negative answer as his boss, and he, too, refused to part with any money.[54]

The most notable aspect of all these developments was the emergent conservatism of the Heidemann combine. Heidemann was frightened by several large-scale American swoop operations conducted during the summer and fall of 1945, code-named 'Tally Ho' and 'Doublecheck,' and he was able to protect himself during this period only with the help of a spy working as a typist in a Military Government office. As a result, he believed that his business success would be threatened by the even more oppressive counter-insurgency sweeps that Werwolf operations would surely provoke, and he quickly turned against any overt display of resistance. Heidemann described violent sabotage in derisory tones as 'fire-and-thunder methods.' Rather, he devoted himself towards the more lofty and long-term goal of the Axmann Plan – that is, the preservation of the 'national essence.' He hoped to achieve this by building his combine into a major economic force in the new Germany, capable of influencing politics and serving as a core for Nazi ideological torch-bearers.[55]

A particularly ready guide to goals of the postwar HJ was provided by Gustav Memminger, whose point-form notes on the movement were found among his belongings after his eventual arrest. In summing up the program of the conspiracy, Memminger noted, in particular, 'preservation of national substance, greater effort to produce. Germany as she existed in 1933 without imperialistic aims, creation of a new German solidarity based on mutual respect. No split between those who are respected and those who are ostracized (*Geachtete und Geächtete*). A Germany intact and able to survive serves also the interest of other nations; the German genius is the last barrier against Bolshevism ... The past twelve years were not in vain, since so many principles and achievements of the National Socialists were incorporated into the parties now in existence.' As for practical matters, the movement was understandably upset by the denazification purges, which they claimed weakened the goal of reconstruction.

In order to count on the strength of National Socialists in the future [Memminger continued], their cohesion and solidarity must be maintained. This requires the organization of all good German elements in solidarity, which will receive their directives from one headquarters (*Führungskopf*). The *Führungskopf* should not be burdened with manifold forms of organization. Camouflage of the *Führungskopf*, in order to exist in illegality. Task of the *Führungskopf* would consist of mobilizing the best known personalities who have not been politically compromised and who can regain for us the respect that had once been gained in battle but which nowadays has been lost through lack of character ... Experts in certain fields who once wore the Party badge must be brought back into their positions, either directly or through middlemen.

According to Memminger, the main means of attaining these objectives was through mutual economic self-help, underground propaganda, the solution of 'problems of camouflage' – meaning the procurement of false papers, the maintenance of secret contact with POWs, and the establishment of relations with sympathetic circles in the homelands of the Western occupying powers.[56]

The politico-military side of the HJ-Werwolf had similar ideals – Heidemann apparently obtained the approval of Franke in shifting the movement away from sabotage – although it is possible that some elements retained a greater commitment to the principle of direct action, and that this caused tension with the economic wing under Heidemann. The Americans believed, for instance, that both Lohel and Badäus had made tentative plans for sabotage, although the British accepted the testimony of these men that they had religiously avoided violent resistance and actually wanted to forge links with the occupying power.[57] At the least, it seems that the German Unification Party (EPD), a group loosely connected with the conspirators, operated in conjunction with such youth gangs as the Edelweiss Piraten, and that they committed sabotage in the Soviet Zone. Even in the British Zone, an EPD agent allegedly destroyed party documents at Bad Öyenhausen in the spring of 1946, and plans were also afoot to blow up a British military headquarters in the same town. Another British Zone conspirator, SS-Lieutenant-Colonel Piemöller, established a 'secret army' composed of several hundred SS men in the Ruhr, who called themselves 'Blue Falcons' and dressed in blue shirts and trousers. Members of this movement established a number of arms caches, and they used the '88' greeting (a code for the eighth letter of the alphabet repeated twice, 'HH,' which in turn signified *'Heil Hitler'*).[58]

Of course, the HJ-Werwolf was such a large network that it soon came to the attention of the Allied counter-intelligence services. Even as early as June 1945, the CIC had suspicions about the Tessmann enterprise, and several undercover agents were sent to infiltrate the company. By the autumn, these agents had grasped the full significance of the Heidemann combine, and the British had also begun efforts to infiltrate the HJ underground in their zone, particularly by 'turning' one of the movement's leaders, Günter Ebeling. By the end of 1945, the Allies had obtained lists of members and sympathizers – a compilation of 1,000 names associated with the southern group, and 1,500 with the northern – and, on this basis, a joint Anglo–American counter-insurgency mission was run during the first winter after the war. Code-named Operation 'Nursery,' a series of raids in 1945–6 netted almost the entire HJ-Werwolf leadership. Axmann and his chief liaison officers, Memminger and Overbeck, were arrested in December 1945, as was one of Heidemann's principal business associates. After the first round of interrogations, an American patrol was also sent into the Alps in order to overrun a hut where HJ conspirators often met, and where they had stored a cache of munitions. After a four-hour climb through a blinding blizzard, the hut was finally found, nearly buried in snow, and two HJ guerrillas were captured. On 7 January, Heidemann and his chief collaborators were arrested – 565,000 marks were found in Heidemann's room, still wrapped in Reichsbank cellophane – and, in February, the remaining leaders of the British Zone conspiracy were also swept into the net. To complete the process, a large-scale raid was conducted in late March, whereby 800 lesser lights were also corralled, occasionally after gun battles between Allied troops and desperate Werewolves.[59] A few nebulous offshoots of the movement survived the Nursery raids – most notably the EPD, the Blue Falcons, and a Schleswig group built around the HJ regional leadership evacuated from East

Prussia[60] – but, within several months, these too were rolled up by the occupation authorities.

The Nursery operation broke the back of the HJ underground, thereby destroying the last major institution of the Third Reich that had retained a degree of organization at senior levels. In many ways, the movement had represented the final flickering of the Hitler regime. Opinion in the newly revived German media was unanimous in harshly condemning the HJ-Werwolf, although it was unclear that public opinion was equally as critical, particularly in the British Zone. British intelligence officers suggested that the Lohel–Badäus–Overbeck wing of the movement was relatively free from the dangers of denunciation or popular hostility, particularly when compared with the relatively harsh environment in the U.S. Zone. In fact, this was precisely why the movement was able to grow faster in the British Zone, even though it had no secret sources of funding analogous to the Heidemann combine. Gustav Memminger told the British Zone conspirators in November 1945 that difficulties had been encountered in the American Zone because of mass arrests. The implication was that the British took security matters less to heart, although Memminger also advised that the northern plotters should view the afflictions of the southerners as a warning, and should take care to obtain false ID documents.[61]

In conclusion, the fact that the HJ made a strong effort to survive – perhaps stronger than any other institution of the Hitler period – is really not much of a surprise. A number of historians maintain that National Socialism originally succeeded because of the fervour of German youth,[62] and that the HJ was designed as a mechanism to maintain the movement's vigour and sustain links to the primary sources of its power. Thus, it was only natural that the regime would return to the well in time of need. Erik Erikson has even argued that part of Hitler's unconscious appeal for the German people was that he was a big kid himself – an overgrown 'Sturm und Drang' adolescent who would *never* give in.[63]

Whether German youth really displayed any eagerness for last-ditch resistance is not entirely clear. Certainly, the preceding pages have shown that, in some areas, a segment of the teenage population was willing to resist the enemy advance and tried to fight on as guerrillas; in other regions, however, there were spectacular breakdowns of morale, even among the young. Martin Niemöller has suggested that German youth who lived through the closing months of the war were cured of their attraction to Naziism by events themselves, and Earl Beck is probably also correct in surmising that the instances of disillusionment and collapse outnumbered the fanatical self-sacrifice of Volkssturm teenagers or Werewolves.[64] Soldiers of the East Lancashire Regiment in northwest Germany were constantly amazed at how German boys could fight fanatically in one locale, but in the next village they had nothing better to do than 'loaf around the streets,' and that they 'cringe[d] and [ran] fawning to obey some order given by a British soldier.'[65]

As for the postwar organization broken by the Nursery operation, it actually did not involve many teenagers, but revolved around adults who were attempting to maintain a structure through which to appeal to German youth in the future. A few leaders of the British Zone conspiracy, mainly centred around HJ-Captain Horst Voigt, made plans to penetrate new youth movements being fostered by the occupying powers, but such operations had barely begun when the net fell upon the leading plotters in February 1946.[66]

Allied polling showed that, after the capitulation, overt Nazi sympathies among former HJ collapsed amazingly quickly. American surveys of German teenagers in July 1945 revealed that, although there was a persistent subconscious attachment to a stock number of National Socialist 'truths,' most adolescents were pro-American and wanted the adoption of a form of semi-authoritarian democracy in Germany. Most important, three-quarters of these kids rejected their former leaders from the HJ, and they suggested that such HJ 'bosses' be prohibited from occupying leadership positions in the new youth movements to be organized under Allied auspices.[67] The most that can be said about a wave of postwar crime and juvenile delinquency – with reference to its 'political' character – is that National Socialism was responsible for eroding the moral underpinnings of German youth, and that most of the teenagers involved in such activity were hostile to the Allies.[68]

Gerhardt Rempel may be correct in arguing that the HJ was successful in imposing a sense of homogeneity upon youth; that the recalcitrants who gathered in oppositional cliques composed only a minor element of about 5 per cent of the teenage population; and that all this regimentation was of considerable benefit to Germany's military capacity, in the sense that it created an enthusiastic and partially trained recruitment pool for the armed forces.[69] However, in the final analysis, the Werwolf was one demand too many upon the spirit and innocence of youth, and the results force us to return to the themes of inefficiency, despair, and heterogeneity that form the underpinnings for much of this study. The spotty performance of HJ guerrillas in 1945 suggests that the attempt to organize and unify an entire generation had failed, and that the overwhelming force brought to bear by the enemy made this failing apparent.

3

A Werwolf War:
The Military and the Kleinkrieg

When a nation sees its national army destroyed or on the very edge of defeat, there is a natural tendency for patriots to rise up, take matters into their own hands, and attack the invaders. Similarly, stragglers and cut-off units of the army often keep fighting, even behind enemy lines, and even though they are detached from the regular chain of command. Such units may be led by fanatics, or they may simply be bound by the same primordial impulses of individual loyalty that had once bound together the ancient *comitatus*.[1] The military authorities may themselves choose to adopt guerrilla tactics, ordering units to infiltrate the enemy rear and operate independently. Once again, the normal chain of command breaks down or contact is maintained only by radio or line-crossers. The officer corps typically distrusts such innovations because they dissolve the tidy line that demarcates military from civilian, war from peace, front from rear. Maintenance of this demarcation serves to protect soldiers under the Geneva Convention, and it provides a sense of order amidst the chaos of war. Thus, guerrilla warfare looms as the military parallel to anarchy. None the less, because the army is in full retreat and final defeat is imminent, the invaders must perforce be attacked along their weakest points, that is, their lines of communication. Even despite their doubts, the professionals of the military establishment are forced to fall back upon the only practicable strategy. This was the situation which faced the German military in 1944–5.

It is, in fact, possible to argue that the Wehrmacht as a whole degenerated into a conglomeration of guerrilla bands during the last four months of the war, particularly during the final weeks of fighting in the West. A British officer later recalled that the German Army seemed to splinter into a collection of small flying columns, which could suddenly appear almost anywhere.[2] Members of such units might surrender *en masse*, or they might fight to the last cartridge. Combat at the tactical level became extremely unpredictable, as is generally the case in guerrilla warfare.

Even as the Wehrmacht retreated from France and Belorussia in the summer of 1944, it began experiments with guerrilla techniques. The paratroop armies that withdrew into northwest Germany were extensively trained in partisan tactics – 'Red Indian war,' the recruits called it – and the new Volksgrenadier regiments were given special courses in sniping. German cadets at the NCO Training School at Heinsberg used the Rhenish village of Birgden, occupied by the 43rd Wessex Division, as a practice-ground for guerrilla tactics, and British soldiers in the town were confronted with a long string of bushwhackings and other mysterious incidents. According to Alsatian and Lorrainais POWs interrogated in 1945, the German Army organized special élite sniper units, modelled in part on the French Forces of the Interior (FFI), and the Waffen-SS set up similar teams. These detachments were supplied with three days' keep and were expected to keep the enemy busy in areas newly overrun. Himmler attempted to encourage the work of such teams by establishing a scale of rewards for snipers: 10 verified kills entitled the sniper to 100 cigarettes; 20, to 20 days' leave; 50, to the Iron Cross (First Class), plus a wrist-watch presented by the Reichsführer-SS; 100, to a hunting gun awarded by Himmler; and 150, to free run of Himmler's private game preserve.[3] Not surprisingly, a nasty series of shootings and sabotage attacks began as soon as enemy troops set foot in the Greater Reich during the fall of 1944, and Military Government officers told journalists that such assaults were 'the work of regular members of the German Army left behind for that purpose.' Sniping was reported in rear areas, where, as *The Stars and Stripes* disdainfully noted, 'legitimate enemy fire would not be expected,' and along the Western Front a number of American troops disappeared. At Roetgen, in the Rhineland, three Military Policemen were ambushed on the night of 20 September, leaving only their bullet-riddled jeep to be found by American investigators the following morning. In several other cases, German reconnaissance troops were discovered snooping around Allied rear areas in civilian clothes, and, in Lorraine, two such agents were tried and shot by the American Third Army.[4]

Guerrilla Warfare on the Eastern Front

This trend towards guerrilla methods was accelerated by the massive Soviet drive in eastern Germany and Poland during early 1945. In truth, the disastrous German collapse caused by this offensive forced the eastern field armies to resort to any expedient capable of slowing the pace of the Soviet advance. Supplied with reports about the sparse distribution of Red Army and Security Force

(NKVD) units in the Soviet rear, Army Group 'Centre' set up a special staff to coordinate guerrilla activities behind Soviet lines. The chief of the Army Group, Field Marshal Schörner, already had experience in this field, having helped to field anti-Soviet Baltic guerrilla groups when he was stationed as commander of German forces in the northwestern USSR.[5] Both Army Groups 'Centre' and 'Vistula' formed 'extermination units of a partisan kind,' which were intended to function along the Russian lines of communication. The first such groups were organized in late January, and by late February a special training course at Höxter, along the Weser River, was busy turning out guerrilla sappers recruited by the eastern *Wehrkreise*. Planning for the Höxter program actually antedated the Soviet Offensive, and it was officially designated as a 'Werwolf' operation, even though it was under full military control.[6] By late March, Naval Special Operations Unit 85 had also arrived in Swinemünde for operations along the lower Oder and the Stettiner Haff, and one group proceeded to Gdynia, which probably served as a base for raids against Memel.[7] Thus, it is possible that German commandos were also transported by sea into the Soviet rear.

The actions of these special teams were varied. In Upper Silesia, units from a 'Landwehr Ranger Battalion' operated behind Soviet lines in civilian clothes in order to carry out reconnaissance and set up radio transmitters.[8] In eastern Brandenburg, a six-man Waffen-SS detachment was purposefully stranded behind the Soviet front in order to carry out 'terrorist–diversionist' activity, and a similar communications team, dressed in camouflage smocks, was left behind in the East Prussian city of Allenstein, although it was overrun and destroyed during an NKVD sweep of the town.[9] A police official involved in the program later recalled that the mass of the population was expected to cooperate, but that very little civilian support actually developed. Moreover, the operation was soon reported to the Soviets, who thereafter took immediate counter-measures. National Socialist 'Commissars' (NSFOs) on the Eastern Front also complained that there was little coordination among the actions of various 'patrol services' maintained by different military and civil agencies.[10]

None the less, various German sources reported in February that extensive partisan warfare had broken out behind Soviet lines in eastern Germany,[11] and it is possible that, along with adverse weather and Luftwaffe air attacks, this was one of the factors involved in the eventual stalling of the Winter Offensive. One NKVD regiment operating in Posen overran more than 8,000 Germans during the first three months of 1945, including 281 'special agents,' and this unit alone killed 225 Germans in armed clashes behind Soviet lines.[12] By March, after the Winter Offensive was blunted, the new rationale for the program was to disrupt Soviet supply lines and thereby break up the impending Soviet onslaught against Berlin. Thus, in early April, the Soviet Sixty-fifth Army, fresh from its conquest of Danzig and redeploying towards the Oder, found it necessary to send forward special detachments in order to cleanse its 200-mile march route of 'small German groups,' even though this ground had been overrun months earlier.[13]

Bypassed bands of German troops also remained a problem for the Soviets, particularly since the Russian Command had recently changed its tactical doctrine and was no longer using front-line combat forces to establish a double inner and outer front around each such isolated group. They now worked on the assumption that, if an overall offensive developed rapidly enough, even large German forces in the rear would no longer pose a threat.[14] Whatever the merits of this logic, cut-off German forces were given a considerable respite in which to reorganize, and they desperately attempted to remain in contact with Army High Command (OKH) by radio or by telephone lines uncut by the Russians. At Sternberg, an NKVD detachment captured a German reconnaissance agent who had the mission of establishing links with German soldier bands, especially in order to gather information and to ascertain the direction of safe paths back through to German lines. According to the one-time *Kreisleiter* of Stargard, the abortive Arnswald Counter-Offensive in February 1945 was aided by cut-off German fragments that were still in contact with the bulk of German forces. The Soviet war communiqué on 12 March told of the destruction of one such band of forty German soldiers near Kolberg. Among the dead was Lieutenant-General Rubel, commander of the 163rd German Infantry Division. A Polish Home Army dispatch from southern Poland on 24 March described the same type of menace: 'The terrain,' they reported, 'has not so far been completely cleared of German soldiers. Many remain in the forests and mountains, and attack Soviet transports and pillage the villages.'[15]

As well as organizing outright guerrilla bands, the German Command also set up tank-destroyer squads, which functioned independently along enemy flanks and lines of communication, and were sometimes coordinated by liaison planes. *Völkischer Beobachter* claimed that the operation of such groups deep in the enemy-occupied hinterland meant that German defensive resiliency was far from being broken in the way that British and French capabilities had been smashed by the German onslaught in the spring of 1940. The most effective of these detachments were recruited among Skorzeny's special commando troops: one such group, 'Dora' II, destroyed more than 125 Soviet tanks during desperate pocket fighting in the last weeks of the conflict. As small, mobile units, these teams were *not* equipped with anti-tank guns, the usual weaponry of tank-destroyer formations; rather, they were supplied with a revolutionary new bazooka called the 'Panzerfaust.'[16] Essentially, the Panzerfaust was a one-shot, shoulder-mounted rocket that was supposed to create parity between an infantryman and a tank. The most interesting aspect of the weapon – and one which reflects vividly on the nature of the Nazi regime – was that it derived its effectiveness from a highly explosive compound called 'cyclonite,' which was used in the warhead. Since cyclonite was unstable, it was usually used only in small quantities as an initiating charge, and the presence of the explosive in the head of the Panzerfaust presented almost as much hazard to the anti-tank troops as to the intended targets.[17] Even when it worked, the Panzerfaust released a flash of flame and a quantity of smoke, thus revealing the location of its user and exposing him or her to counter-fire. Despite these impediments, however, it was broadly assumed that the Panzerfaust was a weapon that made effective guerrilla warfare a real option. 'It seemed at this stage,' remembered one veteran, 'as if every other German soldier was armed with this deadly instrument.'[18]

Improving Relations between the Army and the Werwolf

Much of the OKH's guerrilla effort was coordinated with Skorzeny's commandos,[19] and intimate contacts were also developed between the military and the Werwolf. Such relations were based mainly on the same type of trade-off that existed between Skorzeny's groups and the Werwolf: diminished autonomy for the Werwolf in return for material considerations from the Army. While senior-level cooperation had already been agreed upon in 1944 – with a line running from OKH to the SS-Main Office[20] – the High Command was understandably sceptical of this newfangled organization, as they were of any innovations associated with the SS. By early 1945, however, the need for closer collaboration was obvious: the Werwolf, despite immense problems caused by the Soviet advances and the mass flight from the East, was still accumulating abundant information of tactical importance. Moreover, in a period when the military was rapidly expanding its own capability for partisan warfare, the Werwolf was already in a position to perform many such special functions. The Army, on the other hand, could offer the ill-equipped guerrillas both supply and transport, and could provide a sense of structure and coherence amidst a situation amounting to the wholesale collapse of eastern German society.

Thus it was decided in early February that the Werwolf would place a permanent liaison officer at the various Army unit headquarters along the Eastern Front in order to ensure closer participation by Army Group intelligence officers in the deployment of Werwolf groups, and to increase the cross-flow of information about the enemy. The OKH in return issued an order (6 February) empowering intelligence officers in northeast Germany to meet the Werwolf's need for provisions, and 'regulated' other German groups operating in the enemy rear –

SS-Rangers, FAK units, and SS-Raiding Parties – as a consequence of the Werwolf–Wehrmacht arrangement.[21] The OKH Training Section also requested that the same order be distibuted via the OKW to Army commands in Western Europe.[22] In late February, the importance of a close relationship between military intelligence officers and the Higher SS and Police Leaders (HSSPF) was reiterated, and, on the Werwolf side, 'Werwolf Commissioners' were instructed to report to Military Intelligence once their territories became part of the theatre of operations.[23] In Wehrkreis XIII special transportation and medical units were organized to facilitate Werwolf activity, and in Wehrkreis VII a department called 'Special Abwehr' was set up at district headquarters.[24]

Not only did the military clearly begin to influence Werwolf deployment, but the Army also gained an important function in the guerrilla organization's recruitment and training processes. The OKH Training Section had always taken a healthy interest in these matters,[25] and in early 1945 they suggested a new Werwolf mustering channel be established that was almost entirely in military hands. Desperate for men, the Bureau 'Prützmann' agreed to send out a widely circulated order directing that military recruits for the Werwolf be prepped at the Training Section's own special training facilities, the so-called Army Schools. Although different versions of the order were disseminated, it generally explained that new military recruits were needed in order 'to speed up the establishment of the Werwolf Organization.' Any volunteers who stepped forward were to take part in a spring Werwolf training program at 'Army School' II, located at Turkenburg, in the Carpathian Mountains of western Slovakia, under the command of a leathery, tough infantry officer named Paul Krüger. It was specified that personnel considered for the course should have at least a second-class Iron Cross, and must be non-Catholic. Moreover, recruits were to come from areas only on the eastern and western fringes of the Reich that were already occupied or immediately threatened by the enemy. 'Special emphasis' was placed on the East, and surviving documents show that at least one unit was specifically asked for a man 'whose home town is in Russian-occupied territory.'

The final results were mildly impressive. Although some units either refused the order or ignored it, approximately 300 men passed through the two-week course, two complete cycles of which were conducted before the Soviets overran western Slovakia. It is possible that additional military recruits were trained at 'Army School' I, near Wismar, under the command of Colonel Nobis. Veterans of these courses returned to their units after training. If the home territory of their formations had been overrun, they reported directly to the Bureau 'Prützmann' at Rheinsberg.[26]

Because guerrilla warfare was practically synonymous with demolitions,

Army engineers evinced a particular interest in the Werwolf, especially the Training Subsection of the 'Sapper and Fortifications Staff' of the OKH. Surviving documentation shows that, during 1944, the possibilities of guerrilla warfare were extensively discussed by the faculty at 'Pioneer School' I at Dessau–Rosslau, and that the eventual result of these discussions was a ten-page memorandum titled 'Guerrilla Warfare in Our Own Country,' which was circulated among various senior staffs of the Wehrmacht. After the public proclamation of the Werwolf 'Freedom Movement' on 1 April, Colonel Kemmerich, of the 'Sapper and Fortifications Staff,' suggested that it was time for various offices of the OKH to begin detailed work for the planning and control of Werwolf operations.[27] It was also military engineers who ran the guerrilla training course at Höxter, and once the first cycle of this program was completed in mid-March, some of the teams were transferred to the control of the Bureau 'Prützmann.' The remainder were, in agreement with Prützmann, reserved for the use of the Wehrkreise as 'patrol detachments.'[28]

Although special sapper squads were intended principally for deployment against the Soviets, the Western Allies also overran several such teams in the last weeks of the war. In the Letzlinger Forest and the Harz, American troops encountered elements of a 'Pioneer Special Unit' sent out from a military engineering school east of the Elbe, with orders to infiltrate the Allied front and disrupt supply lines. In the Harz, the Americans captured five of these guerrillas, four in German uniform (even though the unit formally bore a Werwolf designation). They also discovered the group's log book, which gave an account of all the damage it had caused, and the Counter-Intelligence Corps (CIC) raided several local inns that were storing the unit's radio equipment.[29]

In Thuringia, U.S. troops captured documents from a German 'Reconstruction' company showing that it also had orders to convert to partisan activity:

If the enemy should succeed in breaking through our lines, the Code Word 'Wehrwolf' will be disseminated. Upon receipt of this, all soldiers will don civilian dress and continue the fight, working as individual squads. In this case, communication with the Command Leader must be maintained, in order to make an organised assault by the whole Command, in the role of Werewolves, possible. The following must be our device:

Turn day into night, night into day. Hit the enemy wherever you meet him. Be sly! Steal weapons, ammunition and rations! Women helpers, support the battle of the Werewolves wherever you can!

Arrangements were also made to disperse small detachments of 'female helpers' throughout local villages, where they were supposed to disguise themselves in civilian clothing.[30]

Perhaps the most interesting of these units was Pioneer Unit 'Michael,' which was overrun in Carinthia during the last days of the war. The members of this unit were largely radio operators, and, unlike a normal German formation, the ranks did no fatigues and enjoyed friendly relations with their leaders. The detachment's commander, Lieutenant-Colonel Krautzberger, had guerrilla experience as a liaison officer with nationalist Greek guerrillas. Krautzberger, it seems, prepared for operations against the Russians, but he had no desire to fight the Western Powers, and therefore quickly surrendered, although both he and his men subsequently tried to stir up anti-Soviet sentiment among their interrogators.[31]

By the last month of the war, not only engineers, but troops from various services were being hurriedly transferred to the Werwolf, usually with little or no intervening training. In late March, a number of Austrians were released from their regular units, particularly Signals Corps detachments, and quickly trained in Werwolf radio proceedure. Thereafter, they were infiltrated into the Leitha Mountains, southeast of Vienna.[32] Similarly, in Magdeburg, several Wehrmacht officers were reported to have 'gone over' to the Werwolf, including a signals expert who was a forester in civilian life, and who laid a large number of supply stores for German guerrillas.[33] Near Hamburg, British soldiers captured two German officers who were self-confessed Werewolves, one of whom was in charge of a Battle Group below Harburg.[34]

The overall effect of military involvement in the Werwolf was that it crowded out the control machinery previously in charge of the movement. The Bureau 'Prützmann,' for instance, felt an almost inevitable bureaucratic tug that eventually resettled the Werwolf within its most natural command channels. In fact, Prützmann and his staff became largely superfluous to the entire process of fielding and controlling Werwolf groups. The Bureau's intelligence section tried to remain relevant by issuing bimonthly intelligence briefs for the service of those agencies directly controlling Werwolf deployment, but there was little else they could do to involve themselves in the process. Siebel's deputy, Lieutenant-Colonel Sulle, complained to a local Werwolf organizer in April that, as a command centre, the Bureau 'Prützmann' had become paralysed – it could no longer even keep track of its Werwolf groups, because communications throughout Germany had become badly disrupted and because the few remaining wireless stations were so overworked that they could only rarely be used. Thus, in effect, the formations remained only nominally under Prützmann's authority – after February 1945, they had quickly slid under the real control of Army Group intelligence officers and FAK units.

Finally, under the new regime, the nature of work assigned to Werwolf groups altered. Senior military authorities began to insist, for instance, that

Werwolf guerrillas be used to carry out reconnaissance assignments. Thus, detachments intended principally for sabotage and partisan warfare were converted into scouting units. A French report also noted that, by March 1945, groups on the Eastern Front were no longer dispersed in the usual Werwolf fashion, but were concentrated so that the Army could quickly direct them to new tasks wherever their services were required. Along similar lines, Soviet sources report that Werewolves were concentrated much more heavily in the immediate rear of the Red Army than any other pro-German saboteurs who had preceded them in three and a half years of fighting on the Eastern Front: fully 88 per cent of agents and terrorists deployed by the Germans in 1945 were headed directly into the combat zone, versus an average of only 55 per cent for the overall 1941–5 period.[35] This obviously served the short-term requirements of the Army.

One of the main propellants behind this increasing military interest in guerrilla warfare was General Reinhard Gehlen, head of OKH intelligence on the Eastern Front, Foreign Armies East (FHO). Gehlen's main task was the collection of intelligence, although this was a job severely limited by the rapid Soviet advances in 1944–5. In Silesia, for instance, Army Group 'Centre' was pushed back so fast that it had no chance to leave behind an information network.[36] Moreover, the lightning Soviet advance had chewed deep into the original ranks of the Werwolf in the East. Conditions of mass evacuation and the wholesale flight of party and government authorities had momentarily paralysed the Werwolf; meanwhile, the Soviets were able to liquidate many of the Werwolf groups behind Russian lines. Not surprisingly, there were few reports of full-scale Werwolf operations.[37] It was the very magnitude of this disaster, and the dispersion or ineffectiveness of existing organizations, that spawned much of the impetus for the numerous raiding detachments created by the eastern field armies.

Gehlen realized, however, that, in the desperate straits in which Germany and its allies now found themselves, large-scale intelligence operations in the Soviet rear could be motivated only by inculcating a sense of pride in immediate anti-Communist resistance among the operatives. Only by playing an active role in national liberation could morale be maintained. Thus, the FHO began to take intensive interest in the theory and practice of partisan warfare. Even in 1944, the FHO had cooperated closely in SS surveys of anti-German resistance movements, and in December 1944 they circulated throughout the General Staff translated excerpts from The Guerrilla War, Partisanism and Sabotage (1931), a classic work by the Soviet strategist Drasov.[38] In early 1945, Gehlen ordered preparation of a full-scale study investigating the construction of an anti-Soviet underground, using the Polish Home Army as a structural model. The FAK station at Breslau was charged with studying the Warsaw Uprising, and General Bor-Komorowski's archives were translated and brought to the FHO by special courier. The officer charged with this assignment was Captain Friedrich Pop-penberger, a Romanian Volksdeutsch who had already trained anti-Stalinist Russians and Poles for special operations.

On 9 February, Poppenberger submitted a preliminary paper that proposed an eastern underground based upon sixty-man 'Action' units, which would be based in secret hide-outs in the Soviet rear and would perform all the usual Werwolf operations. In truth, the plan called for a whole new phase of the Wer-wolf – a reorganized second stage. Gehlen, however, apparently decided that such a program should be preceded by the organization of a pure intelligence-gathering network, and to suit this purpose he sent a call out for a thousand Wehrmacht volunteers to put themselves at the disposal of FAK units 102 and 103 as line-crossers.[39]

The Poppenberger study produced a mixed reaction, at best, but Gehlen none the less continued to regard partisan warfare as a necessary long-term contin-gency, and he therefore pushed forward. In fact, he drove even harder *after* he had been relieved of command at the FHO for challenging the Führer's depen-dence on intuition as the basis for suppositions about the strength of the Red Army. Gehlen's intelligence reports proved more accurate than Hitler's genius, and, as the bearer of bad news, Gehlen found his services impolitely terminated. Subsequently, Gehlen felt that involvement in Werwolf planning was a safe way to save himself from a post at the front, and thus allow him to kill time and tend a few irons he still had in the fire. Chief among these was a Machiavellian plan to transfer microfilms of the massive files of the FHO westwards, where he hoped they would provide a convenient gift with which to introduce himself to the Americans. It was in this same regard that he viewed the provision of an existing anti-Soviet underground as an added advantage.

With these factors in mind, Gehlen got in touch with his friend in the RSHA, Schellenberg. During a meeting in March 1945, Gehlen told Schellen-berg that the front would hold for only another two months, and that plans soon had to be in place for anti-Soviet resistance *after* the capitulation. As far as Gehlen was concerned, Himmler was 'the only man with the necessary imagination and energy' for such a task. Kaltenbrunner, said Gehlen, had to be frozen out of the scheme, but perhaps Himmler would authorize Schellen-berg himself to establish a movement based upon the Polish Home Army as a model. Gehlen assured his listener that 'the Army had the fullest confidence in Schellenberg as an organizer, and he, Gehlen, and his best general staff officers, as well as many whom Schellenberg did not yet know, would put themselves voluntarily under Schellenberg's command.' Gehlen concluded by telling Schellenberg that he was about to report to an OKW bunker, the Frankenstrupp, for a month-long, marathon planning session in order to bring matters to a state of readiness. Schellenberg, flush with flattery, agreed to use Operation 'Zeppelin' to conduct a parallel study of the Polish Home Army, and several days later he asked the head of 'Zeppelin,' Dr Albert Rapp, to prepare an appropriate paper.

In early April, Schellenberg laid some of these plans before Himmler, suggesting that General Wenck, as commander of Army Group 'Vistula,' should be consulted. Unknowingly, however, Schellenberg had touched a raw nerve with the SS-Reichsführer. Several months earlier, an officer on the Eastern Front had already asked Himmler for a ruling on plans for post-capitulation warfare, and when Himmler had brought the matter to Hitler, the Führer had rudely rebuffed him. Stung by his master's rebuke, and obviously annoyed that the whole idea was still circulating, Himmler reacted with a standard Nazi homily on the taboo of post-capitulation warfare.

'This is complete nonsense,' he bawled. 'If I should discuss this plan with Wenck I would be the first defeatist of the Third Reich. This fact would be served boiling hot to the *Führer*. You need not tell this to your Gehlen. You need only to explain to him that I strictly refuse to accept the plan. Besides – it is typical of the high class general staff officer to sit in the Frankenstrupp nursing post-war plans instead of fighting.'

One can imagine that Himmler immediately recognized that the Gehlen plan called for a restructured Werwolf, no doubt with large-scale military and RSHA influence, which thus removed or diminished his own direct-control channel via the HSSPF. Naturally, he was averse to any shrinkage of his prerogatives, particularly at the behest of a 'high class' general who had been repudiated by the Führer. Gehlen had already alienated Hitler with unpopular ideas; this postwar-resistance concept was sure to be another in that same category, and Himmler had no intention of pursuing it.

Schellenberg, in turn, immediately withdrew the plan, fearing that any useless prolongation of discussion might keep Gehlen's name on Himmler's mind, thus endangering his (Gehlen's) security. Subsequently, he informed both Gehlen and Rapp of Himmler's response, and he later claimed that knew of no further development of the matter.[40] However, Polish sources have since charged that the OKH actually initiated the Gehlen program, at least in part. In fact, Polish Communist historiography blamed the entire Werwolf program on Gehlen, a premise based upon the assertion that during 1944 the FHO played a key role in gathering material on European resistance movements in order to establish models for a similar German organization. While such activity, even if true, hardly qualified Gehlen for paternity of the Werwolf, it no doubt suited

Polish purposes to slander a man who, during the 1950s, became head of the primary West German intelligence agency.

However, the Poles may have been more accurate in charging Gehlen with the organization of a *new* German guerrilla program in the East, which appeared in the wake of the original Werwolf. Even Polish sources admit that the Polish-occupied zones of eastern Germany were relatively passive during the last months of the war, at least until thousands of home-sick refugees began to flood eastwards after the end of large-scale military operations. It was this returning horde, said the Poles, that contained a new wave of Werewolves and was most responsible for organized attacks on Polish colonists. Suspected troublemakers were arrested by Polish authorities and admitted that, prior to the final collapse, the OKH had issued directives for the infiltration and subversion of the new Polish state. Allegedly, Polish-speaking Germans in the Army, the SS, and the SD were told to return to Poland in order to construct a network of German organizations. The Poles claimed that several Volksdeutsche with forged documents were caught in western and central Poland, one even dressed in British military clothing of the sort typically worn by Poles returning home from Germany. As a result, all eastward-bound Germans immediately became suspect.[41] It is therefore possible that the Poppenberger plan, or some modified version of it, was actually undertaken during the last days of the war, largely for the personal benefit of Gehlen and his colleagues.

Guerrilla Warfare along the Western Front

While the original impetus for military interest in guerrilla warfare lay in the East, by March 1945 conditions had so deteriorated in the West that similar tactics also became a necessity on this front. In fact, it was in the West that the Nazi partisan warfare was subsequently developed to its most radical degree. In reality, the Germans had fought and lost the conventional 'Battle for Germany' west of the Rhine: in Alsace, the Saarland, the Rur, the Ardennes, and the Reichswald. Only a thin crust of resistance was left on the east bank of the river, and even the backbone of this force was soon bottled up in the Ruhr, or was weakened attempting to contain the Remagen bridgehead. As a result, the Wehrmacht relied increasingly on unconventional combat measures as they faced vastly superior numbers, armaments, and morale.

Once the Allies breeched the Rhine, they found a superb system of *Autobahnen*, which Hitler had conveniently designed for fast travel. Provided with this incomparable conduit for the invasion of central Germany, Allied units swept through make-shift German defences in typical Blitzkrieg fashion. One must keep in mind, however, that this was an unruly and uneven flood, whose waters were channelled by the roads, by geography, and by the occasional solid rock of German resistance. These rocks were quickly surrounded by the flood waters; eventually they were submerged, and often fragmented under the force of the onrush, but, none the less, they continued to exist, lying below the surface.

The majority of bypassed troops compliantly surrendered, but a significant minority adopted ad hoc guerrilla tactics, at first on their own initiative. Even before the end of March, Wehrmacht stragglers in the Westerwald were changing to civilian clothing and mining roads in the Allied rear.[42] Similar problems developed behind the British sector of the front, where war correspondents reported that the conflict had reached 'the brigand stage.' In one spot, a wire cut found by British soldiers was expertly booby-trapped, and a second breech not far away was accompanied by a small card that announced: 'This cut was done by [the] German *Wehrmacht*.'[43] In the Germersheim Forest, on the west bank of the Rhine, a platoon of German stragglers ambushed a French truck on the night of 8–9 April, and then tried to use the vehicle to cross the Rhine at Speyer, travelling under false colours. The German lieutenant who conducted this abortive mission was caught and executed.[44] Eisenhower, on 31 March, ordered such dispersed German remnants to surrender 'in order to avoid unnecessary bloodshed and sacrifice of human life,' and the U.S. Seventh Army posted proclamations warning that any soldier captured more than twenty-four hours after the occupation of a town would lose the protection of the Geneva Convention, being regarded as a partisan or terrorist.[45]

The Supreme Headquarters, Allied Expeditionary Force (SHAEF) had good reason for worry. By late March, Allied armoured divisions were badly outpacing the advance of the infantry, leaving huge gaps in the rear of the front. Moreover, lines of communication were guarded only by skeletal units, and in some areas the Military Government was practically non-existent, which gave Wehrmacht and SS guerrillas the opportunity for mobility and manoeuvre. Only in late April, once the Americans had reached their strategic objectives along the Elbe and the Saale, were larger numbers of troops redeployed for the purpose of liquidating guerrilla bands. Officers explained that, whereas the task was not debilitating, it was a slow and difficult job because of the vast forests and hill areas that had to be combed. In a few cases, the Germans had even built special underground hide-outs. In the wooded hills along the Weser River, some 300 SS partisans were ensconced in two underground bunkers hidden not far from a German military hospital. American troops in the region were initially too weak to contain this unit, and the SS guerrillas shot at Allied medical personnel, stole American weapons, and victimized local civilians at night. In late April, a battalion arrived from the 102nd Infantry Division with orders to mop up the marauders. 'It takes time, but we are cleaning out places like this every day,' said the battalion commander. 'We don't take any unnecessary chances and it doesn't take long to smoke them out. The regular German soldiers surrender as soon as they can, but we often have a little scrap before the SS has had enough.'[46]

A similar situation developed in Hesse–Nassau, particularly in the woods along the Werra River. The American Third Army vacated this area so completely that, by mid-April, two weeks after the region had been overrun, uniformed SS raiders were seen leisurely sauntering through the streets of Wanfried and Eschwege, where they terrorized the local population. These guerrillas were in contact with German lines via radio, and they communicated with each other by means of signal flares and rockets, which constantly lit up the skies at night. Occasionally they attacked isolated American soldiers; on 18 April a jeep driver was shot and wounded in the shoulder. The few Americans in the area organized sweeps of the woods by counter-guerrilla units composed of liberated Russian slave labourers, but the problem was resolved only by the arrival of 200 American troops on 29 April, by which time the fighting at the front had begun to lag.[47]

Until 1945, standard Wehrmacht policy had been to encourage stranded soldiers or small bands of troops to engage in an armed infiltration back to German lines. In fact, in late 1944, the Army established official standards for the awarding of medals to soldiers who had accomplished such feats. After the further withdrawals in 1945, however, this practice altered: cut-off units were no longer automatically encouraged to fight their way out of encirclement, but were sometimes instructed to devolve into guerrilla detachments. In this respect, German military practice began to resemble methods of warfare used by the Red Army after 1941, as well as the desperate stay-behind tactics adopted by their own Japanese allies. In fact, an officer in the Ruhr, discussing German guerrilla tactics with a Swiss journalist, quite frankly suggested that the Germans had learned a lot in Russia through their experiences with Soviet partisans. On 10 April, General Reinecke told National Socialist Leadership Corps (NSF) officers that 'whoever finds himself behind enemy lines, will conduct guerrilla warfare in the woods and the ruins of the big cities ... Whenever enemy occupation threatens, hand-grenades, munitions, weapons, radio equipment, and medical material will be distributed among activists or buried for future use.'[48] Several days later, the supreme commander in northwest Germany, Field Marshal Busch, noted that 'fighting by bypassed troops behind the enemy front will continue. It is expected of every decent man and woman of the civilian population that they support these forces in every respect.'[49] After the beginning of April, German propaganda promoted such activities under the banner of the Werwolf, cladding the army in the bunting of revolutionary romanticism, whether they wanted it or not.

The first major experiment with such tactics involved the 6th SS Mountain Division, a 15,000–man formation which, in late March 1945, was bypassed and trapped in the rugged forests of the Taunus region, northwest of Frankfurt. After the division was cut off, Army Group 'B' in the Ruhr ordered it to form Werwolf Battle Groups and to harass American supply lines. Apparently this was done directly at Hitler's behest. Elements of the division radiod back on 2 April that this mission was being carried out, and American authorities estimated there were at least two large bands active in the Taunus, each with 2,000 men. These SS detachments were also joined by a considerable number of belligerent civilians and Werewolves, including armed women.[50]

Such partisan groups lay astride the supply routes of several American divisions and were able to cause considerable trouble as they attempted either to harass the Allies or to force their way back to German lines. They killed or captured a number of American drivers, mined Allied supply routes, and besieged the headquarters of an artillery battalion in Geisal. Moreover, they revelled in the brutal code of SS warfare: in one case, recaptured Wehrmacht POWs were machine-gunned; in another instance, several black soldiers belonging to an American ammunition company were murdered. However, what really brought worry to the gentlemanly officers of Twelfth Army Group was that the SS marauders overran a mobile field hospital, which meant that sixteen American nurses fell into the hands of enemy guerrillas. As it turned out, these women were put to work for the Germans, but otherwise were not mauled, or even searched for weapons. Also captured during this same sweep was Lieutenant-Colonel Harold Cohen, who was receiving treatment at the hospital. Cohen was commander of the 10th Armoured Infantry Battalion and was the stable-mate for Colonel Creighton Abrams of the 4th Infantry Division.

Meanwhile, the headquarters of the U.S. First and Third armies realized that there was more fighting in the rear than at the front, and units from three American divisions and a Cavalry Group were recalled in order to deal with the Taunus guerrillas. The hospital unit was rescued, and order was gradually restored. Cohen, despite the fact that his Jewish faith attracted attention among SS officers, was treated correctly, and eventually managed to escape. In the nearby city of Frankfurt, almost 400 underground activists were rounded up and arrested, among them the fourth son of Kaiser Wilhelm II, as well as a major in the Frankfurt police, who was denounced by his collegues. Most of the Nazi partisans either were hunted down or fought their way back to German lines, although a Luftwaffe squadron is on record as late as 17 April inquiring about supply flights for SS elements in the Taunus.[51]

Having achieved a momentary success with the 6th SS Mountain Division, the OKW then decided to repeat the experiment on a larger scale. In mid-April, the huge Army Group 'B,' hopelessly trapped in the Ruhr, was ordered to disintegrate into guerrilla detachments on the model of the Taunus precedent. On 15 April, Field Marshal Model, in command of the Ruhr cauldron, discharged all adolescents and older men under his command and, two days later, demobilized all support troops, and gave combat forces the choice of either returning home as civilians or fighting on as independent Battle Groups. Model himself subsequently fled to the woods and put a pistol to his head, while his second-in-command, General Kortzfleisch, was one of ten Germans killed in a clash on 20 April. Kortzfleisch, too, had fled to the bush, but his band was detected and wiped out by a U.S. patrol.[52]

Allied operations in the Ruhr subsequently degenerated into small-scale counter-guerrilla actions, such as mopping up 'terror bands' of Dutch and French SS troops engaged in sabotage near Recklinghausen, or pursuit of a thirty-man 'Free Corps' detachment spotted on 22 April manning a road barrier on the Westfalendamm in Dortmund. A considerable pocket was contained at Werden, across the Ruhr River from Essen, where a motley assemblage of Werewolves, Volkssturm men, paratroops, and flak crews attempted to carry on the fight. Shooting in this town did not peter out until the night of 6–7 May, two days after the regional armistice in the West. Such stunts made the Americans naturally suspicious of the Ruhr population: 'Why don't the civilians over there rise up against those nuts?' wondered General Matthew Ridgeway, as he observed Werden from a vantage point in Essen. As a counter-measure, U.S. units in the Ruhr rounded up large numbers of men in civilian clothes in order to determine if they were soldiers or Werewolves. Some of these internees were held in concentration pens for up to three days with no food or water.[53]

Patients in German military hospitals behind enemy lines were also encouraged to cause trouble, and some of these men comprised an avid audience for Werwolf radio broadcasts. American troops crushed incipient revolts at hospitals in Pyrmont and Lüdenscheid, both in northwest Germany, and a Werwolf infiltrator was captured in the latter institution. In another case, a convalescent SS man was caught by the French providing direction for a band of teenage terrorists. In Westphalia, the British roared past a military hospital, all bedecked in white flags, only to discover later wounded SS men crawling from their beds and mining nearby roads.[54]

German formations not yet stranded behind enemy lines were also ordered to engage in guerrilla-style operations. On 29 March, Colonel-General Jodl told the Western field armies that Allied tank spearheads could be defeated only by cutting their rearward communication with supply bases,[55] and this order was followed by directives to individual German units which repeatedly hammered home the necessity of infiltration and guerrilla tactics. Near the Aller River, raiding detachments were formed, each with twenty to thirty men. 'The object,' said a captured German order, 'is to deprive the English of the pleasure of sleeping at night with honourless German women and to ensure that they live in a constant state of danger and uncertainty in the villages they have occupied.'[56] Kesselring ordered on 4 April that Allied fuel trucks were to serve as particular targets for guerrilla units, and four days later Jodl quoted Hitler as again insisting on the necessity of attacking Allied flanks, particularly through the deployment of tank-destroyer detachments.

The culmination of this drift towards military atomization was Hitler's order to the Eleventh Army in the Harz 'Fortress,' dated 17 April. A supplement to the order noted that 'these principles are to be made known without delay to *all* the Armies in the West,' and the directive itself is worth quoting in detail: 'Only by attacks against the flank and rear of the Allies, disruption and interruption of their supply lines, can success be guaranteed. Success of the whole is to be won by a total of counterblows to be dealt at all times and in all places in the Allied rear, combined with guerrilla warfare. In such attacks, it is important to exploit to the utmost the wide dispersal of Allied forces. German forces are never to attack the Allies where they are strong ... The most important thing is for German attacking forces to infiltrate through the most forward battle zone. The tactics to be used are those which the Russians taught to the Germans in 1942/44.'[57] In spirit, this order was a wildly amplified form of the so-called Hutier system, the doctrine of infiltration that had brought limited successes for the German Army in 1918. It was also an extension of the standard German tactic of separating enemy tank spearheads from their own 'in-house,' mechanized infantry, only now it was taken as a given that enemy armour would succeed in breaking through, so that German efforts would have to be refocused upon separating these units from their supplies and from the infantry divisions advancing in their wake. There is no doubt, however, that the depth and emphatic nature of this new doctrine made it tantamount to converting the Western field force into bands of skirmishers. In effect, the armies in the West were ordered to convert to partisan warfare on 17 April.

Such tactics naturally became standard fare for German forces. One spot where special use was made of the new doctrines was the Teutoburger Wald, a ridge of forests comprising one of the few elevated points in northern Germany. One of the most famous battles of German history was fought in these hills in A.D. 9, when Teutonic barbarians defeated an invading Roman host, and the Wehrmacht now hoped that a similar punishment could be inflicted upon the Western Allies. The available roads through the Teutoburger Wald passed through narrow defiles, which were easily blocked and defended, and heavy woods provided necessary cover for ambush parties. The last cream of Germany's crop, NCO cadets from Hanover and officer cadets from Ibbenbüren, were thrown into the battle, most of them pledged to win or die. Because of the suitability of the terrain and their own lack of armour or artillery, the Germans broke up into a number of partisan detachments, equipped with small arms and machine-guns, and they conducted, by all accounts, an extraordinary defence. Near Ibbenbüren, which was attacked by the British, adroit raids were staged behind the invader's lines, and when German territory was lost, stay-behind parties often concealed themselves in the woods, and then fired on British soldiers from the rear. At Tecklenburg, NCO cadets led civilians engaged in the fighting, and the town was largely destroyed in a savage battle. One British divisional history credits the Germans with having 'brilliantly fought a sequence of guerrilla battles'; another said that 'seldom in European warfare can there have been a more skillful or more utterly ruthless defence.' Casualties were heavy, and even once the major towns were taken, and Allied spearheads were racing east of the ridge, British units in the area were still engaged in patrol skirmishes and the winkling-out of snipers.[58]

While the northern Teutoburger Wald fell within the British realm of responsibility, the southeast end of the ridge was overrun by units of the U.S. Ninth Army. The fighting, however, bore the same characteristics as the battle in the north: ambushes, sniping, and fanatical resistance were all the order of the day. And, as in areas farther north, cadets also formed the backbone of the German defence force. The tank training schools at Augustdorf and Detmold formed the nursery of the Sixth SS Panzer Army, and the local cadets were therefore some of the last top-rate recruits in Germany.[59] Moreover, after German forces retreated, they left behind special diversionary teams, provisioned with three days' food and equipped with orders to harass Allied supply columns.[60]

Two hundred miles to the south, in Württemberg, the 17th SS Division also had considerable success infiltrating American supply lines along a twenty-five mile salient with its tip at the town of Crailsheim. The U.S. Seventh Army had originally extended this finger from the northwest in hopes of pocketing German forces in the triangle formed by Crailsheim, Heilbronn, and Bad Mergentheim, as well cutting German communications between Stuttgart and Nuremberg and possibly vitiating the entire German position in Bavaria. However, with SS and HJ troops attacking from within occupied Crailsheim, and with small German Battle Groups roaming all over American lines of communication, the entire salient had to be evacuated on 10–11 April. Neuenstein, twenty miles northwest of Crailsheim, was briefly retaken by SS infiltrators in civilian clothes. The commandant of Ansbach reported on 14 April that his garrison's outposts had carried out a merciless harassment of American motorized units, raiding supply routes and occupied villages, particularly at night. He added that 'houses dislaying white flags were burned and the inhabitants shot. The Werwolf fights the enemy and passes judgement on traitors.' At König-shofen, SS teams infiltrated occupied zones of the town in order to blow up or burn down houses that flew the flag of surrender.[61] Crailsheim itself was only subsequently retaken after ten days of Nazi reoccupation, and Ansbach finally fell during the same period, after American spearheads had charged far off to the east and south.

Farther north, Hitler formed a final concentration of reserves fancifully called the Twelfth Army and promoted as a 'liberation force.' This new conglomeration was commanded by General Walter Wenck and composed mainly of ad hoc units of officer cadets. The Führer personally told Wenck and his operations officer, Gunther Reichhelm, that the Twelfth Army had to operate by sneaking through enemy lines at night, with little or no baggage, and would then need to create maximum havoc in Allied rear areas. Hitler also told Speer that the 'Army Wenck' had been formed with the 'specific purpose' of counter-attacking American troops along their flanks, and that all new tanks were allotted to it. One of the Twelfth Army's new scratch units, the Clausewitz 'Division,' crossed the Elbe on 12 April with instructions to infiltrate enemy lines in order to reach the Ruhr and/or harass the flanks of the Twenty-first Army Group. Straggler bands and guerrilla rearguards had already been operating behind Allied lines – using captured Allied equipment – in Altmark, an old NSDAP stronghold. These units were now joined by a thousand riflemen and forty unmarked tanks, which comprised the bulk of the Clausewitz formation. For ten days, Clausewitz predators ambushed American supply columns, mainly in order to capture fuel, and they generally created as much confusion as possible. At one point, all telephone cables between the Ninth Army and its constituent Corps Commands were cut; motor liaison was suspended; contact was maintained only by wireless transmitter and scout planes; and General Bradley announced nervously that enemy disruptions in the rear had caused considerable difficulties. However, by this point, the Clausewitz Battle Group had begun to lurch wildly, as it encountered tough opposition in the north, and hastily began a dash towards the Harz Redoubt, which in turn led them straight into the waiting arms of American units sent back to contain them. By 22 April, most of the Clausewitz bands had been tracked down and destroyed, with the largest battle unfolding in the Klötze Forest north of Magdeburg. The last intact units devolved into straggler bands and attempted to return to German lines, although sniping and sabotage continued in Altmark until May 1945, and a railway bridge at Kaltenhof was blown up by three young soldiers in civilian clothes.[62]

Amid such unsettled conditions, the creation and deployment of Wehrmacht special forces was greatly accelerated. Army intelligence officers were ordered to employ bands of volunteer soldiers for attacks on Allied supply lines and reconnaissance missions. Such activity was made easier by the existence of vast columns of liberated slave labourers and German refugees trudging westwards, which were easy for disguised Wehrmacht personnel to join. In one case, two German soldiers in civilan clothes were overheard by an American war correspondent (who spoke German) discussing their mission. While hanging around an American bivouac in the midst of a group of genuine refugees, one of these men was heard to refer to U.S. soldiers as the 'the killers of our women and children.' They then talked about crossing a nearby river in order to reach a German pocket and report their various observations about the dispositions of American paratroopers and armour.[63]

In the Rhineland, a Polish Volksdeutsch named Richard Jarczyk infiltrated American lines, where he obtained civilian clothing from a sympathetic German woman and, in March 1945, got himself hired by an American Military Government detachment at Bruckweiler. Jarczyk was such a conscientious employee that he was soon considered for an appointment as the *Bürgermeister* of a local town, although his suspicious behaviour eventually gave him away. Since his real mission was sabotage, murder, and espionage, he was persistent in his efforts to obtain travel permits, and this gradually aroused the interest of the CIC. Subsequently he was arrested, tried, and executed on 23 April.[64]

By April 1945 the Army's makeshift anti-tank detachments had also become synonymous with Werwolf units – in fact, six tank-destroyer companies in north Germany were formally subjugated to the Bureau 'Prützmann' in mid-April.[65] German volunteers who reported to the training camp of Anti-Tank Brigade 'Schill,' near Flensburg, expected to be taught how to destroy tanks, but instead found themselves at a full-fledged Werwolf school, where the curriculum concentrated on the martial arts, demolitions, and the use of British and American weapons.[66]

Perhaps the most notable of the Army's guerrilla formations was a stay-behind unit led by Colonel Paul Krüger, former commander of 'Army School' II in Slovakia. Once the original locale of the 'Army School' was threatened by the Soviets, Krüger was ordered to transfer the institution to a new home near Schönsee, in the heart of the Bohemian Forest. It was intended that the school should continue its training mission, and, on 8 April, the OKH ordered several local military commands not to interfere with the school's personnel, but to release them 'for the continuation of highly important Werwolf training.' By late April, however, it was clear that the institution's pedagogical functions were directly imperilled by the American advance, and as a result the OKH ordered the staff to form guerrilla detachments and harass American supply lines, focusing particularly on fuel stocks. Krüger thereupon split up his faculty into four units, designated 'A,' 'B,' and 'C,' each numbering sixty-five men, plus a headquarters staff of thirty soldiers. Each formation had seven officers, many of them disabled veterans released from regular duty. These four units were distributed within a ten-mile radius of Schönsee, at least one of them astride the old pre-war boundary of Czechoslovakia. Moreover, all the detachments were ordered to prepare underground Werwolf galleries, and these bunkers were so well camouflaged that, even once American troops had uncovered the existence and rough location of Battle Group 'Paul,' U.S. patrols stumbled literally within a few feet of these dug-outs without detecting them. The unit was well equipped with small arms and a few months' supply of ammunition, plus 120 horses that were quartered by farmers living in the vicinity.

Krüger's battle plan was to wait ten days until American troops had passed through the area, and then begin sending out ten- to twenty-man detachments with orders to destroy specific targets. In the brief interim, the unit was instructed to confine itself to patrol activity, and a small reconnaissance party led by Krüger himself was sighted by American troops on 2 May. Because of its high standard of training and technical expertise, Krüger's Battle Group was potentially the most dangerous Werwolf formation in all of Europe, although, like many Werwolf operations, it fell strangely flat in the final instance. Unit 'A' in the Sudetenland was detected and wiped out during the initial American advance, and Krüger eventually lost contact with 'B' and 'C.' Worse yet, a deserter provided the Americans with detailed information on the headquarters staff, and it was mainly on the basis of this intelligence that the woods around Schönsee were scoured by American patrols seeking to uncover the hidden galleries. On 4 May, Krüger and some of his staff were captured by an American detachment, and Krüger thereafter ordered his entire headquarters to surrender.[67]

The Navy and the Luftwaffe also poked their fingers deep into the Werwolf pie. In mid-April, Grand Admiral Dönitz offered the Führer 3,000 young men who could be infiltrated through British lines and deployed as guerrilla detachments against the Allied zone of communications. 'As in France,' Dönitz noted, 'the enemy's main problem is one of supplies. Therefore attacks on the enemy's supply lines would hit him in the most vulnerable spot.' Dönitz had hoped to divert this manpower from naval stations in northern Germany, but, while the personnel were available, the weapons to supply them, particularly bazookas, were exceedingly scarce.[68] Given this complication, it is unclear whether these formations were ever actually fielded.

As for the Luftwaffe, Goering apparently had some doubts about the Werwolf, believing that it had no chance of success, but his opinions did not count for much by 1945. We have already noted that paratroop units were trained in guerrilla-style tactics, and these new methods were in full use by the time that enemy forces got to Xanten, where Canadian troops found German units allowing them to pass through forward defences before opening up on them from the rear. In one case, a Canadian officer was captured and evacuated through to German lines by a band of escaped POWs, who in turn had been liberated by a German strike team.[69] Battle Group 'von der Heydte,' the last German parachute unit to actually participate in an airborne operation, was especially schooled in such tactics. The 'von der Heydte' formation had been dropped into the American rear during the Ardennes Offensive in December 1944, although it had enjoyed little success and its commander, Colonel von der Heydte, had been taken prisoner by the Americans. Subsequently, remnants of the unit were reorganized and, as one of its captured officers later admitted, '[it] was intended to operate on similar lines to the "Werewolves."' 'Von der Heydte' partisans aimed at supplying themselves with arms and food from prepared caches, or with goods stolen from the Allies, and they were supposed to blend into the general population. The only problem was that their forged identification papers were sloppy, as was so often the case with phoney German documents and that, since they had been issued no civilian footware, their heavy jumpboots served as a glaring declaration of their true identities.[70]

In April 1945, the Luftwaffe also organized special two-man demolition teams, which were deployed behind Allied lines via light aircraft such as Fieseler Storks. On 14 April, Luftwaffe Command West ordered the establishment of a special detachment of 200 men, based at Puch airfield, near Fürstenfeldbruck. This so-called Death's Head unit, under the control of Pursuit Division Seven, was charged with 'undertakings to be carried out in the rear of the Allies against important targets (installations, bridges, columns, tanks, locomotives, etc.) ... For these tasks,' said Pursuit Division Seven, 'volunteers from the Army and the *Luftwaffe* – courageous men ready to go to their deaths – will be employed as pilots, as *Panzerfaust* men and for demolitions ... When they have completed their tasks, the men will be collected either by a waiting aircraft or [will be picked up] during the following night ... All preparations are to be completed in the shortest space of time, building up from little equipment and drawing upon other units. The motto is "up and at 'em."' Within ten days, 'Death's Head' was ready to operate with a dozen demolition crews, and between 24 and 29 April, they carried out at least twenty-five missions, mainly against objectives at Dillingen, Donauwörth, Ingolstadt, Freudenstadt, and Stuttgart, as well as the Rottweil–Tuttlingen railway. In most of these cases, results were meagre and losses were heavy – at least in part because the Allies had intercepted word of most of the targets through Ultra intercepts – and, by the end of April Operation 'Death's Head' was already forced to suspend operations. 'Fuel stocks,' they reported, 'are exhausted; supply is impossible.' 'Death's Head' ragtag remnants, consisting of twenty-one men and some ammunition, were seconded to tank-destroyer formations.[71]

Despite this limited success, the airborne transmission of demolition teams still seemed like an idea whose time had come, and similar units were also formed along the Eastern Front. In this case, the favourite tactic was to deploy bazooka teams against tanks or railways at dusk, using the low angle of the sun to silhouette the target and exploiting the lengthening shadows for cover. The main detachment engaged in such tactics in the East was a remnant of the German kamikaze 'ramming' unit, Special Command 'Elbe,' under Major Hajo Herrmann. Based at airfields in the Alps, they carried out a number of sabotage attacks against targets in Western Hungary between 2 and 7 May. A final operation, scheduled for 8 May and aimed at a railway switching-yard north of Budapest, was cancelled because of news of the impending capitulation.[72] In late April, an attempt was also made to convert yet another Luftwaffe formation in the West to sabotage activity, although this initiative finally met with vigorous opposition from the OKW.

Military Opinions Change

Before fully discussing the Luftwaffe's final attempt to harass Allied lines of communication, it is perhaps first necessary to retreat several steps and retrace some of the military's developing relationship with the Werwolf. By a peculiar turn of fate, even as the military became increasingly caught up in guerrilla warfare, its relationship with the Werwolf began to undergo a fundamental change. Three crucial elements provided the catalyst for this shift. First of all, while it is clear that the High Command accustomed itself to a Clausewitzian Werwolf, intended mainly for diversion and reconnaissance, and operating strictly as an adjunct to regular operations, they became increasingly disturbed with the kind of political and ideological texture assumed by the movement during the last several months of the war. This development is described in greater detail in subsequent chapters, but at this point suffice it to say that, in March and April 1945, Goebbels and Bormann largely re-created the Werwolf as the instrument of a popular call to arms, or, at the very least, as a political weapon of the party. This had obvious postwar implications that made military men anxious. An armed forces radio broadcast on 2 April tried to imply that civilians would only be 'helpers of the Werwolf,' but this disclaimer did not have much effect. Most German soldiers, irrespective of rank, believed that, in the post-capitulation period, Werwolf activity would degenerate into the uncontained chaos of fanatical banditry, based largely upon a core of irresponsible party and SS desperadoes and almost totally devoid of public support. In this scenario, the guerrillas would scarcely bring about the victory that the mighty Wehrmacht had failed to achieve, but, rather, would merely hinder reconstruction and provoke enemy retaliations upon an already battered German populace. In any case, such activity was well outside the proper bounds of the traditional Clausewitzian ethic; this kind of war would have slipped beyond the realm of rationality, where it served as an instrument of political policy.[73] No less a figure than Colonel General Kesselring, the overall commander in the West, considered the populist Werwolf 'senseless and harmful.' 'Reprisals by the victors,' he reasoned, 'would be the inevitable result. In addition, we have neither the landscape nor the national character for a partisan war.'[74]

Even before Hitler's death, the Army's association with the Werwolf had begun to sour visibly. It is true that there was some genuine Army sympathy for the cause of German guerrillas in Soviet-occupied regions – where there appeared little to lose[75] – and there were several cases in the East where officers resolved to ignore defeat and fight on as partisans. Even in these instances, however, the die-hards were usually junior officers acting independently of senior echelons.[76] In the East Prussian region of Samland, wild schemes for guerrilla warfare swept through the 5th Panzer Division during the last weeks of the war. Officers in this unit believed by mid-April 1945 that they had neither the necessary munitions nor the geographic room to fight any more tank battles against the Russians. Rather, they felt that the division's best bet would be to destroy its tanks and infiltrate southward through Soviet lines in order to launch a partisan campaign, or perhaps to form small Battle Groups and independently march back to German lines. Lieutenant-Colonel Hoppe, the commander of Panzer Regiment 31, believed that his detachment's stock of Russian T-34 tanks would be especially valuable in organizing a breakthrough. When 5th Panzer was ordered into action near Fischhausen by the XXVI Army Corps, some disgruntled officers attempted to carry through the guerrilla option, while others mutineed and fled to the Peyse Peninsula, where they blew up their tanks and desperately attempted to seize landing-craft in order to evacuate themselves by sea.[77]

In other areas along the Eastern Front, factors such as the inherent conservatism of the military, as well as the fear that guerrilla agitation would only make Soviet savagery worse, combined to smother the Werwolf. Moreover, the Soviet-controlled 'Free Germany' movement, with its cadre of captured Wehrmacht officers, began propaganda as early as December 1944 to encourage German officers not to obey orders to go underground.[78] It is questionable whether such urgings played much of a role in decisions made by individual officers, but, none the less feelings against the Werwolf increased in intensity, particularly late in the war. In Pomerania, the staff of II Army Corps expressely forbid cooperation with the Werwolf, and on 20 April they blocked the dissemination of Werwolf recruitment propaganda among reserve forces in Wehrkreis II.[79] Similarly, in Königsberg, the city commandant ordered his staff not to cooperate with the Werwolf, although some of his units attempted to fight on independently after the capitulation of the city.

More generally, as well, the military grew increasingly sticky about cooperation with the Werwolf. Wehrmacht Propaganda Troops refused to collaborate with efforts to encourage active, or even passive, resistance (although their stance may have changed after Günther D'Alquen assumed command of the section towards the end of the war). In a hospital town in Lower Saxony, a Wehrmacht colonel boldly overrode Werwolf instructions from the High Command, arguing that such orders would result in suicide for 'thousands of innocent civilians.'[80] There was similar evidence of hesitancy even at senior levels. On 16 April, the commanders of Army Group 'Vistula,' Generals Kinzl and Heinrici, connived with Speer in a daring plot to seize the main Werwolf radio transmitter and then broadcast a speech by Speer abolishing the Werwolf. This scheme was never executed because of the dangers involved in seizing the station once the Russians were already in range to overrun it, although Speer did secretly record his speech in Hamburg towards the end of April.[81]

A second element affecting the military's approach to guerrilla warfare was the recognition that the Army's capacity for such undertakings had been severly eroded by the spring of 1945. One of the long-time strengths of the German Army was its elaborate replacement system, whereby units (from the division level downward) drew new recruits from the same parts of the country, trained them together, and then marched them to the front together. These measures provided superb unit cohesion, but the system began to unravel in the last weeks of the war.[82] Army Group 'G' noted on 22 April that the meaning of Hitler's new guerrilla tactics was 'fully recognized,' but that there were great difficulties in carrying through these types of manoeuvres. Infantrymen were rarely any longer grouped together in coherent units bonded to their commanding officers. Rather, the bulk of forces were simply a mass haphazardly thrown together, which contained a large proportion of ersatz and training troops. These latter were considered inferior grade, and they could not be expected to perform very well.[83] With its reputation for excellence still relatively intact, the officer corps obviously felt, that if a 'small unit war' could not be launched properly, it ought not to be launched at all.

A third factor involved in the Army's relationship with the Werwolf was the increasing need for negotiating an armistice with the Western Powers. Key elements in the Army had tried to eliminate Hitler in 1943 and 1944, obviously as a necessary precondition for such an armistice, but it was only Hitler's dramatic self-annihilation in Berlin that finally cleared the path to the West. Germany then produced its own Badoglio in the form of Grand Admiral Karl Dönitz, and the centre of power shifted from Berlin to OKW headquarters, first at Plön, and then at Flensburg. Military men effectively became the leading figures in the new constellation of political and military power. Dönitz dominated the north and, as the new head of state, also enjoyed nominal command over all German forces, while Kesselring assumed plenipotentiary powers in the now cut-off regions of southern Germany.

Once the OKW became the authority of last resort, it desperately sought a modus vivendi with the West, and the military therefore showed little further tolerance for Werwolf activity. On 5 May, the day after the proclamation of a regional cease-fire in northwest Europe, two instances of such activity came to light, the most significant of which was evidence of yet another Luftwaffe plot to deploy airborne saboteurs along Allied lines of communication. Even as Operation 'Death's Head' burned through its brief life span in late April, Air Fleet 'Reich' set up a similar unit, based in the Alpine Redoubt, at Muhldorf, composed of 188 personnel and more than 60 aircraft. Organized under the purview of Flight Corps 9, this unit, Detachment 'Beehive,' dispatched a number of demolition crews into Allied-occupied territory. Their orders were to land surreptitiously in the Allied rear, remove their demolition equipment from the aircraft, and then destroy the planes and function as land-bound saboteurs. Some thirty to forty teams were actually dispatched, but in the final analysis they were able to cause limited damage, and a few detachments deserted once they were behind Allied lines – 'Sometimes the saboteurs surrender; sometimes they are shot dead; sometimes they escape.' One unit, however, comprising an officer and three men based at Pocking, did manage to land behind American lines and blow up a bridge over the Danube, near Regensburg. 'Beehive' planes also dropped supplies to HJ and Waffen-SS guerrilla groups behind Soviet lines.[84]

On the afternoon of 5 May, after two captured 'Beehive' crew members had snitched to the Allies, Jodl was gruffly told – via General Eberhardt Kinzel, German liaison at Twenty-first Army Group – to terminate the enterprise. When this matter came to Dönitz's attention, he immediately sent a message to Air Fleet 'Reich,' stating that, 'the situation vis-à-vis the Western Powers having changed fundamentally, any action of this nature is highly injurious to our general interest.' Dönitz then 'requested' that any further Werwolf actions 'be stopped immediately and completely.' To further drive the point home, all Luftwaffe stations were told on 6 May that 'arrangements and instructions concerning the Werwolf are to be cancelled. The discussion of Werwolf activity is to cease.'[85] Fanatical Luftwaffe personnel in Klagenfurt, perhaps upon receipt of this order, threw up their hands in despair and some of them participated in a mass suicide on the night of 8 May.[86]

Dönitz also called into his presence the melancholy figure of Hans Prützmann, who had effectively abandoned his leadership of the Werwolf and probably hoped to hear nothing more of it. The Grand Admiral, however, now rudely addressed Prützmann in his old role as 'Inspector for Special Abwehr.' Dönitz laid down the law, in effect telling Prützmann that the Werwolf was forthwith forbidden because the end of Wehrmacht resistance had rendered it superfluous.[87]

Several hours after the revelations about an aerial Werwolf, the OKW also received a sharp note from Field Marshal Montgomery, claiming that Twenty-first Army Group had monitored a vitriolic speech delivered over Wilhelmshaven Radio, one of the few German stations still broadcasting. Apparently, this wild outburst called for rebellion and resistance against the capitulation agreement. Yet another OKW telegram was sent out, this time to Deputy Gauleiter Joel at Wilhelmshaven, ordering an investigation and authorizing 'drastic measures' against the party functionary who had delivered the offensive speech.[88] On the evening of 5 May, Dönitz held a meeting with Paul Wegener, Gauleiter from the Wilhelmshaven area, 'Supreme Reich Defence Commissâr' and, since 2 May, chief of Dönitz's Civil Private Office (with the rank of state secretary). After again stressing the need for a prohibition of Werwolf activity,[89] Dönitz arranged for a public cancellation to be broadcast over the wavelength of Radio Germany, then based at Flensburg. Wegener, who was responsible for all press and radio announcements, concurred in this decision, and may have prompted Dönitz to make it.[90] At midnight, the station announced that the 'scorched earth' decrees were suspended, and an hour later, Germans were asked to abstain from 'illegal' underground activity either in the Werwolf or in its sister organizations. It is notable, however, that the movement was *never* formally dissolved, *nor did the prohibition apply to Soviet-occupied territory.*[91]

On the following day, Kesselring instructed SS-General Hausser, the ablest and most popular of Waffen-SS leaders, to prevent any guerrilla warfare in the Alps by disgruntled SS units. Several days later the Staff of Army Group 'G' warned that any incipient efforts to construct a 'Free Corps' would constitute a fruitless endangerment of the German people.[92] Thereafter, the Wehrmacht freely provided the Allies with available information on the Werwolf. In Tübingen, the sceptical French were amazed when a lieutenant-colonel in command of military hospitals requested the arrest of one of his non-commissioned officers, who was a Werwolf propagandist.[93] In areas where the defeated Army was given temporary responsibilities for policing and the implementation of control measures, German officers worked scrupulously to prevent sabotage and civilian or military unrest.[94] Radio Flensburg encouraged German troops and civilians to collaborate with the Allies, with the suggestion that this might contribute to the restoration of German lands in the East overrun by the Soviets.[95]

Of course there were various formations in the East that continued to battle on, probably the most important being Ferdinand Schörner's Army Group 'Centre' (about which more will be said in chapter 6). At several spots in Scandinavia, local German commanders spoke of soldiering on, 'even after midnight,' but such declarations usually provoked a flurry of desertions by dispirited troops or sailors who had no desire to play a role in any last-minute, reckless adventures.[96] Overall, the military's association with the Werwolf was terminated. Jodl told Eisenhower on 6 May that individual German soldiers and units might disobey orders to surrender to the Soviets, but he was apparently assured that the OKW would not be held responsible.[97] The only case where official sanction was sought for post-capitulation activities was in the forlorn Courland Pocket in western Latvia, where an 'independent' Latvian regime was organized in early May under an SS officer named Osis. The commanding officer in Courland, General Hilpert, told Dönitz on 5 May that the intent behind the proclamation of Latvian independence was to form volunteers from his 200,000–man Army Group into a 'Free Corps' that could continue operations in aid of a nominally independent Latvian regime. This was not a particularly orginal idea: the same strategy had been undertaken in 1918–19, when remnants of the German Army in the area had fought on with the tacit approval of the Western Allies, ostensibly to preserve the independence of the new Baltic republics. That affair had ended in a fiasco when the Baltic states eventually found themselves forced to dislodge their 'Free Corps' 'allies' in order to secure their independence and prevent ruthless marauding. The OKW probably poured cold water on the scheme, and it was eventually scrapped, mainly because it was impracticable. The 12th Panzer and 19th SS divisions also abandoned plans to independently slash their way back to Germany, although they did fight on for several hours beyond the cease-fire, and thousands of soldiers from Latvian SS units subsequently scattered into the woods and joined partisan bands.[98] Otherwise, the bulk of the Courland garrison surrendered on 9 May, and was rounded up over the course of the following several weeks.

The only place where real trouble occurred was on the eastern Danish island of Bornholm, lying in the Baltic north of Pomerania. This outpost was used by the Germans as a base for seaborne withdrawals from coastal regions in the eastern Baltic, and as such it was heavily bombed, and then invaded by the

Soviets. The OKW believed that the capitulation in all parts of Denmark was to be accepted only by the British, and on 10 May they advised the Bornholm garrison commander, Captain von Kampz, not to concede the island, although they eventually reversed this order after being so instructed by Twenty-first Army Group. However, as a result of this procrastination, the German garrison of 25,000 men wound up resisting the Russians for forty-eight hours, even though the general capitulation had already gone into force. Finally, von Kampz was arrested by three Wehrmacht officers, and the unit formally capitulated, although 4,000 stubborn German troops continued to fight on, and as late as 19 May they were still skirmishing with the Soviets and raiding farmsteads. Von Kampz was handed over to the Russians, whereafter he was tried by a military court at Kolberg and shot.[99]

Although the military's last-minute caution helped the Allies, and even the Soviets, it smelled of posturing and dissimulation. An intelligence assessment by Twenty-first Army Group rightly noted that the OKW was 'playing it safe,' and that their hostile intent had merely been veiled by a screen of cooperation – 'The aim must now be to make themselves indispensable to the Western Allies. That is why there is so little sabotage, so little subversive activity. Only silly little men would do anything like that at this stage. OKW itself has ostentatiously stamped on any attempt, trading in information about Werewolves and clobbering the SS, best of all scapegoats.'[100] While many German officers had initial doubts about the Werwolf, the bald truth is that for several months they happily exploited guerrilla warfare for its short-term benefits, regardless of the resulting anarchy, and they did not change their minds until the end of the war became so immediate that it was impossible not to think about currying favour with the enemy. As late as 8 April, Kesselring himself deployed 'demolition and sabotage teams' in Hesse, specifically to destroy a V-2 missile captured by the Americans, and he promised 'special honours' for the successful team.[101] The military was only one step from the Goebbelsite Werwolf, whose socially destructive impulses will be described in subsequent chapters. Just as the Wehrmacht must share blame for Nazi aggressions and for the Holocaust, so, too, must it share responsibility for the Werwolf.

In the final analysis, of course, the problem of relations between the German military and the Werwolf was solved by the occupying powers, who simply dissolved the Wehrmacht as a corporate entity. There would be no replay of the post–First World War period, when German military officers abetted 'Free Corps' and Vehme activity, as well as collectively snubbing their noses at the Allied Powers. As early as the Tehran Conference, the Big Three had committed themselves to destroying German militarism, a commitment formally outlined at Potsdam, and the OKW was naturally the first target. The Armed Forces High Command was broken up in late May, at the time that the 'Flensburg Government' was dismantled, and OKW personnel were subsequently dispersed and sent to various POW camps outside Germany.[102] Disbanding the rank and file of the Wehrmacht was a more lengthy process, although, within several years, the last remnants of the German Army and Navy had also been demobilized. Of all the occupying powers, the British most dragged their feet, since they made considerable use of uniformed German forces as labour units. It is true that a few individual German personnel still under the colours engaged in Werwolf-like activities – at Altenlunne, a German soldier strung a 'decapitation wire'; at Schmalding, surrendered German troops assaulted a British NCO; in Hamburg, mine-sweeping crews threatened and attacked anti-Nazi Germans – but by 1947 even the British had demobilized the last of these so-called Service Groups.[103] Thus terminated the history of the Prussian/German Army, with its attendent traditions of Landsturm, 'Field Rangers,' and 'Free Corps.'

4

Reign of Terror: The Party and the Werwolf

Aside from the military's intervention into the Werwolf field, there were also some last-minute attempts by party chieftains to promote partisan warfare. This trend particularly centred upon the efforts of two powerful men whose careers had developed within the party bureaucracy and whose bases of power lay within that realm: Martin Bormann, the stocky and sinister head of the party chancellery, who had once gone up against the French as a member of the underground during the Ruhr occupation, but had since switched his expertise to bureaucratic infighting; and Joseph Goebbels, the *Gauleiter* of Berlin and minister of propaganda, who stood out as the only first-rate intellect in the senior Nazi hierarchy. These were the most important of the 'old party comrades' who remained loyal to Hitler's apparent desire for the self-immolation of the Reich, and who during the final months huddled together with their master in the gloomy chancellery bunker. Moreover, they both saw the Werwolf as something more than a strictly Clausewitzian diversionary movement, and Goebbels in particular sought to develop the revolutionary underpinnings of National Socialism as a key motivational element in Werwolf activity.

Of course, Bormann and Goebbels can only loosely be considered a pairing because of the vicious rivalry between the two men, although even this antagonism was dulled in the spring of 1945 because of their agreement on the need to buoy up German resistance by means of fanatical propaganda.[1] Bormann and Goebbels alike indulged in day-dreams about the good old days of the 'Time of Struggle,' and hoped to revive the party as a self-contained political fighting unit:[2] the latter sought by such means to save the ideological aspect of Naziism – or at least to force Germany to undergo the passage of the movement amid a rain of revolutionary fire and brimstone, while the former had the more limited goal of saving himself and the basis of his bureaucratic power. Bormann, in particular, emerged during the final days as the archetypical figure of James Burnham's 'managerial revolution' – that is, the faceless functionary deriving all power from his position in the bureaucracy and existing solely for the will to power. Such a creature was totally unwilling to countenance the collapse of the bureaucracy and was determined to preserve it through dramatic acts of will.

The Volkssturm

Bormann, Goebbels, and various other senior party officials, such as Robert Ley, all fancied having a leftist or 'popular' orientation that naturally led them towards the expedient of a 'people's war.' The parallels with the self-assumed role of the Soviet Communist Party in 1941–2 are obvious. It will be recalled, however, that the main proponents of such a course throughout the early history of the NSDAP had been the Storm Troopers (SA). It was the SA which, in the initial years of the Third Reich, had spoken of organizing a 'people's army' and had actually established training camps for guerrilla fighters, all of which came to an abrupt stop when the paramilitary's leadership was violently suppressed in 1934.[3] Even after the SA's eclipse, it continued to dominate programs such as civilian rifle training, which began in 1939, and for a short period in the spring and summer of 1944 – when the civilian rifle-training course was expanded under the title 'SA Defence Shooting' – it appeared that the SA might emerge from the shadows, although this was only a momentary development.[4] By September 1944, with the Soviets and Western Allies both hovering over Germany's frontiers, the preparation of domestic resistance was suddenly no longer a distant precaution, but a serious business in which the major figures of the Nazi state began to involve themselves. It then became apparent that the Storm Troopers had never really recovered from the blow of the Röhm 'Putsch,' and the SA leadership helplessly found their former sphere of control in adult paramilitary training now poached upon by powers of a higher order. One captured SA official told the Americans that, as a focal point of Nazi resistance warfare, 'the SA may be considered a dead issue.'[5]

With the Wehrmacht on the verge of collapse in August and September 1944, various generals began to demand civilian labour call-ups in borderland regions, mainly for the purpose of constructing defence works. They also requested the formation of a civilian defence militia, perhaps built around the surviving core of the SA.[6] Hitler accepted the basic plan, but rather than allot responsibility to either the SA or the military, he turned to the *Gauleiter*, who by Hitler's order had been appointed 'Reich Defence Commissioners' and whose power and authority had been increasing ever since the declining fortunes of war had seemed to make ideological issues more important for the regime. In this spirit, the most energetic *Gauleiter* had already been attempting to build local home-guard units since 1943, but had been consistently blocked by the Guard Corps (SS), which claimed sole responsibility for security matters.[7] Now, however, party bosses in the borderland *Gaue* were unleashed from prior constraints, and they quickly established themselves as local warlords: Erich Koch, for instance, made early plans to organize a 'Border Guard' in East Prussia;[8] Franz Hofer aided in the call-up of 50,000 Alpine minutemen in the Tyrol–Voralberg;[9] while, in the eastern Ruhr, Albert Hoffmann established a 'Free Corps "Sauerland" ' as a regional paramilitary formation.[10]

In the early fall such regional organizations were incorporated into a new national militia coordinated by the party chancellery.[11] Helmuth Auerbach suggests that both the Werwolf and the new militia, the Volkssturm, were actually mirror images of the same program,[12] with the Volkssturm serving as the component of the 'people's war' at the front, and the Werwolf as its expression in the enemy rear. It was certainly true – in theory, at least – that both the Werwolf and the Volkssturm were supposed to combine party and SS efforts, with the party handling the political and ideological side of matters, and the SS the military side. This new 'people's war' was also launched with a great deal of blustery propaganda, which hinted at the possibility of fighting behind Allied lines but rarely stated this threat directly because of the 'defeatist' implications of such declarations.[13]

At the time of its establishment, there was some doubt about whether members of the Volkssturm were responsible merely for service on the German side of the front, or were also expected to act as *francs-tireurs* and partisans in the enemy rear. Although the Volkssturm was based upon a secret Führer decree of 6 September 1944 (and a formal order issued three weeks later),[14] it was introduced to the public in a speech by Himmler on 18 October. Not incidentally, the speech was given in East Prussia, where Volkssturm units first became operational, and it also commemorated the anniversary of the 1813 Battle of Nations, which was fought in part by the Prussian Landsturm. Himmler continually returned to the inspiration of the Landsturm, but he also made reference to a revival of the Werwolf bands active during the Thirty Years War – 'even in territory which [the enemy] believes they have conquered, the German will to resist will again and again flare-up in their rear, and like Werewolves, death-defying volunteers will injure the enemy and cut his lifelines.'[15]

This statement naturally created considerable alarm among both friend and foe: 'Hitler Rallies Guerrillas' was the banner headline in *The Stars and Stripes*, and at Supreme Headquarters, Allied Expeditionary Forces (SHAEF), Allied officers hinted that unmarked Volkssturm troopers operating in the Allied rear would not be protected by the Hague Rules of War. On the same day that the Volkssturm was announced, SHAEF Civil Affairs/Military Government (G-5) released the legal outline for the Allied Military Government, which contained a well-publicized authorization for firing squads to deal with German civilians blocking the progress of Allied armies.[16] Such declarations reached the ears of many Germans via Allied radio broadcasts.

Thus facing this almost insurmountable barrier to the construction of the Volkssturm, Nazi propagandists immediately began to reverse the signal sent out in Himmler's address. Both domestic and international propaganda heavily stressed that the militia would *not* be a partisan movement. 'The Volkssturm,' said the *12 Uhr Blatt*, 'is no casual heap of poorly armed civilians, but a highly disciplined army of soldiers. It will not fight with flails or ARP [Air Raid Precautions] axes, nor in secret and cowardly ambushes, but with weapons of modern war, and fearlessly, as true soldiers do ...' The same message was conveyed in local newspapers and journals, and also in an important address to foreign journalists by the military propagandist Sündermann, made on the same day as Himmler's speech. To strengthen the claim of such irregular formations to proper treatment, the Germans were also careful to apply the Hague Convention to members of the Polish Home Army captured in the Warsaw Uprising,[17] and they became increasingly lenient with prisoners taken from Yugoslav Partisan formations. They also told the Red Cross that they were now willing to recognize as combatants anyone honouring Article I of the Hague Rules of War (1907), and German units in action against guerrillas were told to stop describing the enemy with pejorative expressions. 'We are compelled to revise our vocabulary in view of our own organisations, such as VS [Volkssturm].'[18]

SHAEF Counter-intelligence (G-2) decided in late October that it had originally misinterpreted the Volkssturm, and a week later the SHAEF chief of staff, General W.B. Smith, issued a directive noting that Volkssturm units would be given appropriate treatment under the Hague Rules, provided that they met the necessary conditions set forth by Articles I and II of the convention (i.e., that they were commanded by a responsible officer, bore a recognizable emblem, and carried their weapons openly).[19] British intelligence had already figured out that Himmler's reference to Werewolves probably did not apply to the main body of the Volkssturm, and on the last day of October, the under-secretary of the Foreign Office told the House of Commons that 'no substantial distinction can be drawn between the position in international law of the *Volkssturm* and of the Local Defence Volunteers when they were formed in 1940 ... they are entitled to be treated as legal combatants.'[20] Subsequent Allied policy was to detain Volkssturm officers, but to release lower ranks with a warning that further interference with Allied personnel or lines of communication would result in the imposition of the death penalty.[21]

The Soviets, however, were not bound by any similar sense of restraint, perhaps because they had earlier employed their own militia units as guerrilla bands, and thus naturally expected that the Germans would do the same. In addition, they were infuriated by anyone captured in a brown uniform – they associated the colour brown with the NSDAP rather than with any proper military formation – and they often encountered Volkssturm members with no uniforms at all. Neither did many of these men have military passbooks or armbands fashioned in a uniform style or colour. As a result, the Soviets routinely massacred captured Volkssturm men on the assumption that they were partisans, particularly in the first months after the formation of the militia.[22] In fact, a Soviet POW told the Germans that a Stalin Order in December 1944 specifically stipulated that Volkssturm troopers be wiped out or summarily executed.[23] Only very late in the war does evidence suggest that the Soviets had begun to erect camps specifically to house 'German partisans,' implying that the shoot-on-sight policy had been amended. One such camp was reportedly established at Insterburg, in East Prussia.[24]

Was, in fact, the Volkssturm meant to have a guerrilla character? Directives from the party chancellery clearly show that the overall organization was regarded mainly as a means of stopping armoured thrusts by the enemy, and that it was intended to operate strictly within the bounds outlined in the Hague Rules. In fact, Bormann even forwarded to the *Gauleiter* summaries of the Hague agreements in order to guide the proper formation and training of local Volkssturm units.[25] Hans Kissel, a former officer in the organization, has also issued a denial that it had any guerrilla character or any association with the Werwolf. Kissel also claims that, in order to maintain order within the militia, a system of military justice was introduced in 1945 which supposedly kept Volkssturm men on the straight and narrow, and prevented the militia from disintegrating into an armed rabble.[26]

Of course, the Volkssturm did have its own 'reconnaissance patrols,' which operated behind the enemy's front lines, and, given the fact that Volkssturm men were typically marked only by armbands, this type of activity veered close to the realm of guerrilla warfare. On 9 April, for instance, Special Unit 'Haupt' infiltrated a number of bicycle-mounted teams behind U.S. lines in the Thuringian Forest, where they collected valuable information on the relationship between American occupation troops and German civilians.[27] In February 1945, the commander of Army Group 'Centre,' Field-Marshal Schörner, suggested that the bulk of the Volkssturm actually be absorbed by the Army, but that special units be left independent for patrol activity, one of the few things that Schörner believed the Volkssturm did well. 'Small, local Volkssturm groups,' he said, '[can] be active in the flank and rear of the enemy.'[28] Overall, this suggestion can be regarded as part of the Army's effort to beef up its capac-

ities for guerrilla warfare behind the Eastern Front, although nothing further
came of it.

Despite Hans Kissel's denials, it is also possible that, according to the preferences of the local *Gauleiter* and *Kreisleiter*, whole battalions were trained for
partisan warfare. Civilians interrogated by the U.S. First Army in Eschweiler
claimed that the newly formed Volkssturm had been trained for sabotage, the
disruption of communications, and sniping. Although organized as military
units, Volkssturm members were instructed to escape enemy scrutiny by posing
as normal civilians.[29] Similarly, German Army POWs from other areas in the
Rhineland reported that, in twice-weekly military training sessions for male
civilians, sabotage was on the curriculum, as well as small-arms proficiency.[30]
It is also known that certain training courses for the Alpine minutemen in
March and April 1945 were in fact programs in sabotage intended to produce
full-fledged Werewolves.[31]

Similar Volkssturm undertakings were launched along the Eastern Front. In
early January 1945, German intelligence officers ran a recruiting campaign in
which they selected a number of Volkssturm officers for 'special training.' As it
turned out, the selectees were mostly SA men, gendarmes, and NSDAP officials. About thirty of these men were transferred to a camp near Landsberg, in
eastern Brandenburg, where they were trained for activity in the Soviet rear.
The head of the program was an Abwehr major named Richard Graven. Before
the arrival of the Red Army, the graduates were divided into cells of five to ten
men each, and were placed under the operational control of another intelligence
officer, named Geldenbrandt. These cells were then prepared to blow up bridges
in the Soviet rear, mine roads and railways, and attack Russian troops. Geldenbrandt even arranged to have two airfields secretly built near Landsberg, so as
to assure a means for the continuing resupply of weapons and ammunition via
Luftwaffe supply flights. Once the Red Army overran Landsberg, several armed
men were uncovered in possession of a radio transmitter, but 'stern treatment'
meted out by a Soviet military court was said to have greatly influenced the
bearing of the civilian populace.

Similar units were fielded in Silesia, consisting mainly of teenagers under the
command of a few qualified Army officers. These teams remained in the rear of
advancing Soviet forces during January and February 1945, and, according to a
Soviet Internal Security (NKVD) report, they terrorized Red Army troops and
contributed to the defence of 'fortresses' such as Breslau and Glogau. As well,
350 to 500 men, nearly half the complement of a Volkssturm-type outfit called
'Free Corps "Upper Silesia,"' were graduates of a Werwolf training school at
Neisse. Arms and supplies were cached in the woods in order to support these
detachments.[32]

As Soviet pressure increased and the Red Army approached Berlin, the attempts to rouse mass resistance became steadily more desperate. 'Hate and Revenge' propaganda in East Prussia called upon the population to use any means at hand to damage the enemy. 'Fight slyly like Indians,' said Kreisleiter Ernst Wagner of Königsberg in an appeal on 1 March; 'all means, fair and foul, are sanctified by the end of destroying Bolshevism.' A captive taken in Fürstenwalde in late April admitted that, shortly before the fall of the city, *all* the male population had been formed into squads which were supposed to operate in the Soviet rear after occupation, and some of these squads were armed at private residences in the eastern part of the city. Hidden Volkssturm arms dumps to support such activity were uncovered in both Fürstenwalde and Frankfurt an der Oder.[33]

On a related theme, it is also true that the Volkssturm had definite associations with the Werwolf, particularly through the limited passage of personnel from the former to the latter. In Cologne, for instance, stalwarts from the local Volkssturm were sent to a five-day Werwolf training course at Osnabrück. The trainees were minor party officials and 'veteran party comrades,' most of whom had no secondary schooling and were generally regarded as the sludge from the bottom of the manpower barrel.[34] In eastern Austria, there was an especially blurred distinction between the Volkssturm and the Werwolf, mainly because both functioned under a single commander, SS-Lieutenant-Colonel Fahrion. A Front Intelligence (FAK) unit that trained a Werwolf group near Graz reported that personnel consisted of Volkssturm men and Hitler Youth (HJ) members, and Fahrion reported to the local HSSPF that he was actively recruiting Werewolves from the ranks of the Volkssturm. Another factor at play in this region was that the Gauleiter of Lower Austria, Hugo Jury, was extremely opposed to the recruitment of HJ members into the Werwolf, thus forcing the organization to look at alternative sources for recruits.[35]

The Party and Werwolf Propaganda

For several months immediately after Himmler's Volkssturm speech, the party tended to keep its focus away from the SS-dominated Werwolf and upon the Volkssturm, where the party was actually gaining influence at the expense of the SS.[36] It will be recalled, for instance, that the *Gauleiter* had been given important tasks relative to Werwolf recruitment, but that this allotment of responsibility had failed because of the tendency of party bosses to direct resources towards the Volkssturm. The *Gauleiter* had also been given extensive local control of Werwolf propaganda (with guiding principles drafted by the Propaganda Ministry) – something of a reversion to the pre-1933 system, in which the *Gauleiter* had dominated party publicity. It was expected that material prepared under this regime would be air-dropped into enemy territory or shot in by means of leaflet shelling. Once again, almost nothing was done in this sphere aside from the air-drop of a few miniature copies of *Völkischer Beobachter*, and the republication of Löns's *Der Werwolf*, which was mandatory reading both for members of the SS guerrilla organization and for so-called worthy men of the Volkssturm.[37]

It is true that the master SS propagandist Günther D'Alquen was attached to Prützmann's staff to handle propaganda matters, and that, in October 1944, D'Alquen published an article on the likelihood of Nazi partisan warfare in his popular SS journal, *Das Schwarze Korps*.[38] However, D'Alquen was subsequently incapacitated by scarlet fever for the winter of 1944–5, and was in hospital from the beginning of November until March.[39] During this period, the Werwolf was thus left without much propaganda punch, although this actually pleased some of the secretive SS officers running the organization, who saw its role as a diversionary force better served by secrecy than by open publicity. Heinz Höhne has rightly described the SS as 'a closed community with its own rules and loyalties'; it is difficult to understand how such a self-consciously élitist movement could have given the Werwolf a popular aspect, particularly when the party, with responsibility for such matters, practically declared its lack of interest.

There were other basic problems also inhibiting Werwolf propaganda. In the first place, consideration of guerrilla warfare would have broken the Nazi taboo on admitting the possible loss of considerable stretches of territory. It also presumed that the Wehrmacht was no longer capable of defending the Reich. Such admissions seemed especially inappropriate during a period when the fronts in both East and West had solidified and the military were in fact preparing a major counter-attack aimed at splitting American and British forces. During the period of panic in September 1944, certain German sources had hinted at the possibility of partisan warfare, as noted above, but even during this period assurances of the Wehrmacht's capability to defend German frontiers easily outnumbered any suggestions of guerrilla fighting occasionally heard or seen in the domestic media.[40] Little or nothing was said about partisan warfare against the Soviets.

A further difficulty was caused by German evacuation policy, according to which the bulk of the loyal citizenry was supposed to leave threatened areas in advance of the enemy's arrival. Although such directives were frequently flouted in western Germany, party and propaganda agencies could hardly report extensive resistance activities in areas that were supposed to be evacuated. In fact, the best they could do was suggest that German civilians would have readily ambushed the invaders, had they been asked to do so. To make matters worse, Goebbels, in early October 1944, made a spectacularly inappropriate radio address, calling all German civilians in the occupied territories 'traitors' who had 'gone over to the Americans,' a depiction that severly demoralized pro-Nazi activists in the occupied borderlands. One such fanatic noted in her diary that Goebbels was a 'parasite,' and that she could never forgive him.[41]

Yet another problem for the Nazis lay in the fact that the limited scale of resistance actually under way in the occupied zones was carried out principally by teenagers. Press and radio outlets occasionally admitted this, and they complained about the harsh sentences meted out to HJ 'martyrs,' but otherwise Nazi opinion-makers probably feared that widespread knowledge of such a children's war would alienate the increasingly irritable home population in unoccupied areas. As late as March 1945, reports of sabotage by teenage HJ members were attributed by the German News Agency to 'systemic' Allied black propaganda.[42]

By the beginning of 1945, however, the factors that had oriented the party away from the Werwolf in favour of the Volkssturm had begun to erode. In the first place, the much-heralded Volkssturm proved both incapable and vastly unpopular. When committed at the front, it performed so poorly that arrangements were made in January to keep Volkssturm battalions constantly stiffened by Army and Waffen-SS troops, lest they collapse and create holes in the front.[43] Moreover, the compulsory mass call-up to the organization caused tremendous resentment, not only because of the demands caused by part-time training, but also because the formation of special battalions for use on the Eastern Front was felt a betrayal of the assurance that the Volkssturm was strictly a measure for local defence.[44] Most important of all, people naturally realized that civilians with pick-up weapons would be slaughtered attempting to succeed where the Wehrmacht had already failed. Himmler's comparison of the Volkssturm to the 1813 'Freedom Fighters' was rejected as totally unrealistic.[45] Many Germans were further convinced by Himmler's inaugural speech that Volkssturm men were in effect guerrillas – notwithstanding Allied assurances of protection under the Hague Convention – and this unsettling suspicion also caused a continual erosion of morale. A government official in Krenau later reported that the Silesians of his homeland would have readily fought the Soviets had they been in the Wehrmacht, but they were not prepared to die for a hopeless cause as partisans or *francs-tireurs*.[46]

Another problem concerned the stubborn presence of the Anglo-American forces, who refused to be pushed back from their narrow beachheads on German soil. There were disturbing signs of timidity and collaboration by the few Rhinelanders under this enemy's thumb, so that, despite the psychological restraints, German propagandists eventually had to admit the need to punish collaborators. By the second week of October both the party chancellery and the Propaganda Ministry were complaining about 'Germans in enemy-occupied areas [who] had not conducted themselves in accord with the principle of national honour,' and they were calling for 'the sharpest measures,' although for the time being they contented themselves with the knowledge 'that the Reichsführer-SS is making the necessary preparations.'[47]

By the end of 1944, however, propaganda policy was being altered to allow for the introduction of an alleged organization called the 'Avengers of German Honour,' which was supposed to combat collaborationism by executing the sentences of Vehme courts. Throughout the first several months of 1945, various Rhenish newspapers carried harrowing reports about the killing of 'dishonourable' Germans, particularly the alleged machine-gunning of three 'informers' near Richterich on the night of 22 December. The increasing activity of the Avengers, said the Nazis, 'made the Americans extremely nervous,' and 'had stiffened the secret resistance of the nationally-minded population.'[48] Some Allied intelligence agencies were doubtful that any such killings actually occurred; SHAEF's Psychological Warfare Division noted that 'no evidence has been received to suggest that the stories are true,' and the 216th Counter-Intelligence Corps (CIC) unit characterized the Avengers as a 'product ... of fancy and fanatical imagination,' although they captured a juvenile wire-cutter who admitted membership in the organization. Various tidbits of information suggest that the movement was sporadically active, if only as a theme for local resisters. A Belgian intelligence report suggested that an Aachen businessman had been riddled with bullets and had a threatening placard pinned to his corpse, a claim also made by a Wehrmacht radio station. The 5th CIC detachment reported, in contrast to the 216th, that the 'Avengers' were functional, at least in the Palatinate, and, similarly, the Political Warfare Executive noted that the 'Avengers' were 'genuinely active in Cologne in March,' although the Americans had previously rejected such reports. Nasty leaflets, bearing the drawing of a man hanging from a gibbet, were shoved under the doors of 'collaborators,' and these were signed 'The Avengers.' An auxiliary policeman was also murdered in Cologne, although it was not certain that the 'Avengers' were responsible. The 'Avengers' apparently consisted of ragtag HJ elements, although rumours in Cologne also suggested that Gestapo men were involved.[49]

Bormann and the Werwolf

By February 1945, the problems posed by the occupied territories had multiplied tenfold, since the Western Allies had further expanded their toe-holds in the Rhineland and the Soviets had also captured large stretches of territory in the wake of their massive Winter Offensive. Party leaders therefore began to take a second look at the Werwolf movement, which the SS was now accused of unconscionably neglecting.[50] Several Bormann minions produced proposals for initiating partisan warfare, particularly 'Senior Section Leader' Hans Dotzler, a Bavarian poultry farmer and former *Kreisleiter* of Landshut, who suddenly bloomed into an expert on guerrilla warfare along the Eastern Front. Dotzler's suggestion for an anti-Soviet underground called for 'all movements from fanatical National Socialism to the national Polish clergy to be employed; varied in their appearance, not absolutely uniform in their lines of thought, and yet shaping an anti-Bolshevist resistance.' Leadership elements, he maintained, 'should be formed from leading personalities of the SD from these territories, who are reliable, and from a few men of the Party Chancellery.' Bormann passed this memorandum on to Himmler, who, in turn, gave the document to Prützmann and ordered the Werwolf leader to report to Bormann and provide the party chief with full details about his work.[51]

By March 1945, Bormann had waded deep into the Werwolf morass. *Gauleiter* in immediately threatened areas were supplied with false identity papers and ordered to go underground in order to help in organizing resistance movements. 'Stay, win or die' became the new motto, and Bormann promised that he would treat as deserters any party officials attempting to leave their *Gaue* without permission.[52] In an operation code-named 'Special Action,' National Socialist Leadership Corps (NSF) officers answerable to the party chancellery were sent out to direct guerrilla preparations and 'to fire up the population for fanatic resistance.' At the same time, local NSDAP officials and *Bürgermeister* were told that the Americans intended to deport all male Germans, which meant that desperate measures were in order. NSDAP officials were also ordered to give up any state or civic posts that might be held concurrently with their party positions, an issue that had long been of concern to Bormann because he feared that local leaders in such offices would lose a sense of party identity. The rationalization for this measure in 1945 was that it would free party hacks for possible underground work and would also create a category of ersatz 'surrender officials' specifically set up by the Nazis for the purpose of later knocking them down, with propaganda, threats, or Werwolf assassination teams.

Bormann also began to warm to the idea of an Alpine redoubt: a memorandum to the Führer suggesting the construction of an Alpine fortress had already been submitted in November 1944 by the Tyrolean *Gauleiter*, Hofer, but it lay gathering dust for four months until Bormann's opinions on the matter had shifted. Only then did he tardily forward the document to Hitler.[53]

Even more important, Dotzler was appointed to head a Werwolf political directorate, which made plans for the re-establishment of secret party nuclei and the spread of Flüsterpropaganda (propaganda through whispers). According to Kurt Tauber, Dotzler's office had big ideas and dedicated itself to organizing the survival of the party as a network of small cells acting clandestinely in pursuit of political ends. Nazi doctrine would be spread by cell members via word of mouth. Since Allied counter-measures were expected to be harsh, leadership would lay in the hands of young and uncompromised men whose names would not appear on Allied or Soviet blacklists. The movement was expected to have a considerable appeal to former members of the Wehrmacht. The main initial aim of the network would be sheer survival, although eventually it was envisioned that the cells might be united under a political front disguised as a Christian-Communist party.[54]

After Bormann's meeting with Prützmann – at which the latter presumably complained about the non-compliance of the *Gauleiter* in aiding Werwolf activities – Bormann also issued a circular to the *Gauleiter* strictly ordering them to appoint a 'Werwolf Commissioner' responsible for recruitment, and thence to forward the names to Dotzler's office at the party chancellery. The immediate posting of such officials, said Bormann, 'was of great importance for this highly significant task.' Soon after, the members of party-affiliated sports organizations were also ordered to maintain their cohesion and prepare for resistance activities in the near future.[55] This effort to encourage the aid of party organizations in Werwolf-related matters had heretofore fallen upon Prützmann, Ley, and the chief of the Party Personnel Office, Marrenbach,[56] but none of these figures could ensure the kind of compliance that Bormann could rightly demand.

It is not unreasonable to surmise that Bormann's increased commitment to Werwolf activism during this period ensured a reciprocal extension of his influence within the organization, and Hugh Trevor-Roper rightly notes that 'the Berlin group' usurped the Werwolf name 'and tried to control the policy.'[57] Several senior German leaders who first came into contact with the Werwolf in March and April 1945 even believed that the organization was directly under Bormann's command and later testified to this effect at the Nuremberg Trials.[58] The conversion of Werwolf into a strong-arm unit for enforcing 'scorched earth' decrees and assassinating 'defeatists' in Nazi-held territory particularly bears the imprint of Bormann's influence. It is notable, for instance, that the posting of threatening Werwolf placards in Wuppertal was done by Kreisleitung functionaries who had taken it upon themselves to organize the local Werwolf.[59] At Schwenningen, in the Black Forest, the Werwolf turned out to be the instrument of Kreisleiter Speck, an ardent Nazi who used the Werwolf to crush political opponents and 'collaborators.'[60] In Brunswick, a Kreisleitung 'hit squad' killed three 'defeatists' and 'cowards,' including a senior government official, and the bodies were pinned with Werwolf warning notes.[61] In Wilhelmshaven, the party's 'Werwolf Commissioner,' Fritz Lotto, personally gunned down three 'traitors' on 2 May 1945, including a police superintendant who had talked about 'going over to the other side.' Similarly, in Dötlingen, a party newssheet claimed on 16 April that a local farmer had been killed by the 'Avengers of German Honour' and his body tagged with a warning note. In actuality, this action was undertaken as part of a larger NSDAP terrorization campaign in southern Oldenburg, and the responsible parties were recruited from a special Volkssturm unit trained in Werwolf tactics.[62]

The worst case of this party-inspired terror occurred in the Alpine mining town of Penzberg, which was affected by the separatist, anti-Nazi rebellion that swept through southern Bavaria on 27–8 April. Although the revolt in Penzberg was suppressed by a Wehrmacht grenadier unit, Gauleiter Giesler quickly dispatched a special para-political unit of the Volkssturm, which was called 'Group Hans' after its leader, the writer and 'veteran party comrade' Hans Zöberlein. 'Group Hans' had already begun to assume a Werwolf aspect by posting up fearsome 'Werwolf Upper Bavaria' placards in Munich, and Zöberlein told members of the detachment, while on their way to Penzberg, that they were now part of an official Werwolf formation. After its arrival, the unit broke up into ten-man teams, each working from lists of suspected rebel sympathizers, and each assigned to track down a particular target. As these squads fanned out throughout Penzberg, announcing their presence by tossing hand-grenades at the doors of unsuspecting victims, eight people were searched out and lynched, two of them women. In one neighbourhood, the avengers got a nasty jolt when they were met by firing from the homes of mine workers, but the only casualty of the skirmish was a miner who was mortally wounded. The terrorists also scattered Werwolf flyers before they slunk out of town under cover of darkness, leaving the burghers of Penzberg to cut down their victims on the following morning. Each body had a placard hung around the neck, marked 'SS-Werwolf Upper Bavaria.'[63]

The party also interested itself in repairing the unpreparedness of the SS by encouraging resistance in territories already overrun. A meeting was held in February between Bormann's deputy, Helmut Friedrichs, and Goebbels's main underling, Werner Naumann, at which such matters were discussed. A suggestion to air-drop sabotage instructions and propaganda into Soviet-occupied areas was rejected on the assumption that the Soviets would react with massive reprisals, and that the measure would therefore be counter-productive. Rather, it was decided to exploit the apparatus of Operation 'Scorpion,' a top-secret project for spreading Vlassovite and Ukrainian nationalist propaganda that was originally launched by Günther D'Alquen's '"Kurt Eggers" Standard' in Poland during the summer of 1944. The 'Scorpion' operation was equipped with loud-speaker trucks and presses organized to produce flyers, and Naumann soon established liaison with the ubiquitous Skorzeny, who had since assumed control of the 'Scorpion' enterprise.[64] According to Polish reports, the Nazis also overcame their squeamishness about Soviet reprisals, and in April 1945 they began air-dropping anti-Soviet propaganda into Silesia.[65]

Such last-minute exertions had a limited effect. In Styria, for instance, the Kreisleitung at Löben began a desperate effort in April 1945 to prepare galleries by employing special groups of NSDAP stalwarts as diggers. Other select recruits were chosen for Werwolf training at a nearby facility at Niederndorf and at a special Werwolf camp near Admont, although not much enthusiasm was generated.[66] In many areas, it was regarded as a foregone conclusion that such efforts would fail because there was not enough time to achieve any chance of success. Kreisleiter Volkert, captured in the Nuremberg area several days after the city's collapse, had plenty of knowledge about resistance activities, and even though he was a devout Nazi, he told American interrogators that the Werwolf was sure to fail. When he himself was charged with Werwolf responsibilities shortly before the American advance, he had been given no personnel, no workable plans, and no material. The *Gauleiter*, he said, 'just told us to do what we could,' and that was the local limit of the party's role in the Werwolf.[67] Similarly, in Heidelberg, the *Kreisleiter* encouraged youths to form Werwolf bands, but it was very unclear whether local boys responded to this appeal, particularly since their main concern was with filling their stomachs.[68]

Party Cadres and Guerrilla Warfare

The direct participation of party functionaries in actual resistance activities was relatively rare. Most such officials ran for cover, committed suicide, or desperately attempted to deal with the advancing enemy. However, there were some scattered instances where party bureaucrats emerged in the resistance movement. In Bremen, for instance, a conspiracy was organized under the control of Max Schumann, a fanatical *Kreisleiter* who in late April actually threatened his own boss, the Deputy Reich Defence Commissioner, with death through a Werwolf execution – his superior had been involved in negotiations to surrender the city to the British. Schumann was subsequently chased from Bremen, but at Wilhelmshaven he was appointed as '*Kreisleiter* on special duty,' and he was apparently engaged in organizing a secret operation when he went to ground on 5 May. Schumann eventually lost heart and committed suicide at Leer in late

June 1945, and Operation 'Schumann' dissolved as the Allies arrested the other leaders of the network.[69]

A similar conspiracy, Organization 'Shepherd,' was launched in the Sudetenland under the control of a local *Kreisleiter*. Like the SS-Werwolf, members of the 'Shepherd' were trained by SS men in methods of propaganda and sabotage, but whereas the SS-Werwolf depended heavily on HJ recruits to fill its ranks, the 'Shepherd' was formed entirely from adult members of the NSDAP. At the group's first meeting on the evening of 1 May 1945, members were told to remaining inactive until the advancing enemy had been in the area for several months. After the initial caution of the occupation forces was relaxed, it was foreseen that 'Shepherd' forces could then strike, working in close concert with the Werwolf. In the first weeks after American troops arrived in the western Sudetenland, 'Shepherd' signs were frequently daubed on walls and sidewalks, but such activity diminished as members of the group were apprehended in June and July 1945.[70]

In Magdeburg, NSDAP die-hards attempted to encourage the outbreak of guerrilla warfare. According to one account (admittedly second-hand), the *Kreisleiter* of Wolmirstedt, a suburb of Magdeburg, undertook leadership of a band of several hundred soldiers hiding in the Letzlingen Heath, northwest of the city. The unit was nourished and supplied from secret weapon depots earlier laid by the *Kreisleiter* in April 1945. When American forces arrived at the Letzlingen Heath, they found it swarming with Nazi bands, and even after they had mopped up Wehrmacht units, the area remained dangerous for small American convoys.[71]

Most reports of NSDAP participation in Werwolf activity came from southwest Germany, a fact that particularly owed to the fanaticism of the Baden *Gauleiter*, Robert Wagner, who was a close associate of Hitler's and a veteran of the Beer-hall Putsch. On 25 March 1945, Wagner was ordered by Bormann to remain behind in his *Gau* and help organize guerrilla warfare in the Black Forest. Unlike many *Gauleiter*, Wagner gave serious attention to this dangerous assignment. On 28 March, even before the Werwolf officially appeared, he launched a public appeal for popular resistance, and he also appointed Deputy Gauleiter Röhn as the party's local 'Werwolf Commissioner.'

There are several conflicting accounts about Wagner's activities after the French stormed through Baden in April 1945. According to his own testimony, Wagner left Lake Constance on 29 April and was on his way north to join one of Röhn's guerrilla detachments when he changed his mind and decided that the scheme was not worth pursuing. On the other hand, a French agent who penetrated the Baden Werwolf reported that Wagner actually led an underground organization in Constance, and that this group was trained for minor sabotage, such as dumping sugar into French fuel stocks and gas tanks. Whatever the truth, Wagner's wife, Annie, was picked up by French troops near Constance and was brought back to Paris for an intense grilling on her husband's activities and whereabouts. Subject to day-and-night questioning, Frau Wagner refused to divulge any information, and on 1 June she took advantage of a few moments inattention by her guards and hurled herself through the fifth-storey window of a French military security headquarters on the rue de Ville. When, in late July, Wagner heard of his wife's dramatic suicide, his spirit collapsed and he surrendered to a CIC unit at Stuttgart. Even then his CIC interrogator regarded him as 'dangerous for Allied security' because of his intelligence and his 'ferocious fidelity to Nazi ideology,' and he subsequently wound up in front of a French firing squad.

Because of directives issued by Wagner in late March and April 1945, there were a number of Party-based guerrilla groups set up by Röhn, who himself led a band near Freudenstadt, containing various senior NSDAP figures. At Freiburg im Breisgau, a shadowy Kreisleitung outfit was organized, based mainly upon HJ members.[72] Leopold Mauch, the Kreisleiter of Waldshut, also created an important detachment of eighty partisans, composed mainly of party members, stragglers, Volkssturm women, along with several HJ employed for reconnaissance. Mauch himself was a former border-patrol officer and therefore had a particularly good knowledge of the terrain of southern Baden. His unit was organized around 10 May and was based in a bunker in the woods north of Bahrenthal. For a week the band was in radio contact with other guerrilla groups at Feldberg and Bad Dürrheim, and elaborate plans for sabotage were developed. Originally, Mauch's partisans had a considerable advantage because of the scarcity of French occupation forces in the area, which was only haphazardly scoured by French motorized patrols. Within weeks, however, the French began to arrive in greater numbers, and by June a severe erosion of morale had set in as the group also realized that the local population was hostile, in part because of a fear of French reprisals. Eventually the band disintegrated in a wave of desertions – thirty in one night – and the remnants were arrested by Allied authorities.[73]

Bormann's Cancellation of the Werwolf

Given Bormann's bluster during the final months of the war, one would naturally have expected him to be at the head of one of these last-ditch bands. The truth is that he was last seen in a desperate attempt to save himself, and that he was probably also animated by the desire to save some of his bureaucratic power by attempting to reach Dönitz's headquarters in Flensburg. A considerable number of party chieftains showed a pronounced tendency to sacrifice the Werwolf in some last-minute bid to preserve a small measure of their power, and Bormann himself led the way.

On 1 May 1945, with the Red Army only several blocks from the chancellery, Bormann reached a last-minute deal with one of Goebbels's deputies, Hans Fritsche. It was Fritsche who had assumed responsibility for surrendering Berlin to the Soviets, and had correctly assumed that the Soviets would demand an end to all 'diversionist' activities and would reserve the right of reprisal. Meanwhile, Bormann and Goebbels's most radical deputy, Werner Naumann, were both planning to flee the Government Quarter and break out of the city, and in their haste they gave little or no thought to the Werwolf plague left in their wake. Fritsche, however, had both the time and the inclination to worry about such matters, and he warned Naumann that he would facilitate an escape attempt only if the Werwolf were cancelled. Naumann, ever the fanatic, gave only a conditional promise of a three-month cessation, but Fritsche made more progress with Bormann.

Bormann, too, at first exploded: 'You should be shot!' he sputtered. But when it became clear that Fritsche would not be intimidated, the voice of reason prevailed. Fritsche suggested that the capitulation of the Berlin garrison could be briefly delayed in order to aid a break-out by Bormann's group, but in return Bormann must agree that further guerrilla warfare was senseless, and he must therefore deactivate the Werwolf. Bormann eventually agreed and, in the presence of Fritsche and Naumann, he assembled several SS officers in the chancellery garden and issued the necessary orders. Bormann also instructed his personal secretary to disseminate the cancellation directive, which, in fact, was his last act as a public official. 'All Werwolf activity,' he reported to Fritsche, 'is to be suspended, including the death sentences. The Werwolf is dissolved!'[74] Bormann himself had presumably dispatched Vehme assassination teams for acts which paled in comparison with this ultimate betrayal of the Werwolf spirit. In any case, he soon ventured off into the smoke and gloom in the company of his fellow escapees, and was never seen again. Postwar rumours suggested that Bormann was hiding out with the Alpine *maquis*, and was inspiring his followers with dramatic radio broadcasts,[75] but more solid evidence suggests that he either died attempting to break out of the Soviet encirclement of Berlin or committed suicide when he realized that escape was impossible.

Party Capacities for Resistance

In the final analysis, the fate of Bormann, and the destiny of the party as a whole, illustrates one of the great failings of Naziism. Hitler and his cohorts had confidently assumed they were building a state to last a millennium; no preparations were made for defeat. The NSDAP was not a conventional political party; rather, it was essentially a propaganda agency which, after 1933, had lost its revolutionary fire and *raison d'être*. With Party cadres unable to totally Nazify the new state or to displace the pen-pushers in the civil service, they became apathetic and corrupt, and thereby alienated traditional élites. The top stratum of the movement survived as an ageing and arthritic group unwilling to clear the decks for the sake of youth and enthusiasm, nor did people of character and ambition care to join the bureaucracy of such an organization. In this regard, the party lagged considerably behind the SS, which had experienced some success in promoting itself as a new élite and in maintaining enthusiasm among fanatics. Thus, despite a limited recovery in authority during the war, as the value of propaganda and indocrination increased, hardly a glimmer of the old 'Battle Party' still remained.[76] Brave words about a return to the 'Time of Struggle' notwithstanding, the party was woefully unprepared for defeat, either organizationally or psychologically, and it was unlikely to leap towards a new stage of revolutionary violence. As a corporate entity, party officialdom sank in this new environment with all the weight of a jumper from a sinking ship, suddenly plunged into freezing waters.

In such circumstances, the Werwolf was a project about which the party did not evince much interest, and only at the last possible minute, in February and March 1945, did Bormann show genuine concern for the possibilities of underground activity. At this late date, party officials were basically faced with two choices: personal destruction or personal survival. The Werwolf, as a sort of extended suicide, did not fit into the calculations of most party cadres. As a result, when the Allies reached central Germany in March and April 1945, there were plenty of instances of suicide, while other party leaders attempted to save themselves either by posing as lackeys to the new conquerors or by hiding. A few party chieftains armed themselves and prepared hide-outs where they could lay low and, if surrounded, sell their lives dearly.[77] However, there were relatively few officials who fled to the woods specifically with the intention of waging guerrilla warfare, nor did many attempt to organize underground conspiracies. One should also note that the NSDAP was itself not a military organization and, apart from supporting guerrilla operations, it did not have much realistic capacity to organize such activity itself.[78]

Although the occupying powers subsequently found little sign of party structures gone underground,[79] there was considerable evidence, from all four occupation zones, of former Nazis engaged in the organized spreading of Flüsterpropaganda, as envisioned by Dotzler. Both the British and the Americans suspected that the NSDAP had left behind a 'rumour-spreading organization,' and a Werwolf captured in Bremen at the end of 1945 admitted that such a network existed. Office of Strategic Services analysts studying Nazi propaganda and posters in Munich and Nuremberg pointed out that themes were 'regionally organized,' and the French also believed that 'the framework for a whispering campaign was left by the departing Nazis,' and that this movement particularly sought a female following.[80] The party, to steal a phrase from Arthur Koestler, was no longer a political organization, but a bleeding mass of pulp, with a thousand arms and a thousand heads, each leading in a different direction, each trying to deliver the message 'We have survived,' but each suffering from a thorough bout of demoralization.[81]

In the final analysis, Hans Mommsen puts his finger on an important point when he notes that the NSDAP of the 'Time of Struggle' had, in general, been little more than a glorified propaganda agency, and that propaganda, rather than organization, always remained the party's strong suit.[82] Thus, while Bormann and Dotzler toyed with a series of half-hearted structural preparations for post-occupation activities, and while they encouraged party hierarchs to play a role in partisan warfare, it was in the encouragement of Flüsterpropaganda that they seem to have achieved their only substantial yield. Moreover, Goebbels eventually threw his ministry into a highly organized Werwolf propaganda campaign, and this was perhaps a more natural line of retreat for the movement than any strictly organizational initiatives.

Goebbels and the Werwolf

Goebbels's interest in the Werwolf lay mainly in its potential in the West, which was perhaps natural since the propaganda minister was a native Rhinelander. It was on this front that the policy of systemic evacuation had broken down during February, a development never paralleled in the East. 'The Führer's continued insistence on his evacuation order is purely academic,' noted Goebbels on 26 March. 'In practice such evacuations simply cannot be carried out.'[83] Meanwhile, Bormann had recommended formally terminating the process because of the confusion it created in the interior, and he openly advised Gauleiter in the West that German civilians left in the wake of the enemy were no longer to be regarded unfavourably.[84] One of the main factors inhibiting a guerrilla propaganda campaign had thus disappeared.

There was also an obvious need for a propaganda jolt to bring western Germans back into line, since most of the population remaining in the Allied rear had been unwilling either to confront the enemy advance or to show hostility to Allied troops once they arrived. Moreover, the party had given an embarrassingly poor account of itself, its functionaries often being the first to flee towns threatened by the enemy, and this too had prejudiced the cause of Nazi resistance.[85] Goebbels, however, did not lose faith in the fortitude of his countrymen. He remained convinced that they had shown courage under aerial bombing, but that this devastating campaign had shattered them both physically and mentally, a condition worsened by the experience of seeing the Wehrmacht routed. In retrospect, it must be noted that Goebbels possessed an amazingly optimistic faith in both the loyalty of Germans to the Nazi cause and in their capacity to maintain a fanatical antagonism towards the occupying powers. 'The people need only a good sleep and release from the scourge of the air war to come to themselves again ... I am of the opinion that slowly the partisan war will start in West Germany. There are already a number of signs of it.'[86]

Goebbels believed that the key to such a turn of events was the anticipated food shortage, and that if such a factor did not cause a rebellion before the loss of the remaining sections of unoccupied territory, it would surely do so afterward. The Western Allies, he surmised, would unwisely attempt a dual-track policy of enforced starvation side by side with democratization:

Should the enemy in their blind hate really allow themselves to be led in such a direction, leaving the defeated German people hungry in a world of plenty, indeed possibly for months and years, then they will never know what hit them. In Germany, they won't lure the dog out from behind the stove with democracy alone. And if democratic theory in practice denotes hunger, they'll see how the emaciated and apparently dull Germans will bear hunger placards through their bombed cities, and how they'll unreservedly throw themselves into the arms of political radicalism. Where Communism cannot reap the fruit of radicalization – and its chance of success in Germany is not very great after all the wrongs and horrors that the Bolsheviks have caused in our eastern provinces – a Neo–National Socialism will be born, pure and honest, uncompromising and strong from the collapse and the following misery as emergence from a purgatory.[87]

As a spark to ignite this conflagration, Goebbels hoped to win control of the Werwolf. After assuming control, he then intended to reorient it in a more radical direction, an initiative which also fit with Goebbels's general effort to get almost all matters of domestic policy under his own control. He approached Hitler with this suggestion in late March 1945, and was rewarded with the transfer of initiative for Werwolf propaganda away from the *Gauleiter* and towards the Propaganda Ministry. Although he had presumably asked for more, Goebbels was pleased with this partial victory, which at least gave him a toehold from which to further expand his grip. In early April he noted that he still had plans 'to get the organization of the Werwolf movement into my own hands,' although he now admitted this must be done gradually. 'Not only do I think myself suited to do it,' he noted, 'but I believe the Werwolf must be led with spirit and enthusiasm.'[88]

Goebbels's intervention into Werwolf affairs naturally created an open rivalry between himself and Prützmann, particularly since the latter was not a party to the new arrangements allowing the Propaganda Ministry to conduct a Werwolf publicity campaign. Goebbels felt that the SS-Werwolf was a failure, and that Prützmann was proceeding far too hesitantly. Prützmann, in defence, argued that the population of occupied districts was apathetic and openly opposed to the NSDAP, which made it necessary to proceed slowly in the organization of partisan warfare.[89] In light of such a position, it is hardly surprising that Prützmann became enraged when the Propaganda Ministry proceeded to surround the Werwolf with a radical and spirited propaganda campaign that did not reflect his views, nor had been previously submitted for the review of his office. In fact, it endangered his guerrillas more than ever, because it eroded their supposed military status. Such an approach, he told Gauleiter Kaufmann, was 'wrong, dangerous and stupid,' and caused 'grave dissentions' between himself and the Goebbels ministry.[90]

Several days after the propaganda campaign had begun, Prützmann burst into Goebbels's office and openly confronted him, claiming that his partisans needed to operate with a certain modicum of secrecy.[91] Goebbels totally rejected such a view: 'We do not intend to hide our light under a bushel and do secret service work,' he noted in his diary. 'On the contrary, the enemy should know precisely what we are planning and doing.'[92] Moreover, the Propaganda Ministry took a particularly broad view of the Werwolf: according to a memorandum circulated by Naumann on 4 April, the full activization of the movement would convert all 'activist fighters' into Werewolves, both in occupied areas and in unoccupied Germany.[93]

Werwolf Radio

The main subject of the Goebbels–Prützmann battle was Werwolf Radio, a broadcasting station that Goebbels began to assemble in March 1945, possibly with Bormann's backing. As early as February, Naumann forwarded instructions to another Goebbels deputy, Hans Fritsche, directing the development of a secret mobile transmitter in order to control Werwolf groups,[94] and it is likely that the matter was discussed during the Naumann–Friedrichs meeting. Naumann himself reintroduced the Werwolf theme in a speech on 23 March 1945, publically calling for a partisan war 'under the sign of the Werewolves,' and praising a boy in Kauderwelsch who had shot a Canadian soldier in the back.[95]

After a considerable rush, Werwolf Radio began to broadcast on Easter Sunday, 1 April (when the symbol of rebirth and the symbol of lunacy appropriately fell upon the same date). In the afternoon, the Home Service broadcast an 'important bulletin' which had supposedly just been received: 'In the German territories of the West which are occupied by the enemy, a German Freedom Movement has come into existence ...' Thereafter, a steady stream of melodramatic reports about the new movement sought to build up excitement, until finally it was announced that the Werwolf possessed its own transmitter behind enemy lines and that an 'effort' would be made to pick up its inaugural proclamation. This was achieved, and the proclamation was broadcast at peak listening time, between 19.00 and 20.00 hours. Thereafter, it was announced that Werwolf Radio would broadcast nightly at 19.00 on 1339 m., the old Radio Germany wavelength.[96]

A Wehrmacht signals expert later pointed out that Goebbels had actually botched the proclamation, since it appealed for a rally of patriots in both the West and the East, but mentioned only one secret, behind-the-lines transmitter. The clever listener would have immediately realized that, to reach both fronts, the station was probably in the mid-section of the country and had to be using broadcasting facilities of considerable output.[97] In truth, the transmitter was located at a Radio Germany station at Nauen, on the western outskirts of Berlin. However, the idea of a secret station on enemy occupied soil was apparently regarded as a necessary ingredient if the proceedings were to develop any decent sense of conspiratorial romance.

To provide an organizational structure for the new station, a special branch called the Werwolf was reportedly organized within the Propaganda Department of the Ministry for Public Enlightenment and Propaganda.[98] The radio station itself was placed in the hands of Horst Slesina, who was transferred from his post as chief of the regional Propaganda Office in Westmark. He was chosen for the position because of his adroit understanding of the situation in western Germany – where Werwolf Radio's main efforts were directed – and because he had made a considerable effort on the Saar Front to rouse civilian resistance to the invading Allied armies.[99] Slesina, however, remained something of a junior manager, since both Goebbels and Naumann took great interest in the day-to-day affairs of the station, as well as regularly writing propaganda copy for its announcers.[100]

Another bureaucratic adjustment was the dismissal of Goebbels's other state secretary, Reich Press Chief Otto Dietrich, whom Goebbels had long despised. Goebbels now got a chance to strike at Dietrich because the latter had not shown sufficient zeal for the latest propaganda developments – 'With men like Dr Dietrich,' Goebbels lamented to the Führer, 'how am I supposed to conduct propaganda, such as that for the Werwolf movement at present, which must be of an extraordinarily radical nature.' Dietrich had particularly angered both Goebbels and Hitler by his dilution of Goebbels's strongly worded announcement on the shooting of the *Oberbürgermeister* of Aachen, especially since he attempted to delete mention of a fictional Vehme trial that was supposed to have condemned the mayor to death.[101] It is notable, however, that with Dietrich on his way out and the Press Department in an uproar, Goebbels failed in his plans to launch a Werwolf newspaper, which was intended to serve as a natural media partner for the radio station.

Claims and Implicit Instructions

For the three weeks after its establishment, Werwolf Radio engaged in two chief operations, other than playing lively pop music. One of these activities was issuing threats, and the other was reporting on various acts of sabotage and murder supposedly committed by the Werwolf movement. Propaganda against native collaborators did not go into great detail, but usually confined itself to general warnings and the naming of lists of individuals under condemnation. Occasionally, accounts of specific killings were given, such as the description on 8 April of the alleged murder of three 'sell-outs,' including a garage proprietor in Osnabrück who was supposedly thrown from a third-storey window as a punishment for having made 'disloyal' utterances. Within the dwindling confines of unoccupied Germany, the station's audience was led to believe that the time had come for 'defeatists' and 'traitors,' even if 'patriots' had to take blood upon their own hands. At Schandelah, HJ officials in the Volkssturm – much influenced by Werwolf propaganda – killed two community leaders who had attempted to remove anti-tank barriers, and, in Kiel, enthusiastic listeners in a maritime flak crew murdered an anti-Nazi grumbler because he had refused to accept a 'Heil Hitler' greeting.[102]

As for the enemy, Werwolf Radio's main targets of abuse were General George Patton and the U.S. financier and presidential adviser Bernard Baruch, who visited occupied Germany in mid-April. Baruch, in particular, was portrayed as an archetypical representative of sinister, behind-the-scenes Jewish influences, and since he was a veteran of the American delegation to Versailles and a key supporter of the Morgenthau Plan, he merited repeated Werwolf death threats while in Europe. In reality, Baruch boldly spent an entire day sitting on a park bench in Frankfurt, where he discussed the city's administration with Military Government officers. Not a 'Werewolf' stirred.[103]

Radio reports also claimed Major-General Maurice Rose as a Werwolf casualty, after Rose was shot and killed on 30 March. Rose, like Patton, was an aggressive advocate of mobile warfare and had the added stigma (from a Werwolf point of view) of being Jewish. In fact, however, Rose was killed along a fluid front near Paderborn when he was trapped by a German Panzer and the tank commander attempted to take him prisoner. Hearing a rapid profusion of German orders, Rose thought he was being told to disarm, and he was shot when he reached for his gunbelt. Nobody even loosely definable as a Werewolf was actually involved in the incident.

Werwolf Radio's other main activity was providing reports on Werwolf success in inflicting damage upon enemy forces. Many of these bulletins were quite fantastic: on 4 April, for instance, the station claimed that Werewolves had captured the secretary of an 'American Extermination Commission' allegedly based in Koblenz. Three weeks later 'Werwolf Commandos' were reported to have blown up part of the Luena Synthetic Petroleum Works, near Leipzig. It was an announcement that must have seemed strange to listeners in the Luena area, where it was well known that most of the plant had already been largely flattened by Allied bombers. Most broadcasts pertained to activity behind the Western Front, although occasional flashes also claimed damage behind Soviet lines, such as a report on the evening of 2 April, which maintained that Werewolves had recently attacked a Russian supply column east of Schneidemühl.[104]

In truth, the Propaganda Ministry admitted in mid-April that 'we know little or nothing of what is happening in these [occupied] areas,' although they did have access to some fragmentary refugee reports. Goebbels himself was the first to admit, at least privately, that Werwolf Radio's output was not actually the news, but 'the news as it should be.' In fact, the propaganda minister personally dictated many of the station's fictional reports, and when he lost inspiration he would wander the corridors of his office, calling out for ideas from his assistants.[105] This was the 'Propaganda of the Deed' in its purest form – all propaganda, no actual deed (or at least no proven deed).

Needless to say, Goebbels and his aides received no help from the Bureau 'Prützmann,' even though that office prepared its own internal reports documenting local successes by Werwolf groups. One Werwolf official noted disapprovingly in mid-April 'that the heroics extolled over the Werwolf radio net were either pure fiction or the accomplishments of small scattered remnants of troops who had no connection with the Prützmann program.'[106]

The purpose of broadcasting largely fictional reports was to create the impression that the Werwolf was widespread, or at least had extensive reach, thus building the proper psychological climate for a real terrorist campaign. It also gave sympathetic listeners in the occupied territories implicit instructions on the kinds of activities they might employ in order to disrupt Allied forces. In fact, Werwolf Radio even broadcast blunt indications of what could be done: 'set up barriers and traps on roads, remove place names and signposts ... remove minefield markings ... take note of the location of the enemy's ammunition and petrol dumps, food stocks and other material. Whenever there is an opportunity – and such opportunities must be brought about by every possible means – the enemy's dumps and stores must be destroyed.' Such instructions formed a large part of the Werwolf 'Sixteen Commandments' broadcast on 7 April. It was admittedly inconvenient that the enemy could listen in and take necessary counter-measures, but Goebbels had already indicated – both to Prützmann and in his diary – that his flights of fancy would remain unaltered by such minor embarrassments.[107] In truth, of course, the public airing of sabotage instructions was actually an admission of extreme weakness. Such a measure would have been unnecessary but for the rapidity of the Allied advance into Germany and Prützmann's inability to get his own agency ready to fully meet this contingency.

Radicalization

Perhaps the most interesting aspect of Werwolf Radio was the highly revolutionary nature of its propaganda output, which recalled both the radical roots of National Socialism and recent political and social trends within the Nazi state. Goebbels repeatedly pointed out that Werwolf Radio represented a return to the essential features of National Socialism, and his favourite title for the underground, 'the Freedom Movement,' was perhaps consciously imitative of the tag adopted by the NSDAP's first successor organization, the 'National Socialist German Freedom Movement,' during the party's one earlier experience with prohibition and disgrace in the wake of the Beer-hall Putsch. Werwolf Radio, Goebbels asserted, would play an extremist role similar to the newspaper *Der Angriff* 'in the good old days of our struggle.' Even the notorious early Nazi rabble-rouser Julius Streicher, whose pathological behaviour had caused his dismissal as *Gauleiter* of Franconia in 1940, was recalled from the wilderness in order to deliver short Werwolf diatribes. However, Werwolf Radio apparently ceased broadcasting before the world was treated to a glimpse of this political comeback. Streicher's presence was not missed, however, since Goebbels himself wrote much wild-eyed copy for the station, which proudly took no account 'of regular methods of conducting war or of wartime foreign policy.' Thus, in terms of radicalism, the station far surpassed the regular propaganda in which Goebbels's authorship was openly acknowledged. This was a great psychological release for the propaganda minister who, after being muzzled since 1934, was finally able to vent his own brand of leftist extremism. 'It is really refreshing,' he said, 'for once to be able to talk as one used to do during our struggle period.' It is interesting to note that, by April 1945, Goebbels liked to place himself in the same category as Stennes, Strasser, and Röhm, except that he was loyal to the Führer, and they supposedly were not.[108]

In line with Goebbels's opinions, Werwolf Radio found the war almost immaterial compared with the fact that a pan-European, anti-bourgeois revolution was under way. It also revived the old SA heresy about the need for 'permanent revolution,' a matter that had cost Röhm his head in 1934.[109] Goebbels believed that, in the course of such a revolutionary struggle, the methods of 'bourgeois' warfare should be totally abandoned, and it was mainly through the intervention of such 'moderates' as Himmler and Goering that his call for a unilateral abrogation of the Geneva Convention went unheeded. Werwolf Radio provided a handy forum for such views, however, and declared on its opening day of broadcasting that Werewolves would happily disregard the rules of war.[110] However, such heady revolutionary declarations were too extreme even for the Werwolf's target audience, and on 5 April the station was forced to broadcast a lengthy apologia. The disavowal of the rules of war was attributed to enemy propaganda and met by the argument that it was the Allies who had broken international law by unleashing a war of aggression and conducting aerial bombing. The Werwolf, said the station, was 'rising to reinstitute the violated law.'[111]

From the very beginning, Werwolf Radio was designed to appeal to 'the unflinching pertinacious political minority which has always formed the steel tip of the popular leaden lance.' This vanguard was believed to consist of about 10 per cent of the German population, but was thought capable of carrying the majority in the direction which it led,[112] a concept which has since become a general article of faith among revolutionaries. In order to build an attitude of tolerance for Werwolf activities beyond the activist minority, however, Werwolf Radio also took the views of the population at large into consideration. Despite publicly divorcing itself from 'stuffy public opinion,' Werwolf Radio displayed a surprising willingness to recognize, and even pardon, the war-weariness of the western German population. 'We Werewolves blame no one for being tired. This weariness will pass. No one can do more than his strength allows.' An early broadcast from the station openly admitted that pressuring civilians to join the Werwolf would be useless, but indicated that 'there will come a time when all will join us, including those who have been tired out by war and the murderous bombing.'[113]

In order to further make itself palatable to the general populace, Werwolf Radio could hardly portray its followers as the cutting edge of the National Socialist revolution – Nazi popularity was, after all, in serious decline. Rather, it sought to portray Werewolves as local vigilantes protecting civilians from the wanton cruelty of Allied soldiers. In Cologne, for instance, a Werewolf was said to have distinguished himself by attacking an American soldier who had pushed an old woman with his gun barrel, and dozens of similar stories were told. Werwolf Radio also claimed that guerrillas stole food from Allied depots in order to foil the enemy 'starvation campaign.'[114] Only in mid-April was it admitted that the Werwolf was not entirely spontaneous, but that trained commandos were being sent into the enemy rear surreptitiously.[115]

Goebbels also injected into Werwolf Radio his repugnance of the western *Gauleiter*. Goebbels had an ongoing grudge against this group because it was their corruption and parochialism that had generally impeded his effort to concentrate domestic power around himself, especially after his appointment as General Plenipotentiary for Total War in July 1944. However, this anti-establishmentarian tendency not only arose from Goebbels's own particular obsession, but was probably inevitable, given the situation in which the Nazi state now found itself. The program of Werwolf Radio, for instance, closely followed the example of the Fascist Republican Party in Italy, when, in the wake of the 1943 armistice, it re-established its credentials as a radical movement by condemning the party 'bosses' who had sacrificed their patriotism for wealth, rank, and a life of comfort.[116] Goebbels, too, realized that the suggestion of a better future – a purer time to come – was the staple of any fanatical movement. Thus, Werwolf Radio proclaimed its intention to 'suffer no careerists, no job-hunters, no doddering place holders, no bosses, for they put their own ends before the common good.'[117] The station's program of 13 April was especially critical of party bosses and corrupt *Bürgermeister*: 'In the good old times they made use of their social position to grow rich at the expense of the people. For years they have been preaching a Spartan life without living it. Their own positions were more important to them than a moral life. Most of them have never come near a real fight in this war; they have never felt the war to the same extent as the masses of the people ... They are lazy and out only for personal power.'[118] In private conversation with his aides, Goebbels went even a step further, claiming that the rising tide of chaos brought about by the Werwolf and enemy occupation was a blessing in disguise. The fire of National Socialism, he said, had 'threatened to smother under the slag of the "bosses' regime" in the Third Reich. The storm wind of enemy rule will rekindle it to a new heat.'[119]

Werwolf propaganda was also remarkable for avoiding the name of the Führer, as if this supreme 'boss' was considered a liability rather than an asset. When Hitler was mentioned, as on his birthday on 20 April, he was presented as a 'revolutionary Socialist,' whose 'historical achievement is to have freed Socialism from all surrounding propaganda, lies, distortions, and misinterpretations and to have led it to victory.' (Only Werwolf Radio had sufficient gall to refer to the situation in April 1945 as a 'victory.') Even Hitler's birthday was used as yet another chance to attack those 'bourgeois souls' who 'loudly proclaimed [Hitler's] name' because 'they feared socialism.'[120] Only during the last few hours of its existence, by which time the Führer had decided to remain in besieged Berlin, did Werwolf Radio present him as the heroic figure so common in Nazi propaganda. 'Hitler,' it was noted, 'did not flee to South Germany ... He stands in Berlin and with him are all those whom he has found worthy to fight beside him.' The 'bosses,' 'reactionary elements,' 'cowards' and other 'impeding elements' had all been sent away, so that 'only the uncompromising revolutionary fighters have remained' – led, of course, by Gauleiter Goebbels, 'the Führer's trusted friend.'[121]

Because of such rhetoric, it is hardly surprising that the werwolf was formally disavowed by the party establishment, which portrayed it as a spontaneous movement of freedom fighters about which little was known. Perhaps the NSDAP leadership felt that such a disclaimer would automatically absolve it of blame for guerrilla activity.[122] After all, it was hardly eager to accept blame for a propaganda movement that was openly hostile to many party officials as well as to the enemy powers. Even the most devout Nazis also had considerable doubts about the whole principle of partisan fighting, since they, like almost all Germans, feared Allied reprisals and an indefinite prolongation of confusion. It is perhaps a measure of Werwolf Radio's distinctiveness – and its contrast to the Nazi establishment – that the term 'neo-Nazi' was first coined in April 1945 as a description of its output.[123]

Werwolf Radio was certainly a harbinger of future trends – most of the distinctive features of postwar Euro-fascism were already apparent in its broadcasts – but it was also a product of radicalizing currents which arose in the several years before it was born. In particular, Werwolf Radio reflected the leftward turn of Naziism and the revival of revolutionary sentiments reminiscent of the 1933–4 period. After the July 1944 putsch, National Socialists increasingly saw themselves as the spearhead of a 'people's war' against not only Jewry, Bolshevism, and Western plutocracy, but also the surviving forces of reaction and defeatism at home – forces which, incidentally, might be expected to reveal their treachery by collaborating with the enemy powers once they had crossed the German frontier.

Another radicalizing trend was the class levelling caused by bombing, rationing, and ground warfare, all of which destroyed the material goods forming the background of bourgeois society. Goebbels and company could barely contain their joy arising from this process of 'proletarianization,' which had begun in the Great War and accelerated through the corrosive interwar years of inflation and depression. This destruction of the bourgeois way of life created new legions of propertyless outcasts and casualties of society, exactly the kind of people who had formed the bedrock support of Naziism before the *Junkers* and industrialists had hitched on to the rising star. In the 1930s, National Socialism had diluted itself by appealing to a middle class that still existed but felt threatened, mainly at the upper level, by communism, and at the *petit bourgeois* level by Jewish economic competition. Werwolf Radio, on the other hand, sought to build a new base among those dispossessed by the bombs of 'Anglo-American plutocracy,' while at the same time not totally neglecting the danger to Germany's 'culture' posed by Russian 'barbarism.'[124]

The rhetoric to stimulate the desired anti-bourgeois impulses reached well beyond the boundaries of socialist radicalism and into the realm of nihilism, equating destruction with the fresh breeze of liberation.

Together with the monuments of culture [said Werwolf Radio], there also crumble the last obstacles separating us from the fulfilment of our revolutionary task. Now that everything is in ruins we are forced to rebuild Europe. In the past private possessions tied us to bourgeois morality and mentality; these possessions have gone now and with them all our bourgeois restraint. Far from killing all Europeans, the bombs have only smashed the prison walls which held them captive ... In trying to destroy Europe's future, the enemy has only succeeded in smashing the past and with it everything old and outward has gone. The crumbling of the facade of tradition has only revealed the inception of a new revolution, and all who are strong and healthy realize their task, which is that of a revolutionary.[125]

Thus was revealed what Hugh Trevor-Roper called 'the authentic voice of Naziism uninhibited' – 'The doctrine of purposeless but gleeful destruction of life and property and all those values of civilization which the German Nazi, though he sometimes tries painfully to imitate them, fundamentally envies and detests.'[126] Hermann Rauschning's 'Revolution of Nihilism' was thus brought full circle.

Adolescent Romanticism

A second main element in Werwolf Radio propaganda was its romantic adventurism, specifically designed for teenage boys and girls. The station gave considerable attention to the adventure stories of Karl May, a nineteenth-century literary hack whose novels about the old American West were eagerly consumed by several generations of German boys. May was favourite reading for Hitler, who, as early as 1942, recommended May's description of 'Red Indian tactics' to his troops on the Eastern Front. Such adolescent romanticism, brought to life, had also inspired the Wandervogel organizations of the Wilhelmine period and, since the beginning of the war, had motivated the independently-minded Edelweiss Piraten groups that fought the HJ and whose members lived a vaguely anarchistic life based on love of adventure. These groups, and a much larger number of teenagers acting alone or in small gangs, were responsible for the steep rise in juvenile delinquency in Germany after 1940. There was also a general increase in misbehaviour and rudeness among German youth during this period. Such problems became worse as teenagers were increasingly drawn further away from the influence of the family, and even the school, as they were drafted into war industries or employed as flak auxiliaries.[127]

Werwolf Radio sought to convert these problems from liabilities into assets by using the spirit of teenage rebellion against the new authority figures in the western occupied zones. The followers of Werwolf Radio were, in effect, Nazified Edelweiss Piraten.[128] This appeal to teenage romanticism was especially apparent in the symbols that Werwolf Radio provided for the resistance movement, and even in its story for the origin of the Werwolf name, which it drew from the ancient berserker legends. 'Werewolves,' said the station, were the 'wild men' of German mythology, 'who clad in the skins of animals bound from the darkness of the woods with the utmost fury upon everything living.'[129] The Werwolf emblem was the Wolfsangel, which was variously explained as either the curve of a werewolf fang, or the hinge of a wolf's trap, a symbol which during the Thirty Years War was supposedly carved into trees where foreign soldiers were hanged. Werwolf Radio also provided the movement with its own theme song, appropriately sung by 'Werwolf Lily':

> I am so savage; I am filled with rage,
> Hoo, Hoo, Hoo
> Lily the werewolf is my name,
> Hoo, Hoo, Hoo,
> I bite, I eat, I am not tame,
> Hoo, Hoo, Hoo,
> My Werwolf teeth bite the enemy,
> and then he's done and then he's gone,
> Hoo, Hoo, Hoo.[130]

This, then, was the sorry stuff with which Werwolf Radio sought to inspire a new generation of German heroes (although it was perhaps not much more ludicrous than the 'Horst Wessel Lied' that had helped to motivate the first wave of the National Socialist movement.)

Surprising as it may seem, Werwolf Radio did make some impact upon young minds already oriented towards Nazi ideology, and it appears to have spurred a last-minute wave of recruits for the SS-Werwolf.[131] Even within several days of the commencement of radio propaganda, German mail captured by the Allies yielded several letters by young girls eager to join the newly revealed Werwolf organization.[132] There was perhaps no better individual example of this last-minute wave than Ruth Thiemann, an embittered true believer who was captured by the CIC in Frankfurt in 1946. Thiemann had been a member of the Federation of German Girls (BdM) since 1938, and in the last few weeks of the war she volunteered for service in the Werwolf. After the capitulation, she also joined a right-wing Edelweiss Piraten group and, as a concurrent member of both organizations, she assisted in hiding SS men, bought and distributed weapons, cut U.S. Army communication wires, and snipped off the hair of women associating with the American occupation troops. 'I am still very much in favour of the Werwolf organization,' she told her CIC interrogators. 'I am and always will be a Nazi; nobody can convince me otherwise.'[133] This was the sort of mentality motivated, or at least focused, by Werwolf Radio.

Throughout the occupied zones, local resistance was also inspired, in theme at least, by Goebbels's publicity campaign. In the American-occupied town of Wetterfeld, in central Hesse, the *Bürgermeister* – much influenced by Werwolf broadcasts – recruited two Hitler Youth to kill a local anti-Nazi, who was gunned down on 10 April. In Hamm, a fear-crazed German civilian, his mind stoked by Goebbelsite propaganda, set fire to his own house and, when two American soldiers showed up to fight the blaze, shot them both. In a panic, he then killed his wife and three children before finally taking his own life. Near Ansbach, the CIC arrested a girl who had been whipped into a frenzy by radio broadcasts, and had contacted at least a dozen families with the aim of forming a Werwolf band. Such spontaneous Werwolf resistance remained a problem until 1947, as individuals and small gangs conducted minor sabotage and propaganda against the occupation forces and harassed the workings of the Communist Party (KPD).[134]

When not preaching to the converted, Werwolf Radio had much less effect, which even the station itself acknowledged: 'Only a small minority,' they admitted, 'refuses to be intimidated and accepts the challenge.' The remainder deeply resented the danger posed by such a general call to arms, and a German soldier who listened to Werwolf Radio's opening broadcast noted that the response was violently negative, at least among his circle of civilian friends – 'Everybody was mad. There is no sense to it, and now civilians will be butchered too. It is a stupid thing to start and it is silly that some stupid people can be found for it.' Others simply found the broadcasts absurd. 'We were sitting in the house of a peasant woman,' remembered another soldier, 'waiting for the Americans to come so we could surrender. The woman was in the kitchen and when she came back we were all laughing heartily. She asked what had happened and we told her what we had just heard, namely the proclamation of the Werwolf.' When the Werwolf was first announced in Berlin, wags in the bomb shelters cavorted around like wolves and howled at the enemy bombers above, all with tongue firmly in cheek.[135] Middle-class elements who had already begun – even as early as 1938 – to fear Nazi threats to property rights and the alleged transformation of the movement into a form of 'Bolshevism,'[136] could hardly have been put at ease by the radical politics of the Werwolf transmitter.

Much of the listenership was also possessed by an abhorrence of guerrilla fighting that Werwolf Radio, despite its best efforts to portray Werewolves as self-defence vigilantes, could not erode. Most Germans, after all, had been taught since the Prussian experience with French *francs-tireurs* in 1870–1 that partisan warfare was dishonourable, and Nazi propaganda since 1940 had reinforced this indoctrination, particularly by equating guerrilla fighters with bandits and criminals.[137] An extrapolation of such attitudes towards their own guerrilla warriors was almost inevitable, at least to some extent, so that in 1945 it was not uncommon to find Germans who believed that Werewolves should suffer the same fate as other partisan-bandits, that is, they should be flogged, imprisoned, or shot. One Rhinelander told American officers that the Allies need not worry themselves with inflicting such punishments – 'We'll take care of that.'[138]

The End of Werwolf Radio

The end for Werwolf Radio came with the final Soviet advance upon Berlin, which prompted a last minute shift of focus away from the West and towards the advancing nemesis in the East. On 23 April, the station announced that Hitler and Goebbels were remaining in Berlin, and that they would be defended by the best surviving forces at Hitler's disposal, even if these had to be withdrawn from the Western Front. Sixteen divisions were said to be already marching towards the threatened capital and were soon expected. 'Herewith,' said the announcer, 'the Reich testifies to its resolve to defend Berlin at all costs.' Moreover, Werwolf Radio noted that, even if the city were lost, 'the Werewolves in it will never be overcome ... We shall fight until the Reich capital is once again the capital of freedom.' Such declarations were supported with a ringing affirmation that 'the main enemy now lay in the east.'[139]

After this final release of bombast, Werwolf Radio ceased broadcasting because its transmitter was overrun by the Red Army, which reached Nauen on 22 April. Only a week later, Goebbels committed suicide in the chancellery bunker, shortly after his appointment as chancellor of the Reich. In the interim between these two events, little more was heard of the Werwolf in any of the Reich's remaining media services, except for a brief notice in the Munich edition of *Völkischer Beobachter* on 24 April. This more reticent approach was apparently dictated by the need to rebuild bridges to the Western Allies and recruit them in the anti-Communist crusade. In any case, the most powerful transmitter yet in Nazi territory was kept out of the hands of fanatics by the shrewd actions of Gauleiter Kaufmann, who on 27 April sent a special Volkssturm company to occupy Radio Hamburg, and thus prevent it from becoming a replacement for the Nauen station.[140] This transmitter, on 30 April, urged not even passive resistance to the occupation, but encouraged only a conscious effort to maintain the German spirit and language.[141]

In late April, however, units of the Luftwaffe Radio Interception Service were given instructions to split up into small groups and infiltrate Allied lines in order to set up auxiliary stations and 'supplement Werwolf activity.' It is also likely that members of the SS Interception Service and the Gestapo Wireless Service were given similar tasks. Little came of these plans to establish truly clandestine propaganda networks, although one such Werwolf unit of about a dozen men was reported in the Andreasberg–Westharz district,[142] and a radio transmitter under the control of SS-General Lindemann in Denmark reportedly kept broadcasting Nazi propaganda until late May 1945. A few underground Nazi transmitters were also sporadically active during the immediate postwar period.[143]

Even Goebbels, who was willing to throw both himself and his family upon the funeral pyre of the regime, made little effort during his final days to maintain Werwolf hostility against the West. Goebbels, however, was much more than a glorified *apparatchik* of the Bormann or Ley type. Rather, he was the archetypical revolutionary rabble-rouser – much more effective at undermining authority than in exercising it. As Joachim Fest notes, Goebbels's power rebounded exactly during the period when the position of the Third Reich became critical, precisely because no one was more psychologically adept at fighting a desperate battle of survival. Only then could his brutal demagogy and revolutionary passions be unleashed without fear of causing offence. 'We have burnt our bridges behind us,' he said in 1943. 'We are forced to proceed to extremes and therefore resolved to proceed to extremes.'[144]

Goebbels was the only senior Nazi leader fully cognizant of the need for a political and ideological foundation for partisan warfare. In fact, he shared much of the spirit of the Marxist and anti-colonial revolutionary warfare that was waged so intensely in the years after 1945. Whereas the SS and the German Army had conceived guerrilla warfare as a process of breakdown and an atomization of existing military forces, Goebbels saw it as part of a build-up of revolutionary potential. He was hostile to a Clausewitzian Werwolf that still fit into the regular order of things. Moreover, while Anglo-American statesmen and soldiers had worried about unleashing the chaos of anti-Nazi guerrilla fighting, Goebbels thought more like Mao Zedong, who exploited partisan warfare, not only as a tactic, but as a means of bonding a revolutionary party to the people it claimed to represent. The Werwolf, in Goebbels's view, emerged as a means of changing society – 'it must not become a mere organization like the SD,' he warned. 'There is no longer much profit in mere organization. Things have gone too far for that.'[145] It was in this sense that Werwolf Radio obviously sought to set the tone for post-capitulation resistance,[146] despite the absence of any explicit admission to this effect.

It has already been shown that Goebbels's propaganda struck the right note for a small minority among the party's dwindling constituency, but for most Germans it lacked any appeal. The anti-materialist and anti-establishmentarian themes were more suited to a mature materialist society beginning to tire of consumerism than to a people who had just grown accustomed to the benefits of the Industrial Revolution, only then to promptly lose them. The bombed-out refugee who had once enjoyed a warm hearth and a comfortable bed was hardly likely to find satisfaction sleeping in the cold, eating turnip soup, or, worst of all, risking violent reprisals for the purpose of prolonging the same violence that had already brought ruin upon his country. Mass resistance is based upon the calculation by a significant segment of the population that present conditions are not much worse than the risks entailed by violent opposition (the latter, of course, gains added attractiveness by idealistic expectations of a better life after the expulsion of the invader). These assumptions did not exist in the occupied Reich, at least not in the West, nor was any amount of nihilistic bombast able to compensate for this lacking, or even to cause a deterioration of conditions to such a degree that the resistance equation would take effect.

It is true that the first bare-cupboard years of enemy occupation caused a spiritual yearning in many Germans, particularly in light of the vacuum that followed the bankruptcy of National Socialism, but this longing was filled largely by religion rather than ideology. In any case, the first signs of economic recovery in 1948 encouraged western Germans to embrace materialism more strongly than ever, and they were joined by literally millions of compatriots from the East who obviously wished to live in the same environment. The revolutionary crisis of confidence in material things that Werwolf Radio sought to create did not occur until the 1960s, and in turn created the impetus for the radical terrorist groups of the following decade.

5

Werwolf Redoubts

Some of the incidents outlined in the previous chapters occurred in heavily wooded and hilly areas to which embittered members of the Guard Corps (SS), Hitler Youth (HJ), Werwolf, and German Army had retreated. Such desperadoes fled to these regions originally because they were ordered to do so by the German High Command, which hoped to use these remote tracts as bases from which to inflict damage upon the Allies or the Soviets. As it turned out, however, many of the elements that holed up in this fashion found themselves unable to accommodate the rapid pace of events of 1945. Like their counterparts in the 'Free Corps' a quarter of a century earlier, some of these men had grown accustomed to the camaraderie and discipline in their units, and they feared the hurly-burly of civilian life. Many had no homes to which to return, thanks to Allied bombing, or their families had been dispersed by the Russians and their physical property now lay behind Soviet lines. Others were interested primarily in escaping confinement, particularly since the leadership cadre among these groups was typically composed of war criminals or Germans who were classed by the enemy in automatic-arrest categories. Some of these men, such as Waffen-SS soldiers and members of other élite formations such as the paratroops, felt that they had no reason to expect 'decent treatment.' They were terrified that Allied cub planes would spot them and call upon them the tanks of which they were even more terrified.[1] It is in this regard – the matter of negative rather than positive intent – that Nazi hold-outs were similar to the bands of young Frenchmen who had, at an earlier stage of the war, fled to the wilderness of their own country rather than perform compulsory labour service in Germany. These German groups were also comparable to the clusters of Soviet troops who had escaped capture during the heady days of the German advance into the USSR in 1941; these groups, too, avoided the enemy not only because they hated him, but because they feared an uncertain future in his hands.

In both the French and Soviet cases, many of these woodland resisters soon became the core of *maquis* or partisan bands, as their sense of fear and persecution was transformed into an active intent to oppose the occupying power. However, the Nazi counterparts of these groups rarely underwent this evolution of purpose. Therefore, they might properly be called embryonic partisans, particularly since they were seldom able to match the main achievement of more motivated guerrillas – namely, the coordination of large-scale, organized resistance. Any of these irregular troops who still had a regard for legalities were affected by the announcement of Hitler's death on 1 May 1945, which released military men from their oaths of loyalty, and they were simlarly influenced by the regional armistice agreements, the formal cancellation of guerrilla warfare on 5 May, and the general capitulation several days later. After these momentous events, many German partisans threw up their hands in despair and either surrendered or made their own way home independently. In southern Germany, huge numbers of isolated troops streamed down from the hills and mountains where they had been hiding, literally begging Wehrmacht units on their way to American-designated assembly points to let them tag along, and to give them something to eat.[2] A much smaller number of die-hards held out for several more months, engaged in minor sabotage and attacks, until they were finally wiped out by the occupation forces or they tired of life in the forests and hills. An American intelligence assessment reported in July 1945 that 'former SS members operating in small groups persist in their occasional harassing activities,' although they added that the importance of such pinpricks was outweighed by the looting and indiscriminate attacks of foreign slave labourers liberated in April and May 1945.[3] Whatever its limitations, however, some sporadic guerrilla resistance did occur, and it is to such activity that this chapter is devoted.

The Lüneburg Heath

In general, the British had fewer guerrillas to worry about than did their American, French, or Soviet allies, although the North German Plain was not entirely without such perils. Granted, with the exception of the Teutoburger Wald, this region was generally flat and was largely cultivated or settled, so that the opportunities for the long-range survival of partisans was poor. Still, there were some HJ groups and bands of SS stragglers that began to harass British supply lines soon after elements of Twenty-first Army Group had crossed the Rhine near Wesel, or had surged into northern Germany from Holland. Near the end of March 1945, 120 HJ marauders near Coesfeld attacked the headquarters of the 6th British Airborne Division, whereafter the majority of the raiders were killed or captured. A week later, a similar HJ partisan group ambushed an ambulance west of Steinhude.[4] On 10 April, a British officer camped near Berge noted laconically in his diary: 'German guerillas pretty active today; 2 i/c Scots Guards wounded while going into wood. Also sergeant never came back.'[5] Later in the month, two Reconnaissance Corps officers were ambushed and killed; a cart-load of liberated slave labourers was massacred; and two rear-echelon officers were killed when their jeep was blown up by a shot from a Panzerfaust.[6] At Steyerberg, a bypassed SS officer took out his fears and resentments on local civilians. On the night of 7 April, he killed a woman who had hoisted a white flag, and, when a neighbour reported this incident to the British Military Government, the SS man shot the informer's brother.[7]

The worst region for such activity in northern Germany was the Lüneburg Heath, a large wasteland of shrubs, heather, and pines, which had a traditional reputation as an abode of witches and evil-doers. In addition, the area was inhabited (thinly) by the kind of middling farmers who had made early converts to National Socialism, and even the region's towns were more trade and administrative loci than industrial centres.[8] Numerous arms and food caches had been laid in this area in order to nourish resisters, and, not surprisingly, it became in April 1945 a point of refuge for 4,000 Nazi fugitives, some of whom busied themselves in sniping at passing Allied forces. Meanwhile, the British, on their way to more important objectives (such as Hamburg), took time to burn large parts of the heath by starting fires with flame-throwers and incendiary shells. They regarded this as a cheap method of clearing an area of secondary importance, but the tactic never entirely succeeded. In fact, well into the postwar period there were still congregations of SS men reportedly roaming the heath, although the British regarded them as 'troublesome individually rather than corporately.' None the less, such elements were perhaps responsible for the sporadic instances of line-cutting, arson, assault, and road obstruction that affected this region in 1945–6.

The most notable of these nasty events was an ambush of two British liaison officers shortly before the end of the war. Both the victims of this attack, John Poston and Peter Earle, were attached to the Twenty-first Army Group, and as such they were close acquaintances of Montgomery and were familiar even with Churchill, who had met them during his frequent trips to the front. Poston, in particular, was one of the legendary 'First Eleven,' who had been with Montgomery since North Africa. On the evening of 21 April, Earle and Poston were returning from a liaison mission when they made the mistake of straying too close to the Lüneburg Heath. While on this dangerous route, their jeep was ambushed by a HJ band, and the two British officers found themselves in the middle of a desperate fire-fight. Earle, wounded in the arm and the temple, and soon out of ammunition, drove the jeep directly towards a machine-gun nest, killing the gunner but throwing both himself and Poston from their vehicle. Just as he looked over at Poston, who was lying prone with his hands behind his head, he heard Poston plead for his life, and then a bayonet was thrust into his comrade, killing him instantly. By the mysterious of chances of war, Earle was spared, and the HJ marauders carried him to a nearby farmhouse, whence he was subsequently evacuated to a German field hospital. On the following day the hospital itself was overrun by British forces, and Earle was rescued by his countrymen.[9]

Schleswig–Holstein

The only other locations in northern Germany to cause the British much concern were the few wooded areas of Schleswig–Holstein. Actually, three-quarters of Schleswig–Holstein was composed of farmland, and since the remainder of the terrain was flat, sandy, well-watered, and lightly wooded, it offered little in the way of hide-outs for guerrillas. None the less, Schleswig–Holstein became a draw for Nazi die-hards because of coincidence: it was the only practical point of collection for German forces being driven northward by the Twenty-first Army Group, like moraine before a glacier. Barely any of the province was occupied before the final German surrender, and there were precious few British personnel on hand until well into the summer of 1945, which meant that, over an extended period, the German Army was responsible for post-capitulation security.

As for the local population, its demographic and cultural character suited the demands of Nazi guerrilla warriors better than any other host group in Germany. The inhabitants of Schleswig–Holstein had a long history of radical, rural populism and reactionary anti-industrialism. Moreover, they had been incensed by the cessation of North Schleswig to Denmark in 1920 and by the Weimar Republic's apparent inability to provide sufficient state aid to deal with the agricultural crisis of the 1920s and 1930s. Not surprisingly, many farmers in the area had sympathized with the Kapp Putschists, paramilitaries had proliferated during the 1920s, and the rural folk of the western marshes and the central moors had thrown their support towards National Socialism at an early date. By the early 1930s, local support for the NSDAP had become overwhelming, and in the election of July 1932 Schleswig–Holstein became the only electoral region in Germany to record an absolute majority of its votes (51 per cent) going to the Nazi Party.[10] Thus, it would be safe to say that National Socialism had a solid base in the area. In addition, by 1945 nearly two-thirds of the population was made up of expellees from Germany's eastern provinces – people who were generally bitter and angry about a fate which they felt had been inflicted upon them by a cruel and dishonourable enemy. Allied observers noted that both soldiers and civilians in Schleswig–Holstein still had 'good morale' and were generally impertinent.[11]

The Segeburg Forest, just north of Hamburg, was a particular focus of concern for the Allies, since in early May a force of warlike individuals gathered in the forest, determined to pay a last homage to the god of battles. Himmler and the Hamburg garrison commander, General Wolf, had both ordered various units to withdraw into the Forest, apparently for a last stand,[12] and a 300-man remnant of this force continued to hold out even after the general capitulation. Among this complement were various Werwolf elements, some of them probably armed from a Wehrmacht dump near Hamburg to which they had been given free access.[13]

On 4 May, a sixty-man SS detachment from Segeburg overran the town of Heiderfeld, ambushing a British jeep in the process. The frightened *Bürgermeister* fled the village and reported to a nearby British unit that this particular SS band had no intention of capitulating. SS raiders also swarmed through other towns in the area, ordering villagers to take down white flags and shooting those who protested. Since a regional ceasefire in northwest Europe had already gone into force, and the general armistice was imminent, the Twenty-first Army Group felt that responsibility for suppressing the Segeburg recalcitrants properly rested with the Wehrmacht, which was expected to guarantee that German elements obeyed the surrender. Local British units were alerted on 7 May that General Zouberzuig and his 8th Parachute Division, one of the Wehrmacht's last battle-worthy formations, were about to undertake a sweep of the forest. This operation began at dawn of 8 May, when British units sealed off the exits of the woods, and Zouberzuig's units approached the eastern extreme of the forest and began driving across the region from east to west. There was some skirmishing with armed bands of 'Displaced Persons,' but the Segeburg *maquis* apparently surrendered to their countrymen without much of a struggle.[14]

Elsewhere in Schleswig–Holstein, considerable bodies of SS men remained in the bush, waiting for a sign from their erstwhile chief. However, after the débâcle of Himmler's capture and suicide, hordes of defeated fanatics meekly surrendered themselves, although a few small bands organized by NCOs continued to lead a 'semi-savage' existence, living mainly through the plunder of local farms. A British Military Government officer at Niebüll, near the Danish frontier, reported in the summer of 1945 that a plot to replace a number of Polish and Russian farm workers with SS men had been uncovered. At Kiel, British officers were fired upon at night, and, after the Kiel Canal was repaired, passing ships were shot at and one of the locks was sabotaged. Near Flensburg, a band of a dozen troops attacked two German housewives because they had allegedly provided the British with information. Throughout 1945–6, there were numerous instances of line-cutting, the stringing of decapitation wires, illegal radio broadcasting, minor sabotage to Allied vehicles, underground pamphleteering, and other forms of illegal activity, and the province was generally considered the most raucous area in the British Zone.[15]

The Sauerland

South of the British sphere of operations in northern Germany, the first place where American units ran into difficulty with guerrillas was in a heavily forested and rainy corner of Westphalia called 'the Sauerland.' U.S. First Army formations advancing from Remagen to Lippstadt managed to cut off most of the Sauerland at the end of March 1945, whereafter they spent the next two weeks gradually boring into the interior of the region as part of a bigger operation to roll up the Ruhr Pocket. However, since the area was topographically suited to partisan warfare, a number of German troops in zones overrun by the Americans fled to the woods rather than giving up, and there is some evidence that SS detachments in the affected areas enforced the adoption of this tactic.[16]

Several surviving documents provide a fascinating look at the action in the Sauerland from the viewpoint of local German guerrillas. On 12 April, a message reached German lines from SS-Captain Dieter Menninger, a war correspondent attached to one of the isolated detachments in the region.

We find ourselves [said Menninger] in the rear of Anglo-American armoured spearheads, in the area between the Lippe and the Sieg. The enemy is all around us, on the roads and on the waterways ... Numerous single warriors from anti-tank units and roadblock squads are breaking out by surprise from the valleys of the Sauerland. *Volkssturm* men, who know each road and pathway of their beloved *Heimat*, lead our brave grenadiers to the hated enemy. Day and night the enemy's supply lines to Thuringia are destroyed, blown up or threatened. The enemy feels the loss of each tank and each supply vehicle that is burned out on the roads of the Sauerland. Enemy troops are uncertain and nervous, since in this rough country quick death awaits them behind each bend in the road.[17]

A less rose-coloured assessment came from the commander of a Waffen-SS group deliberately left behind near the key road hub of Paderborn, where its mission was to mine roads and block Allied supply lines. This report revealed the uncomfortable juxtposition of a squad of fanatics operating amidst an uncaring and potentially hostile population.

[On returning from a road-mining expedition] we were dismayed to find that our ration dump had been looted by the local civilian populace. Anyhow, the attitude of the local civilian population is a chapter all by itself. The civilians are glad the war is over for them. They pander to the Americans in the most revolting way and bar their doors to German soldiers still willing to fight. In Altenbeken the Americans were greeted with the cry 'Welcome to the Liberators.' Paderborn itself is at the moment closed to all civilian traffic because an American Jewish General was got rid of there. A gratifying side-light of which, thank God, there are more ...

The work here is very strenuous. It is extremely hard to obtain any kind of active help, even in the way of goods. But this shall not deprive us of the stimulus for continuing the job. Unfortunately we are entirely without communication with the outside world, due to the breakdown of our radio sets, a state of affairs, however, which cannot be remedied on account of the further advances of the Americans ... We are doing our duty here in such a way that our conscience is clear before ourselves and before Germany.[18]

The population of the Sauerland had never been very sympathetic to National Socialism.

Allied records confirm that there were sporadic difficulties in the areas described by these documents, and that 'German brigands' were shot each night as they snuck into American encampments, attempting to raid ammunition dumps. At Siegen, several American soldiers were shot on the outskirts of the community after it was occupied, and local Military Government detachments were warned to remain alert. At Olpe, a number of U.S. sentries were similarly shot at night, and German informers reported that bands of SS men and Nazi functionaries were active in the forests around the village. Along the Möhne River, two SS bands equipped with radio transmitters were uncovered by patrols from the U.S. Ninth Army. In both cases, these units displayed valour worthy of a better cause, fighting to the last man when surrounded by American detachments.

Even after the Ruhr Pocket collapsed, the U.S. 9th Infantry Division continued to note that, in its area of responsibility, lone vehicles were occasionally fired upon and booby-traps were discovered in isolated localities. Two HJ-Werewolves were arrested at Siegburg, and a former Hitler bodyguard was uncovered at Remscheid in the process of distributing funds for the support of a resistance movement. At Arnsberg, where the Americans had rounded up the entire population of military-age males and marched them off to POW cages, a surviving band of 100 HJ-Werewolves replenished itself from arms caches hidden in caves and engaged in minor sabotage. Their most spectacular stunt was the destruction of a clock tower that served as a belfry for one of Arnsberg's most venerable Catholic churches and was regarded as a local landmark. Several weeks after the arrival of Allied forces, the new authorities removed a gilded swastika that the previous regime had mounted atop the tower, and they replaced this offensive ornament with a Latin cross. On the evening before the new cross was scheduled for unveiling, several boys were seen climbing the scaffolding along the clock tower, and the spire of the roof soon after burst into flames. Fire then consumed the entire structure.[19]

The Odenwald

Again to the south, it was the U.S. Seventh Army that was forced to deal with disturbances in the thick forests of the Odenwald, nestled on a ridge between the three great rivers of the Neckar, the Rhine and the Main. Werwolf organizers did their best to prepare this district for partisan warfare – the Counter-Intelligence Corps (CIC) later uncovered a cache of 1,200 pounds of TNT in the vicinity of Hockenheim – and some civilians in the region rose up in arms against the advancing Americans. Not surprisingly, local woodlands soon became a refuge for bands of bypassed German soldiers attempting to interfere with American supply lines. Their most successful operation was carried out on 2 April 1945, when a group of Germans unbraked a locomotive and some rail coaches near a blasted overpass, and then rolled the train over the edge of the bridge and on to an American armoured column passing on an *Autobahn* below. Several American troops were killed, some equipment was damaged, and the column was delayed several hours until bulldozers were able to clear the road.[20]

Probably the most notable of the isolated German units in the Odenwald was a small battalion of 130 men, under Captain Schwaben, which had been *deliberately* stranded in the Allied rear for the purpose of conducting guerrilla warfare. On the evening of 16 April, outposts of Schwaben's detachment sighted an American vehicle travelling along a nearby road. The occupants of this staff car were two American officers, one a captain in the CIC, the other a Military Government officer, who had lost their bearings and were aimlessly driving around the woods, searching for a familiar landmark. Sensing an easy target, Schwaben's men opened fire on the car, and the two American officers were caught completely off guard. The Military Government officer was killed in the exchange, but the CIC captain was lightly wounded and captured, after which he was marched back to guerrilla headquarters. Schwaben had no use for a captive, so he had the American returned to the scene of the ambush and murdered.[21]

The Harz

Whatever nuisance value was created by various ambushes and guerrilla harassments along American lines of communication, it would be fair to conclude that bypassed bands in the the Odenwald and the Sauerland *never* developed into a major strategic concern for U.S. forces. This casual attitude, however, did not extend to the major geographic obstruction in central Germany – namely, the rough and inhospitable terrain of the Harz Mountains, a natural hurdle between the Weser and the Saale. This formation offered such a good base for German defensive operations or diversionary activities that even the most complacent of American generals was concerned about the prospect of such developments. As a result, several American divisions made a considerable effort, beginning on 10 April 1945, to isolate the Harz and seal off the exits, although they were unable to make much progress in penetrating deeply into the hills. While the U.S. Army rolled on to its geopolitical objectives at Leipzig and Magdeburg, the Harz remained stubbornly stuck in its craw.

Strategically, the Harz was the most important mountain range anywhere in Germany north of the Alps, and there were few other areas in the Reich so perfectly suited for partisan warfare, as had been shown on previous occasions, particularly the Thirty Years War.[22] The landscape consisted of a maze of steep hills, granite cliffs, and extremely thick forest, interspersed with caves and abandoned mines. The roads into the area followed deep valleys, which could be readily blocked, particularly at stream crossings. Compasses were useless because iron deposits distorted magnetic bearings. Aerial spotting was difficult because the Harz, as one of the first major obstacles in the face of moist maritime winds, had a climate that was frequently wet and misty, even in summer.

In a mythological/ideological sense as well, the area was well adapted for the purpose of Nazi partisan warfare. In the Dark Ages, the Harz was the last stronghold of Teutonic paganism, and Mount Brocken was later immortalized by Goethe as the scene of the witches' coven in *Faust*. The Kyffhäusser range, lying immediately south of the Harz, was the mythical resting spot of Frederick Barbarossa, whence, according to lengend, he would someday arise from his slumber and restore Germany's strength. The Nazis recognized the region's value as a centre of German mysticism and, after they rose to power in 1933, they annually commemorated the Walpurgis ceremony, and they consecrated SS standards in Quedlinburg Cathedral. National Socialist candidates did well in elections in the early 1930s, getting over 50 per cent of the vote in Zellerfeld and Goslar, and topping off at 46 per cent in Osterode, although these results were no better than in neighbouring districts outside the hills. Almost all of the local bourgeoisie flocked to the Swastika, although the working class, a considerable presence in the small manufacturing and mining towns of the region, proved resistant. In fact, the Harz had a 'red' reputation dating to the Wilhelmine period, and even in the spring of 1945 the *Kreisleiter* of Blankenburg warned one of his Volkssturm leaders that the Harz was still 'red.'[23] On the other hand, towns such as Nordhausen and Halberstadt were identified by the Americans as 'hotbeds of Naziism,' and in the latter the *Bürgermeister* was so terrified of the Werwolf that he refused to serve the occupation forces.[24]

Whatever the sympathies of the population, the Harz was so attractive geographically that it still proved a tremendous magnet for German units fleeing the débâcles along the Rhine and the Weser. In early April, local *Gauleiter* were ordered to prepare supply depots so that the area could be held as a 'stronghold,' and the *Kreisleiter* of Brunswick was appointed 'Special Commissioner' for the Harz. During the same period, the flotsam that collected in the mountains was formed into the Eleventh Army and was told to maintain the Harz Redoubt at all costs. In orders to this 70,000-man Army on 7 April, the German High Command defined its mission as 'bitter delaying resistance,' thereby holding the mountains as a 'blocking concentration point.' 'Special defences' were to be used to protect the VHF directional transmitter on Mount Brocken. On 8 April, the entire Harz was declared a 'Fortress.' Nine days later, at the height of the battle for the area, Hitler issued his infamous decree to the Eleventh Army, calling for the widespread application of guerrilla tactics and, as we know, this order was subsequently distributed to all units on the Western Front.[25]

Measures were also taken to build up the local Werwolf. In March, a HJ-Lieutenant-General in Mansfeld established a 600-man HJ-Werwolf formation in order to defend the Harz. It was placed under the command of a former HJ official from Posen, who had since become an SS officer and was recuperating from facial wounds suffered on the Eastern Front. The corps of NCOs was composed of wounded SS men from a military hospital in Wernigerode, and the ranks of the battalion were made up of students, HJ members, and a small number of Labour Service men. On 1 April, after a brief period of training, the recruits were sworn into Battle Group 'Ostharz' of the Werwolf, and there were further guerrilla call-ups early in the same month. Military engineers were also set to work in order to prepare mountain caves for habitation or defence by Werwolf units.[26]

Not surprisingly, these prepatory measures contributed to an intense bout of guerrilla fighting that engulfed the Harz after the approach of American forces. There were the usual attemps to terrorize the population. In Osterode, pamphlets called on each inhabitant to kill an American soldier, and when an 'old party comrade' complained about such nonsensical appeals, he was arrested and threatened with death. In Quedlinburg, Werewolves warned townfolk about the consequences of cowardice and treason, and they summarily executed a physician on grounds of 'desertion.' At Everode, HJ-tank destroyer personnel murdered the town *Bürgermeister* because he called them criminals and 'snot-nosed idiots.' At Halberstadt, an engineer named Kleine was arrested because the *Kreisleiter* accused him of telling the Americans about a munitions train in the area. This poor wretch was shot while escaping, but was recaptured and then evacuated to Blankenburg, where he was hanged on a gallows built by Were-wolves in the town square.

Werwolf units and military raiding detachments also made numerous sweeps into the American lines, or they penetrated the enemy front and operated in the rear, laying mines and erecting roadblocks. Groups of anywhere from three to fifty men ambushed American patrols, and on occasion they even retook captured towns. Nazi raiders, for instance, shot up the town of Treseburg after it was overrun by American troops on 17 April, and they also captured American equipment in this area. Less than a week after the battle began, an American officer had been assassinated by a Werwolf, and there were numerous reports of chidren destroying American tanks with Panzerfäuste. At Wernigerode, which was occupied on 11 April, an American officer operating in the rear of the U.S. 83rd Infantry Division discovered a full-scale Nazi meeting in progress, and he fled town in terror. Near the American-occupied village of Eisfelden Talmühle, two German officers on a reconnaissance mission were shot to death while riding in a Red Cross service vehicle.[27]

The Americans themselves often reacted with considerable vindictiveness, particularly since demonizing the enemy became a much easier mental task for the thousands of personnel who had witnessed conditions at the Nazi concentration camp near Nordhausen. Walter Görlitz claims that, at Treseburg, where an American officer was killed by a HJ boy shortly after the arrival of U.S. troops, a dozen German POWs were shot in retaliation. At the town of Heiligthal, the scale of reprisals was even greater. A Volkssturm unit of Labour Service men camouflaged some flak guns and planned to allow forward elements of an American armoured column to pass without a fight, and then ambush the rear echelon. However, a nervous German civilian gave the Americans warning of this impending attack, and the Americans themselves were able to ambush and surround the Volkssturm troopers, although they still lost several tanks in the ensuing battle. Furious about their casualties, the Americans ransacked the Volkssturm encampment, and then gathered together more than a hundred of their prisoners and executed them, although they were wearing Volkssturm arm-bands and brown Labour Service uniforms. The bodies were then laid out in neat rows along the side of the road, as a warning to other would-be partisans.[28] German defenders – possibly SS troopers or HJ minutemen – were also executed in several other instances, particularly around Osterode, in apparent reprisals where the original provocation has long since been forgotten. At

Quedlinburg, the occupiers took a different tack. When a U.S. soldier was shot by a Hitler Youth on the evening of 18 April, shortly after the Americans entered Quedlinburg, the boy was himself killed and the invaders then retreated to the outskirts, whence they spent all night methodically shelling the town. Only in the morning did they return, with a warning that any further 'incidents' would result in the town being burned to the ground in its entirety.[29]

All this mayhem would probably have been worse but for the personality of General Lucht, the commander of the Eleventh Army, who opposed a scorched-earth campaign. In addition, Lucht's troops were demoralized, knowing that the end of the war was at hand, and they were usually uneager to take any more chances than necessary.[30] Werwolf Battle Group 'Ostharz' suffered heavy losses, both from desertions and from enemy fire. Even by 15 April, one American division alone had already killed or captured more than a hundred Werewolves. Near Blankenburg, one band of schoolboy Werewolves, led by a teacher, marched into the woods and disappeared; another group of heavily armed twelve-year-olds was wiped out by the enemy. By the final days of the fight, the Battle Group had been reduced to a desperate rabble near Pansfelde, short of weapons and medicine, and a large part of the remaining band was wiped out by an American ambush on 20 April, while they were in the process of scavenging supplies from a crashed German aircraft.[31]

With the end clearly in sight by 18 April, Kesselring ordered the remnants of the Eleventh Army to make a final stand around Mount Brocken and, if necessary, to form 'separate groups to fight to the last round.'[32] Dispersed German units were still being supplied by Luftwaffe air-drops on 19 April,[33] but by the 21st, with the fall of the last unoccupied village in the area, the final conquest of the Harz was announced confidently by the Allies.

Unfortunately, this happy declaration did not close the book on the Harz fortress. As the collapse of coordinated resistance loomed closer, some German commanders had given their men the option of *either* surrendering *or* carrying on alone or in small groups in order to filter through the Allied ring. American patrols were dispatched into the woods to round up disorganized groupings of German troops, and, on 23 April, Lucht and his headquarters staff were overrun.[34] This raid, however, was only partially successful, and bitter events soon proved that the mountains were still infested with straggler bands and guerrilla detachments committed to causing harm to the Americans. The true pacification of the region had only begun.

Trouble started right away, as malevolent renegades were rousted from their hideaways by the American mop-up campaign. On 23 April, three German stragglers ambushed an equal number of Americans riding in a jeep, one of whom was a medical officer. All three Americans were captured, but since the

German marauders were in no position to take prisoners, they marched the Americans into a nearby house, turned their faces to a wall, and shot them in the back. They then stripped the men of their uniforms, stole their jeep, and began roaming the rear echelon areas of the U.S. Ninth Army. In a separate but similar incident, a small band of German troops attacked an outpost of the 473rd Anti-Aircraft Supply Battalion, killing two guards. They, too, stripped their victims of their uniforms, stole a jeep, and headed off into the night. For the next several weeks, reports of such incidents reached the CIC on a daily basis. The Americans speculated that German partisan units were experiencing a temporary state of grace, in which they had recovered from the shock of being overrun, but still had not yet realized the futility of resistance.[35]

There was also a brief skirmish on 23 April near a Werwolf supply depot, as a CIC detachment tracking down the location of the cache was fired upon by German soldiers left behind to guard it. This sorry little band quickly surrendered, however, after they experienced a return volley. The ammunition dump was destroyed, and, in what seemed an extra bonus, a regional Werwolf chief was also discovered skulking in the area. This malcontent was arrested and was being escorted back to an American command post in Thale when he jumped from a CIC vehicle and was shot while attempting to run.[36]

During this same period, Werwolf activists managed to damage two American observation aircraft, a natural target since spotter planes played a key role in the tracking of guerrilla bands, and American communication lines in the Harz were harassed by wire-cutting. One such case was solved 'by applying pressure on the townspeople of Kinsdorf'; under force, these hapless burghers quickly yielded the names of two HJ members involved in the sabotage. In another incident, American authorities arrested seven underground Nazis and SA men in Wickerode, after these thugs had threatened to kill a policeman appointed by American Military Government.[37]

After the loss of the Mount Brocken radio tower, its recapture or destruction became a primary aim of the local partisan movement, and on 30 April a band of Twenty-five uniformed guerrillas attacked the facility, which had since been converted into a Ninth Army VHF relay station. Divided into four teams and equipped with small arms and grenades, the Germans fought a hard battle. Two guerrillas and two radio-transmitter personnel were wounded before the attackers finally retreated, battered by American tanks and fighter-bombers. A hotel next door to the radio tower was completely destroyed, except for an excellent wine cellar that was brought to light and thereafter looted by the Americans.[38]

On the first day of May, an American patrol searching for Nazi guerrillas stumbled upon a German officer alongside a road near Braunlage. The German was approached and ordered to call out any men in the surrounding forest, but, before he could answer, German partisans behind the trees opened fire. In the ensuing battle, two Americans and four Germans were killed, including the officer initially encountered along the roadside. Two American platoons hurried to the rescue of their comrades, and a subsequent sweep of the area uncovered five civilians who had carried food to German stragglers.

On the following day, yet another incident occurred. At Munschaf, a German powder plant blew up, killing an American officer, Lieutenant John Rosselet, and badly injuring three additional members of a patrol that was in the vicinity. CIC investigators suspected sabotage.[39]

Worst of all, a rump of the Werwolf Battle Group was still running loose, and it caused harm to the Americans as it thrashed out wildly in its death throes. It will be recalled that much of the Battle Group had been wiped out in an American ambush on 20 April, whereafter a number of half-starved survivors had fled in the direction of the Ram Berge, in the Oberharz. By the end of April, the band had been reduced to a strength of only fifty guerrillas. Driven by hunger, these desperadoes built a roadblock on the *Autobahn* between Elbingerode and Wernigerode, where they ambushed an American supply convoy. The Americans, however, beat off the attack, with casualties on both sides, and the Werewolves had to retreat into the woods without any plunder to reward their efforts.[40]

Not surprisingly, this string of incidents tried the patience of the American occupiers. An American OSS team that arrived in the mountains in early May found the local American commander in a sober mood, owing to the fact that a number of his men had recently been wounded in skirmishes with Nazi bands.[41] As a result, yet another series of sweeps was undertaken in order to cleanse the Harz. Broadsheets were posted calling for local civilians to denounce the Werwolf and thus free the area from the scourge of guerrilla warfare. Conclusive success was attained in tracking down the Werwolf Battle Group: its tattered remnants were traced to a refuge near the Hone–Klippen, where they were dug into foxholes, and the Americans deployed against them special counterguerrilla units formed from Polish refugees. Supported by American forces and by fighter-bombers, these Polish detachments methodically blasted their way through the neighbourhood. Ground units lobbed hand-grenades into literally every nook and cranny in the woods. Only five of the adolescent Werewolves were known to have survived this hunt,[42] and the operations of the HJ-Werwolf in the Harz were effectively terminated.

Other small bands and fanatical individuals continued to fight on, but the intensity of partisan warfare began to decline, in part because of the end of the war and the increased illegality of the guerrilla endeavour. None the less, on 11 May, two American riflemen were mysteriously killed and their bodies left in a field near the town of Schierke. Elements of the U.S. 120th Infantry Regiment were sent to scour the woods in search of guerrillas, but the guilty parties were never brought to book. The unit history of the 120th reveals that disgruntled American officers imposed 'prompt and effective reprisal measures,'[43] but these are not described, and it is not clear whether they were any more harsh because the war was officially over.

Elsewhere in the Harz, assaults continued, particularly in the zone occupied by the 8th Armoured Division. One American soldier was severely wounded by a land-mine; another was shot in the back while picking wildflowers in the hills; and, on 21 May, a U.S. officer confronted an axe-wielding German near Osterode, and the American was wounded in the subsequent mêlée. In another case, an American NCO inadvertently discovered three armed HJ members waiting to waylay an unsuspecting member of the occupying forces.[44]

An energetic clique of line-cutters was busy in Nordhausen, where they not only snipped wires, but also composed wordy leaflets and posters intended to shock the local authorities:

To the Gentlemen and Administration of the Town of Nordhausen: Mr. Bürgermeister, Town Major

You will be very interested that only one wire has been cut. We used to cut 5 to 10. This is only tactics. Until now you have omitted to do anything against us. When General Eisenhower will get wind of this you will all be arrested because of showing favours. Perhaps, however, this matter is unimportant because only one wire has been cut; but we do not stop at telephone wires and will do better.

In case you should like my fingerprint I give you the print of my right index finger [a print was impressed upon the note].

On 8 June 1945 we shall inform General Eisenhower.

We beg to salute you.

Heil Hitler
SS-Gestapo-Werwolf[45]

A similar communiqué, more terse in its message, simply said, 'Keep your trap shut or you will be shot, you pigs, MG police and Bürgermeister.'[46]

By mid-June 1945, the incidence of attacks and sabotage had become infrequent.[47] But although the Harz could no longer be described as a theatre of guerrilla warfare, it did remain a problem even for the British and Soviet troops who arrived in the early summer of 1945, as the configuration of forces in Germany was rearranged to fit the limits of the occupation zones decided upon in 1944. British authorities recorded several attacks near Goslar, most particularly the injury of an NCO who was knocked from his motorbike by a decapitation wire in July 1945. Three HJ boys were arrested for this incident.[48]

As for the Soviets, they arrived in the Harz all smiles, and tried to put a fresh face on their occupation policies. A local curfew was removed, German soldiers in military hospitals were given freedom of movement, and the Soviets took measures to counteract plundering raids by Russian and Polish refugee bands.[49] The shine quickly wore off, however, as they too experienced sporadic resistance. In the autumn of 1945, a Werwolf leaflet was discovered in Greussen, and the NKVD bolted into action. Scores of local suspects were arrested, some of whom were released, some of whom disappeared forever into the bowels of the Soviet penal system. Finally, it was discovered that the *Bürgermeister* of Greussen was himself responsible for the propaganda, and that the leaflet had been typed on his machine. At Rossleben, a Werwolf cell in the local *Gymnasium* was crushed by the Russians, although they suspected that surviving remnants were responsible for a poison-pen letter received by an NKVD officer in late February 1946. At Halberstadt, a Soviet officer was ambushed on 14 February, and his pistol and official documents were stolen.

By the spring of 1946, young men from Nordhausen had banded together to cause grief to the Soviets, particularly Russian troublemakers who raped German women and conducted highway robberies. The local military commandant, Colonel Kravchenko, reported in early May that 'attacks on members of the occupation force have been taking place in increasing numbers, whereby German civilian persons have beaten members of the Red Army into insensibility.' Local *Bürgermeister* were warned that, if such assaults continued, they would be held personally responsible and would be tried by military courts. None the less, a heavily armed German band, led by a former Luftwaffe officer, was still reportedly active in the Harz as late as 1947.[50]

The Thuringian Forest

The Thuringian Forest was yet another rugged region that the German High Command hoped to use as a local redoubt. This district had a history as a centre of partisan warfare, having been so used by Communist guerrillas in 1923, and it had been a stronghold of the authoritarian parties of both left and right during the Weimar period. The population had a largely working-class character, but the area's industries were typically small firms whose proprietors formed part of the *petite bourgeoisie,* as did the region's class of middling farmers. Both of these groups had been natural targets for the Nazis, who tapped into a strong local folkish tradition and exploited southern Thuringian particularist sentiment in areas such as Meiningen.[51]

Geographically, the Thuringian massif, like the Harz, suggested intrinsic advantages for defensive troops or guerrillas. It was forested and hilly, and since it was a traditional mining centre, there were lots of unused mining shafts and tunnelways in the district. As American spearheads thundered forward in 1945, Werewolves, cognizant of the region's natural benefits, hurriedly laid ammunition caches, and the local HSSPF engaged in the usual desperate effort to curb 'defeatism' through Werwolf-style killings of 'unreliables.'[52] When the Americans reached the area, the German LXXXV Corps was ordered to hold, and to attack 'again and again in the flank and rear by [deploying] mobile elements' (7 April).[53] Subsequently, German 'flying columns' and partisan teams made life difficult for American ordnance units, and they occasionally retook small towns under the cover of darkness. Rear-echelon columns of the U.S. 26th Division were constantly attacked, with the result that units at the front no longer received fresh meat and other supplies, and were forced back on canned rations. When the city of Suhl was stormed by American units on 4 April, the fanatical *Bürgermeister* refused to surrender the town and insisted that the townspeople fight to the death, which naturally resulted in a considerable spate of sniping. The Americans took reprisals, and they subsequently considered the town a 'probable hotbed of underground activity.'

There was a similarly hostile atmosphere along the northern rim of the forest. Near Ohrdruf, where the population was in a surly mood, civilian guerrillas ambushed a U.S. Third Army jeep on 7 April, after it had smashed into a road blockade. Among the casualties was Colonel Robert Allen, executive officer of the Third Army's G-2 Section. Allen was captured and evacuated back through German lines, but the field hospital where he was laid up was recaptured by American forces on 12 April. General Patton himself arranged for retaliation, noting in his diary that 'the town where [the attack] took place has been removed, together with, I hope, a number of the civilians.'

At Arnstadt, the U.S. 89th Infantry Division established its command post at one end of town and its supply services in a former Siemens factory at the opposite end of the community. One evening in mid-April, small-arms fire began to rain down upon an ordnance company that had settled into the Siemens plant. The quartermaster personnel ran for their weapons and returned fire towards a house across the road, which was the source of the harassment. In the course of the fusillade, the house was destroyed and seven German guerrillas were killed. Investigation showed that the snipers were SS and Luftwaffe troops who had doffed their uniforms in favour of civilian clothes.[54]

Conventional operations in the Thuringian Forest were over by the middle of April, but the woods continued to harbour bands of German stragglers, who functioned under the banner of the Werwolf. One such grouping of thirty men was led by the *Bürgermeister* of Römhild, a Nazi fanatic named Schmidt, and it terrorized the area around Hildburghausen. Each evening, the Schmidt band chose a new suburb to provide their lodging and keep, and they always arrived with weapons drawn in order to ensure the proper measure of hospitality. Another smaller group of SS men similarly foisted itself upon a farm near Weit-ersroda, getting provisions of food and drink each evening before withdrawing back into the woods. The sympathies of local townfolk were ambiguous: they resented Werwolf depredations, but they were also sullen and hostile in the face of the American Military Government. American units in the area were at their wits' end in dealing with such thorny problems.

At Hildburghausen, literally in the eye of the storm, the local 'Antifa' made regular reports about guerrilla activity, and it begged for American arms in order to protect its members and to form posses in order to clear the woods. Per-mission was repeatedly refused, in strict accordance with Allied policy, although the Americans themselves were unable to perform such measures because they had denuded the area of military manpower. As far as the U.S. Third Army was concerned, troop strength should be focused at the front in order to end the greater conflict as quickly as possible. In Hildburghausen, a town of 15,000, which included a Wehrmacht hospital with 400 patients, the American garrison comprised only one officer and a contingent of fifteen NCOs and enlisted men. Moreover, this lone detachment was not a trained Military Government unit, but simply a combat squad pulled from the line, and its only means of contact with the local population was through a fourteen-year-old, English-speaking evacuee from the Rhineland. This lad, in turn, was rattled after his countrymen threatened him with death on grounds of 'collaboration.' In its desperation, the Third Army detachment imposed a strict twenty-hour curfew, which constituted a hardship upon the inhabitants of the town, and fur-ther exacerbated strained relations.

This impossible situation was finally broken by an ugly incident that brought the area to the attention of the ulterior American command. After nightfall on the evening of 22 April, the head of the local American garrison was ambushed and shot while driving without an escort between Schleusingen and Hildburghausen. There were no witnesses, except a farmer who heard two bursts of submachine-gun fire, but the killing was universally attributed to Nazi guerrilla groups oper-ating in the region. Three days later, the Americans were finally provided with reinforcements, allowing for the organization of patrols to round up nearby par-tisan gangs. The new Military Government officer in Hildburghausen reasserted the need for an extended curfew, and he also threatened to shell the town with artillery if any more shots were directed towards American troops.[55]

The Bavarian and Bohemian Forests

As the U.S. Third Army left the Thuringian Forest, most of its components swung in a southeasterly direction and sliced down along the eastern edge of the Bavarian plateau. This area was delineated by several chains of hills, especially the Bavarian Forest and the Bohemian Forest, the latter of which marked the old German–Czech frontier along its divide. Since this region was geographi- cally suited for guerrilla warfare, and was occupied by the Allies relatively late, at the end of April and beginning of May 1945, it formed one of the last redoubts to which Nazi fanatics fled as the war drew to a close. In mid-April, a contingent of Thuringian Gestapo men was led to the Bohemian Forest by SS-Lieutenant Colonel Hans Wolff, the Security Police commander in Weimar, although Wolff admittedly dissolved his band when he heard of Germany's final capitulation. Hans Weibgen's Nuremberg Werwolf similarly planned to use the mountains as a centre for partisan activity, and just before the American advance, an SS officer named Müller toured the area looking for fanatical young Nazis willing to form a stay-behind net. Although an arms depot was set up near Furth im Wald, the vicinity was overrun before Müller could distribute weapons and supplies. SS-Lieutenant Dirschel of the Weiden SD also organized a resistance organization composed of HJ members, which was probably a regional manifestation of the Axmann Plan. Among these boys were fanatics from a Westphalian anti-tank unit already bloodied in combat. These adventur- ers received special training shortly before the American advance, and they then withdrew to mountain huts stocked with food and arms.[56] The only major disincentive to Werwolf warfare was the fact that eastern Bavaria rivalled the Rhineland in its immunity to the Nazi virus. The strongly Catholic majority – over 90 per cent – had rejected National Socialism even as late as the time of the last German elections in 1932 and 1933, and in no other region did support for Bavarian particularism survive so vibrantly. Even after the Nazi rise to power, relatively low 'yes' votes in national plebiscites showed a continuing lack of support for the new order, and by the 1940s resentment against difficult economic circumstances and Nazi anti-Catholicism combined to make the regime extremely unpopular.[57]

Despite this deterrent, the physical features of the Bohemian Forest still made guerrilla warfare an option, and it is hardly surprising that the Americans noted the presence of armed bands in their rear areas, even after the end of the war. On 12 May 1945, a U.S. armoured car fired at a group of German strag- glers attempting to cross the German–Czech frontier; no one was injured in the skirmish, but all the fugitives managed to flee into the woods. Six SS troops were sighted north of Renstein, and a band of four SS stragglers, armed with rifles, was active near Grafenkirchen, where a woman provided them with food. There was a considerable problem in the Landshut area, where 200 SS troops haunted the woods during the daytime and looted towns at night. Information reaching Supreme Headquarters, Allied Expeditionary Force (SHAEF) on 23 May indicated 'much enemy activity in V and XII Corps [areas],' that is, eastern Bavaria and the western Sudetenland.

Naturally, some of these groups were dangerous. Shortly before the end of the war, SS stragglers slithered out of the forest near Roding and machine-gunned forty ex–concentration camp inmates sleeping in a barn, killing all but one. 'What fanaticism,' remembers a survivor. 'They hid in the woods and crept out at night to continue the all-important extermination of the Jews.' In several locations, radical Hitler Youths attacked civilians who were too friendly to the Americans. On the morning of 20 May, American troops were fired upon near Drachselsried, twenty miles north of Deggendorf. In true guerrilla fashion, the snipers fled the scene before they could be engaged in battle. Early on the following morning, a convoy of trucks belonging to a field artillery unit was shot at several miles south of Grafenau. Fire was returned and one German was killed. Four days later, Polish DPs and German civilians in Zfitiarn reported the existence of a band of twenty-one SS troops, armed with machine-pistols. A sweep of the district in question resulted in a skirmish in which one SS man was wounded, although the remainder of the band succeeeded in making good their escape. In early June, an American soldier was shot in Amberg, and the entire town was sealed off and raided by U.S. forces. Near Alsbach, a U.S. soldier disappeared from the 4th Armoured Division on 12 June, only to turn up five days later when his body washed up on the banks of the Danube. He had a wire wrapped around his neck, and a coroner's examination showed that he had been garrotted four days earlier.

Other groups and malevolent individuals seemed interested primarily in sabotage and propaganda. Wires were severed near Regensburg and Neustadt, and in the sector of the U.S. 90th Division, around Eisenstein, line-cutting was widespread and a number of telephone poles were chopped down. A gang of children led by a HJ member was responsible for at least several of these incidents. A similar band of juvenile wire-cutters was caught near Freyung by personnel of the U.S. 5th Infantry Division. On the afternoon of 28 May, a huge fire roared through a Chemical Warfare Dump at Grafenwöhr, near Weiden. Although the exact cause of the blaze was never determined, sabotage was strongly suspected. Several days later, three boys dynamited a bridge near Hakkenagger. The saboteurs were captured and when unmasked, turned out to be twelve-year-olds. Their leader, Robert Weigel, was a former activist in the Pimpfe. At Rottenburg placards were posted declaring, 'Long Live the Führer! Heil Hitler! Long Live Greater Germany! Young Nazi Awakening.'[58] Desultory troubles and round-ups of SS men continued to characterize the situation in the eastern borderlands of Bavaria throughout the remainder of the year.[59]

The Black Forest

On the opposite extremity of the Bavarian plateau, in Baden and Württemberg, lay yet another natural redoubt in the form of the Black Forest. The geography of the area, and its arboraceous character, favoured irregular warfare. There were the fabled dark, evergreen timberlands, which gave the region its name, climbing to a height of 4,000 feet and yet accessible from the mild and cultivated valleys. As well, the rural populace in Protestant pockets of Baden had turned to the Nazis at an early date, in the late 1920s, when the NSDAP had wisely identified itself with debt-ridden farmers, and arrayed its followers behind the traditional 'Bundschuh' ('Peasants' Boot') banner of agrarian revolt. Some of these enclaves in west, north, and southwest Baden went on to provide the Nazis with huge majorities in the elections of the early 1930s.[60] It is probably no coincidence that such localities as Löffingen, Lahr, Lörrach, and Emmendingen – all early bases of National Socialist support – later provided a home for armed bands in the spring of 1945.

These favourable factors should not, however, be overemphasized. Despite the sizeable hills of the Black Forest, it was largely a cultivated woodland with little undergrowth, and was planted with systematic regularity, all of which made the detection of guerrillas easier than might otherwise have been the case. Moreover, the Catholic majority of Baden was noted for its liberal sympathies, and although they had collaborated with the Nazis and much of the Catholic 'milieu' had been destroyed after 1933, it would be true to say that they had tolerated rather than supported the Third Reich. Indeed, the French Military Government reported that most people were 'disciplined and deferent,' particularly in contrast to the much stiffer civilian attitude in Württemberg. In fact, the Allies were well received in Baden, being greeted with wine and feted as 'liberators.' They expected, not without reason, that Werwolf members and sympathizers would be ruthlessly denounced. An American radio commentator who visited Baden near the end of the war noted that there were many 'old men, known for their anti-Nazi feelings, who had never been members of the Party and who are anxious to cooperate with us because they themselves are convinced that the "Werewolves" might cause serious trouble.' Civilians who did wish to carry on the fight had been disheartened by the rout of the Wehrmacht.[61]

However, while the geographic and popular elements favouring partisan warfare were by no means overwhelming, the local Werwolf steeled itself to fight a bitter struggle. Commando squads laid numerous weapons and supply dumps, and no less a figure than Otto Abetz, the former German ambassador to France, was recruited to lend his expertise in helping to prepare the regional Nazi *maquis*.[62] At a number of towns, the movement won itself a notorious reputation in the last few weeks before the arrival of the Allies. At Freudenstadt, it was led by a customs official, and it specialized in menacing the local townfolk. At Rottweil, the Werwolf was formed from the fanatic students of the 'National Political Training Institute' (NAPO), and it was led by twenty professors under the direction of the institution's headmaster. These NAPO boys were primed to become future SS officers, and they were both eager and well trained. At Villingen, Werewolves armed themselves from abandoned Army dumps at Löffingen and Tannheim, and they haunted the woods east of the city. This band managed to detonate five explosive charges at a nearby POW camp, Stalag VB, and they terrorized local civilians. Werwolf gangs at Oberwittstadt and St Trudbert killed parish priests because these men had spoken about the coming occupation in less-than-apocalyptic terms, and had encouraged villagers to take down pictures of the Führer and put away other Nazi symbols. At Freiburg im Breisgau, guerrillas chalked fearsome slogans on walls and fences, and a police captain was kidnapped and murdered after he opposed the infiltration of three Werewolves into the municipal police. At Tübingen, the Werwolf opposed an effort to declare the community an 'open town,' and they warned that they would honour no such agreement. 'Victory or Death' was their motto. They also threatened to kill a university professor accused of 'defeatism.'[63]

The Americans, who in late March overran the first towns at the northern tip of the Black Forest, found that considerable numbers of guerrillas remained in the woods along their lines of communication. The German economist and statesman Heinrich Köhler, reporting from Mudau in late April, a full month after the arrival of the Americans, noted that stragglers, SS men, and Werewolves frequently broke into small villages at night, where they demanded food and a place to sleep. These partisans also had lots to say, assuring their hosts that a turn in the fortunes of war was inevitable, and that all doubters would suffer a 'ruthless vengeance.' Köhler admitted that many farmers were cooperating with the guerrillas, either as a result of fear or from National Socialist sympathies, and that no sense of order could be re-established in these circumstances.[64]

As for the French, who occupied most of the Black Forest, they literally breezed through the area in a rushed effort to push their forces as far east as possible, mainly for political reasons. In the final analysis, this hardly helped their cause. On 21 April, a French drive pocketed the entire forest, and six days later General Lattre de Tassigny concluded that the German units in the trap, mostly the XVIII SS Corps, had been reduced to 'a tangle of fugitives doomed to imminent capture.'[65] A day later, mopping-up operations were concluded and French legions raced off along the northern edge of Lake Constance in order to reach Austria, thereby strengthening France's claim to an Austrian occupation zone.

Actually, conditions were not as positive as the French command liked to believe. On 24 April, Kesselring had ordered SS units in the Black Forest pocket to remain behind as 'rearguards,'[66] and after earlier defeats in Alsace, many of these formations had been restocked with fanatical HJ who were unlikely to give in easily. Even after the forest was supposed to be clear, it was prowled by large and aggressive guerrilla groups. A French patrol bumped into one of these bands on 28 April around the headwaters of the Danube, and there was a fierce clash: one French soldier and six German partisans were killed, and thirty-seven Germans were captured.[67] At Wilferdingen, an SS unit in civilian clothes ambushed a French patrol, but the leader of this detachment was captured and summarily executed by the French.[68] In other areas, Nazi stragglers helped to stir up local revolts. At Marbach, which was occupied by the French on 21 April, the neighbourhood Werwolf leader, a schoolmaster named Fischer, had already made life difficult for the *Bürgermeister* and the village Volkssturm commander, and after the French arrived he remained in contact with German soldiers scattered throughout the surrounding woods. On 25 April, a Wehrmacht column actually recaptured Marbach, an action which the French claimed was assisted by civilian sniping organized by Fischer. French and Moroccan troops retook the town on the evening of the same day, whence they pillaged it and burned a number of buildings, as well as confining the entire male population. As a reprisal, they killed the *Bürgermeister* and the local Volkssturm chief (despite their opposition to the Werwolf); they also caught up to Fischer, who was accused of leading the revolt and was summarily executed on 26 April.[69] The same type of incident also occurred not far away, thirty miles to the northeast, at the village of Bisingen. This town was captured on 21 April by an American special formation, code-named 'ALSOS,' which was looking for technical information on German atomic research. No sooner was the village occupied, however, than it was infiltrated by German stragglers, aided by hostile local inhabitants, and there was some sharp skirmishing between these raiders and American engineering troops. At a nearby hamlet, American forces were warned about the presence of Werwolf bands in the surrounding hills, and some of the villagers appealed for protection.[70]

The worst of these incidents was the violent conquest and pacification of the town of Freudenstadt, an issue around which controversy has swirled for fifty years. Popular German opinion claims that the community was deliberately destroyed by artillery fire as a delayed reprisal for the destruction of the French village of Oradour-sur-Glane, which was wiped off the map by the SS 'Das Reich' Division in June 1944, with the death of more than 600 inhabitants. Moreover, German witnesses claimed that French and Moroccan 'terror troops' subsequently installed themselves in the town and promptly knocked down or burned whatever was still standing. On the other hand, French officers later denied that Freudenstadt was purposefully destroyed, and they claimed that after an artillery bombardment, dictated by tactical necessity, French troops entered the town and did all in their power to suppress blazes that were already under way and were being further spread by high winds. They also pointed out that the town centre of Freudenstadt had many antique wooden buildings that made a fire likely under combat conditions. A French military inquest held after the war cleared French forces of any responsibility for the fires.[71]

Assessments by American liaison officers tell a story less straightforward than either of these stark alternatives. According to these reports, the occupation of the town began amidst the fire and smoke of a last-ditch stand by thirty German troops who refused to surrender. Moreover, French forces were fired upon by several scores of German *francs-tireurs* dressed in civilian clothes, but armed with submachine-guns and Panzerfäuste. A number of tanks were hit by such bazookamen hiding in the trees. The French reacted by heavily and enthusiastically shelling the community, resulting in the destruction of the entire central portion of town, with the exception of the town hall and three or four additional buildings.

After this poor start, conditions deteriorated further. On the late afternoon of 29 April, more than ten days *after* the city was occupied, a fire broke out at the town hall, which was caused by a phosphorous bomb hidden inside a confiscated radio set. The building was completely destroyed and, later the same evening, two other suspicious fires also broke out. As well, there were 20 SS men still hiding in the ruins of the community, and a band of 150 Werewolves was menacing the suburbs. Among the desperadoes on the outskirts of town were Deputy Gauleiter Röhn and other senior party figures.

Amid these conditions, the French Military Government believed they had detected an incipient revolt, and they quickly came to the conclusion that the inhabitants were willing to burn down whatever was left of their town. Under such circumstances, the French First Army ordered the arrest of all males between the ages of sixteen and sixty. After they were rounded up, the arrestees were crammed into a POW enclosure without proper measures to ensure a supply of food or water. For two days, no provisions were available for some 700 prisoners. French troops experienced a delay in receiving their own rations, with the result that they pillaged the town's bakeries and butcher shops, in turn contributing to a local shortage of food. Then, as the problems in the city reached an apex, French combat troops promptly departed the scene – being reassigned to the front – and the entire mess was dumped into the lap of the Corps-level Military Government, which was inadequately staffed.[72]

With such horrific events unfolding in the rear, some French officers worried about the lack of security battalions needed to mop up occupied areas and guard communication lines, and an intelligence report in early May acknowledged that there was a definite problem in Baden, and that, 'in due course,' 'adequate action' would be necessary to break up German groupings.

In the Black Forest, the distinction between 'Maquis' and armed units not yet mopped up is not very clear. The latter description could best apply to the southern tip of the region, while near Lahr a preliminary reconnaissance effected April 27th showed an assemblage of well-armed Wehrmacht, Volkssturm, Werwolf, French miliciens, SS, etc. During its retreat, the German Army abandoned great quantities of ammunition and material of every kind, including complete radio sending and receiving equipment. The Lahr maquis which is said to number anywhere between 3000 and 6000 men, will not lack in supplies ... In view of eventual action against the Maquis of the Black Forest and elsewhere, notices have been posted setting a date and time for the surrender of isolated enemy troops; the population is informed that persons found to have aided all such in avoiding capture shall be tried before a military court and may be liable to capital punishment.

A further report on 20 May noted that 'the weakness of our effectives south of the line Fribourg–Donaueschingen seems to have forced the majority [of Were-wolves] into the region of Feldberg and Belchen, where they appear solidly established.'[73] Gradually, it began to dawn on the French (and everyone else) that the wooded regions of the prospective French Zone were relatively more contaminated with partisans than any other area in western Germany.

As it turned out, the concentrations of men in the Black Forest gradually broke down into smaller, uncoordinated bands, so that by June the French could report that, though the woods were still crawling with SS, Werwolf, and HJ fanatics, 'the existence of a full-fledged *maquis* organization is more and more doubtful.' None the less, groups of various provenance and composition continued to exist across the width and breadth of the forest, usually under the leadership of SS officers or party officials. Small bands of roughly one dozen guerrillas were active near Feldberg, Villingen, Lörrach, and Hammer-Eisenbach, and larger groups of fifty men lurked around the woods near Ober-münsterthal and Rottweil. At Emmendingen, a 'German *maquis*' comprising two twenty-four-man detachments was supplemented by a number of female 'avengers' sworn to inflict retribution in the name of relatives who had been victims of the war. A few of these diverse groups contained French SS men, or *miliciens*, who were typically regarded as the most desperate and savage of the die-hards. Their years of service to the Third Reich made the idea of surrender directly equitable with volunteering for an extended period of imprisonment and hard labour.[74]

Interference with French communications was one of the favourite diversions of these bands. Between Athingen and Haltingen, young boys blocked the road by spreading nails,[75] and in the western Black Forest a Werwolf detachment harassed the French by sabotaging their vehicles.

We really did some pretty dumb things [recalled a former member of the squad] ... We smashed dashboards to pieces, and poured sand by the handfuls into the gas tanks. After a while we decided to change our tactics and began to blow them up. We would ride our bikes the 12 miles to the Siegfried Line, where we knew our soldiers had planted land mines only a few days earlier. There were gaps and holes all over the place, and we could see exactly where the mines had been planted. This was crazy, but we would carefully pull the mines out and take off the lid. Then, holding the pin steady with two fingers, we would deactivate the bomb. Next, we would remove the detonator to take with us. We took hundreds of them and used them to blow up French military vehicles.[76]

A French military correspondent, Roger Baschet, met similar boys who claimed that Hitler was not dead, nor was his philosophy, and that all good Germans counted upon an eventual falling-out among the Allies. 'German youth has not disarmed,' he reported in a dispatch on 28 May. 'The children from five to twelve years do not hide their hate for the soldiers in khaki that they have learned to despise and whom they occasionally greet with stones or even with grenades. As for boys and girls aged thirteen to twenty, they have solid anti-French arguments and manifest their sentiments with a sometimes extraordinary violence.'[77]

The boldest groups attacked the French directly. Isolated vehicles were fired upon at night in remote districts, and, on 10 May, the French Miltary Government delegate at Hugelsheim was waylaid by uniformed SS men.[78] According to a Swiss report – Swiss journalists were the definitive source on conditions in the French Zone[79] – two French soldiers were ambushed and killed on 22 May in a small wood near Tuttlingen. Another report, probably apocryphal, suggested that, on 21 May, a HJ cadre destroyed a tank near Freudenstadt, causing five deaths, and that Freudenstadt was shelled in retaliation.[80] French soldiers reporting back from duty in early June admitted that a number of troops had been killed in Baden, mainly at the hands of 'small groups of SS troops who sifted into the area during the confused period following the German capitulation.'

German 'collaborators' were not safe either: at Mastetten, along the eastern fringe of the Black Forest, several heavily cloaked individuals assassinated the *Bürgermeister*; in the southern Baden town of Lörrach, a woman who had been friendly to French troops was murdered by Werewolves; and in a village near

Freiburg, yet another priest was killed by Werwolf agents. This latter case particularly shocked the archbishop of Freiburg, who was no friend of the French, but showed no patience for Nazi guerrillas either. 'How senseless and suicidal it is,' he admonished in a pastoral letter, 'still to try to engage the victorious army in rearguard skirmishes or, even worse, to hatch plans for revenge; and how criminal it is to terrorize the population from hideouts in the mountains and valleys of the Black Forest and to kill off inconvenient and hated men.'

Foreign workers attracted a particular degree of hostile attention. Near Wolfach, four French prisoners were found buried in a hole originally intended as a Werwolf weapons and supply dump. These unfortunates were killed on 30 March, apparently by a Gestapo officer assigned to dig the pit. At the village of Wiesenthal, in the southern Black Forest, Lieutenant Kurt Rahäuser ordered his Werwolf group to shoot eight Russian and Lithuanian workers. At Offenbach, a delayed-action bomb detonated on 4 May in a German military barracks, killing no fewer than 120 Russian 'Displaced Persons.'[81]

As a result of such outrages, French forces in the Black Forest were placed on a state of alert at night, and they swore 'pitiless justice' for anyone caught committing hostile acts. At Grimmelshofen, where there were a number of minor incidents, the French carried through a wave of arrests and imposed a severe curfew as a reprisal, ordering all Germans indoors during the two hours before midday.[82] Hostages were also shot at several locations, in one case as a reprisal for an escape by German prisoners of war.[83]

Sabotage and instances of murder gradually petered out as the Black Forest guerrillas were rolled up, or as they lost heart and went home. 'We soon realized that our efforts to resist had done absolutely nothing to change anything,' remembered one ex-Werewolf. 'A new era had begun and there was nothing we could do about it.' By the summer of 1945, anti-partisan patrols had found most of the weapons caches, radio posts, and Werwolf galleries, although sporadic attacks upon staff cars and convoys of trucks continued. Even as late as 1947, isolated French detachments and patrols came under occasional attack, and the French suspected that SS men still holed up in the mountains were in contact with small resistance groups in urban areas.[84]

The Alps

On the southern rim of the Bavarian plateau lay the mother of all redoubts, the supposed 'Alpine Fortress.' As the final point of refuge for the detritus of the Third Reich, this mountainous spine, despite its elevation, in effect became a sink-hole that sucked in the odds and ends of a dying regime. Before the region assumed this character, however, the concept of a 'National Redoubt' had been bandied about for over a year, and ideas had run along two parallel lines of thought.

First, there was genuine interest in the possibilities of such a fortress, owing to the topographical advantages of the area for defensive forces. Speculation about such matters began in 1943, when Italy capitulated and it seemed that German armies might be rapidly pushed up through the peninsula. At that time, German Army engineers began to study the possibility of an Alpine stronghold, and in the spring of 1944 preparations were begun to establish a final defence line for the Italian Front. In addition to various fortifications, a large system of storage facilities was also built. These storehouse areas were decentralized to inhibit destruction from bombing, and by the fall of 1944 they had become the main supply sources for the front in Italy. In September 1944, the OKW undertook a further study regarding defence possibilities in the Alpine massif, and in early 1945, after repeated urgings by Gauleiter Hofer of the Tyrol, Hitler authorized work on a system of fortifications. Although the Germans had neither the time nor the resources for a full-scale effort, there was considerable construction under way by the spring of 1945: work had begun on large bunkers in Bad Reichenhall and Berchtesgaden; a large underground installation was carved out of the mountains near Oberau; fieldworks were built in Voralberg, and bridges and roads were mined as a precaution against a possible Allied drive through Switzerland; new railway spurs and cable lines were established in various locations; and huge petrol, ammunition, and tank depots were laid near Innsbruck.

Since supply was recognized as the most crucial problem of any potential redoubt, underground facilities were built for factories at Ebensee, Kufstein, Hallein, Goetzis, Spittal, Theresienweise, and Kirchbichl, although it is probable that this effort was initiated to protect the plants from bombing and originally had little or nothing to do with the 'redoubt' concept. Some of these facilities turned out aircraft parts or V-weapons, but the two most important were the Steyr Works, which manufactured a cheap mass-produced line of small arms, specifically for the Volkssturm and for guerrilla fighters, and the Aschau facility in Oberbayern, which had been set up by I.G. Farben (working in concert with the RSHA) and was supposed to produce explosives for Werwolf operations. The Allies knew about the establishment of many such underground facilities through prisoner interrogations, aerial photography, and Ultra intercepts.[85] In February and March 1945, aerial coverage revealed no fewer than seventy instances of underground construction or the caching of stores.[86]

Quite aside from real plans and real preparations, however, the Germans were also fascinated by the mere threat of a fortified redoubt upon the psychology of the Allied Powers. They hoped that the Western Allies, left momentarily staggered from the hard punch delivered in the Ardennes, would work themselves into a panic about the possibilities of even tougher fighting in the mountains – a prospect that could potentially serve the aim of drawing Germany's enemies to the peace table. As early as the fall and winter of 1943, the Allies had begun receiving intelligence snippets on the possibility of a German redoubt in the Alps, and, in the summer of 1944, a German journalist named von Knyphausen defected to the West, carrying with him stories of Hitler's plans for a southern defensive fortress supporting guerrilla warfare all over Europe. Beginning in September 1944, an SD station in Voralberg began intercepting American reports from Switzerland, and, based upon such reports, the Tyrolean *Gauleiter*, Franz Hofer, developed his own plan for a real redoubt. Moreover, the Propaganda Ministry and the SD also began to feed phoney reports back towards the Allies, hoping thereby to weaken the will of the enemy. Several of the Swiss and Swedish papers carrying reports of the German *maquis* were previously pro-German, or had already been used as channels for Nazi-inspired rumours. By the spring of 1945, there was some suspicion among Allied intelligence officers that information on the redoubt and the underground was being deliberately planted, but, after the intelligence fiasco involved in the Ardennes Offensive, no one was willing to disavow any possibilities.[87]

Based upon this mélange of real and fictional intentions, the RSHA chief, Ernst Kaltenbrunner, was assigned the task in March 1945 of establishing a solid stronghold. Kaltenbrunner subsequently played a complicated double game, strengthening redoubt defences for a final battle, while at the same time establishing lines of contact with an Austrian clique in the RSHA, which wanted to set up an 'independent' Austrian regime as a means of either warding off Allied occupation or ensuring occupation on the easiest terms. Various senior figures in this clique were attempting to negotiate with the Allies, using the alleged redoubt as a bargaining-chip. Kaltenbrunner's heart, however, lay with the former plan of action, and by mid-April the leader of the 'peacemakers,' Wilhelm Höttl, reported to the Allies that Kaltenbrunner was being drawn back into the 'Hitler group' of intransigents. After Kaltenbrunner arrived in the area permanently, in late April, his actions suggest a policy of uncompromising stubbornness. His last messages to Berlin reported the deployment of special commando teams against the roads leading from northern Italy into the Alps; measures to accelerate arms production from the Steyr Works; and efforts to increase food deliveries from Bohemia for storage in the mountains.[88]

Kaltenbrunner's military counterpart was General Ritter von Hengl, the head of the National Socialist Leadership Corps (NSF) and a specialist in mountain warfare, who was appointed as commander of the redoubt in April 1945. Even despite his fanaticism, this officer was immediately overcome with severe doubts about his assignment. Many true believers, like von Hengle, had assumed that credible defences and reserves lay in the Alps; they, too, had been taken in by SD disinformation, which had been intended for the Western Powers, but had leaked back into Germany. When von Hengl actually arrived, however, he found that strong defensive positions had been prepared only on the southern and western edges of the mountains and that, since the penetration of the Western Allies across the Rhine had not been expected so soon, there were only a few tank obstacles and weak field fortifications along the northern approaches. In fact, as late as January 1945, when the Allies were still slogging away in the Ardennes, the OKH had actually cancelled plans to build defences in the Feldkirch–Bregenz district, and the construction of fieldworks in this area in February and March 1945 was apparently undertaken without the approval of the High Command. In addition, construction work had been hampered by the rocky soil of the region, and the transport of building materials such as concrete and blasting powder had been disrupted by intermittent enemy air attacks. It is true that *after* the American Twelfth Army Group breeched the Rhine, suggestions were taken to heart at Führer headquarters to fortify the northern access routes into the mountains, but the resulting directive was not issued until 20 April, two weeks before the final cessation of hostilities.[89] Moreover, the efforts to stockpile supplies and develop essential industries, however much had been achieved for a country in Germany's state, were simply insufficient, and the nation's capacity to do any more was nil. None the less, grandiose plans were still handed down from on high as late as 29 April, calling for the construction of new subterranean ammunition factories and aircraft plants.[90]

On top of these problems, the Alps were overrun by an influx of military and civilian bureaucrats – which the Bavarians and Austrians called contemptuously 'the northern invasion' – and before the southern field armies were pushed back, 90 per cent of the military manpower in the hills comprised rear-echelon personnel. 'I never knew there were so many staffs and so few fighting troops,' noted a bewildered gas-station attendant, as he watched long columns of German vehicles pushing into the mountains. 'No troops have come through, but staffs! Talk about staffs!' A few days before the end of the war, a desperate effort was made to block entrance into the mountains for anything except organized fighting units, and an attempt was also launched to send civilian refugees out of the mountains and back to their home areas in the enemy-occupied lowlands.[91] Both measures were too late to have much practical effect.

Hitler did order, in late April, that von Hengl disband all bureaux of the Wehrmacht not decisively engaged in the war, with the affected personnel being sent to the front, held for the Führer Reserves in the redoubt, or given dismissal papers preparatory to deployment as Werewolves in the enemy rear. In fact, a 'Special Representative' of the Führer Reserves, Lieutenant-Colonel Ehrnsperger, was appointed to tour the redoubt and choose suitable officers to serve as guerrillas. All personnel slated for such special operations were given phoney papers suggesting that they were former soldiers in the non-commissioned or service grades, and that they had been released on grounds of poor health. After discharge, the officers were supposed to report to local *Kreis* and *Gau* offices of the NSDAP in order to get help in immersing themselves in civilian life until military operations passed over the area in question. 'They shall then commence the active Werwolf struggle.'[92] A special SS Demobilization Centre was set up at Schleiseim for the same purpose.[93]

One invalided soldier who volunteered for this program later had little good to say about it. By this stage, he says, everything was being improvised by dilettantes. He personally received no special training, and, aside from civilian clothes and 300 marks, all he was issued was his own service pistol. Weapons and explosives, he was told, had already been cached and would be supplied by his contact, who was the widow of a former Gestapo official. This intrepid individual actually infiltrated American lines, disguising himself as a refugee, and three weeks after the capitulation, he visited his contact. She seemed unhappily surprised, and reported that four of his comrades had already been captured by the Americans. With this news, he quickly excused himself and gave up his embryonic career as a Werewolf. Many others must have done the same, he surmises, because he had heard of no successful attacks or sabotage. None the less, he claims that the enemy still reacted violently to the Werwolf, and that it became 'grounds for many murders and killings of innocents.'[94]

Worse than the problem of trying to forge rear-echelon officers and wounded troops into guerrilla forces, there was was no sign of the ten or twelve fresh Waffen-SS and Gebirgsjäger divisions which could perhaps have defended the passes into the mountains, and helped to maintain a Maoist-style 'liberated zone.' Within the hills, there were only several SS battalions in the Berchtesgaden and Fischhorn areas, plus several thousand troops in training, mostly Mountain Forces, at Hallein, Mittenwald, Villach, Salzburg, and Innsbruck. A 'Corps Group' set up in April to defend the northern passes could muster an effective combat strength of only 3,000 men. By a twist of fate, the thrust of Allied forces into central Germany had driven most of the SS divisions on the Western Front into Bavaria, Württemberg, and Baden, *but* they were severely constrained by Hitler's usual tactic of issuing do-or-die orders aimed at defending forward positions rather than favouring voluntary withdrawals to more defensible terrain. Thus, most of the SS and other German forces in the so-called Alpenvorland were nearly destroyed in the last half of April, before they had a chance to retreat. Along the northern edge of the mountains, two-thirds of this prospective defence force was wiped out before reaching the redoubt proper, and the remaining 300,000 men were dispersed to such an extent that they fled into the hills as a disorganized rabble. The same thing happened on the far side of the mountains, in northern Italy.[95] In the East, Sixth SS Panzer Army had been pushed into the Alps by the Russians, but Hitler had effectively demoralized it by blaming it for failing to force a breakthrough in Hungary in March 1945, and thereafter stripping the troops of their prized SS armbands. As Gerald Reitlinger notes, the rage and resentment thus induced 'effectively prevented the SS playing the role of fanatical candidates for self-immolation, the logical consequence of the role for which Hitler had always intended them.'[96]

With these factors in mind, it is not much of a surprise that the battles for the Alpine passes were lost by 3 May, and by the following day American forces had captured the entire Inn Valley, at the heart of the prospective redoubt. On 2 May, Gauleiter Hofer called for further combat to be restricted solely to the mountains, and this cessation of German control over towns and major thoroughfares in effect reduced the struggle to a guerrilla campaign. Some German officers were annoyed by Hofer's presumptive declaration, but it was a restricted form of mountain warfare, as demanded by Hofer, that nevertheless dominated the last few days of fighting. Meanwhile, some units in Army Group 'G,' manning the German southern front, argued that the capitulation in northern Italy on 2 May also applied to the Tyrol, and their representatives began to dicker with the enemy, being harassed in this process by fanatic SS die-hards. In fact, after early May, the headquarters of Army Group 'G' had itself come under direct American pressure, and, with no further line of retreat, their backs to the wall, they surrendered at Haar on 5 May.

Despite this agreement, many Waffen-SS detachments continued to defy the enemy, and at Wörgl there was heavy fighting *between* the SS 'Greater Germany' Division and a German Army garrison. SS officers claimed that their units were not subject to the compact undertaken by the German Army at Haar, and that they certainly did not regard the capitulation in Italy as having any validity in the Tyrol. Over the next few days, however, many of these formations negotiated their own surrender arrangements with nearby American units, and organized SS resistance came to an end on 8 May, when the leader of the SS in the Alps, Gottlob Berger, gave up his own Battle Group to the 101st Airborne Division.[97]

In a few areas, however, small bands of SS fanatics fled to the wilderness and elected to fight on, even after the arrival of enemy forces, and sometimes even after the piecemeal surrenders of their own units. In the Voralberg, adjacent to the Swiss frontier, the advancing French First Army feared trouble, and one officer groused about the conduct of local civilians, saying that 'they show not the slightest sign of penitence or desire to cooperate.'[98] Indeed, western Austria had a reputation as the heartland of Austrian Pan-Germanism and Naziism: the Austrian NSDAP had already emerged as the strongest party on the political landscape even by 1933, and there is reason to think that it subsequently picked up strength both before and after the union of Austria and Germany in 1938. Despite the Catholic confessional nature of the region, Alpine Austrians hoped for economic advantages from union with the Reich, and it is true that the Tyrol–Voralberg *Gauleiter*, Hofer, had looked after them well and had successfully protected local traditions and autonomy.[99] For these reasons, there was hope that Nazi guerrillas in the area might have some chance of getting support, and with this in mind Hofer's 'Werwolf Commissioner,' an Innsbruck factory manager named Töpper, began work in 1945 organizing such a movement.[100]

An American observer found Tyrolean peasants extremely tight-lipped about SS guerrillas in the surrounding hills; they may have wanted the partisans eliminated, but they were cognizant of the local appeal of National Socialism and wanted blame for betraying no one. A good example of these ambiguous loyalties came from the hills around Salzburg, where the anti-Nazi writer Luise Rinser – just released from prison – had gone to live with her aunt and cousin. Rinser was accustomed to seeing small groups of German soldiers in the surrounding countryside, and one evening she opened the door to two such fugitives, who claimed to be deserters fleeing the vengeance of the SS, but who still wanted to avoid the Americans as well. The older of the two men was injured, and in examining the wound in his arm Rinser determined that her two guests were actually members of the Waffen-SS, and that the older man had cut his blood-group tattoo out of his arm. Rinser pierced the boil over the wound with a knife and, although she briefly considered plunging the blade into her patient, in the long run she proved amazingly affable. On the following morning she led the two desperadoes to a woodshed, where she concealed and fed the pair for the following three days. Once her guests had departed, the older man left a 'thank you' note identifying himself as an SS-general.[101] If someone like Rinser took chances to protect such people, not much could be expected from the rest of the population.

Despite these ambiguities, however, western Austrian traditions also provided the basis for autonomist, anti-Nazi resistance movements, manned largely by Catholics, and the French were happy to find an anti-Werwolf rebellion under way at Oberstdorf, in the Allgau, the only such event encountered in the entire swath of German and Austrian territory that they overran. A small Home Guard had been formed at Oberstdorf in 1943, and by the outset of 1945 the leaders of this organization had decided that their proper duty was to save the Allgau rather than to facilitate useless Nazi efforts to defend it. Members of the Home Guard saw considerable reason for concern: their neighbourhood was home to various SS training units, and it also proved a magnet for Wehrmacht forces seeking to use the Iller Valley as a channel through which to reach the remote highlands of the Austrian Alps. As well, there was a Werwolf training camp at Langenwang, on the outskirts of Oberstdorf, which prepared partisans for action against the Red Army. For several months before the end of the war, the inhabitants of Oberstdorf watched, with increasing trepidation, as secret supply caches were laid away in the surrounding hills. They also saw SS, Gestapo, and SD men disappear into the mountains, which naturally convinced them that a *maquis* was being prepared around remote mountain huts in the region.

In order to prevent Oberstdorf from becoming the epicentre of an Alpine guerrilla war, the Home Guard seized the town in a lightning operation on the night of 30 April–1 May. A band of forty men, marked by armbands in the Bavarian national colours, seized key buildings and arrested the *Bürgermeister*, party functionaries, and SS officers. They also began mopping up groups of armed Nazi resisters in the surrounding highlands. After restoring a measure of order, the leaders of the Home Guard made contact with the French, who had reached Sonthofen, seven miles to the north, and tanks of the French First Army entered Oberstdorf without incident on the afternoon of 1 May. Since the French were short of manpower, they flouted standard SHAEF policy and for five days continued to make use of their German friends. Armed detachments from the Home Guard were employed to clean out the high valleys and pastures of the surrounding mountains; they collected more than 100 prisoners and a large amount of munitions and supplies before they were demobilized.

Even despite the best efforts of the Home Guard, however, not all potential troublemakers in the Allgau were rounded up. Small groups of Werewolves were seen traversing the Laterns Valley, particularly near the Bregenzerwald, and SS contingents were reported around Schoppernau and Schnepfau. It was rumoured that SS-Lieutenant-General von Witzenleben and members of 'Leibstandarte Adolf Hitler' were among these desperadoes. On 15 May, a French patrol stumbled upon a small band in a chalet near Schopernau, touching off an intense fire-fight. Four SS *maquisards* were captured, all slightly wounded; one SS man and a French colonial NCO were killed in the battle. A similar band was ensconced in mountain huts in the Arlberg Mountains, over the headwaters of the Inn River. This group contained approximately twenty-five SS and HJ cadres, armed and equipped for winter, and was led by several officers. The unit was involved in an ambush at St Christophe on 9 May 1945, where the SS suffered two dead and two others wounded. Later, in July 1945, the French convinced a former HJ member to act as a guide, and a final operation was launched against the band.[102]

Numerous groupings of German troops and Volkssturm soldiery remained at large in the Voralberg Alps well into the summer of 1945, some of them dressed in civilian clothes, and some of them concealed by the local population. Many of these outlaws soon tired of being hunted and wished to regularize their status with the French authorities, which in turn led to the conclusion that they were no longer much of a danger to security. Even those still on the run seemed, said the French, 'to be hiding and developing contacts rather than fighting.' None the less, there was a small number of hostile gangs, consisting mainly of HJ members. Such groups were active for several months, and carried out acts of minor sabotage. French authorities were not overly concerned, although they worried that such groups might provide a base for a later recrudescence of full-scale guerrilla warfare.[103]

Next door to the French zone of operations, in the Tyrol and the Salzburg Alps, units of the U.S. Seventh Army first overran the main mountain valleys, and then began to fan out and occupy every town and village up to the limits of human habitation. In some places, patrols penetrated the Alpine snowfields in order to check the remote mountain huts thought to be inhabited by SS guerrillas, and these detachments were aided by aerial detection. 'The partisan war against SS stragglers goes on,' noted a local German observer, two weeks after the ceasefire in the Alps.

These sweeps were accompanied by sporadic violence. On 6 May, HJ troops from Thuringia got into trouble at Mitterweissenbach: one boy was killed after he apparently fired a Panzerfaust at an American tank, and three other teenagers were killed in a fire-fight in a nearby woods. Several days later, a German officer shot an American soldier in Fügen. In direct retaliation, twenty Wehrmacht men were lined up against a wall and shot, and all the towns of the surrounding district, the Zillertal, were placed under a severe curfew.[104] On 13 May, a French correspondent with the American Seventh Army reported that several SS groups in the Salzburg Alps had refused to surrender, and were busy blowing up bridges and conducting nocturnal raids upon local villages in order to obtain food. Another report noted that SS troops were engaged in sniping around the Potschen Pass. Fifty miles to the northeast, guards from Mauthausen concentration camp fled after announcing to the prisoners that they were 'going to the mountains to work for the victory that would not fail to come.' There was some skirmishing between such bands and American patrols or armed detachments of liberated prisoners, and on the night of 23–4 May, the camp commandant, SS-Colonel Ziereis, was mortally wounded in a shoot-out. Other encounters were less confrontational. In the Ausser Land, the Americans used a German officer, General Fabiunke of the III Corps, as an intermediary between themselves and various detachments in the hills. For several weeks, Fabiunke travelled into the mountains, where he established contact with renegade groups of SS men and attempted to convince them to surrender.

As late as the summer of 1945, considerable concentrations of SS troops remained loose in the Salzburg and Tyrolean Alps, and the U.S. Third Army reported that they were 'receiving organized outside support in obtaining supplies.' In a few instances, such bands undertook minor sabotage, such as cutting telephone lines. On 21 July, a bridge near Unken, on the Austro–German frontier, was partially demolished by a charge of explosives. Some of these partisan groups boldly attempted to maintain contact. In September, American authorities discovered an elaborate signal system in the vicinity of Gastein, whereby semiphore and light blinkers were used to maintain communications between the mountain heights. The SS also maintained a reign of terror over the tiny villages clinging to the Alpine hillsides, and Deputy Tyrolean Gauleiter Herbert Parsons, hiding with one of these bands, promised in June 1945 that 'we will be back in three months.' Livestock moved into the high pastures for summer grazing was exposed to the depredations of the SS, and many peasants abandoned this ancient custom in favour of restricting their herds to safer fields. According to an American soldier stationed in the area, SS guerrillas even abducted women to accompany them back to their hide-outs, and those who displeased them were occasionally pushed over the mountain cliffs. On the other hand, young Tyrolean girls were often seen carrying food into the mountains, presumably for the provisionment of SS fugitives.

Stragglers from the SS 'Das Reich' Division offered a special problem. During the last days of the war, the commander of III SS Panzer Corps gave his adjutant orders to organize a Waffen-SS resistance movement, and the key role in this project was played by staff officers of the SS 'Das Reich' Division. Although the adjutant, SS-Lieutenant-Colonel Franz Riedwig, was captured on 3 May, thirty-five members of the SS 'Das Reich' were withdrawn from the division several days before the capitulation, reportedly in order 'to carry out a special assignment.' Their secret hide-out near St Ulrich was overrun by patrols of the U.S. 2nd Infantry Division in June 1945. A SHAEF report in the same month noted that, 'in various areas, small groups of SS troops continue to offer some kind of resistance. In the mountains near Kufstein hidden dumps of weapons, ammunition, explosives and food were discovered and remnants of two SS Panzer Division (*Das Reich*) are still hiding.'[105]

Similar goings-on unfolded across the old Austro–German border, high amidst the narrow ribbon of Alpine territory that framed the southern frontier of Bavaria. At Berchtesgaden, the Führer's summer residence and would-be capital of the National Redoubt, the NSDAP *Kreisleiter* managed to bomb a U.S. command post, injuring an American soldier, and German bands in the mountains fired upon French troops handling flank security for the Americans.[106] Several villages near the Tegernsee were under the thumb of survivors of the 17th SS Division, who menaced local townfolk and assaulted supposed 'collaborators.' After reports of such activity reached Sixth Army Group, a CIC unit and an armoured column were sent to quell these disorders.[107] At Walkenhausen, civilian officials built defence works against SS bands who had fled to the wooded hills nearby. They also took the unusual step of handing out Wehrmacht rifles to local French slave labourers as a means of creating a self-defence force.[108]

Efforts at terrorization by bands in the Bavarian Alps continued long after the end of the war. HJ detachments and whole battalions of SS troops continued to roam the mountains, disrupting the lives of local civilians. Bavarian mountaineers were usually unsympathetic. Although Naziism was born in Upper Bavaria and picked up early support in the region, owing mainly to the inhabitants' anti-communism and to the presence of right-wing activists drawn to Munich by the leniencies of the semi-authoritarian provincial regime, the party soon ran out of opportunities for local expansion. In fact, as the NSDAP established a presence in Germany as a whole, it became more difficult for it to disguise its radical and centralist tendencies, neither of which had much appeal in conservative and particularist southern Bavaria. Thus, even in the early 1930s, the party was barely able to improve on the percentage of the vote that it had garnered in its early heyday in 1924, and its vote-getting appeal slipped well below national averages.[109] Further resentments against centralization built up during the course of the Third Reich, and the townfolk of villages in the Alps were badly alienated by Nazi anti-Catholicism, which by 1941 had already given rise to an 'almost revolutionary mood.' This hate eventually erupted in a violent regionalist revolt in late April 1945. The Upper Bavarian 'Werwolf Commissioner,' Ernst Wagner, knew from the start that the seeds of a Nazi guerrilla movement were being scattered on rocky soil. He noted that any idea coming from Berlin was considered suspect and triggered intense anti-Prussian sentiment.[110]

It is no surprise, therefore, that as the spring of 1945 wore on into the summer, Bavarian mountain folk complained vigorously about being waylaid at night by hungry SS bandits, or about nocturnal attacks on villages, during which SS men held surgeons at gunpoint and forced them to remove blood-group tattoos. In turn, the Americans recruited sympathetic Bavarian guides and mountain climbers to help them search the high country, and anti-partisan patrols scoured the mountains. One Nazi band was ambushed in mid-June, at Prien, while in the process of raiding a farm, and in the autumn the Americans caught up with an outfit of fifty SS men, who were operating a communications network and had established a means of removing tell-tale blood-group markings. In July 1945, the new police chief of Munich, Baron von Godin, formed a 'Special Corps' to battle SS stragglers. Von Godin knew how to handle Nazis, since he was the same police official who had crushed the Beer-hall Putsch in 1923.

By the autumn of 1945 the recalcitrants in the hills had begun to organize wholly new resistance movements: wayward HJ (with homes in the Soviet Zone) identified themselves with the 'Edelweiss' label, while certain SS fugitives organized 'the Grey Wolves.' Nazi propaganda efforts in Bavaria showed signs of being organized on a regional basis, and ragtag desperadoes from 377th SS Brigade infiltrated Munich in order to circulate underground leaflets and post placards. A typical example of this rude propaganda, from September 1945, described the pained reaction of the German soldier who came home to find German women fraternizing with foreigners, especially those with dark pigment – 'It took them five years to beat the German soldier, but a German girl can be had in five minutes ... Just wait, the time will come when even the Negroes will desert you.' Other Alpine resisters contented themselves with the customary Nazi diversion of beating up Jews and, in the autumn of 1945, two young men – one of them a HJ veteran of the Battle of Berlin – were arrested after they attempted to convince some discharged sailors to dynamite a Jewish convalescent home in Mittenwald. During the same period, a group of young men attacked a march by concentration-camp survivors in Garmisch–Partenkirchen, and several of these assailants were found to be armed with explosives.[111] An American intelligence officer estimated at the beginning of August 1945 that there were still 10,000 to 15,000 SS men at large in Bavaria, and in September the Bavarian government reported more than a thousand instances where farmsteads had been raided by armed German bandits or guerrillas.[112]

Most of the Alpine guerrilla groups in Bavaria disintegrated during the winter of 1945–6. The Bavarian minister-president, Wilhelm Högner, was convinced that large bands of Nazi partisans were still active as late as the spring of 1946, and that these groups were responsible for a number of death threats against Bavarian civil officials, including Högner himself.[113] In truth, however, winter in the mountains was so cold and inhospitable that the rigours of the season made guerrillas dependent on the populated valleys controlled by the Allies. The chief of staff of the U.S. Third Army announced in January 1946 that the last big SS partisan groups had disintegrated, and this statement was confirmed by extensive raids undertaken in the spring of 1946. Officers who coordinated these sweeps found that there were no longer any large, well-organized SS bands in the Bavarian Alps, and it was established 'that whatever strength the Edelweiss clique boasted was centered in the towns and not in the mountains.' Even then, however, it was concluded that small groups and fanatical individuals were still running loose, and such elements continued to turn up as late as the summer and autumn of 1946, particularly HJ gangs near Bad Reichenhall and a band of SS men on the Austrian frontier near Rosenheim.[114]

While the last German units in the western Alps were either dissolving or breaking down into guerrilla bands, elements in the eastern mountains were still fighting for their lives, retreating in the face of the Yugoslavs and the Soviets. In particular, elements of General Löhr's Army Group 'E' desperately beat off the advancing Titoists, all the while hoping to back into Allied forces in the German rear. Along this front, guerrilla warfare became the standard tactical doctrine. Fierce fighting in southern Carinthia continued until 15 May, when the Third Yugoslav Army issued its final battle report. Even then SS and Ustasche bands refused to surrender and engaged in desperate last-ditch struggles. Meanwhile, British forces from Italy had begun to displace the Yugoslavs in southern Austria – Carinthia was formally part of British Zone in Austria – and it was they who were left to deal with the remnants of these die-hard forces. According to British reports, ad hoc bands of SS men were still running loose in the vicinity of Moelltal and Lienz, even as late as the summer and fall of 1945. Southern Austrian civilians told a Swiss Red Cross team in June 1945 that 'many thousands of SS are yet free, fleeing in civilian clothes or hiding in the mountains, still armed – and they'll be back.'[115]

Despite this comment, there may have been some degree of local sympathy for Nazi stragglers and partisans, and certainly, at Millstadt, the British in late May 1945 captured a young woman, formerly in the BdM, who was happily carrying food to SS bands in the hills.[116] Carinthia and its next-door neighbour Styria had both been strongholds of the Austrian NSDAP before 1938, mainly because long-standing differences between German- and Slavic-speaking population groups had prompted a sense of 'borderland nationalism,' which in turn had assumed a Pan-German hue. The cession of Lower Styria to Yugoslavia in 1918–9 was especially resented, and its reincorporation in 1941 (as a consequence of the German invasion of Yugoslavia) was greatly appreciated. A British intelligence assessment in May 1945 mentioned that 'Pan-Germanism and the Marchland mentality' still lay not far below the surface of the Carinthian/ Styrian consciousness, and that contemporary Yugoslav encroachments could well cause a recrudescence of such feelings. It should also be noted that the southeastern corner of Austria had been tailor-made for Nazi penetration: living conditions and infrastructure development lagged behind Austrian averages; the Depression had hit these areas with a particular vengeance; there were substantial pockets of Protestants in Middle Carinthia and Upper Styria, and in Carinthia even some of the Catholic clergy had been pro-Nazi.[117]

The Carinthian hills were also a temporary home to a polyglot assortment of

Axis collaborators and allies, most of them seeking to escape vengeful pursuers back in their homelands, and most probably bereft of any sympathy from the local populace. In late May, the notorious 'Bando Spollero,' made up of several scores of Italian Fascist and German stragglers, and led by a former marshal in the Alpini, was believed either to have entered Carinthia or to be lingering along the southern border. This group had earlier been engaged in guerrilla warfare in Friuli–Venezia Giulia, where it had caused at least seven British and Italian casualties through sniping.[118] In addition, there were several thousand pro-German Cossack and Caucasian troops on the run in the Drau Valley, all terrified by the expectation that capture by the British would be followed by repatriation and eventual death, and, for the same reason, there were a number of Hungarian Army and 'Arrow Cross' militia troops still roaming the mountains. Many such bands were mounted, and the damage done to pasture meadows by their horses was a considerable factor hindering recovery of the economy in rural areas of southern Austria. These types of fugitive groups were more interested in evasion than in the active harassment of the enemy, and anti-partisan patrols rarely found themselves involved in gunplay. 'In the summer weather,' remembered one British officer, '[such forays were] more of a pleasure than a business,' and they provided endless opportunities for sightseeing and hunting.[119]

There were, however, some isolated cases of hostility. In the early days of the occupation, there were several cases of sniping and a moderate level of line-cutting. Later in the year, a number of decapitation wires were stretched, including one at Millstadt that was struck by a British vehicle. In 1946, bullets were found scattered with the points upwards over roads in the Lavamund area. The British considered this a successful form of sabotage, noting that one unit suffered thirty punctured tires in a single week. In addition, underground Nazis spread propaganda and held secret meetings. At St Viet, secret NSDAP assemblies were convened in an unoccupied room in the town hall, anti-Nazis were threatened, and the entire village was identified as a centre of continuing Nazi sentiment. At Schwarzach, the work of village government was hampered by a warning to the mayor's interpreter that she would have her throat cut unless she left town. In July, several rallies of Nazi activists were held on Gerlitzen Mountain, in an Alpine hut that had been used in pre-Anschluss days for gatherings of a similar sort. Meetings were also reported in Klagenfurt and Maria Worth.[120]

Events in the mountainous terrain of western and northern Styria also comprised an interesting story. Styria was one of the last areas in the Reich to be occupied, and as a result there was an opportunity for some bitter internecine feuds among the Austrians themselves to flare up. At the village of Hartberg, SS detachments terrorized the inhabitants of the town and, when they were finally forced to retreat, they grabbed twenty-nine prisoners from the local jail and slaughtered them. A type of vicious guerrilla war between the SS and the Austrian anti-Fascist resistance sputtered on for several days after the official capitulation. In fact, Franz Lindmoser, one of the chief leaders of the Styrian patriotic resistance, was killed a day after the official ceasefire. He lost his life in a skirmish with retreating SS troops.[121]

Once the Red Army arrived, with the Bulgarian First Army in tow, they reported sporadic difficulties. The NKVD noted that, as soon as Soviet and Bulgarian units crossed the Austrian frontier, 'there was a considerable step up in diversionist-terrorist activity on the part of German intelligence agents established in our rear, supplied with explosives and guns, whose task was to carry out diversion and the murder of Red Army soldiers.' A Werwolf 'Ranger Commando' was especially active north of Bruck an der Lafnitz, where a 'great number of Bolshevists' were wiped out, and the Styrian HJ chief, Edouard Danziger, was killed in action. At Graz, on the southeastern edge of the Alpine massif, German Army officers who surrendered the city on the night of 8–9 May made clear that they could not vouch for the conduct of SS units in the area, and as a result, the Soviets vested extraordinary powers in the Town Major, declaring that 'drastic measures [were under way] against activities interfering with Red Army operations.' Unlike the cases in Vienna and Lower Austria, the Soviets dissolved the local provincial government and only re-established it on 15 May. On the same day, they also appealed to local townspeople to reveal the locations of soldiers yet fighting Soviet forces, and to avoid reading pamphlets distributed by such elements. Bulgarian units in southeastern Austria also reported in mid-May that they were still battling recalcitrant SS troopers.[122]

In the final analysis, however, the Soviets and Bulgarians did not tire themselves too badly in chasing Nazi guerrillas. Even though the bulk of Styria was overrun by the Soviets (and their lesser allies), according to agreements being negotiated in far-off London, the province actually lay within the formal British sphere of control and would probably have to be soon evacuated by Soviet units. Bearing in mind that their presence in the region was likely a brief one, Soviet commanders did not bother re-establishing civil administrations in localities such as Judenburg, and, worse yet, they informally advised their enemies to make themselves scarce, thus saving themselves the trouble of rounding them up. SS bands found it relatively easy to stay out of Soviet hands, although they clashed with gangs of Russian deserters who had also escaped into the mountains. For months after the capitulation, the eastern Alpine valleys rang with the sound of shots as rival bands fought each other and terrorized the Styrian peasantry.

Not surprisingly, British troops who arrived in the summer of 1945 soon heard news of these scattered SS bands. There were repeated complaints about SS troops in the Seetaler Alpen, and there was also a report of sixty SS men in the Fensteralpen, south of Löben. In the latter case, a police patrol was sent into the hills, but failed to track down the guerrillas.[123]

Most Werwolf groups in Styria either were destroyed by the Soviets or dissolved themselves, particularly after their chief, Franz Steindl, was killed fighting the Russians.[124] However, the Soviets failed to eradicate an active HJ cell near Bruck an der Mur. These Werewolves were believed responsible for at least a dozen mysterious fires in the first months after the war. If anything, this gang became more audacious after the British arrived. During one week in late August, there were five separate instances of incendiarism, three of which were directed at military barracks, although the buildings were empty at the time and little material damage was done. Even as late as November 1945, a sawmill in this area was deliberately destroyed by fire.[125]

In the late summer and fall of 1945, a rash of nasty incidents occurred in Upper Styria. There were wire cuts near Judenburg, several decapitation wires were discovered near Kalwang, and the tires of a British jeep were blown out by sniper fire. Near St Lambrecht, several occasions were noted in which a band of armed men fired at British troops and Austrian civilians, and in the same village two women had their hair cut as a punishment for fraternizing with British soldiers. In Graz, which the British occupied at the end of July 1945, Nazi leaflets circulated and swastikas were frequently daubed upon the walls and pavements of the town. However, British Field Security could be excused for displaying a less than critical concern. When three men were arrested in late August for painting swastikas, British investigations suggested that the culprits were not genuine Nazis at all, but provocateurs connected with the OSNA, the Yugoslav secret police. The Yugoslavs apparently believed that the British were prone to pay little attention to denazification, and such stunts were their way of providing their ally with an incentive for intensifying his efforts.[126]

Forests in Brandenberg

Before concluding this whirlwind account of various Werwolf strongholds, we should perhaps also look briefly at the regions in east–central Germany that were overrun by the Soviets, and which eventually became parts of the Soviet zone of occupation. The worst trouble spots in this area were the extensive pine forests of Brandenburg, particularly in districts adjacent to Berlin, like the Havelland and Mittelmark, where German troops who had escaped the capital in April and May 1945 went into hiding. Army Group 'Vistula' surrendered on 2 May, followed by the Ninth and Twelfth armies three days later, whereafter all bands in the forests were strictly illegal.[127] Brandenburg offered mixed benefits for guerrillas; it was relatively waterlogged, but, on the other hand, it was also flat and was covered by the extensive network of roads leading to and from Berlin. Like the thin woodlands of Schleswig–Holstein, the main advantage of the Brandenburgian timberlands was availability: these forests looked inviting to German troops bypassed by the Soviet advance upon Berlin, whose only other alternative was to pass into captivity in the hands of an unforgiving foe.

On the afternoon of 3 May, one such band of German stragglers was observed in the Forst Schönwalde, immediately north of Berlin, and a fifty-man Soviet patrol was sent to ferret out these recalcitrants. In the course of sweeping the woods, a German captain dressed in civilian clothes was almost immediately captured, and he calmly revealed to the Soviets that he commanded a small group of ten soldiers. The Soviets resumed their sweep, believing their task a relatively easy one, but suddenly one of their squads clashed with a large detachment of armed Germans, who outnumbered the Soviets. The size of the band was estimated at seventy to eighty men, not the ten reassuringly described by the captured officer. In heavy fighting, twenty-two Germans were killed and thirty-five captured, at minimum loss to the better-armed and better-organized Russians. However, a Soviet patrol leader was wounded and evacuated to a Soviet military hospital. Further pursuit of the German band produced sixteen more POWs, who eventually gave up without resistance.[128]

Similar problems cropped up in the woods immediately south of Berlin, particularly the swamplands of the Spreewald. Marshal Ivan Koniev, who advanced upon the Reich capital from the southeast, later noted that his forces' lines of communication were crossed by 'odd groups of Germans ... roving here and there.' When Koniev journeyed to the command post of General Rybalko, commander of Third Guards Tank Army, on the morning of 24 April, the column was terrorized by German bands. 'Enemy gangs that had not surrendered or been disarmed were still lurking in the nearby woods,' noted Koniev. 'They were particularly numerous between Fetschau and Lübben, where the woods were denser. I had good luck all along. Several times our cars were fired upon from the woods, but, thank heavens, we did not run directly into any hostile group, although there were cases when others did.' Near Luckenwalde there were 12,000 dispersed German troops, who harassed Russian lines of communication and hid out in local pine forests, some of them provisioned by neighbouring German families.[129] A British observer noted that 'hardly a day passed on which the Russians were not sniped and local roads cut.'[130]

These guerrilla bands were still active several weeks later. The *Bürgermeister* of a small town near Luckau noted that fires were seen frequently in the nearby woods, which he attributed to Werwolf arsonists. In fact, a suspected Werwolf posing as a medical doctor was actually captured in this village. When he was searched, hidden documents were found indicating that a secret SA rendezvous point existed in a woods near the town.[131]

The presence of large numbers of dispersed German troops in the woods around Berlin continued to pose a problem for the Red Army long after the war ended. Almost a week after the capitulation, several hundred thousand Wehrmacht troops were still roaming loose through the forest, many in civilian clothing, and the 105th NKVD Frontier Regiment reported on 11 May that huge numbers of soldiers in mufti were streaming out of the Berlin amid columns of civilian refugees. A good percentage of these men were simply deserters, many of whom eventually concluded that they would be unable to reach safety. Once they grew sufficiently hungry, they attempted to regularize their status by registering with the Soviet command. On the other hand, a violent minority continued to offer armed resistance. In mid-May, a band of fifty heavily armed soldiers and Volkssturm men were spotted by Soviet aircraft in a woods near Nauen. After surrounding the forest with tanks, artillery, and infantry, the Soviets ran down most of these desperadoes, although at least one Red Army man was killed in the resulting skirmish. A beaten mob of some twenty survivors was overrun by a Polish unit several days later. NKVD troops attached to one formation alone, the forty-seventh Army, engaged in seven armed clashes during May 1945, leaving seventy-eight Germans and two Russians dead. On 28 May, *Tass* announced that bands of German stragglers were still running loose, waging guerrilla warfare against isolated Red Army platoons and plundering remote hamlets for provisionment. Sometimes these units disguised themselves in Soviet uniforms, although there were also numerous groups of Red Army deserters in the woods, so that outlaws in Soviet tunics were not necessarily Germans guilty of dissimulation.[132]

As late as 1946 Soviet security reports continued to describe small 'bandit' groups, whose members lived in the forest and were only gradually rolled up by Russian patrols and German police. At the village of Bremdorf, an NSDAP leader living in the nearby woods was tracked down by the NKVD and accused of 'leading agitation against the Red Army,' and in the suburbs of Eberswalde a five-man German outfit was caught disguising itself in Soviet uniforms and 'trying to defame the Red Army and incite hate among Germans.' Both German gangs and bands of Russian deserters and Vlassovites pillaged the population. In January 1946, the British Military Government complained that supply convoys travelling along the Hanover–Berlin *Autobahn* were repeatedly ambushed and looted as they approached the German capital.[133]

Schwarzenberg

The only other region in the Soviet Zone plagued by guerrilla warfare was the rolling slope of the Erzgebirge (Ore Mountains), which formed the easternmost extension of a network of central German hills that also included the Thuringian Forest and the Harz. The Erzgebirge marked the southern border of the Soviet Zone, but this not an area that received much attention towards the end of the war, mainly because the focus of both sides was on more important sectors of the front, such as Berlin or Prague. The Western Allies and Soviets directed secondary forces towards this region, while the Germans arrayed 'commandos' in the vicinity of Zwickau, and took measures 'to exterminate the enemy in the Bautzen–Kamenz–Konigsbrück–Bischoffswerda region through guerrilla warfare.' In early May, the Russians noted the presence of a 150,000-man German pocket near Kamenz, but, since it was hostile even after other sectors of the front had surrendered, the Red Army was content to sit back and pound the area with long-range artillery.[134]

After the war, the Soviets were so disorganized, and so engaged elsewhere, that they failed even to close up uniformly to the American line of occupation in the mountainous region of Schwarzenberg. As a result, after American patrols withdrew in mid-May, there was a gap of about 600 square miles, populated by 250,000 people, that was controlled by none of the occupying powers until the end of June 1945. The absence of any authority in this area was problematic because it had formed an early and consistent base of support for the NSDAP. The region's socio-economic character had much in common with its neighbour, Thuringia: it was heavily industrialized, but businesses consisted mainly of small firms, particularly textile producers. There were high levels of unemployment even in the 1920s, owing to the collapse of the region's export industries, and farmers in the area typically owned small plots of land. All of this had proved a near-perfect mix for the local rise of National Socialism. In addition, the area had once been characterized as 'red,' but the fracturing of German Social Democracy after the First World War had eroded this temperament.[135]

By May and June 1945, conditions within the region were desperate: a Swiss physician who passed through the district reported that it was plagued by famine; that the population had been doubled by the presence of refugees and dispirited German troops; and that the only authority were some armed 'Antifas.'[136] Given the lack of any external authority in the area, it was a natural magnet for German troops and SS men whose surrender had not been accepted by the Americans, and who so far had not been overrun by the Soviets. Martin Mutschmann, the *Gauleiter* of Saxony, was protected by these bands, and was only captured on 16 May, during a raid on his mountain cabin by armed members of an 'Antifa.' According to the BBC, 'something like a civil war' developed between German troops and civilians – 'These Germans of no-man's land are getting in a pretty desperate state searching for food. They come into towns and villages where they are by no means welcome. They are plundering the countryside and terrorizing the population. It is possible that either we or the Russians will have to take some firm steps.'[137] In truth, local civilians were desperately casting around for help: typically, churchmen appealed to the Americans, hoping that they would occupy the region, while communists looked to the Red Army for security and provision of food. In early June, the Soviets dispatched a force to restore order near Chemnitz, wiping out 'a German gang engaged in sabotage,' and on 21 June they finally began a full-scale occupation of the Schwarzenberg district.[138] Commandants of Soviet garrisons in Saxony reported by the summer of 1945 that there were few further signs of trouble (except from their own undisciplined men), and a security regiment along the Bavarian frontier slowly re-established order by prohibiting illegal passage across the interzonal boundary, and by suppressing small nests of Nazis. However, near Zwickau, where Soviet troops replaced American forces on 19 June, a handful of German snipers remained active, and several Russian troops were shot and killed.[139]

In summing up, it is really not very surprising that a considerable number of German soldiers and civilians gathered in remote areas under conditions conducive to partisan warfare. While it is well known that much desultory fighting followed the end of the First World War, it is not so widely assumed that the ending of the Second World War was also ragged and uneven.[140] However, both before and after 8 May 1945, there was a considerable number of pseudo-guerrilla groups scattered throughout Germany and Austria, a few of them hostile. The post–First World War period is always remembered as the 'Age of the Armed Bands,' but the months (and years) around the end of the Second World War also qualify for such a description. It is true that the bands in this latter period were less organized than the parallel groups from 1918 to 1923; it is true that they were generally more limited to the woods and rural areas than were their antecedents; and it is true that did not make as much political impact as their predecessors; none the less, they were real and they had their own kind of importance.

These forlorn Nazi partisans were not supported by a population that was seeking desperately a return to normalcy, or at least that they were not supported by most German civilians. This made it difficult for the guerrillas to provision themselves or get vital tidbits of information, at least not without exercising coercion. Journalist James Wellard, reporting from the rear areas of the Ninth

Army on 4 May 1945, noted, 'We have German burgomasters complaining about the raids on their towns by SS men who are still holding out in the mountains and forests. These SS and Werewolf bands descend on little towns and villages, strip the place of food and make away before American troops can be called.'[141] This was hardly a process with which any 'freedom movement' would have wanted itself associated. On the other hand, a partisan movement at this tender stage of development could hardly have expected to have had large numbers of sympathizers knocking at its door, proffering help or seeking to join. And the truth is that there was a minority of civilians who did voluntarily aid German bands. Swiss observers noted in late May 1945 that the slow security sweep of wooded areas was in 'some regions,' particularly in the French and Soviet zones, being 'made more difficult by the behavior of the civil population, which continues to make common cause with the National Socialists.'[142]

As for the strength of the guerrilla groups, they obviously reached their peak in April and May 1945, when there were literally hundreds of thousands of desperate troops roaming the woods and mountain pasturelands. However, a few remnants of this diaspora continued to remain in formation even as late as 1946, and U.S. Forces G-2 suggested that some bands were *still* in the process of coalescing at the beginning of 1946.

These groups [they reported] have taken on an aspect of Nomad bands and are living for the most part in mountainous and otherwise inaccessible terrain. There are indications that they have sufficient stores of arms, munitions and food to last them for a considerable period of time ... Indications are that at the present time, these groups, as well as individuals who for the most part are automatic arrestees, are moving southward into Bavaria. It is not yet known what their final destination is or whether these groups have a pre-arranged rendezvous. It has been reported to this Headquarters that in several instances these groups or organizations are well led by men previously trained in espionage and sabotage.[143]

The Americans had not determined whether these bands were being regularly replenished through the recruitment of new members, although, given the fact that we hear little of them after 1946, this seems unlikely.

In the final analysis, we can conclude that the Third Reich left in its wake the necessary cadres for a guerrilla war in the forests and hills, and that some of these elements held on for a protracted period. However, they lacked the psychological and moral climate in which to wage a successful partisan war. Rather than being dynamic groups pledged to the 'liberation' of their homeland, they were really just the ultimate 'stragglers,' isolated in enemy territory, but now with no German lines to regain.

6

The Werwolf along Germany's Periphery

As in Germany proper, Werewolves were also sporadically active in German borderlands populated at least in part by peoples of Germanic origin. The pattern of such resistance also followed the general tendency within Germany itself, where the Western Allies discovered that eastward penetration into the country corresponded with greater evidence of underground warfare and resistance. Werewolfism, it seems, thrived better in an eastern climate.

The limits of this chapter are determined by a consideration of territories with German-speaking inhabitants that still lay outside the Reich's boundaries in mid-1938, that is, after the Anschluss with Austria, but before any further incorporation of foreign lands. In all of these regions, 'Germanness' was an issue. Some of them had been parts of Germany until 1919; the remainder had been stripped away from Austria in the same year. All of these territories had been incorporated into nations with non-German majorities, so that the status of the German language and of German culture was in some measure of doubt. The rise of the Third Reich made the German minorities in these various regions restive, and the group in the South Tyrol was particularly influenced by the Anschluss, which gave Greater Germany a direct border with Italy. In all these cases, the threat of Nazi German physical expansion seemed to empower neighbouring ethnic Germans and gave them a voice and an importance beyond that merited by their numbers. Of course, there were German-speaking Social Democrats, Communists, and liberals in these districts – elements which despised the Nazi regime – but it would be fair to say that, for the most part, a considerable gravitational attraction developed between the minorities and a resurgent and newly proud Germany. The one exception to this general category was a huge swath of the Reich and its attendant population group annexed by Poland in 1945. In this case, local Germans had lived firmly *within* the bounds of the Reich during the interwar and wartime periods, so they were not

Volksdeutsche (or 'foreign Germans'), but full-scale Reichsdeutsche ('domestic Germans'). These provinces had been at least partly inhabited by Germans since the Middle Ages, and had been parts of Prussia since the eighteenth century or earlier.

Alsace–Lorraine

For simplicity's sake, we shall start our review at the French and Belgian border territories and rotate clockwise around the exterior of Germany, leaping to southern Denmark, then to the Reich's eastern borderlands, and finally on to the Alpine frontier between Italy and Austria. In most of western Europe, the Allies were joyously welcomed by local civilians, and the liberators encountered little guerrilla opposition (quite unlike the Soviet experience in the eastern half of the continent). However, the Allies noticed a change in the tone of their reception as they reached the eastern areas of France populated in part by German-speakers. The regions of Alsace and northeastern Lorraine were the shuttlecocks of European geopolitics, having been German in the Middle Ages, then conquered by France in the sixteenth and seventeenth centuries, recovered by Germany in 1871, regained by France in 1919, reannexed by the Reich in 1940, and finally, with the advance of the Allies, about to fly back in the opposite direction again, with the French recovering control. Much of the population was thoroughly sick of this folly, and there is some evidence that its real sentiments were neutral, and that it was equally resentful of all the combatants who seemed intent on fighting their way through an otherwise quiet corner of Europe.[1] On the other hand, many Alsatian and Lorrainais autonomists had definitely hitched their wagons to the German star, and the Nazi regime had done its best to change the character of the population, deporting more than 100,000 ethnic Frenchmen, Jews, and pro-French sympathizers, and replacing them with Reichsdeutsche, who served particularly as minor officials. American troops, without much understanding for the delicacies of this situation, simply regarded the population as unfriendly and not worthy of their trust.[2] A private in the U.S. 10th Infantry Regiment later explained: 'Up till now, the civilians had always been on our side and tickled to death to see us – but Lorraine was different. Even before we caught some of them actually helping the enemy, we were aware of their hostility. It was something you could sense. They were sullen and tried to ignore us as pointedly as possible. They accepted our passage through a town or our presence in one with a sullen, resentful resignation. Some of them were caught harbouring German agents and soldiers in civilian clothes.'[3] General Grow of the U.S. 6th Armoured Division told his men, in frank fashion, 'we are in enemy country and must watch all civilians and treat them as enemy.'[4]

Dirty looks from the local population were an acceptable manifestation of hostility, but sabotage and aid to the enemy were not. There were numerous cases of line-cutting, and at Nousviller, where there was a rash of wire-cuts in early December, the *Bürgermeister* was warned that, unless the town offered up the guilty parties, he personally would be seized as a hostage. In several locations near German-held Kolmar, civilians were suspected of signalling information to German artillery gunners, and two villages, Ostheim and Guemar, were forcibly evacuated as an Allied reprisal. Near Arzwiller, a bomb was placed in a railway tunnel, although an American rail guard discovered the device before it could be detonated by a train. At Falkenburg, two civilians were caught on 23 November trying to booby-trap a jeep. There were also a few cases of sniping, particularly by isolated German officials and NSDAP members. At a small village near Briey, Nazi *francs-tireurs* sniped at Allied sentries, and a security sweep of the area brought in fifty NSDAP functionaries.[5]

One of the most serious problems in Alsace occurred in the provincial capital of Strasbourg, which was captured by French forces on 24 November, and soon became the focal point of a full-scale international incident. French soldiers quickly noted the absence of French flags in liberated Strasbourg, as well as the lack of a friendly reception from the inhabitants. Of course, the ugly fact was that the character of the city had changed dramatically since its occupation by the Germans four years earlier; in a town with a 1939 population of 200,000, more than 40,000 people had been expelled, and a large number of German civilians had arrived in order to take charge of German administration in Alsace. Moreover, as a result of the rapid advance of Allied forces, there were also 10,000 to 15,000 German troops stranded in the city, many of whom had changed into civilian garb. A hurried attempt was made to round up these elements, but many Germans remained at liberty and engaged in a series of fierce sniping attacks against Allied troops, perhaps being aided in this by sympathetic Alsatians. The regimental history of an American unit noted that sniping was still extremely heavy on 29 November: 'it was not safe to traverse the streets unaccompanied or unarmed, especially at nights.'[6] General Jacques LeClerc, the commander of the victorious 2nd French Armoured Division, was forced to shift his headquarters three times because of such dangers, and two of his men were killed at night by German assassins disguised as policemen. In another case, an Algerian soldier was stopped by a man in civilian clothes who asked for a light, and who then killed the Spahi at point-blank range while the latter reached for his lighter. On 9 December a French military chaplain was ambushed on the outskirts of the town; reports on his death specifically mention that he was killed by submachine-gun fire let loose by 'enemy soldiers operating in the rear.'

Notoriously impetuous and undisciplined, LeClerc rashly issued an edict on 25 November to 'suppress all activity of francs-tireurs.' After a deadline two days hence, said LeClerc, five German hostages would be executed in retaliation for every shooting by a sniper or *franc-tireur.* Moreover, LeClerc announced that, after the forthcoming deadline, all persons found in possession of arms, all German soldiers in civilian clothes, and all persons sheltering or aiding snipers would also face summary execution. LeClerc and the civil authorities in Strasbourg believed that the German special services had deliberately left a number of stay-behind agents in Alsace, and that more were currently in the process of infiltrating French lines. This threat seemed to justify especially repressive measures.

LeClerc's edicts considerably exceeded SHAEF's own guidelines for reprisals, particularly since they implied the execution of German POWs, and SHAEF was thereby forced to release a declaration reiterating that it operated strictly along the guidelines of international law: 'In certain circumstances, for instance, if civilians posted on roofs shoot at soldiers, the measures envisaged by General LeClerc can be undertaken in conformity with the Geneva Convention. But they cannot be applied to prisoners-of-war.' The 2nd French Armoured Division was also rushed out of Strasbourg en route to further operations, through which the Allies hoped to imply that LeClerc's edict was automatically cancelled. While this was a wise move diplomatically, it foisted a tremendous burden upon the local civilian authorities, who signalled on 28 November that the bulk of LeClerc's forces had already left the city and that, because of this, it was 'urgent' that 'at least an infantry regiment' be deployed in order to maintain order. American troops were subsequently sent to garrison the town. Four days later, the French government issued a communiqué explaining that LeClerc's threat had applied, *not* to German POWs, but to German civilians in Alsace.

The Germans, of course, could hardly let such an opportunity pass without scoring a few propaganda points. The matter was hushed up at home, no doubt to spare the nerves of the Volkssturm, but on 1 December the German Foreign Office issued an announcement that Gaullists held in Germany would be open to reprisal executions if the LeClerc order was carried through, or, for good measure, if any Alsatian, Lorrainais, or French collaborators were executed. They also denounced the effort to round up German civilians and Alsatian collaborators, calling the measures acts of pure arbitrariness and brutality.' This declaration was followed on 4 December by an official note to the French government delivered via the International Red Cross, which the French dismissed predictably as 'a piece of gross impudence.'[7]

The main trouble spot in Lorraine was the border city of Saareguemines, which was overrun by units of the U.S. Third Army on 6 December, although the American advance subsequently stalled not far beyond the town. The population of Saareguemines was 'apathetic' and their attitude towards the Allies had been influenced adversely by German 'terror bombing' propaganda. Moreover, the locals were suspected of harbouring 300 German deserters, and nearby SS units were busy infiltrating commandos at night into the newly captured town. On top of this unhappy situation, the presence of French policemen and civil officials was minimal, and although French Interior Forces (FFI) auxiliaries were posted on guard duty throughout the city, the Americans felt constrained to impose a harsh curfew and take strict security measures. In the neighbouring community of Remelfing, an entire quarter of the town was evacuated after the inhabitants were accused of providing targeting information for enemy artillery. Not surprisingly, such measures quickly became resented by the Lorrains, and on 20 December the prefect of Moselle complained that the Americans acted like they were already on German soil.

The most serious incidents in Saareguemines occurred at the hands of SS *francs-tireurs* operating in civilian clothes. There were isolated instances of sniping, and an American MP was stabbed. On the night of 15–16 December, a Third Army trooper was overtaken and his throat was slit with a razor. A handful of snipers were arrested with the help of the population, but security remained precarious into the new year, particularly since the local front was frozen until mid-March 1945.[8]

In early 1945, there was something of a crisis in Alsace, as the Germans launched a local counter-offensive code-named 'North Wind,' and it looked briefly as if the Americans might have to evacuate Strasbourg. As the back-and-forth dynamic of Alsatian history seemed about to reassert itself, popular impressions of the Americans and Free French, which had improved since November, soured again. American and French security agencies noted the spread of much underground propaganda, particularly in the Hagenau region.[9] By February, however, the Germans had shot their bolt with the 'North Wind' attack and the crisis ended, as it became clear that the Allies were not about to be chased away.

Some illicit leaflets were circulated subsequently by an outfit calling itself the 'National Alsatian' *maquis*, which may have been a wing of the so-called Alsatian Freedom Front, led by autonomist leader and SS-Colonel Robert Ernst. These pamphlets urged the local populace to prepare for a second coming of Nazi German rule,[10] but not much actually happened. When the U.S. Seventh Army finally broke out on the stalled front near Saareguemines in March 1945, they reached Mosellaise and Alsatian districts on the Palatine border ('Crooked Alsace') that were the heartland of a stridently pro-German brand of autonomism. In the newly occupied town of Rohrbach, a fanatical civilian threw a white phosphorous grenade into an American half-track, burning to death two men and injuring three others. The Americans reacted violently; a cryptic reference in the unit history of the 14th Armoured Division says that the formation 'cleaned that town out,' but leaves all details to the imagination.[11] After the liberation of the final German-held pockets in Alsace–Lorraine during March, there were few further attacks against Allied military personnel. Press reports claim that Nazi 'Freedom Fighters' in Alsace managed to blow up an important bridge over the Rhine in early April, and that they also assaulted the headquarters of General Lattre de Tassigny, causing casualties among the general's staff before five of the six members of the team were overrun by the French Military Police. However, none of this is substantiated by Allied records.[12]

Subsequently, there were still a few instances of internecine conflict in Alsace, mostly cases of 'fifth-columnists' throwing grenades or home-made bombs,[13] but little was heard of such activity after the summer of 1945. Generally, most of the German minority in eastern France got down to the business of acclimatizing themselves – successfully as it turned out – to the restoration of French rule. The autonomist movement seemed hopelessly smashed and did not begin to make a limited revival until the 1960s.

Eupen–Malmedy

A similar sequence of events played out in the areas of eastern Belgium populated by a German-speaking minority. The enclaves of Eupen and Malmedy had a history not unlike that of Alsace–Lorraine, in the sense that they, too, were the subjects of an international tug-of-war. After being parts of the German Reich during the Middle Ages, they were then run by various branches of the Habsburg dynasty for three centuries, were detached from the rest of Belgium and transferred to Prussia in 1815, reannexed by Belgium in 1919, then effectively reincorporated into Germany in 1940, no doubt with the approval of most of the local inhabitants. When elements of the US First Army reached Eupen on 11 September 1944, bringing with them the promise of restored Belgian rule, they noted that white flags were in evidence, but that otherwise the population reacted coldly and was 'strongly pro-German.' A fourteen- year-old boy was caught aiding German stragglers and was sentenced to death in a U.S. Military Court (although the sentence was later commuted). The Army's war diary reported on 17 September that the 'first case of sabotage occurred when wire was stretched across a highway near Eupen. This slowed down and damaged a jeep but the shots which were fired at the driver fortunately went wild.' General Courtney Hodges, head of the First Army, subsequently instructed the local American commander 'to meet violence with violence and to have no qualms about taking the most stringent measures to avoid recurence [*sic*] of such incidents.'[14]

It is perhaps significant, in connection with such events, that the German Seventh Army had organized a number of special guerrilla teams under the leadership of Lieutenant Freiherr von Breisach, and that these units functioned extensively in eastern Belgium. In October 1944, a four-man sabotage detachment blew up a tunnel and rail line near Bocholtz, which was being used as an American supply route, and a different team directed its attentions towards an American tank-repair shop in Eupen. Such units were supported by the HSSPF West and by the Gestapo post in Schleiden, which gave the entire enterprise a semi-Werwolf aspect.[15]

The same deterioration of relations that occurred in Alsace because of the 'North Wind' counter-attack also occurred in eastern Belgium, in this case due to Operation 'Watch on the Rhine,' the Ardennes Counter-Offensive. German- and even Wallonian French–speaking Belgians tore down Allied flags, cast baleful looks at the retreating Americans, and in some places were openly hostile.[16] On the other hand, propaganda specialists with Sixth SS Panzer Army noted that much of the German-speaking population in recovered districts had developed an all-too-favourable view of the Americans,[17] and it is significant that after the territory in question was recaptured by U.S. forces in January 1945, there were no more tales of sabotage or resistance activity. None the less, Reichsdeutsche living in the area sulked about having to wear yellow armbands, and in the immediate postwar period these people were sent back to Germany. As well, pro-Nazi Belgian Germans were stripped of their Belgian nationality and similarly deported.[18]

Denmark

The only other area in northwestern Europe lost by Germany after the First World War was North Schleswig, which passed to Denmark after a plebiscite in 1920, along with a local German-speaking minority that had opposed the transfer but was outvoted. Although this area was not a traditional part of the German Reich, it had been incorporated into the nineteenth century German Federation after a lightning war in 1864, which pitted Prussia and Austria against Denmark, and in 1871 it was included in the new Bismarckian Empire. Like many German-speaking minorities, the 'Folk Group' in Denmark was 'coordinated' in the mid-1930s, coming under the increasing influence of the North Schleswig NSDAP. After the conquests of 1940, which allowed Germany to extend its civil and NSDAP administration to other disputed borderlands, such as Alsace–Lorraine and Eupen–Malmedy, the Nazi regime was also in a position to reincorporate North Schleswig, although they refrained from doing so. This was intended as a concession to the Danish 'Model Protectorate' (although the Germans also toyed with the idea of some day incorporating the entire country within the Reich). British Naval Intelligence estimated in 1944 that there were probably 30,000 to 35,000 'German-minded' people in North Schleswig, about 17 per cent of the area's population, although perhaps only a third of these used German in daily speech.[19]

The situation in Denmark was further complicated by the fact that, in May 1945, there were 290,000 Wehrmacht troops and 230,000 German civilians in Denmark, a group one-seventh as large as the total population of the country.[20] Moreover, these Germans were not concentrated in southern Jutland, but were scattered throughout Denmark. Military personnel were quickly evacuated; by late June there were only 80,000 left, although some of these were engaged in long-term labour duties, such as mine clearance, and were slated to stay on in Denmark as late as 1946. As for the German civilians, most of whom were seaborne refugees from the eastern German provinces, they generally waited until 1946 to be evacuated into Germany.

Naturally these large congregations of embittered Germans provided considerable material for Nazi resistance groups. The first such movement came to light in late May 1945, when a large weapons cache was discovered in a German Army hospital in Copenhagen and a fire-fight broke out between wounded German troops and Danish Home Guardsmen patrolling the grounds. Around the same time, a German Red Cross vehicle was stopped by Danish railway police at Vejle and was found to be carrying fifty rifles, bayonnets, and ammunition. By mid-June, investigations suggested that the German Red Cross in Denmark was being used as a veil for a widespread Nazi underground organization that was involved in shielding wanted Germans and automatic arrestees. The chief of the Danish wing of the German Red Cross, Dr Erhardt, was arrested, along with his deputy, Count Kottulinsky.[21]

The German Werwolf movement also developed a considerable base in Denmark, although it is not clear that this was a remnant of the Prützmann organization, or that Prützmann had been given authority to operate in North Schleswig, seeing as it was not part of the Greater Reich. In any case, by 1946 Danish security agencies were reporting the existence of a widespread and growing network of independent working groups that draped themselves in the Werwolf banner and were based principally in thirteen towns in Jutland. The headquarters of the movement was in Ålborg, and the largest single unit consisted of a hundred activists in Tönder, near the German frontier, where a large Werwolf weapons dump was uncovered by Danish police in May 1946. Different cells of the organization reportedly kept in touch by means of radio receiver-transmitters, and they also maintained courier links with nationalist groups in northern Germany, sometimes via British soldiers doing favours for girlfriends who, unbeknownst to them, were members of the Schleswig Werwolf. The group's main base of support was among disenchanted farmers who had once supported the Schleswig Nazi Party in the 1930s, and now willingly provided financing, stored ammunition, and gave employment to 'wanted' men. The group also had a presence among German POWs in Denmark. The Werwolf in Denmark had some impressive plans for prison break-outs and reprisal murders designed to help ease the Danish backlash against pro-German collaborators, and in July 1945 they were supposed to have raided the Hoerseroed holding camp in northern Jutland, trying to break out some of the 1,000 collaborators and German internees held at the enclosure. The result was a fierce, night-long battle in which sentries at the camp succeeded in deflecting the assailants. Danish Home Guardsmen later found supply caches in the surrounding woods, plus evidence that a fifty-man Werwolf detachment involved in the attack had succeeded in evacuating its dead and wounded by automobile. After this fiasco, the Werewolves were content with posting threatening letters to local courts of law and newspapers.[22]

The fate of this Werwolf network is unknown. Even if we accept at face value everything that the Danes had to say about it, it is still clear that, with the exception of the Hoerseroed attack and one or two other incidents, the Werewolves talked a tougher fight than they provided. It is likely, as with many such organizations, that plans by underground leaders for imminent operations were indefinitely mulled over and deferred until the movement's dangerous future had become its insignificant past.

The Polish 'Western Territories'

If Germans in North Schleswig resented the Danes, Germans in the Reich's eastern provinces hated the Poles with the every fibre of their being. It was Poland, more than any of Germany's other neighbours, that had gained land at the Reich's expense in 1919 (albeit largely from territory seized during the partitions of Poland in the eighteenth century). Evolving partly from the seed of a First World War puppet state created by the Germans themselves, a big Poland was created by the Treaty of Versailles, mainly at the behest of France. The Posen region was captured by the Poles in fighting in 1919 and thereafter incorporated; West Prussia was annexed and became the 'Polish Corridor' to the Baltic, separating East Prussia from the remainder of Germany; Danzig was established as a 'Free State' with its own civic government, under the protection of the League of Nations, but in close economic and political association with

Poland; and Upper Silesia was divided between Germany and Poland in 1921, according to the determinations of a League of Nations plebiscite and amid much heavy fighting between German and Polish militias. As a result of these annexations, as well as the considerable presence of German ethnic groups in the former Russian and Austrian areas of the country, the new Polish state contained 1,750,000 Volksdeutsche in 1920. This number was cut in half over the next two decades due to heavy rates of emigration back to Germany, but during the Second World War it shot back up to nearly the original figure, owing to the resettlement of Volksdeutsch colonists from various areas in the USSR.

Tension over German territorial losses in the east remained extremely high throughout the 1920s, and although these various controversies simmered on a back burner through the mid-1930s, owing to the détente engendered by the German–Polish Non-Aggression Pact of 1934, such issues re-emerged again in the spring of 1939, as German–Polish relations rapidly deteriorated. By the summer of 1939, thousands of Polish Volksdeutsche, both inside and outside Poland, were being secretly prepared for guerrilla and sabotage operations by the Breslau office of the Abwehr, the purpose of which was to provoke anti-Volksdeutsch reprisals that could be claimed as provocations by Berlin. These partisans cooperated with German forces during the Polish campaign and, according to German sources, thousands of them were massacred along with their families and kinsmen, and a large number of Volksdeutsche, some 50,000, were deported to the east.[23]

None the less, after the bitter experiences of 1939, the German minority then found itself in an advantageous position, as Germany reannexed all of the provinces lost in 1919, plus additional ground, and administered the remainder of central Poland as a direct-rule territory called the 'General Government.' The Volksdeutsche played an important role in both zones, lording it over their Polish neighbours. In general, the new order in Poland was characterized a spectacular degree of maliciousness, the tone being set by Hitler's admonition of 22 August 1939, instructing the Wehrmacht to 'kill without pity or mercy' as part of a larger policy to lay the groundwork for a future 'living space' for Germans. SS and police forces systematically decapitated Polish society by killing political and social leaders; they ghettoized and eventually exterminated nearly 5 million Polish Jews; and they steadily worked to eliminate Polish and East European Jewish culture, 'Germanizing' suitable elements.[24] Poland was no longer regarded as a legitimate nation, but simply as a passageway to Germany's eastern empire.

Given this background, it is hardly a surprise that as Poland was liberated in 1944–5, returning Polish officials intended to repay the Germans in kind. In particular, they took aim at the Volksdeutsche, whom they regarded as a most scurrilous breed of traitors, and the repressions typical of the pre-1939 period resumed, albeit much more intensely. In fact, the Poles made it clear that they now intended to eject their entire Volksdeutsch population – a Polish government decree on 28 February 1945 officially subjected these people to collective deportation. The Poles suggested that, if the interwar German minority was allowed to retain its civil rights and remain in Poland, they might 'continue their evil activities, forming clandestine organizations.'[25]

This problem was made infinitely worse by the fact that the Poles also preemptorily annexed *all* of the pre-war German provinces east of the Oder and Lusatian Neisse rivers, plus Danzig, as well as the German port of Stettin, on the left bank of the Oder. The Big Three had signalled approval for these arrangements during the superpower conferences at Tehran and Yalta, principally as a means of winning Polish acquiescence to the cession of the country's eastern provinces, which were coveted by the USSR. The intention was literally to roll Poland 100 to 150 miles westwards, recompensating the country for the loss of its Ukrainian and Belorussian marches with the eastern territories of the Reich. As part of this arrangement, the German ethnographic presence in eastern Europe would also be reduced, pushing the German centre of gravity farther westwards and away from Soviet frontiers. The Western Powers were intially enthusiastic in pursuing this course, although they became more reserved after it became clear, around the turn of 1945, that Polish communists and other proSoviet Poles were likely to play a major role in Poland's future government, and that the Polish exiles in London seemed doomed to oblivion. Concurrently, the Soviets warmed to the whole arrangement, and they egged on the new 'Lublin regime,' which the Soviets had themselves created and manned with Poles obedient to their will. For themselves, the Russians also reserved a direct claim to the northern half of East Prussia, which they hoped to use as the spot for a future naval base on the Baltic. Despite their increasing doubts, the Western Powers gave de facto recognition to these boundary changes in the summer of 1945, at the Potsdam Conference, and they also approved plans for the mass deportations of eastern Germans, although they asked to have these measures postponed briefly until Allied-occupied Germany was ready to accept the expellees.

All of this complicated Polish plans for the expulsion of indigenous Germans because it involved a drastic upward revision of numbers; in addition to the Polish Volksdeutsche, something in the order of 10 million eastern Reichsdeutsche were now slated for permanent removal from provinces that had been transferred to Poland – namely, Silesia, eastern Brandenburg, Hinter Pomerania, and the southern part of East Prussia (Masuria). Although roughly half the Germans in these regions had already fled before the advance of the Red Army, there were still 5 million people in place, and those who had left earlier were now denied the possibility of ever returning home. Reichsdeutsche who had stayed behind in occupied territory were horrified to see the Red Army hoisting Polish flags on public buildings, which was their first indication that their homelands were being transferred to Poland.[26] Large-scale, forced population transfers were supposed to await approval by the Allied Control Council in Germany, which was responsible for receiving the deportees, but the Poles immediately undertook repressions of the Germans in order to encourage supposedly 'voluntary' evacuations, hoping thereby to face the occupying powers with a *fait accompli* and ensure that it would be the Czechs, and not themselves, who be left holding the bag should the Reich's capacity for accepting eastern refugees ever be exceeded.

Amidst this incredible chaos, there was considerable violence and vengeful retribution. Most of this came through the actions of the Red Army and the Poles, although the eastern German population was not entirely blameless. It is true that many Germans had already fled, including some of the most rabid National Socialist elements; it is true that the organizational structures underlaying the Werwolf and the Volkssturm had been badly jolted or destroyed by the lightning Soviet advance; it is true that much of the population that stayed behind was paralysed by fear, owing to the savage behaviour of the Russians. Historians of the German flight from eastern Europe, such as Karl Friedrich Grau and Alfred DeZayas, have emphasized this reality, or perhaps overemphasized it, claiming that an alleged total absence of Nazi underground resistance made Soviet and Polish terror measures even more unfair than they would have been, given conditions of guerrilla warfare.[27] In truth, however, there were at least a few instances of German civilian opposition, and there were also thousands of soldiers from disintegrating Wehrmacht units who fled to the woods and became guerrillas. The Soviets contended that, since German troops often changed to civilian dress once they were surrounded, and since Volkssturm fighters frequently ripped off their brassards in similar situations, the distinction between civilians and soldiers was often academic.[28]

In areas of the 'old Reich,' which the Poles had annexed in 1919, the Volksdeutsche did offer some scattered resistance after the Soviet advance. In February 1945, Kreisleiter Butow of the West Prussian town of Zempelburg was killed by Polish partisans while leading a German reconnaissance team behind Soviet lines. The Soviets took reprisals against the German population in Zempelburg, which they had captured on 27 January, and where many of the townfolk were on hand because Butow had previously prohibited an organized evacuation; such measures, he had said, were 'defeatist.'[29] In the old Polish half of Upper Silesia, HJ boys hid themselves during the evacuation of Kattowitz and later emerged to snipe at Soviet troops as they entered the city. Not far away, at Biala, Werewolves in March 1945 set fire to a factory, but the blaze was extinguished and the arsonists were captured.[30]

It was, however, in the eastern German provinces that the Soviets ran into more serious forms of opposition. East Prussia, 'the bandit's nest of the German landowners,'[31] was repeatedly cited as a hard kernel of Nazi resistance. The province had an ancient tradition of conflict with Slavs and Balts, and it had a long history of right-radical politics; it had been one of the only areas to have provided broad support for the Kapp Putschists of 1920, folkish-nationalist groups later established a firm basis during the 1920s, particularly in Masuria, and the National Socialists scored several early electoral landslides, particularly in frontier districts where the rural populace remembered the brief Russian occupation in 1914 and the referenda on possible transfer of sovereignty in 1920.[32] On the other hand, even staunch National Socialists had been aghast by the precipitate flight of leading SS-Police and party officials in late January 1945, including Gauleiter Koch,[33] and this hardly helped to create an environment conducive to pro-Nazi resistance. The Russians were divided in their assessments: *Izvestia* described the East Prussians as 'servile and accommodating,' but Red Army and NKVD reports denounced them as 'sullen,' 'angry,' 'hostile,' and prone to give cover to Nazi sympathizers and troublemakers. It is also true that NKVD units operating in East Prussia repeatedly discovered German guerrillas, HJ personnel, and intelligence agents lodged in civilian homes or merged with little difficulty into columns of refugees. Civilians caught hiding weapons in their homes were summarily executed.[34] Damning confirmation of such hostility was also provided by a German officer who was momentarily trapped behind the Soviet front in the hills west of Allenstein, although he later broke through to German lines and was thus able to leave his story to posterity. According to his account, he and a group of a dozen soldiers made a conscious decision to convert to partisan warfare, and they were *supported* in this endeavour by the rural folk in the area. Local farmers served as look-outs for the band, and they promised to provide provisionment.[35]

In late January, as Third Belorussian Front surged towards the East Prussian capital of Königsberg, they encountered sniping in the outer suburbs. In one case, two German officers, a Volkssturm man, and three women were extracted from a farmhouse after a half-hour fire-fight, and all six were summarily executed. Near Neuhausen, a Soviet artillery major named Sankov went missing on the night of 28–9 January, while travelling along Soviet rear lines. A Soviet patrol found his body on the following day, noting that his pockets had been rifled and that several secret staff orders and a register of telephone code-names had been stolen, presumably having fallen into the hands of German guerrillas.

In February, a Soviet supply unit in Schreiburg came under attack by a band of German partisans armed with hand-grenades and flame-throwers. As an NKVD patrol subsequently raided and searched Schreiburg, they were sniped at from a small shed, and a heavy return riposte set the structure afire, as explosive material held by the Germans within began to detonate. Three charred and blackened guerrillas eventually staggered from the inferno, and four of their comrades were found dead among the ruins. Subsequent to such incidents, Soviet units were ordered to tighten up security regulations and to enforce non-fraternization directives, and the military newspaper *Red Star* published several editorials advising vigilance in occupied territories.[36]

East Prussia was also the main spot where the Werwolf tried out its mass poisoning tactics, often with deadly effect. Shortly after crossing the East Prussian frontier, troops of Third Belorussian Front began encountering toxic items of liquor and food. One group of Russian soldiers found a barrel containing a beverage which smelled like spirits. One man risked a drink, and the others, seeing that he did not collapse, followed his example. The Germans, of course, had spent considerable time experimenting with various poisons to create this very effect: instead of an immediate and violent reaction, the impact of the poison was delayed. All seventeen men who dipped into this liquor barrel were dead within two days. A similar fate befell three Red Army soldiers who found a jar of liquid in the cellar of a German house. Believing the contents of the bottle to be liquor, they drank it with abandon. Two days later, all three were hospitalized, and soon after all of them died. In yet another case, drink left behind by the Germans was discovered by a Red Army soldier who presented it to Lieutenant Klimetz, his immediate superior. Klimetz and his friends consumed the spirits at a banquet, then fell ill and died in terrible pain, despite expert medical care. Similar incidents were reported by the staff of the 24th Armoured Brigade: their losses amounted to thirteen men, among them several officers.

There was no doubt that such poisonings comprised a deliberate Nazi tactic. At Ladiau, a Red Army patrol ran face to face into members of a German 'special squad,' commanded by a lieutenant, while they were in the process of poisoning food stocks left in a warehouse. All the members of the team were killed by the Soviets. In a number of cases, Third Belorussian officers also sent poisoned alcohol to Red Army laboratories for analysis. The verdict provided by Soviet chemists was inevitably that the liquor had been purposefully poisoned. 'Since the German animals,' said a Soviet circular, 'are not in a position to halt the all-destroying onslaught of the victorious Red Army, they fall back upon the dirtiest, basest, and most hideous means of warfare, such as the poisoning of alcoholic drinks, water, and food. The German monsters reckon that if they succeed in eliminating our soldiers and officers, they will inflict losses on the Red Army and weaken it ... Always keep in mind the danger of poisoning! ... We do not want to offer the despicable enemy even the smallest chance to do us harm or poison our people.'[37]

The German population of Silesia were reputed to be friendlier – or more servile – than their East Prussian cousins, although this province, too, had been an early Nazi stronghold, particularly Lower Silesian districts adjacent to the Polish border. There were a few desultory cases of hostility, and inhabitants emerged only with obvious reluctance in order to work at clearing rubble and debris.[38] Generally, the tone was more hostile in Upper Silesia, which, despite being a region of Catholic coalminers, also had a marked tradition of border-land politics. In the railway town of Schoffets, a handful of Germans were caught tossing hand-grenades into cottages occupied by Soviet troops; at Breitenmark, near Oppeln, the wells were poisoned and a Russian physician confirmed that food and schnapps had also been treated with toxins; and at Zablatsch, civilians on 19 February destroyed a Soviet tank with a Panzerfaust. At a small village near Militsch, in Lower Silesia, a young Polish militiaman was killed on 31 January, probably while in the process of scouting a suitable location for a militia post.[39] Overall, however, there did not seem much prospect for a full Nazi mobilization of the population in occupied Silesia. The commander of a special Battle Group sent behind Soviet lines in February 1945 in order to determine the feasibility of an underground movement concluded that, for the time being, the horrors and outrages associated with the Red Army's advance had sapped most people's will. 'We cannot expect any sudden decision to organize some sort of resistance. Though the rear areas are very thinly garrisoned and insufficiently secured, the Russians have spread such terror by their atrocities that nobody dreams of interfering with the completion of the Russian occupation.'[40]

There was, however, a more severe problem in the form of bypassed German troops hiding in the woods of Silesia. By the time of the 1945 Winter Offensive, the Soviets had mastered Blitzkrieg techniques, and, like the Germans in an earlier stage of the war, they were accustomed to smashing through their foe's front with armoured thrusts, creating large pockets of bypassed enemy troops. However, most Soviet strength was concentrated at the front or in mobile reserves, so that little manpower was left for actually occupying areas that were overrun. Westward-bound columns of motorized infantry did organize hunts for German stragglers, mainly by forming counter-guerrilla bands of former slave workers, but the Russians themselves usually stayed on the main roads and in urban areas. In fact, most towns were permanently occupied only by six-man NKVD units, which spent most of their time terrorizing the local population. German bands therefore had a chance to survive, and even to proliferate.

According to an NKVD report, German straggler groups in Silesia placed before themselves a variety of goals: some intended to conduct a drive back to German lines; others wanted simply to sit out the remainder of the war in relative peace; a few sought to terrorize the Red Army along its lines of communications. In the realization of these aims, such groups attempted to obtain essential uniforms or documents, food, weapons, and ammunition. Frequently, they organized ambushes of lone Red Army soldiers, vehicles, or small units advancing to the front. Not much help for the guerrillas was forthcoming from Silesian-German civilians, since in cases where they were caught aiding stragglers, the guilty parties were shot by the Russians and their houses were set on fire, which presumably provided a lesson for all. In fact, on several occasions congregations of German troops were actually betrayed by local civilians, whereafter these bands were overrun by the Soviets and their members massacred.

Several clashes between the Red Army and cut-off German bands were of a scale rarely equalled on the Western Front. On 23 January, an NKVD detachment of fewer than thirty men bumped into a huge German contingent of troops, who were roaming around the Soviet rear in possession of several cannons and 7 armoured personnel carriers. The Soviets naturally suffered heavy losses in the ensuing battle, including an NKVD officer, but the equation was more than balanced by the fact that 200 Germans were killed and 7 were captured. The ratio of killed to captured in this encounter suggests that many were summarily executed. Nearly a month later, another patrol from the same Soviet regiment discovered a large German band operating in the immediate vicinity of the front. In a sharp skirmish, 42 Germans were killed against the loss of none of their Soviet pursuers. Overall, NKVD and Soviet auxiliary detachments killed almost 700 Germans operating in the Soviet rear during the first two months of the Soviet advance into Silesia.[41]

Army Group 'Centre' also sent various commando detachments into the Soviet rear in Silesia, most of them dressed in civilian clothes. Members of the special Battle Group mentioned above, sent to gauge the possibility of building a resistance movement, spent ten days in the Russian-occupied hinterland north of Bunzlau. At one point during their travels, they got into a fight with a Soviet labour detachment building fortifications near Alt-Öls, although their ability to engage the enemy was limited, owing to the fact that the Soviets used German civilians as a shield. A similar detachment infiltrated Russian lines near Oppeln in order to establish a radio-transmitter outpost along the Soviet lines of communication. On the night of 21 February, another three-man team slipped through the Soviet front near Armenruh and raced fifteen miles to Gröditzberg, where they showed up at the front door of the estate of Herbert von Dirksen, the former German ambassador to the Soviet Union. Both Ribbentrop and Hitler suspected von Dirksen of attemping to dicker with the Russians, and on the basis of this supposition a detachment from Army Group 'Centre' had been given the task of either shooting him or, if he was willing, hauling him back to German lines so that he could be tried by a 'special court.' Faced with this choice, von Dirksen agreed to try the gruelling six-hour march back to German-held territory. He completed the journey, although he was never tried because the strain of the adventure caused Dirksen to have a heart attack, and his pursuers, having snatched him from the clutches of the Soviets and broken his health in the process, apparently believed that enough had been done to guarantee German security.[42]

Similar *sub rosa* activity continued to smoulder in Posen and the trans-Oder sections of Brandenburg, where there were many resettled Volksdeutsche and the advancing Red Army was poorly received.[43] At Zielenzig, a Soviet soldier was shot at the beginning of February 1945, shortly after Russian troops had sacked the town. Several weeks later, an officer with the Thirty-third Soviet Guards Army at Fürstenberg was waylaid, beaten to death, and then, in a gruesome finale, decapitated with a razor. The nature of Soviet reprisals suggest that civilians were responsible in each case: at Zielenzig, thirty male hostages were seized and reportedly shot; at Politsig, where the Russian officer was killed, the NKVD managed to track down the guilty parties, although they also seized twenty-two Volkssturm men, presumably as hostages.[44]

There was also a large number of German straggler bands in these regions, and several surviving German intelligence reports give an excellent account of the composition and psychological state of these groups. These documents were not happy reading for the leaders of the Third Reich, as they suggested that scattered bands of German troops across the Oder suffered from exeedingly poor morale. They regarded the war as irrevocably lost; they wanted peace at all costs; they blamed National Socialism for their plight and were particularly hostile to the SS. In some cases, sergeants told their men that, in case of an encounter with the Russians, no shots were to be fired, but that immediate surrender was the order of the day. The records of an NKVD formation in Eastern Brandenburg confirm this assessment: 'In most cases, enemy individuals and groups of soldiers and officers who remained in the rear of the front and hid in the woods, offered no resistance in surrendering ...'[45] Of course, capitulation was still a considerable risk, considering that, when the Soviets did succeed in rounding up such personnel, they routinely shot them in the nape of the neck, charging that they were partisans. Worst of all, there was little help forthcoming from the remnants of the eastern German population, mainly because civilians were completely terrorized by Russian threats of reprisals.

Such passivity, however, did not always characterize Waffen-SS bands, which retained some degree of loyalty to the National Socialist cause, and which seemed particularly determined to break through to German lines. They also appeared more willing to engage the Red Army: one such band, under the command of SS Sergeant Sass, ambushed some Russian soldiers at a deserted farm in Eastern Brandenburg. In a senseless reprisal, a Soviet patrol later returned and burned the farm to the ground, even though it was uninhabited.

Sass and company were not very sympathetic to complaints by German civilians about the dangers of feeding or housing stragglers. 'Upon meeting or visiting these civilians,' said Sass, 'each soldier is told to quickly go on, lest knowledge of the their presence result in [the civilians] being immediately shot and having their farms burned by the Russians.' Sass and his SS cohorts did not accept such excuses. When they encountered a German landowner who threatened to turn them over to seven Soviet troops quartered at his farm, Sass refused to hurry back into the woods. 'Our first reply,' he recalled, 'was that *we* would immediately burn his farm and butcher the Russians. He then took back his threat, regained his good sense, and produced some bread and coffee.'[46]

The great Hanseatic ports along the Baltic, Königsberg, Danzig, and Stettin, also posed problems for the Russians, not only because they each held out for a long time, but also because, once they were occupied, unrest and disturbances continued for weeks afterwards. For over two months, the East Prussian capital of Königsberg stood fast against heavy Soviet pressure after being nearly taken by storm in late January. However, after the Third Belorussian Front organized a powerful offensive that succeeded, by 9 April, in driving into the heart the city, the German commandant, General Lasch, refused to extend the fighting the usual dozen steps beyond practicality always demanded by Hitler. Rather, after the Red Army broke into the inner city, Lasch quickly ordered the garrison to capitulate. Moreover, since Lasch had strictly ordered his staff *not* to cooperate with the Werwolf,[47] there was not much prospect of further resistance, even of an underground nature.

Unfortunately, this sensible course was greeted with a storm of outrage by party and SS elements, as well as staff officers of the 69th Infantry Division, some of whom elected to fight on. One SS-Police Battle Group was wiped out attempting to escape the Soviet vise, but other fragments of the garrison retreated to the basements and caverns below the city surface, where they were reorganized by SS or NSDAP functionaries and were rallied for a fight to the finish. Shortly after Königsberg's fall, the East Prussian *Gauleiter*, Erich Koch, denounced the capitulation and ordered the local Party Leadership Corps, many members of which were still in the city, to organize German soldiers and Volkssturm men into resistance groups. One of the main figures in this effort was SS-General Siegel, the senior SS officer in Königsberg, who was only captured on 17 April, during a search of the city's cellars. Lasch was singled out for Vehme-style treatment – several days after the surrender, he was officially sentenced to death *in absentia* – and an official from the Gauleitung was also caught attempting to assassinate a Russian negotiator. The German Fourth Army made unsuccessful efforts to contact surviving fragments of the garrison by radio on 10 April, but German aerial reconnaissance on the next day revealed evidence of continued fighting by isolated Battle Groups. German reports claimed that such activity continued for at least a week after the formal surrender of the Fortress headquarters. The Soviets, in turn, answered this threat by calling in NKVD special detachments that had been stationed with the forces advancing upon Königsberg just in case of such an eventuality. They ruthlessly swept the city, and all adolescent Werewolves were rounded up and concentrated in a large holding pen between the headquarters of the police president and the municipal court-house.[48]

In Danzig, there was some limited cooperation between the German Army and the Werwolf. Wehrkreis XX activated the West Prussian Werwolf on 19 February, and, during the last days before the port fell, Werwolf propaganda proliferated and death squads terrorized the city, hanging 'deserters' and 'defeatists.' Most members of the garrison were aghast at such *franc-tireur* tactics, fearing wholesale Soviet reprisals upon the civilian population, but their inherent caution was partially counter-balanced by fanatical NSF cadres, who supported the Werwolf and actually hoped that the Soviets would kill large numbers of hostages, thus forcing public opinion back towards an NSDAP point of view. As a result, some officers and soldiers changed into civilian clothes when Second Belorussian Front overran the city on 27 March, and they continued to snipe at Russian troops. Werwolf saboteurs were also at work after the arrival of the Soviets and, although the city had already burned for several weeks as a result of bombing and shelling, they set alight even more houses, presumably because they belonged to 'collaborators.'

According to the Russians, the newly arrived Danzig commandant, Colonel Ramazanu, 'took decisive measures to safeguard the city from German diversionists.' The population was registered; daily 'inspections' were undertaken; strict traffic controls were implemented at crossroads; guards were stationed at historic buildings of cultural value; and special tribunals worked around the clock, executing or deporting hundreds of suspects, most of them members of the SS, SA, and HJ. Not surprisingly, all the German populace saw was an outbreak of seemingly meaningless and brutal oppression, and they remembered the period as a steady sequence of harassments.[49]

At Danzig's fellow Baltic port of Stettin, HJ-Werwolf detachments under SS-Colonel Hiller were in action against the Soviets, and they performed well around the outer approaches southeast and north of the town, particularly at Pyritz. By the time that the city centre fell to the Russians on 25 April, there were only 6,000 German civilians left, although the fanatical remnants of an SS regiment continued to prowl the ruins for three weeks, sniping, setting fires, and laying booby-traps, until they were at last methodically destroyed. A special naval team of frogmen was also left in the port, and its survivors were preparing to blow up a bridge when, on 12 May, they learned of the final German capitulation and decided to debouch for the western zones of occupation. Thirty miles downstream, at the mouth of the Oder, a 100-man Werwolf Battle Group was active on the island of the Usedom, and was marked for extermination by the Polish Army.[50]

After the final German surrender on 8–9 May 1945, the general state of insecurity in the 'Western Territories' was compounded by forced evacuations, and the situation invited instances of Werwolf activity, particularly in Silesia. As Polish troops and administrators moved into this newly annexed province, they noted a rising current of German opposition, particularly as more than than a million Germans moved back home in June and early July 1945, unable to grasp, as Elizabeth Wiskemann notes, 'that eastern Germany might become western Poland.'[51] Previously it had been the Red Army that had faced sporadic German resistance, but now the focus changed, as Polish militia units fanned out in anti-partisan patrols and thus put themselves in the forefront of the effort to control the Werwolf. Concurrently, the Poles reported an increased rate of attacks and robberies, as well as the first deaths of Polish troops, militiamen, and colonists. Once Polish authorities began keeping records, their casualty lists (albeit incomplete) reflected this shift in the nature of targets fixed upon by German resisters. Throughout the remainder of 1945, forty Polish soldiers and police troops were killed in Silesia, as compared with thirty Red Army men (nineteen of whom perished in a single incident, the explosion of an ammunition train near Steinau in mid-May). Moreover, German guerrillas attacked seventeen Polish militia posts or government offices, as compared with only two Soviet military objectives. The Polish State Railways also reported that seventeen rail workers were killed in sabotage incidents in Silesia during this immediate postwar period.

Some of this violence consisted of raiding and infiltration activity along Silesia's altered frontiers. At the new German–Polish border along the Lusatian Neisse, Polish and Russian patrols skirmished at nights with refugees and German military personnel slipping across the border, headed in either one direction or the other. Several Polish troops were killed in these minor battles, as well as a somewhat larger number of Germans, and in late June 1945 the Poles cleared all Reichsdeutsche out of a wide belt of territory 60 to 120 miles east of the new boundary.[52] Along the southern frontier with Czechoslovakia, there was full-scale guerrilla warfare amidst mountain heights such as the Eulengebirge and the Riesengebirge. Most of these heavily wooded highlands had not been overrun by the Soviets until 8–10 May, and the area quite naturally formed a final haven for forces that could not afford to surrender – that is, Waffen-SS troops, fanatical HJ units, and Vlassovite contingents. The fact that huge supplies of food were hidden near the village of Schreiberau clearly indicates that the SS had made preparations to use the area as a local redoubt, and it is no surprise that an eighty-man guerrilla detachment was later active in the vicinity. Although some skirmishing occurred at the time of the capitulation – SS units at Neurode, for instance, would not surrender – most straggler bands in these hills either headed for the west or withdrew further into the wilderness and prepared themselves for a campaign of harassment and banditry. As the mountain bands began to raid inhabited areas, and the Poles and Soviets simultaneously organized patrols to scour the remote highlands, the first postwar guerrilla clashes took place. On 20 June, three members of a German band murdered a sergeant from the Polish 10th Division near Hirschberg, and nine days later a Polish militiaman was killed in a skirmish with scattered Wehrmacht elements near Waldenburg. During the same period, Polish militiamen were also wounded in shoot-outs with German bands near Schweidnitz and in the Heuscheuer Mountains.[53]

Intermittent battles continued throughout the summer and fall of 1945, and included bold raids on Polish militia posts. At Neurode, a group of armed Germans attacked Polish colonists on 14 August, abducting one and taking him to the forest, where they tortured him in order to extract information about the composition of a nearby Polish militia unit. At night, while the band was busy fighting off an attack by the Poles, their prisoner took advantage of the diversion and escaped. At Liebenthal, northwest of Hirschberg, a Polish militia patrol managed to surprise and overrun a German partisan band. All twelve members were boys of the HJ, armed with automatic weapons and handgrenades. In the neighbourhood of Hirschberg itself, German partisans prowled the woods well into 1946, and the killings continued: in January, a Polish administrator at a local sanitorium was bumped off by German stokers working at the facility; in February, a Polish militiaman was murdered; in September, a German-Silesian pastor was assassinated by Werewolves because he had preached anti-Nazi sermons. In the summer, Polish authorities destroyed a Werwolf detachment that had manifested its presence by calling upon local Germans to snipe at Polish military transports.[54]

Waldenburg, a mining town at the edge of the northern foothills of the Riesengebirge, was another place where trouble continued into 1946, particularly since large numbers of highly trained German miners were exempted from deportation, so that the size of the local German population did not drastically diminish. Several Werwolf groups were surprised and broken up in Waldenburg and its environs, which in one case cost the life of a militiaman in a raiding party. In June 1946 a hundred Germans in the so-called Green Cross organization were also picked up and incarcerated – all these young men were veterans of the SA and the SS, and they had allegedly burned several factories and mined two bridges. On 7 May, a former SS man blew up a building being searched by the Polish militia, killing nineteen people, and three days later a Pole was killed (presumably by Germans) while on the road from Waldenburg to Schweidnitz.[55]

There were problems in other parts of Silesia as well. Breslau, the primary German fortress in the east, had long been a thorn in the side of the Soviets, and the city and its surrounding region was destined to remain a trouble spot. For almost three months in the late winter and spring of 1945, Breslau embarrassed and exasperated Red Army commanders by continuing to hold out, and it capitulated only at the end of the war, when it became apparent that Army Group 'Centre' would not be able to stage an operation to relieve the garrison. Even then, there was a controversy between the 'Fortress' commandant, General Niehoff, who wanted to surrender, and the local Volkssturm chief, SA-General Herzog, who argued that the Western Powers and the USSR would soon be at war, and that a surviving garrison at Breslau could play an important role in this struggle. When Niehoff refused to countenance any such scheme, Herzog committed suicide and the German defence lines around the city collapsed, except for a few rugged battle groups that infiltrated the Soviet ring and fled westwards.[56]

On 7 May, the vengeful Soviet host stormed into a city that was aflame, its defences laid open and the bulk of its remaining population, 200,000 people, cowering in their cellars. The Russians moved through the town like lava, spreading terror before them and burning whatever they touched. In particular, Soviet troops poked through Breslau's basements, searching for troops and weapons, and occasionally they found stragglers hiding amidst the ruins. Several days later the first Polish soldiers arrived, as well as forty gendarmes trained for the maintenance of public security. 'First amongst our tasks,' remembered one militiaman, 'was to clear the terrain of Hitlerite stragglers. To do this we organized nightly traps around the principal road crossings. Every night brought in scores of SS men, Gestapo people, and bandits to the City Command of the MO [militia].' Initially however, security control remained under Russian oversight, and the best the Poles could do was to circle their wagons and hope that resistance would peter out. Until midsummer, Breslau lacked direct contact with Warsaw, since communication cables had been cut and trains only ran as far as Öls, seventeen miles northeast. Moreover, Polish troops and administrators were badly understaffed, and were therefore dependent upon the German inhabitants of the city, who organized their own Communist Party (KPD)–dominated 'Antifa' to handle affairs. Efforts to quell Werwolf activity were heavily reliant upon the cooperation of Communists and Social Democrats among the German population. Occasionally, when the maintenance of order seemed beyond the capabilities of the Polish authorities, Marshal Rokossovsky's headquarters in Leignitz intervened directly. During such operations, an NKVD brigade was sent to surround Breslau, seal off communications, and then methodically sweep the city. Anyone caught in possession of arms or suspected of complicity in attacks or sabotage was subject to immediate execution.

This period of disorder provided a perfect recipe for violence. Soviet troops, passing through Breslau in transit, and not being under the authority of the town commandant, committed a large number of crimes, as did liberated 'Eastern Labourers' and underground Vlassovites. It was, of course, the German resistance movement that was of most concern to the authorities, particularly since it had an appetite for arson no less voracious than that of the Russian soldiery. Throughout May and June, German saboteurs were blamed for between twenty and forty cases of arson *per day*, usually because the effected buildings had been commandeered by the Poles. The storehouse of the Civic Construction Department was the most important of their targets. As late as June 1945, a month after the capitulation, parts of the city were still aflame.

Direct actions against Soviet and Polish personnel also occurred. In the last weeks before Breslau's fall, Werwolf squads had roamed through the city, poisoning food and drink likely to be consumed by Soviet soldiers, and the Deputy Bürgermeister had also directed the preparation of Werwolf galleries, which consisted of oven-like, armour-plated chambers used as firing points beneath destroyed buildings. In at least one instance, Werewolves firing from a such a gallery managed to pin down two Soviet officers. A Polish militiaman came to the rescue by tossing a grenade at the aggressors, although a pitched battle was still necessary before the incident was brought to a successful conclusion. Twelve militiamen were wounded in the skirmish, and the German guerrillas were 'liquidated.'[57]

By the midsummer of 1945, Polish officials were beginning to restore a small measure of order to the Breslau region, although both they and their Soviet allies continued to harbour doubts about their safety. On 17 July, a Polish soldier patrolling the streets of the city was waylaid and murdered, and, a month later, a German band similarly ambushed and killed four Soviet soldiers. During the same period, a German partisan group attacked a Polish militia post, sparking an all-night battle which turned in favour of the Poles only when they were rescued by a Soviet patrol. In a suburb of the city, a German band shot up yet another militia station. The guerrillas involved in this attack then retreated to another village, where they burned the houses of Polish colonists and shot at a group of Russian soldiers, before they finally succeeded in fleeing back to the woods.[58]

At the outlying settlement of Öls, there was a string of threats, attacks, and murders, all of which constituted a good example of the Polish claim that German resistance actually increased *after* the capitulation, due to eastward-bound population movements. During the initial Soviet advance, Öls was heavily damaged and was left practically denuded of inhabitants as a result of German evacuation efforts. At one point, the population was only a quarter of the pre-war figure of 18,000. However, in May and June 1945, German refugees began surging back to their abandoned homes, and the 'Werwolf' – that is, Wehrmacht, stragglers and Nazi Party desperadoes – concurrently became much bolder. At the same time, the few Polish colonists who had ventured into the area fled back to their old homes in pre-1939 Poland.

As part of this renewed surge of Werwolf activity, three Soviet soldiers were waylaid and killed in a village near Öls. An autopsy revealed that they had been bludgeoned to death. With the Red Army yelling for a resolution of this outrage, local Polish authorities determined that a band of about thirty armed Germans was operating in a nearby forest, led by an SD-captain, and it was suggested that this group was responsible for the murders. Local German Communists collaborated with the Polish militia in providing valuable information, but this source quickly dried up once the principal informant was murdered. As the Poles subsequently stumbled around in the dark, German partisans continued to harass the civil life of the surrounding area, and the size of the band increased, reaching a level of fifty men. A break in the case finally came when the Polish authorities discovered a small colony of German civilians who could speak Polish and were willing to provide precise information. These Germans told Polish gendarmes that the Werwolf band had recently split in three: one section that remained in the area, and two splinter groups that had migrated to Trebnitz and Miltsch, respectively. With more exact intelligence now at hand, Polish forces decided to conduct an intense sweep of the local woods. In the course of this operation, the German band was overtaken by surprise in a small hamlet and shots were exchanged. There were no casualties on either side, although several members of the guerrilla group were captured and disarmed. The rest of the band was chased off in the direction of Miltsch, whereafter the Öls militia apparently lost interest since the problem had effectively been dumped in someone else's lap.[59]

A degree of destructive anarchy continued to reign in the Breslau region throughout the autumn and the winter of 1945–6, particularly as right-wing Polish bands moved into the area, bringing with them their own internecine feud with the pro-Soviet Polish government. In November, Polish officials in Breslau received threatening letters warning that German 'agents' had infiltrated back into Silesia, on missions of retribution. An American military observer reported in the fall of 1945 that the nights in the city were full of 'desultory gunfire,' and a Jewish refugee who lived in the town in 1946 also remembered that the hours between sundown and sunrise were punctuated by a steady sequence of screams and shooting. Anti-Semitic outrages and banditry were rampant. A German expellee noted: 'The powerful opposition to the terrorizing elements of the Lublin Government and its powerful instrument, the Militia, shows itself in daily fights. Partisans are busy day and night. Raids are followed by a large number of arrests. As night falls everyone hurries into the sheltering houses. The nights are filled with screams for help and the clattering of machine pistols. Plunderings or political fights are frequent. At dawn, the picture has changed: very few Poles are to be seen. The streets are full of Germans on their way to work. Another report from the same period noted that 'ever since the end of the war, the presence of the Germans in the new Polish areas has caused considerable trouble. There have been frequent shootings and a state of general insecurity has existed.' Around Breslau, there was 'an especially troublesome situation,' and 140 Polish militiamen were killed in skirmishes in the city during the first year after the war.

As late as the spring of 1946, there were still between 100,000 and 200,000 Germans living in the Silesian capital, as compared with 60,000 Poles. The latter kept drifting in and out of the city, often picking up whatever goods they could grab, and then hauling their loot back to pre-war Poland. The Poles, noted one observer, 'do not feel safe yet.'[60]

Another centre for violent opposition was the Bunzlau area. A Nazi guerrilla group was active in this region, composed of Wehrmacht stragglers, Ukrainian collaborators, and local NSDAP notables, and it carried out attacks on Soviet and Polish security units. In July 1945, nine Soviet soldiers were killed in an explosion in a commandeered house outside Bunzlau. Sequestered property was always a favourite target for sabotage throughout occupied Germany, and in this case evidence collected by the Poles suggested that the blast was caused by a land-mine stolen from a Polish pioneer unit in Bunzlau. Several days later, on 21 July, six Polish municipal officials and militiamen were killed in Bunzlau when a wagon ran over a land-mine planted by German saboteurs. Among the victims was Boleslav Kubik, the mayor of Bunzlau and a prominent member of the Polish Socialist Party. A Polish militia report in August noted 'increased activity by German partisans.'[61]

Compared with Silesia, the post-capitulation security problems in most other of the other Polish 'Western Territories' were relatively tame. In Stettin, where by the fall of 1945 the German population had swollen back up to 60,000 (as compared with 35,000 Poles), Deputy Lord Mayor Władysław Kotowski reported a marked recovery of the German spirit of resistance. German underground organizations revived and executed 'a vicious, concerted effort to aggravate the tension between the occupying Russian forces and the Poles moving in to take-over the area from them.' When direct administrative control of the city was handed over to the Poles by the Red Army in early October, the new authorities had to call in a Polish regiment in order to maintain order. According to a British correspondent who visited Stettin during this period, scattered shooting was commonly heard throughout the town, both day and night, although gunmen were tough to track down through the bomb-ruined streets. As a defence of the German inhabitants, however, it should also be noted that the Danish and Swedish consuls in the city reported the systematic starvation of the German population, which was causing deaths at the rate of a thousand per week by the mid-summer of 1945.[62]

In East Prussia, reports from late 1945 tell of German partisans attacking isolated farms and robbing or murdering Polish colonists. In one case in Masauria, a farm steward was killed after he refused shelter to fugitive SS men. In other instances, East Prussian civilians were caught provisioning the guerrillas. The Poles in turn levied their usual heavy hand. In Niedenberg, for instance, there was much abuse and suppression of local Germans on the claim that such measures were necessary to control 'Party comrades' and Nazi guerrillas.[63]

As for the half of East Prussia directly controlled by the Soviet Union, there were some Werwolf remnants in this area, but, by all accounts, anti-guerrilla counter-measures and repression were so intense that the threat of partisan warfare was quickly eradicated. Soviet security troops swept huge stretches of forest with heavy gunfire, killing anyone or anything in the underbrush, and they so terrified German civilians that there were few people brave enough or foolhardy enough to challenge them. By 1946, they were well on their way to destroying the German population itself, which had been diminished by waves of famine, and concurrently swamped by ethnic Russian immigration. From 1947 to 1949 the last important German remnants were deported to the Soviet Zone of Germany. The powerful Lithuanian partisan movement sent several teams into the area, hoping to stir up resistance, but such efforts met uniformly with failure.[64]

In Polish-annexed territories as well, the Werwolf seemed finished by the middle of 1946, although a few cells staggered on into 1947, spreading propaganda. Two factors were crucial in forcing this eventual breakdown. First, the Polish militia and security agencies finally succeeded, by weight of numbers and the dint of perseverance, in dispersing Werwolf groups, even though these organizations had attempted to engage in a vigorous recruitment program. It took quite some time for the postwar Polish militia to get its footing. The force was not renowned for its efficiency, and even Polish Communist historiography admits that it grew too fast, and that it was insufficient in dealing with the heavy responsibilities thrust upon it. Their excuse was that the best elements of Polish society had been systematically decimated by the Germans during the previous six years, and that the only pool of available manpower included a considerable contingent of riff-raff. Moreover, many militia inductees were former slave labourers who had more than the usual Polish grudge against the Germans. In any case, many of these troops were more adept at robbing and abusing eastern German civilians than in dealing with armed opposition, and, although they succeeded in destroying much of the Werwolf in 1945, they were only able to complete the job in 1946.

Second, and even more important, the Poles, like the Soviets, drastically reduced the German population base of their annexed territories. Operation 'Swallow,' the expulsion of the mass of the German population in 1946, negatively affected the Werwolf in a number of ways. The supply and intelligence systems of local groups were destroyed, and many actual resisters were among the Germans physically removed from the country by the resettlement program. Something in the order of 2 million eastern Reichsdeutsche, the bulk of the remaining Germans east of the Oder–Neisse, were on board 'Swallow' transports. Some of the last acts of German resistance in the spring of 1946 are best understood as the final 'scorched earth' measures of a deported population.[65]

Although activity by guerrillas and bandits continued to rock the 'Western Territories' throughout 1947,[66] it is likely that ethnic Germans were responsible for very little of it, if only because most of them were gone and the remaining minority was totally cowed. The Poles in the summer of 1947 accused Werewolves in Stettin of organizing a wave of arson attacks, but the British vice-consul in the city noted that the effect of the dry summer weather, combined with the carelessness of scavengers with matches and cigarettes, was probably the real cause of the fires. This belated wave of Germanophobia quickly blew over after the last fire outbreaks, and there was apparently no action taken against a few Germans arrested on suspicion of incendiarism.[67]

Many eastern German refugees who were driven from the Polish-annexed provinces disclaimed any knowledge of the Werwolf (although not of passive resistance). Admissions of Werwolf activities in Polish courts, they said, were extracted by torture. They claimed that no sabotage acts ever occurred and that any weapons found by the Poles had been 'planted,' mainly as a rational for the levying of retaliatory fines as part of a larger campaign of economic warfare conducted against eastern Germans.[68] It is possible that in a few cases this rejection of Polish claims was a conscious attempt to deny the Poles the main excuse for their program of deportations; people who were loath to confess ever having supported Hitler, or ever having treated the Poles unfairly, were not likely to admit desultory instances of Werwolf activity either. More generally, however, this reluctance arose from an extremely common eastern German tendency to regard Slavs as barbarians, barely fit to govern themselves and certainly unsuitable to rule over Germans. As a result, any collective or individual act by Poles against Germans was by its very nature a transgression of the natural order and hardly needed to be explained by reference to context. Objectively, therefore, it would seem that the expellees exaggerated German passivity, and this misrepresentation, whether unintentional or not, deeply influenced refugee literature and memoirs.[69]

On the other hand, there is no doubt that the Poles cynically exploited Werwolf activity as an excuse for expediting the expulsions. They knew that the availibility of the 'Western Territories' was facilitated by the deportations, which were in turn facilitated by the security threat. The accessibility of these regions was vital for the 'Lublin Poles' as a political shield against attacks by Polish nationalists, who charged that traitorous friends of the Soviet Union had sold out the entirety of eastern Poland for the sake of an onerous Soviet alliance. If anything made the new relationship with the USSR nearly worthwhile, and if anything made the loss of Poland's own eastern territories nearly bearable, it was the annexation of the eastern German provinces, which the influence of the Soviet Union made possible. However, to exploit the 'Western Territories' and to fully incorporate them, the new regime had to pacify these areas and get rid of the German inhabitants, and it was precisely this intention that the Werwolf was attempting to impede.[70] Moreover, they realized that such elements could only take heart from the increasing reluctance of the United States to recognize the new frontiers of Poland, and that this problem was only likely to get worse as long as the eastern Reichsdeutsche were still intact in their old homelands. This was the one of the main motives behind the desire for a quick evacuation of the German population from the 'Western Territories.' As for the domestic Polish opposition, the new rulers of Poland suggested that it was the nationalists who had really betrayed the country through their association with German interests, and they were quick to claim that Werwolf groups in Silesia had contact with General Anders's expatriate nationalist legion and that they worked hand in glove with right-wing Polish bands.[71] It is difficult to comment on the truth of these charges, although Anders did admit in 1946 that, while Poland was fully entitled to Masuria, Danzig, and Upper Silesia, other areas farther to the west were perhaps too much of a meal for Poland to digest.[72]

Czechia and the Sudetenland

Poland's next-door neighbour, Czechoslovakia, did not lay claim to large tracts of Reich territory in the postwar period, although otherwise the parallel with the situation in postwar Poland was very strong. Large Volksdeutsch communities had been included in both countries when they were established in 1918–19, and in both cases the minorities had proven untrustworthy. Both nations exploited the Werwolf menace as a demonstration of the continuing treachery of their German minorities, which in turn was supposed to show the need for expulsion. In Czechoslovakia, anti-Werwolf hysteria was also intended to counteract pro-German propaganda by exiled Sudeten-German Social Democrats based in London.

Geographically and ethnographically, Volksdeutsch regions in Czechoslovakia were well suited for guerrilla warfare. The terrain of the borderlands around Czechia consisted of mountain ranges like the Erzgebirge and the Bohemian Forest, both of which spanned the German–Czech frontier. Farther east, beyond the Elbe Valley, lay the rough contours of the Sudeten Mountains, running through Czech Silesia and northern Moravia. Similar ranges of hills fringed the southern boundary of Czechia, so that the Bohemian Basin, the cradle of the Czech nation, was surrounded by a horseshoe arrangement of highlands, and, through an unfortunate twist of fate, the population in these districts was largely German. These Bohemian-Volksdeutsch groups, who in recent times developed a sense of ethnic cohesion as 'Sudeten Germans,' had come to the Bohemian hills in the Middle Ages, drawn by the region's mineral wealth, and they had traditionally been nurtured on the idea of a historic struggle with the Slavs as part of their cultural mother's milk. After the destruction of the Czech nobility in the early phases of the Thirty Years War, bourgeois elements among the Bohemian Germans had comprised the ruling caste of the realm, as well as being part of the social and economic élite of the Austrian Empire. With such a heritage, it was unlikely they would be happy in the new multi-ethnic state formed in 1918 and dominated by Slavs, although the Czechs, for their part, badly needed the Bohemian highlands for their strategic and economic value. The new Czechoslovak state's capability for autonomous development depended on the possession of these areas. Naturally, when the Czechoslovak Republic seized the borderland districts in 1918–19, Sudeten-German bands skirmished with the interlopers, and similar guerrilla warfare broke out during the Munich Crisis in 1938, at a time when the Third Reich was applying military and diplomatic pressure in order to secure the transfer of the Sudeten borderlands and their population.

After Hitler succeeded in stripping the Sudeten highlands away from Czechoslovakia, the country in effect ceased to be viable, and, as Slovakia went its own way in 1939, Czechia was incorporated into the Reich as the Protectorate of Bohemia–Moravia, under the rule of a German 'Reich Protector.' Like Poland, Czechia too, ceased to have even nominal independence, although its fate was not as terrible as that of its northern neighbour, at least not initially. In the late 1930s and early 1940s, German policy vacillated, lacking a consistent character of repression, and a surviving Czech cabinet was able to act as a buffer between the 'Reich Protector' and the populace. Understandably, there was little active resistance. In 1941, however, the infamous SD chief Reinhard Heydrich was appointed Deputy 'Reich Protector,' and he immediately instituted a tough regime. When Heydrich was assassinated by Czech commandos in May 1942, German rule became even more odious, and retaliations included the wholesale destruction of the town of Lidice, which was burned to the ground and its inhabitants either executed on the spot or sent to concentration camps. This unprecedented act, which was too methodical to be blamed on the desperate savageries of a retreating army, as was the Oradour outrage in France, set the tone for future relations between Germans and Czechs.[73] Moreover, Bohemian Germans covered themselves in shame, cheering news of the Lidice massacre and attempting to lynch Czechs in mixed ethnic areas. Meanwhile, a Czech government in exile, which had formed in London, saw nothing to improve its opinion of the Volksdeutsche in the Sudetenland and the Protectorate. In fact, Czech émigré leaders saw the future of their country based upon a reincorporation of the physical extent of the Sudeten borderlands, albeit without the Sudeten-German inhabitants, who they now wanted to deport to Germany. By 1943, they had wrangled the informal consent of the Big Three in favour of this controversial project.[74]

As the Americans and Soviets advanced on both the Sudetenland and the Protectorate in April 1945, the political arrangements of 1938–9 began to crumble, and the Czechoslovak exile regime returned to liberated Slovakia. They announced, on 5 April, that the national recovery program included a stipulation for expelling all Sudeten Germans, except the few who could prove their loyalty. Naturally, everyone anticipated that, as the exile regime restored its authority in Bohemia, the type of skirmishing that had taken place in 1918–19 and 1938 would probably recur, perhaps being worse this time because the promise of expulsions now hung heavy.[75] So surely did the Czechoslovak government expect such difficulties, that, in late April, they sent a special team

behind German lines to the western Sudetenland, where they pleaded with German civil officials not to wage a last-ditch stand or conduct Werwolf warfare.[76]
To further complicate matters, Bohemia and its Sudeten borderlands, *unlike* the
eastern German territories seized by Poland, were never evacuated by the Nazis
themselves, so the Czechoslovaks lacked the Polish advantage of dealing with
regions that were half empty. In fact, National Socialist extremists fleeing other
areas of Germany, particularly in the east, were bottled up in Bohemia in the
spring of 1945, since it was the last secure spot in the quickly declining confines of the Third Reich. Not all of these fanatics were ready to give up the
fight. This meant that a considerable number of sympathetic civilians were on
hand to offer eventual succour for guerrilla groups, or to provide raw but ready
recruits, particularly teenagers.

The Sudeten Werwolf did its best to exploit these favourable factors. They
portrayed themselves as the champions of Germandom, and they expected, on
the basis of experience in the 1930s, that they could win support from the
majority of the population. They also looked forward to a collapse of relations
between the Great Powers, which they believed would strengthen their own
position. In a short period prior to the surrender, more than 1,100 Werewolves
were trained at numerous camps in Czechoslovakia, and thousands of underground dumps were laid by German commando units. One of these groups
alone established nearly 1,000 caches, another laid more than 500, and a dozen
such squads operated in the Pilsen area alone.[77] Swiss observers noted in early
1945 that the Sudeten Germans were arming themselves for a showdown with
the Czechoslovaks, and a journalist who travelled through the region in May
and June pointed out that, in small villages especially, 'the idea of resistance
has taken form and thousands of young Sudetens are organizing to oppose the
eviction by force, preferring death to the abandonment of their farms.'[78]

In March 1945, Hans Prützmann also ordered that a regional Werwolf organization be set up in the Protectorate under the control of 'Reich Protector' Karl
Frank, who was the area's HSSPF. Within Frank's command, Werwolf responsibilities were probably delegated to his BdS, Dr Weinmann, or to one of Weinmann's staff members. The Abwehr also drew up plans were for both 'active'
and 'passive' resistance, and various supplies of weapons and food were cached
as part of 'Operation Marabu.' Primary efforts were devoted towards finding
volunteers among the 400,000 Volksdeutsche in the Protectorate and among
the large number of German refugees, although Weinmann also considered recruiting right-wing Czechs, and the Soviets eventually overran several Czech
reconnaissance teams in Moravia.[79]

Both the Soviets and Americans encountered hostile civilians and belligerent
Werwolf formations. When the Red Army began to pressure the Slovakian

capital of Pressburg, a four-man guerrilla unit from Austria succeeded in slipping behind their lines in eastern Moravia, with orders to collect intelligence. In early April, this detachment succeeded in ambushing a column of Soviet motorized infantry that was passing through a narrow gorge. A mine blew up the lead vehicle, and when the last driver in the convoy attempted to shift into reverse, his truck was also demolished by a mine. All the vehicles caught between these smoking wrecks were then shot up by the Werewolves positioned along the walls of the ravine.[80] The typical Soviet answer to such problems was to form counter-guerrilla detachments (with the aid of Czech partisans), to reconnoitre the woods with PO-2 airplanes, and to rake with heavy gunfire the forests in problem areas. Captured German irregulars and SS men were shot as a matter of course.[81]

The Americans faced similar difficulties in western Bohemia. In April, American units arriving at Asch got baleful looks from local townspeople, and children threw stones at passing troops and vehicles. Ethnic Czechs around Asch seemed terrified, begging Americans not to show favours or give them packets of sweets and cigarettes, lest their Sudeten-German neighbours inflict reprisals for consorting with the enemy.[82] Forward patrols pushing into unoccupied areas were occasionally ambushed by Werwolf and Volkssturm units equipped with small arms and Panzerfäuste. As late as 7 May, American units were engaged in fierce fire-fights with German detachments, such as the Marienbad Volkssturm. In Pilsen, a huge Czech crowd gathered in the city square to greet the Americans, but German snipers organized a vicious spate of shooting after American tanks had rolled through the town. Third Army forces were extremely cautious, not wishing to sustain last-minute casualties, and they typically reacted to ambushes by calling forth air strikes and heavy-artillery bombardment. The fury of such attacks was expected to bring opposition to heel without undue risk of life or limb on the American side. Czech sources claim that such last-minute resistance was widespread, even after the capitulation, and that Sudeten Nazi elements enthusiastically aided nearby Wehrmacht units that refused to surrender.[83]

Not only were civilians and paramilitary personnel in an ugly mood, but Bohemia was also the refuge of the last large concentration of German troops who refused to yield. A big part of this problem was that Hitler, mistakenly expecting a Soviet offensive against Prague rather than Berlin, had sent many of his remaining élite units to reinforce Army Group 'Centre,' stationed in Bohemia. Under the (initial) leadership of the fanatical Field Marshal Schörner, these elements continued to offer resistance to the Soviets until 19 May, eleven days after the formal German capitulation.[84] Many German soldiers had a justifiable fear of Soviet captivity, and they desperately sought to reach American lines, which they equated with safety and comfort. In particular, SS men and Vlasso-vite legionnaires believed that surrender was tantamount to a death sentence at the hands of Soviet troops or victorious Czech partisans. Others claimed that their comrades in American POW camps would be freed and rearmed for a con-frontation with the Russians, and their efforts to reach the West were based at least in part upon the expectation of playing a role in this final struggle.

With such assumptions in mind, Schörner decided to hold out as long as pos-sible, and this sense of resolve was reinforced when the commander of the Luft-waffe, Ritter von Greim, arrived in Bohemia on 3 May, with suggestions that Schörner should ignore any capitulation order. Greim had flown south after attending a Dönitz war council two days earlier, so his advice bore the stamp of official approval. Delegates sent from Schörner's command post to Dönitz headquarters in Flensburg got the same message, being told by Colonel General Jodl 'to organize their positions so as to gain time.' At midnight on 7 May, Schörner made a radio address denouncing reports of total capitulation as 'an evil rumour,' and claiming that the battle in the East continued. 'There would never be any question of capitulating to the Bolsheviks,' he said, 'since that would be the death of us all.' On 8 May, Schörner's headquarters was destroyed after a Soviet armoured breakthrough, and the field marshal, now on the run, released his troops from active service and gave them permission to flee to the west, in lieu of surrendering to the Russians. The OKW meanwhile fobbed off the Allied Powers with the excuse that Czech partisans had destroyed vital lines of communication and that the dissemination of the surrender order was thus problematic.[85]

The reaction of Schörner's forces was mixed. Some surrendered despite their commander's advice: in Prague, the garrison commander capitulated and, in acknowledging that his control over Waffen-SS and Schörner troops was lim-ited, he promised to use his own forces to clean up recalcitrant nests of resis-tance. Many soldiers slipped into the woods and undertook a wholesale flight westwards, only engaging the enemy in self-defence. A week after the capitula-tion, large groupings of soldiers still held out in the Brda Forest, the Sudeten Highlands, and the forests west and southwest of Prague, and, as late as June 1945, NKVD units operating in the rear of Fourth Ukrainian Front rolled up over 2,700 soldiers and 750 Volkssturm men, many of them clad in civilian clothes and responsible for pillaging the local population. More aggressive ele-ments actively harassed the enemy: near Kutna Hora, saboteurs blew up a bridge in mid-May, several days after this area was overrun by a column of the Fourth Ukrainian Front, and for weeks after the capitulation shooting was heard in the Sudeten hills as German stragglers clashed with Red Army and Czech partisan detachments. The road between Prague and Vienna was still blocked on 18 May by hostile German action. In Prague, SS desperadoes set last-minute delayed-action charges, striking a final blow at the hated Czechs, and sporadic skirmishes continued until 20 May. On the evening of 24 May, Czech authorities overran an illicit broadcasting station: this underground transmitter had already announced that German forces would eventually recapture Prague, and that St Wenceslas Square would then be paved with Czech skulls.[86] Even in U.S.–occupied Sudeten-German areas, there were a few instances in which Waffen-SS guerrilla bands were sighted after the capitulation, and near Mount Kleinberg an American NCO was shot by a sniper on 10 May while his platoon was in the process of suppressing 'unorganized resistance.' In mid-May, a train carrying Czech partisans was derailed at Komotau, and on 20 May six U.S. officers were ambushed near Horazdowitz. One man was wounded.[87]

Perhaps typical was the experience of an SS counter-insurgency company, which was stranded at Reichenberg, some 200 miles behind Soviet lines. At the time of the general capitulation, officers from this unit decided that any process of surrender would terminate in death, particularly since they themselves had summarily killed thousands of Czech guerrillas. An Army battalion commander attempted to get the SS men to surrender, advising them that otherwise they would themselves be no better than guerrillas and bandits, and that, even if they reached Bavaria, the Americans would regard this behaviour as a clear breech of the rules of war. Despite such advice, the SS and some German Army dissidents decided to launch a desperate trek to the west. After a final battle with a nearby Soviet unit, the SS group destroyed their tanks and artillery, and resolved to break through by using only their light weapons. Seven weeks of fighting and walking followed. In the course of this odyssey, the SS company plundered a Czech village, liberated more than twenty German POWs from a forced-labour detail, wiped out four Soviet and Czech patrols who had the misfortune to cross their path, and overran numerous enemy checkpoints and blockades. At the height of the summer, they finally reached the Bavarian Forest, where they quickly captured several members of an American patrol, and then just as quickly released them. After a final bivouac near Cham, the group broke up, with each member resolved to reach home on his own. There were only 42 survivors from a band that originally numbered 360.[88]

Such security problems were considered so serious that American and Soviet forces agreed to temporarily maintain occupation zones in Czechoslovakia 'in order to assist the Zecho people in the elimination of remnants of Nazi forces ...'[89] The Czechs were supposed to employ this interregnum to prepare their own army and security forces, although (like the Poles) they had considerable difficulty in obtaining satisfactory and disciplined personnel. As soon as the German administration was bowled over in early May, the new regime began a sweep of Sudeten-German areas in order to disarm the population, prevent anticipated uprisings, and stop the Werwolf from developing into a genuine self-defence force capable of interfering with the forthcoming expulsions. Germans with experience of bearing arms were automatically arrested, and weapons and radio receivers were confiscated.[90] Because of manpower shortages and inadequate preparation, this initial house-cleaning was superficial, although it was carried through with an extremely heavy hand.

While the Czechoslovaks were not particularly commendable in dealing with their Sudeten problems, it must be admitted that they were in a difficult situation. Having committed themselves to a policy of expulsion, they had hoped in the spring of 1945 that both the Americans and Soviets would impose a full Military Government in occupied Sudeten territories. However, both powers demurred, and although they both agreed to keep military forces in Czechoslovakia temporarily, they immediately thrust civil-affairs responsibilities upon the Czechoslovaks, which left the latter scrambling. The new regime desperately recruited security troops and police auxiliaries from among former concentration-camp inmates, repatriated slave labourers, and various types of adventurers and juvenile delinquents, which guaranteed that the Sudeten Volksdeutsche would hardly be treated with kid gloves. At the time of the German capitulation, the Czechoslovak authorities addressed the truculence of Army Group 'Centre' by announcing that any Germans caught resisting after the ceasefire would forfeit the protection of the Geneva Convention, and that Czechoslovakia would fight 'until the last German *franc-tireur* is rendered harmless, disarmed or killed.' And they immediately gave teeth to this policy by summarily executing all German troops taken in a post-capitulation skirmish at Riwitz, where Sudeten-German civilians were subsequently forced to bury the bodies, and threats were issued to shoot all Silesian refugees in the region should another Czech be attacked.[91]

For several weeks, particularly in June 1945, the situation in the Sudetenland seemed to quiet down: on 27 June, Premier Fierlinger announced in Prague that there was 'no special problem' in the Sudeten borderlands, although there were 'individual cases of sabotage,' and several underground radio transmitters had been monitored.[92] In July, however, reports of Werwolf activity rebounded in number, and the Czechoslovaks suddenly seemed faced with a problem of crisis proportions in certain areas. The embryonic Czechoslovak Army took its knocks; there were panicky appeals to Prague for reinforcements; and, by the end of July, representations had been directed even towards the Red Army, asking for help in the maintenance of order.[93]

There were two reasons for this sudden escalation of the conflict. First, it was only in the summer of 1945 that Czechoslovak administrators and 'Revolutionary Guards' began to stream into Sudeten-German areas in truly significant numbers. Their arrival, and their frequently atrocious behaviour, could be interpreted as a 'provocation' of the German-Sudeten population, which in turn seemed to demand retaliatory violence. As a third stage in this vicious cycle, the Czechoslovaks then engaged in counter-reprisals that were so brutal, and involved such large numbers of people, that they seemed part of a policy of repression with aims far greater than the mere containment of underground resistance. The worst aspects of this contest of wills were the so-called wild expulsions that began in June 1945. Put simply, these were ad hoc evacuations of whole towns, with only a few hours' notice, whereby Sudeten-German burghers were literally chased to the German frontier.

As the Czechoslovaks gradually pried open the closed structures of Sudeten-German society, the Communist-dominated security services claimed to find evidence of a conspiracy that their cursory disarmament sweeps of May and June had failed to disclose. It might be argued that they saw *more* signs of organization and coherency than actually existed, although there is little doubt that remnants of the Werwolf were still there to be uncovered, and that such elements may have even gained a measure of credibility due to the brutal behavior of Czechoslovak security forces after the end of the war. In mid-July, the authorities discovered a Werwolf net in the vicinity of Reinerz, complete with secret caches of weapons and supplies, and they claimed that there were many other places where Sudeten Germans had a continuing involvement in the underground. In other words, the conspiracy was not isolated, 'but there was reason to believe it had ramifications throughout the country.' The Czechoslovaks were particularly aghast that Sudeten German 'Antifas' apparently had liaison with Werwolf groups, and that the two movements were cooperating in the forging of identification papers to protect Sudeten Germans against forced deportation, particularly phoney membership cards in the Communist Party.[94] This seemed to suggest that the Werwolf was seen as a valuable instrument even by anti-Nazi Sudeten Germans, who, despite their anti-Fascism, still had autonomist and anti-Czech inclinations. From there, the stigma of involvement spread like an ugly stain, and, in Czechoslovak eyes, *all* Germans were blemished. In this kind of atmosphere, random acts came to seem part of a larger design, and innocuous events were misinterpreted so that a number of undoubtedly innocent Sudeten German civilians were imagined culpable in regard to underground activity.[95]

Despite a strong streak of Czechoslovak paranoia, there is also evidence that some genuine resistance was actually under way. A British intelligence summary set the proper tone by noting that outbreaks of violence were real enough, although there was no evidence of 'any long-term resistance plan' – 'It seems more likely that it is merely an example of the petty, unorganized sabotage common in occupied Germany, though perhaps exacerbated by the political situation in the Sudetenland.'[96] In several cases, Czechoslovak administrators and military officials were attacked; there were raids on Czechoslovak internment camps in order to aid mass break-out attempts; secret radio transmitters were monitored (particulary at Tetschen); Sudeten German youths pulled down Czechoslovak flags and harassed Czechoslovak administrators; Werwolf and 'Shepherd' signs were chalked on doors and walls; and Nazi rumour-mongers spread unrest and created the impression that the Western Powers were preparing to intervene in favour of the Sudeten Germans.[97] Even the Americans experienced sabotage and attacks, and the history of the U.S. 94th Infantry Division notes that 'there was considerable hostility toward the occupation troops.' On the other hand, it must be admitted that American relations with the Sudeten Germans rapidly improved, and the Americans even began to complain about the tendency of the Czechoslovak security services to torture and otherwise abuse their prisoners.[98] By the late summer and fall of 1945, the last thing most Sudeten Germans wanted was to drive away the Americans and let the Czechoslovak administration have full sway.

Some of the most disruptive acts of violence involved attacks against Czechoslovak civil and military officials, since these were outright challenges to Prague's capacity to extend its authority over Sudeten-German districts. In one case, two Czechoslovak soldiers trapped in an ambush were shot in the back of the head by their guerrilla captors. In several other instances, shots were fired into the homes of Czechoslovak district administrators or militia officers; in one case the bullets lodged in a bedstead inches above the head of the intended victim. According to an American intelligence report, at least five Czechoslovaks were killed in an outburst of shooting incidents in late July. The most prominent victim was Dr Rychlik, the manager of a government program to transfer industry from the Sudetenland to Slovakia. Rychlik was kidnapped and murdered by German terrorists.[99]

There was also a considerable amount of partisan activity in the Sudetenland. The woods were rife with Werwolf groups composed of HJ teenagers and led by SS men or German Army officers. 'They lived from pillage,' said a Czechoslovak militia commander, and they 'attacked new colonists and set fires.' In June 1945, large stretches of northern Moravia were sealed off and swept by Czechoslovak militiamen mopping up these bands.[100] In the same month, the NKVD 'liquidated' Werwolf groups at Waltersdorf and Grulich, in northern Bohemia. Most of the personnel in these detachments had been trained at a German sabotage school at Grossgerlitz, and they were well equipped with arms and ammunition. In July, Czechoslovak militiamen arrested fourteen HJ-

Werewolves in the Broumov district, and in the same area, elements of the Czechoslovak 14th Division overran a thirty-seven-man Werwolf unit led by a renegade Dutch Nazi. 'The Broumov region,' reported the Ministry of Information in August 1945, 'is a part of the country where werewolves still exist and terrorize the local population.'[101]

The area around Kaaden was a special trouble spot. Although Sudeten German refugees later claimed that 'not one shot' was fired by civilians in the Kaaden region,[102] this was hardly the case. In truth, a Werwolf training course had been held in a HJ camp near Kaaden, and the whole district had been terrorized even before the capitulation, especially through fiery slogans chalked upon the walls: 'Better Dead than Red'; 'The Way to the Reich Lays Only Over Our Dead Bodies.' 'These sayings,' remembered one inhabitant, 'grinned at us like ghosts week after week.'[103] Worse yet, the local *Kreisleiter* and other NSDAP hacks headed for the woods at the time of the final collapse, and their flight subsequently posed some intractable problems for the district.

On 25 May, two Czechoslovak gendarmes were dispatched to search the village of Totzau, near Kaaden, looking for the errant *Kreisleiter*. Although the *Bürgermeister* assured the authorities that there were no strangers in the town, the two Czechoslovaks were then fired at by a hidden SA man. One of the Czechoslovaks was killed instantly, while the other was wounded in the shoulder. Bleeding profusely, the injured gendarme staggered back to the *Bürgermeister*, yelled, 'Why didn't you tell us?,' and then shot the mayor in the chest. Subsequently, he managed to reach the post office and called in reinforcements. Totzau was then ringed by Czechoslovak military units, and was swept by security troops amid much tumult and shouting.

After this raid, and yet another one several days later, the villagers of Totzau were horrified when Czechoslovak gendarmes once again rushed into the town in early June. A gendarmerie captain barked out an announcement, declaring that a Czechoslovak patrol had just been attacked in a nearby forest by German guerrillas armed with hand-grenades. The villagers claimed that they knew nothing, and had not even heard the attack, but the Czechoslovaks sealed the village and once again swept it in rough fashion. Shortly before noon, weapons were discovered, although the local authorities once again tried to slip an ever-tightening noose by claiming that the American headquarters in Karlsbad had approved their possession of a few weapons for self-defence. The Czechoslovaks would hear nothing of such excuses, and they ordered the entire population of the village to form up in front of a local inn. Once gathered, six NSDAP members were sorted out of the crowd and set aside for special treatment, as the gendarmerie officer meanwhile strode through the multitude, arbitrarily selecting male hostages with such remarks as, 'You'll have to die too, you Blonde

Beast.' Finally, twenty men were lined up in two rows and mercilessly beaten. Once they were half dead, a clatter of machine-gun and pistol shots finished them off, amidst the screams and wailing of the assembled inhabitants of the village. 'We could hardly bear to watch it,' remembered the wife of one of the hostages, 'but we were forced to keep our eyes on what was taking place.'

Meanwhile, the local Nazi Party chieftains who were at least indirectly responsible for such mayhem continued to remain at large, and the Czechoslovaks grew ever more vicious in their pursuit. At Totzau, where a local burgher was suspected of lodging the *Kreisleiter*, the man and his entire family were killed by the Czechoslovaks, and their bullet-peppered bodies were left adorning the front hall of their home. On the night of 2–3 June, five Sudeten Germans were also executed at Kottersdorf because of Czechoslovak suspicions that they had dared to contact the fugitive. Shortly thereafter, a Sudeten German anti-Fascist offered to venture into the woods and track down the malevolent *Kreisleiter*, but good intentions were no match for bullets, and in the final analysis it was this intrepid Nazi-hunter who was shot and killed by his nemesis.[104]

The most disruptive kind of event in the newly liberated Sudetenland was the sequence of an alleged bomb attack, followed by a brutal knee-jerk reaction from the Czechoslovaks, often wholly disproportionate to the seriousness of the original incident. The first such event occurred in late June 1945 at Teplitz, where several missiles held in an arsenal blew up and killed two Czechoslovak guards. Actually, the cause of this blast was (and is) unclear. Much unfused ammunition was held at a depot in the town, and Sudeten Germans later claimed that Czechoslovak militiamen were careless in handling this volatile material. The Czechoslovaks countercharged that German saboteurs had blown up the rockets. The authorities also had evidence that there had been a Werwolf training camp near Teplitz, which (for them) seemed the final piece of the puzzle. One thing that is clear is that the consequences of this explosion were severe. Accused of 'an act of resistance,' all the Volksdeutsch villagers of Teplitz were rounded up and forcibly evacuated from the area,[105] one of the first so-called wild expulsions.

Next, on 6 July, came an explosion at the police station at Freudenthal, in the eastern Sudetenland. This blast cost the Czechoslovak militia, which was using the building as a command post, several dead and several more injured. The Czechoslovak authorities claimed that a time bomb had been concealed in a confiscated radio set. As a reprisal, they shot twenty prisoners held in a local concentration camp, all of whom were described as NSDAP members or SA men. The other prisoners in the Freudenthal holding camp were forced to watch the shootings and were warned that, if there were any further instances of sabotage, fifty Germans would be executed instead of twenty.

As usual, Sudeten German refugees from Freudenthal had their own versions of this incident, which varied considerably from the Czechoslovak story. Several reports claimed that the bombing was faked and that the charges of sabotage were entirely false. One former resident of the town claimed that the explosion was real enough, but that a Czechoslovak soldier had confidentially revealed the 'true cause' of the blast: several Czechoslovak militiamen had supposedly been playing with a hand-grenade when it accidentally detonated.[106]

In mid-July, there was yet another mysterious explosion. Reports varied, but it appears that there was a blast at a munitions cache in an old chocolate plant at the small village of Khotine, which killed eleven Czechoslovak guards and a number of German workers. The police chief of nearby Liberec immediately smelled sabotage, claiming that a German bomber had touched off the burst. Apparently, the remains of an explosive device were found littering the body of one of the Germans killed in the disaster. 'Since the people of Khotine won't tell us who blew up the ammunition dump,' said the police chief, '... the entire German population – anti-Fascists excepted – will be evicted at three hours' notice.' Soon after the blast, Czechoslovak military police herded the town's inhibitants onto the village common. Luggage was searched, and many in the crowd were robbed, particularly of jewels and silver, although they were able to hold on to paper money. English journalist Peter Smollett was invited to witness this evacuation, and his report on 20 July gives a good sense of the event:

I spent all day yesterday [said Smollett] with 518 Germans walking under a blazing sun from Sudetenland into Soviet-occupied Germany. They were old and young, men and women, little children. They pulled barrows and pushed prams with their belongings. None was allowed to take more than he could carry. The very old and the very young could ride on horse-drawn carts. The rest must walk. They were accompanied by Czechoslovak guards, who took them 12 miles beyond the border. I was with them from 5.30 a.m., the moment when the Czech police called them out of bed and told them to pack up and leave within three hours. I left them at 6 p.m. at Hartau, in Saxony, in the Soviet Zone ...

We struck out at 11 a.m. and reached the border at five. Some of the old people had been pushed off the carts by stronger, younger ones. Occasionally I saw a Czech guard push a cart for an old woman straggler. I saw no German help another. On the other side of the border a Czech told them: 'You are among your own people now. You can even take off the white armlet here.'

Smollett was continually told along the way that the expellees had done nothing against the Czechoslovaks.[107]

The worst such case occurred in the Schönpriesen industrial suburb of Aussig an der Elbe, although the consequences were far more serious than in any previous incident. On the afternoon of 30 July 1945, a deafening roar shook Schönpriesen, shattering windows within a two-mile radius. The material that had detonated comprised about 2 million items of arms and munitions abandoned by the Schörner Army Group in May 1945, all of which was stored in the cellars of a cable works. The initial explosion naturally touched off a fire and, owing to high winds, this blaze spread to nearby factories and caused several additional explosions. Eventually, the flames also reached workers' housing adjacent to the industrial district. According to Czechoslovak estimates, 50 people were killed in this initial chain of detonations and fires, including some Sudeten Germans; another 160 people were injured; and property damage amounted to nearly $1.8 million. Thus began the most important of all 'Werwolf' incidents, although it is by no means clear that the Werwolf was directly involved. In the final analysis, only the tension and irrascibility that they provoked may have been to blame for what occurred.

The original blast in Schönpriesen was quickly followed by a sort of psychological explosion, which resulted from the rumour that German Werewolves had blown up the arsenal. Off-duty Czechoslovak soldiers recently arrived in the town had already begun to amuse themselves by beating up hapless Germans, and now, in the company of black-uniformed Czechoslovak security forces and occasional Red Army troopers, they unleashed a full-scale reign of terror. The huge clouds of black smoke billowing over the city from Schönpriesen seemed a signal for the outbreak of a pogrom. Within an hour of the explosion, a large mob of Czechoslovak security personnel had collected at a bridge over the Elbe. Here they waylaid workers streaming across the bridge from the Schicht factory in Schreckenstein, on the south bank of the river. Most of these labourers, on their way home after the 4:30 shift, never again saw their houses or their kin. Czechoslovak marauders armed with iron bars and pick handles beat the German workers senseless, and then tossed their bodies into the Elbe. A machine-gun set up on a nearby hill shot at the heads of any unfortunates who bobbed to the surface. Several other groups of young men were arrested and carted away to local holding camps at Theresienstadt and Lerchenfelde, where they were either beaten to death or slowly starved and tortured.

Workers from the Schicht plant were not the only victims. Women and children were also beaten and tossed into the Elbe; even young mothers with perambulators suffered this gruesome fate. Other civilians were thrown into water reserve tanks in Aussig's main square, where Czechoslovaks with poles pushed down any victims who struggled to the surface. Elsewhere, Czechoslovak mobs roamed the streets, assaulting Germans or breaking into their homes and hauling the inhabitants out for a beating. Sudeten Germans were easily identifiable because most were forced to wear white armbands, signifying that they were subject to eventual deportation. However, attacks were also directed towards Volksdeutsche with yellow armlets, showing that their status was undecided, or even red armlets, showing that they were active anti-Fascists.

This mayhem raged unchecked for several hours, until a few responsible authorities finally succeeded in restoring a semblance of order. The Czechoslovak mayor of Aussig, Josef Vondra, risked being thrown into the Elbe himself in an attempt to stop the violence. By early evening, Vondra had received Soviet help, and the virulence of the attacks decreased, although even on the following day German civilians were still pushed from the sidewalks and beaten in the streets. On 31 July, Vondra posted notices announcing a curfew and the imposition of the death penalty for anyone on the streets after eight o'clock.

The sorrows of the local Sudeten Germans, however, were still not over. The sentiments of the new Czechoslovak inhabitants of the town had been raised to a fever pitch by the explosions and the riots, and they now demanded that all local Germans be summarily expelled from their homes. Thus, in addition to suffering casualities estimated at anywhere from 200 killed and injured to 4,000 dead (the highest German estimate), the remaining 20,000 Volksdeutsche in the area were uprooted and forced to trek to Germany. Half the German Aussiger population had already been expelled, so this final push effectively ended the history of Aussig as a German settlement – henceforth it would exist as the Czech city of Ústí nad Labem. As for the Czechoslovak and foreign press, they were fobbed off with the declaration that the disorder had been caused by the Germans themselves, and it was claimed that Czechoslovak special forces had merely been rushed to the town in order to 'secure' the German ethnic inhabitants.[108]

Basically, there were three competing theories about what actually happened at Aussig. The first was merely an extension of the initial Czechoslovak rumour about Werwolf incendiarism. Soon after the riot a special commission composed of Defence Minister Svaboda, Interior Minister Nosek, and the chief of Czechoslovak intelligence, Colonel Bartak, arrived in Aussig with a mandate to restore calm and determine the cause of the blast. After investigation, and several tortuous internal debates, the authorities confirmed that German saboteurs had actually touched off the explosion. Fragments of bombs, they said, had been found among the debris, and they also hinted some of the fires that broke out were set separately and were not attributable to the original blast. There were several factors favouring such an explanation: German political captives had been employed stacking munitions in the Schönpriesen depot, and a squad of such prisoners had finished its shift shortly before the explosion. As well, the Czechoslovak premier, Fierlinger, had been in Aussig earlier on 30 July, where he had made some typically severe remarks about the sort of treatment that Sudeten Germans had a right to expect, and this, when combined with the undisciplined behaviour of Czechoslovak troops on the morning of 30 July, could well be interpreted as an event demanding some sort of retaliatory act on behalf of the German population. Hardened Nazis thus had both an opportunity and a motive to blow up the weapons depot. Sudeten-German refugees later tried to claim that there were actually no Werewolves in this area at all, but, several days after the Aussig incident, the Czechoslovaks produced a local Werwolf leader named Lange. Paraded before journalists at a press conference in Aussig, Lange admitted to being an ex-DAF official, an NSDAP member, a Volkssturm volunteer, and the graduate of a local Werwolf training course. The Werwolf, said Lange, was operating in expectation of an imminent conflict between East and West, and German guerrillas were prepared to march against the Russians.[109]

Publicizing the Aussig incident had definite advantages for the Czechoslovaks. They naturally said nothing about the pogrom, but they pointed to the initial explosion as a prime example of the dangers that the Sudeten-German population still posed for the Czechoslovak state. Throughout early August, the press blustered about Aussig as an outrage against Czechoslovak authority, and they emphasized that it was not an isolated event, but part of an ongoing current of opposition that provided extra incentive for accelerating the rate of expulsion. This press campaign was obviously linked to the concurrent discussions by the Big Three at Potsdam, where formal approval for Czechoslovak expulsion plans was pending. Once the final communiqué at the Great Power Conference made it clear that the Czechoslovaks had a fundamental right to effect mass deportations, but that the timing of further expulsions was still in the air, even the Czechoslovak government joined the chorus seeking to use Aussig as a vehicle to discredit the country's ethnic German minority. 'The transfer must proceed ... ,' said Defence Minister Svaboda on 12 August. 'We will not tolerate half-measures and the recent acts of terror at Ústí must be a final warning to one and all.' Hubert Ripka, the Minister of Foreign Trade, noted on 20 August: Our people are worried ... by the postponement of the transfer. We are fully conscious of the technical and food difficulties which the Allies have to overcome in connection with the deportation of the Germans from Czechoslovakia and Poland to Germany, but one should understand the feeling of our people who are being constantly attacked by Werwolf organizations, and whose property is still being destroyed. We witness large-scale sabotage as was recently the case at Ústí nad Labem. Many of our people do not feel safe until they know that the Germans will go away.[110]

As far as Sudeten Germans were concerned, the fortunate timing of the blast (from the point of view of Czechoslovak propaganda) was far too convenient. Not only did they see themselves as entirely blameless – not one among their number lifted a finger against their oppressors – but they also believed that the Czechoslovaks had conspired to besmirch the otherwise stainless record of Sudeten-German passivity. 'A favourite trick of the Czechs in the Sudetenland,' noted one refugee, 'was ... to set a house afire and lay the blame for "sabotage" at the door of the Germans. Such was the case with the factory explosion in Aussig.' There were the usual pieces of second-hand evidence to support this claim: a Czechoslovak, met on the train in the fall of 1945, told a Volksdeutsch acquaintance that a camarilla had staged the explosion and that they had prepared the massacre well in advance of 30 July; a Viennese opera singer, who was in Aussig on the day of the catastrophe, claimed that her Czechoslovak porter told her to remain indoors all day, since something bad was about to occur. Sudeten-German Social Democrats tried to expose the timing of the pogrom as evidence of premeditation. Some claimed that the disturbances broke out before the explosion, although this in itself proved nothing, and actually provided the Germans with a possible motive. Others noted that Vondra's proclamations declaring a curfew were composed, printed, and posted within a few hours of the blast, timing they claimed was physically impossible. But this was a weak argument because it assumed that the explosion was on 31 July, whereas several of the most reliable witnesses categorically testified that the initial blast occurred on 30 July. One Sudeten witness clearly remembered that, on the evening of 30 July, the curfew was announced by loudspeaker trucks, and that the printed posters did not appear until the following day. Moreover, Vondra risked his life to stop the pogrom, so it was unlikely that he was involved in any conspiracy to incite it.[111]

A third theory, rather more satisfactory than either of the first two, was that the explosion was simply an accident. Many Sudeten-German refugees suggested this was the case: the explosion, they said, was touched off by reckless Russian soldiers searching for alcohol in a nearby brewery, or was ignited by Czechoslovak guards who carelessly smoked near the arsenal.[112] However, the best evidence was submitted by a former Czechoslovak official in Aussig, who fled Czechoslovakia at the time of the pro-Soviet *coup d'etat* in 1948, and later told his story to a Czechoslovak exile journal in London. According to this witness, the guards and supervisors at the Schönpriesen depot paid little attention to their work, although they did have an inordinate interest in consuming the products of a distillery next door. Thus, according to this former government bureaucrat, arms and munitions were simply thrown together in a hopeless jumble – 'This,' he said, 'was the cause of the catastrophe.' Moreover, there were severe debates among government officials about where to point the fin-

ger of blame, particularly since it was clear that both the explosion and the subsequent riot had occurred as a result of negligence on the part of the military.
But the Army, which was already badly overstrained and faced intense problems in recruitment, refused to bear its share of responsibility.[113]

According to Czechoslovak sources, Werwolf outrages in Bohemia reached
their peak with the Aussig incident, whereafter the Czechoslovak Army and
security forces finally began to gain the upper hand. By August, the majority of
reports told of the successful liquidation of armed bands by Czechoslovak units,
and the situation in the Sudetenland subsequently grew quieter. Even as early as
the beginning of August, the trade-union organ *Prace* reported that conditions
in the frontier districts were already growing calmer, and a trade-union official
who toured the Sudeten districts in the same month reported that the spirit of
the Volksdeutsche, once so militant, was now crushed. 'The feeling,' he said,
'... resembles a cemetery. The Germans wear white armlets and walk about
silently, and even at home they do not dare to speak. It is difficult to imagine
that they would still have spirit to offer forcible resistance, though reports of
sabotage are many.'[114] Towards the end of 1945, at the suggestion of President
Truman, U.S. and Soviet forces were evacuated from Czechoslovakia. 'There
is,' Truman said, 'no longer any necessity to protect the Zecho people against
any Nazi depredations, and since the presence of our troops undoubtedly constitutes a drain on their economy, [such forces] should be withdrawn as soon as
practicable ... .'[115] Nevertheless, a minor level of Werwolf activity did continue
into the fall of 1945. In the town of Tyssa, a local industrialist was arrested,
along with thirty of his workers, on charges of Werwolf sympathies, and in
September this same individual was executed when a hidden machine-gun was
discovered on the premises of his factory. In Teplitz, Werwolf leaflets warned,
'we are on the alert. We are waiting and fighting,' and further radio broadcasts
continued to urge murder and mayhem aimed at the Czechoslovaks. In Eger,
four adolescent Werewolves were arrested on charges of planning to blow up a
Czechoslovak military barracks, and another plot was uncovered where the goal
was to destroy eighty railway engines. Spikes were found scattered over various
roads, and dumps of arms, explosives, and medical equipment continued to be
unearthed.[116]

One such incident of late-blooming Werwolf activity was witnessed by an
American journalist in Marienbad during the autumn of 1945. In this case, a
yellow-armleted German complained to the authorities that he had been
attacked by a man wearing a red star and armed with a revolver. Investigation
showed that the culprit was *not* a Communist, but a Werwolf agent provocateur
named Rudolf Hergeth. Under interrogation, Hergeth's will crumbled and he
quickly revealed all that he knew, which included the location of an arms cache

and the names of fellow members in his Werwolf cell. In turn, one of these confederates admitted training at two special Werwolf schools, while another proved to have successfully disguised himself as an accredited anti-Fascist and was serving as an employee in a Czechoslovak municipal office. Even the Czechoslovaks hastened to add, however, that the number of Werewolves was not large, and that the majority of the Sudeten-German population peaceably went about its business.[117]

The final resolution of the Werwolf problem corresponded with the ultimate expulsion of the German minority, as was also the case in Poland. Nearly 2.3 million Sudeten Germans were deported to the U.S. and Soviet zones of Germany in 1946, leaving only 200,000 ethnic Germans in Czechoslovakia by 1947. Czech reports from 1946 claimed that overall there had been 314 cases of underground activity in Bohemia, including sabotage; arson; and damage to railway lines, bridges, and communication cables. Included among these incidents were 84 assaults upon Czechoslovak soldiers, administrators, and colonists, most of which took the form of sniping and grenade attacks.[118]

However, while Sudeten-German unrest within Czechoslovakia was all but over, there were still some continuing difficulties with raiding activity along Czechia's frontiers, which particularly involved bands of Sudeten-German expellees. This was a form of activity similar to the Palestinian fedayeen raids that disrupted the civil life of Israel during the early 1950s, and, like the fedayeen parallel, many of these incidents were essentially looting expeditions, although they had a definite political flavour that was recognized by the country whose borders had been violated. The raids were usually conducted by Sudeten-German expellees, who organized armed bands in the land of their exile, and then infiltrated back into their homeland, usually in order to recover their livestock and material goods, or to steal from farms expropriated by Czechoslovak colonists. As early as the fall of 1945, five armed Germans were captured as they attempted to enter Czechoslovakia illegally, and such problems grew worse as the numbers of deportees got larger. Near Aussig, raiders left postcards warning Czechoslovak settlers to take good care of 'their' property, or they spread leaflets calling upon the few remaining Volksdeutsche to engage in sabotage, and promising that the Western Allies would soon arrive to champion the Sudeten-German cause. In a few cases, Sudeten-German trespassers set fires, or they killed Czechoslovak border guards – in early April 1947, a customs official was murdered by a German band operating just inside the Czechoslovak frontier at Görkau. A year later, a prominent Sudeten-German Communist, Augustin Schramm, was shot and killed, allegedly by a 'terrorist band' based at Regensburg. According to Sudeten-German opinion, Schramm was a traitor because he had served as an officer in the Red Army and had organized pro-Soviet guerrilla units in Czechoslovakia. At the time of his assassination, Schramm was the chief of a special intelligence apparatus connected with the Central Committee of the Czechoslovak Communist Party.[119]

The most serious incident along the frontier occurred on the night of 6–7 September 1946. On this evening, 200 Sudeten-German refugees crossed the border between Moravia and the Soviet Zone of Austria, and they pillaged the town of Schossenburg, near Feldsburg, whence many of them had originally been expelled. During the attack, the band was encountered by Czechoslovak customs officials, and a battle broke out before the raiders succeeded in slipping back into Austrian territory. There were several casualties, and fourteen prisoners were taken by the Czechoslovaks, although only one person was killed.

Such events caused considerable tension between the Czechoslovaks and their neighbours, including even their Soviet and Polish allies. After the Schossenburg incident, the Czechoslovaks lodged a vigorous protest, charging that Austrian officials had connived with the raiders, and that a few local bureaucrats and gendarmerie officials had even joined the expedition. The raid, they pointed out, was actually led by the *Bürgermeister* of the nearby Austrian town of Schrattenberg. The Czechoslovaks also complained that 'a Werwolf organisation,' the 'Sudeten-German Freedom Corps,' was operating from the Soviet Zone in Austria, after having shifted its headquarters from Polish Silesia.[120]

Special invective was reserved for the Americans, who were suspected of turning a blind eye to Sudeten revanchism. There was considerable tension along the border, owing to the Czech habit of surging across the frontier in hot pursuit of raiders – General Clay complained to the War Department about this matter in April 1946 – and Sudeten German border-crossers captured in Czechoslovakia were questioned in detail about Werwolf activities and potentialities. The Czechs also suspected that the Americans were keeping German Army and SS units in existence.[121] The CIC did confirm that the Edelweiss Piraten in Regensburg were organized for violence against the Czechs, and that considerable underground agitation among the refugees was attributable to right-wing Sudeten German Social Democrats led by Wenzel Jaksch, who in turn was linked with General Prchala and his 'Czech Resistance Movement.'[122] To soothe the ruffled feathers of the Czechoslovaks, *all* Sudeten-German political activity was banned by the American Military Government, although this was not enough to please Prague.[123]

The South Tyrol

Finally, moving southwestwards, we come to the last important German borderland – namely, the South Tyrolean region of northern Italy. Unlike Czechoslovakia, Italy was an Axis state, and therefore did not possess the moral high ground in its claims for effective restoration of control over the South Tyrol and its pocket of 200,000 ethnic Germans. In fact, there was a real question in 1945–6 whether the territory and its population might return to Austria, which had run the area until 1919. Certainly there was no talk of Polish- and Czech-style deportations.

There is no doubt that the Italians had treated the province poorly during the interwar period, regarding South Tyrolean Germans as wayward 'Teutonized' Latins, in desperate need of Italianization. The South Tyrolean Volksdeutsche deeply resented these policies, and in the 1930s some of them began to stake their hopes on Mussolini's rival, Adolf Hitler. However, the Nazi regime, despite its much-ballyhooed dedication to German ethnic minorities, was ready to blithely sell out the interests of the South Tyroleans for the sake of a German alliance with Italy. Berlin's studied lack of interest in the problem was one of the few things weighing down the fortunes of regional Nazis in both the South Tyrol and western Austria, and as a result they frequently ignored official policy and made the cession of the area a major feature of their propaganda. The only saving grace for the movement was that other local alternatives on the right were just as pro-Italian as the Nazis themselves. Hitler was loath to acknowledge such regional discontents, and in 1939 he negotiated a pact with Mussolini that arranged for a mass evacuation of German-speakers from northeastern Italy; those who wished to maintain their German identity were invited to emigrate to the Greater Reich; those willing to bear Italian assimilation could stay. Over a quarter of the Volksdeutsch population decided in favour of Germany and actually left the region, although some later filtered back. Another large block of the population chose to leave, but then remained on hand, hoping to outwait the evacuation in the expectation of a radical change in the balance of Italo–German relations. A third group chose to remain behind permanently, even though this meant accepting Italianization. Naturally, this sequence of events produced a deep cleavage between Nazified elements that 'opted' for the Third Reich ('Optants'), and the portion of the population that decided to remain ('Stay-Behinders').

The 'Optants' came into their own in 1943, when Italy capitulated and the Germans organized a special operational zone in northeastern Italy called the 'Alpenvorland,' bringing back many 'Optants' as administrators and officials. Although the fig leaf of Italian sovereignty was maintained as a concession to Mussolini's new pro-German government in northern Italy, in many ways the South Tyrol was effectively annexed to the Reich. The NSDAP was still prohibited, but the civilian high commissioner of the operational zone was Franz Hofer, *Gauleiter* of the Tyrol–Voralberg and primary advocate of full South

Tyrolese reincorporation. Many South Tyroleans were enthusiastic about this de facto Anschluss with their Austrian motherland, and the suspicion that the Americans might overturn this state of affairs served to make South Tyroleans cool, 'non-cooperative,' and in some instances openly hostile to the Allies.[124]

Another big problem was that the South Tyrol played a large role in various scenarios regarding the Alpine Redoubt, mainly because of its position as a secure place of retreat for the German armies in Italy. In fact, during the last weeks of the war, the Germans managed to withdraw 600,000 soldiers into the area, so that the military population of the region was three times as large as its ethnic German civil populace. When the first Allied troops arrived in the province in the wake of the 2 May capitulation, they were outnumbered by German forces at a rate of sixty to one. In a few cases – that of 1st Parachute Division, for instance – German units refused to surrender, and there were skirmishes with the approaching Allies. According to one German soldier, SS hold-outs sniped at German armies retreating through the Brenner Pass, and many troops were turned aside and forced to search for open passes, often leaving behind their sick and wounded in the process. A regiment of Italian Fascists was active in the same region, also opposing the Allied advance.

In areas where they did surrender, the German forces made the most of their momentary advantage in numbers. A wilful and arrogant tone was set by Himmler's man on the spot, SS-General Karl Wolff, known to history as the man who arranged the early surrender of German forces in Italy. To put Wolff in context, however, it is important to note that he was a native Tyrolean who entertained a patriotic interest in retaining the South Tyrol for his Austrian homeland. Wolff had been involved in underground Nazi agitations during the late 1930s, and he may have been connected with similar schemes for the postwar period. He and his staff swore to Allied interrogators that no directives concerning the Werwolf were ever sent to the 'Alpenvorland,' but this was a lie: Werwolf orders were in fact dispatched to the SS-Police Command in Italy as early as the fall of 1944, and the Werwolf actively recruited among the German soldiery in northern Italy. Moreover, the HJ-Werwolf was used as a source of sabotage and espionnage agents, and it was led by a rabid Nazi suspected of killing an American airman who had bailed out over the Brenner Pass. On top of all this, a Werwolf training camp was established at Schlanders, whence recruits went on to a demolitions course in Innsbruck. Thus, it is boundlessly apparent that the Wehrmacht was implicated in Werwolf-type activity, just as it was elsewhere in the Greater Reich.

German forces were confined to barracks in mid-May, but thousands of Wehrmacht troops paraded around the South Tyrol under the protection of passes ostensibly issued by the International Red Cross. Eventually, a printing press was discovered in Meran that had been producing large numbers of these passes; some 20,000 cards were seized. Moreover, Germans operating under Red Cross colours were discovered loading machine-guns into ambulances. German troops and HJ also roamed the streets, singing Nazi marching songs, and a riot nearly began when a German unit was prevented from holding a ceremony for the presentation of service medals.

The worst problem faced by the Allies was the fact that many German soldiers and SS men were hidden by the local populace, or were posing as wounded veterans in various military hospitals. On several occasions German commanders were unable to muster their forces in mid-May, when the Allies began evacuating German troops down to the North Italian plain. A Luftwaffe unit, for example, was originally numbered at 2,000; its evacuation staff then provided a revised strength of 600; and, when the men were called to the parade-ground for evacuation, only 230 appeared. Owing to such contrivances, American forces formed special raiding patrols, which swept local mountain villages and bagged renegade Nazis. Most of the desperadoes gave up quietly, but occasionally shooting broke out: Italy's top Waffen-SS officer, SS-Major Mario Carita, was killed in such a fight on 20 May, after he managed to shoot an American soldier.[125]

Obviously, an explosive situation existed for several weeks, and it is hardly surprising that it occasionally developed into instances of active resistance. As early as 3 May, an American soldier was poisoned with toxic wine in the largely Italian town of Riva, an incident which left the dead man's comrades wondering how the townfolk could treat them as liberating heroes on the day before, and then attempt to kill them on the following night. Several days later, German troops blew up a barracks in Brixon, which had been chosen as an American billet. Although no one was injured in the Brixon incident, a time bomb also blew up in Eisack, wounding twenty-two American soldiers. The charge had been left in the cellar of an American billet, and it completely demolished a battalion command post. Another incident occurred when Allied troops, using captured German flare guns to celebrate VE day, found to their dismay that SS troops, as a last act of defiance, had extracted the normal cartridges and replaced them with TNT charges.[126] Such outrages continued until the end of May, by which time most German troops had been evacuated.

Meanwhile, relations between the occupiers and the indigenous South Tyroleans warmed several degrees,[127] but it is important to note that there was a much larger potential for friction between native Tyrolean Germans and incoming Italians. Considering the recent history of the area, it was almost natural that skirmishes broke out, and, when a large mass of Wehrmacht troops were still in the area during May, they regarded themselves as the appointed protectors of the local German populace. From 1943 to 1945, the Wehrmacht had waged a ruthless war against Italian partisans, and fighting between the two sides continued even beyond the German capitulation on 2 May. Under the armistice agreement, anti-Fascist Italian partisan units were supposed to accept the surrender of German detachments in the South Tyrol, and to occupy the major towns of the region. There was scattered German resistance: on 2 May, SS troops fired on partisans preparing to assume the administration of Laas, killing nine, and on the following day a battle was fought in the downtown portion of Meran, resulting in the deaths of fifteen more partisans. In mid-May, a newly arrived CIC unit in Meran arrested SS-Lieutenant Colonel Horst Eller, on charges of killing three Italian Partisans in the post-capitulation period. Gradually, however, the relative balance of this struggle altered: German troops were disarmed and evacuated, and subsequently Italian troops of the Gruppo Folgore moved into the region.

By June 1945, civilians were still skirmishing with well-armed troops, but now it was German civilians and Italian soldiers, rather than vice versa. The Americans had entertained plans to withdraw their forces after the advance of the Gruppo Folgore, but it now became necessary to leave behind troops to act as a buffer between the local German populace and the Italian units. Even with these precautions, there was still a rash of attacks against Italian forces, which by mid-June had resulted in the deaths of two soldiers. There was also an inevitable series of Italian retaliatory actions against German-speaking inhabitants. Sparks were still flying as late as midsummer 1945, when a train carrying former Italian concentration-camp inmates from Germany was shot at as it passed through the Alps. Several passengers were wounded.[128] It is true that the German population organized its own legitimate, pro-Austrian political movement, the South Tyrolean People's Party (SVP), which signed an agreement of limited cooperation with the Italian partisans in late May, but the Allies still suspected that each side was stockpiling arms for a showdown. *Avanti* also reported that 'reactionaries' were doing their best to disrupt the People's Party–Partisan accord.

Another source of tension was a divide within the Tyrolean-German population itself, with 'Optants' and 'Stay-Behinders' at opposite poles. When the Werwolf was set up in the autumn of 1944, it naturally drew recruits from a radical fringe of the 'Optants.' There was some question whether the Werwolf had been established at all, due to the fact that the 'Alpenvorland' had never been formally annexed by Germany, and the development of a regional wing of the NSDAP had remained forbidden. Thus, as noted above, Wolff and his captured staff solemnly swore to Allied interrogators that the guerrilla program had been restricted to Germany proper and had never spread to northeastern Italy. However, documentary evidence leaves no doubt that a South Tyrolean chapter of the Werwolf *was* organized, probably with the handy rationalization that it was a military agency rather than a parapolitical adjunct of the NSDAP. In fact the first Ultra intercept concerning the overall program, dated 19 November 1944, was an instruction for the HSSPF Italy to send his indents for Werwolf arms and equipment directly to the Bureau 'Prützmann.'[129] It must be noted, on the other hand, that the SVP was mainly an organ of the 'Stay-Behinders,' and that it alienated Nazi opinion by agreeing in its May 1945 pact with the Italian partisans to cooperate in a denazification purge.

It was this current of fratricidal animosity that formed the background to a report in early July 1945, which suggested a continuing level of Werwolf activity in the South Tyrol. According to the French news service AFP, an entire family of Tyrolean Germans was massacred by Werewolves. The head of the family had been a prominent anti-Nazi.[130]

After a few initial incidents in the liberated South Tyrol, signs of unrest diminished, but they just as quickly re-merged when it became clear that the new Austrian Republic was prepared to actively demand the region's reincorporation. American intelligence sources reported that in December 1945 there had been a conference in Innsbruck between South Tyrolean leaders and officers from Austrian military battalions that had been retained in formation by the French as labour units. Arrangements were made that these labour battalions would infiltrate into the South Tyrol and launch an armed rising in case the Great Powers should decide that the region would remain Italian. Communication channels were established between the North and South Tyrol, travelled by armed couriers, and a secret SS weapons cache was exploited in order to send arms southward in anticipation of an impending clash.[131] As well, an underground radio station was established in order to broadcast to the German population of South Tyrol from Austria, and illegal nationalist propaganda was smuggled across the frontier by the 'Federation of South Tyroleans,' based in Innsbruck.[132]

When the decision at the Paris Peace Conference in 1946 approved Italy's claim to retain the South Tyrol, there were strikes, demonstrations, and armed clashes in Bozen, Meran, and Brixon, and fighting between South Tyrolese and Italian *carabinieri* was also reported in the Pustertal. On 1 July came the first of a long string of sabotage attacks aimed at railway transmission cables and transformer pylons. Near Ora, one of the steel structures supporting railway electric lines was blown up by saboteurs. Special importance was attached to this incident by the fact that General Mark Clark, the commander of American occupation forces in Austria, had travelled along this line only twenty-four hours earlier.[133] Attacks on power transformers with dynamite were also a favourite tactic of the German resistance, particularly since Italy wished to retain the South Tyrol in part because of its promise of hydro-electric power for a country starved of fossil fuels. A series of outrages in Bozen Province was accompanied by letters signed by the 'We-Wo' (Werwolf), which threatened to continue such attacks until the South Tyrol was returned to Austria.[134]

Unlike the case in other Germanic borderlands, resistance activity continued in South Tyrol for decades, based upon succeeding generations of terrorists. Although many South Tyroleans reconciled themselves to their fate, the Italian government hedged on its commitment to acknowledge South Tyrolean autonomy, and among German radicals the flame of resistance flickered on. Bombings and sabotage continued throughout the 1950s, and actually increased in the 1960s, particularly as the newly sovereign Austrian government was woefully unable (or unwilling) to control Fenian-type skullduggery along its Italian frontier. Nationalist guerrilla groups based themselves in Innsbruck and found a considerable degree of safe haven in Austria. For two and half decades after the end of the war, the problem remained a major irritant in Italo-Austrian relations, and periodically threatened to provoke a regional crisis between the two states. Although such activity might not qualify as true Werwolf operations, and the core of the original movement was long gone, many of the 'German nationalist' groups continued to have a markedly neo-Nazi character. On the other hand, National Socialism was not the best organizing principle for revanchist terrorism – given Hitler's lengthy appeasement of the Italians – and there was some effort during the 1950s and 1960s to give the movement a broader character, particularly by appealing to the tradition of Andreas Hofer and his 1809 Tyrolean 'freedom movement.'[135]

In all these borderland cases, from the South Tyrol to the western frontiers, to the eastern provinces and the Sudetenland, several salient points are apparent. Obviously, the Werwolf was defeated in all these instances, although it was typically exploited by anti-German ultra-patriots and Communists seeking to inhibit, harass, or even to expel Volksdeutsch minorities. In eastern Europe, Werwolf resistance at least equalled the level of such activity within Germany itself, and was inflamed by forced deportations and intense repression. However, in all these cases (with the exception of Denmark), the Werwolf drew heavily upon a so-called borderland mentality, which can be interpreted as an attitude of confrontation between an allegedly superior culture and the philistines living beyond the watchtowers.

Perhaps the final word on these movements should address their National Socialist character or, more specifically, their lack of it. Although much of their rhetoric and aesthetic was framed in terms of National Socialism, in truth troublesome groups and individuals in the German boundary districts seem to have drawn their sense of purpose more from local patriotism than from anything identifiable as Nazi ideology. One Silesian Werwolf who made his way across the Soviet Zone and was captured by British authorities at Lübeck seemed motivated primarily by attachment to his home region (*Heimat*). 'I find it hardest of all,' he lamented, 'to bear the thought of our lovely Silesia being handed over to the Poles.'[136] As Celia Applegate notes, '*Volk*' and 'Nation' had long since become just empty words, and only '*Heimat*' still had a resonance. During the 'Zero Hour,' loyalties were reduced from the ephemeral Third Reich down to the concrete world of one's own immediate environment,[137] which in truth represented a revival of the brands of local patriotism that had been an important element in early Naziism. Naturally, this process was most marked in the outer regions that had always had less of a relationship with the centre. It was this shrinkage of the German consciousness that most characterized the borderland Werwolf.

7

Western Allied and Soviet Reactions to the Werwolf

Examination of the German side of the story does not, of course, tell the entire tale. No one can have read this account without wondering about the reactions of the Allies and Soviets, and it is perhaps fitting to offer a few final observations on this matter before closing. In short, it might be concluded that the threat of Nazi partisan warfare had a generally unhealthy effect on broad issues of policy among the occupying powers. As well, it prompted the development of Draconian reprisal measures that resulted in the destruction of much German property and the deaths of thousands of civilians and soldiers.

Allied Occupation Policy

From the beginning, General Eisenhower considered the Germans a warlike race who would never surrender, and he suggested that the German Army would break down into individual centres of resistance, possibly anchored in an Alpine Redoubt, rather than capitulate.[1] Based on such expectations, he contributed to the hardening of American occupation policy in the late summer and fall of 1944. In August, he anticipated Treasury Secretary Morgenthau's quest for a so-called hard peace,[2] and soon after he also asked for the revision of a Combined Chiefs of Staff directive that had made Allied forces initially responsible for the maintenance of public services and utilities in occupied Germany: 'it may well be that the German Army as a whole will never actually surrender and that we shall enter the country finding no central German authority in control, with the situation chaotic, probably guerrilla fighting and possibly even civil war in certain districts ... If conditions in Germany turn out to be as described it will be utterly impossible effectively to control or save the economic structure of the country ... and we feel we should not assume the responsibility for its support and control.'[3] The pragmatic British were mortified by such a suggestion,[4] but the American War Department naturally took considerable account of the Supreme Commander's opinions, and for some time was quite amenable to suggestions from the Treasury that occupation policy should be more harsh.[5]

The eventual outcome of these changes in policy was Joint Chiefs of Staff Directive 1067 (for U.S. forces only), the SHAEF Occupation Directive of 9 November 1944, and the much-revised *Handbook for Military Government in Germany*, a final version of which was published in December 1944.[6] These documents called for severe denazification guidelines, non-fraternization between Allied troops and German civilians, and the schooling and re-education of German youth – all measures intended to safeguard the immediate security of the occupation forces, as well as to lay the groundwork for a long-term solution of 'the German Problem.'[7]

Thus, when Allied forces arrived in Germany, they brought with them a number of harshly negative commandments, all prefaced with the injunction 'Thou shalt not ...' General John Hilldring, director of the U.S. Civil Affairs Division, set the tone in August 1944, noting that 'a policy of severe control, carried out with fairness and discipline, is deemed the only effective method of ensuring protection against sabotage and fifth column activity.'[8] This system of rules and regulations governed the day-to-day existence of Germans well into the summer of 1945, and in some cases much longer. German life, for instance, was regulated by a curfew and by strict travel restrictions (which damaged agricultural production);[9] all meetings of more than five persons were banned (which effectively eliminated *all* political activity);[10] Germans had to surrender hunting rifles and ceremonial arms (which meant that farmers could not protect crops from wild animals);[11] German mail services and news media were closed and, when reopened, were subject to strict censorship (which suffocated freedom of communication and expression);[12] and German children were prohibited from forming Boy Scout troops[13] or clubs engaged in so-called militaristic sports[14] (which put the onus on ill-equipped Allied troops to entertain and remould German youth).[15] 'German civilians have to mould their lives to a massive series of regulations,' noted a British journalist in June 1945. '[These] are pasted up in shop windows along every district. Side by side with these rules are often pictures of Belsen and other camp victims, so that thousands of Germans have been compelled to look at them now.'[16]

In addition, German POWs were held by the victorious powers for several years after the conclusion of the war, in open contravention of international law. Winston Churchill announced in April 1945 that Allied policy was to hold all German officers as long as the threat of Nazi guerrilla warfare existed.[17] Hundreds of thousands of German scratch troops captured in the last weeks of the fighting were also held for four months in make-shift camps along the Rhine, mainly in order to prevent Werwolf activity. Conditions in these facilities were bad, as food, water, and shelter were lacking.[18] In addition, the number of civilian detainees held by the Americans alone shot up from 1,000 in late March 1945 to more than 30,000 by late June, and exceeded 100,000 by the end of the year. Once again, conditions in the internment camps in which these prisoners were held were frequently poor.[19]

Allied Justice

Assuming that these measures, even despite their severity, might still fail to preempt underground operations, SHAEF also drafted a series of stiff ordinances to deal with die-hard activity. Armed resistance, sabotage, and possession of weapons were all defined as capital crimes in SHAEF's Proclamation no.1, and although General W.B. Smith removed from that document an outright threat of death for Nazi recalcitrants, Eisenhower in late March 1945 made a plain promise of swift execution for all German *francs-tireurs*.[20] 'I have told my Army Commanders,' said Eisenhower, 'that resistance of that kind will be dealt with sternly and on the spot. I will not tolerate civilians, people out of uniform, bearing arms, firing on our troops.'[21] This declaration came as an obvious response to increased German partisan resistance east of the Rhine, particularly in the Main Valley.

Noting Eisenhower's toleration for frontier justice, some American officers felt increasingly free to order the killing of belligerent German civilians, even without the formality of a trial. In the Hardt Forest, American tankmen shot several civilians who were caught in combat and had guided Wehrmacht tank-destroyer teams. Similarly, a number of snipers were hanged near Schweinfurt, where American forces faced intense hostility, and vehicles 'were ambushed by isolated German resistance groups.' In Offenbach, where an American tank driver was killed by a civilian with a Panzerfaust, the guilty party was hauled from his house and shot, and at Rupboden, a fanatical Nazi was gunned down by a U.S. armoured-division commander after he had encouraged the inhabitants of the town to tear down white flags.[22] Three Werwolves captured after assassinating an Allied officer were dispatched in similar fashion.[23] It should be pointed out that, while such summary killings were dubious in a moral sense, they were not contraventions of international law because neither the Hague nor the Geneva conventions provided any protection for combatants, such as partisans, who failed to meet the criteria set forth in Article I of the Hague rules.

A number of Germans were also sentenced to death in a more judicial way, by Allied military courts, beginning with two line-crossers who were tried and shot in mid-April 1945, and a Hitler Youth executed several days later.[24] Britain was the only major power which made any complaint about the Draconian nature of such sentences, with criticism coming mainly from elements on the left. Students from the University of London objected to the execution of two teenage members of the Hitler Youth on 1 June 1945; both of these boys had been recruited by the Nazis from a reformatory and had been promised a chance to rehabilitate themselves if they undertook a mission behind the lines of the U.S. Ninth Army. Publisher Victor Gollancz also complained about the severity of the sentences meted out to these adolescents.[25] On a different tack, the pro-Labour *Daily Herald* made an oblique protest about the prospect of British troops being chosen by ballot to act as executioners in cases where resisters were to be put to death by the traditional German method of beheading. A senior British officer denied that any English personnel would be involved in guillotinings, and one soldier who volunteered for such assignments was denied permission.[26]

The procedural mechanisms of Allied military courts were hardly familiar, at least to Anglo-American sensibilities. First, these tribunals did not proceed on an assumption of innocence, even though this assumption was made by Allied military courts operating in Italy. Second, there was no regulation preventing Allied security services from holding detainees even if they were acquitted, and this was frequently done. Third, 'technicalities' raised by the defending counsel were not allowed to sway cases, and if the defence attorney discovered facts prejudicial to military security, he could report this information to Allied counter-intelligence agencies. Fourth, there was no set age at which a juvenile could not be tried as an adult.[27] And, fifth, the parents of adolescents were made legally responsible for the conduct of their children and could be charged for failing to prevent offences against the occupation forces. This suggestion first came up in October 1944, when four boys in Aachen were caught sniping at an American artillery position. Although these children were eventually released after a lengthy detention, and neither they nor their parents were prosecuted,[28] SHAEF G-5 battened upon the idea of parental culpability, particularly once they discovered that it had been provided for by the German criminal code since 1940. In early February 1945, General A.E. Grasett, the Assistant G-5 chief of staff, recommended the procedure to Military Government detachments. In a number of subsequent cases, German fathers and mothers were prosecuted under this provision and, when found guilty, were typically saddled with suspended sentences made dependent upon the future behaviour of their offspring.[29]

Allied Reprisals

While military courts were sufficient to deal with resisters who were caught, an infinitely more difficult problem involved German guerrillas, stragglers, and *francs-tireurs* who disappeared after launching sudden ambush attacks, presumably because they were hidden by the civilian population. The unfortunate answer to such situations was collective punishments, even despite the questionable legality of such expedients. SHAEF had announced, during the 'Strasbourg Incident' of November 1944, that Allied forces would act strictly in accord with 'international law,' although this they did not do. Article L of the Hague Rules of War (1907) specifically stated that 'no general penalty, pecuniary or otherwise, shall be inflicted on the population on account of the acts of individuals for which they cannot be regarded as jointly or severally responsible.' In addition, Article XXV prohibited bombardments of undefended towns, Articles XXVIII and XLVII prohibited pillage, and Article XLVI committed occupation forces to respecting civilian lives and private property. The SHAEF counter-insurgency manual, *Combatting the Guerrilla*, implicitly recommended contravention of these principles under certain circumstances. The handbook stressed that, while it was desirable to isolate partisans from the population, there was a proper time for 'stern measures,' including forced labour and the seizure of hostages. 'Prompt, efficient and effective counter-measures,' it advised, would be necessary to suppress partisan activity – 'Ineffective or half-hearted measures in the early stages will tend to be the greatest incentive and encouragement not only to the guerrillas, but also to all potential guerrillas and active sympathizers.' Similarly, a SHAEF Joint Intelligence Committee paper noted that it was 'important that the most drastic measures be taken whenever the Werewolves achieve a success or when any are captured.'[30]

Two factors seem to have been involved in this deliberate breech of the rules. First of all, Allied thinking was influenced by a revival of the ancient classical concept of a 'war between peoples,' which suggested that the entire population of a state contributed to its belligerent character. This theme has been revisited periodically throughout history, most notably by Hugo Grotius and Emmerich de Vattel, and in the 1940s it was combined with elements of the 'just war' doctrine to produce the idea of enemy 'collective guilt.' Since Allied forces advancing into Germany were taught that all Germans bore a measure of responsibility for the criminal deeds of the National Socialist leadership (and its agents), it is hardly surprising that Allied officers were willing to hold the entire population to blame for the desperate acts of small groups or individuals attempting to fight a rearguard action for the beleaguered regime. In fact, this assumption of common responsibility, even despite any breeches of the Hague Convention, was one of the main implications of the 'collective guilt' idea.

Second, SHAEF actually looked to the practices of the hated enemy as a precedent, even though German security services had recently proven themselves willing to act outside all set norms of civilized conduct. For the most part, this was *not* intended as a kind of extended reprisal, based on the assumption that Germans should get a dose of their own medicine (although some French troops regarded it in this sense). Rather, most SHAEF officers saw the German precedent solely in terms of technical applicability, as they felt that German control measures in occupied Europe had achieved considerable results. With this in mind, a program was launched in November 1944 to interview former French, Belgian, Polish, and Czech resisters in order to ascertain how the Germans had kept order, and to find out about any mistakes they had made so that the Allies could avoid repeating them. Only on one recorded occasion did the SHAEF G-2 counter-intelligence chief, Colonel H.G. Sheen, attempt to deal with the moral aspects of copying this precedent, warning near the outset of the project that 'we should never, as a matter of policy, employ the more brutal methods of repression as practiced by the Germans.'[31] Even despite this caveat, knowing that such research formed the background to *Combatting the Guerrilla* helps to explain why SHAEF policies assumed such a hard edge.

Within the broad parameters suggested by SHAEF, the precise nature of retaliations was usually dictated by local conditions, the preferences of individual Allied commanders, and the national traditions of the various armies joined together in the Allied Expeditionary Force. The British, for instance, seemed uncomfortable with policies that encouraged blood-letting or even the wilful demolition of property. In the autumn of 1944, Rear-Admiral H.T. Baillie-Grohman complained that the shooting of hostages was 'not in accordance with our usual methods,' and in December the Foreign Office frowned upon a proposal that reprisals should be visited upon civilian property, noting that such conduct was foreign to British customs.[32] Owing to such tendencies, British forces in northwest Germany were seldom responsible for summary killings or punitive property damage, and this state of affairs was no doubt helped by the fact that the Twenty-first Army Group faced a relatively less significant guerrilla problem than its allies operating to the south and east. There were only two minor exceptions to this rule: at Seedorf, north of Bremen, British armoured cavalry burned two cottages, chosen at random, on the morning of 26 April, after villagers had hidden German bazookamen in their cellars; and near Osnabrück, British officers threatened unnamed retaliations against local civic leaders unless they rounded up the leader of a vigilante group that had murdered two East European slave labourers on 14 April.[33]

Although part of the Twenty-first Army Group, the Canadian First Army took a tougher line, particularly the 4th Armoured Division under General Chris Vokes, an officer who put the stamp of his own rugged personality upon reprisal policies. Vokes saw the destruction of property as the most effective answer to civilian resistance, even though he knew that this measure violated the Hague Rules and that it put him on such shaky legal ground that he prudently avoided issuing written proclamations whenever the policy went into force. The first place to suffer under Voke's heavy hand was the northwest German town of Sogel, where a number of civilians harboured Wehrmacht bazookamen and participated in a revolt against Canadian troops on 10 April, the day after the community was captured. After five Canadian soldiers lost their lives suppressing this disturbance, civilians were ordered to leave their homes, and the centre of town was systematically blown into rubble. Similar measures were undertaken in Freisoythe, where a Canadian battalion commander was killed in a battle with fifty cut-off German troops (although it was believed at the time that the officer had been killed by a *franc-tireur*), and, in Mittelsten, where an unnamed transgression caused the Canadians to send out a 'punitive expedition' with orders to burn down the village. In this latter case, the town was saved after only three houses were put to the torch, mainly because a nearby Canadian sapper unit intervened. They argued that the local inhabitants were engaged in vital tasks at an army sawmill and that this work could not be disrupted.[34] Near Wilhelmshaven, where a Canadian soldier lost his arm to a booby-trap strung to his tank hatch by a civilian saboteur, the houses of three suspected culprits were demolished by bulldozers and armoured recovery tanks.[35]

The Americans often conducted themselves with a similar aggressiveness, thus reiterating the fact – shown so vividly in the American West, in the Philippines, and in Vietnam – that American citizen-soldiers have traditionally been uncomfortable in an environment of partisan warfare. They engaged in summary executions, took hostages, and destroyed private property, although their bark was sometimes worse than their bite. The first controversy involving American forces centred upon the borderland village of Wallendorf, which was overrun by the U.S. Third Army on 14 September 1944. Most of Wallendorf was demolished in an artillery duel between American and German gunners, but the British and American press wrongly reported that the town had been burned down by American occupiers as a reprisal for persistent sniping activity. The interesting aspect of this affair is that SHAEF allowed this story to stand unchallenged, even though their own Psychological Warfare Division was aghast at an account that they regarded as supporting German propaganda, and even though the faulty report was openly questioned in late September by *Stars and Stripes* reporter Andy Rooney.[36] Obviously, some American generals thought that the existing story set the right mood for the occupation, whether it was true or not.

By the spring of 1945, Third Army soldiers were being issued with genuine orders to burn all dwellings containing SS *francs-tireurs*, and units of the U.S.

Seventh Army were instructed to demolish with artillery any houses containing snipers, 'rather than risking the lives of Allied soldiers in reducing them.'[37] Some units warned *Bürgermeister* in threatened towns that a single shot fired into the backs of American troops would result in the affected community being destroyed by fighter-bombers. At Stuppach, in northern Württemberg, townfolk were suspected of harbouring a wounded German officer, but they were instructed to produce within three hours either the officer or a good explanation; otherwise, all male inhabitants would be shot, women and children would be driven into the hinterland, and the town would be levelled. In the same region, two U.S. soldiers were garrotted by German stragglers. American authorities mistakenly believed that surly local civilians were responsible, and on 18 April they conducted a brutal security sweep, arresting the entire military-age, male populations of villages such as Brüchlingen. In northern Baden, combat troops destroyed the town of Bruchsal, apparently in response to some unnamed atrocity by the SS.[38]

The French at least equalled the severity of American and Canadian reprisal measures, and in some ways they led the way in imposing a Carthaginian peace. Their demeanor in Germany was affected by their peculiar status as the only occupying power to have itself been totally overrun by the enemy, and by the acute economic and political weaknesses of the new French regime. 'Their own insecurity as conquerors,' as James Warburg rightly notes, 'made them jumpy and vindictive.'

First of all, as a revenge for the humiliations of 1940, and as a means of hindering the 'natural affability' of French troops, the French Army in early April organized a deliberate attempt to whip up the anti-German sentiments of its fighting men. Needless to say, the Army subsequently found themselves faced with a riot of pillage and rape once the troops rolled into southwestern Germany. Like the Soviets on the Eastern Front, who made the same series of mistakes, the French, too, were forced to undertake severe measures to restore order and prevent any further deterioration in the prestige of the First Army.[39]

Second, certain French officers felt that, because of their country's recent fate, they enjoyed a special insight into the resistance mentality, and they were thoroughly familiar with ruthless German methods of suppressing unrest. Ironically, they believed that severe German retaliations had been effective in France, and they fully intended to copy such tactics and turn them back upon the country of their origin – 'the law of Oradour,' as they called it.[40] Their intentions in this regard considerably exceeded those of SHAEF, and by the end of April 1945 the French had already come under fire by SHAEF for threatening civilians with fearsome reprisals and putting the onus of non-fraternization on the German populace.[41] French officers of the old school, now derided by leftist *résistants* as Vichyites, had to keep their heads low until later phases of the occupation, when they were able to moderate some previously tough policies.

A third factor, which was largely a corollary of the first two, was that the French flooded their zone with men, mainly because of their security mania, but also in order to foist hungry mouths upon the resources of the Germans (a practice originally developed by the Revolutionary French in the 1790s, during the first Wars of the Coalition). By the autumn of 1945, there were at least 300,000 men crowded into Germany in order to perform a job that could have been handled by two mobile divisions and a combat command. By 1946, France maintained a ratio of 118 soldiers per 10,000 civilians, whereas the British had 66, and the Americans 90.[42] France's meagre and overstretched capacities could ill-afford to feed large numbers of soldiers at home or to provide their keep in Germany, so this was another reason that there was widespread looting in the French Zone, right from the initial point of entry onward. Huge numbers of French troops lived off the land, which imposed a tremendous burden upon the crippled economy of southwest Germany, and the inevitable result was that, by the late summer of 1945, there were signs of developing malnutrition among German civilians.[43]

A fourth disruptive factor also developed out of French weakness – namely, the shortage of trained Military Government personnel. France, like the Soviet Union, had neither the time nor the resources to prepare properly for the occupation, so their presence in Germany assumed a largely ad hoc character. Unlike the Soviets however, the French were not willing to allow a rapid devolution of political power to their German charges, thus delaying any chance to free themselves of innumerable administrative burdens. As well, they garrisoned troops from Africa who had only a rudimentary knowledge of the proper duties of occupation forces, and the Germans, many of them still secure in their own sense of racial superiority, accused these colonial forces of pillage and rape. Even France's allies could not fail to note such problems – 'It is natural enough that in these circumstances Germans are resentful ... ,' sniffed a British assessment. 'There is a real danger that a sore spot will develop in Western Germany which might be difficult to localize.'[44]

The walking incarnation of this whole complex of fears and inabilities, masked beneath a veil of bravado, was the military governor of the French Zone, Marshal Lattre de Tassigny. The marshal got his first chance to bluster in mid-May during a tour of Constance, a town where the French had originally been received joyfully in late April. Since the German capitulation, however, Constance had been plagued by repeated acts of minor sabotage, including the destruction of French proclamations and damage to telephone lines. A nearby

Werwolf band prowled the forest and received food from local women. Much of the German population was 'cunningly hostile,' and engaged in passive resistance, although they were also terrified of possible reprisals, not without reason since the French had already seized 400 hostages, and had actually shot 2 people who had resisted French orders. German civil authorities half-heartedly endeavoured to render the Werwolf harmless, although active anti-Nazis were not accorded any measure of protection by the French.

It was into this situation that Lattre intervened. During his passage through Constance, the marshal noted that many French posters were in a poor state, although it was unclear whether these proclamations had actually been damaged by hostile Germans, or were simply worn by the weather. Whatever the truth, the marshal saw evidence of German impudence and swore revenge. On his orders, a small quarter of the town was cleared of civilians and occupied by the French gendarmerie. New proclamations posted on the walls of the city threatened to burn down the evacuated neighbourhood in the event of further resistance. During the same night, the *Oberbürgermeister*, his deputy, several former mayors, and the chief of police were all summoned and arrested. Both the police president and the mayor were Nazi hold-overs, and the latter, Dr Mager, had been a close associate of Gauleiter Wagner. Both men were blamed for the alleged leniency of the administration and the insolence of the German police in the town. Over the next month, no fewer than four successors would attempt to hold the *Oberbürgermeister*'s post, each of them appointed and then sacked when he ran afoul of the French.[45]

This was the first application of what Lattre came to call 'the Constance method,' but it was far from the last. In truth, the French assembled a considerable catalogue of repressions, particularly through the forced evacuation of villages and towns, which involved more than 25,000 people and bore a distinct resemblance to the 'wild expulsions' under way in the former eastern provinces of the Reich. On the evening of 15 May, the inhabitants of six towns in the Jastetter 'Tip' were deported because they had hidden German Army and SS stragglers from French authorities; on 17 May, most of the island of Reichenau was evacuated due to the 'disloyal behaviour' of the local population; two weeks later, the majority of the inhabitants of Gailingen am Rhein were expelled from their homes; and, in early June, farm families from the country hamlets of Weichs and Randen were similarly uprooted. Some of these evacuees eventually wound up in Alsace, where they were employed in clearing minefields; others gradually seeped back to their home villages as the wariness of the French diminished. With such incidents in mind, Swiss observers concluded that, whereas local public opinion had originally been relieved that French forces had arrived in advance of the Russians, sentiment towards the occupying power had quickly soured. This development was, they said, directly related to the forced evacuations, which seemed a policy no worse than could be imposed by the Soviets. Comparisons to Nazi policies were also unavoidable. 'The oppression by the French seems far worse than by Hitler [noted the *Berner Tagblatt* on 30 May]. The original atmosphere of liberation has turned to the reverse: the people are depressed and irritated and hatred against the victors who were at first welcomed as liberators seems to be increasing ... It is not understood why on account of a few hooligans who will not come to heel the whole population should pay a hard penalty, why even a whole village should be evacuated on account of a single individual.'

The most serious such case occurred in the south Bavarian town of Lindau, which in mid-May 1945 was the scene of a deteriorating security situation. Up to 60 per cent of the population was regarded as pro-Nazi, and at night pot shots were frequently directly towards French troops. On 23 May, a French officer was shot and killed by a member of the HJ, fourteen years of age, who was himself captured and executed summarily. Notices posted by the *Bürgermeister* warned that Werwolf or NSDAP inscriptions had to be washed away within half an hour of appearing, lest the walls of the affected structure be torn down and the proprietors arrested. As well, a number of buildings burned down under mysterious circumstances, particularly a French supply depot that was thought to have been destroyed by an act of arson.

The French command was sensitive to such disruptions, particularly since it was preparing to transfer the headquarters of First French Army to Lindau, and with the assassination on 23 May their patience snapped. A loudspeaker truck was dispatched to make a round of the community, announcing that a collective punishment was to be imposed in response to recent acts of ill discipline: with only a few hours' warning, the great majority of the town's population would be forcibly evacuated. According to the French, the inhabitants would be replaced by refugees from Alsace, and (coincidentally) the displacement would also open up billet space for French forces flooding into the town in conjunction with their transfer of headquarters. According to a German account, French troops streamed ashore from two ships recently docked at Lindau, and they freely looted the residential quarters of the town in the absence of its inhabitants.

After this man-made disaster, both the Catholic and Evangelical ministers in the community petitioned Lattre for a pardon, and the *Bürgermeister*, Franz Ebarth, also bowed and scraped to the French command, literally begging for clemency. All these parties promised to do everything in their power to prevent future disorders, and this plea had considerable effect. In particular, the Protestant chaplain with the headquarters staff of the First Army, Captain Jean Cadier, intervened to win a reprieve for the local burghers. Annulment of the measure was probably also related to the fact that the affair had shocked American and Swiss observers, which was an embarrassment to the French. After two days of roaming the neighbouring countryside, the inhabitants were allowed to return to their homes.[46]

Some French commanders preferred alternate punishments that caused less social dislocation than forced evacuations. At a number of spots where there were shooting affrays, such as Markdorf and Reutlingen, the French seized and killed hostages.[47] At Lichtenthal, where the French encountered hard resistance from the Volkssturm, they sacked the town and pillaged or raped the population.[48] At Busingen, a small enclave near Schaffhausen, entirely surrounded by Swiss territory, shots fired at French officers on the night of 16 June 1945 were answered by the imposition of a severe curfew and a warning that, if the incident was repeated, ten hostages would be executed *and* the community would be cleared.[49] In the newly occupied French sector of Berlin, gendarmes responded to the theft of several service revolvers by storming into the streets and beating everyone in sight, even including the *Bürgermeister* of Tegel.[50] In Speyer, where the population was unsettled and the French captured four Werewolves, they seized a number of old men and forced them to stand at attention, for many long hours, outside the main Military Government building. At Lustnau and Tübingen, the French imposed stiff collective fines – in the first case because of the presence of unsurrendered German soldiers, in the second because of wire cuts – while, at Überlingen, on Lake Constance, the occupiers threatened to blow up buildings defaced with Werwolf slogans unless the offensive inscriptions were erased within an hour of their appearance. When the French occupied Koblenz in July 1945, taking over from the Americans, they kept their options open, warning town fathers that resistance would result in *either* the evacuation of the affected area, more restrictive curfews, limitation of circulation, fines, internment of draft-age men, *or* the execution of hostages at a ten-to-one ratio for French casualties.[51]

There is little doubt that such harsh Allied measures contributed to the successful suppression of underground activity in Germany, although this was achieved at a considerable price: treating the German nation as a uniformly hostile entity not only made life difficult for Werwolf die-hards, but also undermined the confidence of anti-Nazi Germans. Moreover, it was an approach that created a vast gulf between the occupation forces and the German people during a brief period of profound psychological and social dislocation, when German society might otherwise have been most open to new influences. German civilians claimed that measures like non-fraternization had 'soured' them, and one anti-Nazi who hoped to work for the Military Government reported that the screening process by British Field Security was 'inclined to leave even the most harmless of civilians with feelings worthy of an incipient Werwolf.' Revolutionary committees, or 'Antifas,' were broken up, and the first major anti-Nazi demonstration in postwar Germany – a rally in Cologne for homecoming concentration camp prisoners (20 May 1945) – was dispersed by Allied military police, who fired above the heads of the demonstrators.[52]

It must be emphasized that such incidents resulted, *not* from a conscious fear of the Left, as is sometimes suggested,[53] but from a zealous application of measures specifically meant to smother Nazi opposition. Allied security mania was evident in an American intelligence summary from the summer of 1945, which noted that even seemingly legitimate political movements could be a cloak for subversives, or in a British directive that warned, 'It is ... necessary to ensure that [Naziism's] place is not taken by other more disguised anti-democratic, reactionary, and militarist movements.'[54] In a memo on 18 May 1945, the Political Warfare Executive denounced German anti-Fascists as 'tear-wolves' – 'penitent pacifists in civilian suits who claim the martyr's crown and the right to lead German reconstruction.'[55] The results of such fears were soon obvious: the postwar premier of Schleswig–Holstein, Theodor Steltzer, noted in December 1946 that Allied expectations of Werwolf resistance had led to an attempt at bureaucratic overcontrol, and had thus resulted in a reign of debilitating inefficiency. Once this 'vast apparatus' was in place, claimed Steltzer, it became an end in itself and worked 'so negatively' that it crushed any hope of a German recovery and generally convinced Germans that it was an instrument for the 'annihilation or enslavement' of the country.[56]

Postwar Allied Control Measures

Having instituted Draconian policies while the war was still under way, there is no evidence that these policies got even tougher in the post-capitulation period, despite the even more clearly illegal nature of guerrilla and underground resistance. It is true that several dozen Germans were executed *after* the war, mainly on charges of sniping or hiding weapons,[57] but even the severity of penalties for such serious offences as these became much more lenient after August 1945.[58] Except for the situation in the French Zone, collective punishments inflicted by the Allies almost invariably got lighter after the German surrender. The Americans levied their first collective fine upon a German town in the summer of 1945, and all of the Allies extended curfew hours at the first sign of trouble. In dealing with a rash of wire-cuts in the summer of 1945, the Americans warned property owners that they were responsible for the security of communication cables lying on their lands, and at Westhofen, in the Rhineland, the mayor was told that 'he would be held responsible' for any further interference with tele-phone lines. In the Bavarian town of Schönwald, all the male inhabitants of the community between the ages of eighteen and thirty-eight were assembled and searched after a U.S. Constabulary trooper was assaulted and severely beaten by four Germans. In Berlin, the weight of reprisals fell upon former members of the NSDAP: when resisters scrawled 'Kill the Red Beasts! Werwolf catches all traitors!' upon walls and pavements in Neukölln, German police called upon former party members and forced them to scrub away the inscriptions. By 1947–8, even the French had given up on extreme measures, but were forcing communities affected by wire-cutting to provide civilian patrols in order to prevent sabotage at night.[59]

The first important security measures to be rescinded were strict travel and curfew limits that damaged the German economy. By midsummer 1945, postal services had also been restored on a zonal scale, although correspondence was subject to spot-checks by censors, and use of the system was denied to ex-mem-bers of the Wehrmacht.[60] It was only after the Potsdam Conference, however, that a general thaw began, first in the removal of bans on political activity,[61] and then in the cancellation of formal non-fraternization rules.[62] Cinemas opened in the British Zone in August 1945, although this was done against the protests of the Political Warfare Executive, which argued that it was too soon.[63] Even then, security measures remained strict,[64] and American replacement troops arriving in Germany were reminded that they were on hostile terrain. 'You are a soldier fighting a war,' said one orientation pamphlet. 'The shooting is over but there is still a lot to be done ... Look out, the people are still a formidable enemy.'[65] Not surprisingly, collective punishments such as fines and curfews were still being imposed upon German communities as late as 1948, and in 1947 the inhabitants of a town in the Tyrol were crisply informed that they could face the death penalty if interference with communication wires did not cease.[66] Numerous restrictions also remained in place. Even in 1948, the British were still extremely careful about releasing 'security detainees,' and the American Civil Liberties Union complained that restrictive licensing and censorship regulations were still being enforced in western Germany.[67]

The French remained particularly skittish, especially since they thought that some of the Werwolf's command centres had survived the end of the war, and that the movement itself reflected the incorrigible nature of the German 'national character.'[68] They believed that more liberal policies on German com-munications and travel would help the Nazi underground coordinate its opera-tions,[69] and this was one of the considerations that led to their delegate's repeated veto of Control Council proposals to restore the economic unity of the country.

Despite all this negativity, it might also be noted that fear of guerrilla warfare had at least one positive implication: as early as June 1945, it was realized that food would necessarily have to be imported into Germany in order to prevent starvation and the resultant breakdown in law and order, particularly since it was suspected that many of the arms and sabotage caches secreted by Nazi commandos were not yet uncovered. Allied authorities estimated that several million firearms had been stowed away by German civilians, Werewolves, and former military personnel, a suspicion partially confirmed by U.S. Zone raids in July and November 1945, which turned up no fewer than 1,770 Germans in possession of unauthorized weapons. 'If they're hungry this winter,' said one Military Government officer, 'they'll dig up the guns and start shooting.'[70]

Allied Military Strategy and the Threat of Guerrilla Warfare

Fear of Nazi guerrilla warfare also influenced Allied military strategy during the final months of the war. As the Allies advanced into Germany, General Eisenhower specifically instructed that no towns be left unoccupied and that no pockets be left in the Allied rear, a policy that naturally complemented the broad-front strategy and attempted to avoid the kind of mistakes made by the Germans themselves in Russia and Yugoslavia – mistakes that had eventually yielded large-scale guerrilla resistance. Rather than reaching geographic targets, Eisenhower constantly emphasized the destruction of the Wehrmacht and the Nazi capability for resistance. Thus, the Allies rarely ignored bypassed straggler/guerrilla bands, but constantly employed troops to double back and eliminate these dangers.[71]

As wise as this policy was, it grew threadbare after huge stretches of German territory were overrun in April 1945, particularly as Eisenhower lacked one of the main instruments needed to make it work. The principal weaknesses of the U.S. Army in a Blitzkrieg environment was its lack of motorized infantry. Although the Americans had once experimented with setting up independent motorized infantry divisions, the concept had been scrapped, and when infantry divisions were called upon to rush forward at high speed, as they were in 1944–5, they were forced to scrounge trucks from the quartermaster services. As a result, huge gaps typically opened up between the rear and the front and, although this situation was not debilitating while American forces were operating in friendly territory (like France), it became a big problem in hostile territory (like Germany).

Given this failing, however, the Americans did the best they could with existing resources and patterns of organization. In the autumn of 1944, five teams, of two officers and seventeen men each, were organized by SHAEF in order to tour the front and provide training in counter-guerrilla operations for Allied combat units and rear-echelon forces.[72] Although SHAEF was extremely reluctant to divert combat forces from the front,[73] in March 1945 an entire army, the Fifteenth, was activated as a garrison force in the Rhineland, specifically for the purpose of blocking possible efforts at raiding activity and sabotage by German units.[74] Marshal de Lattre also created a number of French anti-partisan formations, called 'unités C.M.,' manned by former members of the Resistance, and after mid-April the French began running anti-guerrilla aerial-spotting missions and motorized patrols in Baden.[75]

Eisenhower's decisions to eliminate the Alpine Redoubt and the Ruhr Pocket rather than to drive upon Berlin comprised a natural culmination of the broad-front strategy and the desire to eliminate any pockets of possible resistance. The last-minute switch of emphasis away from Berlin and towards Berchtesgaden was a particularly difficult choice, and was influenced by a flood of low-grade intelligence that had been surging into SHAEF since 1943, and which told of extensive preparations for German guerrilla warfare, possibly based upon strongholds in an Alpine base area.[76] In March 1945 came the first Ultra confirmations of the German withdrawal of military headquarters into the Alps and of the attempts to establish a widespread Werwolf guerrilla movement.[77]

Around this same period, the SHAEF Joint Intelligence Committee warned that, if the Alps were not rapidly occupied, 'guerrilla or dissident movements will gain ground and the Nazis may be able to put into effect some of their plans for establishing subversive organizations in Germany and other countries.' The conclusion was obvious: 'We should ... be prepared to undertake operations in Southern Germany in order to overcome rapidly any organised resistance by the German Armed Forces or by guerrilla movements which may have retreated to the inner zone and to this redoubt.'[78]

Based upon such advice, Eisenhower and Bradley decided in mid-March to shift the focus of Allied operations away from a northern drive towards Berlin, in favour of a push into central Germany in order to cut Germany in two by linking up with the Soviets. In the bargain, the Allies would also get the Thuringian industrial complex, which was a centre of German small-arms production and was thought to play an important role in the manufacture of weapons for Nazi guerrilla warfare. A second step would then be to destroy Nazi forces in southern Germany before they could withdraw into the National Redoubt. Eisenhower reported to Roosevelt on 31 March, 'I am hopeful of launching operations that should partially prevent a guerrilla control of any large area, such as the southern mountain bastion.'[79]

It has often been argued, of course, that Eisenhower's central and southern drives resulted from a faulty strategy that overemphasized the threat of the

Alpine Redoubt and underemphasized the political value of Berlin. However, given the fact that, within several weeks of Eisenhower's decision, numerous German partisan bands had actually congregated in the Allied rear; given the fact that the Werwolf and the SS 'Rangers' actually did attempt to turn the mountains into a guerrilla stronghold; and given the fact that Hitler decided only on 22 April to stay in Berlin and forgo the option of personally rallying his troops in the mountains,[80] Eisenhower's decision was perhaps not totally misguided after all. Moreover, the inadequacy of preparations in the Alps should not obscure the fact that the Germans had a consistent record of muddling through such disabilities and achieving more with less, particularly when given a breathing space in which to recoup. In their postwar memoirs, both Eisenhower and his intelligence chief, General Kenneth Strong, recalled that the Nazi guerrilla movement was a real threat that may well have posed a considerable danger to Allied forces had it not been speedily neutralized.[81]

Soviet Occupation and Reprisal Policies

It is likely that Soviet strategy and occupation policy was also influenced by the Werwolf danger, although the outline of this story is not as clear as in the West. We do know, however, that, like the Western Allies, the Soviets were exercised by the possibility of a guerrilla stronghold in the Alps (or in East Prussia);[82] that, like the Western Allies, the Soviets were deeply suspicious of German groups claiming socialist or democratic leanings on the suspicion that they had been penetrated by Nazis; and that, like the Western Allies, the Soviets maintained stringent security measures, and even added an extra element by the deployment of full-scale NKVD divisions organized to maintain security in the rear.[83]

Although the evidence is thin, it appears that the development of Soviet policy in Germany was a mirror image of the same process in the West. First came a reactive policy designed in part to crush Nazi underground resistance, although this policy was more dependent on the indigenous population than was its Western counterpart. Once the Werwolf failed to bloom into a major threat to the occupation forces, this improvised policy was gradually replaced by an ideological attempt to mould the Germans in the image of their occupiers, as also occurred (to some degree) in the West.

During the early part of 1945, Soviet policy in Germany was disorganized, short-term, and dualistic, although the two major trends were both influenced by security concerns. The dark side of Soviet policy was probably conditioned by two factors. First, since the Red Army had now freed nearly all of the USSR, the 'liberate the motherland' motivational theme was no longer valid and there was a need to find a new means through which to energize the soldiery. Second, and of more direct interest to us, there was an obvious desire to terrorize the German population into a state of dumb, animalistic fear, with the presumption that this would make active, and even passive, resistance impossible. The answer to both of these problems was to whip up the troops with a desire for revenge, and to inspire a simultaneous fear and loathing of the German population.

It was widely rumoured in 1945 that a Stalin Order had given permission for Soviet soldiers to do as they pleased on German soil, but a study by German military intelligence could find no firm evidence that this order ever existed. Instead, they concluded that early wartime speeches by Stalin – very inflammatory in nature – were quoted by Red Army political officers in order to create the same impression as the apocryphal 'Stalin Order,' and that this was combined with the widespread dissemination of hate propaganda by the rabid Germanophobe writer Ilya Ehrenburg. Soviet officers and troops were also terrified by predictions of guerrilla warfare on German territory, a spectre that particularly haunted the forces earmarked for service in East Prussia.[84] Since much of the population left in the German eastern provinces was female, Soviet incitements also assumed a distinct misogynistic character, as suggested by Ehrenburg's cry for Russian troops to 'break the racial pride of German women.' Feminist theorists such as Susan Brownmiller have touched on an important point by emphasizing that wartime rape has traditionally resulted, not from sexual urges, but from a desire to express power and domination. Brownmiller rightly claims that rape was the ultimate physical intimidation of women;[85] mass rape was thus the ultimate intimidation of an entire society, meant to induce collective shock and a resultant paralysis.

As a result of such factors, when the Red Army slashed its way across the frontiers of eastern Germany, its personnel were overtaken by a frenzy of bloodlust and a savage craving for destruction. Many units, particularly in the Soviet second wave, degenerated into simple bands of marauders, engaged in an endlessly repeated sequence of pillage, rape, and murder. German civilians who failed to flee found that (for once) the Nazi authorities had painted a realistic picture of the probable behaviour of the foe, something that had been possible to gauge since October 1944, when German troops had recaptured the East Prussian town of Nemmersdorf and had found abundant evidence of Soviet atrocities.[86] Beaten, robbed, and sexually tortured, eastern German civilians were in no position to offer opposition, although there were a few instances where Soviet brutalities backfired and stirred up resistance that otherwise might have been absent. In several Upper Silesian towns, Russian soldiers were shot by rape victims or by relatives of the abused, although such incidents typically resulted in Red Army reprisals that then involved even more large-scale mal-treatment of civilians. At the village of Kupp, where a member of the HJ killed a Soviet officer who had violated the boy's sister, Red Army detachments responded by burning approximately seventy buildings and massacreing numerous civilians, who were eventually buried in a mass pit. As for the killer, he was forced to dig graves for himself and his parents, and then all three were toppled into these holes after being shot.[87]

Not only were many Soviet troops cruel, but they were also uneasy, reli-giously avoiding the woods and keeping their weapons in firing position.[88] 'Certainly we do not like [German civilians],' admitted one officer. 'How can a soldier like people who might shoot him tomorrow.'[89] Anyone suspected of resistance or guerrilla activity was shot on the spot, as was anyone holding weapons, even forest rangers and huntsmen.[90]

As for collective reprisals, Stalin had reportedly issued orders stipulating that the killing of any Red Army trooper be answered immediately by the execution of the perpetrator and the destruction of his or her town, which was usually the course of action pursued in such cases.[91] At Jarmin, in Pomerania, the commu-nity was cleared of its inhabitants and demolished after two Soviet officers were killed in a nearby guerrilla ambush.[92] Similarly, at the town of Schivelbein, a HJ armed with a Panzerfaust blew off the head of a Russian general, after which all the men in the neighbourhood were shot, and all the women and girls raped.[93] And yet again, in the Mecklenburg town of Malchin, the same sequence repeated itself when HJ-Werewolves sniped at Red Army troops on 30 April, prompting the destruction of the town by fire.[94] In Upper Silesia, at Plieschnitz, twenty German civilians were executed in retaliation for the death of a Soviet officer in a skirmish, and in Mark Brandenburg, the Soviets similarly killed five hostages in a public display of ferocity.[95] At the Bohemian town of Gabloncz, Sudeten-German burghers were ordered on an extended 'hunger march' after a Russian officer was murdered.[96] In northern Masuria the entire population of a village was rounded up and sent to a concentration camp, the Russians claiming that several bridges had been blown up in the vicinity.[97]

The occupation of Berlin posed a special problem, even though the capital's population of 2 million was much reduced from the pre-war level. On 28 April 1945, with Soviet formations hammering on the gates of the inner city, the newly appointed town commandant issued a proclamation guaranteeing swift execution for all 'Hitlerite agents, terrorists and diversionists.' He also prom-ised that, in cases where guilty parties could not be found, the occupying power reserved the right to seize hostages and, if necessary, to hang them. In the Nowawes–Potsdam area, where HJ guerrillas shot at a Soviet officer, the house in which they had hidden was destroyed, and some 400 hostages were taken.

According to a Vatican report, 'Russian reprisals to certain reactions of the Werwolf were terrible. Using flame-throwers the Russians destroyed entire blocks of houses causing the deaths of hundreds of the inhabitants.'[98]

Even in the first months after the German capitulation, the sword of Damocles continued to hover above the heads of Berliners. In fact, Soviet forces now had better legal grounds for bitter retaliation precisely because the war was over, and all Germans were supposed to have laid down their arms. When the middle-class borough of Charlottenburg was wracked by sniping and arson attacks, in which several Red Army soldiers were killed, the Soviets responded by cutting off food rations to the entire district, and they threatened worse reprisals in answer to any future troubles.[99] Convinced that organized HJ and Werwolf nests lay behind such violence, the Russians recruited the new *Oberbürgermeister* of Berlin, Arthur Werner, to direct a threatening radio address to this consituency.

Criminal and deluded persons are still to be found [said Werner], who by acts of madness want to prevent a return of law and order. Human lives and property which the war had spared have already fallen victim to their treacherous activity. So far as such attacks are directed against members of the Red Army, they constitute a provocation of the Occupying Power which is as senseless as it is criminal ... I warn all deluded and misguided persons, particularly former members of the Hitler Youth, against a continuation of such acts. Parents and teachers, make it clear to your children what a senseless and harmful crime against the nation all kinds of outrages constitute in these days ... Anyone making an attempt against the life of a member of the Red Army or an official functionary, or who commits arson for reasons of political hostility, will drag into disaster in addition to himself 50 former members of the Nazi Party who will forfeit their lives, together with that of the perpetrator or incendiary.[100]

In June 1945, rumours reached the British Zone suggesting that a group of fifty NSDAP hostages had already been executed.[101]

Meanwhile, many Russian officers had been shamed by the wilder and more purposeless outrages of their troops, and anyone with a political sensibility had realized that such behaviour was endangering the possibility of any future reconciliation with the Germans. Moreover, Soviet leaders had become aware that valuable property – a resource needed for the future reconstruction of the Soviet Union – was being needlessly ransacked and destroyed.[102] Worst of all, it had become increasingly difficult for the Red Army to maintain the necessary order, discipline, and sobriety needed to get any fighting done. Since January, a rash of directives had been issued in an attempt to moderate plundering, and though the wink-and-a-nod atmosphere during the Soviet Winter Offensive had rendered these directives superfluous, this leniency had begun to abate by the spring of 1945. During the lull on the Oder, intense ideological reorientation was done among the soldiery in an attempt to refocus their enthusiasms, and, in April, Ilya Ehrenburg's hate propaganda was officially denounced by a senior Soviet Communist Party official. Thereafter, looting and rapes continued as an unfortunate aspect of the Soviet presence in Germany, even as late as 1947, but outright killings of civilians declined. By June and July 1945, when the Red Army moved into portions of the Soviet Zone that had been briefly occupied by the Anglo-Americans, Russian troop behaviour had improved another step and had nearly come within the range usually expected of occupation forces.[103]

Aside from the destructive side of Soviet policy, the official Russian approach towards Germany was based upon a 'liberation' of the German people,[104] and the final destruction of Fascism through the continued unity of the Grand Alliance, only with the stipulation that Germans admit a sense of guilt for Nazi crimes. German Communist cadres were trained to aid the occupation forces, but were told *not* to expect the immediate establishment of socialism. Rather, their task was to 'democratize' the German people and to construct an anti-Fascist, democratic mass organization. The very prospect of such an anti-Fascist coalition implies an expectation that National Socialism would still play such an important role in German life that all other political forces would need to subsume their differences in a continuing rally against 'Hitlerism.' One of the main themes was 'to convince [the population] that the extermination of Naziism is in the interest of the German people, and that therefore all honest Germans must help with the tracking and elimination of war criminals, fascist terrorists, and saboteurs' (5 April 1945).[105] Soviet propaganda appealed to Germans for help in eliminating Nazi resisters, and threats to kill hostages were funnelled through newly appointed German civil officials in order to keep such declarations one step removed from Soviet military authorities.[106]

When several German Communist special teams were actually sent into eastern Germany in early May 1945, they aided in liquidation of secret Nazi resistance cells, and reportedly attempted to prevent 'excesses' in German–Soviet relations. In fact, the Berlin team was encouraged by Marshal Zhukov to be even more vigilant in such matters, and its chief, Walter Ulbricht, testily replied that it was Soviet military intelligence which was failing to hold Nazi activists even after they had been identified and apprehended. 'In the Ulbricht group,' noted one member, 'we greatly overestimated the influence of the Nazis.'[107]

By June 1945, however, the contours of Soviet and German Communist policy had begun to change. Although there had been scattered sniping, arson attacks, and guerrilla warfare, there had been no major outbreaks of insurgency (which defied all expectations). Not surprisingly, it was at this point that Soviet policy showed signs of turning away from a solely reactive, security-conscious position, and towards a more ideologically oriented policy: the possibility of dismembering Germany was now rejected, the KPD was officially refounded, a Communist press was established, and directives from Moscow ordered an acceleration of mildly leftist policies such as land reform. Although this change was clothed as part of a general democratic revival, in which major bourgeois parties were also allowed to reorganize, the real shift in policy was impossible to ignore: the monolithic anti-Fascist movement, which had earlier been posited as a weapon against the Nazi underground, was now replaced before it even appeared, mainly by a re-established Communist Party that was expected to outpoll its rivals.[108] This development paralleled a much-heralded Communist Party renaissance within the Soviet Union itself, also beginning in 1945.

Even then, however, Soviet security manias continued to hinder their political strategies in Germany. The Americans learned from German teenagers, as early as the spring of 1946, that the typical Russian response to an outbreak of resistance was to systematically arrest *all* the adolescent males in the affected area and dispatch the boys to concentration camps or to the interior of the USSR. Worse yet, the teenagers detained in such fashion seemed to disappear from the face of earth; rarely, if ever, did they retain contact with their families, nor were their parents informed of their whereabouts. The Soviets claimed that only a limited number of 'subversive agents of the Hitler Youth' were involved, but actually the deportations were of such scale that they discredited the Soviets and anyone associated with them. Leaders of the KPD and the Socialist Unity Party complained repeatedly – in Saxony, local party chief Otto Buchwitz succeeded in getting about 400 to 500 young people released – and even the Propaganda Department of the Soviet Military Government lamented to Moscow about the adverse impact of Russian security forces in the zone, and the dangerous propaganda opportunities that this offered to the Western Allies.[109]

Seen in dialectical terms, it might thus be concluded that it was the antithesis to the Werwolf that gave the Nazi guerrilla movement its greatest historical significance: the Werwolf had an impact, not because it succeeded, but merely because it existed. As a diversion, it drew Allied troops away from Berlin – only to allow the capital to fall to the Soviets – and it also momentarily diverted the occupying powers from the long-term task of imposing their own political beliefs and value systems upon Germany. In both west and east, the first months of the occupation quite obviously formed the counter-insurgency phase of the operation. After a brief interim, during which it became clear that the occupation forces would not have to function under a continuous state of siege, the occupying powers got back to the work of achieving their own long-term goals within the truncated Reich. The main themes of the occupation thereafter became re-education, democratization and (in the Soviet Zone) socialization, although a trace of the early negativism never entirely disappeared. The reactive influence of the Werwolf threat thus dates mainly to a half-year in the spring and summer of 1945, the so-called Zero Hour, although, once again, the significance of this brief period for the overall history of the occupation should not be underestimated.

There is no doubt that the tough aspects of the occupation in 1944–5 prejudiced the political and social goals of the occupiers, and that the Russians and French, in particular, were never forgiven for the excesses of their troops. Whether this was avoidable is another question. Certainly, the Soviets went overboard in efforts to terrorize the population, and the wisdom even of the Western Allies, in basing security measures on Nazi models, is questionable. None the less, given what the Werwolf was doing, or trying to do, the responses of the occupiers do not lay beyond the realm of comprehension. As Richard Holmes notes, unless troops are exceptionally well trained and controlled, 'it only needs a few partisan attacks for soldiers to overreact to the slightest provocation.'[110]

8

Consequences and Significance of the Werwolf

Overall, a great deal of ground has been covered in this work, but from this mass of material a few primary conclusions arise. Perhaps the most basic of these points is the very existence in 1944–5 of a significant Werwolf movement, which comprised one of the chief initiatives of the dying Nazi Reich, and which was intended to harass the invading Allied and Soviet armies to such a degree that the Nazi regime could save some semblance of its power and authority. In some ways, the Werwolf represented a continuation of classic Nazi trends, such as in its emphasis on youth. In other ways, it marked a dramatic *volte-face*, particularly with regard to girls and women, who in the Werwolf finally slipped the reins of National Socialist paternalism and were assigned combat or near-combat roles. On the Eastern Front, Nazi guerrilla warfare represented a natural culmination of the savage mode of fighting that had already characterized combat on that front; in the West, it reflected the increasing abandonment of more civilized norms, a development also signalled by unrestricted submarine warfare and by the aerial bombing of civilian targets.

The Werwolf was also sporadically active, particularly if we accept Goebbels's expanded definition of the movement; that is, that any German who committed an act of resistance, even if solely on his or her own initiative, was in fact a Werewolf. We now know, for instance, that civilian *francs-tireurs* occasionally fired at Allied troops; that bypassed groups of soldiers and SS men harassed Allied supply lines (and were occasionally bolstered by special stay-behind sabotage teams); that scores of German 'defeatists' and collaborators were liquidated by Werwolf assassins; that Werewolves attempted to disrupt the Soviet rear behind the Eastern Front; and that minor sabotage and attacks continued for several years after the end of the war. The Werwolf was also venomous, and Prützmann's headquarters was in charge of various mass-poisoning projects. There is little doubt that this escalating terror scared Germans into a stiffer attitude towards foreign occupation, but there is also little doubt that it helped to further discredit National Socialism. The barbarity of Naziism had previously been hidden behind prison walls and concentration-camp wire; with the Werwolf it became manifest.[1]

The final number of casualties caused by such violence is unknown, but must certainly extend into the thousands. In addition to persons killed directly as a result of Werwolf activity, the toll must also include many hundreds who died in reprisal killings or in anti-partisan raids such as that at Aussig an der Elbe in late July 1945. A final total of 3,000-5,500 dead ranks the Werwolf as a final drop in the torrent of blood spilled during the Second World War, but it is more significant if considered in its own right as an example of recent partisan warfare and terrorism in Europe.

As for the geographic configuration of Werwolf activity, there is no doubt that long-time NSDAP strongholds such as the Thuringian Forest, the Lüneburg Heath, southwestern Saxony, Altmark, and Masuria all became trouble spots in 1945. In a few other areas that were also traditional Nazi bastions but were lacking in terrain features favouring guerrilla warfare, such as the Frisian coast, there was also evidence of heightened civilian hostility and sporadic resistance. Although it is impossible to prove conclusively, it *seems* as though central Germany posed more difficulties for the Allies than did the Rhineland; certainly, five of seven *Bürgermeister* killed by the Werwolf were laid low east of the Rhine, and, with several exceptions, nearly all other civil and party officials murdered by Werewolves similarly met their fates east of the river. Furthermore, most guerrilla ambushes of enemy forces occurred in central or eastern Germany. What is interesting, however, is the lack of sources suggesting that the Nazi leadership had carefully planned to exploit its political bases for the success of the Werwolf, or that their understanding of partisan warfare was sufficiently sophisticated to concentrate attention upon demographically favourable regions or population groups. Rather, the fact that German forces, including guerrillas, were eventually drawn to the Sauerland, the Thuringian Forest, the Harz, the Alps, or the Ore Mountains was due to the favourable terrain features of those areas and to the axis of Allied and Soviet advances and corresponding German retreats. Certainly, in the case of Schleswig–Holstein, the latter factor was almost solely operative. The failure of Nazi agencies to target favourable regions was indicated by their try at launching the Werwolf in the Rhineland, which fizzled, and by their similarly misbegotten, albeit ad hoc, attempt to turn the wooded mountains of eastern Bavaria into a partisan redoubt. Both projects were determined solely by geographic and military factors and took no account of the character of local populations – namely, the fact that the Catholic inhabitants of these regions comprised the two most 'Naziproof' population clusters in the entire Reich. The only exceptions to this rule were Franconia and East Prussia, where the Nazi leadership admittedly did take note of the 'special relationship' between people and the party.

Overall, a considerable degree of Nazi underground warfare must be granted, although the final note on the Werwolf must also address why it fell short of its objectives. The most obvious determinants of this breakdown appear repeatedly throughout this study and comprise the debilitating structural faults in the movement. Recall, for instance, the absence of strong leadership; the lack of independent access to weapons and personnel by the Prützmann agency; and the employment of middle-aged policemen who often had no idea how to organize guerrilla warfare. It is likely that, whatever the condition of the Werwolf, die-hard members of the Waffen-SS and other Nazi auxiliary organizations would have resisted the occupation unless specifically instructed not to do so. Thus, to some extent, the Werwolf was superfluous. There was also a bitter competition between rival agencies, and as the Werwolf loop grew larger, Prützmann's control correspondingly diminished: the military took over Werwolf groups for use in tactical or reconnaissance missions; Bormann expanded the Werwolf as a domestic terror force; and Goebbels established a propaganda channel that launched a call to arms aimed mainly at teenagers.

Perhaps worst of all, Prützmann was stuck in a frame of mind outlined by Clausewitz more than a century before, which considered guerrilla warfare strictly as an adjunct to regular military operations. The Werwolf was originally conceived only as an instrument of reach (i.e., into the occupied territories), not as a vehicle for succession (or even survival). Only at the last desperate minute was guerrilla warfare given consideration as a post-capitulation, revolutionary sort of tactic, and even these hasty plans were mere wisps of smoke that disappeared during the final scramble for safety. Only Axmann had the verve to actually carry through an attempt to bring the Werwolf into the post-capitulation period. Among the most senior echelons of the Nazi leadership, it was Goebbels alone who perceived the vast revolutionary possibilities of guerrilla warfare, although he lacked either the time or the means to shape such a movement.

This prejudice against postwar partisan activity was also caused by an obvious fear of defeatism. As ironic as it seems, the whole idea of carrying on – of infusing National Socialism as the leading element in a future German resistance struggle – was itself considered a betrayal of the cause. The NSDAP was a paradoxical movement that refused to abet its survival simply because it assumed that it could not die. When it finally became apparent that death was imminent (or, at least, that a fall from power was close at hand), the primary impulse was one of self-annihilation.

Evidence of such chaos and confusion within the Nazi regime adds extra weight to the so-called structuralist or functionalist school of historiography, which regards the Third Reich as a 'polycracy' of competing centres of power. The Werwolf, in fact, was the penultimate act in the bureaucratic anarchy that resulted in a black night of lawlessness and self-destruction. On the other hand, not even the staunchest advocates of a 'programmatic' point of view would deny that Hitler's position had drastically weakened by 1944–5, and that any 'program' advocated by the Führer had already failed, thus allowing the bureaucratic factions within the regime to spiral into a whirlwind of confusion and barbarism.

Whether the 'functionalist' nature of the Third Reich should be interpreted as a tragic erosion of traditional ruling élites is another question, although one senior bureaucrat fleeing from Berlin, and captured by the U.S. First Army, explained it this way. This official warned his interrogators about the Werwolf, which he saw as a product of fanatical youth. He suggested that the movement was allowed to exist because of the absence of any moderating influences – 'For the past 12 years all leading people of the middle class and the nobility have been killed off and Hitler's experiment has destroyed most of the constructive forces in Germany. Life doesn't mean a thing. You are shot right away or hanged. The organization surpasses imagination. I wonder myself that I am still living.'[2]

'Functionalists' also portray Hitler as a figure strangely remote from the day-to-day operations of the civil and party bureaucracies, and this too is suggested by this study. There is scant evidence to suggest that the initiative for the Werwolf came from Hitler, and it is quite clear that his heart did not lay with the project, apart from a late-blooming interest in introducing guerrilla-style tactics into the Army. Hitler adopted Louis XIV's motto of 'Après moi, le déluge,' and he viewed his own personal defeat as the end of German history. In March 1945, the Führer was heard to groan that, because Germany had lost a war of extermination, the welfare of the surviving populace no longer mattered. In fact, on 29 March, in a directive ordering 'fanatical' attacks upon lines of communication behind enemy spearheads, he specifically noted that 'no regard [is] to be paid ... to the civilian population.' When Hitler's mood occasionally lightened a degree or two, he would suggest that the German people actually wanted a fight to the death, and that it was only foreign labourers who were hoisting white flags. He also spoke of the survival of his 'idea,' with the hope that by sacrificing himself in Berlin he could somehow provide a myth for his country in the distant future. The announcement of his death by German Radio (1 May) certainly attempted to lay the necessary groundwork by portraying Hitler as a brave fighter who had died in battle.[3] In a more immediate sense, however, he had little belief in the organizational survival of his movement, and a Wehrmacht radio operator who had handled communications in the Berlin Bunker during the final week of Hitler's life later recalled that he had heard or seen nothing concerning stay-behind organizations.[4]

Of course, while we may conclude that the fractured nature of Nazi authority weakened the Werwolf, it is also true that, when the final collapse came, some fragments of the movement were able to struggle onward independently. Even once the head had been cut off, a few limbs continued to twitch. This was a natural corollary of the fact that the Third Reich was not really an Arendtian, totalitarian state. However, this type of resistance was strongly reactive rather than proactive. Essentially, there are two types of partisans: those who fight for an idea, and those who hide out for a number of reasons, most of them involved with escaping from one or another form of authority. The former are often very difficult to crush, while the latter typically provide far fewer problems. The Werwolf was supposed to be the first kind of movement, but in actual fact most German resisters fell into the second category.

Because of the Werwolf's multiple weaknesses, it never survived its immature stage, when it could only reasonably have expected to carry a minority of the population with it. In fact, many Germans were eager to point out Nazi saboteurs to the occupation authorities, since failure to eliminate this danger in a quick and efficient fashion seemed to promise reprisals as a consequence. German POWs familiar with the Werwolf told Allied interrogators that the partisans also had a very difficult time in securing provisions from farmers and merchants.[5]

Six principal factors contributed to the widespread public disillusionment with Werwolf warfare. First, the entire Werwolf program was based on a faulty premise, at least in western Germany, where the Allies were the only potential force standing in the way of Soviet occupation. The average German could hardly have relished the prospect of a continual Soviet push westwards should Allied forces slow up the pace of their advance in order to deal with harassments in the rear. Since considerable public support has traditionally been regarded as a necessary prerequisite for large-scale guerrilla warfare – a point repeatedly made even in the Werwolf instruction manual itself – the Werwolf must be regarded as a misbegotten effort.

Second, the Werwolf was irrevocably associated with the National Socialist Party, despite propaganda efforts to prevent this association, and by 1945 the movement was discredited in the eyes of many Germans. The NSDAP, as Edward Peterson notes, was a populist party dependent upon success, and in this sense it could not sustain the terrible failure that it had incurred. Ian Kershaw notes that the party's popularity even in rural Germany, once the National Socialist heartland, was nil by 1944–5, and that, in truth, 'detestation of the

Nazi regime was ... almost universal in country areas.'[6] In addition, most party officials made a bad situation worse by shamelessly scrambling for safety in the face of the Allied advance. Had the NSDAP leadership stood fast, thereby giving the population at least some small reason to believe in the continuing legitimacy of the system, the Werwolf might have developed more popular appeal. It is thus clearly evident that the collapse of the Third Reich marked a reassertion of the centuries-old German tradition of aversion to politics, rather than a wave of final loyalty to either the party or the Führer.[7] (This is not to argue, of course, that the party's ideas and teachings were also quickly discarded.)

Given these circumstances, the best chance of success for the Werwolf would have been to convert itself into a strictly patriotic rally against the occupiers, portray itself as a self-defence mechanism, or depict itself as a European reaction against 'barbaric' outsiders. All these strategies were in fact applied – usually without much effect – although it is perhaps significant that the Soviets and French, the least benevolent of the conquerors, probably also experienced the most trouble. It is also interesting to note that Nazi efforts to stir up a spirit of vengeance based upon the Allied air attacks usually backfired: although the majority of the populace in heavily bombed areas resented the Allies, they felt even more strongly that their own government's failure to clear the skies of the Reich was inexcusable and they staunchly refused, at least on these grounds, to become cannon-fodder for resistance efforts.[8]

Third, Germany's moment of final defeat was much worse than that of such countries as France or Yugoslavia, in the sense that partisans in those nations had foreign sources of supply, and a justified hope for eventual victory. Even in these cases, it is significant that resistance was minimal until well after the entry of the USSR and the United States into the war. Alternately, Nazi guerrillas had no foreign supply bases, nor were they able to preserve the so-called Alpine Redoubt as a base area (another prerequisite of successful partisan warfare).[9] Considering that most Werewolves assumed on Clausewitzian grounds that guerrillas alone were incapable of defeating a regular military force, they were left with no belief in the possibility of eventual victory. The only flicker of hope was provided by an expected clash between the Western Allies and the Soviet Union, and the continued survival of Naziism even amidst the flames of such a conflict appeared unlikely. The desperation of this situation was realized by the bulk of the population and made the Werwolf seem like an entirely hopeless effort.

Fourth, the German people were too tired, both physically and psychologically, to respond to Werwolf appeals, a factor which even Werwolf Radio was forced to acknowledge. People who worked ten hours per day, who spent almost all their spare time in food queues, and who suffered under a constant barrage of aerial bombardment could hardly have been expected to oppose the final end of the conflict which had created these conditions in the first place. 'The war-weary population,' said one German general, 'will prove to be a poor breeding ground for guerrilla activities of any kind other than of irresponsible and sporadic nature.' According to the SHAEF Joint Intelligence Committee (11 April 1945), 'all reports from Allied occupied Germany state that, while there may be bitterness and resentment against the attitude of Allied troops and Allied bombing, the mass of the people are apathetic and desperately war-weary.'[10]

Similarly, in the immediate post-capitulation period, the average German was too concerned with his own survival and that of his family to find time to engage in resistance activities – foraging and black market operations necessarily consumed spare time. In fact, Allied intelligence reports noted in 1946 and 1947 that resistance to foreign rule was a reasonable expectation, but for the factors of cold and hunger that largely governed German behaviour.[11] One is reminded of the maxim that revolutions are made not by the desperate, but by the marginally well-off. On the other hand, it is certainly no coincidence that the spirit of Nazi underground resistance flourished most among children and teenagers, the segment of the population least affected by the demands of war, and – in the postwar period – the only generational group with spare time to fill.

Fifth, there was a great fear of enemy reprisals against anyone harbouring resisters. As noted in a British assessment, German 'knowledge of the ruthless way in which their armies have always treated saboteurs and francs-tireurs in occupied territories' created a certain set of assumptions about what to expect if the tables were ever reversed.[12] Even in Soviet-occupied territory, where deep hatred of the conqueror created a considerable psychological basis for guerrilla warfare, the intense savagery of the occupation troops largely paralysed the populace and sapped any capacity for vigorous activity. A Wehrmacht report from eastern Austria, dated 7 April 1945, noted that 'fear of Russian reprisals' dissuaded civilians from fighting, and that 'white flags [are] held ready in town and country.'[13] With no obvious point as a strategy, the Werwolf's only real value was as a gesture, and the threat of retaliation made the price far too high. Thus, captured Werewolves told Allied interrogators that they often had as much difficulty evading German civilians as in dodging Allied troops, and many Germans were sorely tempted to attack or disarm Werewolves in order to prevent any possible disturbances.[14] Werwolf supply dumps were frequently plundered or betrayed to the occupation authorities.

A sixth and final factor mitigating against resistance was that the social and political climate of the Reich had conditioned several successive generations of Germans to regard partisan warfare as an illegitimate tactic. Werwolf propaganda desperately sought to reverse this belief by appealing to strong traditions of German 'popular' warfare, but, given the short time in which Werwolf Radio could influence opinion, it is hardly surprising that little was accomplished. In the final analysis, most Germans retained almost as much contempt for their own guerrilla fighters as for the 'bandits' and 'Reds' who had harassed the Wehrmacht. It would be incorrect to conclude, however, that Germans were unsuited for partisan warfare on 'racial' grounds, or even that the fundamental nature of German culture was somehow barren of such roots. As Erik Erikson noted, 'national culture' existed as a definite factor in German behaviour, but it was partially created by immediate historical or geographical experiences that influenced child-rearing, and it was by no means an unchanging, absolute force.[15]

In the final analysis, however, we ought not to overemphasize the German public's snubbing of the Werwolf. While there is no doubt that a majority of the population consciously rejected guerrilla-warfare measures – precisely for the reasons listed above – there was also a minority of some 10 to 15 per cent who were regarded by the Allies as the core of public support for the movement.[16] Given the right conditions, this minority, and its Werwolf champions, could no doubt have succeeded in bullying the huge, apathetic mass that comprised the majority of the population, and in terrorizing the small minority of anti-Nazis on the opposite extreme of the ideological spectrum. Certainly such situations had developed in some Allied POW camps for German prisoners,[17] and it was perhaps only the vigilance and rigid controls imposed by the Allies that prevented such an outcome. One can only speculate, but had the Werwolf (despite its myriad difficulties) managed to terrorize the public into tolerating its efforts, then its potential to mount effective resistance would have increased exponentially.

The conventional wisdom on guerrillas is that they fail unless sustained by a genuinely sympathetic population. A significant pool of popular support creates an environment where the partisans can function like 'fish in water,' as suggested by Mao Zedong's famous aphorism. However, the French 'guerre révolutionnaire' theorists of the 1950s – learning from their own experiences with the Vietminh and the Algerian Mujahadeen – argued that guerrillas force much of the population's 'sympathy' through the ruthless use of terror.[18] The dividing lines among 'support,' 'tolerance,' and 'opposition' are ambiguous and easily traversed. Viewed from this perspective, which is not without merit, the importance of a band of isolated fanatics such as the Werwolf gains added importance.

There was also a considerable tendency among the Allies to regard the widespread German mood of tractability as an occasional veil for hostility. Almost everyone who visited Germany in 1945 was impressed by the apparent 'scarcity' of Nazis and by the German lack of willingness to admit past sins. From these observations, it was not much of a leap to assume that German civilians were also responsible for hiding attempts at sabotage and subversion by their more militant compatriots. The American journalist Martha Gellhorn, reporting from the Rhine Front in March 1945, claimed that local Germans were like chameleons who changed their colours according to the hour of the day. 'At night,' she claimed, 'the Germans take pot shots at Americans, or string wires across the roads, which is apt to be fatal to men driving jeeps, or they burn the houses of Germans who accept posts in our Military Government, or they booby trap ammunition dumps or motorcycles or anything that is likely to be touched. But that is at night. In the daytime we are the answer to the German prayer, according to them.'[19] An American soldier advancing up the Lahn Valley in Hesse also claimed that the attitude of the local inhabitants depended on how dark it was – 'The treacherous populations, which amazed us by cheering us as we entered their towns and then shot us in the back at nightfall, acquainted us with one of the fruits of Nazi ideology.'[20] Similarly, the unit history of the U.S. 90th Division, published in 1945, noted that 'all Germans despised the Nazis and loved the Americans passionately, a phenomenon which the troops accepted with a sceptical grain of salt.' No sooner had the 90th driven into Hesse than 'wooded areas ... began to disgorge roving bands of "guerillas" whose self-assigned mission was to harass the perilously-stretched lines of communication.'[21] And in the same spirit, a Red Cross official who toured Germany in May 1945 reported numerous instances where tires on Allied vehicles were blown out by tacks, or where wires were cut, even though most Germans were seemingly willing to obey Military Government rules. 'They are docile and have to be obedient,' she added, 'but I know they hate us.'[22]

Moreover, resentment against the Nazis did not necessarily mean sympathy for the Allies. Many German conservatives regarded the war from a patriotic point of view, wholly independent of National Socialist interpretations. A good example was Archbishop Count von Galen of Munster, a virulent critic of the Nazis who none the less told British journalists, in an interview in early April 1945, that he was 'loyal to the Fatherland' and regarded the Allies as enemies.[23] A Dutch interpreter working for the Allies in Cologne reported in March 1945 that although the city's inhabitants cheered the Americans, 'in their hearts they hate them. They will do anything to get the Allies out of here. Some Germans may have hated the Nazis, but they are still Germans.'[24]

Undoubtedly some such reactions were too strong and were conditioned by wartime hatreds. On the other hand, it is also true that the lethargic mood among many Germans during the 'Zero Hour' was caused more by shock than by a lack of willingness to stand up for National Socialist values, and that if the NSDAP was rejected as an organization, many of its ideas were not so quickly cast aside. 'We found,' said a British security specialist, 'resignation along with resentment, and arrogance mixed with envy ... The spirit of rebellion was something to be reckoned with from time to time.'[25] Assessments of public opinion in the U.S. Zone indicated that, within a half-year of the surrender, German morale had begun to revive, and that attitudes had crystallized into an enmity that was only scarcely concealed. 'Casual conversation in private among German civilians,' warned a year-end report, 'shows not only dislike of occupation troops but a narrow and bellicose nationalism which is not encouraging for the future.'[26] A similar report from the same period identified Bavarians as the people most likely to revolt in the U.S. Zone, owing to the fact that their relative lack of concern with basic issues like food and housing left them time to think about 'resistance possibilities.' 'It must [also] be admitted that the further a German in our Zone lives from the Russians, the more he resents the presence of American troops.'[27] A clear indication of German sensibilities was provided by a conversation among the passengers of a train that was reported to American authorities in December 1945, and which convinced the occupiers that, when Germans talked among themselves, out of earshot of Allied monitors, 'they do not hesitate to discuss their hostile feelings quite openly or to intimidate those who dare to take the opposite view.' In this case, almost all the passengers objected vigorously when someone noted that the conduct of American troops had been exemplary. Open resistance was advocated – 'It is high time that we take action' – and a former concentration-camp inmate was threatened with violence when he said than any current abuses were no worse than those perpetrated by the Wehrmacht when it had occupied foreign territories.[28]

Once again, we can only conclude that, given our knowledge of the simultaneous activities of Nazi fanatics eager to stampede public opinion, it was fortunate that sufficient occupation forces were on hand to keep the populace on a straight and narrow path. One Foreign Office bureaucrat concluded that even the limited scope of German resistance demonstrated 'the complete futility of piously hoping that the Germans will "in due course" convert themselves, by their own efforts, into right-thinking Europeans, without our doing anything very definite to help them.'[29]

Finally, we must briefly consider how the Werwolf influenced the nature of the occupation. Although it has been claimed that the prospect of Werwolf resistance caused the Western Allies to advance with 'unnecessary violence,'[30] the unfortunate truth is that the threat of partisan warfare created a setting conducive to the abuse of ordinary folk, principally because the guerrillas attempted to hide themselves among civilians, and thus endangered all noncombatants. As the war devolved into guerrilla combat during its final phase, this gave rise (in certain areas) to the savageries typical of such a struggle, and the occupation got off to a rough start. As Manfred Bosch observes, even the period after 8 May had 'a postwar character, but yet there was no peace.'[31] It is true that Allied commanders authorized breeches of the Hague Regulations, and that they occasionally carried through such transgressions, although to keep this issue in perspective it is necessary to note that, throughout this century, most invasion and occupation forces have similarly broken the rules when it suited their purposes to do so.

It is also clear that, while the Allies planned even as early as 1942–3 to enter Germany as conquerors rather than liberators, the Werwolf threat magnified the force of this intention. The result was Military Governments that had a twofold purpose: to maintain security and to promote the cause of democratic change. Even as early as May 1945, a War Office expert, Brigadier H.E. Balthin, recognized the essence of the contradiction implied by this dualism. 'There is,' he observed, 'an immediate conflict between our demand for absolute and unquestioning obedience to our orders and our requirement that the Germans shall develop a sense of civic responsibility, the lack of which has led to their subservience to the Nazi regime and their failure to accept responsibility for its acts.'[32] Although the incompatibility between these two functions diminished over the course of time, it never entirely disappeared, and there is little doubt that security concerns hindered the more positive aspects of the Allied program, such as democratization and re-education. Western Germany, at least, would eventually emerge as a stable democracy, but only after an important transitional phase in the 1950s and early 1960s, once both the Werwolf and the occupiers had long ceased to tussle over the remains of the Reich.

APPENDICES

The Werwolf as a Research Problem:
A Historiographical Essay

One has to wonder how a story as important as that of the Werwolf has nearly slipped through the cracks of written history. Walter Struve, for one, notes that themes such as the Nazi attempt to fanaticize part of the population and mobilize youth against the advancing enemy have attracted surprisingly little attention in the existing literature.[1] Several factors have combined to produce this curious omission.

One major assumption that has prejudiced research is the common fallacy that guerrilla warfare supposedly had no hope of success in Germany because certain deeply ingrained aspects of German 'national character' did not favour such tactics, a misconception often repeated by Germans themselves. Thus, the German people have been regarded as too orderly, too steeped in a tradition of strict obedience to authority, too chivalrous (in a hollow sense), and too lacking in individual initiative to resort to any sort of popular or partisan warfare.[2] One German general noted that Germanic 'common sense' did not permit acceptance of a tactic more appropriate to hot-blooded Latins and Slavs. This sort of biased commentary has been given serious consideration by the British military writer Kenneth MacKsey, who claims that such 'racial aspects' are significant and 'worthy of further study.'[3]

Such ideas can be quickly laid to rest. In truth, partisan warfare has a long and important tradition in Germany. For centuries, the armed *canaille* was responsible for guerrilla-style raiding, or 'social banditry,' in mountains and heavily wooded areas, such as the Harz, the Thuringian Forest, and the country bordering the Rhine Valley.[4] Medieval jurisprudence actually allowed for peasants' uprisings,[5] and the Thirty Years War was a classic example of a war without limits, pitting peasant guerrillas against various princes, mercenaries, and foreign occupation armies. According to Hermann Löns, bands operating against the Swedes during the 1630s adopted the name 'Wehrwolf' and chose as their emblem the *Wolfsangel*, which resembled an inverted 'N.'[6] Another classic example of such peasant forces took shape in the Alps, where geographic and social conditions gave rise to an independently-minded armed peasantry and a number of autonomous republics. The tactics of these Alpine warriors – harassment of the enemy both behind and forward of earthen or masonry barricades[7] – eventually evolved into a kind of national strategy for the Swiss, and their 'National Redoubt' in turn served as an intriguing model for the leaders of the Third Reich, who were themselves faced in the last months of the Second World War with the prospect of being chased into the Alps. The rise of modern nationalism also added a crucial new element to 'popular' risings, such as the 'People's War' of 1813,[8] or the paramilitary resistance campaigns waged from 1918 to 1923 in the face of the Poles, the Bolsheviks, and the Western Allies.[9]

These traditions lent themselves well to the ideological fixations of National Socialism. The image of the partisan, for instance, fit into the romantic Nazi ideal of the individual warrior, an idea borrowed from Ernst Jünger: that is, an élite man of action and subjectivist, rather than a modern soldier-as-manager. This was exactly the spirit used to deify Leo Schlageter, the one-time leader of a Nazi sabotage team in the Ruhr who was captured and executed by the French in 1923. Schlageter subsequently became honoured as the so-called first soldier of the Third Reich, and 'Schlageter Memorial Day' was celebrated annually with appropriate panoply and fanfare.[10] Partisan warfare was also a logical extension of the Hitlerian interpretation of war as a struggle of races, with no holds barred, as opposed to the traditional concept that war was a clash of legally organized armed forces. Given this view, it was hardly a surprise that Hitler anticipated anti-German guerrilla operations in occupied areas, particularly Poland and Russia, and that he accepted the need for Nazi-inspired partisan warfare in case the Reich was itself threatened. This appreciation for the totality of war, with its supposed web of interrelated racial, cultural, economic, and ideological elements, suggested the breakdown of any meaningful distinction between soldiers and civilians.[11] Furthermore, the prospect of fighting in forests and wildlands appealed to the romantic naturalism of the German Youth Movement, a feeling eventually inherent by National Socialism.[12] As a result, it is no surprise to find the military forces of the Third Reich exploiting guerrilla tactics on a systematic basis, particularly through the deployment of paramilitary formations recruited among the Volksdeutsche. Irregular formations of Nazified foreign volunteers helped to precipitate the conquests of Austria, Czechoslovakia, Poland, and Yugoslavia,[13] and they also played a role in the campaign against the Soviet Union.[14]

Germany also has a vigorous history of vigilantism, ranging from 'oat field actions' undertaken in medieval Bavaria to the 'self-protection' forces of the post–First World War period. However, the 'Vehme' of the late Middle Ages was probably the most famous and vibrant of these traditions. Because of the medieval Balkanization of the Reich and the absence of a strong central power, certain Westphalian courts in the thirteenth century, adopted clandestine practices as a means of preserving justice in the face of local princes who were otherwise disposed to tamper with the normal execution of law. The proceedings of these courts were carried out in true cloak-and-dagger fashion, and free jurymen – who both decided the cases and carried out the verdicts – established a secret fraternity among themselves. In the fourteenth century, the Vehme courts were recognized by the emperor, mainly as a means of counteracting the unbridled power of the regional lords, and the jurisdiction of the courts expanded into other areas of Germany. As time passed, of course, the Vehme began to exercise their authority in an increasingly arbitrary fashion, which eventually aroused criticism, not only from the local princes, but also from the rising burgher class. Thus, in the late fifteenth century, the power of the courts was broken, although they survived in much weakened form until the end of the Holy Roman Reich.[15] It is important for our purposes to note, however, that, even as the courts declined, they were remembered and romanticized in German popular culture, and such writers as Goethe and Kleist made the Vehme a standard prop in the new genre of *Romanliteratur*. As a result, the Vehme tradition was fondly remembered by members of the post–First World War paramilitaries, many of whom declared war on the 'inner enemy' – that is, German liberals, Socialists, and Communists – and revived the medieval rituals of the Vehme. Politicians who had dickered with the enemy or flirted with Bolshevist Russia, such as Matthias Erzberger and Walther Rathenau, were ruthlessly eliminated, and overall more than 400 victims fell to this virulent new form of vigilantism. The National Socialists inherited many of these violent habits.[16]

The most that can be said for the argument that Germans were too 'orderly' for partisan warfare is that the whole idea of guerrilla fighting momentarily fell under a dark cloud during the late nineteenth and early twentieth centuries. Unlike the case in such countries as Greece or Italy, partisan warfare did not play a significant role in the saga of German national consolidation, mainly because the unification of the German state was orchestrated from above, by Bismarck and William I, and did not arise from popular initiative. Bismarck and his contemporaries were happy to convert nationalism into a prop for the new Wilhelmine Empire, thus stealing the thunder of German liberals, but they were certainly not prepared to favour the doctrine of a 'people's war' as well. War in the Bismarckian view remained what it had long been in the eyes of European reactionaries and conservatives – namely, a sole prerogative of the state and the

professional army. Moreover, the popular culture of a dynamic state with considerable political, economic, and imperial aspirations bore little sympathy for a
form of warfare that was a natural weapon of the weak. Thus, the French *francs-
tireurs* of 1870–1, the Belgian partisans of 1914, and the Yugoslavian and Russian guerrillas of 1941–2 all received short shrift in Germany, and Geoffrey
Best rightly speaks of the German Army's 'ingrained detestation of guerrillas.'[17] When this situation had finally reversed itself by 1944, and the Germans
were forced to establish their own partisan movement, Nazi ideologists and propagandists were left scrambling, desperately searching for traditional sources of
inspiration that could rouse a 'popular rising' and erode recent prejudices.
Guerrilla tactics, as a military study tactfully noted, comprised, 'not a bandit
war, but a people's war.' This is not to argue, however, that Germans had no
capacity for guerrilla warfare – the only inhibitors were certain limited aspects
of Imperial-era culture that continued to echo as late as the 1930s and 1940s.

A second major research problem vis-à-vis the Werwolf concerns lack of
sources, particularly the fact that there is no central collection of original Werwolf documents. There was a considerable paper flow in the SS and HJ wings
of the Werwolf, consisting of directives, monthly situation reports by regional
Werwolf organizers, and a headquarters serial called 'Werwolf News East and
West,' which kept track of events in the occupied territories and documented
Werwolf actions.[19] However, almost all of these records were destroyed during
the German retreat in 1944–5, largely because the Germans continued to regard
guerrilla warfare as an illegal tactic, and therefore feared that any surviving evidence would be used by the enemy to prosecute breeches of the rules of war. It
is also true that many sensitive messages related to Werwolf operations and
organizational matters were probably only orally communicated: 'Nothing written,' it seems, was the watchword of many Werwolf elements.[20]

In addition to the scarcity of documents, few former Werwolves have rushed
forward to publish their wartime diaries or memoirs, a hesitancy that probably
owes something to the fact that the topic still leaves a bad taste in the mouths of
many Germans and that fear of prosecution continues. Most Werewolves who
have bothered to recount their stories have sworn that their orders were undertaken reluctantly and that operations were never pursued vigorously.[21] The
major exception is Fred Borth, the one-time chief of a HJ-Werwolf detachment
that functioned in Eastern Austria. After the war, Borth was so ready to spill the
details of his mission that he was actually arrested while giving evidence at a
trial in 1948, mainly on the assumption that his lively description of guerrilla
actions comprised an implicit attempt to kick-start the Austrian Werwolf.[22]
Borth's subsequent memoirs, *Nicht zu Jung zum Sterben*, were supposed to
illustrate the horror of deploying children in war, but the author fondly remem-

bered youthful exploits and made no real attempt to hide that fact. Even Borth, however, felt constrained to explain that he was *not* part of Goebbels's terrorist Werwolf, but was a member of Prützmann's 'Special Abwehr,' which was supposed to have had a strict guerrilla character.[23]

Given the absence of many Werwolf documents or much voluntary evidence by former participants, we are left with Allied and Soviet appreciations of the Werwolf. In truth, the fact that is possible to form a picture of the movement at all owes mainly to the work of the counter-intelligence agencies of the occupying powers, which gathered information on the movement in order to destroy it. However, the reverberatory and indirect nature of this evidence comprises a third research problem. First of all, Allied and Soviet impressions were built largely on the basis of interrogations, which are invaluable sources in reference to any organization loath to create a written record of incriminating details,[24] but which are problematic for various reasons. Typically, the captured guerrillas most willing to talk were usually those least committed to the movement, and they were eager to tell their questioners what they thought they wanted to hear. Less-talkative prisoners either denied membership in the Werwolf or swore that it was inactive, quite correctly fearing that their captors would show an adverse reaction as a result of open admissions of murder or sabotage directed against the occupying forces. Thus, it is correct to assume that facts about the Werwolf revealed through interrogation constituted a bare minimum, particularly with regard to Werwolf operations.

Interrogations were also influenced by the mind-set of the interrogators, mainly through the type of questions that they asked and the way in which they filtered answers through the screen of their own perceptions and prejudices. Considering the generally warped view of all things German which existed in 1945; considering the then-prevalent image of National Socialism as a pure and inseparable extension of 'German Nationalist philosophy,' and considering the inability of many Allied authorities to distinguish among different German age groups and social classes in their relationship to Naziism, it is scarcely surprising that various Allied and Soviet 'experts' either underestimated or overestimated the movement, each according to his own particular biases. Popular assumptions about German 'national character' deeply influenced considerations about German guerrilla warfare, especially the conclusion that such tactics demanded a degree of independent enterprise supposedly alien to the German nature. 'I thought from the first,' said General George Patton, 'that the threat of "werewolves," and murder was inconsequential because the German is incapable of individual initiative action.'[25] On the other hand, this type of stereotyping could also point to the opposite conclusion, specifically on the grounds that the Germans were an inherently warlike race tied by a mystical bond to their Führer, and that the latter would demand – and receive – die-hard fanaticism. Thus, in March 1945, when Allied officers first encountered unarmed German soldiers surrendering in great masses, they could hardly believe the claim of these men that they had destroyed their weapons, rather leaping to the more paranoid supposition that the defeated troops had given their arms to German civilians for use in partisan warfare.[26]

Not only did such prejudices interfere with the objective exercise of judgment, but the occupiers were also bedevilled by problems in the dissemination of the type of information needed to make accurate assessments. Such difficulties are most clearly shown by the fact that various incidents of violent resistance are *not* uniformly reported in the different sources of information available to the present-day researcher, particularly Allied intelligence reports and summaries. For instance, unit histories contain abundant information that apparently never reached the central intelligence departments at SHAEF, the Army Groups, and the headquarters of the various occupation forces. Colonel H.G. Sheen, the head of SHAEF Counter-Intelligence, is on record in mid-April 1945 pleading with the Army Groups for an adequate flow of information on the Werwolf – 'it is urgently requested that your lower echelons be impressed with the importance of sending back material back though you [to us] at the earliest practicable moment.'[27]

Of course, collecting timely information from subordinate units is the kind of problem that inevitably faces every superior headquarters, but collecting intelligence about guerrillas poses a special difficulty because of the inherent hostility and disdain towards such forces exhibited by the professional military. R.F. Weigley rightly notes that 'guerrilla warfare is so incongruous to the natural methods and habits of a stable and well-to-do society that the American Army has tended to regard it as abnormal and to forget about it whenever possible.'[28] Liberated French political prisoners in Hesse were shocked when they brought a report on Werwolf bands to a local American combat commander, and he tore it up before their eyes. He was sympathetic, he said, but he did not feel that many of his fellow officers would be similarly inclined – 'You don't understand the mentality of our officers. They have no political make-up; they are military, that's all ... You have involved yourself in something they ignore and nothing will be done against these Werewolves.'[29] Difficult to categorize and assess, full of political undercurrents foreign to military thinking, partisan warfare was frequently ignored.

In addition, whatever measures were undertaken to combat guerrillas sometimes involved fierce reprisals that few military officers were willing to commit to a paper record or to later remember in their memoirs. When preparing to level the northwest German town of Freisoythe, Canadian General Chris Vokes was convinced by his executive officer not to post proclamations or issue a written order outlining the nature of the operation. To his credit, Vokes was later bold enough to record the incident in his memoirs, perhaps because he was certain of the moral and functional rectitude of his actions. Vokes admitted that he had acted outside of the rules of war, but he bore no regrets.[30]

Eventually, the initial concern shown by the Allies over the possibility of guerrilla warfare began to dissipate as it became apparent that the extravagant claims of 'Werwolf Radio' were verifiably false, which tended to throw doubt on all accounts of Werwolf activity, no matter how authentic. Moreover, it gradually became apparent that most actual guerrilla attacks and attempts to provoke unrest were *uncoordinated*, and that the Werwolf had failed to lay a strong basis for concerted action. After the massive blood-letting of a world war, sporadic incidents resulting in minor inconveniences and a handful of casualties seemingly did not inspire much worry. Having originally focused an exaggerated fear upon the Werwolf, the pendulum subsequently swung to the opposite extreme, and there was a marked tendency to write off the Werwolf entirely. Professional officers were keen to get to the Pacific, where there was still potential for real career-building, while civilians in uniform were anxious to demobilize. Thus, harassments of Allied troops and communication lines were routinely denied importance in American and British intelligence reports because they were uncoordinated and supposedly posed no long-term threat to the occupation forces. Thus, one finds SHAEF calmly asserting that numerous instances of sniping and sabotage in the Allied rear were usually the work of bypassed German soldiers and *not* Werewolves per se, which they saw as a good thing.[31]

Werwolf attacks upon other Germans warranted even less attention, in part because Allied troops had difficulty envisioning the victims as martyrs, or even as normal human beings deserving of justice. As Earl Ziemke notes, a great many Germans died in the spring of 1945, most of them in forgotten circumstances and most without many questions asked.[32] A callous Allied position on German 'collaborators' took shape around the turn of 1945, when it was feared that, as a result of the Ardennes Counter-Offensive, the Allies might lose their toe-holds in the Rhineland. In the case of such an eventuality, several British newspapers pushed for German 'collaborators' to be evacuated, or at least for the Allied High Command to warn returning Nazis not to retaliate against such people, and the U.S. First Army actually blurted out a promise to do everything possible within the bounds of practicality and military necessity. However, SHAEF said and did nothing, owing to the advice of its G-5 Legal Branch that anti-Nazi 'collaborators' might actually be traitors 'under existing German law,' and the contention of G-5's Operations Branch that any statement in favour of German 'collaborators' would potentially undercut the French government in dealing with pro-German French collaborators as it saw fit.[33]

On top of all these contemporary factors underplaying the Werwolf, one must also note the censorship imposed by Allied authorities, a factor which – perhaps more than any other – created the popular impression that the Werwolf was dormant and that Germans were uniformally docile. The Twelfth Army Group suggested in early April 1945 that press accounts of the fighting should avoid extensive reportage of Werwolf activity, mainly on the grounds that any publicity would magnify the movement and win it new recruits. 'Likewise,' they noted, '[we] must avoid [a] heroic martyr myth similar to Schlageter of the last occupation.' This policy was subsequently adopted by the relevant SHAEF censorship and public-relations authorities,[34] and such strictures lasted until September.[35] As late as midsummer 1945, a *Washington Post* correspondent investigating SS bands in the Alps found it impossible to get any information from the relevant military authorities, and one officer to whom he spoke said he feared court-martial if he even acknowledged the issue.[36] By the time that censorship measures were rescinded, the American press, at least, had lost interest in Germany and had shifted its collective gaze elsewhere.[37]

Even less information filtered out of the Soviet Zone or areas east, although, for many months after the war, each Soviet commandant in occupied areas drew up his own censorship regulations – only in August 1945 was the process centralized in the hands of the Soviet Military Administration at Karlshorst.[38] None the less, despite evidence of initial disorganization, news reports from the Eastern Zone were usually controlled, or at least influenced, by Soviet political and military authorities, and are thus suspect. We know, for instance, that the Soviets and their allies had much to say about 'Werewolves' and Vlassovite guerrillas committing crimes while dressed in Russian tunics, allegedly in order to defame the Red Army.[39] While such things no doubt happened,[40] this was also an all-too-easy excuse for the fact that Soviet hordes were involved in pillaging, rape, and murder, crimes to which the Russians were loath to admit. It is also true that the Poles and Czechs released considerable information on Werwolf outrages, but this was clearly part of an effort to expedite the forced expulsion of ethnic Germans from reannexed territories, which in turn involved proving the perfidy of German populations. Considering that the provision of such information obviously served the designs of Polish, Czech, and Soviet policy, reports from the east must be treated with due caution. None the less, such data have some value; certainly information from Eastern Europe has been given enough credence to serve as evidence in war-crimes cases tried in American courts.

Of course, there have been lots of instances where neither the questionable nature of evidence, nor a shortage of primary sources has deterred investigation, and it is similarly true that historians have rarely let the conventional wisdom of a past era determine research agendas. With regard to the Werwolf, however, there has been no strong motive for original scholarship, and this constitutes a fourth and final factor discouraging work on the topic. In Germany, the Werwolf does not fit easily into the semi-official view of modern German history, which sees the resistance *against* Hitler as a basis of legitimacy for the Federal Republic, and as a means of redemption for the German people. After the revelations about the Nuremberg Laws, Munich, the 'Night of Crystal,' the T4 Program, Coventry, Babi Yar, Operation Reinhard, the Commando Order, Auschwitz, the Malmedy Massacre, – there was no desire to search for anything else to add to this list. Germans already had enough difficulties in their ongoing struggle to deal with the past, where every wound was still raw. Truth, as Rousseau notes, does not lead to fortune.

For many years, the only group of historians with a deep and abiding interest in the intricate workings of the Third Reich was the Institute for Contemporary History in Munich. Not incidentally, this institution produced the only German research on the Werwolf published until the 1980s, which was a short summary article by Hellmuth Auerbach.[41] A seminal history, *Werwolf, 1944–1945*,[42] has since been written by military historian Arno Rose, but it is still a significant comment on modern German historiography that there are only several German works on the Werwolf, whereas one could literally fill a library with books on the underground resistance *against* Hitler. Rose's book was a ground-breaker and a solid piece of work, although it was not without its faults, most of which were related to its exclusively German research base. This limited range of primary sources led to an overemphasis on the Werwolf's crimes against fellow Germans – almost to the exclusion of other parts of the story – and it determined that the narrative came to a screeching halt when it reached May 1945, the chronological point at which the supply of German documents runs out. Moreover, Rose's text betrays a marked right-wing tone,[43] and his failure to use Soviet, Polish, or Czech sources leaves his depiction of the Werwolf uneven.

Only in 1995 can we register the first general study to accord the Werwolf much attention: in the magisterial *Die amerikanische Besetzung Deutschlands*,[44] Klaus-Dietmar Henke certainly avoided the trap of using only German sources, and as a result he showed a full understanding of the impact of the movement upon American mentalities and policies. Henke's chapters on German guerrillas are the best published source on the movement in the American Zone, although even he underplays the activities of Werwolf groups.

The Soviets and East Germans, meanwhile, were admittedly shy about acknowledging any popular resistance to the triumph of Socialism. Soviet and

East European historians usually gave primary attention to the survival of 'fascist' industrial and military élites, which in turn served as a convenient means of discrediting the German Federal Republic. It was obviously difficult to fit such a self-destructive impulse as the Werwolf into an historiography that regarded the Third Reich as a creature of German capitalism, although some passing attempts were made in this direction. Certain Soviet and Czech sources suggested, for instance, that the Werwolf was intended mainly to survive the defeat of the Reich,[45] or that it comprised Nazi politicians and industrialists who later received the patronage of the Western Powers. 'The fascist "werewolves",' said *Izvestia* in 1949, 'are becoming the allies and servants of Wall Street and the City.'[46] This merely reflected a more general inability among Marxist historians to deal with the irrational, neo-barbaric nature of National Socialism, as opposed to regarding the movement as an outgrowth of capitalist decline.

It also seems likely that the usual Communist portrayal of partisan fighting as a rallying of patriots to Soviet Socialism made it difficult to subsequently reverse the positive connotations of this type of endeavour by focusing attention upon a specifically Nazi version of guerrilla warfare, even if it failed. The logical conclusions of such a study might have seemed, in a totalitarian society, to diminish the contrast between the forces of light (i.e., Soviet Socialism) and those of darkness (i.e., Hitlerite fascism). Thus, even though the Red Army clearly recognized in 1945 that the Werwolf was supposed to have a popular character, and was meant 'to draw people into armed struggle against the Soviet forces,'[47] the appropriate term 'partisan' was never bestowed upon Werewolves, either in intelligence reports or in subsequent literature. Rather, Werwolf guerrillas were always referred to as 'diversionists,' which in Soviet usage denoted personnel dispatched into enemy territory for a limited period in order to perform specific tasks, and therefore less significant than true partisans with a mass base.[48]

Western historians have long laboured under the assumption that the Werwolf was a non-starter, a perception that has held sway since the second half of the 1940s. The only significant work has been done by several British specialists in popular war narratives, such as Charles Whiting and James Lucas,[49] and even these studies are poorly referenced and fail to attempt any sustained analysis of the entire movement. In fact, Whiting's book, *Hitler's Werewolves*, is mainly an account of one Werwolf operation, the murder of the *Oberbürgermeister* of Aachen. Moreover, as Roderick Watt notes, these studies indulge in much speculation and novelistic reconstruction of dialogue – 'they tend to read like racy "faction" rather than reliable history.'[50] Some of the same limitations also characterize the chapter on the Werewolves in E.H. Cookridge's biography of

Reinhard Gehlen.[51] Apart from these few works, it seems that inhibitions similar to those operative in Germany and Eastern Europe also exist in the West. In Western Europe and the Anglo-American world, the popular view of non-Communist partisan warfare has long been influenced by the lingering romantic aura of Second World War–era anti-Nazi resistance and the associated trend of humanist existentialism. It was generally felt – and still is – that an individual sense of morality and courage was the engine that had supposedly propelled a brave minority of *résistants*, and that the absence of such an ethical gyroscope was one of the key markers of the Nazi character type. Following this line of reasoning, National Socialists lacked the psychological ability to create a resistance movement analagous to the groups that had so resolutely fought the Nazis themselves. French historian Jean Hugonnot, for instance, argues that the German guerrilla movement 'was a denial of history's teachings, in forgetting that an army of Resistance is essentially an army of free men, an army in the service of national independence and liberty; that is to say, the exact antithesis of this artificial *maquis*, this paper *maquis* ... '[52] Not surprisingly, given this premise, he concluded that the Werwolf was a total bust.

The main assumption of this brief essay is certainly not that there has been an overt suppression of the facts, nor that there has been any nefarious effort to cover up the Werwolf. Rather, there has simply been an absence of interest – the sort of historiographical forces that typically focus the attention of historians on a topic have so far been missing. This monograph is an attempt to reddress that failure.

APPENDIX B:

Charts and Tables

CHART 1: Dienststelle Prützmann

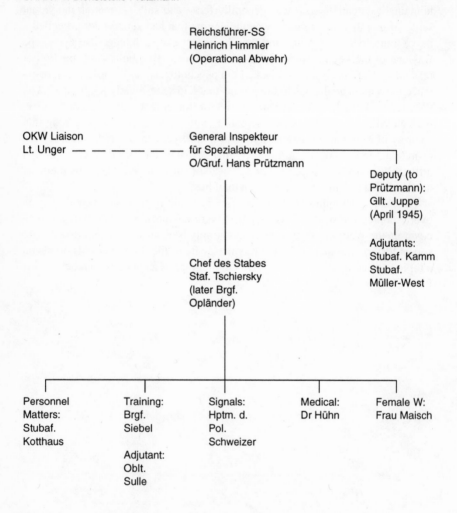

Reichsführer-SS
Heinrich Himmler
(Operational Abwehr)

OKW Liaison
Lt. Unger — — — — — — —

General Inspekteur
für Spezialabwehr
O/Gruf. Hans Prützmann

Deputy (to
Prützmann):
Gllt. Juppe
(April 1945)

Adjutants:
Stubaf. Kamm
Stubaf.
Müller-West

Chef des Stabes
Staf. Tschiersky
(later Brgf.
Opländer)

Personnel
Matters:
Stubaf.
Kotthaus

Training:
Brgf.
Siebel

Adjutant:
Oblt.
Sulle

Signals:
Hptm. d.
Pol.
Schweizer

Medical:
Dr Hühn

Female W:
Frau Maisch

Source: CSDIC/WEA BAOR 'Second Interim Report on SS Obergruf. Karl Gutenberger,'
IR no. 34, 1 Nov. 1945, OSS 123190, NA

CHART 2: The SS-Police Command Structure

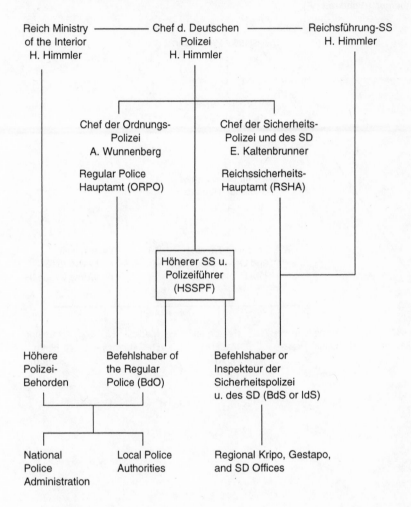

Source: Finding Guide to the Records of the Reich Leader of the SS and Chief of
      German Police, German Military Records, NA

CHART 3: An Example of Regional Werwolf Organization – The Werwolf Staff of HSSPF Gutenberger (Wehrkreis VI)

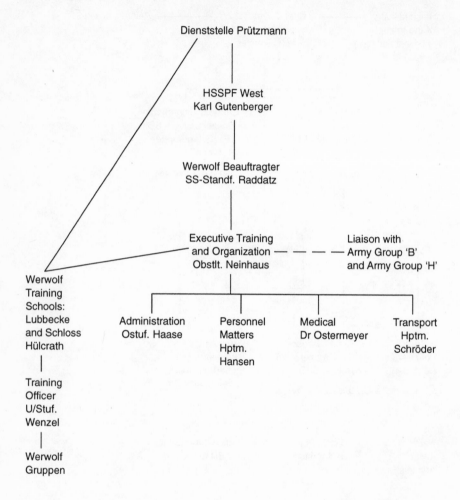

Dienststelle Prützmann

HSSPF West
Karl Gutenberger

Werwolf Beauftragter
SS-Standf. Raddatz

Executive Training
and Organization — — — —
Obstlt. Neinhaus

Liaison with
Army Group 'B'
and Army Group 'H'

Werwolf
Training
Schools:
Lubbecke
and Schloss
Hülcrath

Administration
Ostuf. Haase

Personnel
Matters
Hptm.
Hansen

Medical
Dr Ostermeyer

Transport
Hptm.
Schröder

Training
Officer
U/Stuf.
Wenzel

Werwolf
Gruppen

Source: CSDIC/WEA BAOR 'Second Interim Report on SS-Obergruf. Karl Gutenberger,'
        IR no. 34, 1 Nov. 1945, OSS 123190, NA

TABLE 1: HSSPF in the Greater Reich, Autumn 1944

Wehrkreis	HSSPF	Headquarters	Extent of Influence
I (Nordost)	O/Gruf. Georg Ebrecht (later replaced by Prützmann)	Königsburg	East Prussia, Memel
II (Ostsee)	O/Gruf. Emil Mazew	Stettin	Mecklenberg, Pomerania
III (Spree)	O/Gruf. August Heissmeyer	Berlin	Brandenberg, Altmark, Neumark
IV (Elbe)	Gruf. Rudolf von Alvensleben	Dresden	Saxony, Thuringia, Northwest Sudetenland
V (Südwest)	O/Gruf. Otto Hofmann	Stuttgart	Württemberg, Baden, Alsace
VI (West)	O/Gruf. Karl Gutenburger	Düsseldorf	Westphalia, Rhineland, Eastern Belgium
VII (Süd)	O/Gruf. Karl von Eberstein	Munich	Southern Bavaria
VIII (Südost)	O/Gruf. Heinrich Schmauser	Breslau	Silesia, Sudetenland
IX (Fulda-Werra)	O/Gruf. Josias Erbprinz zu Waldeck und Pyrmont	Kassel	Hessen, Western Thuringia
X (Nordsee)	Gruf. Georg von Bassewitz-Behr	Hamburg	Frisia, Schleswig
XI (Mitte)	Gruf. Hermann Höfle (later replaced by Querner)	Hanover	Hanover Prov., Brunswick, Anhalt
XII (Rhein–Westmark)	Gruf Jürgen Stroop	Wiesbaden	Southwest Hesse, Eifel, Palatinate, Saar, Lorraine
XIII (Main)	Gruf. Benno Martin	Nuremberg	Northern Bavaria, Western Bohemia
XVII (Donau)	O/Gruf. Rudolf Querner (later replaced by Schimana)	Vienna	Nothern Austria, Southern Sudetenland
XVIII (Alpenland)	Gruf. Erwin Rösener	Salzburg	Southern Austria, Northern Slovenia
XX (Weichsel)	Gruf. Fritz Katzmann	Danzig	Polish Corridor, Danzig, Western East Prussia
XXI (Warthe)	Brgf. Heinz Reinefarth	Posen	Western Poland
General-Government (Ost)	O/Gruf. Wilhelm Koppe	Cracow	Central and Southern Poland
Bohemia–Moravia	O/Gruf. Karl Frank	Prague	Central Bohemia, Moravia
Bialystock (under Wkr. Nordost)	Brfg. Otto Hellwig	Bialystock	Northeast Poland

Source: 'Liste der Höchsten und Höheren SS– und Polizeiführer sowie der SS– und Polizeiführer,' 20 Oct. 1944, NS 19/1637, BA

TABLE 2: *Gauleiter* in the Greater Reich, Summer 1944

Gau	Gauleiter	Headquarters
Baden	Robert Wagner	Karlsruhe
Bayreuth	Fritz Wächtler	Bayreuth
Berlin	Joseph Goebbels	Berlin
Düsseldorf	Friedrich Karl Florian	Düsseldorf
Essen	Josef Terboven	Essen
Franconia	Karl Holz	Nuremburg
Hamburg	Karl Kaufmann	Hamburg
Hessen–Nassau	Jakob Sprenger	Frankfurt am Main
Cologne–Aachen	Joseph Grohe	Cologne
Kurhessen	Karl Weinrich	Kassel
Magdeburg–Anhalt	Rudolf Jordan	Dessau
Main–Franconia	Otto Hellmuth	Würzburg
Moselland	Gustav Simon	Koblenz
Munich–Upper Bavaria	Paul Giesler	Munich
East Hanover	Otto Telschow	Lüneberg
Schleswig–Holstein	Heinrich Lohse	Kiel
Swabia	Karl Wahl	Augsburg
South Hanover–Brunswick	Hartmann Lauterbacher	Hanover
Thuringia	Fritz Sauckel	Weimar
Weser–Ems	Paul Wegener	Oldenburg
North Westphalia	Alfred Meyer	Münster
South Westphalia	Albert Hoffmann	Bochum
Westmark	Josef Burckel	Neustadt
Württemberg–Hohenzollern	Wilhelm Murr	Stuttgart

Source: Werner Haupt, *Das Ende im Westen*, 1945, 213

Notes

Abbreviations

ACA (BE)	Allied Commission, Austria (British Element)
ACC	Allied Control Council
ACoS	Assistant Chief of Staff
AN	Archives Nationales, Paris
AOK	Armee Oberkommando
BA	Bundesarchiv, Koblenz
BAOR	British Army of the Rhine
BLA	British Liberation Army
BLPES	British Library of Political and Economic Science, London
BMA	Bundesmilitärarchiv, Freiburg
CCG (BE)	Control Commission Germany (British Element)
CFM	Council of Foreign Ministers
CSDIC	Combined Services Detailed Interrogation Centre
DIC	Detailed Interrogation Centre
DNB	Deutschesnachrichtenbüro
ECAD	European Civil Affairs Division
EDS	Evaluation and Dissemination Section (of SHAEF G-2)
ETO	European Theatre of Operations
ETOUSA	European Theatre of Operations, United States Army
Eucom	European Command
FO	Foreign Office
FORD	Foreign Office Research Division
GSI	General Staff Intelligence
Int.	Intelligence
IRR	Investigative Records Repository

IWM	Imperial War Museum, London
JIC	Joint Intelligence Committee
MFI (U)	Mobile Field Interrogation (Unit)
MI-14	German Section of the Military Intelligence Directorate
MI-6	Military Intelligence designation of the Secret Intelligence Service
MIS	Military Intelligence Service
NA	National Archives, Washington, DC, and Suitland MD
OSS	Office of Strategic Services
OWI	Office of War Information
PID	Political Intelligence Division
PRO	Public Records Office, Kew Gardens, London
PWD	Psychological Warfare Division
PWE	Political Warfare Executive
SHAT	Service Historique de l'Armée de Terre, Vincennes, Paris
SSU	Strategic Services Unit
USFET	United States Forces, European Theatre
USSBS	United States Strategic Bombing Survey
WFST	Wehrmachtführungstab
WO	War Office

Introduction

1 See, for instance, Willi Frischauer, *Himmler* (London 1953), 229–30; Aubrey Dixon and Otto Heilbrunn, *Communist Guerrilla Warfare* (London 1954), xiii; Eugene Davidson, *The Death and Life of Germany* (New York 1959), 49; Trevor-Roper, *The Last Days of Hitler*, 49, 51; Jurgen Thorwald, *Defeat in the East* (New York 1967), 211; Klaus Hildebrandt, *The Third Reich* (London 1984), 83; Dietrich Orlow, *The History of the Nazi Party* (Pittsburgh 1973), 481; Jay Baird, *The Mythical World of Nazi War Propaganda* (Minneapolis 1974), 307; Minott, *The Fortress That Never Was*, 93; Peter Black, *Ernst Kaltenbrunner* (Princeton 1984), 234; Walter Laqueur, *Young Germany: A History of the German Youth Movement* (London 1962), 214–15; Marguerite Higgins, 'What Price Cooperation?' in *This Is Germany* (Freeport 1971), 298–9; Douglas Botting, *In the Ruins of the Reich* (London 1985), 17; and Ivor Montagu, *Germany's New Nazis* (London 1967), 117.

2 The term 'Zero Hour' is used throughout this text as a convenient reference for the months around the collapse of the Third Reich. The term does not necessarily imply that the period comprises a dramatic caesura in German history.

3 Eugen Weber, *Peasants into Frenchmen* (Stanford 1976), 101–12, 519.

4 Curt Jany, *Geschichte der Preussischen Armee* (Osnabrück 1967), vol 4, 73, 86–7; Paul von Schmidt, *Der Werdegang des Preussischen Heeres* (Krefeld 1975), 212–13,

218, 300, 314, 317–18; Rose, *Werwolf*, 42–7, 49–66; Friedrich Meinecke, 'Landwehr und Landsturm seit 1814,' in *Friedrich Meinecke Werke* (Stuttgart 1979), vol. 9, 538, 544, 547–50; Obstl. von Voss, 'Denkschrift über den Feldjägerdienst,' 1 Apr. 1928; Obstl. von Voss to the Leiter der Heeres-Abteilung, 1 May 1928; 'Ausländersarbeit,' 31 Mar. 1928, all in RH 2/418, BMA; *Jugend Contra Nationalsozialismus*, 193–4; Peter Merkl, *Political Violence under the Swastika* (Princeton 1975), 80, 127, 141, 202, 237–8, 244–5, 318–19, 373–4; Robert Waite, *Vanguard of Nazism* (Cambridge, MA, 1952), 50, 56, 190–1, 193, 228–9, 232, 248; Heydebreck, *Wir Wehr-Wölfe*, 123–49, 158–62; and Nigel Jones, *Hitler's Heralds* (London 1987), 221.

5 Lieutenant-General Heinrich Kirchheim, quoted in *The New York Times*, 26 Apr. 1945

6 Edwin Hoyt, *Guerilla: Colonel von Lettow-Vorbeck and Germany's East African Empire* (New York 1981), and Leonard Mosely, *Duel for Kilimanjaro* (New York 1963)

7 Watt, 'Wehrwolf or Werwolf?' 892–3.

8 Henri Schmidt, the former Gestapo chief of Dresden, was arrested in 1987 after he had addressed a group of young people with the salutation 'Heil Hitler Werewolves!' Schmidt wound up in an East German prison, where he met and influenced the leaders of a new generation of radical neo-Nazis. One of Schmidt's disciples, Ingo Haselbach, later printed excerpts from *Werwolf: Winke für Jagdeinheiten* for members of his group, the 'National Alternative': Ingo Haselbach, *Führer-Ex* (New York 1996), 60–1; and 'The "Einblick" Trial: Notes from the Nazi Underground,' http://burn.ucsd.edu/archive/ats1/1995/oct/0024.html, as of 25 Nov. 1996. One of Germany's most notorious neo-Nazis, Detlev Bender, is the main force behind an organization called 'Defence Sports Group *Wehrwolf* 21.' Between 1989 and 1995, Bender was arrested on numerous occasions for possession of illegal weapons, breach of the peace, display of prohibited symbols, and attacks against Turkish guest workers. Gottfried Küssel, intellectual godfather of the so-called Young German Barbarians, cites as a model the 'volunteer Hitler Youth formations' fielded in 1944–5: 'Unimut: Zeitung (an) der Uni Heidelberg' #103 – E-Version http://ftp.urz.uni-heidelberg....p/fsk/unimut/unimut.103_081195, as of 25 Nov. 1996; and *Der Spiegel* 50 / 45 (7 Dec. 1992), 28.

9 Kirill Buketov, 'Russian Fascism and Russian Fascists,' gopher://gopher.etext.org/oo/p...antifa/russia.fascism.overview, as of 25 Nov. 1996; 'Jewish Bulletin of Northern California Online – News,' http://www.jewish.com/bk960216/iworld.htm, as of 25 Nov. 1996; and 'Antifa Info-Bulletin, Supplement 22,' http://burn.uscd.edu/archive/ats-1/1996.apr/0000.html. as of 25 Nov. 1996

10 These categories are from H. Jon Rosenbaum and Peter Sederberg, 'Vigilantism: An Analysis of Establishment Violence,' in *Vigilante Politics*, ed., H. Jon Rosenbaum and Peter Sederberg (Pittsburgh 1976), 5–6.

1: Gothic Guerrillas

1 Friedrich Meineke, *The Age of German Liberation, 1795–1815* (Berkeley 1977), 114; and Walter Simon, *The Failure of the Prussian Reform Movement* (New York 1971), 180. For a discussion of 'conservative' guerrilla warfare, see Karl Metz, 'Der Kleine Krieg im grossen Krieg: Die Guerilla,' *Militärgeschichtliche Mitteilungen* 33 (1983), 12–14. For a more general discussion of the 1813 Liberation War and its revolutionary implications, see Emil Oberman, *Soldaten – Bürger – Militäristen* (Stuttgart 1958), 151–6.

2 Carl von Clausewitz, *On War* (Princeton 1976), 479–80, 482.

3 For German appreciations of Allied intentions, see Steinert, *Capitulation 1945*, 56, 87; and OWI Memo 'Special Report on Enemy Handling of the Morgenthau Plan for Germany,' 10 Oct. 1944, General Records of the Treasury, Office of the Secretary, General Correspondence 1933–45, RG 56, NA.

4 Ian Kershaw, *Popular Opinion and Political Dissent in the Third Reich* (Oxford 1983), 329.

5 ECAD 'General Intelligence Bulletin' no. 31, 11 Dec. 1944, WO 219/371A, PRO; and *Pogranichnye Voiska SSSR Mai, 1945–1950*, 699.

6 Peter Hüttenberger, 'Nationalsozialistische Polykratie,' *Geschichte und Gesellschaft* 2 (1976), 423–37, 442.

7 Trevor-Roper, *The Last Days of Hitler*, 54. For commentary on Hitler's management style, see Sebastian Haffner, *The Meaning of Hitler* (London 1979), 43–4; Hüttenberger, 'Nationalsozialistische Polykratie,' 431–2; Edward Peterson, *The Limits of Hitler's Power* (London 1979), 4, 15; Martin Broszat, *The Hitler State* (London 1981), 283–6; Michael Geyer, 'The Nazi State Reconsidered,' in *Life in the Third Reich*, ed. Richard Bessel (Oxford 1987), 61, 64–6; Karl Dietrich Bracher, 'Stages of Totalitarian "Integration" (Gleichschaltung): The Consolidation of National Socialist Rule in 1933 and 1934,' in *Republic to Reich*, ed. Hajo Holborn (New York 1972), 127–8; Joseph Nyomorkay, *Charisma and Factionalism in the Nazi Party* (Minneapolis 1967), 41–3; Hans Mommsen, 'National Socialism: Continuity and Change,' in *Fascism: A Reader's Guide*, ed. Walter Lagueur (Beverly Hills 1976), 195–7; Hans Mommsen, 'Hitlers Stellung im nationalsozialistichen Herrschaftssystem,' and Klaus Hildebrand, 'Monokratie oder Polykratie? Hitlers Herrschaft und das Dritte Reich,' both in *Der 'Führerstaat': Mythos und Realität*, eds. Gerhard Hirschfeld and Lothar Kettenacker (Stuttgart 1981), 67–8, 73–96; *Nazism: A History in Documents and Eyewitness Accounts, 1919–1945* (New York 1988), vol. 2, 205–8; and Martin Kitchen, *Nazi Germany at War* (London 1995), ch. 1.

8 ACA Intelligence Organization 'Joint Weekly Intelligence Summary' no. 16, 27 Oct. 1945, FO 1007/300, PRO. See also British Troops Austria 'Joint Weekly Intelligence Summary' no. 9, 31 Aug. 1945, FO 1007/300, PRO.

9 Rose, *Werwolf, 1944–1945*, 24–6, 29–31, 61, 65; Obstl. von Voss, 'Denkschrift über den Feldjägerdienst,' 1 Apr. 1928; Obstl. von Voss to the Leiter der Heeres-Abteilung, 1 May 1928, both in RH 2/418, BMA; and PWE 'German Propaganda and the German,' 2 Oct. 1944, FO 898/187, PRO. For public citations from Clausewitz's work on guerrilla warfare, see PWE 'German Propaganda and the German,' 23 Oct. 1944 and 30 Oct. 1944, both in FO 898/187, PRO. A German garrison officer in Briançon observed in March 1944 that it was not only the French who would produce *maquisards*: 'When Germany is invaded we also will have many partisans, many francs-tireurs': *Libération*, 10 Sep. 1944. This suggests that such possibilities were being discussed at this time, even in provincial outposts.

10 Moczarski, *Conversations with an Executioner*, 240; and Gołąbek and Tryc, 'Z Genezy Powstania i Działalności Werwolfu,' 126–7. For information reaching Sweden about SS guerrillas observing the Warsaw fighting, see Twenty-first Army Group 'CI News Sheet' no. 7, 5 Oct. 1944. Part I, WO 205/997, PRO.

11 The first mention of the organization was in a Himmler memorandum of 16 September 1944, in which he notes that 'the responsibility for the resistance movement in the German border provinces is disseminated in one of my verbal orders': Himmler to Kaltenbrunner, 16 Sep. 1944, Records of the Reich Leader of the SS and Chief of the German Police, Microcopy no. T-175, Roll 122, frame 2648215, NA. A French intelligence bulletin noted that a written order from Himmler creating an inspectorate to oversee guerrilla warfare 'on German soil behind enemy lines' was captured at Nuremberg, although no trace of it remains: Direction des Services de Documentation Allemagne 'Note sur la formation du Werwolf,' 6 Jul. 1945, IRR File XE 049 888 'Werewolf activities Vol. I,' RG 319, NA.

12 Hildebrandt to Himmler, 19 Sep. 1944, NS 19/2884, BA; and Steinert, *Capitulation 1945*, 125.

13 Watt, 'Wehrwolf or Werwolf,' 879, 882–3, 887–92, 895; J.M. Ritchie, *German Literature under National Socialism* (London 1983), 14–17; Waite, *Vanguard of Nazism*, 252, 279; Jones, *Hitler's Heralds*, 78, 220, 245; and *Jugend unter Nationalsozialismus*, 154–7, 189, 199–200. For the origin of the werewolf legend in ancient German mythology, see Jakob Grimm, *Teutonic Mythology* (New York 1966), vol. 3, 1093–7, and vol. 4, 1629–30. For the wearing of wolf cloaks by the ancient Teutons, see H.R. Ellis Davidson, *Gods and Myths of Northern Europe* (Harmondsworth 1964), 67–8.

14 The first mention of the 'Werwolf' title was in a speech by Himmler on 18 October and an SS-Police organizational chart of 20 October 1944, which referred to the 'Werwolf Organization for Germany': *Völkischer Beobachter*, 19 Oct. 1944; and 'Liste der Höchsten- und Höheren SS und Polizeiführer sowie de SS- und Polizeiführer,' 20 Oct. 1944, NS 19/1637, BA. See also Watt, 'Wehrwolf or Werwolf,' 888.

15 Skorzeny, *La Guerre inconnue*, 196; M. Bormann, Partei-Kanzlei 'Rundschreiben'

410/44, 23 Nov. 1944, NS 6/349, BA; Watt, 'Wehrwolf or Werwolf,' 882; Hasenclever, *Ihr Werdet Deutschland nicht wiederkennen*, 86; U.S. Twelfth Army 'Werewolves.' 31 May 1945, IRR File XE 049 888 'Werewolf Activities Vol. I,' RG 319, NA; CSDIC WEA BAOR 'Second Interim Report on SS Obergruf. Karl Gutenberger,' IR 34, 1 Nov. 1945, OSS 123190, RG 226, NA; and Rose, *Werwolf*, 35, 128.

16 Twenty-first Army Group 'CI News Sheet' no. 24, 27 Jun. 1945, Part I, WO 205/ 997, PRO; and BAOR Int. 'Appreciation of the Werwolf Movement,' IRR File XE 049 888 'Werewolf Activities Vol. I,' RG 319, NA. Schellenberg, the powerful head of the RSHA's foreign bureau and a personal confidant of Himmler's, loudly complained to the Reichsführer about the 'weakness' and 'inefficiency' of the Werwolf, claiming that it should be terminated: Trevor-Roper, *The Last Days of Hitler*, 52; Whiting, *Hitler's Werewolves*, 67; and Walter Schellenberg, *The Schellenberg Memoirs* (London 1960), 440.

17 Whiting, *Hitler's Werewolves*, 147; Trevor-Roper, *The Last Days of Hitler*, 51–2; Gołąbek and Tryc,'Z Genezy Powstania i Działalności Werwolfu,' 129–30; BAOR Int. 'Appreciation of the Werwolf Movement,' 29 Aug. 1945, IRR File XE 049 888 'Werewolf Activities Vol. I,' RG 319, NA; and British Troops Austria 'Joint Weekly Intelligence Summary' no. 9, 31 Aug. 1945, FO 1007/300, PRO. The Werwolf manual defined 'guerrilla warfare' in purely Clausewitzian terms: a partisan war, it said, 'is an effective means to aid one's own military and political struggle ... In desperate situations it is the last means to defend to the utmost freedom and life of the people. Conducted in conjunction with general military operations, clear political objectives and qualified means, partisan warfare can lead to success of decisive importance': *Werwolf: Winke für Jagdeinheiten*, 1.

18 Whiting, *Hitler's Werewolves*, 66, 180; Jean de Lattre, *Reconquérir*, 329; Direction Générale des Études et Recherches 'Bulletin d'Information de CE' no. 66; BAOR Int. 'Appreciation of the Werwolf Movement,' 29 Aug. 1945; EDS Report no. 34 'Notes on the "Werewolves"'; Direction des Services de Documentation Allemagne 'Note sur la formation du Werwolf,' 6 Jul. 1945, all in IRR File XE 049 888 'Werewolf Activities Vol. I,' RG 319, NA; Oberst Kemmerich 'Kleinkrieg in eigenen Land,' RH 11 III/34, BMA; M. Bormann 'Rundschreiben' 128/45: 'Durchführing von Sonderaufgaben im Rücken des Feindes,' 10 Mar. 1945, NS 6/354, BA; Rose, *Werwolf*, 131–5; Moczarski, *Conversations with an Executioner*, 239; and *Werwolf: Winke für Jagdeinheiten*, 1, 4–5, 29–32, 35–42, 47–8.

19 *Völkischer Beobachter*, 8 Apr. 1945.

20 Whiting, *Hitler's Werewolves*, 180; de Lattre, *Reconquérir*, 326–8; Oberst Kemmerich 'Kleinkrieg in eigenen Land,' RH 11 III/34, BMA; and *Werwolf: Winke für Jagdeinheiten*, 2, 4.

21 Letter to the author from K. Schikorski, 23 Feb. 1945; USFET MIS Center 'CI Inter-

mediate Interrogation Report (CI-IIR) no. 24 – O/Gruf. Jürgen Stroop,' 10 Oct. 1945, OSS XL 22157, NA; SHAEF CI War Room 'The SS Guerrilla Movement,' 9 Apr. 1945, ETO MIS-Y-Sect. Miscellaneous Interrogation Reports 1944–6, RG 332, NA; BAOR Int. 'Appreciation of the Werwolf Movement'; EDS Report no. 34 'Notes on the "Werewolves"'; U.S. Twelfth Army 'Werewolves,' 31 May 1945; MFI 5/752 Note on Werwolf equipment, 27 Apr. 1945; USFET MIS Center 'CI Intermediate Interrogation Report (CI-IIR) #18 – Krim. Rat. Stubaf. Ernst Wagner,' 30 Aug. 1945; and Twenty-first Army Group Int. 'Appendix "C" to 2 Can. Corps Sitrep,' 22 Jun. 1945, all IRR File XE 049 888 'Werewolf Activities Vol. I,' RG 319, NA; Moczarski, *Conversations with an Executioner*, 241–2; Rose, *Werwolf*, 136, 153; Hugonnet, 'La Preparation du "maquis" allemand,' 58; and *Werwolf: Winke für Jagdeinheiten*, 8–10.

22 Rose, *Werwolf*, 152; and *Werwolf: Winke für Jagdeinheiten*, 10. Several Werewolves captured in the Rhineland were clothed in Waffen-SS uniforms: *History of the Counter Intelligence Corps*, vol. 19, 59, NA.

23 Twelfth Army Group, Office of ACoS G-2 to ACoS G-2, U.S. Third Army, ACoS G-2 U.S. Ninth Army, and ACoS G-2 U.S. Fifteenth Army, 13 May 1945, WO 219/1602, PRO.

24 Enemy Personnel Exploitation Sect., Field Information Agency Technical CCG (BE) 'Two Brief Discussions of German CW Policy with Albert Speer,' 12 Oct. 1945, FO 1031/141, PRO.

25 SHAEF CI War Room 'The SS Guerrilla Movement,' 9 Apr. 1945, ETO MIS-Y-Sect. Miscellaneous Interrogation Reports 1944–6, RG 332, NA; CSDIC WEA BAOR 'Second Interim Report on SS Obergruf. Karl M. Gutenberger' IR 34, ETO MIS-Y-Sect. CSDIC/WEA Interim Interrogation Reports 1945–6, RG 332, NA; USFET MIS Center 'CI Intermediate Interrogation Report (CI-IIR) no. 24 – O/Gruf. Jürgen Stroop,' 10 Oct. 1945, OSS XL 22157, RG 226, NA; Twelfth Army Group 'Unternehmen W,' 12 Jun. 1945; U.S. Ninth Army, Report 1658 'Fritz Georg Schlessmann,' 30 May 1945; Twenty-first Army Group BLA, Extract from 'Current Notes on Enemy Espionage,' 26 May 1945, Part III; Twelfth Army Group 'Werewolves,' 31 May 1945; BAOR Int. 'Appreciation of the Werwolf Movement,' 29 Aug. 1945; Direction des Services de Documentation Allemagne 'Note sur la formation du Werwolf,' 6 Jul. 1945, all in IRR File XE 049 888 'Werewolf Activities Vol. I,' RG 319, NA; and *Werwolf: Winke für Jagdeinheiten*, 49–50.

26 Rose, *Werwolf*, 26, 29; Moczarski, *Conversations with an Executioner*, 23; CSDIC WEA BAOR 'Final Report on SA Brgf. u. HDL Fritz Marrenbach,' FR 29, 21 Jan. 1946, Appendix 'A,' ETO MIS-Y-Sect. Final Interrogation Reports 1945–9, RG 332, NA; and U.S. Ninth Army Report 1658, 'Schlessmann, Fritz Georg,' 30 May 1945, IRR File XE 049 888 'Werewolf Activities Vol. I,' RG 319, NA.

27 Birn, *Die Höheren SS- und Polizeiführer*, 342; William Coombs, *The Voice of the SS*

(New York 1986), 370; Wenck, OKH to the Heeresgruppen and Armeen, 6 Feb. 1945, RH 2/1930, BMA; CSDIC WEA BAOR 'Second Interim Report on SS Obergruf. Karl Gutenberger' IR 34, 1 Nov. 1945, ETO MIS-Y-Sect. CSDIC/WEA Interim Interrogation Reports 1945–6, RG 332, NA; CSDIC WEA BAOR 'Final Report on SA Brgf. u. HDL Marrenbach' FR 29, 21 Jan. 1946, 'Appendix A,' ETO MIS-Y-Sect. Final Interrogation Reports, 1945–9, RG 332, NA; USFET MIS Center 'CI Intermediate Interrogation Report (CI-IIR)' no. 24, 10 Oct. 1944, OSS XL 22157, RG 226, NA; BIMO 'Résumé traduction d'un document de l'I.S. Anglais en Suisse,' 29 Oct. 1945, 7P 125, SHAT; British Troops Austria 'Joint Weekly Intelligence Summary' no. 31 Aug. 1945, FO 1007/300, PRO; USFET MIS Center 'Intermediate Interrogation Report (IIR)' no. 18, 30 Aug. 1945; CI Bureau Twenty-first Army Group BLA, 'The Werwolf Movement' 29 Aug. 1945; EDS Report no. 34 'Notes on the "Werewolves"'; 2677th Regt., OSS (Prov.) Det. A, 'The Werwolf Organization, Salzburg Area,' 16 Jul. 1945; 'Weekly Intelligence Summary' no. 42, 29 May 1945, all in IRR File XE 049 888 'Werewolf Activities Vol. I,' RG 319, NA; Trevor-Roper, *The Last Days of Hitler*, 52; SHAEF CI War Room 'Supplement to "The SS Guerrilla Movement,"' 23 Apr. 1945, ETO MIS-Y-Sect. Misc. Interrogation Reports, 1944–6, RG 332, NA; SSU Report no. LP/2-13, 31 Aug. 1945, OSS XL 27108, RG 226, NA; Peter Padfield, *Himmler: Reichsführer SS* (London 1991), 462; Rose, *Werwolf*, 26–7; and Moczarski, *Conversations with an Executioner*, 102, 238–9.

28 'Liste der Höchsten- und Höheren SS und Polizeiführer sowie der SS- und Polizeiführer,' 20 Oct. 1944, NS 19/1637, BA.

29 Birn, *Die Höheren SS- und Polizeiführer*, 62.

30 CSDIC (UK) 'SS Hauptamt and the Waffen SS,' 23 Aug. 1945, OSS 144337, RG 226, NA; USFET Interrogation Center 'Final Interrogation Report (FIR) #6 – O/Gruf. Karl Frank,' 7 Jul. 1945, OSS 138456, RG 226, NA; USFET MIS Center 'Intermediate Interrogation Report (IIR) #18 – Krim. Rat. Stubaf. Ernst Wagner,' 30 Aug. 1945; BAOR/Int. 'Appreciation of the Werwolf Movement'; EDS Report no. 34 'Notes on the "Werewolves"'; 'Weekly Intelligence Summary' no. 42, 29 May 1945; SHAEF EDS CI/G-2 'Extract from Report of Interrogation of POW, US Ninth Army,' 28 Apr. 1945, all in IRR File XE 049 888 'Werewolf Activities Vol. I,' RG 319, NA; CSDIC WEA BAOR 'Final Report on Dr. Gerhardt Willi Teich,' FR 31, 21 Jan. 1946, 'Appendix B – Unternehmen Zeppelin,' ETO MIS-Y-Sect. CSDIC/WEA Final Interrogation Reports 1945–7, RG 332, NA; BIMO 'Résumé traduction d'un document de l'I.S. Anglais en Suisse,' 29 Oct. 1945, 7P 125, SHAT; British Troops Austria 'Joint Weekly Intelligence Summary' no. 9, 31 Aug. 1945, FO 1007/300, PRO; USFET Interrogation Center 'Final Interrogation Report' (FIR) no. 11, Annex IV, 31 Jul. 1945, OSS 13775, RG 226, NA; ETO MIS-Y-Sect. CSDIC/WEA Interim Int. Reports, 1945–6, RG 332, NA; USFET Interrogation Center 'Intermediate Interrogation Report (IIR) #9 – H/Stuf. Hans Gerlach,' 11 Aug. 1945, OSS XL 13744,

RG 226, NA; David Kahn, *Hitler's Spies* (New York 1978), 262, 266; Rose, *Werwolf,* 32, 35–6, 128, 153–4; and Ultra Document BT 9509, 5 Apr. 1945, Ultra Documents Collection, Reel 69.

31 BAOR/Int. 'Appreciation of the Werwolf Movement'; EDS Report no. 34 'Notes on the "Werewolves"'; U.S. Twelfth Army 'Werewolves'; Direction des Services de Documentation Allemagne 'Note sur la formation du Werwolf,' 6 Jul. 1945, all in IRR File XE 049 888 'Werewolf Activities Vol. I,' RG 319, NA; and SHAEF CI War Room 'The SS Guerrilla Movement,' 9 Apr. 1945, ETO MIS-Y-Sect. Misc. Interrogation Reports, 1944–6, RG 332, NA.

32 USFET Interrogation Center 'Intermediate Interrogation Report (IIR) #5 – O/Gruf. Freiherr Friedrich K. von Eberstein,' 27 Jul. 1945, IRR File XE 049 888 'Werewolf Activities Vol. I,' RG 319, NA. One party official later noted that it was unlikely that local party *Gauleiter* uniformly appointed a 'Werwolf Commissioner,' although they were ordered to do so in November 1944 and the order was repeated by Bormann in March 1945: CSDIC WEA BAOR 'Final Report on SA Brigf. u. HDL Fritz Marrenbach,' FR 29, 21 Jan. 1946, Appendix 'A,' ETO MIS-Y-Sect. Final Interrogation Reports, 1945–9, RG 332, NA.

33 Helmuth Krausnik et al., *Anatomy of the SS State* (London 1968), 213–41; and Birn, *Die Höheren SS- und Polizeiführer,* 9–14, 41–2, 58–60, 79–80, 83–93, 96–105, 323–9. For Himmler's tendency to adopt Hitler's administrative tactics of organized disorder, see Felix Kersten, *The Kirsten Memoirs, 1940–1945* (London 1956), 216–17. For the appointment of representatives for 'special tasks' as a general characteristic of the Hitlerian system of administration, see Mommsen, 'Hitlers Stellung im nationalsozialistischen Herrschaftssystem,' 53.

34 Oberst Bonin, OKH, Memo 'Kampf in Rücken des Feindes' 12 Nov. 1944, RH 2/1929, BMA.

35 Krausnik et al., *Anatomy of the SS State,* 232, 237–8; Birn, *Die Höheren SS- und Polizeiführer,* 106–31, 308–16; Peter Hüttenberger, *Die Gauleiter* (Stuttgart 1969), 178; and Kitchen, *Nazi Germany at War,* 22.

36 U.S. Twelfth Army 'Werewolves,' 31 May 1945, p. 1, IRR File XE 049 888 'Werewolf Activities Vol. I,' RG 319, NA; and *Pogranichnye Voiska SSSR v Velikoi Otechestvennoi Voine, 1942–1945,* 550.

37 SS O/Gruf. von Herff, Chef des SS Personalhauptamtes to RFSS Persönlicher Stab, 11 Sep. 1944, NS 34/12, BA; and Liste der Höchsten- und Höheren SS- und Polizeiführer sowie der SS- und Polizeiführer, 20 Oct. 1944, NS 19/1637, BA.

38 U.S. Twelfth Army 'Werewolves,' 31 May 1945, p. 1, IRR File XE 049 888 'Werewolf Activities Vol. 1,' RG 319, NA.

39 Gołąbek and Tryc, 'Z Genezy Powstania i Działności Werwolfu,' 134, 135; Rose, *Werwolf,* 169; *History of the Counter Intelligence Corps,* vol. 20, 4, NA; MI-14 'Mitropa' no. 5, 22 Sep. 1945, FO 371/46967, PRO; Ewan Butler and Gordon

Young, *Marshal without Glory* (London 1951), 247; and U.S. Twelfth Army 'Werewolves,' 31 May 1945, IRR File XE 049 888 'Werewolf Activities Vol. I,' RG 319, NA.

40 Korovin and Shibalin, 'Gitlerovskii Abwehr Terpit Parazhenie,' 104; and *The Times*, 12 Mar. 1945.

41 Siomash to Izugenev, 1 Apr. 1945, *Pogranichnye Voiska SSSR v Velikoi Otechestvennoi, 1942–1945*, 509; and Lucas, *Kommando*, 318–19.

42 Chuikov, *The End of the Third Reich*; Kuby, *The Russians and Berlin, 1945*, 47; and Blond, *The Death of Hitler's Germany*, 252.

43 Vselodod Vishnevesky, 'Street Fighting in Berlin,' and Boris Gorbatov, 'Around Berlin,' both in *World War II: Dispatches from the Soviet Front*, 331, 337; Konev, *Year of Victory*, 170, 176; and Andreas-Friedrich, *Berlin Underground*, 302–12.

44 *The St Louis Post–Dispatch*, 9 May 1945.

45 Rose, *Werwolf*, 115, 324; Whiting, *Hitler's Werewolves*, 189; and Lucas, *Kommando*, 331.

46 Harry C. Butcher, 'Notes on Berlin Surrender,' in *David Irving, Papers Relating to the Allied High Command, 1943/45*, Reel no. 3; *Trud*, 11 May 1945; PID 'Germany: Weekly Background Notes' no. 4, 4 Jul. 1945, FO 371/46933, PRO; *The Manchester Guardian*, 31 Jul. and 1 Aug. 1945; *The Washington Post*, 31 Jul. 1945; *The Times*, 31 Jul. 1945; *The Age* (Melbourne), 1 Aug. 1945; Rysanov to Gavrikov, 30 May 1945; Mashin to Alexeev, 14 May, 9 Jun., 1 Jul. 1945, all in *Pogranichnye Voiska SSSR Mai, 1945–1950*, 66, 77, 80, 82; HQ Berlin Area 'Intelligence Summary' no. 1, 8 Jul. 1945, WO 205/1078, PRO; no. 5, 30 Jul. 1945, FO 1005/1706, PRO; MI-14 'Mitropa' no. 2, 11 Aug. 1945, FO 371/46967, PRO; John Erickson, *The Road to Berlin* (London 1983), 779; and Albert Seaton, *Stalin as Warlord* (London 1976), 254.

47 Rose, *Werwolf*, 324; and H. Buettler, 'Niederschrift über Flucht aus Ostpreussen,' 25 Oct. 1950, Ost Dok. 2/13, BA.

48 CSDIC WEA BAOR 'Second Interim Report on SS Obergruf. Karl Gutenberger,' IR 34, 1 Nov. 1945, ETO MIS-Y-Sect. CSDIC/WEA Interim Interrogation Reports, 1945–6, RG 332, NA; USFET MIS Center 'CI Intermediate Interrogation Report (CI-IIR) #24 – O/Gruf. Jürgen Stroop,' 10 Oct. 1945, OSS XL 22157, RG 226, NA; Direction Générale des Études et Recherches 'Bulletin de Renseignements – Allemagne: Organisation du Werwolf,' 20 Aug. 1945; 1ère Armée Française, 2ème Bureau 'Bulletin de Renseignements,' 16 May 1945, Annex no. II, both in 7P 125, SHAT; U.S. Twelfth Army, 'Report on Unternehmen Werwolf,' 12 Jun. 1945, IRR File XE 049 888 'Werwolf Activities Vol. I,' RG 319, NA; Whiting, *Hitler's Werewolves*, 70; USFET Interrogation Center 'Intermediate Interrogation Report (IRR) #9 – H/Stuf. Hans Gerlach,' 11 Aug. 1945, OSS XL 13744, RG 226, NA; Rose, *Werwolf*, 28–9; and *Justiz und NS-Verbrechen*, vol. 3, 300, 302.

49 Extract from Twelfth Army Group 'Interrogation of Hans Karl Gustav Kaleske,' 12
Jun. 1945, IRR File XE 049 888 'Werewolf Activities Vol. I,' RG 319, NA; USFET
Interrogation Center 'Intermediate Interrogation Report (IRR) no. 9 – H/Stuf. Hans
Gerlach,' 11 Aug. 1945, OSS XL 13744, RG 226, NA; and Hugonnot, 'La Prépara-
tion du "Maquis" allemand,' 58.

50 Rose, *Werwolf*, 135–6. As early as 2 February 1945, a German unit in the Rur inadvertently discovered a Werwolf gallery manned by three heavily armed guerrillas.
Mobile Field Interrogation Unit no. 1 'PW Intelligence Bulletin' no. 1/51, 24 Mar.
1945, OSS 125027, RG 226, NA. For examples of Werwolves air-dropped along
Allied lines of communication, see *History of the XVI Corps* (Washington 1947), 38;
and 'Report from Captured Personnel and Material Branch, Military Intelligence
Division, U.S. War Department,' 13 May 1945, State Dept. Decimal Files 1945–9,
740.00119 Control (Germany), RG 59, NA.

51 Arnold Brecht, *Federalism and Regionalism in Germany* (London 1945), 32, 39, 41.

52 Gerhard Brunn, 'Köln in den Jahren 1945 und 1946: Die Rahmenbedingungen des
gesellschaftlichen Lebens,' *Köln nach dem Nationalisozialismus*, ed. Otto Dann
(Wuppertal 1981), 37; and *Die Nationalsozialistische Zeit (1933–1945) in Neuss*
(Neuss 1988), 323, 333.

53 Merkl, *Political Violence under the Swastika*, 189–206.

54 For Allied appreciations of the Rhenish capacities for guerrilla warfare, see OSS
'European Political Report' RAL-3-33, 20 Oct. 1944, WO 219/3761A, PRO; and 'CI
News Sheet' no. 9, 5 Nov. 1944, Part III, WO 205/997, PRO.

55 BAOR Int. 'Appreciation of the Werwolf Movement,' IRR File XE 049 888 'Werewolf Activities Vol. I,' RG 319, NA; CCG (BE) 'Intelligence Review' no. 12, Sep.
1946, FO 1005/1700, PRO; *History of the Counter Intelligence Corps*, vol. 19, 57,
78; vol. 20, 18, 26, 45, 59–60, 72, 125–6, 144–7, 152, NA; P. de Tristan, First French
Army, 5th Bureau 'Monthly Historical Report,' 1 May 1945, WO 219/2587, PRO;
History of the Fifteenth United States Army: 21 August 1944 to 11 July 1945 (Bad
Neuenahr 1945), 27; SHAEF PWD – 'Reactions to "Werwolf" in Cologne,' 26 Apr.
1945, OSS 128265, RG 226, NA; Charles Leach, *In Tornado's Wake: A History of
the 8th Armoured Division* (Chicago 1956), 136; ECAD 'General Intelligence Bulletin' no. 34, 13 Jan. 1945, WO 219/3760A, PRO; and Henke, *Die amerikanische
Besetzung Deutschlands*, 337.

56 Jonathan Osmond, *Rural Protest in the Weimar Republic* (New York 1993), 142–52,
and Celia Applegate, *A Nation of Provincials* (Berkeley 1990), 182–9.

57 For Allied intelligence on the state of public opinion in the Saarland and the Palati-
nate, see P.R. Sweet, Adv. Det. P & PW Detachment, Twelfth Army Group to P &
PW Officer, Twelfth Army Group, 22 Sep. 1944, OSS 118484, RG 226, NA; A.
Stein to P & PW Officer, Twelfth Army Group, 23 Sep. 1944, OSS 116632, RG 226,
NA; P.C. Surrt to PW Officer, Twelfth Army Group, 27 Sep. 1944, OSS 116633, RG

226, NA; G. Hallgarten, Adv. Sect. PWB, P & PW, Twelfth Army Group to PWO, P & PW, Twelfth Army Group, OSS 116842, RG 226, NA; P.R. Surrt to P & PW Officer, Twelfth Army Group, 27 Sep. 1944, OSS 116845, RG 226, NA; and OSS 116846, RG 226, NA. See also *Le Monde*, 13 Sep. 1945. For the postwar discovery of Werwolf weapons caches in the Saar, see Fifteenth Army ACoS G-2 'Periodic Report' no. 58, 20 Jun. 1945, OSS XL 11747, RG 226, NA.

58 *The Stars and Stripes*, 15 Jan. 1945; and *History of the Counter Intelligence Corps*, vol. 20, 70, NA.

59 *The New York Times*, 3 Apr. 1945; *The Manchester Guardian*, 21 Mar. 1945; *Völkischer Beobachter*, 5 Apr. 1945; Sheen, SHAEF G-2 to British Pol. Off., U.S. Pol. Off., and Sec. JIC, 11 Apr. 1945, WO 219/1603, PRO; and SHAEF JIC 'Political Intelligence Report,' 14 Apr. 1945, WO 219/1700, PRO. For Werwolf cells in Bad Kreuznach and the surrounding area, see *History of the Counter Intelligence Corps*, vol. 20, 125–6, NA.

60 Infield, *Skorzeny*, 110. For the absence of Werwolf prepatory measures in the Ruhr conurbation and other areas lying immediately east of the Rhine, see USFET MIS Center 'CI Intermediate Interrogation Report (CI-IIR) #24-O/Gruf. Jürgen Stroop,' 10 Oct. 1945, OSS XL 22157, RG 226, NA; and CSDIC WEA BAOR, 'Second Interim Report on SS Obergruf. Karl M. Gutenberger,' IR 34, 1 Nov. 1945, ETO MIS-Y-Sect. CSDIC/WEA Interim Interrogation Reports 1945–6, RG 332, NA.

61 *Trial of the Major War Criminals before the International Military Tribunal*, vol. 14, 448, 580; Jochen von Lang, *Der Hitler-Junge – Baldur von Schirach* (Hamburg 1988), 380–1; Karl Wahl, *'... es ist das deutsche Herz'* (Augsburg 1954), 405; Office of the U.S. Chief Counsel, Subs. Proceedings Div. Interrogations Branch 'Summary #166 – Baldur von Schirach,' IWM; Arthur Zechel, *Die Geschichte der Stadt Peine* (Hanover 1982); and Generalmajor der Polizei Wilhelm von Grolmann, Polizeipräsident von Leipzig 'The Collapse of the German Reich as Seen from Leipzig,' *World War II German Military Studies*, 24.

62 GSI Eighth Army 'Joint Weekly Intelligence Summary' no. 5, 3 Aug. 1945, FO 371/46611, PRO; and GSI British Troops Austria 'Joint Weekly Intelligence Summary' no. 7, Part I, FO 371/46612, PRO.

63 CDSIC WEA BAOR 'Second Interim Report on SS Obergruf Karl Gutenberger' IR 34, OSS 123190, RG 226, NA. Once the Ruhr was surrounded at the end of March 1945, some hasty measures in support of the Werwolf were undertaken. Underground bunkers were dug, and explosives were handed out to fanatics who were left more or less to their own initiative. U.S. Fifteenth Army Triumph Interrogation Center 'Connections with the Werwolf, Party Officials Hideout,' 19 Jun, 1945; U.S Fifteenth Army Interrogation Report 'Friedrich Hollweg' 4 Jun. 1945, both in IRR File XE 049 888 'Werwolf Activities Vol. I,' RG 319, NA; and German Directorate 'Weekly Intelligence Summary' no. 36, 11 Jul. 1945, OSS 140955, RG 226, NA.

64 Jeremy Noakes, *The Nazi Party in Lower Saxony, 1921–1933* (Oxford 1971), chs.
6–13; Hans Fenske, *Wahlrecht und Parteiensystem* (Frankfurt am Main 1972),
268–81; Merkl, *Political Violence Under the Swastica*, 84–7; John O'Loughlin,
Colin Flint, and Luc Anselin, 'The Geography of the Nazi Vote: Context, Confes-
sion, and Class in the Reichstag Election of 1930,' *Annals of the Association of
American Geographers* 84/3 (1994), 360–2; and Klaus Schaap, *Die Endphase der
Weimarer Republik im Freistaat Oldenburg, 1928–1933* (Düsseldorf 1978), 27–39,
46–7, 94–126, 137–9, 141–51, 183–265, 269–71, 273–8.

65 Theodore Draper, *The 18th Infantry Division* (New York 1946), 229; *The Daily Her-
ald*, 7 Apr. 1945; *The New York Times*, 1 Apr. and 25 Jul. 1945; ECAD 'General
Intelligence Bulletin' no. 46, 1 Jun. 1945, WO 219/3760A, PRO; SHAEF JIC (45)
16 (Final) 'Political Intelligence Report,' 14 Apr. 1945, WO 219/1700, PRO; *Conquer: The Story of the Ninth Army* (Washington 1947), 340–1; SHAEF G-5 'Military
Government–Civil Affairs Weekly Field Report' no. 48, 12 May 1945, State Dept.
Decimal File 1945–9, 740.00119 Control (Germany), RG 59, NA; and P. de Tristan,
First French Army, 5th Bureau 'Monthly Historical Report,' 1 May 1945, WO 219/
2587, PRO.

66 Allan Mick, ed., *With the 102d Infantry Division through Germany,* (Washington
1947), 211. For the 'bomb happy' population of Bremen, most of whom were
'beyond resisting,' see George Blake, *Mountain and Flood: The History of the 52nd
(Lowland) Division, 1939–1946* (Glasgow 1950), 203.

67 Kershaw, *Popular Opinion and Political Dissent in the Third Reich*, 154–5, 375.

68 *The Daily Express*, 5 Apr. 1945; James Huston, *Biography of a Battalion* (Gering
1950), 258; *The Daily Herald*, 1 May 1945; and *The Manchester Guardian*, 1 May
1945.

69 *The Daily Express*, 5 Apr. 1945; *The Christian Science Monitor*, 6 Apr. 1945; and
The Daily Herald, 7 Apr. 1945.

70 ECAD 'General Intelligence Bulletin' no. 44, 5 May 1945, WO 219/3760A, PRO;
and Percy Knauth, 'The German People,' *Life* 18/19 (7 May 1945), 69–70. D.L.
Charters, a British POW liberated near Frankfurt, noted that 'the Americans are having a lot of trouble with German children ten years of age and upwards. For months
they have been taught in school how to plant mines on the roads. They allow the
American spearheads to pass through and then, under cover of darkness, the children
go out and lay the mines': *The Manchester Guardian*, 14 Apr. 1945.

71 Joseph Binkoski and Arthur Plaut, *The 115th Infantry Regiment in World War 2*
(Washington 1984), 340–1; and SHAEF G-5 'Military Government-Civil Affairs
Weekly Field Report' no. 50, 26 May 1945, State Dept. Decimal File 1945–9,
740.00119 Control (Germany), RG 59, NA.

72 *The Manchester Guardian*, 27 Apr. 1945.

73 Confidential information; Lord Russell, *Return of the Swastika?* (London 1968),

183; Earl Ziemke, *The U.S. Army in the Occupation of Germany, 1944–1946* (Washington 1975), 245–6; and Laurence Byrnes, ed., *History of the 94th Infantry Division in World War Two* (Washington 1948), 469, 471. For the story of a Werwolf unit which had plans to blow up a number of bridges in the Lahn Valley, see *History of the Counter Intelligence Corps*, vol 20, 32, NA.

74 Kershaw, *Popular Opinion and Political Dissent in the Third Reich*, 17–18, 23, 25–7; Fenske, *Wahlrecht und Parteiensystem*, 269–70; Geoffrey Pridham, *Hitler's Rise to Power* (London 1973), 321; and SHAEF G-5 'Military Government-Civil Affairs Weekly Field Report' no. 46, 28 Apr. 1945, State Dept. Decimal File 1945–9, 740.00119 Control (Germany), RG 59, NA.

75 USFET Interrogation Center 'Preliminary Interrogation Report (PIR) #40 – Benno Martin,' 3 Aug. 1945, OSS 141752, RG 226, NA; Twenty-first Army Group 'Weekly CI News Sheet' no. 81, IRR File XE 049 888 'Werwolf Activities Vol. I,' RG 319, NA; U.S. Third Army Interrogation Center (Prov.) 'Interrogation Report' no. 39, 8 Sep. 1945, OSS XL 19643, RG 226, NA; Henke, *Die amerikanische Besetzung Deutschlands*, 949; and *History of the Counter Intelligence Corps*, vol. 20, 97, NA.

76 *Völkischer Beobachter* (Munich), 26 Apr. 1945; Charles MacDonald, *The Last Offensive* (Washington 1973), 410; John Turner and Robert Jackson, *Destination Berchtesgaden: The Story of the United States Seventh Army in World War Two* (London 1975), 157; *The Fighting Forty-Fifth: The Combat Report of an Infantry Division* (Baton Rouge 1946), 160-5; *The Seventh US Army in France and Germany, 1944–1945* (Heidelberg 1946), vol. 3, 766–7; *The New York Times*, 3 Apr. 1945; *Time* 45/16, (9 Apr. 1945), 18; *The St Louis Post–Dispatch*, 3 Apr. 1945; *The Washington Post*, 3 Apr. and 4 Apr. 1945.

77 W. Dettelbacher, *Würzburg: ein Gang durch seine Vergangenheit* (Würzburg 1974), 180; MacDonald, *The Last Offensive*, 420; *The Seventh United States Army in France and Germany*, vol. 3, 770; Turner and Jackson, *Destination Berchtesgaden*, 157–8; Hugh Daley, *42nd 'Rainbow' Infantry Division: A Combat History of World War II* (Baton Rouge 1946); and Haupt, *Das Ende im Westen*, 160–1.

78 Haupt, *Das Ende im Westen*, 170–1; Holzträger, *Der Wehrertüchtigungslager*, 101; U.S. Third Army Interrogation Center (Prov.) 'Interrogation Report' no. 39, 8 Sep. 1945, OSS XL 19643, RG 226, NA; Ultra Document KO 729, 18 Apr. 1945, Ultra Document Collection, Reel 71; and Allied Intelligence Report, *c.* May 1945, IRR File XE 049 888 'Werewolf Activities Vol. I,' RG 39, NA.

79 Turner and Jackson, *Destination Berchtesgaden*, 163; *The Fighting Forty-Fifth*, 181; *The Seventh United States Army in France and Germany*, vol. 3, 795; *History of the Third Infantry Division*, 356; *The New York Times*, 20 Apr. and 21 Apr. 1945; *The St Louis Post–Dispatch*, 27 Apr. 1945; and Haupt, *Das Ende im Westen*, 172–3.

80 Infield, *Skorzeny*, 110.

81 MI-6 'CX-Report,' 16 Jun. 1945; CSDIC/CMF 'The Werwolf Organisation,' 10 Jun.

1945; 2677th Regt., OSS (Prov.) Det. 'A' 'The Werwolf Organization(s), Salzburg
Area,' 16 Jul. 1945, all in IRR File XE 049 888 'Werewolf Activities Vol. I,' RG
319, NA; GSI British Troops Austria 'Joint Weekly Intelligence Summary' no. 7,
Part I, FO 371/46612, PRO; and CSDIC WEA BAOR 'Final Report on Dr. Gerhardt
Willi Teich,' FR 31, 21 Jan. 1946, 'Appendix B – Unternehmen Zeppelin,' ETO
MIS-Y-Sect. CSDIC/WEA, Final Interrogation Reports 1945–7, RG 332, NA.

82 USFET Interrogation Center 'Intermediate Interrogation Report (IIR) no. 6 – HSSPF
Walter Schimana,' 31 Jul. 1945, OSS 142090, RG 226, NA.

83 Allied Intelligence Report, c. May 1945; USFET Interrogation Center 'Intermediate
Interrogation Report (IIR) #5 – O/Gruf. Freiherr Friedrich K. von Eberstein,' 27 Jul.
1945; USFET MIS Center 'Intermediate Interrogation Report (IIR) #18 – Krim. Rat.
Stubaf. Ernst Wagner,' 30 Aug. 1945, all in IRR File XE 049 888 'Werewolf Activi-
ties Vol. I,' RG 319, NA; USFET Interrogation Center 'Preliminary Interrogation
Report (PIR) #36 – Krim. Rat. Ernst Wagner,' 27 Jul. 1945, OSS 140564, RG 226,
NA; USFET Interrogation Center 'Intermediate Interrogation Report (IIR) #4 –
Obst. d. Pol. Paul Schmitz-Voigt,' 23 Jul. 1945, OSS XL 13822, RG 226, NA; U.S.
Third Army G-2 'Information Bulletin' no. 72, 27 May 1945, WO 219/1602, PRO;
History of the Counter Intelligence Corps, vol. 20, 97, NA; Henke, *Die amerika-
nische Besetzung Deutschlands*, 949; and Birn, *Die Höheren SS- und Polizeiführer*,
332.

84 Wenck, OKH to the Heeresgruppen and Armeen, 6 Feb. 1945, RH 2/1930, BMA.

85 Auerbach, 'Die Organisation des "Werwolf,"' 353; EDS Report no. 34 'Notes on the
"Werewolves"'; USFET MIS Center 'Intermediate Interrogation Report (IIR) #18 –
Krim. Rat. Stubaf. Ernst Wagner,' 30 Aug. 1945, both in IRR File XE 049 888
'Werewolf Activities Vol. I,' RG 319, NA; CSDIC/WEA BAOR 'Second Interim
Report on SS Obergruf. Karl M. Gutenberger,' IR 34, 1 Nov. 1945, ETO MIS-Y-
Sect. CSDIC/WEA Interim Interrogation Reports 1945–6, RG 332, NA; Simon
Wiesenthal, *Justice, Not Vengeance* (London 1991), 37; and Rose, *Werwolf*, 153–4.
According to a system devised by Himmler's Home Army headquarters in the fall of
1944, all requests by the HSSPFs for equipment, weapons, and ammunition flowed
through the Bureau 'Prützmann'; allocations were supposed to be made via the mili-
tary Wehrkreis offices: Ultra Document BT 7004, 12 Mar. 1945, Ultra Document
Collection, Reel 65.

86 British Troops Austria 'Joint Weekly Intelligence Summary' no. 9, 31 Aug. 1945, FO
1007/300, PRO; BAOR/Int. 'Appreciation of the Werwolf Movement'; and U.S.
Twelfth Army 'Werewolves,' 31 May 1945, p. 2, both in IRR File XE 049 888 'Werewolf Activities Vol. I,' RG 319 NA. Prützmann also begged supplies from the RSHA
central ordnance service, which was run by his old protégé, Josef Spacil, but was
reportedly refused in all such requests USFET MIS Center 'Intermediate Interrogation
Report (IIR) #16 – 0/Führer Josef Spacil,' 28 Aug. 1945, OSS 15135, RG 226, NA.

87 CSDIC WEA BAOR. 'Second Interim Report on SS Obergruf. Karl M. Gutenberger' IR 34, 1 Nov. 1945, ETO MIS-Y-Sect. CSDIC/WEA Interim Interrogation
   Reports 1945–6, RG332, NA; USFET MIS Center 'Intermediate Interrogation
   Report (IIR) #18 – Krim. Rat. Stubaf. Ernst Wagner,' 30 Aug. 1945; USFET Interro-
   gation Center 'Intermediate Interrogation Report (IIR) #5 – O/Gruf. Freiherr Karl
   von Eberstein,' 27 Jul. 1945; Twelfth Army Group Mobile Field Interrogation Unit
   no. 4 'Gen. Lt. Walter Schimana,' 27 May 1945; MI-6 'CX Report,' 16 Jun. 1945;
   CSDIC/CMF 'The Werwolf Organization,' 10 Jun. 1945, all in IRR File XE 049 888
   'Werwolf Activities Vol. I,' RG 319, NA; USFET Interrogation Center 'Intermediate
   Interrogation Report (IRR) #6 – Walter Schimana,' 31 Jul. 1945, OSS 142090, RG
   226, NA; CSDIC (UK) 'SS Hauptamt and the Waffen SS,' 23 Aug. 1945, OSS
   144337, RG 226, NA; *The Stars and Stripes*, 31 May 1945; USFET 'Weekly Intelli-
   gence Summary' no. 50, 27 Jun. 1946, and no. 69, 7 Nov. 1946, both in State Dept.
   Decimal File 1945–9, 740.00119 Control (Germany), RG 59, NA. For the transfer of
   Reichsbank financial resources into the Alps in order to fund resistance activity, see
   Ian Sayer and Douglas Botting, *Nazi Gold* (London 1985), 24, 29–38.
88 EDS Report no. 34 'Notes on the "Werewolves,"' IRR File XE 049 888 'Werewolf
   Activities Vol I,' RG 319, NA.
89 U.S. Twelfth Army 'Werewolves,' 31 May 1945, and MFI Report on Werwolf Sabotage Equipment 5/752, 27 Apr. 1945, both in IRR File XE 049 888 'Werewolf Activities Vol. I,' RG 319, NA; and USFET MIS Center 'CI Intermediate Interrogation
   Report (CI-IIR) #24 – O/Gruf. Jürgen Stroop,' 10 Oct. 1945, OSS XL 22157, RG
   228, NA.
90 One example of transport difficulties: supplies were actually set aside in Berlin,
   Hamburg, and Breslau for the use of Stroop's Werwolf section in Wehrkreis XII, but
   the regional Werwolf organizations were responsible for transport and in this case
   there was only enough fuel to send supply trucks to and from Berlin. Available supplies in the other two cities were never utilized, at least not by the intended
   Wehrkreis: Twelfth Army Group 'Unternehmen W.,' 12 Jun. 1945, IRR File XE 049
   888 'Werwolf Activities Vol I,' RG 319, NA.
91 Rose, *Werwolf*, 154; and J.P. Nettl, *The Eastern Zone and Soviet Policy in Germany,
   1945–50* (Oxford 1951), 3–4.
92 USFET Interrogation Center 'Intermediate Interrogation Report (IIR) #5 – O/Gruf.
   Friedrich K. von Eberstein,' IRR File XE 049 888 'Werwolf Activities Vol. I,' RG
   319, NA.
93 CSDIC WEA BAOR 'Second Interim Report on SS Obergruf. Karl M. Gutenberger'
   IR 34, 1 Nov. 1945, ETO MIS-Y-Sect. CSDIC/WEA Interim Interrogation. Reports
   1945–6, RG 332, NA; EDS Report no. 34 'Notes on the "Werewolves"'; BAOR Int.
   'Appreciation of the Werewolf Movement,' both in IRR File XE 049 888 'Werwolf
   Activities Vol. I,' RG 319, NA; USFET MIS Center 'CI Intermediate Interrogation

Report CI-IRR #24 – O/Gruf Jürgen Stroop,' 10 Oct. 1945, OSS XL 22157, RG 226, NA; SHAEF CI War Room 'The SS Guerrilla Movement,' 9 Apr. 1945, ETO MIS-Y-Sect. Misc. Interrogation Reports 1944–6, RG 332, NA; 'Entlassungstelle der Waffen SS, Lustheim and Other Locations,' 17 Apr. 1945, ETO MIS-Y-Sect. CSDIC (UK) Special Interrogation Reports 1943–5, RG 332, NA; *The Daily Express*, 21 Apr. 1945; and interview with R. Jussenhofen, 30 Dec. 1991.

94 CSDIC WEA BAOR 'Final Report on SA Brgf. u. HDL Fritz Marrenbach' FR 29, 21 Jan. 1946, Appendix 'A,' ETO MIS-Y-Sect. Final Interrogation Reports 1945–9, RG 332, NA.

95 CSDIC (UK) 'SS Hauptamt and the Waffen-SS,' 23 Aug. 1945, OSS 144337, RG 226, NA.

96 CSDIC WEA BAOR 'Second Interim Report on SS Obergruf, Karl M. Gutenberger,' IR 34, 1 Nov. 1945, ETO MIS-T-Sect. CSDIC/WEA Interim Interrogation Reports 1945–6, RG 332, NA. An OKW memo noted that soldiers within the Werwolf were volunteers and were employed as leaders of Werwolf 'troops': Winter, memo from WFST./Op (H)/Ia to Chef WFST., Stellv. Chef, Op(H), Ia, Ic, Qu, 28 Feb. 1945, RW 4/v. 702, BMA.

97 PWE 'German Propaganda and the German,' 23 Apr. 1945, FO 898/187, PRO; CSDIC (UK) Interrogation Report 'Amt III (SD Inland) RSHA,' 30 Sep. 1945, ETO MIS-Y-Sect. Special Interrogation Reports 1943–5, RG 332, NA; EDS Report no. 34, 'Notes on the "Werewolves,"' and BAOR/Int. 'Appreciation of the Werwolf Movement,' both in IRR File XE 049 888 'Werewolf Activities Vol. I,' RG 319, NA; Rose, *Werwolf*, 301; and Third Army G-2 'Interrogation Report' no. 2, 14 May 1945, OSS XL 11132, RG 226, NA.

98 Direction des Documentions Allemagne 'Note sur la formation de Werwolf,' 6 Jul. 1945, IRR File XE 049 888 'Werewolf Activities Vol. I,' RG 319, NA; and USFET Interrogation Center 'Final Interrogation Report (FIR) #6 – Karl–Frank,' 7 Jul. 1945, OSS 138456, RG226, NA.

99 Rose, *Werwolf*, 112; Jurgen Thorwald, *Defeat in the East* (New York 1967), 192; and Kurt Schilde, *Vom Columbia-Haus zum Schulenburgring* (Berlin 1987), 306.

100 Dotzler, 'Vorschlage zum Aufbau einer Widerstandsbewegung in den von den Bolschewisten besetzten deutschen Ostgebeiten,' 23 Jan. 1945, NS 19/832, BA; and *History of the Counter Intelligence Corps*, vol. 20, NA. For Polish and Soviet arrests of presbyters, priests, and cantors on charges of association with the Werwolf, see *The Tragedy of Silesia, 1945–46*, 363, 444, 488; *Vertreibung und Vertreibungsbrechen*, 255; Pastor Weichert 'An der grossen und kleinen Brennpunkten der Schlesischen Kirche vom 25.5.1943 bis 31.12.1946,' Ost Dok. 2/177, BA; G. Thomas 'Verbrechen im Schlaup, Kr. Jauer,' 9 Oct. 1952, Ost Dok. 2/189, BA; and *The Manchester Guardian*, 27 Apr. 1945. For arms hidden in Sudeten monasteries, see W. Hoffmann 'Bericht über meine Erlebnisse in Sudetenland,' 1956–7, Ost

Dok. 2/279, BA; Gustav Beuer, *New Czechoslovakia and Her Historical Background* (London 1947), 188; and XXII Corps, Pilsen, ACoS G-2 'Periodic Report' no. 47, 18 Sep. 1945, OSS XL 18718, RG 226, NA.

101 SHAEF intelligence reports quoted German sources as citing a total Werwolf membership of 1,000 to 2,000, while a number of published accounts settle upon a figure of 3,000 to 5,000: EDS Report no. 34 'Notes on the "Werewolves,"' IRR File XE 049 888 'Werewolf Activities Vol I,' RG 319, NA; Twelfth Army Group from Sands from Sibert sgnd. Bradley to SHAEF Main for G-2, 9 Apr. 1945, WO 219/1602, PRO; Rose, *Werwolf*, 104, 107; Lucas, *Kommando*, 332; Isreal Gutman, ed., *Encyclopedia of the Holocaust* (New York 1990), vol. 4, 1645; Whiting, *Hitler's Werewolves*, 70, 190; and Kenneth Macksey, *The Partisans of Europe in World War II* (London 1975), 247. The output of the main Werwolf schools does not give the impression of a mass organization – for instance, Lubbecke graduated 220 trained Werewolves; Esslingen, 200; Kloster Tiefenthal, 150 to 200; Mariazell, 15 to 20; and Neustrelitz, 300 to 400: CSDIC WEA BAOR 'Second Interim Report on SS Obergruf. Karl M. Gutenberger,' IR 34, 1 Nov. 1945, OSS 123190, RG 226, NA; l^{ère} Armée française, 2ème Bureau 'Bulletin de Renseignements,' 16 May 1945, Annex II, 7P 125, SHAT; USFET Interrogation Center 'Intermediate Interrogation Report (IIR) #6 – Schimana, Walter,' 31 Jul. 1946, OSS 142090, RG 226, NA; USFET MIS Center 'CI Intermediate Interrogation Report (CI-IIR) #24 – O/Gruf. Jürgen Stroop,' 10 Oct. 1945, OSS XL 22157, RG 226, NA; U.S. Twelfth Army 'Werewolves' 31 May 1945, and Twelfth Army Group 'Unternehmen W,' 12 Jun. 1945, both in IRR File XE 049 888 'Werewolf Activities Vol I,' RG 319, NA. Orders placed at factories for Werwolf supplies – such as 5,000 containers for Werwolf sabotage kits (March 1945), or 2,000 radio receiver-transmitter sets (October 1944) – seem to support a membership total of at least 5,000 men and women: MFI no. 5/752, Note on Werwolf Equipment, *c.* Apr. 1945, IRR File XE 049 888 'Werewolf Activities Vol I,' RG 319, NA.

102 U.S. Ninth Army 'Fritz Georg Schlessmann,' Report no. 1658, 30 May 1945, IRR File XE 049 888 'Werewolf Activities Vol. I,' RG 319, NA; CSDIC/WEA BAOR 'Second Interim Report on SS Obergruf. Karl M. Gutenberger,' IR 34, 1 Nov. 1945, ETO MIS-Y-Sect. CSDIC/WEA Interim Interrogation Reports 1945–6, RG 332, NA; and PWE 'German Propaganda and the German,' 30 Apr. 1945, FO 898/198, PRO. For problems in the recruitment of suitable group leaders in Austria, see USFET Interrogation Center 'Intermediate Interrogation Report (IIR) #6 – Schimana, Walter,' 31 Jul. 1946, OSS 142090, RG 260, NA.

103 EDS Report no. 34 'Notes on the "Werewolves,"' IRR File XE 049 888 'Werewolf Activities Vol. I,' RG 319, NA.

104 USFET MIS Center 'Intermediate Interrogation Report (IIR) #18,' 30 Aug. 1945; BAOR/Int. 'Appreciation of the Werwolf Movement,' both in IRR File XE 049

888 'Werewolf Activities Vol. I,' RG 319, NA; Allied Intelligence Report, *c.* Aug. 1945, OSS OB 28993, NA; and 'Report from Captured Personnel and Material Branch, MID, US War Dept.,' 9 May 1945, State Dept. Decimal Files 1945–9, 740.00119 Control (Germany), RG 59, NA.

105 Trevor-Roper, *The Last Days of Hitler*, 52; SHAEF CI War Room 'The SS Guerrilla Movement,' 9 Apr. 1945, ETO MIS-Y-Sect. Misc. Interrogation Reports 1944–6, RG 332, NA; and CSDIC/WEA BAOR 'Second Interim Report on SS Obergruf. Karl M. Gutenberger IR 34,' 1 Nov. 1945, ETO MIS-Y-Sect. CSDIC/WEA Interim Interrogation Reports 1945–6, RG 332, NA. Gutenberger later claimed that, although a high standard of physical fitness was maintained for Werwolf entrants, less attention was paid to strength of character, and as a result 'a fairly large percentage of undesirables merely working for their own gain appeared in the ranks of the W Movement.' This, he surmised, was one of the causes of the organization's failure.

106 Ière Armée Française, 2ème Bureau 'Bulletin de Renseignements,' 16 May 1945, Annex II; 'Organisation du "Werwolf,"' 19 Jun. 1945; Direction Générale des Études et Recherches 'Bulletin de Renseignements – Allemagne: Wehrwolf,' 23 Jun. 1945; 'Bulletin du Renseignements – Allemagne: Organisation du Werwolf,' 20 Aug. 1945; and 'Bulletin de Renseignements' no. 9, 8 Nov. 1945, all in 7P 125, SHAT; Borth, *Nicht zu Jung zum Sterben*, 58–68; Smirnov to Blumin, 10 May 1945, *Pogranichnye Voiska SSSR Mai, 1945–1950*, 65; Gołąbek and Tryc, 'Z Genezy Powstania i Działalności Werwolfu,' 136; USFET Interrogation Center 'Intermediate Interrogation Report (IIR) no. 11 – Obst. Paul Krüger,' 31 Jul. 1945, Annex II, OSS XL 13775, RG 226, NA; USFET Interrogation Center 'Intermediate Interrogation Report (IRR) #6 – Walter Schimana,' 31 Jul. 1945, OSS 142090, RG 226, NA; Drška, *Československá Armadá v Národní a Democratické Revoluci*, 63; Rose, *Werwolf*, 66, 128–30, 133–4, 138–40; Lucas, *Kommando*, 311, 314–16; BAOR/Int. 'Appreciation of the Werwolf Movement,' Jul. 1945; Twenty-first Army Group/Int. 'Appendix C' to Cdn. Corps Sitrep, 22 Jun. 1945; U.S. Twelfth Army 'Werewolves,' 31 May 1945; EDS Report no. 34 'Notes on the "Werewolves"'; 6th AG 'Resistance Organizations (Germany)'; Twenty-first Army Group BLA 'Extract from "Current Notes on Enemy Espionage,"' 26 May 1945; U.S. Twelfth Army 'Report on Unternehmen Werwolf,' 12 Jun. 1945, all in IRR File XE 049 888 'Werewolf Activities Vol. I,' RG 319, NA; USFET MIS Center 'Intermediate Interrogation Report (CI-IIR) #24 – O/Gruf. Jürgen Stroop,' 10 Oct. 1945, OSS XL 22157, RG 226, NA; Auerbach, 'Die Organisation des "Werwolf,"' 353; British Troops Austria 'Joint Weekly Intelligence Summary' no. 9, 31 Aug. 1945, FO 1007/300, PRO; USFET Interrogation Center 'Intermediate Interrogation Report (IIR) #9 – H/Stuf. Hans Gerlach,' 11 Aug. 1945, OSS XL 13744, RG 226, NA; SHAEF CI War Room 'The SS Guerrilla Movement,' 9 Apr. 1945, ETO MIS-Y-

Sect. Misc. Interrogation Reports, 1944–6, RG 332, NA; CSDIC/WEA BAOR
'Second Interrogation Report on SS Obergruf. Karl M. Gutenberger' IR 34, 1 Nov.
1945, ETO MIS-Y-Sect. CSDIC/WEA, Interim Interrogation Reports 1945–6, RG
332, NA; Twelfth Army Group from Sands from Sibert and Bradley to SHAEF
Main G-2 (CIB), 9 Apr. 1945, and from Sands from Sibert sgnd. Bradley to SHAEF
Rear for Robertson for G-2 (CI), 19 Apr. 1945, both in WO 219/1602, PRO; Whit-
ing, *Hitler's Werewolves*, 73–4, 189; *History of the Counter Intelligence Corps* vol.
20, 37, NA; MIS Center 'CI Intermediate Interrogation Report (CI-IIR) #24,' OSS
XL 22157, RG 226, NA; CSDIC (WEA) BAOR 'Final Report on Gunther
Haubold' FR 94, ETO MIS-Y-Sect. CSDIC/WEA Final Interrogation Records
1945–7, RG 332, NA; Allied Intelligence Report, *c.* Aug. 1945, OSS OB 28993,
RG 226, NA; and *Werwolf: Winke für Jagdeinheiten*, 11–26.

107 U.S. Fifteenth Army, Office of ACoS G-2 'Periodic Report' no. 60, Annex 3, OSS
     XL 12362, RG 226, NA.

108 SHAEF CI War Room 'The SS Guerrilla Movement' 9 Apr. 1945, ETO MIS-Y-
     Sect. Misc. Interrogation Reports, 1944–6, RG 332, NA; and *Istoriya Velikoy
     Otechestvennoy Voyny Sovetskogo Soyuza, 1941–1945*, ed. Piotr Pospelev et al.
     (Moscow; distributed by Office of the Chief of Military History, U.S. Army,
     1960–5), vol. 6, 136.

109 U.S. Twelfth Army 'Werewolves,' 31 May 1945, IRR File XE 049 888 'Werewolf
     Activities Vol. I,' RG 319, NA.

110 Sig. illegible, Leitstelle II Ost für FAK to OKH/Genst. d. H/Fremde Heere Ost,
     20 Mar. 1945, Records of OKH, Microcopy no. T-78, Roll 565, frame 915, NA; and
     W. Hoffman 'Bericht über meine Erlebnisse in Sudetenland' (1956–7), Ost Dok.
     2/279, BA.

111 Direction des Services de Documentation Allemagne 'Note sur la formation du
     Werwolf,' 6 Jul. 1945, IRR File XE 049 888 'Werewolf Activities Vol. I,' RG 319,
     NA; Skorzeny, *La Guerre inconnue*, 196–7; Whiting, *Hitler's Werewolves*, 68–9;
     and Rose, *Werwolf*, 28.

112 British Troops Austria 'Joint Weekly Intelligence Summary' no. 9, 31 Aug. 1945,
     FO 1007/300, PRO.

113 Direction des Services des Documentation Allemagne 'Note sur la formation du
     Werwolf,' 6 Jul. 1945; EDS Report no. 34 'Notes on the "Werewolves"'; and U.S.
     Twelfth Army 'Werewolves,' 31 May 1945, all in IRR File XE 049 888 'Werewolf
     Activities Vol. I,' RG 319, NA.

114 Canadian First Army 'Intelligence Periodical' no. 3, 30 May 1945, WO 205/1072,
     PRO; CSDIC WEA BAOR, 'Sixth Combined Interim Report – Stubaf. Kopkow,
     Stubaf. Thomsen, Stubaf. Noske' IR no. 62, 31 May 1946, ETO MIS-Y-Sect.
     CSDIC (UK) Interim Interrogation Reports 1945–6, NA; and USFET MIS Center
     'CI Intermediate Interrogation Report (CI-IIR) #24 – O/Gruf. Jürgen Stroop,' 10
     Oct. 1945, OSS XL 22157, RG 226, NA.

115 Benton Wallace, *Patton and His Third Army* (Harrisburg 1946), 188; *The New York Times*, 29 Mar., 1 Apr., and 17 Apr. 1945; *The Daily Express*, 29 Mar. 1945; SHAEF G-5 'Weekly Journal of Information' no. 7, 4 Apr. 1945, WO 219/3918, PRO; and *The Washington Post*, 17 Apr. 1945. A French intelligence report noted that techniques for the poisoning of food and water were taught at Werwolf training schools: l^{ère} Armée Française, 2ème Bureau 'Bulletin de Renseignements,' 16 May 1945, Annex no. II, 7P 125, SHAT. See also Whiting, *Hitler's Werewolves*, 148.

116 *The Globe and Mail*, 24 Jul. 1945; *The Washington Post*, 16 Apr. 1945; V Corps 'Weekly Intelligence Summary' no. 6, 17 Aug. 1945, FO 1007/299, PRO; and USFET 'Weekly Intelligence Summary' no. 61, 12 Sep. 1946, State Dept. Decimal File 1945–9, 740.00119 Control (Germany), RG 59, NA.

117 Brig. Davis, SHAEF Memos, 29 Mar. 1945; 8 Apr. 1945, both in WO 219/3513, PRO; and *Final Entries, 1945*, 311.

118 Enemy Personnel Exploitation Sect., Field Information Agency Technical CC (BE) 'Two Brief Discussions of German CW Policy with Albert Speer,' 12 Oct. 1945, OSS XL 22959, RG 226, NA. Speer's remarks in an interrogation on 21 September 1945 are the matter of some dispute. His own typed transcript of the interrogation stated that chemical-warfare supplies *may* have been provided to the Werwolf and 'Free Corps "Adolf Hitler,"' while his two interrogators claimed that, during the actual conversation, Speer had unequivocally admitted the transfer of such material. Speer's interrogators later charged that his written statement had deliberately muddied the waters in order to leave an air of ambiguity over his admission that poison gas had in fact been supplied to the guerrillas. Maj. E. Tilley to Lt.-Col. G.L. Harrison, FO 1031/150, PRO. For secret caches and production facilities for poison gas, see Office of the U.S. Chief of Counsel for War Crimes, Evidence Division, Interrogation Branch 'Interrogation Summary #819 – George R. Gerhard,' 31 Dec. 1946, IWM.

119 PWE 'German Propaganda and the German,' 25 Feb. 1945, FO 898/187, PRO; Himmler to Gutenberger, 18 Oct. 1944, Microcopy no. T-580, Reel 78; Rose, *Werwolf*, 13; Whiting, *Hitler's Werewolves*, 179–80; *Final Entries, 1945*, 94–5, 105, 258, 279; Trees and Whiting, *Unternehmen Karnival*, 261–2; and P. de Tristan, First French Army, 5th Bureau 'Monthly Historical Report,' 1 May 1945, WO 219/2587, PRO. For Nazi propaganda treatment of Winkler, see *Völkischer Beobachter* (Munich), 23 Mar. 1945; and 25 Apr. 1945.

120 Twelfth Army Group to SHAEF Main for G-2 (CIB), 7 Apr. 1945, WO 219/1602, PRO; SHAEF JIC (45) 14 (Draft) 'Security Problems Facing the Allies in Germany,' 11 Apr. 1945, 'Annex A,' WO 219/1659, PRO; *The History of the Counter Intelligence Corps*, vol. 20, 85–6, NA; *The New York Times*, 11 Apr. 1945; *The St Louis Post–Dispatch*, 20 May 1945; Henke, *Die amerikanische Besetzung Deutschlands*, 950; and Bruno Brehm, *Wehe den Bestiegten Allen* (Graz 1962), 361.

121 *Justiz und NS-Verbrechen*, vol. 5, 418–17; vol. 10, 80–91; vol. 12, 203–6; USFET Interrogation Center 'Intermediate Interrogation Report (IIR) no. 9 – H/Stuf. Hans

Gerlach,' 11 Aug. 1945, OSS XL 13744, RG 226, NA; CSDIC WEA BAOR
'Interim Report on SS-Obergruppenführer Karl M. Gutenberger' IR 8, 8 Oct. 1945;
CSDIC WEA BAOR 'Third Interim Report on SS-Obergruppenführer Karl M.
Gutenberger,' IR 38, both in ETO MIS-Y-Sect. CSDIC/WEA Interim Interrogation
Reports 1945–6, RG 332, NA; 'Intelligence Bulletin' no. 28, 20 Nov. 1944, FO
115/3614, PRO; Whiting, *Hitler's Werewolves*, 3–17, 72, 74–5, 96–7, 103–10,
115–27, 131–7, 157–68, 190–2; Rose, *Werwolf*, 13–21; Ziemke, *The U.S. Army in
the Occupation of Germany*, 184; Julius Mader, *Hitlers Spionagegenerale sagen
aus* (Berlin 1971), 15; Sayer and Botting, *America's Secret Army*, 218–19; Herbert
Kriegsheim, *Getarnt, Getäuscht und Doch Getrue* (Berlin 1958), 274–9; SHAEF
PWD Intelligence Sect. 'Murder of Franz Oppenhoff, Mayor of Aachen,' 29 Mar.
1945; 'Public Reaction to the Murder of Dr. Oppenhoff, Mayor of Aachen,' 29 Mar.
1945, both in OSS 124475, RG 226, NA; Jones, Mil. Gov. Det. F1 G2, Co. 'G,' 2nd
ECAD to Commanding General, U.S Fifteenth Army, 30 Apr. 1945, WO 219/1602,
PRO; *The Times*, 29 March 1945; PWE 'German Propaganda and the German,' 2
Apr. 1945, FO 898/189, PRO; *The New York Times*, 2 Apr. 1945; and DNB Report
'Sühne für ehrlosen Verrat,' 29 Mar. 1945, R 34/270, BA.

122 OSS Paris Report 'City Government of Aachen,' 16 Dec. 1945, WO 219/1648A,
PRO; *The Daily Express*, 30 Jan. 1945; 1 Feb. 1945; 7 Mar. 1945; *History of the
Counter Intelligence Corps*, vol. 16, 22–4, NA; and Henke, *Die amerikanische
Besetzung Deutschlands*, 284–97.

123 Ulrich Borsdorf and Lutz Niethammer, eds., *Zwischen Befreiung und Besatzung*
(Wuppertal 1976), 153; Georg Bönisch, 'Alles leer, oder, zerstörte: Köln 1945,' 75;
Henry Taylor, *Men and Power* (New York 1946), 188–9; Peter Hüttenberger,
*Düsseldorf: Geschichte von den Anfang bis ins 20. Jahrhundert – Die Industrie und
Verwaltungsstadt (20. Jahrhundert)* (Düsseldorf 1989), vol. 3, 648; Hans Kösters,
Essen Stunde Null (Düsseldorf 1982), 97; *The New York Times*, 3 Apr. and 17 Apr.
1945; *The Manchester Guardian*, 11 May 1945; *History of the Counter Intelligence
Corps*, vol. 20, 97, NA; and ECAD 'General Intelligence Bulletin' no. 44, 5 May
1945, WO 219/3760A, PRO. Reports about a widespread fear of Nazi retaliation
also came from French and Soviet occupied areas: P. de Tristan, First French Army,
5th Bureau 'Monthly Historical Report,' 1 May 1945, WO 219/2587, PRO; and PID
'Germany: Weekly Background Notes' no. 4, 4 Jul. 1945, FO 371/46933, PRO.

124 K. Strölin, Der Oberbürgermeister der Stadt der Auslandsdeutschen to HSSPF Hofmann, 5 Apr. 1945, Records of the Reich Leader of the SS and Chief of the German
Police, Microcopy no. T-175, Roll 223, NA; and Karl Strölin, *Stuttgart im Endstadium des Krieges* (Stuttgart 1950), 52–3.

125 Strölin was in fact on an SS 'Blacklist,': Lutz Niethammer, 'Activität und Grenzen
der Antifa-Ausschusse 1945: Das Bespiel Stuttgart,' *Vierteljahrshefte für Zeitgeschichte* 25/3 (1975), 305.

126 *Justiz und NS-Verbrechen*, vol. 3, 302.

127 Donald McKale, *The Nazi Party Courts* (Lawrence 1974), 183–4.

128 Von Lang, *Bormann*, 315; *Völkischer Beobachter*, 17 Feb. 1945; Ingo Müller, *Hitler's Justice* (Cambridge 1991), 188–9; and Henke, *Die amerikanische Besetzung Deutschlands*, 845–6. See also Ultra Document BT 4666, 12 Feb. 1945, Ultra Document Collection, Reel 61. For a 'civilian summary court' convened at Lohr, supposedly under the conditions of the 13 February edict, see *Justiz und NS-Verbrechen*, vol. 7, 171–86.

129 Joachim Fest, *Hitler* (New York 1974), 731; Hohenecker, 'Das Kriegsende 1945 im Raum Fischbach,' 203; Hildebrand Troll, 'Aktionen zur Kriegsbeendigung in Frühjahr 1945,' 657; Friedrich Blumenstock, *Der Einmarsch der Amerikaner und Franzosen im Nordlichen Württemberg im April 1945*, (Stuttgart 1957), 29–30; Schwardzwälder, *Bremen und Nordwestdeutschland am Kriegsende 1945*, vol. 2, 70–3; *Justiz und NS-Verbrechen*, vol. 2, 647; and Dieter Rebentisch, 'Nationalsozialistische Revolution, Parteiherrschaft und totaler Krieg,' in *Die Geschichte Hessens*, ed. Uwe Schultz (Stuttgart 1983), 248.

130 Haffner, *The Meaning of Hitler*, 158–62.

131 Henke, *Die amerikanische Besetzung Deutschlands*, 950; Hermann Vietzen, *Chronik der Stadt: Stuttgart, 1945–1948* (Stuttgart 1972), 16–17; Strölin, *Stuttgart in Endstadium des Krieges*, 25; *Zwischen Befreiung und Besatzung*, 58–9; Desmond Flower and James Reeves, eds., *The War, 1939–1945* (London 1960), 1011; Tully, *Berlin: Story of a Battle*, 218; W. Hoffmann 'Bericht über meine Erlebnisse in Sudetenland,' 1956–7, Ost Dok. 2/279, BA; Zolling, ' "Was machen wir am Tag nach unserem Sieg?," ' 121; and *History of the Counter Intelligence Corps*, vol. 20, 134, NA. At Hartmannsdorf, the local Werwolf chief forced townspeople to take down white flags which had been hoisted in anticipation of the arrival of American troops: Ralph Pearson, *Enroute to the Redoubt* (Chicago 1958), vol. 3, 189.

132 CSDIC WEA BAOR 'Interim Report on SS Obergruppenführer Karl M. Gutenberger' IR no. 8, 8 Oct. 1945, ETO MIS-Y-Sect. CSDIC/WEA Interim Interrogation Reports 1945–6, RG 332, NA; Schwarzwälder, *Bremen und Nordwestdeutschland am Kriegsende 1945*, vol. 2, 69; *The New York Times*, 3 Apr. 1945; *Time* 45/15, (9 Apr. 1945), 25; *Kriegsende und Neuanfang in Augsburg 1945: Erinnerungen und Berichte*, ed. Karl-Ulrich Gelberg (Munich 1996), 118, 128; and *Justiz und NS-Verbrechen*, vol 3, 695–709.

133 *Final Entries, 1945*, 105.

134 For Werwolf threats against priests and pastors, see SHAEF G-5 'Civil Affairs – Military Government Weekly Field Report,' 19 May 1945, State Dept. Decimal File 1945–9, 740.00119 Control (Germany), RG 59, NA; Kuby, *The Russians and Berlin*, 104; and PID 'Germany: Weekly Background Notes' no. 1, 8 Jun. 1945, FO 371/46933, PRO

135 Ernst Jünger, *Jahre der Okkupation* (Stuttgart 1958), 16. For mention of an SS guerrilla unit tracking a cowardly Nazi Party official in the Ruhr, see Allied Intelligence Report, OSS 133195, RG 226, NA.

136 *Justiz und NS-Verbrechen*, vol. 1, 411–30; vol. 5, 361–9; and Pearson, *Enroute to the Redoubt*, vol. 3, 168–9.

137 Franz Hofer, 'National Redoubt' MS no. B-488, *World War II German Military Studies*, 24.

138 Wahl, ... *es ist das deutsche Herz*, 418.

139 Albert Speer, *Inside the Third Reich* (London 1970), 469, 475; and SHAEF G-2 'Interrogation of Albert Speer – 7th Session, 1st Jun. 1945 – Part Two,' FO 1031/141, PRO.

140 Speer, *Inside the Third Reich*, 442, 562; Jochen von Lang, *Bormann* (London 1979), 310; Henke, *Die amerikanische Besetzung Deutschlands*, 424–7; and Infield, *Skorzeny*, 110.

141 SS-Partei Kanzlei-Wehrmacht 'Verwendung des Deutschen Volkssturms,' 28 Mar. 1944, NS 6/99, BA; Rose, *Werwolf*, 227–8; and Kuby, *The Russians and Berlin*, 104–5.

142 Gołąbek and Tryc, 'Z Genezy i Działalności Werwolfu,' 138.

143 *Justiz und NS-Verbrechen*, vol. 4, 208; Speer, *Inside the Third Reich*, 446–7; Kösters, *Essen Stunde Null*, 84; *Die Nationalsozialistische Zeit (1933–1945) in Neuss*, 69; SHAEF G-2 'Interrogation of Albert Speer, Former Reich Minister of Armaments and War Production,' 7th Session, 1 Jun. 1945, FO 1031/141, PRO; SHAEF G-5 'Military Government–Civil Affairs Weekly Field Report' no. 46, 28 Apr. 1945, State Dept. Decimal Files 1945–9, 740.00119 Control (Germany), RG 59, NA; SHAEF PWD 'Guidance Notes for Output in German for the Week 30 Apr.–7 May 1945,' 29 Apr. 1945, FO 371/46894, PRO; and *History of the XVI Corps*, 76–7.

144 Twenty-first Army Group 'CI News Sheet' no. 27, 14 Aug. 1945, Part III, WO 205/997, PRO; and SHAEF JIC 'Political Intelligence Report,' 3 Apr. 1945, WO 219/1659, PRO.

145 *History of the Counter Intelligence Corps*, vol. 19, 83–4, NA.

146 *The Daily Express*, 22 Feb. 1945.

147 George Dyer, *XII Corps: Spearhead of Patton's Third Army* (Baton Rouge 1947), 262; Wallace, *Patton and His Third Army*, 127; and Twenty-first Army Group 'CI News Sheet' no. 14, Part I, WO 205/997, PRO.

148 Rose, *Werwolf*, 304; PWE 'German Propaganda and the German,' 2 Apr. 1945, FO 898/187, PRO; *The New York Times*, 30 Mar. 1945; Leonard Rapport and Arthur Northwood, Jr, *Rendezvous with Destiny: A History of the 101st Airborne Division* (Greenville 1965), 716; 'Report from Captured Personnel and Material Branch, Military Intelligence Division, U.S. War Department,' 13 May 1945, State Dept.

Decimal File 1945–9, 740.00119 Control (Germany), RG 59, NA; Will Bird, *No Retreating Footsteps: The Story of the North Nova Scotia Highlanders* (Kentville, n.d.), 391; SHAEF JIC 'Political Intelligence Report,' 20 Jun. 1945, WO 219/1700, PRO; Enclave Mil. Dist. ACoS G-2 'CI Periodic Report' no. 3, 18 Jul. 1945, OSS XL 12926, RG 226, NA; Henke, *Die amerikanische Besetzung Deutschlands*, 951; Binkoski and Plaut, *The 115th Infantry Regiment in World War II*, 349, 351; *The Stars and Stripes*, 10 Jun. 1945; *The Christian Science Monitor*, 5 Jun. 1945; *The Manchester Guardian*, 5 Jun. 1945; *Journal de Genève*, 5 Jun. 1945; *The Washington Post*, 5 Jun. and 23 Jun. 1945; and Anthony Cave Brown, *The Last Hero: Wild Bill Donovan* (New York 1982), 769.

149 Abt. Fremde Heere Ost (III f) 'Übersetzung einer Anordnung des Obersten Befehlshabers aus einem Beutepapier des 195. Garde–A.R. der 91. Garde-S.D. Duchowschtschina vom August 1944,' 8 Mar. 1945, Records of OKH, Microform no. T-78, Reel 488, frame 6474481, NA.

150 Memo for Dienststelle Obergruppenführer Prützmann 'Verbereitungen für den Werwolf in Karinhall,' Records of the Reich Leader of the SS and Chief of the German Police, Microfilm no. T 175, Roll 452, frame 2967661, NA.

151 Schade, 'Verluste Berliner Museumgüter während des zweiten Weltkrieges,' 496–7.

152 Thomas Carr Howe, *Salt Mines and Castles* (Indianapolis 1946), 62–3, 154–5, 216.

153 Erich Kästner, *Notabene 45* (Berlin 1945), 79; Jünger, *Jahre der Okkupation*, 16; and Bornemann, *Die letzten Tage in der Festung Harz*, 17, 20.

154 *History of the Counter Intelligence Corps*, vol. 20, 72, 152; vol. 19, 59, NA; Whiting, *Hitler's Werewolves*, 189; Inge Sbosny and Karl Schabrod, *Widerstand in Solingen* (Frankfurt am Main 1975), 120, 123; *Neue Zürcher Zeitung*, 5 Jun. 1945; and Bornemann, *Die letzten Tage in der Festung Harz*, 87. For denunciations of Werwolves at Worpswede, see Schwarzwälder, *Bremen und Nordwestdeutschland am Kriegsende 1945*, vol. 2, 69.

155 U.S. Constabulary G-2 'Weekly Intelligence Summary' no. 98, 19 Apr. 1948, WWII Operations Reports 1940–8, RG 407, NA; *History of the Counter Intelligence Corps*, vol. 20, 144, NA; and Tully, *Berlin*, 178–9.

156 *Justiz und NS-Verbrechen*, vol. 4, 195–257; Hüttenberger, *Düsseldorf*, 647–8; Walter Görlitz, *Der Zweite Weltkrieg, 1939–1945* (Stuttgart 1952), vol. 2, 551; and SHAEF JIC 'Political Intelligence Report,' 30 Apr. 1945, WO 219/1700, PRO. For last-minute attempts to organize Werwolf activity, see U.S. Fifteenth Army Triumph Interrogation Center 'Connections with Werewolf, Party Officials Hideout,' 19 Jun. 1945, and U.S. Fifteenth Army Interrogation Report 'Friedrich Hollweg,' 4 Jun. 1945, both in IRR File XE 049 888 'Werewolf Activities Vol. I,' RG 319, NA; and German Directorate 'Weekly Intelligence Summary' no. 36, 11 Jul. 1945, OSS 140955, RG 226, NA. For Werwolf pamphleteering and wire cutting in Düsseldorf, see *The Manchester Guardian*, 1 May 1945.

157 According to an account by a former Allied prisoner in Germany, who was marched passed a HJ training camp in Apr. 1945, adolescent Werewolves ran out to greet the POW column and readily expressed their anxiety about being committed to combat. Their officers did nothing to interfere with the conversation: Aidan Crawley, *Spoils of War* (Indianapolis 1973), 15.

158 Whiting, *Hitler's Werewolves*, 147.

159 Ibid., 184–6; and Rose, *Werwolf*, 319.

160 Frank Bojohr, 'Gauleiter in Hamburg: Zur Person und Tätigkeit Karl Kaufmanns,' *Vierteljahrshefte für Zeitgeschichte* 43/2 (Apr. 1996), 267–95.

161 'Extract from Interrogation of Karl Kaufmann,' 11 Jun. 1945, Appendix 'A' – 'The Werwolf Organisation in Hamburg,' IRR File XE 049 888 'Werewolf Activities Vol. I,' RG319, NA.

162 'Die Deutsche Freiheitsbewegung (Volksgenossische Bewegung),' 3 Apr. 1945, Records of OKW, Microfilm no. T-77, Reel 775, frames 5500617–5500621, NA; and Steinert, *Capitulation 1945*, 5.

163 Werner Baumbach, *Zu Spät: Aufstieg und Untergang der deutschen Luftwaffe* (Munich 1949), 291; and Count Folke Bernadotte, *The Curtain Falls* (New York 1945), 93.

164 Letter to the author from K. Schikorski, 23 Feb. 1992.

165 Schellenberg, *The Schellenberg Memoirs*, 440; and Moczarski, *Conversations with an Executioner*, 23.

166 Air Div. U.S. Forces in Austria 'The Last Days in Hitler's Air Raid Shelter,' 8 Oct. 1945, *Covert Warfare* 14.

167 Ultra Documents BT 9696, 7 Apr. 1945 (Reel 69); KO 729, 18 Apr. 1945 (Reel 71), both in Ultra Document Collection; *History of the Counter Intelligence Corps* vol. 20, 55, NA; and CSDIC WEA BAOR 'Second Interim Report on SS Obergruf Karl Michael Gutenberger,' IR 34, 1 Nov. 1945, OSS 123190, RG 226, NA.

168 'Extract from Interrogation of Karl Kaufmann,' 11 Jun. 1945, Appendix 'A' – 'The Werwolf Organisation in Hamburg', Twenty-first Army Group/Int. 'Appendix C' to 2 Cdn. Corps Sitrep, 22 Jun. 1945, both in IRR File XE 049 888 'Werewolf Activities Vol. I,' RG 319, NA. For the reaction of the Hamburg military garrison to the Werwolf, see Schwarzwälder, *Bremen und Nordwestdeutschland am Kriegsende 1945*, vol. 2, 68.

169 Whiting, *Hitler's Werewolves*, 187; 'Extract from Interrogation of Karl Kaufmann,' 11 Jun. 1945, Appendix 'A' – 'The Werwolf Organisation in Hamburg,' IRR File XE 049 888 'Werewolf Activities Vol. I,' RG 319, NA; British Troops Austria 'Joint Weekly Intelligence Summary' no. 9, 31 Aug. 1945, FO 1007/300, PRO; BIMO 'Résumé traduction d'un document de l'I.S.Anglais en Suisse,' 29 Oct. 1945, 7P 125, SHAT; and Steinart, *Capitulation 1945*, 60.

170 Rose, *Werwolf*, 327.

171 'Report from Captured Personnel and Material Branch issued by MID, US War Dept.,' 4 Aug. 1945, OSS XL 15506, RG226, NA; Pip Roberts, *From the Desert to the Baltic* (London 1987), 242–3; and Roger Manville and Heinrich Fraenkel, *Heinrich Himmler* (London 1965), 247–8. For the caching of arms by Himmler's adjutants, see DIC/CCG (BE) FR 111 'Final Report on W/SS Stubaf. Heinrich Adolf Springer,' ETO MIS-Y-Sect. CSDIC WEA Final Interrogation Reports 1945–7, RG 332, NA.

172 *The Stars and Stripes*, 3 Jun. and 16 Jun. 1945; *Journal de Genève*, 2–3 Jun. 1945; and *The Manchester Guardian*, 2 Jun. 1945. For the Arenholz raid, see Steinert, *Capitulation 1945*, 120.

173 'Report from Captured Personnel and Material Branch issued by MID, US War Dept.,' 4 Aug. 1945, OSS XL 15506, RG 226, NA; CSDIC (UK) Interrogation Report 'Amt III (SD Inland) RSHA,' 30 Sep. 1945, ETO MIS-Y-Sect. Special Interrogation Reports 1943–5, RG 332, NA; Whiting, *Hitler's Werewolves*, 192; Rose, *Werwolf*, 326–8; and Frischauer, *Himmler*, 253–5.

174 Whiting, *Hitler's Werewolves*, 193–6; Reitlinger, *The SS*, 447–8; EDS Report no. 34 'Notes on the "Werewolves,"' in IRR File XE 049 888 'Werewolf Activities Vol. I,' RG 319, NA; Rose, *Werwolf*, 328; Frischauer, *Himmler*, 9, 255, 257; and Padfield, *Himmler*, 606, 611.

175 USFET Interrogation Center 'Final Interrogation Report (FIR) – Karl Frank' no. 6, 7 Jul. 1945, OSS 138456, RG 226, NA; and Tauber, *The Eagle and the Swastika*, vol. 1, 23–4. Prützmann's family was also evacuated into the Salzburg area in early Apr.

176 Rose, *Werwolf*, 326–8; and Trees and Whiting, *Unternehmen Karnival*, 275.

177 ACA Intelligence Organisation 'Joint Weekly Intelligence Summary' no. 16, 27 Oct. 1945, FO 1007/300, PRO; and Birn, *Die Höheren SS- und Polizeiführer*, 338–9. For the break-out of Reinefarth's 'Battle Group' from Küstrin, see Körner to Bormann, 5 Apr. 1945, Biographical Records, Microcopy T-580, Reel 78; W. Pahl 'Bericht über die lezten Monate von und um Küstrin,' Ost Dok. 8/713, BA; J. Huir 'Einsatz des Volkssturmbatt. Küstrin,' 4 Oct. 1954, Ost Dok. 8/710, BA; and Christopher Duffy, *Red Storm on the Reich* (New York 1991), 247.

178 V Corps 'Weekly Intelligence Summary' no. 7, 30 Aug. 1945, FO 1007/299, PRO.

179 Prokhopenko to Smirnov, 1 Oct. 1945, *Pogranichnye Voiska SSSR Mai, 1945–1950*, 140–1.

180 SHAEF ACoS G-2 'Minutes of a Secret Discussion of the Wehrwolf Untergruppe VII a, Section 4e,' 28 May 1945, IRR File XE 049 888 'Werewolf Activities Vol. I,' RG 319, NA. German officers told Allied interrogators 'that guerrillas were ordered to remain quiet for a few months after the German collapse and then go into action.' A Werwolf officer captured by the French in the Black Forest claimed that it would take the Werwolf three years 'to become active on a large scale': *The*

Washington Post, 1 Jul. 1945; and German Directorate 'Weekly Intelligence Summary' no. 38, 23 Jul. 1945, OSS 142218, RG 226, NA.

181 Interrogation Report no. 5 'Werwolf Organization in Bayern,' OSS XL 11218, RG 226, NA.

182 *Neue Zürcher Zeitung*, 30 May 1945; and Intelligence Report, Intelligence Division, Office of Chief of Naval Operations, 25 Jun. 1945, OSS XL 12705, RG 226, NA.

183 USFET 'Weekly Intelligence Summary' no. 58, 22 Aug. 1946, State Dept. Decimal File 1945–9, 740. 00119 Control (Germany), RG 59, NA.

184 USFET 'Weekly Intelligence Summary' no. 74, 12 Dec. 1946, State Dept. Decimal File 1945–9, 740.00119 Control (Germany), RG 59, NA.

185 Interview with R. Jussenhofen, 30 Dec. 1991.

186 Tauber, *The Eagle and the Swastika*, vol. 1, 404–5. For details on various bombings in Nuremberg in 1947–8, all involving similar devices and possibly connected to Zitzmann's detachment, see Constabulary G-2, 'Weekly Intelligence Summary' no. 31, 11 Jan. 1947, Annex no. 1; no. 86, 26 Jan. 1948, Annex no. 1, both in WWII Operations Reports 1940–8, RG 407, NA; USFET 'Weekly Intelligence Summary' no. 81, 30 Jan. 1947; Eucom 'Intelligence Summary' no. 1, 13 Feb. 1947; no. 2, 27 Feb. 1947; no. 5, 14 Apr. 1947; no. 21, 18 Nov. 1947; USFET 'Theatre Commander's Weekly Staff Conference' no. 2, 14 Jan. 1947; no. 5, 4 Feb. 1947; no. 6, 11 Feb. 1947, all in State Dept. Decimal File 1945–9, 740.00119 Control (Germany), RG 59, NA; *The New York Times*, 2 Feb, 3 Feb, 28 Mar; and 21 Apr. 1947; *The Times*, 3 Feb. 1947; *The Stars and Stripes*, 9 Jan, 3 Feb, and 5 Feb. 1947; British Consulate, Munich, 'Political and Economic Reports' no. 3, Jan.–Mar. 1947, FO 371/64272, PRO; and FORD 'Digest for Germany and Austria' no. 704, 27 Jan 1948, FO 371/70791, PRO.

187 Vietzen, *Chronik der Stadt*, 36; *FO Weekly Political Intelligence Summaries* 11, Summary no. 298, 20 Jun. 1945; *History of the Counter Intelligence Corps*, vol. 26, 13, 74, NA; ACA (BE) Intelligence Organization 'Joint Weekly Intelligence Summary' no. 21, 1 Dec. 1945, and no. 28, 2 Feb. 1946, both in FO 1007/300, PRO; ACA(BE) Intelligence Organization 'Joint Fortnightly Intelligence Summary' no. 21, 30 Nov. 1946, FO 1007/301, PRO; CCG (BE) 'Intelligence Bulletin' no. 7, 28 Feb. 1946, and no. 13, 24 May 1946, both in FO 1005/1701, PRO; *The Stars and Stripes*, 16 Jan. 1946; *Neue Zürcher Zeitung*, 14 Jun. 1945; *The Manchester Guardian*, 14 Jun. 1945; USFET 'Weekly Intelligence Summary' no. 22, 13 Dec. 1945; no. 24, 27 Dec. 1945; no. 26, 1 Jan. 1946; no. 30, 7 Feb. 1946; no. 31, 14 Feb. 1946; no. 45, 23 May 1946; no. 50, 27 Jun. 1946; no. 62, 19 Sep. 1946; USFET MG Office 'Bi-Weekly Political Summary' no. 4, 15 Oct. 1945, all in State Dept. Decimal File 1945–9, 740.00119 Control (Germany), RG 59, NA; US Constabulary 'Weekly Intelligence Summary' no. 96, 5 Apr. 1948 Annex no. 1, WWII Operations

Reports 1940–8, RG 407, NA; Office of British Naval Commander-in-Chief, Germany, 'Periodical Security Report,' Jan. 1946, ETO MIS-Y-Sect., Miscellaneous Interrogation Records, 1944–6, RG 332, NA; and ECAD 'General Intelligence Bulletin' no. 46, 1 Jun. 1945, WO 219/3760A, PRO.

188 USFET G-5 'Bi-Weekly Political Summary' no. 3, 29 Sep. 1945, OSS XL 20917, RG 226, NA; *Le Monde*, 19 Sep. 1945; *L'Aurore*, 2 Sep. 1945; MI-14 'Mitropa' no. 4, 8 Sep. 1945, FO 371/46967, PRO; U.S. Fifteenth Army G-2 'Periodic Report' no. 60, 4 Jul. 1945, OSS XL 12362, RG 226, NA; and *The Christian Science Monitor*, 22 Dec. 1945.

189 USFET G-2 'Weekly Intelligence Summary' no. 16, 1 Nov. 1945, State Dept. Decimal File 1945–9, 740.00119 Control (Germany), RG 59, NA.

190 For the crash of Montgomery's plane, see Kirby, *1100 Miles with Montgomery*, 169. For the Aurich case, see MI-14 'Mitropa' no. 5, 22 Sep. 1945, FO 371/46967, PRO. For the Hartshorne murder, see James Tent, *Mission on the Rhine: Reeducation and Denazification in American Occupied Germany* (Chicago 1982), 80–1, 95, 97–8; *The New York Times*, 1 Sep. and 6 Sep. 1946; *The Washington Post*, 4 Sep. and 5 Sep. 1946; USFET G-2 'Weekly Intelligence Summary' no. 63, 26 Sep. 1946, State Dept. Decimal File 1945–9, 740.00119 Control (Germany), RG 59, NA; Peter Merkyl, review of Tent's *Mission on the Rhine*, *The Political Science Quarterly* 99/1 (Spring 1984), 169–70; and Gordon Argyle, 'Banishing the Past: The Failure of US Denazification and Reeducation Policies,' MA thesis, University of Victoria, 1996, 96–7.

191 *History of the Fifteenth United States Army, 21 August 1944 to 11 Jul. 1945* (Bad Neuenahr 1945), 72; ECAD 'General Intelligence Bulletin' no. 46, 1 Jun. 1945, WO 219/3760A, PRO; *The Stars and Stripes*, 28 Jan. 1946; *Neue Zürcher Zeitung*, 29 May 1945; Cookridge, *Gehlen*, 100; and 250 British Liaison Mission Report no. 7, Apr. 1947, FO 371/64350, PRO. For the sentencing of a Werewolf to death in the spring of 1946, see *The Times*, 10 Apr. 1946.

192 *History of the XVI Corps*, 79.

193 *The Stars and Stripes*, 25 Jul., 30 Jul., and 4 Aug. 1945; *The Times*, 28 Jul. 1945; *The Manchester Guardian*, 28 Jul. 1945; SHAEF JIC (45) 'Political Intelligence Report,' 9 Jul. 1945, *Documents on British Policy Overseas* Series I, vol. 1, 97; GSI British Troops Austria 'Joint Weekly Intelligence Summary' no. 8, Part I, 24 Aug. 1945, FO 371/46612, PRO; and *The Globe and Mail*, 28 Jul. 1945.

194 Whiting, *Hitler's Werewolves*, 189; Lucas, *Kommando*, 333; and Hans Fritsche, *The Sword in the Scales* (London 1953), 304.

195 *Pogranichnye Voiska SSSR Mai, 1945–1950*, 699.

196 Murawski, *Die Eroberung Pommerns durch die Rote Armee*, 38.

197 6 SFSS HQ V Corps 'Notes on the Political Situation in Carinthia and Western Styria, May 1945'; 22 May 1945, FO 371/46610, PRO; Reg Hershy, *Freedom at*

Midnight (Upton upon Severn 1989), 144; and Rozkhov to Pavlov, 1 Jul. 1945, *Pogranichnye Voiska SSSR Mai, 1945–1950*, 89–90.

198 British Troops Austria 'Joint Weekly Intelligence Summary' no. 10, 7 Sept 1945, FO 1007/300, PRO; MI-14 'Mitropa' no. 4, 8 Sep. 1945; and no. 5, 22 Sep. 1945, both in FO 371/46967, PRO. An NKVD officer reported in August 1945 that isolated SS and Volkssturm detachments were still active in Vienna, where they were responsible for 'individual cases of hostility displayed against the Soviet Union and the Red Army': Smirnov, Report of 25 Aug. 1945, *Pogranichnye Voiska SSSR Mai, 1945–1950*, 128.

199 Naimark, *The Russians in Germany*, 376–80, 382–5, 395–6, 558; Puchev to Tselikov, 13 Aug. 1945; Gavrikov to Izugenev, 15 Aug. 1945; Prokhopenko to Smirnov, 1 Oct. 1945; Antonyuk to Zimin, 9 Mar. 1946; 10 May 1946; Antonyuk to Abyzov, 10 Apr. 1946; Morozov to Blyumin, 1 Jan. 1947, all in *Pogranichnye Voiska SSSR Mai, 1945–1950*, 124–5, 128–9, 140, 157, 162, 164, 166–7; *The Stars and Stripes*, 14 Jan. 1946; and *The New York Times*, 23 Nov. 1946. For internment camps in the Soviet Zone, see Wember, *Umerziehung im Lager*, 89–91; and Naimark, *The Russians in Germany*, 246, 381, 386, 557.

200 Report by Polkovnik Antonyuk, 12 Mar. 1946, *Pogranichnye Voiska SSSR Mai, 1945–1950*, 157; Jan Misztal, 'Działalności Propagandowa Podziemia Poniemieckiego na Śląsku Opolskim w Latach, 1945–1949,' 52, 55–63; ... *By Inni Mogli Żyč Spokojne*, 26–9, 45–53; *Encyclopedia of the Holocaust*, 1645; USFET 'Weekly Intelligence Summary' no. 64, 3 Oct. 1946, State Dept. Decimal File 1945–9, 740.00119 Control (Germany), RG 59, NA; and Arthur Dickens, *Lübeck Diary* (London 1948), 217–19.

201 Drška, *Československá Armáda v Národní a Demokratické Revoluci*, 65.

202 Gołąbek and Tryc, 'Z Genezy Powstania i Działalności Werwolfu,' 139. As early as January 1945, a party expert on the Werwolf advised the SS to recruit 'reliable National Socialists who were former members of the KPD or the *Rotfront*,' and he suggested that these people be infiltrated into 'illegal *Grossdeutschland* groups. These groups must attempt direct contact with Bolshevik groups or with Seydlitz units,': Dotzler 'Vorschläge zum Aufbau einer Widerstandsbewegung in den von den Bolschewisten besetzten deutschen Ostgebieten,' 23 Jan. 1945, NS 19/832, BA. For Soviet suspicions of 'Antifa' groups, see Wolfgang Leonhard, *Child of the Revolution* (London 1957), 318–19; and Ernst-Joachim Krüger, 'Zur Arbeit der Initiativgruppe Sobottka in Mecklenburg unter besonderer Berücksichtigung ihrer Hilfe für die Kommunisten und andrere Antifaschisten in Greifswald in den ersten Wochen nach der Befreiung vom faschistischen Joch (Mai 1945),' *Wissenschaftliche Zeitschrift der Ernst-Moritz-Arndt-Universität Greifswald*, 13/112 (1964), 106–7.

203 V Corps 'Weekly Intelligence Summary' no. 5, 10 Aug. 1945; no. 6, 17 Aug. 1945, both in FO 1007/299, PRO.

204 Gorbatovski to Korchagin, 5 May 1946, *Pogranichnye Voiska SSSR Mai, 1945–1950*, 161.

205 FORD 'Digest for Germany and Austria' no. 693, 10 Jan. 1948, FO 371/70791, PRO.

206 Report by General-Maior Zubarev, 8 Apr. 1945, *Pogranichnye Voiska v Velikoi Otechestvennoi Voine, 1942–1945*, 554–5.

207 Gołąbek and Tryc, 'Z Genezy Powstania i Działalności Werwolfu,' 140–1.

208 ACA (BE) Intelligence Organisation 'Joint Weekly Intelligence Summary' no. 27, 19 Jan. 1946, FO 1007/30, PRO.

209 15 Schleswig-Holstein Intelligence Office Monthly Summary, Dec. 1947, Part II, FO 371/70613A, PRO.

210 Antonyuk to Zimin, 9 Mar. 1946; Gorbatovski to Korchagin, 5 May 1946; Morozov to Blyumin, 1 Jan. 1947, all in *Pogranichnye Voiska SSSR Mai, 1945–1950*, 157, 162, 166; and Cookridge, *Gehlen*, 101, 106, 152–3.

211 Chuikov, *The End of the Third Reich*, 187; Sig. illegible, 'Kockendorf,' 13 Apr. 1953, Ost Dok. 2/1, BA; Lucas, *Kommando*, 331; *The Washington Post*, 8 May 1945; and Pastor Weichert 'An der grossen und kleinen Brennpunkten der Schlesischen Kirche vom 25.5.1943 bis 31.12.1946,' Ost Dok. 2/177, BA. For the necessity of stationing strong Red Army guard detachments in the rear, see *The Christian Science Monitor*, 12 Feb. 1945; and Lt.-Gen Ludnikov 'Befehl für den Truppen der 39. Armee' no. 05/011 (Germ. transl.), 6 Feb., Records of OKW, Microcopy no. T-78, Roll 488, frames 6474409–6474410, NA. For Soviet efforts to scour forests in the rear, see SD Report 'Verhalten der Sowjets in den von ihnen besetzten Gebeiten des Gaues Mark Brandenburg,' 20 Feb. 1945; and 'Auszug aus Schilderungen des Meisters d. Gen. d. Friedrich Riekeheer – Verhaltnisse hinter des Sowj. Front,' 11 Mar. 1945, both in RH 2/2129, BA.

212 FAK officers inspecting a Werwolf unit on the Eastern Front specifically complained about the lack of mobility, and they advised using motorcycles for reconnaissance and communications: Leitstelle II Ost für Frontaufklärung to OKH/Fremde Heere Ost, 20 Mar. 1945, Records of OKH, Microcopy no. T-78, Reel 565, frame 915, NA.

213 Col. F.O. Miksche, quoted in Ladislas Farago, *Spymaster* (New York 1962), 192–3.

2: A Nursery Tale

1 Whiting, *Hitler's Werewolves*, 4–5, 80–7, 103–10; and Hasenclever, *Ihr Werdet Deutschland nicht wiederkennen*, 86.

2 Holzträger, *Der Wehrertüchtigunslager*, 14–20, 25–35, 43–73; Hans Christian Brandenburg, *Die Geschichte der HJ* (Köln 1982), 228–31; H.W. Koch, *The Hitler Youth* (New York 1976), 232–4, 236, 239–41, 243–4; Rempel, *Hitler's Children*, 36, 41,

63–5, 76, 177–204, 216–17; and *Jugend Contra Nationalsozialismus*, 71–4, 136–40. For questions over the legal status of HJ flak gunners, see Hans-Dietrich Nicolaisen, *Die Flakhelfer* (Berlin 1981), 183–7.

3 Jahnke, *Hitlers letztes Aufgebot*, 11–15, 44–72; Alfons Heck, *The Burden of Hitler's Legacy* (Frederick 1988), 153; ECAD 'General Intelligence Bulletin' no. 26, 13 Nov. 1944, WO 219/3761A, PRO; Allied Intelligence Report, *c.* May 1945, IRR File XE 049 888 'Werewolf Activities, Vol. I,' RG 319, NA; and *Justiz und NS-Verbrechen*, vol. 3, 415–18.

4 Jahnke, *Hitlers letztes Aufgebot*, 15–27, 78–173; Holzträger, *Der Wehrertüchtigungslager*, 93–102; Koch, *The Hitler Youth*, 248–51; Rempel, *Hitler's Children*, 235–43; Seidler, '*Deutscher Volkssturm*,' 65–6, 89; Brandenburg, *Die Geschichte der HJ*, 233; and Rose, *Werwolf*, 114.

5 PWE 'German Propaganda and the German,' 30 Apr. and 7 May 1945, both in FO 898/187, PRO; USFET MIS Center 'CI Intermediate Interrogation Report (CI-IIR) #24 – O/Gruf. Jürgen Stroop,' 10 Oct. 1945, OSS XL 22157, NA; Auerbach, 'Die Organisation des "Werwolf,"' 354; Twenty-first Army Group 'CI News Sheet' no. 10, Part I, WO 205/997, PRO; Extract from SHAEF Cable, 17 Feb. 1945; EDS Report no. 34 'Notes on the "Werewolves"'; USFET MIS Center 'Intermediate Interrogation Report (IIR) no. 18 – Krim. Rat. Stubaf. Ernst Wagner,' 30 Aug. 1945, all in IRR File XE 049 888 'Werewolf Activities Vol I,' RG 319, NA; Office of U.S. Chief Counsel, Evidence Div. Interrogation Br. 'Summary #789 – Hans Schweizer,' IWM; CSDIC/WEA BAOR 'Second Interim Report on SS Obergruf. Karl Gutenberger' IR 34, ETO MIS-Y-Sect. CSDIC/WEA Interim Interrogation Reports, 1945–6, RG 332, NA; BIMO 'Résumé traduction d'un document de l'I.S. Anglais en Suisse,' 29 Oct. 1945; État-Major Général de la Défense Nationale 'Note de Renseignements,' 2 May 1945; Direction des Services de Documentation Allemagne 'Note sur la formation de Werwolf,' 6 Jul. 1945, all in 7P 125, SHAT; Rose, *Werwolf*, 122, 135; Moczarski, *Conversations with an Executioner*, 241; Ultra Document BT 7004, 12 Mar. 1945, Ultra Document Collection, Reel 65; 'Report from Captured Personnel and Material Branch, MID, US War Dept.,' 9 May 1945, State Dept. Decimal File 1945–9, 740.00119 Control (Germany), RG 59, NA; CSDIC Misc. Interrogation Report 'Werwolf,' 27 Apr. 1945, ETO MIS-Y-Sect. CSDIC (UK) Special Interrogation Reports, 1943–5, RG 332, NA; von Lang, *Der Hitler-Junge*, 380; and Leitstelle II Ost für Frontaufklärung to OKH/Genst.d.H./Fremde Heere Ost, 20 Mar. 1945, Records of OKH, Microcopy no. T-78, frame 915, Reel 565, NA.

6 CSDIC WEA BAOR 'Final Report on Günter Haubold,' FR 94, 18 Sep. 1946, ETO MIS-Y-Sect. CSDIC/WEA Final Interrogation Records 1945–7, RG 332, NA; Etat-Major Général de la Defence Nationale 'Note de Renseignements,' 2 May 1945, 7P 125, SHAT; 'Report from Captured Personnel and Material Branch, MID, US War Dept.,' 9 May 1945, State Dept. Decimal File 1945–9, 740.00119 Control (Germany)

1945–9, 740.00119 Control (Germany), RG 59, NA; EDS Report no. 34 'Notes on the "Werewolves"'; Twenty-first Army Group extract from 'News Sheet no. 20'; USFET MIS Center 'Intermediate Interrogation Report (IIR) no. 18 – Krim. Rat. Stubaf. Ernst Wagner,' 30 Aug. 1945, all in IRR File XE 049 888 'Werewolf Activities Vol. I,' RG 319, NA; Rose, *Werwolf*, 122; *History of the Counter Intelligence Corps*, vol. 20, 37, NA; *The Christian Science Monitor*, 31 Mar. 1945; *The New York Times*, 1 Apr. 1945; Jahnke, *Hitlers letztes Aufgebot*, 25, 165–7; Kröner, 'Nahkampf-bataillon "Werwolf,"' 210, 213; and Hasenclever, *Ihr Werdet Deutschland nicht wiederkennen*, 86. For a faded set of instructions for HJ line-crossers, see 409/R58, BA. For the description of guerrilla-training materials found by advancing Canadian troops in a schoolhouse in Üdem, see Donald Pearce, *Journal of a War: Northwest Europe, 1944–1945* (Toronto 1965), 148–9.

7 *History of the Counter Intelligence Corps*, vol. 18, 14, 18, 20–1, 47, 56–7, 64, NA; *The Stars and Stripes*, 12 Jan. 1945; *Le Figaro*, 12 Jan. 1945; and Twenty-first Army Group 'CI News Sheet' no. 23, Jan. 1945, WO 205/997, PRO.

8 *History of the Counter Intelligence Corps* vol. 18, 95–7, 101–2, NA.

9 Ibid., vol. 19, 40, 67, 71–2, 84, 98, 108–9; 'After Action Report: Section II – Intelligence,' 31 Mar. 1945, *Covert Warfare* 12; *The Washington Post*, 19 Apr. 1945; and 13 Jun. 1945.

10 'Werwolf,' CSDIC (UK) Miscellaneous Interrogation Report, 27 Apr. 1945, ETO MIS-Y-Sect. CSDIC (UK) Special Interrogation Reports 1943–5, RG 332, NA; Rose, *Werwolf*, 121; *History of the Counter Intelligence Corps*, vol. 20, 64–5, NA; Sixth Army Group 'Resistance Organizations (Germany)' *c*. Jun. 1945, IRR File XE 049 888 'Werwolf Activities Vol. I,' RG 319, NA; Allied Intelligence Report, OSS 134 791, RG 226, NA; PWE 'German Propaganda and the German,' 7 May 1945, FO 898/187, PRO; and *The New York Times*, 4 Apr. 1945.

11 *History of the Counter Intelligence Corps*, vol. 20, 31–2.

12 *The Age* (Melbourne), 20 Apr. 1945; *The Daily Express*, 19 Apr. 1945; *Libération* (Paris), 19 Apr. 1945; *The Washington Post*, 20 Apr. 1945; and James de Coquet, *Nous sommes les occupants* (Paris 1945), 147.

13 *L'Aurore*, 12 Apr. 1945; George Moreton, *Doctor in Chains* (London 1970), 231–6; *History of the Counter Intelligence Corps* vol. 20, 74, NA; SHAEF G-5 'Weekly Journal of Information' vol. 9, 19 Apr. 1945, WO 219/3918, PRO; *The Christian Science Monitor*, 6 Apr. 1945; *The Daily Express*, 26 Mar. and 10 Apr. 1945; *The Daily Herald*, 9 Apr. 1945; and Laurence Byrnes, ed., *History of the 94th Infantry Division in World War Two* (Washington 1948), 480–1.

14 *The St Louis Post–Dispatch*, 27 Apr. 1945; *With the 102nd Infantry Division through Germany*, 218, 235, 241; and Marianne MacKinnon, *The Naked Years: Growing Up in Nazi Germany* (London 1987), 218–22.

15 M. Florheim 'Der Einmarsch der Russen in mein Heimatgebiet Forst/Lausitz im

Früjahr 1945 und die dort durchgeführten Kämpfe,' 11 Jan. 1956, Ost Dok. 8/711, BA; and *Völkischer Beobachter*, 25 Feb. 1945.

16 E. Schöpffer 'Der Kampf in Elbing,' Ost Dok. 8/247, BA; Gavrikov to Izugenev, 7 Apr. 1945, *Pogranichnye Voiska SSSR v Velikoi Otechestvennoi Voine, 1942–1945*, 557; *Völkischer Beobachter*, 9 Feb. (Munich) and 14 Mar. 1945. For confirmation that HJ units fought on in Hindenburg even after the German Army had evacuated the city and the Soviets had arrived, see Wolfgang Schwarz, *Die Flucht und Vertreibung Oberschlesien, 1945/46* (Bad Nauheim, 1965), 107.

17 'Report from Captured Personnel and Material Branch, Military Intelligence Division, U.S. War Department,' 9 May 1945, State Dept. Decimal Files 1945–9, 740.00119 Control (Germany), RG 59, NA.

18 Moczarski, *Conversations with an Executioner*, 243; CSDIC (UK) 'SS Hauptamt and the Waffen-SS,' 23 Aug. 1945, OSS 144337, RG 226, NA; Rose, *Werwolf*, 164–6; and USFET MIS Center 'CI Intermediate Interrogation Report (CI-IIR) #25 – O/Gruf. Juergen Stroop,' 10 Oct. 1945, OSS XL 22157, RG 226, NA.

19 CSDIC WEA BAOR 'Final Report on Günter Haubold,' FR 94, 18 Sep. 1946, ETO, MIS-Y-Sect. CSDIC/WEA Final Interrogation Records 1945–7, RG 332, NA; and *The Stars and Stripes*, 23 Oct. 1945.

20 Prokherenko to Smirnov, 6 Oct. 1945, *Pogranichnye Voiska SSSR Mai, 1945–1950*, 142–3.

21 Scholz, 'Fortuna ist ihr Name,' 65–8.

22 Von Lang, *Der Hitler-Junge*, 380; *The Daily Express*, 23 Mar. 1945; *The New York Times*, 26 Mar. 1945; PWE 'German Propaganda and the German,' 23 Apr. 1945, FO 898/187, PRO; 'Werwolf Movement,' IRR File XE 049 888 'Werewolf Activities Vol. I,' RG 319, NA; Ramsbotham to ACoS SHAEF G-2, 17 Apr. 1945; Robertson to McLeod, 2 Jun. 1945, both in WO 219/1602, PRO; Tauber, *The Eagle and the Swastika*, vol. 2, 1040–1; von Lang, *Bormann*, 315; and Derr to Klähn, 16 Mar. 1945, Biographical Records, Microcopy no. T-580, Reel 78, NA.

23 *History of the Counter Intelligence Corps*, vol. 20, 26, NA.

24 PWE 'German Propaganda and the German,' 23 Apr. 1945, FO 818/187, PRO.

25 Allied intelligence report, OSS XL 7836, RG 226, NA; *Völkischer Beobachter*, 27 Mar. 1945; Leo Heogh and Howard Doyle, *Timberland Tracks: The History of the 104th Infantry Division, 1942–1945* (Washington 1946), 318–19; Jahnke, *Hitlers letztes Aufgebot*, 166–7; and Koch, *The Hitler Youth*, 249. For the belief in late victory by some adolescents, see *Jugend unterm Schicksal*, 24–5, 205, 210, 216–17.

26 Hasenclever, *Ihr Werdet Deutschland nicht wiederkennen*, 27; interview with John Wietz, 26 Jul. 1993; Paul Carell and Günter Böddeker, *Die Gefangenen* (Ullstein 1990), 148, 155; Steinhoff, Pechel, and Showalter, *Voices from the Third Reich*, 490–1; Schenck, *Ich Sah Berlin Sterben*, 92; Nicolaisen, *Die Flakhelfer*, 186; *Die Nationalsozialistische Zeit (1933–1945) in Neuss*, 327; *The Washington Post*, 1 Sep.

1946; and Joel Agee, *Twelve Years: An American Boyhood in East Germany* (New York 1981), 59–60.

27 Ogmore, 'A Journey to Berlin, 1944–45 – Part II,' 88–9; and Fayard, 'L'Allemagne sous la Croix de Lorraine,' 72.

28 PWE 'German Propaganda and the German,' 30 Apr. 1945, FO 898/187, PRO.

29 *History of the Counter Intelligence Corps*, vol. 20, 18, 134, NA; *The New York Times*, 15 Apr. 1945; Kirby, *1100 Miles with Monty*, 108; and Kröner, 'Nahkampfbataillon "Werwolf"'; 221–12.

30 SHAEF PWD Intelligence Sect. 'A Volkssturm Company Commander,' 15 Mar. 1945, OSS 120243, RG 226, NA; Blumenstock, *Der Einmarsch der Amerikaner und Franzosen im Nordlichen Württemberg im April 1945*, 31–2; Henke, *Die amerikanische Besetzung Deutschlands*, 837; Brückner, 'Als der Rote Turm brannte,' 99; *Justiz und NS-Verbrechen*, vol. 13, 359–72; and sig. illegible, 'Beiblatt zu Erhebungsbogen,' Ost Dok. 2/264, BA.

31 PWE 'German Propaganda and the German,' 30 Apr. 1945, FO 898/187, PRO; and EDS Report no. 34 'Notes on the "Werewolves,"' IRR File XE 049 888 'Werewolf Activities Vol. I,' RG 319, NA.

32 Ogmore, 'A Journey to Berlin, 1944–1945 – Part I,' 30; SHAEF G-5 'Weekly Journal of Information' no. 9, 19 Apr. 1945, WO 219/3918, PRO; *The Daily Express*, 19 Apr. 1945; Bornemann, *Die letzten Tage in der Festung Harz*, 92; Hasenclever, *Ihr Werdet Deutschland nicht wiederkennen*, 86–7; Henke, *Die amerikanische Besetzung Deutschlands*, 163–9; and *Le Figaro*, 12 Jan. 1945.

33 Joachim Fest, *The Face of the Third Reich* (London 1970), 233.

34 Aurel Ende, 'Battering and Neglect: Children in Germany, 1860–1978,' *The Journal of Psychohistory* 7/3 (Winter 1979–80), 266; and Christian Büttner, *Kriegsängste bei Kindern* (Munich 1982).

35 Twenty-first Army Group 'Weekly Political Intelligence Summary' no. 9, 1 Sep. 1945, FO 371/46934, PRO; Daniel Horn, 'Youth Resistance in the Third Reich: A Social Portrait,' *The Journal of Social History* 7/1 (Fall 1973), 31; *The St Louis Post–Dispatch*, 9 Apr. 1945; *Völkischer Beobachter*, 27 Mar. 1945; OSS Det. (Main) 'R & A Interviews with Friendly Prisoners of War,' 15 Jan. 1945, OSS XL 5580, RG 226, NA; Paul Kecskemeti and Nathan Leites, 'Some Psychological Hypotheses on Nazi Germany: I,' *The Journal of Social Psychology* 26 (1947), 177; Alexander Mitscherlich, *Society without the Father* (London 1969), 142–3, 277–88; and Eric Hoffer, *The True Believer* (New York 1951), 31–2. For examples of youthful psychological confusion at the time of the German collapse, see *Jugend unterm Schicksal*, 22, 28, 147.

36 *Neue Zürcher Zeitung*, 29 May 1945; *Journal de Genève*, 25 May 1945; *Le Monde*, 29 May 1945; *The Stars and Stripes*, 27 May 1945; Vietzen, *Chronik der Stadt Stuttgart*, 36; *History of the Counter Intelligence Corps*, vol. 26, 87–8, NA; *The*

Times, 9 Feb. 1946; USFET G-2 'Weekly Intelligence Summary' no. 30, 7 Feb. 1946; no. 32, 21 Feb. 1946; Office of MG for Greater Hesse, 'Weekly Military Government Summary' no .32, 18 May 1946, all in State Dept. Decimal Files 1945–9, 740.00119 Control (Germany), RG 59, NA; *The Manchester Guardian*, 4 Sep. 1945; and *The New York Times*, 25 Jul. 1945.

37 *History of the Counter Intelligence Corps*, vol. 26, 74, NA; and USFET G-2 'Weekly Intelligence Summary' no. 2, 24 Jul. 1945, State Dept. Decimal File 1945–9, 740.00119 Control (Germany), RG 59, NA.

38 Interview with John Weitz, 26 Jul. 1993; Anthony Cave Brown, *The Last Hero: Wild Bill Donovan* (New York 1982), 769–70; and Larry Adler, *It Ain't Necessarily So* (London 1984), 7–9.

39 USFET G-2 'Weekly Intelligence Summary' no. 14, 18 Oct. 1945, State Dept. Decimal File 1945–9, 740.00119 Control (Germany), RG 59, NA. See also General McNarney's comments in *The Stars and Stripes*, 10 Apr. 1946.

40 Filin to Chirkov, 28 Apr. 1946; Morozov to Blyumin, 1 Jan. 1947, both in *Pogranichnye Voiska SSSR Mai, 1945–1950*, 161, 165–6; and *The New York Times*, 8 Jul. 1945.

41 USFET G-2 'Weekly Intelligence Summary' no. 33, 28 Feb. 1946, State Dept. Decimal File 1945–9, 740.00119 Control (Germany), RG 59, NA; CCG (BE) 'Intelligence Review' no. 13, Oct. 1946, FO 100/1700, PRO; CSDIC (WEA) BAOR 'Report on Nursery' SIR 28, 18 Apr. 1946, ETO MIS-Y-Sect. Intelligence and Interrogation Records, 1945–6, RG 332, NA; and USFET MIS Center 'Intermediate Interrogation Report (IIR) #18 – Krim. Rat. Stubaf. Wagner,' 30 Aug. 1945, IRR File 049 888 'Werewolf Activities Vol. I,' RG 319, NA; and Moczarski, *Conversations with an Executioner*, 243–4.

42 Tauber, *The Eagle and the Swastika*, vol. 2, 1040–1; Werner Brockdorff, *Flucht vor Nürnberg* (Wels 1969), 12; and Rose, *Werwolf*, 109. An underground movement, headed by Griesmayr, was still in existence in 1947: HQ U.S. Forces Austria 'Intelligence Summary' no. 155, 28 May 1948, FO 371/70402, PRO.

43 For the testimony of HJ leaders who ran the gamut and reached the Alps during the final days of the war, see Maschmann, *Account Rendered*, 167–8, and Kästner, *Notabene 45*, 94. Some abandoned children headed south because they regarded the mountains as a safe place to hide from the Soviets and the Western Allies: Charlotte Kahn, 'The Different Ways of Being a German,' *The Journal of Psychohistory* 20/4 (Spring 1993), 384.

44 USFET MIS Center 'Intermediate Interrogation Report (IIR) no. 18 – Krim. Rat. Stubaf. Wagner,' 30 Aug. 1945, IRR File 049 888 'Werewolf Activities Vol. I,' RG 319, NA; Maschmann, *Account Rendered*, 169; and Ernst von Salomon, *Fragebogen* (New York 1955), 397–8.

45 USFET Interrogation Center 'Intermediate Interrogation Report (IIR) #5 – O/Gruf.

Friedrich K. von Eberstein,' 27 Jul. 1945, OSS XL 13016, RG 226, NA; and USFET MIS Center 'CI Intermediate Interrogation Report (CI-IIR) #24 – O/Gruf. J. Stroop,' 10 Oct. 1945, OSS XL 22157, RG 226, NA; and Memo for the Commanding Officer, Garmisch Sub-Region, HQ CIC Region IV, 10 Sep. 1946, IRR File XE 049 888 'Werewolf Activities Vol. I,' RG 319, NA.

46 2677th Regt. OSS (Prov.) Det. 'A' 'The Werwolf Organization(s), Salzburg Area,' 16 Jul. 1945, IRR File XE 049 888 'Werewolf Activities Vol. I,' RG 319, NA; 6 SFSS HQ V Corps 'Notes on the Political Situation in Carinthia and Western Styria,' May 1945,' 22 May 1945, FO 371/46610, PRO; and Ultra Document KO 476, 15 Apr. 1945, Ultra Document Collection, Reel 70. An HJ élite school at Rokitzan, in Bohemia-Moravia, was also ordered in late Apr. to fight its way to Upper Bavaria: Ultra Document KO 1716, 30 Apr. 1945, Ultra Document Collection, Reel 73.

47 Borth, *Nicht zu Jung zum Sterben*, 15–16, 55, 56–7, 130–211, 219–20, 231, 233, 264, 283–4, 294–5.

48 Ibid., 16, 212, 220–5, 235–46, 253–63, 266–82, 284–8, 301–6, 317; Lucas, *Kommando*, 319–20, 329–30; von Lang, *Der Hitler-Junge*, 395–6; and Ultra Document KO 1702, 30 Apr. 1945, Roll 73, Ultra Document Collection.

49 *Die Verhinderte Alpenfestung Berchtesgaden 1945*, 30; Von Salomon, *Fragebogen*, 334–5; 'CX Report,' 16 Jun. 1945, and CSDIC/CMF/SD 21 'The Werwolf Organisation,' 10 Jun. 1945, both in IRR File XE 049 888 'Werewolf Activities Vol. I,' RG 319, NA.

50 Lucas, *Last Days of the Reich*, 203, 205–6; Evelyn Le Chêne, *Mauthausen* (London 1971), 161; Turner and Jackson, *Destination Berchtesgaden*, 182; Dyer, *XII Corps*, 420; and Haupt, *Das Ende im Westen*, 176.

51 Borth, *Nicht zu Jung zum Sterben*, 289, 298.

52 Sussmann, Memo for the Commanding Officer, Garmisch Sub-Region, CIC Region IV, 10 Sep. 1946, IRR File 049 888 'Werewolf Activities Vol. I,' RG 319, NA; Pearson, *Enroute to the Redoubt*, vol. 3, 252; and *History of the Counter Intelligence Corps*, vol. 25, 18–19.

53 Trevor-Roper, *The Last Days of Hitler*, 245; *The New York Times*, 1 Apr. 1946; *The Stars and Stripes*, 1 Apr. 1946; USFET G-2 'Weekly Intelligence Summary' no. 33, 28 Feb. 1946, State Dept. Decimal File 1945–9, 740.00119 Control (Germany), RG 59, NA; CCG (BE) 'Intelligence Review' no. 13, Oct. 1946, FO 100/1700, PRO; and MI-14 'Mitropa' no. 19, 6 Apr. 1946, FO 371/55630, PRO.

54 CSDIC WEA BAOR 'Report on Nursery' SIR 28, 18 Apr. 1946, Appendix 'A,' and Appendix 'B,' ETO MIS-Y-Sect. Intelligence and Interrogation Records 1945–6, RG 332, NA; USFET G-2 'Weekly Intelligence Summary' no. 33, 28 Feb. 1946, State Dept. Decimal File 1945–9, 740.00119 Control (Germany), RG 59, NA; CCG (BE) 'Intelligence Review' no. 13, Oct. 1946, FO 100/1700, PRO; *The Stars and Stripes*,

31 Mar. 1946; *The New York Times*, 31 Mar. 1946; Brown, *The Last Hero*, 766–7; MI-14 'Mitropa' no. 18, 23 Mar. 1946, FO 371/55630, PRO; and *The Times*, 1 Apr. 1946.

55 CSDIC WEA BAOR 'Report on Nursery' SIR 28, 18 Apr. 1946, ETO MIS-Y-Sect. Intelligence and Interrogation Records 1945–6, RG 332, NA; *The Times*, 1 Apr. 1946; Brown, *The Last Hero*, 767; CCG (BE) 'Intelligence Review' no. 13, Oct. 1946, FO 100/1700, PRO; MI-14 'Mitropa' no. 18, 23 Mar. 1946, FO 371/55630, PRO; USFET G-2 'Weekly Intelligence Summary' no. 33, 28 Feb. 1946, State Dept. Decimal File 1945–9, 740.00119 Control (Germany), RG 59, NA; *The Stars and Stripes*, 31 Mar. and 1 Apr. 1946; and ACC Report for the Moscow Meeting of the CFM, Feb. 1947, Sect. II 'Denazification,' Part 9, British Zone Report, American Zone Report, FO 371/64352, PRO.

56 USFET G-2 'Weekly Intelligence Summary' no. 34, 7 March 1946, State Dept. Decimal File 1945–9, 740.00119 Control (Germany), RG 59, NA.

57 USFET G-2 'Weekly Intelligence Summary' no. 33, 28 Feb. 1946, State Dept. Decimal File 1945–9, 740.00119 Control (Germany), RG 59, NA; CCG (BE) 'Intelligence Review' no. 13, Oct. 1946, FO 100/1700, PRO; and CSDIC (WEA) BAOR, 'Report on Nursery' SIR 28, 18 Apr. 1946, ETO MIS-Y-Sect. Intelligence and Interrogation Records 1945–6, RG 332, NA.

58 CCG (BE) Intelligence Division 'Summary' no. 1, 8 Jul. 1946 and no. 12, 31 Dec. 1946, both in FO 1005/1702, PRO; CCG (BE) 'Intelligence Bulletin' no. 9, 28 March 1946; no. 10, 10 Apr. 1946; no. 12, 10 May 1946, all in FO 1005/1701, PRO; and MI-14 'Mitropa' no. 21, 7 May 1946, FO 371/55630, PRO.

59 *The New York Times*, 31 Mar. 1946, 1 Apr. and 2 Apr. 1945; *The Times*, 1 Apr. and 3 Apr. 1946; MI-14 'Mitropa' no. 18, 23 Mar. 1946, and no. 19, 6 Apr. 1946, both in FO 371 55630, PRO; von Lang, *Der Hitler-Junge*, 443–5; CCG (BE) 'Intelligence Review' no. 13, Oct. 1946, FO 100/1700, PRO; USFET G-2 'Weekly Intelligence Summary' no. 33, 28 Feb. 1946, and Eucom 'Intelligence Summary' no. 1, 13 Feb. 1947, both in State Dept. Decimal File 1945–9, 740.00119 Control (Germany), RG 59, NA; *The Stars and Stripes*, 31 Mar., 1 Apr., and 2 Apr. 1946; and Brown, *The Last Hero*, 767–70.

60 CCG (BE) Intelligence Division 'Summary' no. 9, 15 Nov. 1946, and no. 12, 31 Dec. 1946, both in FO 1005/1702, PRO.

61 'Monthly Report of the Military Governor, US Zone: Information Control' no. 10, 20 May 1946, FO 371/55665, PRO; *The New York Times*, 2 Apr. 1946; MI-14 'Mitropa' no. 23, 5 Jun. 1946, FO 371/55630, PRO; and CSDIC (WEA) BAOR 'Report on Nursery' SIR 28, 18 Apr. 1946, ETO MIS-Y-Sect. Intelligence and Interrogation Records 1945–6, RG 332, NA.

62 Walter Laqueur, *Young Germany* (London 1962); Peter Loewenberg, 'Psychological Origins of the Nazi Youth Cohort,' *The American Historical Review* 76/5 (Dec.

1971), 1457–1502; Richard Grunberger, *A Social History of the Third Reich* (Harmondsworth 1971); Peter Stachura, *Nazi Youth in the Weimar Republic* (Oxford 1975); and Rempel, *Hitler's Children.*

63 E.H. Erikson, quoted in Kecskemeti and Leites, 'Some Psychological Hypotheses on Nazi Germany: I,' 176.

64 *The Manchester Guardian*, 4 Sep. 1945; and Earl Beck, 'The Anti-Nazi "Swing Youth," 1942–1945,' *The Journal of Popular Culture* 19/3 (Winter 1985), 50–1.

65 *The Manchester Guardian*, 13 Apr. 1945.

66 CSDIC WEA BAOR 'Report on Nursery' SIR 28, 18 Apr. 1946, ETO MIS-Y-Sect. Intelligence and Interrogation Records 1945–6, RG 332, NA; and CSDIC WEA BAOR 'Final Report on Hauptgefolgschaftsführer Horst Voigt,' 15 Aug. 1946, ETO MIS-Y-Sect. CSDIC/WEA Final Interrogation Records, 1945–7, RG 332, NA.

67 Donald McGranahan and Morris Janowitz, 'Studies of German Youth,' *The Journal of Abnormal and Social Psychology* 41 (1946), 4–5.

68 *The Stars and Stripes*, 2 Apr. 1947.

69 Rempel, *Hitler's Children*, 203.

3: A Werwolf War

1 For the factors behind small-unit cohesiveness in the Wehrmacht, see Morris Janowitz and Edward Shils, 'Cohesion and Disintegration in the Wehrmacht in World War II,' in *Military Conflict: Essays in the Institutional Analysis of War and Peace* (Beverly Hills 1975); and Edward Shils, 'Primordial, Personal, Sacred and Civil Ties,' *The British Journal of Sociology* 8 (1957), 135–6. For an analysis that stresses the role of National Socialist ideology in German Army cohesiveness, see Omer Bartov, *Hitler's Soldiers* (New York 1991).

2 William McElwee, *History of the Argyll and Sutherland Highlanders, 2nd Battalion (Reconstituted) – European Campaign, 1944–45* (Edinburgh 1949), 185.

3 Steinhoff, Pechel, and Showalter, *Voices from the Third Reich*, 412–13; Lord Birdwood, *The Worcestershire Regiment, 1922–1950* (Aldershot 1952), 72; H. Essame, *The 43rd Wessex Division at War, 1944–1945* (London 1952), 182; *The Times*, 19 Sep. 1944; Direction Générale des Études et Recherche 'Rapport sur les Organisations des Partisans en Allemagne,' 23 Apr. 1945, 7P 125, SHAT; and PWE 'German Propaganda and the German,' 18 Feb. 1945, FO 898/187, PRO. For a description of an SS team sent behind American lines for four days in order to tap telephone lines, see *History of the Counter Intelligence Corps*, vol. 182, NA.

4 *The New York Times*, 22 Sep. 1944; *The Stars and Stripes*, 25 Sep. 1944; *The Washington Post*, 14 Sep. 1944; 23 Sep. 1945; *The Washington Post*, 12 Nov. 1944; PID 'News Digest' no. 1574, 10 Oct. 1944, Bramstedt Coll., BLPES; *From England to the Elbe: Troop B, US 113 Cavalry Reconnaissance Squadron* (1945), 6; *History of*

the 120th Infantry Regiment, 96; OSS 'European Political Report' RAL-3-33, 20 Oct. 1944, WO 219/3761A, PRO; and CAD Poster and covering letter to SHAEF, 18 Dec. 1944, CAD 250.1, RG 165, NA. For mention of 'dangerous SS *francs-tireurs*' encountered by a French-Canadian regiment while occupying Xanten, see Gerard March and, *Le Régiment de Maisonneuve vers la Victoire, 1944–1945* (Montreal 1980), 203–4. An SS sniper in civilian clothes was captured at Velfing, in Lorraine, and German snipers in civilian garb were also caught in the Geldern–Kevelaar area. Houses containing such snipers were downed by tank fire. In the Vosges, French North African troops encountered female auxiliaries who donned uniforms and sniped during the daytime and at night posed as civilians: Edward Cranz, *Ninety-Fifth Infantry Division – History, 1918–1946* (Atlanta); *The New York Times*, 4 Mar. 1945; and *Paris-Presse*, 19 Nov. 1944.

5 Gołąbek and Tryc, 'Z Genezy Powstania i Działalności Werwolfu,' 134. For an example of a favourable report about conditions in the Soviet rear, see 'Bericht des Rittmeisters v. Loeben von der 17. Panzerdivision über Verhaltnisse im feindbesetzen Hinterland,' 11 Mar. 1945, Records of OKH, Microcopy no. T-78, Roll 565, frame 804, NA

6 Maj. Percy Schramm, 'The Wehrmacht in the Last Days of the War (1 January–7 May 1945),' 454–5, in *World War II German Military Studies* vol. 2; Rose, *Werwolf*, 171–2; Murawski, *Conversations with an Executioner*, 38; Ultra Documents BT 5156, 19 Feb. 1945 (Reel 62), and BT 1789, 9 Jan. 1945 (Reel 57), both in Ultra Document Collection.

7 Ultra Document BT 7444, 17 Mar. 1945, Ultra Document Collection, Reel 65.

8 *Silesian Inferno*, 45–7.

9 Zolotvskii to Gavrikov, Jul. 1945, *Pogranichnye Voiska Mai, 1945–1950*, 113.

10 M. Florheim 'Der Einmarsch der Russen im mein Heimatgebiet Forst/Lausitz im Früjahr 1945 und die dort durchgeführten Kämpfe,' 11 Jan. 1956, Ost Dok. 8/711, BA; Lt. Stempel 'Tätigkeits- und Erfahrunsbericht,' 15 Mar. 1945, and Oblt. Gutjahr 'Einsatzbericht' no. 2, 15 Feb. 1945, both in Biographical Records, Microform no. T-580, Reel 78.

11 Schramm, 'The Wehrmacht in the Last Days of the War,' 455; and PWE 'German Propaganda and the German,' 12 Feb. 1945, FO 898/187, PRO.

12 Report by Gavrikov, Jul. 1945, *Pogranichnye Voiska SSSR v Velikoi Otechestvennoi Voine, 1942–1945*, 567.

13 Max Florheim 'Der Einmarsch der Russen im mein Heimatgebiet Forst/Lausitz im Früjahr 1945 und die durchgeführten Kämpfe,' 11 Jan. 1956, Ost Dok. 8/711, BA; and Pavel I. Batov, *V Pokhodakh i Boiakh* (Moscow 1974), 485.

14 Konev, *Year of Victory*, 23.

15 Siegfried Schug 'Bericht über die Kreise Stargard-Saatzig und Pyritz,' 12 Mar. 1954, Ost Dok. 8/637, BA; Gavrikov to Izugenev, 7 Apr. 1945, *Pogranichnye Voiska SSSR*

v Velikoi Otechestvennoi Voine, 1942–1945, 557; Jahn, *Pommersche Passion*, 89; and AK to Polish Government (London), 24 Mar. 1945, *Documents on Polish-Soviet Relations, 1939–1945*, vol. 2, 560.

16 *Völkischer Beobachter* (Munich), 25 Apr. and 26 Apr. 1945; Schramm, 'The Wehrmacht in the Last Days of the War,' 451; Seidler, *'Deutscher Volkssturm'*, 150–3; James Lucas, *War on the Eastern Front, 1941–1945* (London 1979), 23–7; Rose, *Werwolf*, 171–2, 202; Ultra Document BT 8169, 24 Mar. 1945, Ultra Document Collection, Reel 67; Helmuth Spaeter, ed., *Die Geschichte des Panzerkorps Grossdeutschland* (Duisberg–Ruhrort 1958), 287–9; Duffy, *Red Storm on the Reich*, 370; and Georg Gunter, *Letzter Lorbeer* (Darmstadt 1974), 187.

17 John Weeks, *Men against Tanks: A History of Anti-Tank Warfare* (New York 1975), 70, 73; Seidler, *'Deutscher Volkssturm,'* 145–7, 151, 321–2; and Duffy, *Red Storm on the Reich*, 369–70.

18 Roden Orde, *The Household Cavalry at War: Second Household Cavalry Regiment* (Aldershot 1953), 502.

19 Skorzeny, *La Guerre inconnue*, 364.

20 Oberst von Bonin, OKH OP. Abt./Fest., Memo 'Kampf in Rücken des Feindes,' 21 Nov. 1944, RH 2/1929, BMA.

21 Gołąbek and Tryc, 'Z Genezy Powstania i Działalności Werwolfu,' 134; Wenck, OKH to the Heeresgruppen and Armeen, 6 Feb. 1945, RH 2/19930, BMA; and Direction des Services de Documentation Allemagne 'Note sur la formation du Werwolf,' 6 Jul. 1945, IRR File XE 049 888 'Werewolf Activities Vol. I,' RG 319, NA. During this same period, the OKW published guidelines for the establishment of sabotage dumps for the use of commando groups or military units cut off in the enemy's rear: 'Richtlinien für die Anlage von S-Depots,' Records of OKW, Microcopy no. T-77, Roll 1441, frames 652–660, NA.

22 Sig. illegible, OKH Gen. Std. H/Ausb. Abt. (I) to OKW/WFSt., 6 Feb. 1945, RH 2/1523, BMA.

23 Memo from WFSt./Op.(H)/Ia to Chef WFSt., Stellv. Chef. OP(H), Ia, Ic, Qu, 28 Feb. 1945, RW 4/v.7022, BMA; Rose, *Werwolf*, 168–9; USFET MIS Center 'Intermediate Interrogation Report (IIR) – Ernst Wagner,' 30 Aug. 1945, IRR File XE 049 888 'Werewolf Activities Vol. I,' RG 319, NA; and USFET Interrogation Center 'Intermediate Interrogation Report (IIR) no. 6 – Walter Schimana,' 31 Jul. 1945, OSS 1422090, RG 226, NA.

24 'Transportation,' IPW-14, 28 Apr. 1945, IRR File XE 049 888 'Werewolf Activities Vol. I,' RG 319, NA; and USFET Interrogation Center 'Intermediate Interrogation Report (IRR) no. 5 – O/Gruf. Friedrich Karl von Eberstein,' 27 Jul. 1945, OSS XL 13016, RG 226, NA.

25 'Weekly Intelligence Summary' no. 42, 29 May 1945, IRR File XE 049 888 'Werewolf Activities Vol. I,' RG 319, NA.

26 PWE 'German Propaganda and the German,' 9 Apr. 1945, FO 898/187, PRO;
Mobile Field Interrogation Unit no. 1 'PW Intelligence Bulletin' no. 47, 13 Mar.
1945; Mobile Field Interrogation Unit no. 1 'PW Intelligence Bulletin' no. 1/48,
16 Mar. 1945, both in G-2 Int. Div. Captured Personnel and Material Branch Enemy
POW Interrogation File (MIS-Y), 1943–5, RG 165, NA; Mobile Field Interrogation
Unit no. 1 'PW Intelligence Bulletin' no. 1/51, 24 Mar. 1945, OSS 125027, RG 226,
NA; USFET Interrogation Center 'Final Interrogation Report (FIR) no. 11 – Obst.
Paul Krüger,' 31 Jul. 1945, XL 13775, RG 226, NA; SHAEF G-5 'Weekly Journal of
Information' no. 10, 26 Apr. 1945, WO 219/3918, PRO; OSS R&A 'European Polit-
ical Report' no. 14, II, 6 Apr. 1945, OSS XL 7262, RG 226, NA; CSDIC (UK)
'Interrogation Report,' 20 Apr. 1945; SHAEF Report 'Observations Concerning
Occupied Germany,' 5 May 1945, both in State Dept. Decimal Files 1945–9,
740.00119 Control (Germany), RG 599, NA; EDS Report no. 34 'Notes on the
"Werewolf"'; 'The Werewolf Movement,' IRR File XE 049 888 'Werewolf Activi-
ties Vol. I,' RG 319, NA; and Rose, Werwolf, 129, 167–8.
27 Oberst Kemmerich, Stabe Gen. d. Pi. u. Fest. im OKH, Staffel to Oberst Mayer-
Detring, Chef Op. Abt.-Wehrmachtfahrungstab, 1 Apr. 1945, RH 11 III/34,
BMA.
28 Ultra Documents BT 7004, 12 Mar. 1945 (Reel 65); and BT 7689, 19 Mar. 1945
(Reel 62), both in Ultra Document Collection.
29 History of the Counter Intelligence Corps, vol. 22, 84–5, NA; and Robert Hewitt,
Work Horse of the Western Front: The Story of the 30th Infantry Division (Washington 1946), 265.
30 Third Army G-2 Documents Sect., translations of captured Werwolf orders, 19 Apr.
1945, IRR File XE 049 888 'Werewolf Activities Vol. I,' RG 319, NA.
31 6 SFSS HQ V Corps 'Notes on the Political Situation in Carinthia and Western
Styria, May 1945,' 22 May 1945, FO 371/46610, PRO.
32 Lucas, Kommando, 329–30.
33 Twelfth Army Group Mobile Field Interrogation Unit no. 4, PW Intelligence Bulletin
no. 4/2, Annex 'Notes on Werwolf,' 7 May 1945, OSS OB 27836, RG 226, NA.
34 The New York Times, 23 Apr. 1945.
35 Direction des Services de Documentation Allemagne 'Note sur la formation du Werwolf,' 6 Jul. 1945; USFET MIS Center 'Intermediate Interrogation Report (IIR) no.
18 – Krim. Rat Stubaf. Ernst Wagner,' 30 Aug. 1945, both in IRR File XE 049 888
'Werewolf Activities Vol. I,' RG 319, NA; CSDIC WEA BAOR 'Second Interim
Report on SS Obergruf. Karl M. Gutenberger' IR 34, 1 Nov. 1945, OSS 123120, RG
226, NA; and Istoriya Velikoy Otechestvennoy Voyny Sovetskogo Soyuza, 1941–
1945, 6, 137.
36 Sig. illegible, Heerwesen-Abt. to FHO, 4 Apr. 1945, RH 13/v. 52, BMA.
37 ... By Inni Mogli Żyč Spokojne, 26–7; Encyclopedia of the Holocaust, vol. 4, 1645;
and The New York Times, 21 Apr. 1945.

38 Abt. Fremde Heere Ost (III F) 'Teilübersetzung – Der Kleinkrieg, Partisanentum und Sabotage von Drasow, 1931,' Records of OKH, Microcopy no. T-78, Roll 565, frames 835–839, NA.

39 General-major Gehlen, Abt. FHO 'Vortragsnotiz über zur Aktivierung der Frontaufklärung,' 25 Feb. 1945, RH 2/1930, BMA; Cookridge, *Gehlen*, 96–8, 152; Report by General-Major Gehlen, Generalstab des Heeres/Abt. FHO, Records of the Reich Leader of the SS and Chief of the German Police, Microcopy no. T-175, Roll 580, frames 1–8, NA; Gołąbek and Tryc, 'Z Genezy Powstania i Działalności Werwolfu,' 127–9; Höhne and Zolling, *The General Was a Spy*, 44, 47–8, 50; and Julius Mader, *Die Graue Hand* (Berlin 1960), 48–9.

40 Letter to the author from K. Schikorski, 23 Feb. 1992; Gehlen, *Der Dienst*, 126; 'Report on Interrogation of Walter Schellenberg, 27th Jun.–12th Jul. 1945,' ETO MIS-Y-Sect. Miscellaneous Intelligence and Interrogation Reports, 1945–6, RG 332, NA; and Gołąbek and Tryc, 'Z Genezy Powstania i Działalnósc Werwolfu,' 129.

41 ... *By Inni Mogli Żyč Spokojne*, 25–7; Gołąbek and Tryc, 'Z Genezy Powstania i Działalności Werwolfu,' 127, 130; Misztal, 'Działalnóść Propagandowa Podziemia Poniemieckiego na Śląsku Opolskim,' 57; MI-14 'Mitropa' no. 5, 22 Sep. 1945, FO 371/46967, PRO; and no. 12, 29 Dec. 1945, FO 371/55630, PRO. For the testimony of an eastward-bound East Prussian Volkssturm man who was arrested in August 1945 and accused by the NKVD of being a Werwolf, see F. Hermann, untitled report, 28 Oct. 1951, Ost Dok. 2/1, BA.

42 *The New York Times*, 28 Mar. 1945.

43 *Spearhead in the West: The Third Armoured Division, 1941–45* (Nashville 1980), 441–2; *A History of the 90th Division in World War II* (1945), 78; Sayward Farnum, *'The Five by Five': A History of the 555th Anti-Aircraft Automatic Weapons Battalion* (Boston 1946), 36–7; and *The Daily Herald*, 23 Apr. 1945.

44 P. de Tristan, First French Army 5th Bureau 'Monthly Historical Report,' 1 May 1945, WO 219/2587, PRO.

45 *The Washington Post*, 1 Apr. 1945; and Henry Metalmann, *Through Hell for Hitler* (Wellingborough 1990), 185. SHAEF also issued fliers to this same effect: *Die Letzten Hundert Tage* (Munich 1965), 117.

46 *The Washington Post*, 23 Apr. 1945; *With the 102d Infantry Division through Germany*, 190–200, and *Conquer*, 300.

47 Agnès Humbert, *Notre Guerre* (Paris 1946), 357–8, 361–3, 369–70, 373–4, 376, 378–80, 383–5.

48 *Journal de Genève*, 9 Apr. 1945; and Gen. Reinecke 'Schnelldienst' no. 31, 9 Apr. 1945, Biographical Records, Microcopy no. T-580, Reel 78.

49 Haupt, *Das Ende im Westen*, 135; and Schwarzwälder, *Bremen und Nordwestdeutschland am Kriegsende*, vol. 2, 81.

50 Gerhardt Boldt, *Die Letzten Tage der Reichskanzlei* (Reinbeck bei Hamburg 1964),

52–3; Ultra Document BT 9333, 3 Apr. 1945, Ultra Document Collection, reel 68; *XX Corps: Assault Crossing of the Rhine and into Germany* (1945), 9; *History of the Counter Intelligence Corps*, vol. 20, 16, 31–2, 64–5, NA; *Neue Zürcher Zeitung*, 19 Apr. 1945; U.S. Third Army, Office of ACoS G-2 'Interrogation Report' no. 2, 14 May 1945, OSS XL 11132, RG 226, NA; Extract from 'Weekly Intelligence Summary' no. 42, 29 May 1945, IRR File XE 049 888 'Werewolf Activities vol. I,' RG 319, NA; *Zwischen Befreiung und Besatzung*, 152; and Adolf Diamant, *Gestapo: Frankfurt am Main* (Franfurt am Main. 1988), 298.

51 MacDonald, *The Last Offensive*, 349–50; Dyer, *XII Corps*, 392–3; *The New York Times*, 4 Apr. and 20 Apr. 1945; *The Daily Herald*, 4 Apr. 1945; *The Fifth Infantry Division in the ETO*; *The Times*, 3 Apr., 4 Apr., and 20 Apr. 1945; *The St Louis Post–Dispatch*, 3 Apr., 5 Apr., and 10 Apr. 1945; Whiting, *Hitler's Werewolves*, 180–1; Nat Frankel and Larry Smith, *Patton's Best: An Informal History of the 4th Armoured Division* (New York 1978), 126–7; Kenneth Koyen, *The Fourth Armoured Division: From the Beach to Bavaria* (Munich 1946), 113; Ultra Documents KO 26, 10 Apr. 1946 (Reel 70); KO 654, 17 Apr. 1945 (Reel 71), both in Ultra Document Collection; *XX Corps* (Halstead 1984), 9; ECAD 'General Intelligence Bulletin' no. 44, 5 May 1945, WO 219/3760A, PRO; and Patton Diary, 308, in *David Irving, Papers Relating to the Allied High Command, 1943/45*, Reel no. 4.

52 *The Washington Post*, 23 Apr. 1945; *The St Louis Post–Dispatch*, 21 Apr. 1945; and *The Fifth Infantry Division in the ETO* (Vilshofen 1945).

53 'An Interview with Genobst. Alfred Jodl,' Enthint 52, 2 Aug. 1945, *World War II German Military Studies* 3; *The Fifth Infantry Division in the ETO*; Willy Timm, *Freikorps 'Sauerland,' 1944–1945* (Hagen 1976), 24; MacDonald, *The Last Offensive*, 369–70, 372; Charles Whiting, *Battle of the Ruhr Pocket* (New York 1970), 140, 145; William Manchester, *The Arms of Krupp, 1587–1968* (Boston 1968), 595, 603, 609–11; Haupt, *Das Ende im Westen*, 112–13; *History of the XVI Corps*, 76; Kösters, *Essen Stunde Null*, 107–8; and Reckitt, *Diary of Military Government in Germany*, 46.

54 Charles Whiting, *Patton's Last Battle* (New York 1990), 146–7; *History of the 120th Infantry Regiment*, 227; PID German/Austrian Intelligence 'Analysis of French Output to Germany, 25 May to 20 Jun. 1945,' FO 371/46728, PRO; and *The Daily Express*, 4 Apr. 1945. For postwar underground activity in a network of Luftwaffe hospitals in Carinthia, see GSI Eighth Army 'Joint Weekly Intelligence Summary' no. 3, 20 Jul. 1945, FO 371/46611, PRO.

55 Ultra Document BT 9227, 2 Apr. 1945, Ultra Document Collection, Reel 68.

56 *History of the East Lancashire Regiment in the War, 1939–1945* (Manchester 1953), 202.

57 Ultra Documents BT 9648, 6 Apr. 1945 (Reel 69); and KO 4, 10 Apr. 1945 (Reel 70), both in Ultra Document Collection.

58 George Blake, *Mountain and Flood: The History of the 52nd (Lowland) Division* (Glasgow 1950), 184, 186; *The Daily Express*, 5 Apr. 1945; *The St Louis Post–Dispatch*, 6 Apr. 1945; G.L. Verney, *The Desert Rats: The History of the 7th Armoured Division, 1938–1945* (London 1954), 272–3; Dudley Clarke, *The Eleventh at War: The Story of the XIth Hussars (Prince Albert's Own), 1934–1945* (London 1952), 451–2; David Russik, *The DLI at War: The History of the Durham Light Infantry, 1939–1945* (Durham c. 1954), 296–7; Augustus Muir, *The First of Foot: The History of the Royal Scots* (Edinburgh 1961), 414–15; R.J.B. Sellar, *The Fife and Forfar Yeomanry, 1919–1956* (Edinburgh 1960), 230–1; R.H.W.S. Hastings, *The Rifle Brigade in the Second World War, 1939–1945* (Aldershot 1950), 401, 406; and H.T.M. Durand and R.H.W.S. Hastings, *The London Rifle Brigade, 1919–1950* (Aldershot 1952), 277.

59 Hewitt, *Work Horse of the Western Front*, 254–7; *History of the 120th Infantry Regiment*, 219–25; and *Völkischer Beobachter*, 11 Apr. 1945.

60 Direction Générale des Études et Recherches 'Rapport sur les Organisations de Partisans en Allemagne,' 23 Apr. 1945, 7P 125, SHAT.

61 SHAEF G-2 'Weekly Intelligence Summary' no. 56, 15 Apr. 1945, Part I; Rose, *Werwolf*, 246–7; Blumenstock, *Der Einmarsch der Amerikaner und Franzosen im nordlichen Württemberg*, 32–3, 59–64, 67–71, 73–8; Henke, *Die amerikanische Besetzung Deutschlands*, 783–4; Lester Nichols, *Impact: The Battle Story of the Tenth Armoured Division* (New York 1954), 230–3; *The Seventh United States Army in France and Germany*, vol. 3, 787; *The Washington Post*, 9 Apr. 1945; and Haupt, *Das Ende im Westen*, 161–2.

62 Franz Kurowski, *Armee Wenck* (Neckargemund 1967), 31, 47–56, 96–100; Enemy Personnel Exploitation, Field Information Agency Technical CC (BE) 'Two Brief Discussions of German CW Policy with Albert Speer,' 12 Oct. 1945, OSS XL 22959, RG 226, NA; Whiting, *Battle of the Ruhr Pocket*, 130; *Conquer*, 306–8; Draper, *The 84th Infantry Division in the Battle of Germany*, 236–9; *With the 102d Infantry Division through Germany*, 211, 217–20, 235, 241; Binkoski and Plaut, *The 115th Infantry Regiment in World War II*, 328–31; Huston, *Biography of a Battalion*, 258–9; Zofia Kruk, *The Taste of Fear: A Polish Childhood in Germany, 1939–1946* (London 1973), 136–8; SHAEF G-2 'Weekly Intelligence Summary' no. 57, 22 Apr. 1945, Part I; *The New York Times*, 20 Apr., 22 Apr., and 23 Apr. 1945; *The St Louis Post–Dispatch*, 24 Apr. 1945; *The Daily Herald*, 20 Apr. 1945 'First US Army Diary (Courtney H. Hodges),' *David Irving, Papers Relating to the Allied High Command, 1943/45*, Reel 8; and *History of the Counter Intelligence Corps*, vol. 20, 68, NA. For the early strength of the NSDAP in Altmark, see Fenske, *Wahlrecht und Parteiensystem*, 270, 275.

63 Ultra Document KO 780, 19 Apr. 1945, Ultra Document Collection, Reel 72, and *The Daily Express*, 5 Apr. 1945.

64 *History of the Counter Intelligence Corps*, vol. 19, 57; vol. 16, NA; and *The Washington Post*, 24 Apr. 1945.

65 Ultra Document KO 387, 14 Apr. 1945, Ultra Document Collection, Reel 70; and Rose, *Werwolf*, 282.

66 Allied Intelligence Report, OSS OB 28993, RG 226, NA.

67 USFET Interrogation Center 'Final Interrogation Report (FIR) no. 11 – Obst. Paul Krueger,' 31 Jul. 1945, OSS XL 13775, RG 226, NA; SHAEF G-5 'Weekly Journal of Information' no. 13, 16 May 1945, WO 219/3918, PRO; Ultra Document KO 563, 16 Apr. 1945, Ultra Document Collection, Reel 71; and *History and Mission of the Counter Intelligence Corps in World War II*, 47.

68 *Fuehrer Conferences on Naval Affairs, 1939–1945* (London 1990), 484–5.

69 Butler and Young, *Marshal without Glory*, 247; and Kingsley Brown, Sr, Kingsley Brown, Jr, and Brereton Greenhaus, *Semper Paratus: The History of the Royal Hamilton Light Infantry (Wentworth Regiment), 1862–1977* (Hamilton 1977), 322–5.

70 Field Interrogation Report 'Lt. Erich von Hundt,' 21AG/Int/2428(116), 29 Apr. 1945, IRR File XE 049 888 'Werewolf Activities vol. I,' RG 319, NA. See also *Journal de Genève*, 2–3 Jun. 1945. For the experience of the 'von der Heydte' unit in the Ardennes, see Peter Elstob, *Hitler's Last Offensive* (New York 1971), 143–4; Milton Schuman, *Defeat in the West* (London 1986), 263; and Gen. von der Heydte 'German Paratroops in the Ardennes,' EThint 75, 31 Oct. 1945, *World War II German Military Studies* 3.

71 Ultra Documents KO 786, 11 Apr. 1945 (Reel 72); KO 919, 20 Apr. 1945 (Reel 71); KO 1139, 23 Apr. 1945 (Reel 72); KO 1255, 24 Apr. 1945 (Reel 73); KO 1349, 25 Apr. 1945 (Reel 72); KO 1351, 25 Apr. 1945 (Reel 72); KO 1860, 2 May 1945 (Reel 73); and KO 1877, 2 May 1945 (Reel 73), all in Ultra Document Collection. Air Force officers in southern Germany also used He 111s to provision some mountain huts on Gross-Glockner Mountain, with the eventual aim of housing resistant Luftwaffe personnel high in the hills: Karl Koller, *Der letzte Monat* (Mannheim 1949), 89–90.

72 Ultra Document KO 918, 20 Apr. 1945, Ultra Document Collection, Reel 71; and Dahl, *Rammjäger*, 205–8.

73 MID Report, 16 Sep. 1944, OSS L 45595, RG 226, NA; SHAEF G-5 'Weekly Intelligence Summary' no. 1, 22 Feb. 1945, WO 219/3918, PRO; ECAD 'General Intelligence Bulletin' no. 39, 12 Mar. 1945, WO 219/3513, PRO; DIC (MIS) Detailed Interrogation Report 'Opinions of Generalleutnant Schimpf,' 26 Mar. 1945, OSS 122312, RG 226, NA; SHAEF PWD Intelligence Sect. 'Consolidated Report on Reaction of 18 P/War on the "Werwolf,"' 16 Apr. 1945, WO 219/1602, PRO; PWE 'German Propaganda and the German' 9 Jun. 1945, FO 898/187, PRO; Twenty-first Army Group Int. 'Enemy Resistance Organisations,' 30 Apr. 1945, IRR File XE 049 888 'Werewolf Activities vol. I,' RG 319, NA; DIC (MIS) Detailed Interrogation Report 'Possibilities of Guerrilla Warfare in Germany as Seen by a Group of Seven-

teen German Generals,' 17 May 1945, OSS 130749, RG 226, NA; and Whiting, *Hitler's Werewolves*, 208.

74 Siegfried Westphal, *Erinnerungen* (Mainz 1975), 339.

75 SHAEF G-5 'Weekly Intelligence Summary' no. 1, 22 Feb. 1945, WO 219/3918, PRO; ECAD 'General Intelligence Bulletin' no. 39, 12 Mar. 1945, WO 219/3513; and DIC (MIS) Detailed Interrogation Report 'Possibilities of Guerrilla Warfare in Germany as Seen by a Group of Seventeen German Generals,' 17 May 1945, OSS 130749, RG 226, NA.

76 For the case of the 5th Infantry Regiment, a Pomeranian formation, see Murawski, *Die Eroberung Pommerns durch die Rote Armee*, 38.

77 Klaus von der Groeben 'Das Ende in Ostpreussen – der Ablauf des Geschehnisse im Samland (1944–45),' 1 Oct. 1952, Ost Dok. 8/531, NA; *Abwehrkämpfe am Nordflügel der Ostfront 1944–1945* (Stuttgart 1963), 389–90; Duffy, *Red Storm on the Reich*, 218–19, 372; and *Die Letzten Hundert Tage*, 156.

78 Twenty-first Army Group 'News Sheet' no. 14, Jan. 1945, WO 205/997, PRO; and G-2 Periodoc Report no. 152, Annex no. 4, OSS 114151, RG 226, NA.

79 Murawski, *Die Eroberung Pommerns durch die Rote Armee*, 38.

80 Hasso von Wedel, *Propagandatruppen der Deutschen Wehrmacht* (Neckargemund 1962), 151; and *The St Louis Post–Dispatch*, 9 Apr. 1945.

81 Trevor-Roper, *Hitler's Last Days*, 126–7; SHAEF G-2 'Interrogation of Albert Speer: Seventh Session 1st Jun. 1945 – Part Two,' FO 1031/141, PRO; and Speer, *Inside the Third Reich*, 626–7.

82 Martin van Creveld, *Fighting Power: German and U.S. Army Performance, 1939–1945* (Westport 1982), 45, 75–6.

83 Ultra Document KO 1215, 24 Apr. 1945, Ultra Document Collection, Reel 72.

84 *History of the Counter Intelligence Corps*, vol. 20, 146, NA; SHAEF G-2 'Weekly Intelligence Summary' no. 59, 6 May 1945, Part II, WO 219/5170, PRO; Sayer and Botting, *America's Secret Army*, 209; *The Daily Express*, 5 May 1945; Ultra Documents KO 1721, 30 Apr. 1945 (Reel 73); KO 1726, 30 Apr. 1945 (Reel 73); KO 1736, 30 Apr. (Reel 73); KO 1822 (1 May 1945); KO 1988, 4 May 1945 (Reel 73), all in Ultra Document Collection; and Dahl, *Rammjäger*,

85 Steinart, *Capitulation 1945*, 179; Görlitz, *Der Zweite Weltkrieg*, 577; Ultra Document KO 2082, 8 May 1945, Ultra Document Collection, Reel 73; and Schultz-Naumann, *Die Letzten dreissig Tage*, 89.

86 Rose, *Werwolf*, 97–9.

87 Gerald Reitlinger, *The SS: Alibi of a Nation* (London 1981), 445.

88 Wegener to Joel, 5 May 1945, Records of OKW, Microcopy no. T-77, Reel 864, frame 5611864, NA; and Joachim Schultz-Naumann, *Die Letzten dreissig Tage* (Munich 1980), 89. See also *FO Weekly Political Intelligence Summary* 11, Summary no. 292, 9 May 1945.

89 Walter Lüdde-Neurath, *Regierung Dönitz* (Leoni am Starnberger See 1980), 180.

90 Wegener's role in the final prohibition of Werwolf activity is difficult to determine. Although he claimed in the early 1950s that he had already prohibited guerrilla operations in North Germany, and then 'obtained' the same prohibition for the entire Reich, a mere three weeks earlier he had attempted to get some Volkssturm troopers to conduct a reign of terror in the southern part of his *Gau*, calling them 'Avengers of German Honour.' His deputy, Joel, had himself made a recent speech lauding 'tenacious resistance' and berating the Allies, and had attended a Werwolf organizational meeting in early May. As well, Wegener's 'Werwolf Commissar,' Fritz Lotto, told one his officers shortly *after* the capitulation that he should continue to follow orders and carry out commands, 'even if the Allied Occupation Troops shoot fifty German women in retaliation.' If Wegener did actually move to cancel Werwolf activity, which seems likely, he was clearly not in control of his *Gau* staff: *Justiz und NS-Verbrechen*, vol. 11, 107; vol. 3, 390–1; *The Daily Express*, 5 May 1945; and Appendix 'C' to 2 Cdn. Corps Sitrep, 7 Jun. 1945, IRR File XE 049 888 'Werewolf Activities vol. I,' RG 319, NA. For Wegener's position and responsibilities, see Steinart, *Capitulation 1945*, 127.

91 PWE 'Propaganda and the German,' 7 May 1945, FO 898/187, PRO; *The New York Times*, 6 May 1945; PID 'Background Notes,' 12 May 1945, FO 371/46790, PRO; Auerbach, 'Die Organisation des "Werwolf," ' 355; Whiting, *Hitler's Werewolves*, 190; and Padfield, *Dönitz*, 420.

92 Albert von Kesselring, *The Memoirs of Field-Marshal Kesselring* (London 1953), 290. See also ibid., 286, and Rose, *Werwolf*, 293–4. Hauser met with a number of HSSPF at Taxenbach on 7 May, where it was decided that Kesselring's surrender order would be obeyed: USFET MIS Center 'CI Intermediate Interrogation Report 24 – O/Gruf. J. Stroop,' 10 Oct. 1945, OSS XL 22157, RG 226, NA.

93 P. de Tristan, First French Army, 5th Bureau 'Monthly Historical Report,' 1 May 1945, WO 219/2587, PRO. Similarly, a Werwolf cache discovered in May 1945 by the staff of a Wehrmacht field hospital near Eutin was almost immediately reported to the British authorities, who dismantled it: CSDIC WEA BAOR 'Final Report on Gunter Haubold' FR 94, ETO MIS-Y-Sect. CSDIC/WEA Final Interrogation Records 1945–7, RG 332, NA.

94 'Administration and Military Government,' Report by British Second Army, Jun. 1945, WO 205/1084, PRO; and *The Manchester Guardian*, 19 May 1945. Two examples of the military's strict measures against sabotage and unrest: several Germans who fired upon members of the Norwegian Home Army on 22 May were later sentenced to death by a Wehrmacht military court at Trondheim; similarly, a German in Holland who accidentally blew up some gasoline containers after lighting a cigarette was shot on the spot by his own officer. Canadian officers were told: 'We mustn't run the risk of sabotage at this stage. We must make an example,': PID 'News Digest' no. 1770, 29 May 1945, Bramstedt Collection, BLPES; and *The Stars*

and Stripes, 20 May 1945. Thousands of armed Wehrmacht personnel were still responsible for security in over 1,000 square miles of northern Germany as late as the mid-summer of 1945: *The Age* (Melbourne), 31 Jul. 1945.

95 Arthur Smith, *Churchill's German Army* (Beverly Hills 1977), 68.

96 Müller, *Hitler's Justice,* 190; W. Wonderley and S.J. Arneson, Asst. Mil. Attachés, MID Military Attaché Report, Stockholm, 5 Jun. 1945, OSS XL 11965, NA; *Justiz und NS-Verbrechen,* vol. 5. 195–205, and vol. 10, 446–511.

97 Steinart, *Capitulation 1945,* 168.

98 *Borba Latyshskogo Naroda v Gody Velikoi, Otechestvennoi Voiny, 1941–1945* (Riga 1970), 903, 915–16; Steinart, *Capitulation 1945,* 182–3; Müller to Dönitz, 5 May 1945, Records of OKW, Microcopy no. T-77, Reel 864, frame 5611862; NA; Hilpert to Keitel, 6 May 1945, R62/18, BA; and Visvaldis Mangulis, *Latvia: In the Wars of the 20th Century* (Princeton 1983), 151–4. In late May, two Red Army men were shot by fugitive German officers: Carell and Böddeker, *Die Gefangenen,* 344.

99 Steinart, *Capitulation 1945,* 183–4; *The New York Times,* 19 May and 20 May 1945; *The Washington Post,* 19 May 1945; *Journal de Genève,* 19–20–21 May 1945; *The Manchester Guardian,* 17 May 18 May, 19 May, and 25 Jun. 1945; *The Daily Express,* 17 May and 19 May 1945. For Bornholm's role in German maritime evacuations, see Ultra Document KO 2043, 6 May 1945; and KO 2055, 6 May 1945, both in Ultra Document Collection.

100 Canadian First Army 'Intelligence Periodical' no. 1, 14 May 1945 (citing Twenty-first Army Group Review no. 189, 8 May 1945), WO 205/1072, PRO.

101 Ultra Document KO 15, 10 Apr. 1945; and KO 369, 13 Apr. 1945, both in Ultra Document Collection, Reel 70.

102 Steinart, *Capitulation 1945;* 280; *The St Louis Post–Dispatch,* 23 May 1945; and *The Age* (Melbourne), 23 Jun. 1945. An SD man, who had served in Spain during the war, later told the American CIC that he had personally carried money to Spain – around 15 million Goldmarks – as part of an effort by the military to preserve the core of an Army General Staff. Apparently, the military had long seen Germany's impending defeat, and had sought to bridge the period of enforced disarmament by building a structure that could ensure a sense of continuity in military thought and planning. This secret staff was also supposed to serve as a nucleus for future activity against the Russians: Hasenclever, *Ihr Werdet Deutschland nicht wiederkennen,* 96–7. A similar organization was formed by the Naval High Command in 1944, which was known in Germany under the code-name 'Caesar' and abroad under that of 'Siegfried': CCG(BE) 'Intellience Review' no. 5, 6 Feb. 1946, FO 371/55807, PRO.

103 Smith, *Churchill's German Army,* 89–125; ACA Intelligence Organization 'Joint Fortnightly Intelligence Summary' no. 11, 13 Jul. 1946, FO 1007/301, PRO; CCG (BE) 'Intelligence Division Summary' no. 6, 27 Sep. 1946, FO 1005/1702, PRO;

and Twenty-first Army Group 'CI News Sheet' no. 26, Part III, 30 Jul. 1945, WO 205/997, PRO.

4: Reign of Terror

1 Baird, 'La Campaign de propagande nazie en 1945,' 75.
2 Mommsen, 'National Socialism: Continuity and Change,' 204.
3 Rose, *Werwolf*, 25.
4 PWE 'German Propaganda and the German,' 3 Apr., 22 May, 28 May, 12 Jun., 26 Jun., 1944; 3 Jul., 10 Jul. 1944, all in FO 898/187, PRO; *The Times*, 31 Mar. 1944; OSS R & A no. 1934 'The Problem of the Nazi Underground,' 21 Aug. 1944, *OSS/ State Department Intelligence and Research Reports,* Micf. Roll XIII; and OSS R & A no. 1934.1 'The Clandestine Nazi Movement in Post-War Germany,' 13 Oct. 1944, *OSS/State Department Intelligence and Research Reports*, Micf. Roll XIV.
5 Seidler, *'Deutscher Volkssturm'*, 36–7, 42, 44–7; and U.S. First Army Interrogation Report Extract 'Lorenz's Opinions on the Occupation of Germany,' OSS XL 5732, RG 226, NA.
6 Seidler, *'Deutscher Volkssturm'*, 38–9; Hugh Trevor-Roper, ed., *Blitzkrieg to Defeat: Hitler's War Directives, 1939–1945* (New York 1971), 172, 179, 182–4; Heinz Guderian, *Panzer Leader* (New York 1967), 288; Kissel, *Der deutsche Volkssturm*, 16–19; and Henke, *Die amerikanische Besetzung Deutschlands*, 128–9.
7 Hüttenberger, *Die Gauleiter*, 162–5, and Seidler, *'Deutscher Volkssturm'*, 36–8, 42, 44–7, 54–5.
8 Kissel, *Der deutsche Volkssturm*, 61; Seidler, *'Deutscher Volkssturm'*, 35, 297–8; Otto Lasch, *So Fiel Königsberg* (Stuttgart 1976), 29–30; Thorwald, *Defeat in the East*, 20–1; and Heinz Höhne, *The Order of the Death's Head* (London 1969), 550–1.
9 Hofer, 'National Redoubt,' *World War II German Military Studies* 24.
10 Timm, *Freikorps 'Sauerland'*, 8–11; FO 'German Intelligence Report' no. 107, 14 Jan. 1945, FO 371/46764, PRO; PWE 'German Propaganda and the German,' 15 Jan. and 9 Apr. 1945, FO 898/187, PRO; and Mobile Field Interrogation Unit no. 1 'PW Intelligence Bulletin' no. 1/32, 30 Jan. 1945, G-2 Intelligence Division Captured Personnel and Material Branch Enemy POW Interrogation File (MIS-Y) 1943–5, RG 165 NA.
11 Timm, *Freikorps 'Sauerland'*, 9–12; Seidler, *'Deutscher Volkssturm'*, 113–14; *Review of the Foreign Press*, Memorandum no. 266, 2 Jan. 1945, Series A, IX; Mobile Field Interrogation Unit no. 2 'PW Intelligence Bulletin #2/44,' 12 Mar. 1945, OSS 124057, RG 226, NA; CC (BE) 'Intermediate Resistance in Germany,' *c.* April–May 1945, WO 219/1602, PRO; and Klietmann, 'Der Deutsche Volkssturm in Tirol–Voralberg,' 157–8.

12 Auerbach, 'Die Organisation des "Werwolf,"' 354.

13 OSS R & A no. 1934.1 'The Clandestine Nazi Movement in Post-War Germany,' 13 Oct. 1944, *OSS/State Department Intelligence and Research Reports*, Micf. Roll XIV; OSS Report from Switzerland no. TB 206, 5 Sep. 1944, RG 226, OSS 90852, NA; OSS Report from North Italy no. J-2594, 15 Oct. 1944, OSS 101229, RG 226, NA; *The Times*, 5 Sep. and 5 Oct. 1944; *FO Weekly Political Intelligence Summaries* 10, Summary no. 258, 13 Sep. 1944; PWE 'German Propaganda and the German,' 4 Sep., 11 Sep., 18 Sep., 9 Oct., 16 Oct., and 23 Oct. 1944, all in FO 898/187, PRO.

14 A. Hitler 'Erlass über die Bildung des Deutschen Volkssturmes,' 25 Sep. 1944, NS 6/78, BA; and Kissel, 20. The original decree is cited in SS-H/Stuf. and Adj. Eppenaur to Persönlichen Stab Reichsführer-SS, 7 Oct. 1944, Records of the Reich Leader of the SS and Chief of the German Police, Microcopy no. T-175, Roll 122, frame 2648068, NA.

15 'Ansprache an Volkssturmänner in Bartenstein am 18.10.1944,' NS 19/4016, BA; *Völkischer Beobachter*, 19 Oct. 1944; and PWE 'German Propaganda and the German,' 23 Oct. 1944, FO 898/187, PRO.

16 *The Stars and Stripes*, 19 Oct. and 20 Oct. 1944.

17 Watt, 'Wehrwolf or Werwolf,' 889; Kissel, *Der deutsche Volkssturm*, 45, 124–5; Seidler, *'Deutscher Volkssturm'*, 246, 271–2; PWE 'German Propaganda and the German,' 23 Oct. and 30 Oct. 1944, both in FO 898/187, PRO; *The Times*, 19 Oct. 1944; *Review of the Foreign Press, 1939–1945*, Memorandum no. 262, 12 Dec. 1944, Series A, IX; OSS R & A 'European Political Report – RAL-3-33,' 20 Oct. 1944, WO 219/3761A, PRO; and *The New York Times*, 14 Mar. 1945.

18 Geoffrey Best, *Humanity in Warfare* (London 1980), 239–40; and FO German Intelligence Report no. 108, 16 Jan. 1945, FO 371/46764, PRO.

19 *The Law of War*, vol. 1, 224–5, 313–14; Seidler, *'Deutscher Volkssturm'*, 247; SHAEF G-2 'Weekly Intelligence Summary' no. 32, 29 Oct. 1944, Part I, WO 219/5168, PRO; and SHAEF CoS Lt.-Gen. W.B. Smith, memo on 'Treatment of Partisans in Germany,' 6 Nov. 1944, WO 219/1602, PRO.

20 *FO Weekly Political Intelligence Summaries* 10, Summary no. 264, 25 Oct. 1944; and *The Times*, 1 Nov. 1944.

21 Seventh Army 'Small Unit Commander's Guide to Military Government,' 3 Apr. 1945, WO 219/3499, PRO; and *Conquer*, 195, 287–8. For French Communist criticism of this tolerance of 'the German terrorists of the *Volkssturm*,' see *L'Humanité*, 4 Nov. 1944.

22 John Armstrong, ed., *Soviet Partisans in World War II* (Madison 1964), 79; Seidler, *'Deutscher Volkssturm'*, 247–8, 342–3; *Silesian Inferno*, 55, 192; Thorwald, *Defeat in the East*, 72, 135; Lucas, *The Last Days of the Reich*, 28, 59; RSHA Amt VI C2b '36 Wochenbericht über Aussen- und Innenpolitik der SU,' 10 Mar. 1945, RH

2/2330, BMA; Adolf Fischer 'Insterburg und Ostpreussen in der Zeit vom 1.6.44 bis 10.2.1945,' 8 Mar. 1950, and Frau Traum 'Mein Erlebnis, 1892–1951,' both in Ost Dok. 2/18, BA; W. Magunia 'Der Volkssturm in Ostpreussen, 1944/45,' 10 Apr. 1955, Ost Dok. 8/592, BA; Dr Carl Brenke 'Die Vorgänge in Königsberg seit Bedrohung der Stadt,' 7 Mar. 1953, Ost Dok. 8/518, BA; Walter Petzel 'Militärische Vorbereitungen für Verteidigung des Warthegaus,' 15 Jun. 1949, Ost Dok. 8/399–400, BA; Oberstl. Kahl 'Ostwallbau u. Volkssturm in Ost Brandenburg,' Ost Dok 8/712, BA; Dr Münde 'Organisation und Einsatz des Volkssturms in und um Landsberg/Warthe,' Jan. 1953, Ost Dok. 8/704, BA; Kissel, *Der deutsche Volkssturm*, 46; Kurt Dieckert and Horst Grossmann, *Der Kampf um Ostpreussen* (Munich 1960), 67; and Gunter, *Letzter Lorbeer*, 127.

23 'Auszug aus V.O. St. O. Pro. H. Gr. Mitte,' Records of OKH, Microcopy no. T-78, Roll 488, frame 6474434, NA.

24 Hans von Lehndorf, *East Prussian Diary* (London 1963), 97, 114.

25 M. Bormann, Partei-Kanzlei 'Anordnung' 290/44, 1 Oct. 1944, 'Auszug aus der Haager Landkriegsordnung,' Annex to 'Anordnung' 277/44, 27 Sep. 1944, both in NS 6/98, BA; and *Das Dienstagebuch des deutschen Generalgouverners in Polen, 1939–1945* (Stuttgart 1975), 918. For an official list of the Volkssturm's responsibilities, see SS-Parteikanzlei-Wehrmacht 'Verwendung des Deutschen Volkssturms,' 28 Mar. 1945, NS 6/99, BA. For a précis from the Volkssturm training *Stab*, see Kissel, *Der deutsche Volkssturm*, 122–4.

26 Kissel, *Der deutsche Volkssturm*, 46–7, 56, 126–34; Seidler, *'Deutscher Volkssturm,'* 249–55; and *Völkischer Beobachter* (Munich), 14 Apr. 1945.

27 Sig. illegible 'Meldung,' Apr. 1945, NS 6/135, BA. For actions on the Eastern Front by Volkssturm reconnaissance patrols, see Seidler, *'Deutscher Volkssturm,'* 139–40, and Dieckert and Grossmann, *Der Kampf um Ostpreussen*, 64–5.

28 Kissel, *Der deutsche Volkssturm*, 86.

29 U.S. First Army 'Intelligence Bulletin' no. 2, 6 Nov. 1944, WO 219/3761A, PRO.

30 *The Stars and Stripes*, 28 Dec. 1944.

31 Direction Générale des Études et Recherches 'Bulletin de Renseignements – Allemagne: Wehrwolf,' 23 Jun. 1945, P7 125, SHAT.

32 Report by General-Maior Zubarev, 8 Apr. 1945, *Pogranichnye Voiska SSSR v Velikoi Otechestvennoi Voine 1942–1945*, 550–1, 554; *The Manchester Guardian*, 17 Mar. 1945; and Gołąbek and Tryc, 'Z Genezy Powstania i Działalności Werwolfu,' 133, 136.

33 Von Lehndorf, *East Prussian Diary*, 22–3; *Völkischer Beobachter*, 2 Mar. 1945; and Gavrikov to Izugenev, 30 Apr. 1945, *Pogranichnye Voiska SSSR v Velikoi Otechestvenoi Voine, 1942–1945*, 564–5.

34 EDS Report no. 34 'Notes on the "Werewolves,"' and Twenty-first Army Group 'News Sheet' no. 20 Extract, both in IRR File XE 049 888 'Werewolf Activities vol.

I,' RG 319, NA. A Werwolf officer in northern Germany told Allied interrogators that senior Volkssturm officers either were Werwolves or knew of its members: Twenty-first Army Group/Int. 'Appendix "C" to 2 Cdn. Corps Sitrep,' 22 Jun. 1945, in IRR File XE 049 888 'Werewolf Activities vol. I,' RG 319, NA.

35 Twelfth Army Group Mobile Field Interrogation Unit no. 4 – 'Schimana, Walter, Gen/Lt.,' 27 May 1945, IRR File XE 049 888 'Werewolf Activities vol. 1,' RG 319, NA; USFET Interrogation Center 'Intermediate Interrogation Report (IIR) #6 – Walter Schimana,' 31 Jul. 1946, OSS 142090, RG 226, NA; USFET MIS Center 'Interrogation Report (CI-IRR/42) – SS-H/Stuf. Wolfram Kirchner,' 3 Jan. 1946, OSS XL 40257, RG 226, NA; and *Trial of the Major War Criminals before the International Military Tribunal*, vol. 14, 448.

36 The matter of declining SS involvement in the Volkssturm was touched upon by the former police president in Leipzig, who claimed that in December 1944 Himmler confided that he was withdrawing from deep involvement in the Volkssturm because it had become an instrument of power for Bormann: Grolmann 'The Collapse of the German Reich as Seen from Leipzig,' *World War II German Military Studies* 24. See also Seidler, *'Deutscher Volkssturm,'* 60–1.

37 M. Bormann, Partei-Kanzlei 'Rundschreiben' 410/44, 23 Nov. 1944, NS 6/349, BA; CSDIC WEA BAOR 'Second Interim Report on SS Obergruf. Karl Gutenberger,' OSS 123190, RG 226, NA; CSDIC WEA BAOR 'Final Report on SA Brgf. u. HDL Fritz Marrenbach,' FR no. 29, 21 Jan. 1946, ETO/MIS-Y-Sect. Final Interrogation Reports 1945–9 RG 332, NA; *Völkischer Beobachter*, 16 Nov. 1944; and PWE 'German Propaganda and the German,' 23 Oct. 1944, FO 898/187, PRO. As early as 1943, there was increased discussion in Nazi journals about partisan warfare. Werner Best, for instance, published a series of articles in *Zeitschrift für völkische Verfassung und Verwaltung* concerning the methods used by the German underground opposed to Allied forces in the Rhineland after the First World War: OSS R & A no. 1934 'The Problem of the Nazi Underground,' 21 Aug. 1944, *OSS/State Department Intelligence and Research Reports*, Micf. Roll XIII. Arthur Erhardt's *Kleinkrieg* was also republished in 1944. (The copy held by the Library of Congress is a 1944 edition.)

38 Brown, *The Last Hero*, 739; *FO Weekly Political Intelligence Summaries* 10, Summary no. 262, 11 Oct. 1944; and PWE 'German Propaganda and the German,' 9 Oct. 1944, FO 898/187, PRO.

39 For reference to D'Alquen's hospitalization, see Sven Steenberg, *Vlasov* (New York 1970), 149; and Jurgen Thorwald, *The Illusion: Soviet Soldiers in Hitler's Armies* (New York 1974), 230–1. D'Alquen was back on active service by mid-March 1945. See Pavlo Shandruk, *Arms of Valor* (New York 1959), 237.

40 PWE 'German Propaganda and the German,' 18 Sep. and 9 Oct. 1944, FO 898/187, PRO.

41 *FO Weekly Political Intelligence Summaries* 11, Summary no. 288, 11 Apr. 1945; and Henke, *Die amerikanische Besetzung Deutschlands*, 167.

42 FO 'German Intelligence Report' no. 162, 20 Mar. 1945, FO 371/46764, PRO. For German press complaints about executions and harsh sentences meted out to the HJ by Allied Military Courts, see *Rhein Mainische Zeitung*, 13 Jan.1945; *Völkischer Beobachter*, 13 Jan., 21 Feb., 24 Feb., and 1 Mar. 1945; DNB 'Zwangsarbeit für Hitlerjungen,' 22 Feb. 1945, R 34/270, BA; FO German Intelligence Report no. 105, 12 Jan. 1945, FO 371/46764, PRO; *FO Weekly Political Intelligence Summaries* 11, Summary no. 276, 17 Jan. 1945; *The Daily Express*, 7 Feb. and 22 Feb. 1945.

43 *Blitzkrieg to Defeat*, 204; Seidler, *'Deutscher Volkssturm,'* 343–4; Kesselring, *Memoirs*, 73; CSDIC (UK) 'Entlassungstelle der Waffen SS,' 17 Apr. 1945, ETO MIS-Y-Sect. CSDIC (UK) Special Interrogation Reports 1943–5, RG 332, NA; Ultra Document BT 4210, 6 Feb. 1945, Ultra Document Collection, Reel 60; Barbara Selz, *Das grüne Regiment* (Freiburg 1970), 235; and Wilhelm Prüller, *Diary of a German Soldier* (London 1963), 178. For the ineffectiveness of the Volkssturm, see Seidler, *'Deutscher Volkssturm,'* 323–4, 338, 340–4, 365–8, 372–4; and SHAEF PWD 'The Volkssturm in Action,' 15 Mar. 1945, FO 371/46894, PRO.

44 USSBS 'The Effects of Strategic Bombing on German Morale' (May 1947), no. I, 51, in *The United States Strategic Bombing Survey*, vol. 4 (New York 1976).

45 PWE 'German Propaganda and the German,' 27 Nov. 1944, 8 Jan. and 12 Mar. 1945, all in FO 898/187, PRO; SS Ostuf. to SDRF-SS-SD Leitabschnitt Stuttgart 'Stimmen zum Erlass des Führers über die Bildung des Deutschen Volkssturms,' 8 Nov. 1944, Records of the NSDAP, Microcopy no. T-81, Roll 95, frames 108117–108119, NA; and OSS Report 'Germany – Morale, the Volkssturm, etc.,' 27 Nov. 1944, OSS L 50687, RG 226, NA.

46 SS O/Stuf. to SDRR-SS-SD Leitabschnitte Stuttgart 'Stimmen zum Erlass des Führers über die Bildung des Deutschen Volkssturms,' 8 Nov. 1944, Records of the NSDAP, Microcopy no. T-81, Roll 95, frames 108118–108120, NA; *The New York Times*, 14 Mar. 1945; Marlis Steinert, *Hitlers Krieg und die Deutschen* (Dusseldorf 1970), 506–7, 553; Seidler, *'Deutscher Volkssturm,'* 248; *The Christian Science Monitor*, 14 Mar. 1945; *The Times*, 13 Mar. 1945; Dr Heinrich Gröll, 'Die Ereignisse im Kreise Kranau O/S während der russichen Offensive auf Oberschlesien in Januar 1945' (1953), Ost Dok. 2/768, BA; and Ultra Document, KO 340, 13 Apr. 1945, Ultra Document Collection, Reel 70. Shortly after the Himmler address, one brave Alsatian wrote an open letter to his local Kreisleiter, claiming that his countrymen were dubious of protection under international law for the Volkssturm. He requested dissemination of the relevant Hague texts protecting the militia: 'If the Alsatians – against all international law – are being forced to fight, let them at least be honest soldiers, and not terrorists or bandits': Annex 'A' to SHAEF G-2 'Report' no. 178, 14 Dec. 1944, WO 219/1602, PRO.

47 'Verhalten deutschen Volksgennosen in den besetzten deutschen Ortschaften,' 12 Oct. 1944, Microcopy no. T-580, Reel 78, NA.

48 *Rhein-Mainische Zeitung*, 6 Feb. 1945; *Essener National Zeitung*, 2 Feb. 1945; *FO Weekly Political Intelligence Summaries* 10, Summary no. 271, 13 Dec. 1944; 10, Summary no. 273, 27 Dec. 1944; PWE 'German Propaganda and the German,' 27 Dec. 1944 29 Jan. and 12 Feb. 1945, all in FO 898/187, PRO; and FO 'German Intelligence Report' no. 222, 24 Feb. 1945, FO 371/46764, PRO.

49 SHAEF PWD 'Weekly Intelligence Summary for Psychological Warfare' no. 22, 24 Feb. 1945; and no. 25, 19 Mar. 1945, both in FO 371/46894, PRO; *History of the Counter Intelligence Corps*, vol. 19, 62, 73, NA; *The New York Times*, 4 Apr. 1945; and PWE 'German Propaganda and the German,' 7 May 1945, FO 898/187, PRO. For the Aachen case, see PWE 'German Propaganda and the German,' 11 Dec. 1944, FO 898/187, PRO; and OSS (Paris) Report 'City Government of Aachen' no. FR-698, 16 Dec. 1944, WO 219/1648, PRO. The Belgian report was a controversial one. OSS officers were told by the head of the Belgian Sûreté de la État that, while the substance of the report was probably correct, its compiler was a former member of the Resistance who 'more than once had too strong reactions towards events and persons.' Moreover, the German sources for the report, although reliable, could not be construed as 'trained observers in the exact sense of the word': Bihan to Coster, 21 Mar. 1945 and Gamble to Sheen, 27 Mar. 1945, both in WO 219/1648A, PRO.

50 In a note to Himmler on 8 February, Bormann strongly implied that the SS had allowed preparation of guerrilla warfare to fall behind: M. Bormann to H. Himmler, 8 Feb. 1945, NS 19/3705, BA.

51 Noack to Rüder 'Richtlinien für das Verhalten der deutschen Zivilbevölkerung in den vom Feind besetzten Gebeiten,' 14 Feb. 1945, NS 6/135, BA; Dotzler 'Vorschläge zum Aufbau einer Widerstandsbewegung in den von den Bolschewisten besetzten deutschen Ostgebeiten,' 23 Jan. 1945; M. Bormann to H. Himmler, 27 Jan. 1945; H. Himmler to M. Bormann, 8 Feb. 1945; SS-Staf. (sig. illegible) to O/Gruf. Prützmann, all in NS 19/832, BA; and Michael Kater, *The Nazi Party: A Social Profile of Members and Leaders, 1919–1945* (Cambridge 1983), 227.

52 M. Bormann 'Anordnung,' 1 Apr. 1945, Biographical Records, Microcopy no. T-580, Reel 78; and *The Manchester Guardian*, 17 Mar. 1945.

53 Memo to K. Henlein 'Sondereinsatz der Partei-Kanzlei in frontnahen Gebeiten,' 15 Mar. 1945, Microcopy no. T-580, Reel 78; Seidler, '*Deutscher Volkssturm*,' 346–7; Von Lang, *Bormann*, 319; Rauchensteiner, *Krieg in Österreich 1945*, 242; Rose, *Werwolf*, 231–2; A. Hitler 'Verfügung 1/45,' 14 Feb. 1945, NS 6/78, BA; SHAEF G-5 'Weekly Journal of Information' no. 7, 4 Apr. 1945, no. 9, 19 Apr. 1945, both in WO 219/3918, PRO; *The New York Times*, 8 Apr. 1945; *Neue Zürcher Zeitung*, 10 Apr. and 11 Apr. 1945; Henke, *Die amerikanische Besetzung Deutschlands*, 830, 937–8; Nettle, *The Eastern Zone and Soviet Policy in Germany, 1945–50* (London

1951), 2–10; and Hofer 'National Redoubt,' *World War II German Military Studies* vol. 24.

54 Taüber, *The Eagle and the Swastika*, 23–4.

55 M. Bormann 'Rundschreiben 128/45 – Durchführung von Sonderaufgaben in Rücken des Feindes,' 10 Mar. 1945, NS 6/354, BA; CSDIC WEA BAOR 'Final Report on SA Brgf. u. HDL Fritz Marrenbach' FR no. 29, 21 Jan. 1946, Appendix 'A,' ETO MIS-Y-Sect. Final Interrogation Reports 1945–9, RG 332, NA; USFET MIS Center 'Intermediate Interrogation Report (IIR) no. 18 – Stubaf. Ernst Wagner,' 30 Aug. 1945, IRR File XE 049 888 'Werewolf Activities vol. I,' RG 319, NA; and Rose, *Werwolf*, 231–2.

56 CSDIC WEA BAOR 'Final Report on SA Brgf. u. HDL Fritz Marrenbach' FR no. 29, 21 Jan. 1946, Appendix 'A,' ETO MIS-Y-Sect. Final Interrogation Reports 1945–9, RG 332, NA; and U.S. Ninth Army 'Report no. 1658 – Fritz Georg Schlessmann,' 30 May 1945, IRR File XE 049 888 'Werewolf Activities vol. I,' RG 319, NA.

57 Trevor-Roper, *The Last Days of Hitler*, 53.

58 *Trial of the Major War Criminals before the International Military Tribunal*, vol. 17, 230; Rose, *Werwolf*, 218; Watt, 'Wehrwolf or Werwolf,' 885; Enemy Personnel Exploitation Sect., Field Information Agency Technical CC (BE) 'Two Brief Discussions of German CW Policy with Albert Speer,' 12 Oct. 1945, OSS XL 22959, RG 226, NA; Wahl, ... *es ist das deutsche Herz*, 404–5; Tauber, *The Eagle and the Swastika*, vol. 1, 23; and Trevor-Roper, *The Last Days of Hitler*, 53. Speer believed that Bormann attempted to form the Werwolf as a mass, popular movement, which was a jealous reaction to the formation of an élite NSDAP unit within the Volkssturm, the 'Free Corps "Adolf Hitler,"' controlled by Robert Ley. Speer's information on the Werwolf was second-hand, however, provided mainly by his own Armaments Ministry section heads and by several of Bormann's deputies.

59 Rose, *Werwolf*, 232–7; and U.S. Fifteenth Army HQ Interrogation Report on 'Hellwig, Friedrich,' 4 Jun. 1945, IRR File XE 049 888 'Werewolf Activities vol. I,' RG 319, NA.

60 1ère Armée Française, 2ème Bureau 'Bulletin de Renseignements,' 16 May 1945, Annex no. II, 7P 125, SHAT.

61 *Justiz und NS-Verbrechen*, vol. 1, 383–98, 433–68; vol. 3, 33–53; and Vol. 5, 517–34.

62 Ibid., vol. 2, 135–75; vol. 3, 299–322, 383–409; vol. 6, 141–51; vol. 10, 188–201; vol. 11, 97–142; Schwärzwalder, *Bremen und Nordwestdeutschland am Kriegsende*, vol. 2, 67–8, and vol. 3, 137–8.

63 Tenfelde, 'Proletärische Province. Radikalisierung und Widerstand in Penzberg/ Oberbayern,' 375–7, 380–1; Troll, 'Aktionen zur Kriegsbeendung in Frühjahr 1945,' 671–2; *Justiz und NS-Verbrechen*, vol. 3, 67–128; vol. 6, 439–45; vol. 7, 560–657;

vol. 13, 478–582; Hallig, *Festung Alpen*, 120; and Heike Bretschneider, *Der Widerstand gegen den Nationalsozialismus in München 1933 bis 1945* (Munich 1968), 236.

64 Sig. illegible to Noack, 24 Feb. 1945, NS 6/135, BA. For the background and capabilities of Operation 'Scorpion,' see O/Stubaf. Grothman to Staf. D'Alquen, Kommandeur SS-Standarte 'Kurt Eggers,' 23 Jun. 1944, NS 19/2451, BA; Lt. Stempel 'Tätigkeit- und Erfahrungsbericht,' 15 Mar. 1945, and Oblt. Gutjahr 'Einsatzbericht' no. 2, 15 Feb. 1945, both in Geographical Records, Microcopy no. T-580, Reel 78; Thorwald, *Defeat in the East*, 202–3; Steenberg, *Vlasov*, 135–7; Alexander Dallin, *German Rule in Russia, 1941–1945* (London 1957), 604–5; and Von Wedel, *Die Propagandatruppen der Deutschen Wehrmacht*, 86. A call went out in Apr. 1945 for volunteer wireless transmitters 'urgently required for special employment' with the 'Kurt Eggers' unit, although it was not clear that this involved partisan warfare: Ultra Document KO 386, 14 Apr. 1945, Ultra Document Collection, Reel 70.

65 Misztal, 'Działalność Propagandowa Podziemia Poniemieckiego na Śląsku Opolskim,' 53–4.

66 V Corps 'Weekly Intelligence Summary' no. 1, 11 Jul. 1945, and no. 5, 10 Aug. 1945, FO 1007/299, PRO.

67 *History of the Counter Intelligence Corps*, vol. 20, 97–8, NA; and Holzträger, *Der Wehrertüchtigungslager*, 101.

68 Theodore Heuss, *Aufzeichnungen, 1945–1947* (Tübingen 1966), 48–9.

69 HQ Enclave Military District, Office of ACoS G-2 'CI Periodic Report' no. 3, 18 Jul. 1945, OSS XL 12926, RG 226, NA; and Schwarzwälder, *Bremen und Nordwestdeutschland am Kriegsende*, vol. 2, 64, 69, 71, 190; vol. 3, 98–9, 146.

70 *The History of the Counter Intelligence Corps*, vol. 26, 76–7, NA.

71 HQ Twelfth Army Group, Mobile Field Interrogation Unit no. 4 'PW Intelligence Bulletin' no. 4/2, Annex 'Notes on Werwolf,' 7 May 1945, OSS OB 27836, RG 226, NA; and Hewitt, *Work Horse of the Western Front*, 265.

72 PWE 'German Propaganda and the German,' 9 Apr. 1945, FO 898/187, PRO; 'Maquis Allemands,' 7P 125, SHAT; and Philip Charles Farwell Bankwitz, *Alsatian Autonomist Leaders, 1919–1947* (Lawrence 1978), 102–3. For the eventual fate of Wagner and Röhn, see Ueberschär, "Volkssturm" und "Werwolf",' 36; Grill, *The Nazi Movement in Baden*, 518–19; Bankwitz, *Alsatian Autonomist Leaders*, 105–6; and Peter Sauer, 'Staat, Politik, Aktuere,' in *Das Dritte Reich in Baden und Württemberg*, ed. Otto Borst (Stuttgart 1988), 25. For the story of Annie Wagner's suicide, see *The Daily Express*, 7 Jun. 1945.

73 Direction Générale des Études et Recherches 'Bulletin des Renseignements – Allemagne: Wehrwolf,' 26 Jun. 1945, 7P 125, SHAT.

74 Von Lang, *Bormann*, 333; Rose, *Werwolf*, 319–20; Thorwald, *Defeat in the East*, 211; Peter Gosztony, ed., *Der Kampf um Berlin 1945* (Düsseldorf 1970), 368–9;

Simon Wiesenthal, *The Murderers among Us* (London 1967), 279; and Tully, *Berlin*, 272. For Soviet prohibitions on 'diversionist' activities, see Chuikov, *The End of the Third Reich*, 252.

75 *The Stars and Stripes*, 21 Sep. 1945 and 24 Feb. 1946; *Le Monde*, 4 Sep. 1945; *The Manchester Guardian*, 8 Sep. 1945; ACA(BE) Intelligence Organisation 'Joint Fort-nightly Intelligence Summary' no. 10, 29 Jun. 1946, FO 1007/301, PRO; CCG(BE) 'Intelligence Bulletin' no. 10, 10 Apr. 1946, FO 1005/1701, PRO; USFET 'Weekly Intelligence Summary' no. 62, 19 Sep. 1946, no. 67, 24 Oct. 1946, and no. 68, 31 Oct. 1946, all in State Dept. Decimal File 1945–9, 740.00119 Control (Germany), RG 59, NA.

76 Herbert Ziegler, *Nazi Germany's New Aristocracy: The SS Leadership, 1925–1939* (Princeton 1989), 128. See also Hüttenberger, *Die Gauleiter*, 174; and 'National-sozialistische Polykratie,' 427–8.

77 Fifteenth Army Interrogation Report 'Hellwig, Friedrich,' 4 Jun. 1945; and U.S. Fif-teenth Army Triumph Interrogation Center, 19 Jun. 1945, both in IRR File XE 049 888 'Werewolf Activities, vol. I,' RG 319, NA.

78 U.S. First Army Interrogation Report Extract 'Lorenz's Opinions on the Occupation of Germany,' OSS XL 5732, RG 226, NA.

79 ECAD 'General Intelligence Bulletin' no. 49, 11 Jul. 1945, State Dept. Decimal File 1945–9, 740.00119 Control (Germany), RG 59, NA; and CCG (BE) 'Intelligence Review' no. 5, 6 Feb. 1946, FO 371/55807, PRO.

80 SHAEF G-5 'Political Intelligence Letter' no. 10, 19 Jun. 1945, FO 371/46933, PRO; *The Stars and Stripes*, 28 May and 30 Jul. 1945; *The New York Times*, 19 Jul. 1945, and 13 Jul. 1946; *The Daily Express*, 14 Jun. 1945; *Zwischen Befreiung und Besetzung*, 94, 122; OSS Report from Germany (Munich and Nuremberg), LP/8–163, 158, 160, LP/7–19, Sep. 1945, OSS XL 23770, RG 226, NA; 3 Cdn. Inf. Div. CAOF 'Internal Security Exercise,' 14 Jan. 1946, Appendix 'A,' D Hist. 581.009 (D 103), Op. Orders and Instructions, PAC; Kiselev to Drozdov, 19 Nov. 1945, *Pogran-ichnye Voiska SSSR Mai, 1945–1950*, 147–8; 'Intelligence Summary' no. 8, 22 May 1947; and P. de Tristan, First French Army 5th Bureau 'Monthly Historical Report,' 1 Jun. 1945, both in State Dept. Decimal File 1945–9, 740.00119 Control (Ger-many), RG 59, NA. For Nazi rumour-mongering in immediate postwar Austria, see *History of the Counter Intelligence Corps*, vol. 25, 20, NA; and PWB British Units (Austria) 'Consolidated Intelligence Report' no. 4, 14 Aug. 1945, FO 1007/296, PRO.

81 Arthur Koestler, *Darkness at Noon*. Koestler's comments pertained to the plight of the KPD in 1933.

82 Mommson, 'National Socialism: Continuity and Change,' 182.

83 *Final Entries, 1945: The Diaries of Joseph Goebbels*, ed. Hugh Trever-Roper, 233.

84 Bormann to Himmler, 8 Feb. 1945; Bormann, Memo to Ten Western Gauleiter 'Vorbereitungen auf Feindoffensive im Westen,' both in NS 19/3705, BA; and Ultra Document BT 4666, 12 Feb. 1945, Ultra Document Collection, Reel 61.

85 *Final Entries*, 38, 49, 68, 76, 94–5, 105, 114–15, 121, 134–5, 149, 233–4, 237, 244–5, 258, 271; Heinz to Bormann, 15 Mar. 1945, 51/NS6, BA; and *The St Louis Post–Dispatch*, 8 Apr. 1945. For the example of Kassel, see 6824 DIC (MIS)/M.1136 Detailed Interrogation Report 'German Signals Counter-Intelligence,' 23 Apr. 1945, OSS 126394, RG 226, NA.

86 *Final Entries*, 188–9, 286–7. See also 170–1, 195. For the same view in a circular signed by Naumann, see Rose, *Werwolf*, 266.

87 Wilfred von Oven, *Final Furioso: Mit Goebbels bis zum Ende* (Tübingen 1974), 619–20.

88 *Final Entries*, 258, 269, 277, 296; and 'Report from Captured Personnel and Material Branch issued by MID, US War Dept., by Combined Personnel of US and British Services for the Use of Allied Forces,' 4 Aug. 1945, OSS XL 15506, RG 226, NA.

89 *Final Entries*, 258, 269, 289; and Rose, *Werwolf*, 253.

90 'Extract from Interrogation of Karl Kaufmann,' 11 Jun. 1945, Appendix 'A' – 'The Werewolf Organization in Hamburg,' IRR File XE 049 888 'Werewolf Activities vol. I,' RG 319, NA. Arno Rose claims that great unease was caused among the Prützmann Werewolves by the work of Werwolf Radio, mainly because these para-military commandos now found themselves lumped together with Goebbels's spon-taneous 'Werewolves.' This, in turn, further increased the chances of dying a humiliating death at the end of a hangman's rope: Rose: *Werwolf*, 265.

91 Curt Reiss, *Joseph Goebbels* (London 1949), 400–1.

92 *Final Entries*, 234.

93 Rose, *Werwolf*, 265–6.

94 Auerbach, 'Die Organisation des "Werwolf,"' 354, and *The Trial of the Major War Criminals before the International Tribunal*, vol. 17, 229.

95 *Die Letzten Hundert Tage*, 78, 117.

96 *Final Entries*, 296; *Völkischer Beobachter*, 3 Apr. 1945; PID Background Notes, 5 Apr. 1945, FO 371/46790, PRO; and PWE 'German Propaganda and the German,' 2 Apr. 1945, FO 898/187, PRO.

97 Detailed Interrogation Report 'German Signals Counter-Intelligence,' 6824 DIC (MIS)/M.1136, 23 Apr. 1945, OSS 126394, RG 226, NA.

98 U.S. Seventh Army Interrogation Center '"Wehrwolf Section" of Propaganda Ministry,' 10 Jul. 1945, IRR File XE 049 888 'Werewolf Activities Vol. I,' RG 319, NA.

99 *Final Entries*, 232–3, 289.

100 Ibid., 296; and Special Detention Center 'Ashcan,' 'Detailed Interrogation Report – Friedrich Wilhelm Kritzinger,' 27 Jul. 1945, OSS XL 13731, RG 226, NA.

101 *Final Entries*, 277, 280; Von Oven, *Final Furioso*, 611; and Otto Dietrich, *The Hitler I Knew* (London 1957), 101–2.

102 PWE 'German Propaganda and the German,' 9 Apr. 1945, FO 898/187, PRO; Bornemann, *Die letzten Tage in der Festung Harz*, 18–20; *The Daily Herald*, 9 Apr. 1945; *Justiz und NS-Verbrechen*, vol. 5, 319–57, and vol. 8, 139–50.

103 Bernard Baruch, *The Public Years* (New York 1960), 351; Jordan Schwarz, *The Speculator: Bernard M. Baruch in Washington* (Chapell Hill 1981), 478; SHAEF G-5 'Weekly Journal of Information' no. 11, May 1945, WO 219/3918, PRO; *The New York Times*, 3 Apr. and 12 Apr. 1945; *The St Louis Post–Dispatch*, 2 Apr. and 20 May 1945; and *The Nation* 160/16 (21 Apr. 1945), 445.

104 *Völkischer Beobachter*, 8 Apr. 1945; *The Daily Express*, 4 Apr. 1945; *The Daily Herald*, 3 Apr. 1945; *The Nation* 160/16 (21 Apr. 1945), 445; *The New York Times*, 23 Apr. 1945; *The Times*, 4 Apr. 1945; and Bornemann, *Die letzten Tage in der Festung Harz*, 17–18.

105 PWE 'German Propaganda and the German,' 23 Apr. 1945, FO 898/187, PRO; Von Lang, *Bormann*, 313; Rose, *Werwolf*, 261; and Reiss, *Joseph Goebbels*, 401–2.

106 USFET MIS Center 'Intermediate Interrogation Report (IIR) #18 – Krim. Rat. Stubaf. Ernst Wagner,' 30 Aug. 1945, IRR File XE 049 888 'Werewolf Activities vol. I,' RG 319, NA.

107 PWE 'German Propaganda and the German,' 9 Apr. 1945, FO 898/187, PRO; and *The Nation* 160/16 (21 Apr. 1945), 445.

108 *Final Entries*, 269, 277–8, 280, 296, 310; and Von Oven, *Final Furioso*, 641.

109 PWE 'German Propaganda and the German,' 16 Apr. and 23 Apr. 1945, both in FO 898/187, PRO; and SHAEF G-5 'Journal of Information' no. 10, 26 Apr. 1945, WO 219/3918, PRO.

110 PWE 'German Propaganda and the German,' 2 Apr. 1945, FO 898/187, PRO; *FO Weekly Political Intelligence Summaries*, vol. 11, Summary no. 187, 4 Apr. 1945; and FORD 'Review of the Foreign Press, Series A #319 – The German Home Front and the War (Apr. 1945)' *Review of the Foreign Press, 1939–1945*, Series A, IX.

111 PWE 'German Propaganda and the German,' 9 Apr. 1945, FO 898/187, PRO.

112 *Final Entries*, 296, 304; PWE 'German Propaganda and the German,' 9 Apr. and 16 Apr. 1945, both in FO 898/187, PRO; ECAD 'General Intelligence Bulletin' no. 43, 26 Apr. 1945, WO 219/3760A, PRO; and CX Report 'Werewolf Personnel,' 24 Apr. 1945, IRR File XE 049 888 'Werewolf Activities vol. I,' RG 319, NA.

113 PWE 'German Propaganda and the German,' 9 Apr., 16 Apr., and 23 Apr. 1945, all in FO 898/187, PRO.

114 SHAEF G-5 'Weekly Journal of Information' no. 9, 19 Apr. 1945, WO 219/3918, PRO; OSS Report, OSS XL 7836, RG 226, NA; and EDS Report no. 34 'Notes on the "Werewolves,"' IRR File XE 049 888 'Werewolf Activities vol. I,' RG 319, NA.
115 PWE 'German Propaganda and the German,' 23 Apr. 1945, FO 898/187, PRO.
116 SHAEF Report 'Observations Concerning Occupied Germany,' 5 May 1945, State Dept. Decimal Files 1945–9, 740.00119 Control (Germany), RG 59, NA.
117 PWE 'German Propaganda and the German,' 9 Apr. 1945, FO 898/187, PRO.
118 Ibid., 16 Apr. 1945, FO 898/187, PRO.
119 Von Oven, *Final Furioso*, 620.
120 PWE 'German Propaganda and the German,' 23 Apr. 1945, FO 898/187, PRO; and *FO Weekly Political Intelligence Summaries* 11, Summary no. 290, 25 Apr. 1945.
121 EDS 'Extract from PID Daily Intelligence Summary for Germany and Austria, #211 of 24 Apr. 1945,' IRR File XE 049 888 'Werewolf Activities vol. I,' RG 319, NA; and *The Globe and Mail*, 24 Apr. 1945.
122 Henke, *Die amerikanische Besetzung Deutschlands*, 944; *Neue Zürcher Zeitung*, 3 Apr. 1945; *The Daily Express*, 3 Apr. 1945; *FO Weekly Political Intelligence Summaries* 11, Summary no. 287, 4 Apr. 1945; OSS Report, OSS XL 7777, RG 226, NA; ECAD 'General Intelligence Bulletin' no. 42, 11 Apr. 1945, WO 219/3760A, PRO; and *The Times*, 3 Apr. 1945.
123 PWE 'German Propaganda and the German,' 23 Apr. 1945, FO 898/187, PRO; and PID 'Background Notes,' 26 Apr. 1945, FO 371/46790, PRO.
124 PWE 'German Propaganda and the German,' 23 Apr. 1945, FO 898/187, PRO; Trevor-Roper, *The Last Days of Hitler*, 57–8; and SHAEF G-5 'Weekly Journal of Information' no. 10, 26 Apr. 1945, WO 219/3918, PRO.
125 PWE 'German Propaganda and the German,' 16 Apr. and 23 Apr. 1945, both in FO 898/187, PRO.
126 Trevor-Roper, *The Last Days of Hitler*, 57.
127 PWE Report 'Edelweiss-Piraten and Similar Oppositional Groups,' 4 Dec. 1944, FO 898/187, PRO; Twenty-first Army Group 'CI News Sheet' no. 7, 5 Oct. 1944, Part I, WO 205/997, PRO; SHAEF PWD 'Guidance Notes for Output in German for the Week 30 April–7 May 1945,' 29 Apr. 1945, FO 371/46894, PRO; and EDS Report no. 34 'Notes on the "Werewolves,"' IRR File XE 049 888 'Werewolf Activities vol. I,' RG 319, NA.
128 SHAEF PWD 'Guidance Notes for Output in German for the Week 30 Apr.–7 May 1945,' 29 Apr. 1945, FO 371/46894, PRO.
129 *FO Weekly Political Intelligence Summaries* 11, Summary no. 287, 4 Apr. 1945.
130 *The New York Times*, 6 Apr. and 8 Apr. 1945; and *Time* 45/16 (16 Apr. 1945), 26. For the Werwolf's 'Hymn of Hate,' broadcast on the evening of 6 April, see *The*

Daily Herald, 7 Apr. 1945. For the best history of the *Wolfsangel* symbol, see Watt, 'Wehrwolf or Werwolf,' 881–2.

131 Whiting, *Hitler's Werewolves*, 146–7.

132 PID Background Notes, 19 May 1945, FO 371/46790, PRO.

133 USFET 'Weekly Intelligence Summary' no. 58, 22 Aug. 1946, State Dept. Decimal File 1945–9, 740.00119 Control (Germany), RG 59, NA.

134 *Justiz und NS-Verbrechen*, vol. 1, 1–9; *The Daily Herald*, 9 Apr. 1945; Intelligence Office, Chief of Naval Operations 'Intelligence Report,' 26 Jul. 1945; C.M. Culp, Acting Chief CIC, USFET to E. Sibert, 13 Apr. 1946, both in IRR File XE 049 888 'Werewolf Activities vol. I,' RG 319, NA; Allied Intelligence Report, OSS 137491, RG 229, NA; Intelligence Division, Chief of Naval Operations 'Intelligence Report,' 1 Aug. 1945, OSS XL 14154, RG 226, NA; ACA (BE) CMF 'Joint Weekly Intelligence Summary' no. 21, 1 Dec. 1945, FO 1007/300, PRO; *History of the Counter Intelligence Corps*, vol. 20, 126, NA; USFET 'Weekly Intelligence Summary' no. 18, 15 Nov. 1945; no. 74, 12 Dec. 1945; Eucom 'Intelligence Summary' no. 8, 22 May 1947, all in State Dept. Decimal File 1945–9, 740.00119 Control (Germany), NA; CCG (BE) 'Intelligence Review' no. 5, 6 Feb. 1945, FO 371/55807, PRO; MI-14 'Mitropa' no. 21, 7 May 1946, p. 10, FO 371/55630, PRO; 250 British Liaison Mission Report no. 8, Jul. 1947, FO 1005/1615, PRO; Report by Polkovnik Antonyuk, 12 Mar. 1946 and Kisilev to Drozdov, 19 Nov. 1945, both in *Pogranichnye Voiska SSSR Mai, 1945–1950*, 147–57.

135 Baird, 'La Campagne de Propagande Nazie en 1945,' 84; SHAEF PWD Intelligence Section 'Consolidated report on the reaction of 18 Ps/W on the "Werewolf,"' 16 Apr. 1945, WO 219/1602, PRO; Bornemann, *Die letzten tage in der Festung Harz*, 17–18; and *The Washington Post*, 10 Apr. 1945.

136 Kershaw, *Popular Opinion and Political Dissent in the Third Reich*, 151, 153, 322, 351.

137 PWE 'German Propaganda and the German,' 9 Apr. and 16 Apr. 1945, both in FO 898/187, PRO; Baird, 'La Campagne de Propagande Nazie en 1945,' 84; Rose, *Werwolf*, 260–1; Heuss, *Aufzeichnungen*, 48; and Kästner, *Notabene 45*, 79.

138 SHAEF PWD Intelligence Div. 'Reactions to "Werewolf" in Cologne,' 18 Apr. 1945, OSS 128265, RG 226, NA.

139 *Völkischer Beobachter* (Munich), 24 Apr. 1945; *The Daily Herald*, 23 Apr. 1945; PID Background Notes, 26 Apr. 1945, FO 371/46790, PRO; *FO Weekly Political Intelligence Summaries* 11, Summary no. 290, 25 Apr. 1945; *The New York Times*, 24 Apr. 1945; *The Globe and Mail*, 24 Apr. 1945; PWE 'German Propaganda and the German,' 30 Apr. 1945, FO 898/187, PRO; Amb. Johnson, Stockholm to Sec. of State, 24 Apr. 1945, State Dept. Decimal Files 740.0011 EW, Micf. no. M982, Roll 217, NA; SHAEF G-5 'Journal of Information' no. 12, 11 May 1945, WO 219/3918, PRO; and EDS 'Extracts from PID Daily Intelligence Summary for Germany and

Austria #211 of 24 Apr. 1945,' IRR File XE 049 888 'Werewolf Activities Vol I,' RG 319, NA.

140 *Völkischer Beobachter,* 24 Apr. 1945; and Kurt Detlev Müller, *Das letzte Kapital: Geschichte der Kapitulation Hamburgs* (Hamburg 1947), 114. A pamphlet widely circulated through Hamburg in late April warned that the city was 'no place for the criminal errors of the Goebbelsite Werwolf,' and said that anyone 'sabotaging peace' would forfeit his life: Haupt, *Das Ende im Westen,* 142.

141 EDS Report no. 34 'Notes on the "Werewolves,"' IRR File XE 049 888 'Werewolf Activities Vol. I,' RG 319, NA; Twenty-first Army group 'CI News Sheet' no. 25, 13 Jul. 1945, Part III, and no. 28, 9 Sep. 1945, both in WO 205/997, PRO.

142 EDS Report no. 34 'Notes on the "Werewolves,"' IRR File XE 049 888 'Werewolf Activities Vol. I,' RG 319, NA; Twenty-first Army group 'CI News Sheet' no. 25, 13 Jul. 1945, Part III; and no. 28, 9 Sep. 1945, both in WO 205/997, PRO.

143 *The Manchester Guardian,* 31 May 1945. For specific instances of illicit postwar radio broadcasting, see PID 'News Digest' no. 1767, 25 May 1945, Bramstedt Collection, BLPES; HQ U.S. Third Army, 'Military Government Weekly Report,' 11 Jun. 1945, OSS 137425, RG 226, NA; *The Stars and Stripes,* 14 Jun. 1945; PWD Liaison Sect. SHAEF to SHAEF G-2, 30 Jun. 1945; H.G. Sheen, Office of ACoS SHAEF G-2 to ACoS, Twelfth Army Group G-2, 1 Jul. 1945; Lt.-Col. Sassard, Office of ACoS USFET G-2 to ACoS SHAEF G-2, 10 Jul. 1945; H.G. Sheen, SHAEF G-2 to PWD Liaison Sect. SHAEF, 12 Jul. 1945, WO 219/1602, PRO; *FO Weekly Political Intelligence Summaries* 11, Summary no. 298, 20 Jun. 1945; 'Allemagne – Activité du Werwolf,' 15 Jun. 1945, 7P 125, SHAT; Intelligence Office, Chief of Naval Operations 'Intelligence Report,' 26 Jul. 1945, IRR File 'Werewolf Activities Vol. I,' RG 319, NA; *The Times,* 7 Aug. 1945; USFET G-5 'Political Intelligence Letter' no. 1, 3 Aug. 1946; SHAEF JIC 'Political Intelligence Report,' 2 Jul. 1945; USFET 'Weekly Intelligence Summary' no. 30, 7 Feb. 1946, to no. 56, 8 Aug. 1946, all in State Dept. Decimal File 1945–9, 740.00119 Control (Germany), RG 59, NA; CCG (BE) 'Intelligence Bulletin' no. 7, 28 Feb. 1946; no. 8, 13 Mar. 1946; no. 10, 10 Apr. 1946, all in FO 1005/1701, PRO; 12 (Berlin) Intelligence Staff 'Monthly Summary' no. 7, 30 Sep. 1947, FO 1005/1708, PRO; Constabulary G-2 'Weekly Intelligence Report' no. 9, 18 Oct. 1946, Annex no. 1, WWII Operations Reports 1940–8, RG 407, NA; Livingston to Bevin, 25 Jul. 1947, FO 371/64351, PRO; ACA Intelligence Organisation 'Joint Fortnightly Intelligence Summary' no. 51, 7 Feb. 1948, FO 1007/303, PRO; *The Daily Express,* 13 Jun. 1945; *The Washington Post,* 13 Jun., and 26 Jun. 1945.

144 Fest, *The Face of the Third Reich,* 94–7.

145 *Final Entries,* 297.

146 PWE 'German Propaganda and the German,' 16 Apr. 1945, FO 898/187, PRO; Rose, *Werwolf,* 148–9; and Reiss, *Joseph Goebbels,* 402.

5: Werwolf Redoubts

1 PWE 'German Propaganda and the German,' 9 Oct. 1944, FO 898/187, PRO; and Draper, *The 84th Infantry Division in the Battle of Germany*, 236.

2 *The Daily Express*, 30 May 1945.

3 USFET G-2 'Weekly Intelligence Summary' no. 2, 24 Jul. 1945, State Dept. Decimal File 1945–9, 740.00119 Control (Germany), RG 59, NA.

4 Desmond Flower, *History of the Argyll and Sutherland Highlanders, 5th Battalion: 91st Anti-Tank Regiment, 1939–45* (London 1950) 328, 332, 353; *The Age* (Melbourne), 3 Apr. and 4 Apr. 1945; *The Daily Herald*, 10 Apr. 1945; and *The Manchester Guardian*, 16 Apr. 1945.

5 Orde, *The Household Cavalry at War*, 490.

6 Nigel Hamilton, *Monty: The Field Marshal, 1944–1976* (London 1986), 490; and L.C. Gates, *The History of the Tenth Foot, 1919–1950* (Aldershot 1953) 202.

7 *The Manchester Guardian*, 10 Apr. 1945.

8 Fenske, *Wahlrecht und Parteiensystem*, 268, 270, 275.

9 Kirby, *1100 Miles with Monty*, 127–9; Hamilton, *Monty*, 489–90; CCG (BE) 'Intelligence Review' no. 5, 6 Feb. 1946, FO 371/55807, PRO; interview with Lord Nöel Annon, 29 Apr. 1986; Whiting, *Hitler's Werewolves*, 182; Giovanni Guareschi, *My Secret Diary, 1943–1945* (New York 1958), 173–83; *The Daily Herald*, 23 Apr. 1945; *The Daily Express*, 20 Apr. and 26 Apr. 1945; and Rose, *Werwolf*, 316–17. For operations against this pocket, see G.L. Verney, *The Desert Rats* (London 1954), 227–8. For minor sabotage and attacks in the Lüneburg area, see *The Stars and Stripes*, 31 Oct. 1945; CCG (BE) 'Intelligence Bulletin' no. 7, 28 Feb. 1946; no. 9, 28 Mar. 1946, both in FO 1005/1701, PRO; and CCG (BE) Intelligence Division 'Summary' no. 12, 31 Dec. 1946, FO 1005/1702, PRO.

10 Timothy Alan Tilton, *Nazism, Neo-Nazism and the Peasantry* (Bloomington 1975), 40–1, 51–71; Lawrence Stokes, *Kleinstadt und Nationalsozialismus: Ausgewählte Dokumente zur Geschichte von Eutin 1918–1945* (Neumünster 1984), 34–42, 317–24; and Rudolph Heberle, *From Democracy to Nazism* (New York 1970), Chs. 3–5.

11 Richard Brett-Smith, *Berlin '45* (London 1946), 11, 24, 32; and MI-14 'Mitropa' no. 13, 12 Jan. 1946, FO 371/55630, PRO.

12 Reitlinger, *The SS*, 442–3; Müller, *Das letzte Kapital*, 144; and Leon Degrelle, *Front de l'Est, 1941–1945* (Paris 1969), 420–5.

13 Whiting, *Hitler's Werewolves*, 189; Twenty-first Army Group/Int. 'Appendix "C" to 2nd Cdn. Corps Sitrep,' 22 Jun. 1945, IRR File XE 049 888 'Werewolf Activities Vol. I,' RG 319, NA; CSDIC WEA BAOR 'Final Report on Gunter Haubold' FR 94, ETO MIS-Y-Sect. CSDIC/WEA Final Interrogation Records, 1945–7, RG 332, NA; and Allied Intelligence Report, *c.* Aug. 1945, OSS OB 28993, RG 226, NA.

14 Kemsley and Riesco, *The Scottish Lion on Patrol*, 218–19; Charles Whiting, *Hunters*

from the Sky: The German Parachute Corps, 1940–1945 (New York 1974), 231;
H.G. Martin, *The History of the Fifteenth Scottish Division* (Edinburgh 1948),
338–9; Dickens, *Lübeck Diary*, 235–6; *The Manchester Guardian*, 7 May 1945; *The New York Times*, 10 May 1945; *The St Louis Post–Dispatch*, 9 May 1945; *The Age* (Melbourne), 12 May 1945; and *The Washington Post*, 10 May 1945.

15 Roberts, *From the Desert to the Baltic*, 242–3; Jordan Vause, *U-Boat Ace: The Story of Wolfgang Lüth* (Annapolis 1990), 201–8; Sir W. Strong 'Diary of a Tour through Germany, 1–6 Jul. 1945,' FO 371/46933, PRO; *The Stars and Stripes*, 6 Jul. 1945 and 11 Apr. 1946; *The Globe and Mail*, 11 Jul. 1945; *The New York Times*, 11 Jul. 1945; *The Daily Express*, 11 Jul. 1945; *The Manchester Guardian*, 3 Jul. and 7 Jul. 1945; *Le Figaro*, 30 May 1945; *Le Monde*, 17 Jan. 1946; CCG (BE) 'Intelligence Bulletin' no. 7, 28 Feb. 1946; no. 8, 13 Mar. 1946; no. 9, 28 Mar. 1946; no. 11, 26 Apr. 1946; no. 13, 24 May 1946; no. 14, 7 Jun. 1946, all in FO 1005/1701, PRO; and MI-14 'Mitropa' no. 13, 12 Jan. 1946, FO 371/55630, PRO.

16 FHO (IIa) 'Zusammenstellung von Chi-Nachrichten' no. 1023, 5 Apr. 1945, Records of OKH, Microcopy no. T-78, Reel 496, frame 6484378, NA; *Historical and Pictorial Review of the 28th Infantry Division in World War II* (Nashville 1980), 171; and *The New York Times*, 4 Apr. 1945.

17 *Völkischer Beobachter*, 12 Apr. 1945.

18 American Intelligence Report, OSS 133195, RG 226, NA.

19 Reckitt, *Diary of Military Government in Germany*, 25, 31–3, 46, 54; *Journal de Genève*, 5 Apr. 1945; *The Daily Herald*, 7 Apr. 1945; *History of the Counter Intelligence Corps*, vol. 20, 9, 37, NA; *History of the 94th Infantry Division in World War Two*, 481; ECAD 'General Intelligence Bulletin' no. 46, 1 Jun. 1945, WO 219/3760, PRO; Twenty-first Army Group 'CI News Sheet' no. 25, 13 Jul. 1945, WO 205/997, PRO; and CCG(BE) 'Intelligence Division Summary' no. 2, 22 Jul. 1945, FO 1005/1702, PRO.

20 'Intelligence Summary' no. 10, 19 Jun. 1947, State Dept. Decimal File 1945–9, 740.00119 Control (Germany), RG 59, NA; Nathan White, *From Fedala to Berchtesgaden: A History of the Seventh United States Infantry in World War II* (Brockton 1947), 257, 260; *History of the Counter Intelligence Corps*, vol. 20, 116, NA; and *The New York Times*, 3 Apr. 1945. For civilian participation in combat in (and near) the Odenwald, see SHAEF G-2 'Weekly Intelligence Summary' no. 54, 1 Apr. 1945, Part I, WO 219/5170, PRO; Joseph Hasson, *With the 114th in the ETO* (1945), 103; and *The 106th Cavalry Group in Europe, 1944–1945* (Augsburg 1945), 107.

21 *History of the Counter Intelligence Corps*, vol. 20, 110–11; and Sayer and Botting, *America's Secret Army*, 233–4.

22 For the role of guerrillas in the Harz during the Thirty Years War, see Öle Stender-Petersen, 'Harzskytterne: Et glemt Kapital Christian 4.s Nedersachsiske Krig,' *Historie* 13/3 (1980), 49–70.

23 Struve, *Aufstieg und Herrschaft des Nationalsozialismus in einer industriellen Klein-*

stadt, 34, 44, 100–4, 115–18, 125, 153–7, 161–5; and *Justiz und NS-Verbrechen*, vol. 19, 639.

24 Kehm to SHAEF ACoS G-2, 28 May 1945, WO 219/1651, PRO; SHAEF G-5 'Civil Affairs-Military Government Weekly Field Report,' 19 May 1945, State Dept. Decimal File 1945–9, 740.00119 Control (Germany), RG 59, NA; and *The New York Times*, 17 Apr. 1945.

25 Ultra Documents BT 9894, 9 Apr. 1945; BT 9943, 9 Apr. 1945 (both Reel 69); KO 62, 10 Apr. 1945 (Reel 70); and KO 758, 18 Apr. 1945 (Reel 72), all in Ultra Document Collection; Bornemann, *Die letzten Tage in der Festung Harz*, 10–11, 22–3; Hartmann Lauterbacher, *Erlebt und mitgestaltet: Kronzeuge einer Epoch, 1923–1945. Zu neuen Ufern nach Kriegsende* (Preussisch Oldendorf 1984), 318–19; Struve, *Aufstieg und Herrschaft des Nationalsozialismus in einer industriellen Kleinstadt*, 491–2, 494; *Justiz und NS-Verbrechen*, vol. 20, 819; Kesselring, *Memoirs*, 267; and MacDonald, *The Last Offensive*, 390–1.

26 Rose, *Werwolf*, 119–20; Bornemann, *Die letzten Tage in der Festung Harz*, 17; Struve, *Aufstieg und Herrschaft des Nationalsozialismus in einer industrielen Kleinstadt*, 493; Schneider, 'Der Frieden begann mit Süssigkeit – Wernigerode/Harz 1945,' 177; *The St Louis Post–Dispatch*, 22 Apr. 1945; and *The Washington Post*, 22 Apr. 1945.

27 Struve, *Aufstieg und Herrschaft des Nationalsozialismus in einer industriellen Kleinstadt*, 502–3; *Justiz und NS-Verbrechen*, vol. 3, 57–64; vol. 13, 708–21; Bornemann, *Die letzten Tage in der Festung Harz*, 28, 58–9, 102; Leach, *In Tornado's Wake*, 179–80; MacDonald, *The Last Offensive*, 404; Joseph Mittelman, *Eight Stars to Victory: The History of the Veteran Ninth US Infantry Division* (Washington 1948), 364–5; and *The New York Times*, 17 Apr. 1945.

28 Görlitz, *Der Zweite Weltkrieg*, vol. 2, 544; and Steinhoff, Pechel and Showalter, *Voices from the Third Reich*, 497–8.

29 Struve, *Aufstieg und Herrschaft des Nationalsozialismus in einer industriellen Kleinstadt*, 509; and Bornemann, *Die letzten Tage in der Festung Harz*, 29–30, 41–2.

30 Lawton Collins, *Lighting Joe: An Autobiography* (Baton Rouge 1979), 322; and MacDonald, *The Last Offensive*, 403–4.

31 Rose, *Werwolf*, 120; *The New York Times*, 17 Apr. 1945; and Bornemann, *Die letzten Tage in der Festung Harz*, 78–9.

32 Ultra Document KO 946, 21 Apr. 1945, Ultra Document Collection, Reel no. 71.

33 Mittelman, *Eight Stars to Victory*, 370; and KO 985, 21 Apr. 1945, Ultra Document Collection, Reel no. 71.

34 Mittelman, *Eight Stars to Victory*, 371; Leach, *In Tornado's Wake*, 184–5; MacDonald, *The Last Offensive*, 405; *Spearhead in the West: The Third Armoured Division, 1941–45* (Nashville 1980), 155; Bornemann, *Die letzten Tage in der Festung Harz*, 75–6, 88; Struve, *Aufstieg und Herrschaft des Nationalsozialismus in einer*

industriellen Kleinstadt, 510; and Nikolaus Ritter, *Deckname Dr. Rantzau* (Hamburg 1972), 295.

35 *The New York Times*, 25 Apr. 1945; *The Washington Post*, 25 Apr. 1945; Leach, *In Tornado's Wake*, 186; Bornemann, *Die letzten Tage in der Festung Harz*, 87; and *History of the Counter Intelligence Corps*, vol. 20, 9, NA.

36 *History of the Counter Intelligence Corps*, vol. 20, 54–5, NA.

37 Ibid., vol. 20, 9, 84, 105, NA. For mention of isolated wire-cutting incidents near Sangerhausen, see *Spearhead in the West*, 155.

38 Leach, *In Tornado's Wake*, 186–7.

39 Ibid., 187; and *History of the Counter Intelligence Corps*, vol. 20, 50, NA.

40 Rose, *Werwolf*, 120–1.

41 Felix Gilbert, *A European Past: Memoirs, 1905–1945* (New York 1988), 197.

42 Rose, *Werwolf*, 121. For the testimony of a German straggler captured by Poles in the Harz on 27 Apr. 1945, see *Jugend unterm Schicksal*, 46.

43 *History of the 120th Infantry Regiment*, 253.

44 *The Stars and Stripes*, 27 May 1945; and Leach, *In Tornado's Wake*, 187.

45 SHAEF JIC 'Political Intelligence Report,' 20 Jun. 1945, WO 219/1700, PRO.

46 Leach, *In Tornado's Wake*, 187.

47 *The Wartime Journals of Charles A. Lindbergh* (New York 1970), 991.

48 Twenty-first Army Group 'News Sheet' no. 26, 30 Jul. 1945, WO 205/997, PRO; and CCG (BE) Intelligence Division 'Summary' no. 2, 22 Jul. 1946, FO 1005/1702, PRO.

49 William Hughes, *Those Human Russians* (London 1950), 86–7. For confirmation that the Soviets arrived in Western Saxony and Thuringia with a comparative degree of order and civility, see Louis Weisner, Memo no. 119 'Conditions of Political Life in the Soviet Zone of Germany and in Berlin,' 18 Mar. 1946, State Dept. Decimal File 1945–9, 740.00119 Control (Germany), RG 59, NA.

50 Fritz Löwenthal, *News from Soviet Germany* (London 1950), 147–8; Naimark, *The Russians in Germany*, 558; Antonyuk to Abyzov, 10 Apr. 1946; Gorbatovskii to Korchagin, 5 May 1946, both in *Pogranichnye Voiska SSSR Mai, 1945–1950*, 160–1; and CCG (BE) Intelligence Division 'Summary' no. 2, 15 Nov. 1947, FO 1005/1703, PRO.

51 Donald Tracey, 'The Development of the National Socialist Party in Thuringia, 1924–30,' *Central European History* 8/1 (Mar. 1975), 23–5; and Fenske, *Wahlrecht und Parteiensystem*, 304–5, 313.

52 'Kretschmar, Gerhard,' IRR File XE 049 888 'Werewolf Activities Vol. I,' RG 319, NA; and USFET MIS Center 'CI Intermediate Interrogation Report (CI-IIR) no. 46 – O/Stubaf. Hans Wolff,' 22 Jan. 1946, in *Covert Warfare* 13.

53 Ultra Document KO 57, 10 Apr. 1945, Ultra Document Collection, Reel 70.

54 German War Communiqués, 8 Apr., 9 Apr., 10 Apr., and 12 Apr. 1945; SHAEF G-5

'Military Government – Civil Affairs Weekly Field Report' no. 46, 28 Apr. 1945, State Dept. Decimal Files 1945–9, 740.00119 Control (Germany), RG 59, NA; *The Story of the 11th Armoured Division* (1945), 19; Patton Diary, 310, 315, 322–32, *David Irving, Papers Relating to the Allied High Command, 1943/45*, Reel no. 4; *The Washington Post*, 25 Apr. 1945; *The St Louis Post–Dispatch*, 8 Apr., 15 Apr., and 25 Apr. 1945; and *The 89th Infantry Division, 1942–1945* (Washinton 1947), 130.

55 SHAEF PID Intelligence Section 'Citizen's Security Organization in Hildburghausen, Thüringen,' 23 May 1945, OSS 131771, RG 226, NA.

56 Twenty-first Army Group 'Weekly CI News Sheet' no. 20, IRR File XE 049 888 'Werewolf Activities Vol. I,' RG 319, NA; USFET MIS Center 'Consolidated Interrogation Report (CIR)' no. 8, 31 Aug. 1945, OSS XL 15368, RG 226, NA; and U.S. Third Army, ACoS G-2 Intelligence Center 'Interrogation Report' no. 26, 2 Aug. 1945, OSS XL 15457, RG 226, NA.

57 Kershaw, *Popular Opinion and Political Dissent in the Third Reich*, 20, 23, 27, 48, 342; and Pridham, *Hitler's Rise to Power*, 321–3.

58 Paul, 'Veränderungen aus dem Tagebuch 1945,' 92; Jack Eisner, *The Survivor* (New York 1980), 300; E.G.C. Beckwith, ed., *The Mansel Diaries: The Diaries of Captain John Mansel, Prisoner-of-War – and Camp Forager – in Germany, 1940–45* (London 1977), 144–7; Peter Seewald, 'Grüss Gott, ihr seid frei,' 105; Dyer, *XII Corps*, 460; *The Stars and Stripes*, 18 Jun. and 29 Jun. 1945; U.S. Third Army 'Military Government Weekly Report,' 11 Jun. 1945, OSS 137425, RG 226, NA; *The Washington Post*, 18 Jun. 1945; and Diary of Maj.-Gen. Everrett Hughes, 304, *David Irving, Papers Relating to the Allied High Command, 1943/45*, Reel no. 5.

59 USFET G-2 'Weekly Intelligence Summary' no. 16, 1 Nov. 1945, State Dept. Decimal File 1945–9, 740.00119 Control (Germany), RG 59, NA.

60 Johnpeter Horst Grill, *The Nazi Movement in Baden, 1920–1945* (Chapel Hill 1983), 135–41, 144–50, 165–8, 190–1, 229–30, 237–8, 240; and O'Laughlin, Flint and Anselin, 'The Geography of the Nazi Vote,' 355–6.

61 P. de Tristan, First French Army, 5th Bureau 'Monthly Historical Report,' 1 May 1945, WO 219/2587, PRO; ibid., 1 Jun. 1945, State Dept. Decimal File 1945–9, 740.00119 Control (Germany), RG 59, NA; R. Smith, Military Attaché, Paris, MID Military Attaché Report, 9 Jun. 1945, OSS 133586, RG 226, NA; and *L'Aube*, 23 Apr. 1945. For the evolution of Catholic opinion on Naziism in Baden, see Cornelia Rauh-Kühne, *Katholisches Milieu und Kleinstadtgesellschaft: Ettlingen, 1918–1939* (Sigmaringen 1991), 423–5.

62 Direction Générale des Études et Recherches 'Bulletin de Renseignements – Allemagne: Depot de Werwolf en Forêt Noire,' 20 Aug. 1945, 7P 125, SHAT; P. de Tristan, First French Army, 5th Bureau 'Monthly Historical Report,' 1 May 1945, WO 219/2587, PRO; and Otto Abetz, *Das Offene Problem* (Cologne 1951), 300–1.

63 Direction Générale des Études et Recherches 'Bulletin de Renseignements – Alle-
    magne: Services Speciaux. Wehrwolf,' 23 Jun. 1945, P7 125, SHAT; Rose, *Werwolf*,
    207–10, 304–5; Zolling, '"Was machen wir am Tag nach unserum Sieg?,"' 121;
    Justiz und NS-Verbrechen, vol. 12, 545–71; G-2 (OSS) 6th AG to R & A Branch
    Paris, 1 May 1945, 'Werewolf Propaganda,' OSS 128942, RG 226, NA; and Ueber-
    schär, '"Volkssturm" und "Werwolf",' 34.

64 Heinrich Köhler, *Lebenserinnerungen des Politikers und Staatsmannes, 1878–1949*
    (Stuttgart 1964), 349–50.

65 Marshal Lattre de Tassigny, *The History of the French First Army* (London 1952),
    480; and SHAEF G-2 'Weekly Intelligence Summary' no. 58, Part I, 29 Apr. 1945.

66 Ultra Document 1333, 25 Apr. 1945, Ultra Document Collection, Reel 72.

67 'Maquis Allemands,' 7P 125, SHAT.

68 *Avant-Garde*, 5 Sep. 1945.

69 Riedel, *Marbach*, 15, 18, 23–5, 35–48.

70 Samuel Goudsmit, *ALSOS: The Failure of German Science* (London 1977), 98;
    Alfred Beck et al., *The Corps of Engineers: The War Against Germany* (Washington
    1975), 556–8; and R.V. Jones, *The Wizard War* (New York 1978), 478, 486.

71 Marc Hillel, *L'Occupation Française en Allemagne, 1945–9* (Paris 1983), 125–30;
    De Coquet, *Nous sommes les occupants*, 98–100, 111–113; and Henri Navarre, *Le
    Temps des vérités* (Paris 1979), 184. Some French units made a general practice of
    shelling each German town before they entered it, mainly with the intent of pre-
    empting civilian resistance: Pierre Lyautey, *Carnets d'un goumier: Allemagne 1945*
    (Paris 1945), 97–8.

72 Capt. Memmendinger to ACoS, G-5, Sixth Army Group, 26 Jun. 1945, State Dept.
    Decimal Files 1945–9, 940.00119 Control (Germany), RG 59, NA; SHAEF JIC G-2
    'Political Intelligence Report,' 14 May 1945, WO 219/1659, PRO; Navarre, *Le
    Temps des vérités*, 183; and 'Maquis Allemands,' 7P 125, SHAEF.

73 P. de Tristan, First French Army, 5th Bureau 'Monthly Historical Report,' 1 May
    1945, WO 219/2587, PRO; and de Lattre, *Reconquérir*, 329–30.

74 P. de Tristan, First French Army, 5th Bureau 'Monthly Historical Report,' 1 Jun.
    1945, State Dept. Decimal Files 1945–9, 740.00119 Control (Germany), RG 59, NA;
    Sixth Army Group 'Civil Security,' IRR File XE 049 888 'Werewolf Activities Vol.
    I,' RG 319, NA; Rose, *Werwolf*, 325; 'Maquis Allemands'; 1ère Armée Française,
    2ème Bureau 'Bulletin de Renseignments,' 16 May 1945, 'Annex 3,' both in 7P 125,
    SHAT; Henri Amouroux, *La Page n'est pas encore tournée* (Paris 1993), 279; and
    The New York Times, 4 Jun. 1945.

75 'Maquis Allemands,' 7P 125, SHAT.

76 Steinhoff, Pechel, and Showalter, *Voices from the Third Reich*, 492–3.

77 *L'Aube*, 27–8 May 1945.

78 P. de Tristan, First French Army, 5th Bureau 'Monthly Historical Report,' 1 Jun.

1945, State Dept. Decimal Files 1945–9, 740.00119 Control (Germany), RG 59, NA; and 'Maquis Allemands,' 7P 125, SHAT.

79 American Legation, Bern, 'Recent Swiss Press Comment on Allied Occupation Policy,' 20 Nov. 1945, State Dept. Decimal Files 1945–9, 740.00119 Control (Germany), RG 59, NA.

80 OSS Report from Switzerland, F-2320, 25 May 1945, OSS L 57490, RG 226, NA.

81 'Maquis Allemands,' 7P 125, SHAT; *The New York Times*, 3 Jun. and 4 Jun. 1945; *L'Aurore*, 25 May 1945; Allied Intelligence Report, p. 6, OSS 134791, RG 226, NA; Christian Zentner and Friedemann Bedürftig, eds., *Encyclopedia of the Third Reich*, vol. 2 (New York 1991), 1042; *Justiz und NS-Verbrechen*, vol. 17, 618, 627–8, 630; Maj.-Gen. Smith, Military Attaché at Paris, MID Military Attaché Report, 9 Jun. 1945, OSS 133586, RG 226, NA; PID 'Germany: Weekly Background Notes' no. 4, 4 Jul. 1945, FO 371/46933, PRO; and Ueberschär, '"Volkssturm" und "Werwolf",' 34–5.

82 *Neue Zürcher Zeitung*, 16 Jun. 1945.

83 Görlitz, *Der Zweite Weltkrieg*, 545; and Hillel, *L'Occupation française*, 235.

84 Steinhoff, Pechel, and Shawalter, *Voices from the Third Reich*, 493; *Neue Zürcher Zeitung*, 1 Jul. 1945; Ministre de l'Information 'Articles et Documents,' 17 Sep. 1945, Nouvelle série no. 274, 7P 125, SHAT; *The Stars and Stripes*, 24 Feb. 1946; and 250 British Liaison Mission 'Report' no. 8, Jul. 1947; and no. 9, Dec. 1947, both in FO 1005/1615, PRO.

85 Peter Black, *Ernst Kaltenbrunner* (Princeton 1984), 235–6; Rauchensteiner, *Krieg in Österreich, 1945*, 239–40, 256; Eigruber to Speer, 25 Jan. 1945, Records of the NSDAP, Microcopy no. T-81, Roll 94, frame 107905, NA; Franz Hofer 'The National Redoubt'; Georg Ritter von Hengl 'The Alpine Redoubt'; Georg Ritter von Hengl 'Report on the Alpine Fortress,' all in *World War Two German Military Studies*, vol. 24; DIC (MIS)/M.1116 Summary Interrogation Report 'The "National Redoubt,"' 10 Apr. 1945, OSS 124431, RG 226, NA; Mobile Field Interrogation Unit no. 2 'PW Intelligence Bulletin' no. 2/44, 12 Mar. 1945, OSS 124057, RG 226, NA; MFIU no. 1 'PW Intelligence Bulletin' no. 1/56, 9 Apr. 1945, OSS 126114, RG 226, NA; Office of U.S. Chief Counsel, Evidence Div., Interrogation Br. 'Summary #673 – G.R. Gerhardt'; 'Summary #819 – G.R. Gerhardt,' both in IWM; Ultra Document BT 4477, 10 Feb. 1945, Ultra Document Collection, Reel 61; *Blitzkrieg to Defeat*, 176–81; *Die Verhinderte Alpenfestung Berchtesgaden 1945*, 44; SHAEF G-2 'Weekly Intelligence Summary' no. 51, 11 Mar. 1945, Part I; no. 56, 15 Apr. 1945, Part I; *Libération*, 16 May 1945; *The Manchester Guardian*, 8 Jun. 1945; and *Le Monde*, 16 May 1945.

86 SHAEF G-2 'Weekly Intelligence Summary' no. 57, 22 Apr. 1945, Part I.

87 Jenkins, 'The Battle of the German National Redoubt – Planning Phase,' 3; OSS R & A no. 1934.1 'The Clandestine Nazi Movement in Post-War Germany,' 13 Oct. 1944,

OSS/State Department Intelligence and Research Reports, Micf. Reel XIV; Minott, *The Fortress That Never Was*, 15–26; Rauchensteiner, *Krieg in Österreich 1945*, 240–1; PID 'German Propaganda and the German,' 9 Oct. 1944, FO 898/187, PRO; Franz Hofer 'The National Redoubt'; Franz Hofer 'The Alpine Fortification – & Defence Line: A Report on German and US Views of the Alpine Redoubt in 1944'; Georg Ritter von Hengl 'The Alpine Redoubt,' all in *World War II German Military Studies*, vol. 24; SHAEF G-5 'Weekly Journal of Information' no. 3, 7 Mar. 1945, WO 219/3918, PRO; and Conrad to MIS, War Dept., 27 Mar. 1945, Army-Intelligence Project Decimal File 1941–5, 370.64 (Germany), RG 319, NA.

88 Wilhelm Höttl, *The Secret Front* (New York 1954), 312–13; Manfred Rauchensteiner, *Der Sonderfall* (Graz 1979), 99–100; Black, *Ernst Kaltenbrunner*, 258–9; and Minott, *The Fortress That Never Was*, 127.

89 Franz Hofer 'The Alpine Redoubt'; Georg Ritter von Hengl 'Report on the Alpine Fortress,' 25 Apr. 1946; George Ritter von Hengl 'The Alpine Redoubt,' all in *World War II German Military Studies*, vol. 24; Rauchensteiner, *Krieg in Österreich 1945*, 242–3; Koller, *Der letzte Monat*, 71; SHAEF G-2 'Weekly Intelligence Summary' no. 58, 29 Apr. 1945, Part I; and Ultra Document, KO 1674, 29 Apr. 1945, Ultra Document Collection, Roll 73.

90 ACA (BE) CMF 'Joint Weekly Intelligence Summary' no. 23, 15 Dec. 1945, FO 1007/300, PRO.

91 Ultra Document, KO 12858, 2 May 1945, Ultra Document Collection, Roll 73; Black, *Ernst Kaltenbrunner*, 257; and von Salomon *Fragebogen*, 319, 333.

92 I.A. Maisal to OB West, AOK 1, AOK 19, Wkr. VII, and Wkr. XVIII, 28 Apr. 1945 (frames 5610751–5610752); and I.A. Maisal 'Vortragsnotiz für Chef HPA,' 29 Apr. 1945 (frame 5610750), both in Records of OKW, Microcopy no. T-77, Roll 863, NA. These documents directly contradict von Hengl's later claim to American interrogators that 'I never received any orders concerning guerrilla warfare in the Alpine region': Georg Ritter von Hengl 'Report on the Alpine Fortress,' 25 Apr. 1946, *World War II German Military Studies*, vol. 24. Von Hengl's interrogation reports have formed an important source for much of the literature on the redoubt, including Rodney Minott's *The Fortress That Never Was*.

93 FID IPW Team – PWE no. 1, ETO PWE Interrogation Def. no. 2016 'Summary Report on the "Redoubt Area" of Austria and SE Bavaria,' 1 May 1945, OSS XL 8961, RG 226, NA.

94 Letter to the author from Josef Dax, 26 Feb. 1992.

95 James, 'The Battle of the German National Redoubt – Planning Phase,' 6–8; James, 'The Battle of the German National Redoubt – Operational Phase,' 24–6; Kesselring, *Memoirs*, 276; Georg Ritter von Hengl 'Report on the Alpine Fortress,' 25 Apr. 1946, 2–4, *World War Two German Military Studies*, vol. 24; Mark Clark, *Calculated Risk* (New York 1950), 440–1; SHAEF JIC (45) 14 'Enemy Capacity to Con-

tinue the War,' 27 Apr. 1945; and SHAEF JIC (45) 17(Final) 'Disposition of German Forces after the Junction of the Allied and Russian Armies,' 20 Apr. 1945, both in WO 219/1700, PRO. For the numbers of training troops in the Alps, see Rauchensteiner, *Krieg in Österreich, 1945*, 257, 262, 268, 270–1; Mobile Field Interrogation Unit no. 2 'PW Intelligence Bulletin' no. 2144, 12 Mar. 1945, OSS 124057, RG 226, NA; and MFIU no. 1 'PW Intelligence Bulletin' no. 1/56, 9 Apr. 1945, OSS 126114, RG 226, NA.

96 Reitlinger, *The SS*, 370–1.

97 Georg Ritter von Hengl 'Report on the Alpine Fortress,' 25 Apr. 1946; Franz Hofer 'The National Redoubt,' both in *World War Two German Military Studies*, vol. 24; *The Seventh United States Army in France and Germany*, vol. 3, 845, 860–1; Walter Maass, *Country without a Name* (New York 1979), 146; Turner and Jackson, *Destination Berchtesgaden*, 187; Weibel-Altmeyer, *Alpenfestung*, 229–35; Amouroux, *La Page n'est pas tournée*, 415–16; Minott, *The Fortress That Never Was*, 126; *L'Aurore*, 9 May 1945; Paul Reynaud, *In the Thick of the Fight* (New York 1955), 653–5; Radomir Luza, *The Resistance in Austria, 1938–1945* (Minneapolis 1984), 253–4, 256–7; and Edouard Daladier, *Journal de Captivité, 1940–45* (1991), 349–51.

98 *The Manchester Guardian*, 19 May 1945.

99 Harald Walser, *Die illegale NSDAP in Tirol und Voralberg, 1933–1938* (Vienna 1983), 1–22, 31–4; Ernst Hanisch, 'Westösterreich,' in *NS-Herrschaft in Österreich, 1938–1945*, ed. Emmerich Talos, Ernst Hanisch, Wolfgang Neugebauer, 442–3 (Vienna 1988); and Radomir Luza, *Austro-German Relations in the Anschluss Era* (Princeton 1975), 119–20, 308, 318–19.

100 U.S. Seventh Army Interrogation Centre, 24 May 1945, IRR File XE 049 888 'Werewolf Activities, Vol. I,' RG 319, NA.

101 *The Christian Science Monitor*, 7 Jul. 1945; and Rinser, 'Zwischen den Zeiten,' 213–14.

102 Twenty-first Army Group 'Weekly Political Intelligence Summary' no. 3, 21 Jul. 1945, FO 371/46933, PRO; Troll, 'Aktionen zur Kriegsbeendigung in Früjahr 1945,' 685–6; USFET Interrogation Center 'Intermediate Interrogation Report (IIR) #9 – H/Stut. Hans Gerlach,' 11 Aug. 1945, OSS XL 13744, RG 226 NA; ACA(BE) Intelligence Organisation 'Joint Weekly Intelligence Summary' no. 27, 19 Jan. 1946, FO 1007/300, PRO; SHAEF JIC 'Political Intelligence Report,' 2 Jul. 1945, WO 219/1700, PRO; and 1ère Armée Française, 2ème Bureau 'Bulletin de Renseignements,' 16 May, Annex 4; Direction Générale des Études et Recherches 'Bulletin de Renseignements – Allemagne: Activité clandestin dans le Voralberg,' 2 Jul. 1945, both in 7P 125, SHAT.

103 1ère Armée Française, 2ème Bureau 'Bulletin de Renseignements,' 16 May 1945, Annex '4,' 7P 125, SHAT; *Le Monde*, 13 Sep. 1945; and ACA Intelligence Organi-

sation 'Joint Weekly Intelligence Summary' no. 11, 14 Sep. 1945, FO 1007/300, PRO.

104 *The Seventh United States Army in France and Germany*, vol. 3, 850; Hugh Daley, *42nd "Rainbow" Infantry Division: A Combat History of World War II* (Baton Rouge 1946); Joseph Hasson, *With the 114th in the ETO* (1945), 123; Hallig, *Festung Alpen*, 118–24; and Kästner, *Notabene 45*, 150, 158.

105 *Le Monde*, 15 May 1945; *FO Weekly Political Intelligence Summaries* 11, Summary no. 293, 16 May 1945; Pearson, *Enroute to the Redoubt*, vol. 3, 221, 223, 235–6, 244, 260; Weibel-Altmeyer, *Alpenfestung*, 264; *History of the Counter Intelligence Corps*, vol. 25, 17; Howe, *Salt Mines and Castles*, 162; USFET G-5 'Political Intelligence Letter' no. 1, 3 Aug. 1945; USFET G-2 'Weekly Intelligence Summary' no. 11, 27 Sep. 1945, both in State Dept. Decimal File 1945–9, 740.00119 Control (Germany), RG 59, NA; *The Christian Science Monitor*, 7 Jul. 1945; Rapport and Northwood, 756; *The Globe and Mail*, 30 Jun. 1945; SHAEF JIC 'Political Intelligence Report,' 20 Jun. 1945, WO 219/1700, PRO; *The Washington Post*, 18 Jun. and 24 Jun. 1945. For interrogation information on the '*Das Reich*' SS-'Resistance Movement,' see CSDIC WEA BAOR 'Final Report on Ostubaf Franz Riedwig and Hptstuf Arthur Gratwohl,' 18 Sep. 1946; DIC/CCG (BE) FR no. 102 'Final Report on Ernst Müller, Wolfgang Wegener, and Heinrich Wolpert,' 5 Oct. 1946; CSDIC WEA BAOR FR no. 96 'Final Report on Robert Rathke, Otto Specht, Albert Horschemeyer, Theodor Butke,' 30 Sep. 1946; CSDIC WEA BAOR FR no. 99 'Final Report on Willi Theile,' 21 Sep. 1946; and HQ BAOR 'Fortnightly Military Intelligence Summary' no. 4, 15 Jun. 1946, all in ETO MIS-Y-Sect. CSDIC/WEA Final Interrogation Records 1945–7, RG 332, NA. For a confirmation of heavy fighting around Salzburg until 11 May, see David Max Eichhorn, 'Sabbath Service in Dachau Concentration Camp,' *Dachau Review* 1 (1989), 104. For the events around Mauthausen, see Christian Bernadac, *Le Neuvième Cercle* (Montreal 1982), 256; Evelyn Le Chêne, *Mauthausen: The History of a Death Camp* (London 1971), 163, 170–1, 173–4, 218; *The Daily Herald*, 8 Jun. 1945; and Tom Segev, *Soldiers of Evil* (New York 1987), 155.

106 *Die Verhinderte Alpenfestung Berchtesgaden, 1945*, 25–7, 39–40, 42, 45–6, 102; and *The St Louis Post–Dispatch*, 7 May 1945.

107 Sixth Army Group, Office of Asst. CoS G-2 'Monthly Counter-Intelligence Report' no. 14, 30 May 1945, OSS 134791, RG 226, NA.

108 Ralph Mueller and Jerry Turk, *Report after Action: The Story of the 103rd Infantry Division* (Innsbruck 1945), 135–6.

109 Pridham, *Hitler's Rise to Power*, 322–3; Kershaw, *Popular Opinion and Political Dissent in the Third Reich*, 18, 21, 23; and Michael Kater, *The Nazi Party* (Cambridge 1983), 22–9.

110 Kershaw, *Popular Opinion and Political Opinion in the Third Reich*, 207, 341–57; and USFET MIS Center 'Intermediate Interrogation Report (IIR) #18 – Krm. Rat. Wagner, Ernst,' 30 Aug. 1945, IRR File XE 049 888 'Werewolf Activities Vol. I,' RG 319, NA.

111 R. Murphy, Pol. Adv. Germany to J. Caffrey to Sec. of State, 29 May 1945; Heath, Office of Pol. Adv. Germany via J. Caffrey to Sec. of State, 2 Jun. 1945; USGCC 'Observations on the Situation in Munich,' 16 Jul. 1945; USFET G-5 'Political Intelligence Letter' no. 1, 3 Aug. 1945; USFET MG Office 'Bi-Weekly Political Summary' no. 7, 1 Dec. 1945; USFET G-2 'Weekly Intelligence Summary' no. 22, 13 Dec. 1945, all in State Dept. Decimal File 1945–9, 740.00119 Control (Germany), RG 59, NA; *History of the Counter Intelligence Corps*, vol. 26, 68, NA; MI-14 'Mitropa' no. 15, 9 Feb. 1946, FO 371/55630, PRO; Howe, *Salt Mines and Castles*, 72; OSS Report from Germany, LP 8-163, 158, 160, LP/7-19, Sep. 1945, OSS 23770, RG 226, NA; OSS Report from Germany, L-991, 29 Nov. 1945, OSS 31522, RG 226, NA; *Le Monde*, 26 Jul. 1945; *Neue Zürcher Zeitung*, 23 Jul. 1935; *The New York Times*, 30 Sep. 1945; and *The Washington Post*, 23 Jul. 1945.

112 'Minutes of Special Staff Meeting, US Group CC,' 1 Aug. 1945, State Dept. Decimal File 1945–9, 740.00119 Control (Germany), RG 59, NA; and *The Washington Post*, 1 Oct. 1945.

113 OMGUS, Office of Political Affairs, Political R & A Br. 'Daily Information Summary' no. 231, 15 May 1946, State Dept. Decimal File 1945–9, 740.00119 Control (Germany), RG 59, NA; and *The New York Times*, 22 Apr. 1946.

114 'Comments of Russian Correspondents on the American Zone Appearing in the German Press,' 11 Feb. 1946; USFET G-2 'Weekly Intelligence Summary' no. 32, 21 Feb. 1946; no. 40, 18 Apr. 1946; no. 42, 2 May 1946; no. 56, 8 Aug. 1945; no. 61, 12 Sep. 1946; no. 63, 26 Sep. 1946; no. 65, 10 Oct. 1946; and Office of MG for Germany, Press Release, 9 May 1946, all in State Dept. Decimal File 1945–9, 740.00119 Control (Germany), RG 59, NA.

115 Karl Hnilicka, *Das Ende auf dem Balkan, 1944/45* (Göttingen 1970), 156; Lucas, *Last Days of the Reich*, 110–12; Rauchensteiner, *Krieg in Österreich, 1945*, 323–5; *Operation Slaughterhouse,* John Prcela and Stanko Guldescu, eds. (Philadelphia 1970), 78–9; Reg Herschy, *Freedom at Midnight* (Upton upon Severn 1989), 143; British Troops Austria 'Joint Weekly Intelligence Summary' no. 7, 17 August 1945, FO 371/46612, PRO; MI-14 'Mitropa' no. 4, 8 Sep. 1945, FO 371/46967, PRO; and *Neue Zürcher Zeitung*, 17 Jun. 1945.

116 Fifteenth Army Group 'Security Summary,' 16 Jun. 1945, WO 204/831, PRO.

117 Stephan Karner, '"... des Reiches Südmark,"' in *NS-Herrschaft in Österreich, 1938–1945*, ed. Emmerich Talos, Ernst Hanisch, Wolfgang Neugebauer, 458–66 (Vienna 1988); and 6 SFSS HQ V Corps 'Notes on the Political Situation in Carinthia and Western Styria, May 1945,' 22 May 1945, FO 371/46610, PRO.

118 Fifteenth Army Group 'Security Summary for May 1945,' 16 Jun. 1945, WO 204/
     831, PRO.
119 A.D. Malcolm, *History of the Argyll and Sutherland Highlanders 8th Battalion*
     (London 1949), 256; *The Manchester Guardian*, 5 Jul. 1945; R.L.V. Ffrench Blake,
     A History of the 17th/21st Lancers, 1922–1959 (London 1962), 227–8, 230; and
     Nikolai Tolstoy, *Victims of Yalta* (London 1979), 274–5, 331.
120 Herschy, *Freedom at Midnight*, 143; Fifteenth Army Group 'Security Summary for
     May 1945,' 16 Jun. 1945, WO 204/831, PRO; ACA(BE) CMF 'Joint Weekly Intel-
     ligence Summary' no. 19, 17 Nov. 1945, FO 1007/300, PRO; AFP 'Découverte
     d'une organisation Nazie en Carinthie,' 19 Jul. 1945, 7P 125, SHAT; ACA(BE)
     Intelligence Organization 'Joint Fortnightly Intelligence Summary' no. 11, 13 Jul.
     1946, FO 1007/301, PRO; Eighth Army 'Joint Weekly Intelligence Summary,' no.
     3, 20 Jul. 1945; no. 4, 27 Jul. 1945; no. 5, 3 Aug. 1945, all in FO 371/46611, PRO;
     MI-14 'Mitropa' no. 1, 29 Jul. 1945, FO 371/46967, PRO; PWB British Units
     (Austria) 'Consolidated Intelligence Report' no. 15, 31 Oct. 1945, FO 1007/297,
     PRO; GSI British Troops Austria 'Joint Weekly Intelligence Summary' no. 7, 17
     Aug. 1945, FO 371/46612, PRO; and PID 'Austria: Weekly Background Notes'
     no. 1, FO 371/46933, PRO.
121 Walter Maass, *Country without a Name: Austria under Nazi Rule, 1938–1945* (New
     York 1979), 149–50.
122 'Background Notes Annex: Calender of Recent Events in Austria,' 18 May 1945,
     FO 371/46790, PRO; *Neue Zürcher Zeitung*, 16 May and 29 May 1945; Logvinov
     to Chernyshev, 30 May 1945; Rozhkov to Pavlov, 1 Jul. and 30 Sep. 1945, all in
     Pogranichnye Voiska SSSR Mai, 1945–1950, 69, 88–9, 133; Rauchensteiner, *Der
     Sonderfall*, 84; and *Le Monde*, 19 May 1945.
123 Lucas, *Last Days of the Reich*, 113; V Corps 'Weekly Intelligence Summary' no. 1,
     11 Jul. 1945; no. 6, 17 Aug. 1945, both in FO 1007/299, PRO; and Rauchensteiner,
     Der Sonderfall, 85.
124 V Corps 'Weekly Intelligence Summary' no. 6, 17 Aug. 1945; no. 7, 30 Aug. 1945;
     British Troops Austria 'Joint Weekly Intelligence Summary' no. 7, 17 Aug. 1945,
     all in FO 1007/300, PRO.
125 ACA Intelligence Organisation 'Joint Weekly Intelligence Summary' no. 12, 27
     Sep. 1945; no. 14, 13 Oct. 1945; no. 15, 20 Oct. 1945; no. 16, 27 Oct. 1945, all in
     FO 1007/300, PRO.
126 ACA Intelligence Organisation 'Joint Weekly Intelligence Summary' no. 12, 27
     Sep. 1945; no. 14, 13 Oct. 1945; no. 15, 20 Oct. 1945; no. 16, 27 Oct. 1945; no. 20,
     24 Nov. 1945, all in FO 1007/300, PRO; PWB Branch Units (British) 'Intelligence
     Summary,' 22 Nov. 1945, FO 1007/297, PRO; and V Corps 'Weekly Intelligence
     Summary' no. 7, 30 Aug. 1945, FO 1007/299, PRO.
127 Steinert, *Capitulation, 1945*, 150.

128 Rysanov to Gavrikov, 30 May 1945, *Pogranichnye Voiska SSSR Mai, 1945–1950*, 74–5.

129 Koniev, *Year of Victory*, 151; and Kingsley Brown, *Bonds of Wire: A Memoir* (Toronto 1989), 239, 246–8, 250, 252.

130 *The Daily Express*, 8 Jun. 1945.

131 Weisenborn, 'Reich Street,' 210–11.

132 Rysanov to Gavrikov, 30 May 1945; Mashin to Alexeev, 11 May and 1 Jul. 1945, all in *Pogranichnye Voiska SSSR Mai, 1945–1950*, 66, 72–4, 82; *Le Monde*, 12 May 1945; *The Washington Post*, 14 May 1945; Hildegard Knef, *The Gift Horse* (New York 1971), 86–8; Erich Honecker, *From My Life* (Oxford 1981), 119; *The Daily Express*, 28 May 1945; and *FO Weekly Political Intelligence Summaries* 12, Summary no. 296, 6 Jun. 1945.

133 Naimark, *The Russians in Germany*, 357–8; Gavrikov to Izugenev, 15 Aug. 1945; Antonyuk to Zimin, 9 Mar. 1946; Antonyuk to Abyzov, 10 Apr. 1946; Morozov to Blyumin, 1 Jan. 1947, all in *Pogranichnye Voiska SSSR Mai, 1945–1950*, 125, 157, 160, 166–7; *The Manchester Guardian*, 30 Oct. 1945; and *Tägliche Rundschau*, 8 Jan. 1946.

134 German War Communique, 21 Apr. 1945; 'Tagesmeldungen vom 21 Apr. 1945,' in *Die Geheimentagesbuch der Deutschen Wehrmachtfuhrüng im Zweiten Weltkrieg, 1939–1945* 12, 399; and *Neue Zürcher Zeitung*, 5 May 1945. For reference to SS bands in the woods northeast of Chemnitz, see P.R. Reid, *The Last Days at Colditz* (London 1965), 318.

135 Fenske, *Wahlrecht und Parteiensystem*, 268–70, 285–8.

136 PID 'Germany: Weekly Background Notes' no. 1, 8 Jun. 1945, FO 371/46933, PRO; and *The Daily Express*, 5 Jun. 1945. For a report on 'thousands of sick and homeless children' wandering in the no man's land in southern Germany, see *The Daily Herald*, 29 May 1945.

137 Naimark, *The Russians in Germany*, 268–9; *The Stars and Stripes*, 28 May 1945; and *The Washington Post*, 28 May 1945.

138 Naimark, *The Russians in Germany*, 269; and *The New York Times*, 3 Jun. 1945.

139 Gregory Klimov, *The Terror Machine* (New York 1953), 121; Kiselev to Drozdov, 19 Nov. 1945; and Report by Lt. Turin, 14 Mar. 1946, both in *Pogranichnye Voiska SSSR Mai, 1945–1950*, 147, 158.

140 A.J.P. Taylor argues that the Second World War ended more 'raggedly' than the Great War, but what he meant was that there was no comprehensive peace treaty, and that all the Axis powers bowed out at different intervals: A.J.P. Taylor, *How Wars End* (London 1985), 83, 103–18.

141 *Daily Express*, 5 May 1945.

142 *Neue Zürcher Zeitung*, 29 May 1945.

143 USFET G-2 'Weekly Intelligence Summary' no. 29, 31 Jan. 1946, State Dept. Decimal File 1945–9, 740.00119 Control (Germany), RG 59, NA. For an example of a radical HJ group that had formed in northern Germany, but had plans for a march to the Alps in order to join larger guerrilla bands in that area, see USFET G-2 'Weekly Intelligence Summary' no. 11, 27 Sep. 1945, State Dept. Decimal Files 1945–9, 740.00119 Control (Germany), RG 59, NA.

6: The Werwolf along Germany's Periphery

1 Der Kommandeur der Orpo im Elsass to Schlierbach, Gestapo Aussenstelle Kolmar, 14 Dec. 1944, 25/R70, Elsass, BA.
2 White, *From Fedala to Berchtesgaden*, 195; Jack Colbaugh, *The Bloody Patch: A True Story of the Daring 28th Infantry Division* (New York 1973), 115; and *Five Years – Five Countries – Five Campaigns: An Account of the One-Hundred-Forty-First Infantry in World War II* (1945), 66.
3 *History of the Tenth Infantry Regiment, United States Army* (Birmingham 1946), 65.
4 George Hoffman, *The Super Sixth: History of the 6th Armoured Division in World War II and Its Post-war Association* (Louisville 1975), 262.
5 *History of the Counter Intelligence Corps*, vol. 17, 32, 46–8, 52; vol. 18, 75, 89, NA; White, *From Fedala to Berchtesgaden*, 199; *Five Years – Five Countries – Five Campaigns*, 89; Hasson, *With the 114th in the ETO*, 29; *L'Humanité*, 26 Sep. 1944; Pearson, *Enroute to the Redoubt*, vol. 2, 100; and *Combat Record of the Sixth Armoured Division – In the European Theatre of Operations, 18 Jul. 1944 – 8 May 1945* (Aschaffenburg 1945), 128.
6 *Libération*, 1 Dec. 1944; White, *From Fedala to Berchtesgaden*, 188; and *The New York Times*, 1 Dec. 1944.
7 *L'Aube*, 2 Dec., 5 Dec., 6 Dec., and 10/11 Dec. 1944; Fernand L'Huillier, *Libération de l'Alsace* (Paris 1975), 91–3; de Lattre, *Reconquérir*, 119–21; Général Vézinet, *Le Général LeClerc de Hauteclocque, Maréchal de France* (Paris 1974), 166; *The Times*, 2 Dec., 4 Dec., 5 Dec., and 6 Dec. 1944; *The Stars and Stripes*, 30 Nov. 1944; *The New York Times*, 2 Dec., and 3 Dec. 1944; *FO Weekly Political Intelligence Summaries* 10, Summary no. 270, 6 Dec. 1944; Summary no. 271, 13 Dec. 1944; FORD 'Review of the Foreign Press: Series F: France and the French Empire,' 11 Dec. 1944, no. 48, *Review of the Foreign Press, 1939–1945* Series F, France, no. 1–62; PWE 'German Propaganda and the German,' 4 Dec. 1944, FO 898/187, PRO; Maja Destrem, *L'Aventure de LeClerc* (1984), 323; and the Commissaire Régional de la République à Strasbourg to M. le Ministre de l'Intérieur, 28 Nov. 1944, F/1a/4024, AN.
8 Eugène Heiser, *La Tragédie lorraine* (1983) vol. 2, 364; vol. 3, 124, 134–5, 140, 142,

150, 154; Huston, *Biography of a Battalion*, 152; Commissariat de la République, Region de Nancy 'Rapport Bi-mensuel,' 16 Nov. 1944, Part XII; 1 Dec. 1944, Part XII, F/1a/4024, AN; and Préfecture de la Moselle 'Rapport,' 20 Dec. 1944, Part XII, F/1cIII/1222, AN.

9 *History of the Counter Intelligence Corps*, vol. 18, 81, NA; and Minister de la Guerre, 5^{éme} Bureau 'Renseignements – Alsace,' 8 Jan 1945, 7P 125, SHAT.

10 *News Review* 19/17 (26 Apr. 1945), 13. For descriptions of the 'Alsatian Freedom Front,' see L'Huillier, *Libération de l'Alsace*, 107; Bankwitz, *Alsatian Autonomist Leaders*, 103; and Grill, *The Nazi Movement in Baden*, 516–17.

11 Joseph Carter, *The History of the 14th Armoured Division* (Atlanta 1946).

12 *The Daily Mirror*, 11 Apr. 1945; and *Völkischer Beobachter*, 13 Apr. 1945.

13 *La Croix*, 8 Jun. 1945; *L'Humanité*, 7 Jun. and 5 Jul. 1945; and *Journal de Genève*, 20 Jul. 1945.

14 'Diary of First US Army (Courtney Hodges),' *David Irving, Papers Relating to the Allied High Command, 1943/45*, Reel no. 8; and Conrad Latour and Thilo Vogelsang, *Okkupation und Wiederaufbau* (Stuttgart 1973), 50.

15 Einsatzkommando I Geheime Staatspolizei Köln to Hoffmann, 26 Oct. 1944, Records of the Reich Leader and Chief of the German Police, Microcopy no. T-175, Roll 577, frames 379–381, NA.

16 Desmond Hawkins, ed., *War Report: D-Day to V-E Day* (London 1985), 243; and Minister de la Guerre 5^{éme} Bureau 'Renseignements – Belgique,' 17 Jan. 1945, 7P 125, SHAT.

17 SS Panzerarmee-Oberkommando 6 Führungsabteilung VI (NSFO), 'Führungshinweis zum Flugblatt "Kameraden wir marschieren wieder,"' 30 Dec. 1944, Records of the Waffen-SS, Microcopy no. T-354, Reel 116, frame 3750130, NA.

18 *Neue Zürcher Zeitung*, 12 Jul. 1945.

19 Sven Tägil, *Deutschland und die deutsche Minderheit in Nordschleswig* (Stockholm 1970), ch. 4; and Naval Intelligence Division 'Denmark' (Jan. 1944), BR no. 509 Geographical Handbook Series.

20 For the numbers of Germans in Denmark, see Steinert, *Capitulation, 1945*, 143–4.

21 *The New York Times*, 29 May 1945, *The Daily Express*, 29 May and 13 Jun. 1945; PID 'News Digest' no. 1769, 28 May 1945, Bramstedt Collection, BLPES; and *The Manchester Guardian*, 13 Jun. 1945.

22 Strategic Services Unit, War Dept. Mission to Germany, Report no. H-10 'Werewolf Activities in Denmark,' IRR File 'Werewolf Activities Vol. I,' XE 049 888, RG 319, NA; *The News Chronicle*, 9 Feb. 1946; *The Stars and Stripes*, 12 Feb. 1946; Intelligence Division, Office of Naval Operations, 'Intelligence Report,' 12 Feb. 1946, State Dept. Decimal File 1945–9, 740.00119 Control (Germany), RG 59, NA; *Le Populaire*, 10 Jul. 1945; *L'Aurore*, 10 Jul. 1945; and *The New York Times*, 15 Jul.

1945. U.S. Strategic Services in Germany believed that the Danes probably exaggerated the importance of the Werwolf movement, and sceptics also suggested that the Hoerseroed skirmish was probably a case of camp guards firing aimlessly into the air and then falsely claiming that they had been attacked. Oslo Radio reported on 22 Jul. 1945 that Werewolves had launched a raid against Danish border guards, and that British troops with armoured cars had been called out to restore order, but there is no confirmation of this from British sources.

23 See, for instance, Edwin Erich Dwinger, *Der Tod in Polen: Die Volksdeutsch Passion* (Jena 1940).

24 Jan Tomasz Gross, *Polish Society under German Occupation* (Princeton 1979); and Richard Lukas, *The Forgotten Holocaust* (Lexington 1986).

25 Wiskemann, *Germany's Eastern Neighbours*, 96; and PID 'News Digest' no. 1767, 25 May 1945, Bramstedt Collection, BLPES.

26 O. Durig 'Polish Hordes in Silesia and the County of Glatz (after the armistice),' 20 May 1946, FO 371/55824, PRO.

27 *Silesian Inferno*, 11, 36, 44; and DeZayas, *Nemesis at Potsdam* (Lincoln 1989), 98, 202.

28 *The Christian Science Monitor*, 12 Feb. 1945. In Memel, the first city in Greater Germany to fall into Russian hands, the Soviets treated all male civilians capable of bearing weapons as POWs: Fremde Heere Ost (III/Prop.), Memo, Records of OKH, Reel 488, frame 6474504, BA. For confirmation that some bypassed troops and Volkssturm fighters changed into civilian clothes, see GFP 729, Interrogation Report on Gefr. W. Hager, 27 Feb. 1945, RH 2/2129, BMA; and M. La Ramee 'Der Kreis Pyritz im letzten Kriegsjahr,' 17 Dec. 1953, Ost Dok. 8/657, BA.

29 H. von Wilckens 'Die Raumung und Besetzung des Kreises Zempelburg (West Preussen) im Januar/Februar 1945,' Ost Dok. 8/218, BA; and *Die Vertreibung der deutschen Bevölkerung aus der Gebeiten östlich der Oder Neisse*, 174–5.

30 *Völkischer Beobachter*, 9 Feb. 1945; 'Wichstige Ereignisse vor H. Gr. Mitte,' 12 Mar. 1945, RH 2/2008, BMA; and *The Daily Mail*, 19 Mar. 1945.

31 *Izvestia*, 6 Feb. 1945.

32 Merkl, *Political Violence*, 78–83, 189; O'Laughlin, Flint and Anselin, 'The Geography of the Nazi Vote,' 360, 362; and Fenske, *Wahlrecht und Parteiensystem*, 268, 270.

33 'Koch, ein 'wackerer Kämpfer' – und wie es wirklich war,' 16 Mar. 1953, Ost Dok. 8/523, BA.

34 *Izvestia*, 31 Jan. 1945; *Istoriya Velikoi Otechestvennoi Voiny Sovetskogo Soyuza, 1941–1945*, vol. 5, 118; *The Christian Science Monitor*, 12 Feb. 1945; *The Times*, 7 Mar. 1945; Nikolaev to Lyubyi, 12 Apr. 1945, in *Pogranichnye Voiska SSSR v Velikoi Otechestvennoi Voine, 1942–1945*, 558, 560; and Christin Andree 'Die Heimat in der Händen der Roten Armee und der Polen,' Ost Dok. 2/1, BA.

35 Bruno Georg Kirschbaum 'Kennwort Gneisenau für Allenstein!,' Ost Dok. 8/550, BA.
36 Lt.-Gen. Lidnikov 'Befehl für die Truppen der 39. Armee,' no. o5/o11, 6 Feb. 1945
    (Germ. transl.) (frames 6474409–6474410); FHO (III Prop.), Memo (frame
    6474505), both in Records of OKH, Microcopy no. T-78, Reel 488, NA; Lasch, *So
    Fiel Breslau*, 69; Nikolaev to Lyubyi, 12 Apr. 1945, *Pogranichnye Voiska SSSR v
    Velikoi Otechestvennoi Voine, 1942–1945*, 559; *The Christian Science Monitor*,
    12 Feb. 1945; and *The Times*, 12 Mar. 1945.
37 Memo by Political Office by the 3rd Belorussian Front, 22 Feb. 1945 (Germ. transl.)
    (frames 6474493–6474494); Gen. Susaikov to Troops of the 2nd Ukrainian Front,
    no. 17, 8 Feb. 1945 (Germ. transl.) (frame 6474401); and 'Auszug aus Frd. Heere
    Ost (IIIg) Az. 6b Kgf. no. 1291 v.17.2.1945, Kgf. Vern' (frame 6474473), all in
    Records of OKH, Microcopy no. T-78, Reel 488, NA; *The Daily Express*, 7 Feb.
    1945; and *Der Kampf um Berlin 1945*, 64.
38 O'Laughlin, Flint and Anselin, 'The Geography of the Nazi Vote,' 360, 362; Shpa-
    kov to Zubarev, 8 Apr. 1945, in *Pogranichnye Voiska SSSR v Velikoi Otechestvennoi
    Voine, 1942–1945*, 553; Michael Radziwill, *One of the Radziwills* (London 1971),
    204; and *The Times*, 7 Mar. 1945.
39 *The Daily Express*, 25 Jan. 1945; Oberkommando der Heeresgruppe Mitte, Abt. Ic/
    AO 'Ic-Tagesmeldung vom 1.3.45,' RH 2/2008, BMA; and ... *By Inni Mogli Żyč
    Spkojnie*, 192.
40 *Silesian Inferno*, 79.
41 Shpakov to Zubarev, 8 Apr. 1945; and Polyakov to Shambarov, 31 Jan. 1945, both
    in *Pogranichnye Voiska SSR v Velikoi Otechestvennoi Voine, 1942–1945*, 500–1,
    553–5. For the testimony of a survivor from a squad of bypassed German stragglers,
    which spent nineteen days in the Soviet hinterland in this same area, and lost nine of
    its twelve-man complement, see Rothenburger to Bormann, NS 6/132, BA. For
    reprisals or threats against German civilians, see Heinrich Kober, untitled report,
    7 Feb. 1951, Ost Dok. 189, BA; Wilhelm Heinel 'Anlage: Schilderung der in Lauen-
    brunn,' 3 Jul. 1952, Ost Dok. 2/177, BA; and 'Bericht des Rittmeisters v. Loeben von
    der 17 Panzerdivision über Verhältnisse im feindbesetzen Hinderland,' 11 Mar. 1945,
    Records of OKH, Microcopy no. T-78, Roll 565, frame 804, NA. For the massacre of
    stragglers betrayed by German civilians and wiped out by the Soviets, see *Silesian
    Inferno*, 37–8.
42 *Silesian Inferno*, 45–7, 78–9; Alexander Stahlberg, *Bounden Duty* (London 1990),
    386–7; and Herbert von Dirksen, *Moscow, Tokyo, London* (London 1951), 263–71.
43 'Auszug aus Kgf. Vern. FHO (IIIa) Nr. 1290 v. 19.2.45 – Schtz. Ssarkissjan, Magar-
    ditsch Aramowitsch,' 16 Mar. 1945, Records of OKH, Microcopy no. T-78, Reel
    565, frame 802, NA.
44 *Vertreibung und Vertreibungsverbrechen, 1945–1948*, 244–5; and Siomash to
    Izugenev, 1 Apr. 1945, *Pogranichnye Voiska SSSR v Velikoi Otechestvennoi Voine,
    1942–1945*, 505.

45 Gavrikov to Izugenev, 30 Apr. 1945, in *Pogranichnye Voiska SSSR v Velikoi Otechestvennoi Voine, 1942–1945*, 563.

46 SD Report 'Verhalten der Sowjets in den von ihnen besetzten Gebeiten des Gaues Mark Brandenburg,' 20 Feb. 1945; 'Auszug aus Bericht über die Erlebnisse des SS-Sturmscharführers Sass in dem von den Russen besetzten Gebeit und die dort gemachten Beobachtungen,' 17 Feb. 1945; 'Bericht des Rittmeisters v. Loeben von der 17.Panzerdivision über Verhaltnisse im feindbesetzen Hinterland,' 11 Mar. 1945; 'Auszug aus Schilderungen des Meisters d. Gend. Friedrich Riekeheer – Verhaltnisse hinter der Sowj. Front,' 11 Mar. 1945; and GFP 729, Interrogation Report on Gefreiter Willi Hager, 27 Feb. 1945, all in RH 2/2129, BMA. For accounts of a series of skirmishes from the 7th to the 9th February, in which NKVD patrols killed twenty-five German stragglers, see Siomash to Izugenev, 1 Apr. 1945, *Pogranichnye Voiska SSSR v Velikoi Otechestvennoi Voine, 1942–1945*, 506, 508.

47 Dr V. Werbke 'Austellung neuer Truppenteile in Königsberg; Verhaltnis zwischen Stab Lasch (Gen. d. Inf.) u. Kommandant d. Festg. Königsberg und Parteianstellen, 1945,' Ost Dok. 8/586, BA.

48 P.G. Ianovski, 'Kapituliatsiia Gitlerovtsev v Kenigsberge,' *Voenno-Istoricheskii Zhurnal* no. 2 (1986), 72–4; Otto Lasch, *So Fiel Königsberg* (Stuttgart 1976), 108–11; *Völkischer Beobachter*, 17 Apr. 1945; Ultra Document KO 452, 15 Apr. 1945, Ultra Document Collection, Reel 70; Duffy, *Red Storm over the Reich*, 215; *Istoriya Velikoi Otechestvennoi Voiny Sovetskogo Soyuza, 1941–1945*, vol. 5, 175; Soviet War Communiqué Supplement, 9 Apr. 1945; Soviet War Communiqué , 10 Apr. 1945; German War Communiqué, 12 Apr. 1945; Soviet War Communiqué Supplement, 17 Apr. 1945; *Abwehrkampf am Nordflügel der Ostfront, 1944–1945*, 384–5; 'Tagesmeldungen vom 11. Apr. 1945,' *Die Geheimentagesbuch der Deutschen Wehrmachtführung im Zweite Weltkrieg, 1939–1945* 12, 369; *Pogranichnye Voiska SSSR v Velikoi Otechestvennoi Voine, 1942–1945*, 552–3; and Lucy Falk, *Ich bleib in Königsberg: Tagebuchblätter aus dunkeln Nachkriegsjahren* (Munich 1966), 44–5.

49 *Izvestia*, 3 Apr. 1945; FHO (IIa) 'Zusammenstelleng von Chi-Nachrichten' no. 1022, 4 Apr. 1945, Records of OKH, Microcopy no. T-78, Reel 496, frame 6484380, NA; Ultra Document BT 7004, 12 Mar. 1945, Ultra Document Collection, Reel 65; Duffy, *Red Storm over the Reich*, 228; and *Die Vertreibung der deutschen Bevölkerung aus der Gebeiten östlich der Oder-Neisse*, vol. 1, 285–6, 297–305.

50 Leitstelle II Ost für Frontaufklärung to OKH/Genst. d. H/Fremde Heere Ost, 20 Mar. 1945, Records of OKH, Microcopy no. T-78, Reel 565, frame 000915, NA; Rose, *Werwolf*, 114–16; *The New York Times*, 6 Aug. 1945; C.D. Bekker, *K-Men: The Story of the German Frogmen and Midget Submarines* (Maidstone 1973), 187–91; and Ignacy Blum, *Z Dziejow Wojska Polskiego w Latach, 1945–1948* (Warszawa 1960), 34.

51 Wiskemann, *Germany's Eastern Neighbours*, 97.

52 Pferrer W. Grabsch 'Augenzeugenbericht über die Vorgange bei der Räumung Schlesiens 1945/46,' 22 Aug. 1949, Ost Dok. 2/177, BA; *Silesian Inferno*, 64–5; *The Tragedy of Silesia*, 405; and Marion Wojciechowski, 'The Exodus of the Germans from the Odra and Lusatian Nysa Territories,' *Polish Western Affairs/La Pologne et les Affairs Occidentales* no. 1–2 (1990), 10; ... *By Inni Mogli Żyč Spokojne*, 65–6, 68, 70–1, 73, 75, 182, 186, 194; Wiskemann, *Germany's Eastern Neighbours*, 97–8; and Gołąbek and Tryc, 'Z Genezy Powstania i Działalności Werwolfu,' 140.

53 *The Tragedy of Silesia*, 398, 500; Gołąbek and Tryc, 'Z Genezy Powstania i Działalności Werwolfu,' 136; and ... *By Inni Mogli Żyč Spokajne*, 71, 99, 184, 196.

54 ... *By Inni Mogli Żyč Spokojne*, 71, 77–8, 97–9, 183, 191; *The Christian Science Monitor*, 12 Sep. 1946; MI-14 'Mitropa' no. 28, 12 Aug. 1946, 7, FO 371/55630, PRO; and Bourdillon, Minute on file folder N14024, 12 Dec. 1947, FO 371/66217, PRO.

55 ... *By Inni Mogli Żyč Spokojne*, 79, 126–30, 197; and *The New York Times*, 20 Jun. 1946.

56 Kissel, *Der deutsche Volkssturm*, 81; *Istoriya Velikoi Otechestvennoi voiny Sovetskogo Soyuza, 1941–1945*, vol. 5, 318; *The New York Times*, 9 May 1945; and Duffy, *Red Storm over the Reich*, 228.

57 ... *By Inni Mogli Żyč Spokojne*, 66, 68, 84–5, 95–7, 146–7; and *The Washington Post*, 17 Apr. 1945.

58 ... *By Inni Mogli Żyč Spokojne*, 71–2, 96, 149, 199.

59 Ibid., 130–3.

60 USFET 'Weekly Intelligence Summary' no. 44, 16 May 1946; no. 45, 23 May 1946; no. 73, 5 Dec. 1946, all in State Dept. Decimal File 1945–9, 740.00119 Control (Germany), RG 59, NA; *The Stars and Stripes*, 19 Oct. 1945; Joachim Schoenfeld, *Holocaust Memoirs* (Hoboken 1985), 168; and Gołąbek and Tryc, 'Z Genezy Powstania i Działalności Werwolfu,' 140.

61 ... *By Inni Mogli Żyč Spokojne*, 66, 72–3, 181, 186, 189, 193.

62 *The New York Times*, 10 Oct. 1945; *The Washington Post*, 6 Aug. and 10 Oct. 1945.

63 MI-14 'Mitropa' no. 12, 29 Dec. 1945, FO 371/55630, PRO; and *Vertreibung und Vertreibungsverbrechen, 1945–1948*, 206.

64 Von Lehndorf, *East Prussian Diary*, 76, 114; E. Ames 'Interview with a Red Army Political Officer Returned from Germany,' 9 Jul. 1945, State Dept. Decimal File 1945–9, 740.00119 Control (Germany), RG 59, NA; and Juozas Daumantas, *Fighters for Freedom: Lithuanian Partisans versus the USSR (1944–1947)* (New York 1975), 198.

65 Mieczysław Sodel, 'Kształtowanie sie Organow Słuzby Bezpieczenstwa Publicznego na Dolnym Śląsku w 1945 Roku,' *Ślaski Kwartalnik Historyczny Sabotka* 25/3 (1970), 425–33; Wiskemann, *Germany's Eastern Neighbours*, 89, 94–5; ... *By Inni Mogli Żyč Spokojne*, 79, 97; and Gołąbek and Tryc, 'Z Genezy Powstania i

Działalności Werwolfu,' 140–1. For references to a Werwolf group that came to light in Frankenstein at the time of the 'Swallow' evacuations, see M. Pawlowski 'Bericht über die Ermorderung des Millermesiters Bernhard Pawlowski,' 21 May 1951; and 'Verhandlung gegen Max Gottwald,' 9 Feb. 1952, both in Ost Dok. 2/177, BA.

66 Contrôle de la Sûreté du Württemberg 'La Silesie sous l'Occupation Polonaise,' 22 Oct. 1947, OMGUS ODI Excerpts of Miscellaneous Reports, 92 (Poland), RG 260, NA.

67 J. Walters, British Vice-Consulate, Stettin to Russell, British Embassy, Warsaw, 21 Nov. 1947, FO 371/66217, PRO.

68 G. Krömer, untitled report, 8 May 1951, and W. Grabsch 'Augenzeugenbericht über die Vorgänge bei der Raumung Schlesiens, 1945/1946,' 22 Aug. 1949, both in Ost Dok. 2/177, BA.

69 Bourdillon, Minute on file folder N14024, 12 Dec. 1947, FO 371/66217, PRO. For commentary on the extreme selectivity of refugee memoirs, see Robert Moeller, 'War Stories: The Search for a Usuable Past in the Federal Republic of Germany,' *The American Historical Review* 101/4 (Oct. 1996), 1026–8.

70 Radio Warsaw broadcast, PID Summary, 20 Dec. 1945, FO 371/46990, PRO.

71 USFET G-2 'Weekly Intelligence Summary' no. 55, 1 Aug, 1946; no. 56, 8 Aug. 1946; and no. 73, 5 Dec. 1946, all in State Dept. Decimal File 1945–9, 740.00119 Control (Germany), RG 59, NA.

72 Wiskemann, *Germany's Eastern Neighbours*, 135.

73 Detlef Brandes, *Die Tschechen unter deutschen Protektorat* (Munich 1969), vols. 1 and 2; and Vojtech Mastny, *The Czechs under Nazi Rule* (New York 1971).

74 *Die Vertreibung der Deutschen Bevölkerung aus der Tschechoslovakei*, vol. 4, pt. 2, 38–49; Wiskemann, *Germany's Eastern Neighbours*, 65–7; and Edward Taborsky, *President Eduard Benes: Between East and West, 1938–1948* (Stanford 1981), 125–6, 156.

75 The Sudeten-German Social Democrats in exile warned the Czech émigré regime in 1942 that any intention to carry through large-scale population transfers would cause a civil war: Wiskemann, *Germany's Eastern Neighbours*, 66.

76 'Erlebnisbericht des Landrates a. D. Dr. Karl Utischell, jetzt in Lindau/Bodensee,' *c.* 1950, Ost Dok. 2/263, BA.

77 Drška, *Československá Armáda v Národní a Demokratické Revoluci*, 63; *The Times*, 28 Jul. 1945; *The Globe and Mail*, 28 May 1945; and *The Stars and Stripes*, 31 May 1945.

78 PID 'News Digest' no. 1692, 24 Feb. 1945, Bramstedt Collection, BLPES; and *Journal de Genève*, 13 Jun. 1945. Czech assessments confirm that it was particularly teenage Sudeten-Germans 'who, with their usual megalomania, will not submit to the new order of work and duty,': PID 'News Digest' no. 1763, 21 May 1945, Bramstedt Collection, BLPES.

79 USFET Interrogation Center 'Final Interrogation Report (FIR) #6 – Karl Frank,'
    7 Jul. 1945, OSS 138456, RG 226, NA; Bleidung to FHO, 15 Feb. and 17 Feb. 1945,
    both in RH 2/2129, BMA; USFET MIS Center 'KdM Prague,' CI-IIR/11, 10 Jan.
    1946, *Covert Warfare* 13; Smirnov to Blumin, 10 May 1945, and Anisimov to
    Padzhev, 30 May 1945, both in *Pogranichnye Voiska SSSR Mai, 1945–1950*, 65, 71;
    and AFP Bulletin 'Découverte d'une organisation "Werwolf" dans les Sudetes,'
    13 Jul. 1945, 7P 125, SHAT.

80 Lucas, *Kommando*, 317.

81 Fritz Jokolo Metzler, *Stacheldraht und Sonnenblumen: Auf der Flucht aus Russis-
    cher Gefangenschaft* (Düsseldorf 1974), 35, 40, and Otto Weidinger, *Division Das
    Reich*, vol. 5 (Osnabrück 1982), 548.

82 *The New York Times*, 23 Apr. and 24 Apr. 1945; and *The Daily Express*, 19 Apr. 1945.

83 *The Fifth Infantry Division in the ETO*; Lucas, *Last Days of the Reich*, 79, 198; *The
    St Louis Post–Dispatch*, 8 May 1945; F. Nitsch 'Beiblatt zur Erhebung über den
    Volkssturm,' Ost Dok. 2/770, BA; and Gustav Beuer, *New Czechoslovakia, and Her
    Historical Background* (London 1947), 187. For Sudeten-German denials regarding
    post-capitulation activity by the Volkssturm, see the various documents headed 'Bei-
    blatt zur Erhebung über den Volkssturm,' filed in Ost Dok. 2/245, 2/253, 2/262, 2/
    263, 2/270, 2/285, 2/288, and 2/289, all in BA.

84 Kiril Moskalenko, 'The Liberation of Prague,' in Igor Vitukhin, ed., *Soviet Generals
    Recall World War II* (New York 1981), 392.

85 Ultra Document KO 2083, 8 May 1945, Ultra Document Collection, PRO; *Istoriya
    Velikoi Otechestvennoi Voiny Sovetskogo Soyuza, 1941–1945*, 322–3; S.M. Shte-
    menko, *The Last Six Months* (New York 1977), 403, 415; Steinert, *Capitulation
    1945*, 153–4, 167–8, 180–1; Koller, *Der Letzte Monat*, 93; and Air. Div. U.S. Forces
    in Austria 'The Last Days in Hitler's Air Raid Shelter,' *Covert Warfare* 14. For Ger-
    man assumptions about the willingness of the Americans to employ them in an anti-
    Soviet struggle, see Klaus Granzow, *Tagebuch eines Hitlerjungen: Kriegsjugend in
    Pommern, 1945* (Hamburg 1974), 276, 278; and *The Ottawa Journal*, 12 May 1945.

86 Brandes, *Die Tschechen unter deutschen Protektorat*, 144–5; Thorwald, *Defeat in the
    East*, 247; *Journal de Genève*, 10 May and 20 Jun. 1945; Bosyi to Fadaev, 30 Jun.
    1945, *Pogranichnye Voiska SSSR Mai, 1945–1950*, 91; Steenberg, *Vlasov*, 208; *Ein
    Tagebuch aus Prag, 1945–46: Aufzeichnungen von Margarete Schell* (1957), 30;
    Thorwald, *The Illusion: Soviet Soldiers in Hitler's Armies*, 301, 312; *The New York
    Times*, 12 May, 21 May, and 3 Aug. 1945; Petro Grigorenko, *Memoirs* (New York
    1982), 196–9; Koniev, *Year of Victory*, 230, 235; *The Washington Post*, 14 May
    1945; *Le Monde*, 12 May 1945; and 15 May 1945; *The Manchester Guardian*,
    12 May and 21 May 1945; untitled and anonymous report on Prague, 1945, Ost Dok.
    2/312, BA; *The Times*, 26 May 1945; and PID 'News Digest' no. 1767, 25 May
    1945, Bramstedt Collection, BLPES.

87 *The Stars and Stripes*, 2 Jul. 1945; *The New York Times*, 3 Aug. 1945; and Dyer, *XII Corps*, 460.

88 George Elford, *Devil's Guard* (New York 1988), 15–48.

89 *Foreign Relations of the United States, 1945*, vol. 14, 506.

90 Horecky to Caritasverband für Diozese Fulda, 13 Jul. 1952, Ost Dok. 2/262, BA; Prof. E. Hanke 'Erlebnisbericht von 1945,' 27 Nov. 1955; Moldner to Staatskommissariat für das Flüchtlingswesen, both in Ost Dok. 2/288, BA; F/O A. Reitzner 'Reports on his Observations in the Sudeten Territory,' FO 371/46901, PRO; A. Knoll, 'Ein unvergessliches Jahr,' Ost Dok. 2/245, BA; and Raymund Klofat 'Plan bei Marienbad, eine ausgestorbene Stadt,' 27 Jun. 1946, Ost Dok. 2/270, BA.

91 H. Ripka to P. Nicholls, 20 Apr. 1945; P. Nicholls to C.F.A. Warner, FO, 20 Apr. 1945; Eisenhower, SHAEF to CCS for CCAC, VOG 425, 6 May 1945; JSM Washington to AMSSO, DON 728, 7 May 1945; AMSSO to JSM Washington, NOD 772, 19 May 1945, all in FO 371/47154, PRO; CCAC/CCS to SHAEF Main for SHGE (GOV 296), 21 Apr. 1945; SHAEF Frwd. to CCS for CCAC (VOG 400), 21 Apr. 1945; JSM Washington to AMSSO, 21 Apr. 1945, DON 693, all in FO 371/47085, PRO; Wiskemann, *Germany's Eastern Neighbours*, 103; *The Expulsion of the German People from the Territories East of the Oder-Neisse Line*, 151–2; *The Globe and Mail*, 8 May 1945; Sig. illegible, '"Pozar!" Cella 6,' Ost Dok. 2/263, BA; Dr W. Kreissel 'Erlebnisbericht aus Komotau über die Zeit vom 10.5.45–13.11.45,' Ost Dok. 2/264, BA; and *The Daily Express*, 20 Jul. 1945.

92 *The Washington Post*, 28 Jun. 1945.

93 Drška, *Československá Armáda v Národní a Demokratické Revoluci*, 65–6; *The Christian Science Monitor*, 25 Jul. 1945; and *The Times*, 28 Jul. 1945.

94 *Die Vertreibung der Deutschen Bevölkerung aus der Tschechoslovakei*, vol. 4, pt. 2, 69–70; *The Christian Science Monitor*, 25 Jul. 1945; *Londynsky Listy* 2/14 (15 Jul. 1948), 143; AFP Bulletin 'Decouverte d'une organisation "Werwolf" dans les Sudetes,' 13 Jul. 1945; AFP Bulletin 'L'Activité du "Werwolf" dans les Sudetes,' 16 Jul. 1945, both in 7P 125, SHAT; and *Neue Zürcher Zeitung*, 30 Jul. 1945.

95 For examples, see *The Times*, 28 Jul. 1945; *Neue Zürcher Zeitung*, 25 Jul. 1945; MI-14 'Mitropa' no. 2, 11 Aug. 1945, FO 371/46967, PRO; H. Pilz 'Bericht über die Erlebnisse und unmenschliche Behandlung bei der Vertreibung aus der Heimat: Schondtalen und Tetschen, 1945–6,' 22 Mar. 1947, Ost Dok. 2/288, BA; C. Gregor 'So sind die Tschechen! Ein Tatsachenbericht,' Ost Dok. 2/289, BA; Wilhelmine Hoffmann 'Bericht über meine Erlebnisse in Sudetenland,' 1956–7, Ost Dok. 2/279, BA; Sig. illegible to Dr Renner, 11 Aug. 1945, Ost Dok. 2/240, BA; J. Schumann 'Erlebnis-Protokoll,' 1 Sep. 1947; and 'Erlebnisberichte des Landrates a. D. Dr. Karl Utischell in Lindau,' *c.* 1950, both in Ost Dok. 2/263, BA.

96 MI-14 'Mitropa' no. 3, 25 Aug. 1945, FO 371/46967, PRO.

97 *The Times*, 28 Jul. and 7 Aug. 1945; Wiskemann, *Germany's Eastern Neighbours*, 102; PID 'News Digest' no. 1763, 21 May 1945, Bramstedt Collection, BLPES; *FO Weekly Intelligence Summaries* 12, Summary no. 307, 22 Aug.; *History of the Counter Intelligence Corps*, vol. 26, 77, NA; and XII Corps G-2 (Pilsen) 'G-2 Periodic Report' no. 47, 18 Sep. 1945, OSS XL 18718, RG 226, NA. For the eye-witness account of a Werwolf raid on the Czech holding camp at Adelshof, see *Dokumente zur Austreibung der Sudetendeutschen*, 244–5. Interestingly, the witness, who was within the camp and heard the battle raging outside the perimeter fences, could never accept that his fellow countrymen had actually raided the camp. Instead, he blamed the incident on Czech duplicity and the trigger-happy folly of the guards, even though one of the guards later indicated (in confidence) that they had really been attacked.

98 American Intelligence Report, *c.* Aug. 1945, OSS OB 28993, RG 226, NA; XXII Corps, ACoS G-2 'Periodic Report' no. 47, 18 Sep. 1945, OSS XL 18718, RG 226, NA; OMGUS Director of Intelligence Chart for Deputy Military Governor, 22 Oct. 1945, OMGUS Adjutant General's Office Decimal File, 1947, 091.411, RG 260, NA; *History of the 94th Infantry Division in World War Two*, 495; *Documents on the Expulsion of the Sudeten Germans*, 119–20; Drška, *Československá Armáda v Národní a Demokratické Revoluci*, 64–5; Wenzel Jaksch, *Europas Weg Nach Potsdam* (Cologne 1967), 438; *Foreign Relations of the United States, 1945*, Vol. 4, 488; and *The Washington Post*, 1 Jul. 1945.

99 *The New York Times*, 29 Jul. 1945; *FO Weekly Political Intelligence Summaries* 12, Summary no. 304, 1 Aug. 1945; *The Christian Science Monitor*, 9 Oct. 1945; and USFET G-5 'Political Intelligence Letter' no. 1, 3 Aug. 1945, State Dept. Decimal File 1945–9, 740.00119 Control (Germany), RG 59, NA.

100 Drška, *Československá Armáda v Národní a Demokratické Revoluci*, 65.

101 Smirnov to Blyumin, 30 Jun. 1945, *Pogranichnye Voiska SSSR Mai, 1945–1950*, 92–3; *The Globe and Mail*, 12 Jul. 1945; and Bulletin of the Czechoslovak Ministry of Information, 1st Dept., no. 8, 18 Aug. 1945, State Dept. Decimal Files 1945–9, 860F.00, RG 59, NA.

102 *Dokumente zur Austreibung der Sudetendeutschen*, 327.

103 W. Hoffmann 'Bericht über meine Erlebnisse in Sudetenland,' 1956–7, Ost Dok. 2/279, BA; and *Die Vertreibung der deutschen Bevölkerung aus den Gebeiten ostlich der Ober–Neisse*, 463.

104 Weisbach to the Staatskommissariat für das Flüchtlingswesen, 28 Mar. 1947; H. Happ 'Verhandlungsschrift,' 3 Jul. 1945, both in Ost Dok. 2/262, BA; W. Hoffmann 'Bericht über meine Erlebnisse im Sudetenland,' 1956–7, Ost Dok. 2/279, BA; *Documents on the Expulsion of the Sudeten Germans* (Munich 1953), 117–18, 221–6; and *Vertreibung und Vertreibungsverbrechen*, 86–7.

105 Sig. illegible to Dr Renner, 11 Aug. 1945, Ost Dok. 2/240, BA; and *The New York Times*, 3 Aug. 1945.

106 F. Dresler, untitled report, 5 Mar. 1953; E. Kiranke 'Bericht über die Austreibung 1945/45,' 8 Dec. 1955; J. Wildner 'Schreckensregiment und Blutgericht in Freudenthal KZ,' 28 Aug. 1947, all in Ost. Dok. 2/253, BA; and Sig. illegible 'Meine Erlebnisse in der Tschechoslovakei nach Beendigung des Krieges,' Ost Dok. 2/313, BA.

107 *The Daily Express*, 20 Jul. 1945; *The Stars and Stripes*, 23 Jul. 1945; and *The Washington Post*, 28 Jul. 1945.

108 *The Times*, 3 Aug. 1945; *The Manchester Guardian*, 2 Aug. 1945; *The Washington Post*, 5 Aug. 1945; *FO Weekly Political Intelligence Summaries* 12, Summary no. 305, 8 Aug. 1945; Bardachzi to Korb, 22 May 1946; F. Bardachzi 'Schilderung der Ereignisse in Aussig/Elbe nach dem Umsturz 1945,' 31 Oct. 1948; A. Köhler 'Gesamtdokumentation über Ausweisung der Deutschen aus der Czechoslowakei,' 9 Mar. 1947; Sig. illegible to Dr Renner, 11 Aug. 1945; Schindler to Arbeitsgemeinschaft zur Wahrung Sudetendeutschen Interessen, *c.* Jun. 1947, all in Ost Dok. 2/240, BA; E. Richtler 'Dokumente der Vertreibung aus Bodenbach-Tetschen a/Elbe (CSR) im Jahre 1945–46,' Nov. 1952, Ost Dok. 2/288, BA; *Die Vertreibung der Deutschen Bevölkerung aus der Tschechoslovakei*, 626; Erich Kern, *Das Andere Lidice* (Wels 1950), 80, 100–1; Emil Franzel, *Die Vertreibung Sudetenland, 1945–1946* (Munich 1980), 249–53; *Geflohen und Vertrieben*, 217–18, 221; *Dokumente zur Austreibung der Sudetendeutschen*, 121–5, 151–2, 397; and *The New York Times*, 3 Aug. 1945. Most casualty estimates by Sudeten Germans ran between 800 and 3,000. The most authoritative estimate, by a former member of the local Czech administration, was that 2,000 German-Aussiger were killed in the pogrom.

109 Drška, *Československá Armáda v Národní a demokratické Revoluci*, 66; Beuer, *New Czechoslovakia*, 187; MI-14 'Mitropa' no. 2, 11 Aug. 1945, FO 371/46967, PRO; *Journal de Genève*, 2 Aug. 1945; *The Manchester Guardian*, 3 Aug. 1945; and Wiskemann, *Germany's Eastern Neighbours*, 104. The labour Kommando actually at work at the Schönpriesen depot on 30 July never returned to its home camp at Theresienstadt. Members were either killed in the blast or beaten to death by the mob: *Dokumente zur Austreibung der Sudetendeutschen*, 131. For Fierlinger's remarks at Aussig, see *Neue Zürcher Zeitung*, 31 Jul. 1945.

110 *Die Vertreibung der Deutschen Bevölkerung aus der Tschechoslowakei*, 71–2; *FO Weekly Political Intelligence Summaries* 12, Summary no. 305, 8 Aug. 1945; Bulletin of the Czechoslovak Ministry of Information no. 4, 13 Aug. 1945, State Dept. Decimal File 1945–9, 860F.00, RG 59, NA; and *War and Peace Aims of the United Nations*, vol. 2 (Boston 1948), 1048.

111 K. Lehmann 'Augenzeugenbericht über die Behandlung der Deutschen in der Tschechei nach der Kapitulation 1945,' 1946, Ost Dok. 2/313, BA; Kern, *Das Andere Lidice*, 80; Theresia Mager 'Augenzeugen-Bericht über das Blutbad von Schönpriesen am 30. Juli 1945,' 11 Aug. 1946; 'Die Evakuierung der Deutschen aus der Tschechoslowakischen Republik von Apr. 1945 bis Dezember 1947,' both in Ost Dok. 2/240, BA; *Geflohen und Vertrieben*, 218; *Dokumente zur Austreibung der Sudetendeutschen*, 123; Franzel, *Die Vertreibung Sudetenland*, 250–1; F/O A. Reitzner (RAF) 'Reports on His Observations in Sudeten Territory' and 'Deportation Drama in Czechoslovakia: The Case of a Dying People,' both in FO 371/46901, PRO.

112 Horejschi to Jaksch, 21 Jun. 1947; F. Schneider 'Das Blutbad von Aussig-Schreckenstein am 31.7.1945,' 1 Aug. 1945, both in Ost Dok. 2/240, BA; Kern, *Das Andere Lidice*, 103; and F/O Reitzner (RAF) 'Reports on his Observations in Sudeten Territory,' FO 371/46901, PRO.

113 *Londynske Listy* 2/14 (15 Jul. 1948), 143–4. (A copy is filed in Ost Dok. 2/240, BA.)

114 Drška, *Československá Armáda v Národní a Demokratické Revoluci*, 65–6; *FO Weekly Political Intelligence Summaries* 12, Summary no. 305, 8 Aug. 1945; and Report by the Parliamentray Delegation of Sudeten Labour in England 'The "Prodigious Drama" of the Sudeten People,' Oct. 1945, FO 371/46901, PRO.

115 *Foreign Relations of the United States, 1945*, vol. 4, 507. USFET reported on 3 September 1945 that 'the Sudeten German-Czech situation [is] at present quiet and should remain so since the Czech Government in the area has a firm hold'; JCS Memo for SWN Coordinating Committee, 6 Sep. 1945, Enclosure 'C,' *Records of the JCS: Part I, 1942–45, European Theatre*, Roll 13.

116 Sig. illegible 'Geheim!! Da noch Verwandte in den besetzt. Gebeiten Sudetenland, Tyssa, Tetschen,' 21 Jan. 1952, Ost Dok. 2/288, BA; Beuer, *New Czechoslovakia*, 188; W. Stich 'Meine Erlebnisse im Jahre 1945,' 21 Feb. 1947, Ost Dok. 2/240, BA; MI-14 'Mitropa,' no. 5, 22 Sep. 1945, FO 371/46967, PRO; and MI-14 'Mitropa' no. 9, 16 Nov. 1945, FO 371/46935, PRO.

117 *The Christian Science Monitor*, 9 Oct. 1945.

118 Drška, *Československa Armáda v Národní a Demoktratické Revoluci*, 66–7.

119 *The Washington Post*, 1 Oct. 1945; USFET MG Office 'Bi-Weekly Political Summary' no. 6, 16 Nov. 1945, State Dept. Decimal File 1945–9, 740.00119 Control (Germany), RG 59, NA; *The New York Times*, 14 Apr. 1947; FORD 'Digest for Germany and Austria' no. 690, 7 Jan. 1948, FO 371/70791, PRO; ACA (BE) 'Joint Fortnightly Intelligence Summary' no. 58, 15 May 1948, FO 1007/303, PRO; *The Times*, 19 Jul. 1948; and Jan Foitzik, 'Kadertransfer: Der Organisierte Einstaz sudetendeutscher Kommunisten in der SBZ 1945/46,' *Vierteljahrshefte für Zeitgeschichte* 31/2 (1983), 316.

120 *The Times*, 9 Sep. 1946; and *The Christian Science Monitor*, 11 Sep. 1946.

121 *The Times*, 30 Apr. 1945; USFET 'Weekly Intelligence Summary' no. 57, 15 Aug. 1946, State Dept. Decimal File 1945–9, 740.00119 Control (Germany), RG 59, NA; U.S. Constabulary 'Report' no. 9, 12 Apr. 1947, WWII Operations Reports, RG 407, NA; and Grenzkommissar H. Roeschen, Report, 30 Mar. 1951, Ost Dok. 2/245, BA.

122 USFET G-2 'Weekly Intelligence Summary' no. 32, 21 Feb. 1946, and no. 81, 30 Jan. 1947, State Dept. Decimal File 1945–9, 740.00119 Control (Germany), RG 59, NA. Propaganda leaflets addressed 'to the Silesians and the German Population of Bohemia' circulated heavily in the vicinities of Stuttgart and Bamberg: USFET 'Weekly Intelligence Summary' no. 68, 31 Oct. 1946, State Dept. Decimal File 1945–9, 740.00119 Control (Germany), RG 59, NA.

123 FORD 'Digest for Germany and Austria' no. 729, 2 Mar. 1948, FO 371/70792, PRO.

124 John Delaney, *The Blue Devils in Italy* (Washington 1947), 225; and Rgnl. Cmssr. Dunlop, Report for May 1945, in Harry Coles and Albert Weinburg, *Civil Affairs: Soldiers become Governors* (Washington 1964), 57–8.

125 Chester Starr, *From Salerno to the Alps: A History of the Fifth Army, 1943–1945* (Washington 1948), 438–9; Kästner, *Notabene 45*, 143; Direction Générale des Études et Recherches 'Bulletin de Renseignements – Allemagne: Wehrwolf,' 23 Jun. 1945, 7P 125, SHAT; Fifth Army G-2 'General Security Report,' 4 Sept. 1945, WO 204/805, PRO; CSDIC/CFM/SD 21 'The Werwolf Organisation,' 10 Jun. 1945, IRR File XE 049 888 'Werewolf Activities Vol. I,' RG 319, NA; Ultra Document BT 7004, 12 Mar. 1945, Ultra Document Collection, Reel no. 65; *The Times*, 26 Mar. 1945; *The Washington Post*, 16 May, 21 May 1945; *Combat*, 5 May 1945; *Neue Zürcher Zeitung*, 22 May 1945; *The Daily Herald*, 21 May 1945; Delaney, *The Blue Devils in Italy*, 225–6, 230, 239; Fifteenth Army Group 'Security Summary for May 1945,' 16 Jun. 1945, WO 204/831, PRO; and *The Daily Herald*, 30 May 1945. For Wolff's background, see Antony Evelyn Alcock, *The History of the South Tyrol Question* (London 1970), 51.

126 John Bassett, *War Journal of an Innocent Soldier* (New York 1989), 139–40; and Delaney, *The Blue Devils in Italy*, 226–7.

127 Fifteenth Army Group 'Security Summary for May 1945,' 16 Jun. 1945, WO 204/831, PRO.

128 Alcock, *The History of the South Tyrol Question*, 76; H. L. d'A. Hopkinson, 'Report on a Visit to Bolzano and Trento,' 2 Jun. 1945; H.L. d'A. Hopkinson to HQ AC, 9 Jun. 1945, both in Coles and Weinburg, *Civil Affairs*, 573–4; *Neue Zürcher Zeitung*, 18 Jun. 1945; *History of the Counter Intelligence Corps*, vol. 25, 58, NA; Delaney, *The Blue Devils in Italy*, 234; *Journal de Genève*, 16–17 Jun. and 18 Jun. 1945; and *The Globe and Mail*, 7 Aug. 1945.

129 Alcock, *The History of the South Tyrol Question*, 82; and Fifteenth Army Group 'Security Summary,' 16 Jun. 1945, WO 204/831, PRO; Ultra Document BT 7004, 12 Mar. 1945, in Ultra Document Collection, Reel no. 65; CSDIC/CMF/SD21 'The Werwolf Organisation,' 10 Jun. 1945, IRR File XE 049 888 'Werewolf Activities Vol. I,' RG 319, NA; and Fifth Army G-2 'General Security Report,' 4 Sep. 1945, WO 204/805, PRO. For tension in 1943 and 1944 between the 'Optants' and the 'Stay-Behinders,' see Dennison Rusinow, *Italy's Austrian Heritage, 1919–1946* (Oxford 1969), 314–16.

130 German Directorate 'Weekly Intelligence Summary' no. 36, 11 Jul. 1945, OSS 140955, RG 226, NA.

131 SSU Report no. LA-255, 2 Jan. 1946, OMGUS AG Security-Classified Decimal File 1945–9, 350.09 (Intelligence, General), RG 260, NA.

132 *FO Weekly Political Intelligence Summaries* 12, Summary no. 303, 25 Jul. 1945; *The Manchester Guardian*, 22 Nov. 1945; and PWB British Units (Austria) 'Weekly Summary of Political Developments' no. 33, 2 Mar. 1946, FO 1007/298, PRO.

133 MI-14 'Mitropa' no. 22, 20 May 1946, FO 371/55630, PRO; Rusinow, *Italy's Austrian Heritage*, 389; *The Times*, 3 May 1946; and *The New York Times*, 3 Jul. 1946.

134 Alcock, *The History of the South Tyrol Question*, 224.

135 Toscano, *Alto Adige – South Tyrol* (Baltimore 1975), 143–245; and Werner Wolf, *Südtirol in Österreich* (Würzburg 1972), 75–6, 138–41.

136 Dickens, *Lübeck Diary*, 217–19.

137 Applegate, *A Nation of Provincials*, 226.

7: Western Allied and Soviet Reactions to the Werwolf

 1 *The Papers of Dwight David Eisenhower – The War Years* (Baltimore 1970), vol. 4, 2107, 2119, 2187; Henke, *Die amerikanische Besetzung Deutschlands*, 160; *The Times*, 13 Oct. 1944; *The New York Times*, 6 Apr. 1945; and *The Globe and Mail*, 17 Apr. 1945.

 2 Fred Smith, 'Rise and Fall of the Morgenthau Plan,' *U.N. World* 1 (Mar. 1947), 32; Henry Morgenthau, 'Our Policy toward Germany,' *The New York Post*, 24 Nov. 1947; *The Morgenthau Diary (Germany)* (Washington 1967), 424; Stephen Ambrose, *Eisenhower the Soldier* (London 1984), 422; Dwight D. Eisenhower, *Crusade in Europe* (Garden City 1948), 287; Bradley Smith, *The Road to Nuremberg* (London 1981), 21; and *Foreign Relations of the United States, 1945* (Washington 1968), vol. 3, 390.

 3 SCAF 68, SHAEF to AGWAR for CCS, 23 Aug. 1944, CAD 014 Germany, RG 165, NA. One of Eisenhower's main advisers on military government policy, General Julius Holmes, noted in September 1944 that SHAEF's rejection of mandatory resus-

citation of the German economic infrastructure had actually anticipated Henry Morgenthau's new policy – ' ... we were the first to become aware of the fact that it would be not only dangerous but futile for us to attempt to prop up the rickety economic and financial structure of Germany,': J. Holmes to J. Hilldring, 11 Sep. 1944, CAD 014 Germany, RG 165, NA.

4 Draft telegram to the JSM in Washington, Annex II to Note by Secretariat, APW, 29 Aug. 1944, CAB 87/8, PRO. Churchill, on 26 Jul. 1944, advised the War Cabinet that Germany would submit 'totally' once organized resistance ceased, and that there would be little SS guerrilla warfare in mountainous areas of the Reich: Ben Pimlott, ed., *The Second World War Diary of Hugh Dalton* (London 1986), 774.

5 Ziemke, *The U.S. Army in the Occupation of Germany*, 105; *Foreign Relations of the United States, 1944* (Washington 1966), vol. 1, 420; *Foreign Relations of the United States, 1945*, vol. 3, 457; *The New York Times*, 20 May 1949; and Edward Peterson, *The American Occupation of Germany: Retreat to Victory* (Detroit 1977), 33, 39.

6 *Foreign Relations of the United States: The Conferences at Malta and Yalta* (Washington 1955), 143–54; SHAEF Directive for Military Government of Germany Prior to Defeat or Surrender, 9 Nov. 1945, WO 219/1634, PRO; and *The Handbook for Military Government in Germany*, Part III, Dec. 1944, WO 219/2920, PRO.

7 For the immediate security aspect of denazification, see Twenty-first Army Group 'Counter Intelligence Instruction No. 4: The Occupation of Germany,' 1944, WO 205/1086, PRO; and Robertson to Jenkins, Control Office, 7 Mar. 1947, FO 371/64352, PRO. For the relationship of nonfraternization to security against Nazi terrorists, see SHAEF G-5 Historical Sect. Analysis Sheet, 2 Aug. 1944, Hilldring to Troops in Germany, WO 219/3652, PRO; Paraphrase of State Dept. cable information War Dept., 13 Jul. 1945; Maj.-Gen. R.B. Lord, Comm. Zone ETO, Memo on 'Relations with German Clergy,' 9 Apr. 1945, both in CAD 250.1, RG 165, NA; and *The Washington Post*, 17 Sep. 1944. For the desire to get German children back into school in order to occupy their time and remove any residual influences leading them towards resistance activities, see SHAEF G-5 'Educational Technical Manual Advanced Edition,' Jan. 1945, WO 219/2587, PRO.

8 Memo by Maj.-Gen. Hilldring, Enclosure 'A,' 2 Aug. 1944, WO 219/3652, PRO.

9 Sayer and Botting, *America's Secret Army*, 203–4; Signature X, SHAEF G-5 to Chief, Post-Hostilities Planning Sub-Section, SHAEF G-3, 29 Jul. 1944, WO 219/3868, PRO; Twenty-first Army Group 'CI News Sheet' no. 13, Part III, WO 205/997, PRO; 'CI News Sheet no. 5 – Provisional Policy for the Advance through France, Holland and Belgium and the Occupation of Germany,' WO 205/997, PRO; SHAEF CAD (Govt. Affairs Br.) 'Staff Study – Travel Restrictions and Exemptions in Liberated and Occupied Territories,' 27 Feb. 1944; Seventh Army to Sixth Army Group G-5, 11 May 1945; Col. H.G. Sheen, SHAEF G-2 (CI) to Col. O'Rorque, SHAEF G-5 Public Safety Sect.; Lt.-Col. R.E. McLeod, SHAEF G-2 to Army Group

Int. Staffs, 18 May 1945; Col. S.B. Story, Chief SHAEF G-5 Internal Affairs to ACoS SHAEF G-2, 1 Jul. 1945, all in WO 219/1648A, PRO; SHAEF sigd. SCAEF to AMSSO for JIC, 17 Mar. 1945, WO 219/1651, PRO; SHAEF G-5 'Political Intelligence Letter' no. 9, 4 Jun. 1945, FO 371/46933, PRO; Peterson, *The American Occupation of Germany*, 157; and Dyer, *XII Corps*, 462. Extensive restrictions of movement were also placed upon north German fishermen, since the Allies were well aware of the value of fishing vessels in providing escape routes and aiding subversion. Again, however, this restriction curtailed food production: SHAEF G-5 'Political Intelligence Letter' no. 9, 4 Jun. 1945, FO 371/46933, PRO; and Twenty-first Army Group 'News Sheet' no. 26, 30 Jul. 1945, Part III, WO 205/997, PRO.

10 John Gimbel, *A German Community Under American Occupation: Marburg, 1945–52* (Stanford 1961), 49; S.F.V. Donnison, *Civil Affairs and Military Government: Northwest Europe* (London 1961), 240–1; and John D. Montgomery, *Forced to Be Free: The Artificial Revolution in Germany and Japan* (Chicago 1957), 36–69. Even once the establishment of political parties was approved by the Western Allies, strict provisions were imposed to prevent the use of such organizations by underground Nazis: *The Manchester Guardian*, 15 Sep. 1945.

11 Peterson, *The American Occupation of Germany*, 138; Eugene Davidson, *The Death and Life of Germany* (London 1959), 137; *The Stars and Stripes*, 9 Mar. 1947; James Warburg, *Germany – Bridge or Battleground* (London 1947), 7; and Zonal Advisory Council, Minutes of the 3rd Meeting Held in Hamburg, 2/3 May 1946, FO 371/55614, PRO.

12 MG Notice for Reichspost Officials, WO 219/3499, PRO; 'Plan for Censorship in Germany' (Goldcup) WO 219/1826, PRO; Col. H.G. Sheen, SHAEF G-2 (CI) to CI War Room, 1 Apr. 1945; SHAEF Signal Div. Memo on Monitoring of German Telecommunications, 7 Jan. 1945, both in WO 219/1561, PRO; Report by British Second Army 'Administration and Military Government,' WO 205/1084, PRO; MG Law no. 76 – 'Post, Telephones, Telegraphs and Radio,' filed under SHAEF Directive for Military Government of Germany Prior to Defeat or Surrender, 9 Nov. 1944, WO 219/1634, PRO; SHAEF Counter-Intelligence Directive – Pre-Surrender Period, Sep. 1944, WO 219/1634, PRO; Peterson, *The American Occupation of Germany*, 157; *The New York Times*, 11 May 1945; and *FO Weekly Political Intelligence Summaries* 11, Summary no. 298, 20 Jun. 1945. The French did not revive mail service in their zone until the fall of 1945: *Le Monde*, 2 Oct. 1945.

13 W. Strang 'Diary of a Tour through Westphalia and the North Rhine Province, 15–17 October 1945,' FO 371/46935, PRO; U.S. Berlin District 'The Problem of German Youth,' 3 Dec. 1945, State Dept. Decimal Files 1945–9, 740.00119 Control (Germany), RG 59, NA; R. Murphy, Pol. Adv. Germany to Sec. of State, 10 Aug. 1945, State Dept. Decimal Files 1945–9, 862.4081/1–145, RG 59, NA; and CG, USFET from Clay sgd. Eisenhower to War Dept. CAD, 3 Aug. 1945, CAD 080 Boy Scouts

of America, RG 165, NA. The Scouting Movement was initially prohibited by the
Allies and Soviets because of the fear that local Scout groups might metamorphose
into neo-HJ cells.

14 MI-14 'Mitropa' no. 10, 1 Dec. 1945, FO 371/46967, PRO; and FORD 'Digest for
Germany and Austria' no. 726, 26 Feb. 1948, FO 371/70792, PRO.

15 For reference to the mediocre youth-training programs fostered in the Western
Zones, see Libby, 'Policing Germany,' 123–8; USFET MG Office 'Weekly Intelligence Summary' no. 19, 21 Nov. 1945; USFET 'Weekly Intelligence Summary' no.
13, 11 Oct. 1945; no. 22, 13 Dec. 1945; no. 30, 7 Feb. 1946; no. 37, 28 Mar. 1946;
no. 38, 4 Apr. 1946; no. 42, 2 May 1946; no. 44, 16 May 1946; no. 45, 23 May 1946;
USFET 'Theatre Commander's Weekly Staff Conference' no. 16, 9 Apr. 1946; State
Dept. Div. of Foreign Activity Correlation Memo, 16 May 1946; OMGUS Informa-
tion Control 'Intelligence Summary' no. 23, 15 Dec. 1945; no. 45, 8 Jun. 1946, all in
State Dept Decimal Files 1945–9, 740.00119 Control (Germany), RG 59, NA; *The
New York Times*, 17 Apr. and 11 Aug. 1946; *Mission Accomplished: Third US Army
Occupation of Germany* (Munich 1947), 22, 28; *The Stars and Stripes*, 13 Sep. 1945,
10 Feb., 7 Mar., and 6 Apr. 1947.

16 *The Daily Herald*, 6 Jun. 1945.

17 Davidson, *The Death and Life of Germany*, 168; and *The New York Times*, 25 Apr.
1945. The French also put great stock in the holding of German officers as a means
of preventing German guerrilla warfare. M. Hahn, Memorandum to ACoS G-2 –
'Visit to French Headquarters in Baden-Baden,' 20 Sep. 1945, State Dept. Decimal
Files 1945–9, 740.00119 Control (Germany), RG 59, NA.

18 Carell and Böddeker, *Die Gefangenen*, 162.

19 'Draft: Outline for Instructions for the Organizational Administration of Internment
Camps in Germany'; Twenty-first Army Group to First Canadian Army and Second
British Army, 12 May 1945, both in WO 205/388, PRO; Childs, 'The Far Right in
Germany since 1945,' 292; C.O. Debate 29/vii/46, FO 898/386, PRO; W. Griffiths,
cited in Peterson, *The American Occupation of Germany*, 146, 168; Tom Bower,
Blind Eye to Murder (London 1983), 485; Donnison, *Civil Affairs and Military Government*, 360–2; Wember, *Umerziehung im Lager*, 14, 20, 47, 85, 100, 117–18; ACC
Report for the Moscow Meeting of the CFM, 21 Feb. 1947, Sect. II – 'Denazification,' Part 5, FO 371/64352, PRO; *The Times*, 5 Jun. 1946; *The New York Times*,
2 Apr. 1946; *The Observer*, 26 May 1946; and Montgomery, *Forced to Be Free*,
38–9. For numbers of detainees and conditions in the camps in western Germany and
Austria, see Wember, *Umerziehung im Lager*, 88–9, 91, 93, 96–101, 109–16, 132–3;
and Henke, *Die amerikanische Besetzung Deutschlands*, 254.

20 MG Ordinance no. 1 – 'Crimes and Offences,' filed under SHAEF Directive for Military Government in Germany Prior to Defeat or Surrender, 9 Nov. 1944, WO 219/
1634, PRO; SHAEF Hist. Sect. Analysis Sheet, 6 Nov. 1944, containing draft Procla-

mation no. 1, WO 219/3761A, PRO; *The New York Times*, 26 Mar. and 28 Mar. 1945; *The Daily Express*, 5 May 1945; and Wallace, *Patton and His Third Army*, 184. For American ordinances in newly occupied Leipzig, see Friedrich Michael, 'Letzte Wochen in Leipzig,' *Städte 1945*, ed. Ingeborg Drewitz (Düsseldorf 1970), 104.

21 Harry Butcher, *My Three Years with Eisenhower* (New York 1946), 784.

22 *The New York Times*, 1 Apr. and 2 Apr. 1945; *History of the Third Infantry Division in World War II*, 351; Hoffman, *The Super Sixth: History of the 6th Armoured Division in World War II and Its Postwar Association*, 362–3; Carter, *The History of the 14th Armoured Division*; and John Ausland, *Letters Home: A War Memoir (Europe 1944–1945)*, ch. 17, 5; http://www.pagesz.net/jbdavis/ww2_ausland.html, as of 30 Dec. 1996.

23 SHAEF JIC (45) 16 (Final) 'Political Intelligence Report,' 14 Apr. 1945, WO 219/1700, PRO.

24 *The Daily Express*, 14 Apr. 1945; and Henke, *Die amerikanische Besetzung Deutschlands*, 948. See also *The New York Times*, 1 Apr. 1945; Blumenstock, *Der Einmarsch der Amerikaner und Franzosen in Nordlichen Württemberg*, 224; Rose, *Werwolf*, 121; Trees and Whiting, *Unternehmen Karnival*, 263; and *Conquer*, 342.

25 *The Times*, 14 Jun. 1945; and *The Manchester Guardian*, 6 Jul. 1945.

26 *The Daily Herald*, 7 Jun. 1945; and *The Daily Express*, 25 Jul. 1945.

27 'Memo re memo from Mr. Seavey dated 9 Feb. with regard to the CA Manuel OPNAV 13–23 issued by the CoNO, Nov. 15, 1944,' CAD 250.401, RG 165, NA; and Kurt Tweraser, 'Military Justice as an Instrument of American Occupation Policy in Austria 1945–1950: From Total Control to Limited Tutelage,' *Austria History Yearbook* 24 (1993), 158.

28 OSS 'European Political Report' RAL-3–35, 3 Nov. 1944, WO 219/3761A, PRO; *Prevent World War Three* I, no. 6 (Dec. 1944), 32; *Libération* (Paris), 2 Nov. 1944; and Trees and Whiting, *Unternehmen Karnival*, 262–3.

29 Grasett, SHAEF G-5 to DCCAO Twenty-first Army Group, ACoS G-5 Twelfth Army Group, and ACoS G-5 Sixth Army Group, 1 Feb. 1945, CAD 014 Germany, RG 165, NA. For examples of sentences, see *The Stars and Stripes*, 29 Jun. 1945; USFET 'Military Government Weekly Field Report' no. 4, 11 Aug. 1945, State Dept. Decimal File 1945–9, 740.00119 Control (Germany), RG 59, NA; and The Twenty-first Army Group 'CI News Sheet' no. 25, 13 Jul. 1945, Part III, WO 205/997, PRO.

30 *The Law of War*, vol. 1, 229–33, 318–23; SHAEF G-3 'Combatting the Guerrilla,' WO 219/2921, PRO; and SHAEF JIC (45) 14 (JIC Draft) 'Security Problems Facing the Allies in Germany,' 11 Apr. 1945, WO 219/1659, PRO.

31 Sheen to SHAEF Mission to Belgium, 5 Nov. 1944; Sheen to Wise, ACos G-2 SHAEF (France), 8 Nov. 1944; Bull to Deputy CoS SHAEF G-3 (Main); Jervis-Reed to SHAEF G-3 (Training), 14 Nov. and 5 Dec. 1944; Blake to Head of CI, ACoS G-2

SHAEF, 15 Jan 1945; Sheen to WO, SOE, 16 Jan. 1945; Sheen to ACoS G-2 SHAEF (France), 4 Feb. 1945; Blake to Head of CI, ACoS G-2 SHAEF, 11 Feb. 1945; SHAEF Mission (Belgium) to SHAEF G-2 (CI), 22 Feb. 1945; McLeod to Furnival-Jones, 2 Mar. 1945, all in WO 219/1602, PRO; and JCS 'Memorandum for Information No. 385 – German Controls in Occupied Countries,' 9 Apr. 1945, WO 219/1651, PRO.

32 H.T. Baillie-Grohman 'Proposals for the Protection of Personnel of Allied Forces of Occupation in Germany and for the Hastening of German Disarmament,' 26 Sep. 1944, WO 219/1659, PRO; Hoare to Cadogan, 6 Dec. 1944; and Registry Sheet, 9 Dec. 1944, both in FO 371/39203, PRO.

33 Orde, *The Household Cavalry at War*, 519; and *Justiz und NS-Verbrechen*, Vol. XX, 507–15.

34 C.P. Stacey, *The Victory Campaign: Operations in Northwest Europe, 1944–45* (Ottawa 1960), 558; Chris Vokes, *Vokes: My Story* (Ottawa 1985), 194–5; R. Spencer, *History of the Fifteenth Canadian Field Regiment* (Amsterdam 1945), 248–51; R.A. Paterson, *A Short History: The Tenth Canadian Infantry BDE* (1945), 66; Tony Foster, *Meeting of Generals* (Toronto 1986), 436–7, 489; *The New York Times*, 20 Apr. 1945; *The Globe and Mail*, 20 Apr. and 23 Apr. 1945; Geoffrey Hayes, *The Lincs: A History of the Lincoln and Welland Regiment at War* (Alma 1986), 121; H.M. Jackson, *The Story of the Royal Canadian Dental Corps* (1956), 266; *Green Route Up: 4th Canadian Armoured Division* (The Hague 1945), 83, 86–7; and Brereton Greenhous, *Dragoon: The Centennial History of the Royal Canadian Dragoons, 1883–1983* (Ottawa 1983), 392–3.

35 Douglas Harker, *The Story of the Men Who Have Served in Peace and War with the British Columbia Regiment (DCO), 1883–1973* (1974), 293.

36 *Historical and Pictorial Review of the 28th Infantry Division in World War II* (Nashville 1980), 84–5; Henke, *Die amerikanische Besetzung Deutschlands*, 152–3; *The Washington Post*, 17 Sep. 1945; *The Stars and Stripes*, 20 Sep. and 29 Sep. 1944; and *FO Weekly Poltical Intelligence Summaries* 10, Summary no. 265, 1 Nov. 1945.

37 *The Manchester Guardian*, 6 Apr. 1945; *The Daily Express*, 6 Apr. 1945; and HQ Seventh Army 'Military Operations in German Territory,' 10 Apr. 1945, WO 219/3513, PRO.

38 *With the 102d Infantry Division through Germany*, 206; Blumenstock, *Der Einmarsch der Amerikaner und Franzosen im Nordlichen Württemberg*, 224–6; Hassan, *With the 114th in the ETO*, 112; and Carl Friedrich, 'The Three Phases of Field Operations in Germany, 1945–1946,' in *American Experiences in Military Government in World War II*, ed. Carl Friedrich (New York 1948), 241.

39 James Warburg, *Germany – Bridge or Battleground* (London 1947), 62; Amouroux, *La Page n'est pas encore tournée*, 276–8; and Michael Müller, 'Zum Verhaltnis von

Kirche und Besatzung,' in *Franzosen und Deutsche am Rhein 1789–1918–1945* (Essen 1989).

40 Hillel, *L'Occupation française en Allemagne*.

41 Heyman to Parkman, 20 Apr. 1945; Gerry to Chief, 5eme Bureau, First French Army, 28 Apr. 1945; Gerry to ACoS G-5, Sixth Army Group, 28 Apr. 1945; and Parkman to Heyman, 29 Apr. 1945, all in WO 219/3499, PRO.

42 *Le Monde*, 2 Oct. 1945; *Paris-Matin*, 25 Nov. 1945; and R.F. Ennis, Memo 'Nazi Underground Movement in Germany,' 10 Feb. 1947, Army-Intelligence Project Decimal File 1946–8, 370.64 (Germany), RG 319, NA.

43 Pol. Adv. Office (Germany) 'Military Government in the French Zone of Württemburg,' 12 Jul. 1945, State Dept. Decimal Files 1945–9, 740.00119 Control (Germany), RG 59, NA; Minute by Troutbeck on a verbal report by Capt. Scott, 17 Aug. 1945, FO 371/46934, PRO; and J.E. Bell 'Report on Visit to Baden-Baden,' 11 Sep. 1945, FD 371/46935, PRO.

44 Richard Scammon, 'Political Parties,' in *Governing Postwar Germany*, ed. Edward Litchfield (Ithaca 1953), 478; MI-14 'Mitropa' no. 5, 22 Sep. 1945, FO 371/46967, PRO; and *The New York Times*, 3 Jun. 1945.

45 De Lattre, *Reconquérir*, 325–6; *Le Monde*, 1 Jun. 1945; *The Manchester Guardian*, 19 May 1945; *The New York Times*, 21 May 1945; *Neue Zürcher Zeitung*, 29 Apr., 18 May, 20 May, and 29 May 1945; *Journal de Genève*, 29 Apr., 19–20–21 May, 19 Jun. 1945; OSS Report from Switzerland, F-2320, 25 May 1945, OSS L 57490, RG 226, NA; Amouroux, *La Page n'est pas encore tournée*, 273–4; Georges Ferber, 'Vicissitudes ou les debuts de la presse a Constance en 1945–46,' *La denazification par les Vainqueurs* (Lille 1981), 65–6; Strang to Bevin, 14 Sep. 1945, 'Political Summary' no. 5, in *Documents on British Policy Overseas*, ed. M.E. Pelly and H.J. Yasamee (London 1990), Series I, 5, 129; and Bosch, Der *Neubeginn*, 24-7

46 Amouroux, *La Page n'est pas encore tournée*, 274–5; *Journal de Genève*, 12–13 May, 26–7 May, and 20 Jul. 1945; *Daily Express*, 16 May 1945; *L'Aurore*, 21 Jun. 1945; *The New York Times*, 26 May 1945; Deutsch to Merkt, 11 Jun. 1945, WO 219/3513, PRO; PID 'Germany: Weekly Background Notes' no. 1, 8 Jun. 1945; 'Swiss Press Extracts on Germany,' 26 Jul. 1945, both in FO 371/46933, PRO; *Neue Zürcher Zeitung*, 16 May, 20 May, 25 May, 27 May, 29 May, 1 Jun., 3 Jun., 21 Jun., and 12 Jul. 1945; *The Manchester Guardian*, 19 May 1945; *The Washington Post*, 2 Jul. 1945; and Ferber, 'Vicissitudes ou les debuts de la presse a Constance en 1945–46,' 66.

47 Hillel, *L'Occupation française en Allemagne*, 236; Hermann, *Tübingen 1945*, 94, 96; and Görlitz, *Der Zweite Weltkrieg*, 545. For a firsthand account by a former HJ leader who was seized as a hostage for twelve days in Jul. 1945, see Heck, *The Burden of Hitler's Legacy*, 2.

48 Hillel, *L'Occupation française en Allemagne*, 85.
49 PID 'Germany: Weekly Background Notes' no. 4, 4 Jul. 1945, FO 371/46933, PRO; and *Neue Zürcher Zeitung*, 20 Jun. 1945.
50 Fenner Brockway, *German Diary* (London 1946), 90–1.
51 P. de Tristan, First French Army, 5th Bureau 'Monthly Historical Report,' 1 May 1945, WO 219/2587, PRO; Roy Willis, *The French in Germany, 1945–1949* (Stanford 1962), 262; Peter Brommer ed., *Quellen zur Geschichte von Rheinland-Pfalz während der französischen Besatzung* (Mainz 1985), 24; Hermann, *Tübingen 1945*, 86, 94; and Bosch, *Der Neubeginn*, 24.
52 Gimbel, *A German Community under American Occupation*, 52–3; Brett-Smith, *Berlin '45*, 25; Harold Zink, *American Military Government in Germany* (New York 1947), 241–2; *The Daily Express*, 17 Jul. 1945; Elisabeth Hömberg, *Thy People, My People* (London 1950), 223; R.W.B. Izzard, 'Situation Report on Conditions in Germany,' 17 Aug. 1945, FO 371/46934, PRO; PID 'Background Notes,' 26 May and 2 Jun. 1946, both in FO 371/46790, PRO; and M.E. Lockyer, Twelfth Army Group G-5 to ACoS SHEAF G-5, 29 May 1945, WO 219/1648A, PRO; and Bosch, *Der Neubeginn*, 24.
53 Balfour, 'Four Power Control in Germany,' 68; and Gabriel Kolko, *The Politics of War: Allied Diplomacy and the World Crises of 1943–1945* (London 1969), 509–10.
54 Berlin Dist. 'Weekly Intelligence Summary,' 26 Jul. 1945; and 'Guidance for Output in German for the Week 23–30 Apr. 1945,' 21 Apr. 1945, FO 371/46894, PRO. See also *The Washington Post*, 24 Sep. 1944, Part II; and PWE 'German Propaganda and the German,' 9 Apr. 1945, FO 898/187, PRO. Even the Danish autonomy movement in South Schleswig was suppressed under the heavy hand of the Military Government. British authorities suspected it was a disguised Nazi movement: Twenty-first Army Group 'Weekly Political Intelligence Summary' no. 4, 28 Jul. 1945, FO 371/46933, PRO.
55 PWE 'Central Directive – Information and Publicity to Germany and Austria,' 18 May 1945, FO 371/46790, PRO.
56 Seltzer interview in *Der Zeit*, 5 Dec. 1946 (press extract); and FORD 'Germany Weekly Background Notes' no. 74, 2 Jan. 1947, both in FO 371/64389, PRO.
57 *The Daily Express*, 18 May, 19 May, 5 Jun., 6 Jun., and 25 Jun. 1945; *The New York Times*, 18 May, 11 Jun., 20 Jun., 25 Jun., 1 Jul., and 25 Jul. 1945; *The Globe and Mail*, 18 May, 11 Jun., and 25 Jun. 1945; *The Washington Post*, 7 Jun., 11 Jun., 20 Jun., 23 Jun., 25 Jun., and 2 Jul. 1945; *The Manchester Guardian*, 18 May, 5 Jun., and 2 Aug. 1945; *The Daily Herald*, 5 Jun. 1945; *Le Monde*, 23 Jun. 1945; Latour and Vogelsang, *Okkupation und Wiederaufbau*, 77, 200; *News of Germany*, 21 Jul. 1945, 2; PID 'Germany: Weekly Background Notes' no. 2, 15 Jun. 1945, FO 371/46933, PRO; Dickens, *Lübeck Diary*, 163, 252; *The Stars and Stripes*, 28 Jun. and 3 Jul. 1945; SHAEF G-5 'Civil Affairs – Military Government Weekly Field

Report' no. 54, 23 Jun. 1945, State Dept. Decimal Files 1945–9, 740.00119 Control (Germany), RG 59, NA; Gen. Devers HQ Communications Zone ETO to WD, 19 Jun. 1945; Gen. Bradley, HQ Communications Zone ETO to WD, 26 Jun. 1945, both in CAD 250.401, RG 165, NA; and Ogmore, 'A Journey to Berlin, 1944–45 – Part II,' 88–9.

58 USFET 'Military Government Weekly Field Report' no. 4, 11 Aug. 1945, State Dept. Decimal File 1945–9, 740.00119 Control (Germany), RG 59, NA.

59 Enclave Military District G-2 'CI Periodic Report' no. 3, OSS 12926, RG 226, NA; *History of the Counter Intelligence Corps*, vol. 26, 48, NA; Fifteenth Army G-2 'Periodic Report' no. 58, 20 Jun. 1945, OSS XL 11747, RG 226, NA; *The Stars and Stripes*, 8 Jan. 1946; USFET G-2 'Weekly Intelligence Summary' no. 26, 1 Jan. 1946; no. 71, 21 Nov. 1946, both in State Dept. Decimal File 1945–9, 740.00119 Control (Germany), RG 59, NA; FORD 'Weekly Background Notes' no. 111, 9 Oct. 1947, FO 371/46392, PRO; FORD 'Germany: Fortnightly Background Notes' no. 134, 15 Apr. 1948, FO 371/70617, PRO; and GMZFO Direction de la Sûreté 'Bulletin de Renseignements,' no. 48, 31 Mar. 1948, OMGUS ODI Miscellaneous Reports, RG 260, NA.

60 Twenty-first Army Group 'Weekly Political Intelligence Summary' no. 1, 7 Jul. 1945; W. Strang 'Diary of a Tour through Germany, 1–6 Jul. 1945,' both in FO 371/46933, PRO; and Nichol to CIC/HS, 8 Jul. 1945, WO 219/1561, PRO.

61 R. Murphy, U.S. Pol. Adv. (Frankfurt) to Berlin, 8 Aug. 1945, State Dept. Decimal Files 1945–9, 740.00119 Control (Germany), RG 59, NA.

62 For the gradual loosening of non-fraternization rules, see Libby, 'Policing Germany,' 53; I. Kirkpatrick, SHAEF Pol. Off. to A. Eden, Sec. of State for Foreign Affairs, 18 Jun. 1945, FO 371/46933, PRO; F. Matthews, State Dept. Eur. to Gen. J. Hilldring, Dir. CAD, 20 Jun. 1945, CAD 250.1, RG 165, NA; *FO Weekly Political Intelligence Summaries* 12, Summary no. 302, 18 Jul. 1945; *The Stars and Stripes*, 14 Jun., 15 Jul., 22 Aug., 8 Sep., and 21 Sep. 1945.

63 Minute on file jacket C5205, 13 Sep. 1945, FO 371/46934, PRO.

64 American troop compounds were guarded and ringed with barbed-wire fences until the spring of 1947, and there were complaints even when these measures were abandoned. *The Stars and Stripes*, 14 Apr. and 16 Apr. 1947.

65 Davidson, *The Death and Life of Germany*, 81.

66 For security problems and British counter-measures in the Eastern Tyrol, see ACA(BE) Intelligence Organisation 'Joint Fortnightly Intelligence Summary' no. 29, 5 Apr. 1947; no. 30, 20 Apr. 1947; no. 33, 31 May 1947; no. 38, 9 Aug. 1947; no. 43, 18 Oct. 1947; no. 45, 15 Nov. 1947, all in FO 1007/302, PRO.

67 Wember, *Umerziehung im Lager*, 20; and Peterson, *The American Occupation of Germany*, 157.

68 Direction Générale des Études et Recherches 'Bulletin de Renseignements –

Allemagne – Wehrwolf,' 23 Jun. 1945, P7 125, SHAT; and PID German/Austrian Intelligence 'Analysis of French Output to and about Germany and Austria,' 16 Jul. 1945, FO 371/46728, PRO.

69 M. Hahn, Memo to ACoS G-2 'Visit to French Headquarters in Baden-Baden,' 20 Sep. 1945, State Dept. Decimal File 1945–9, 740.00119 Control (Germany), RG 59, NA.

70 *The New York Times*, 26 Jun. 1945. For American security sweeps in the summer and fall of 1945, see Ibid., 24 Jul. 1945; and USFET G-2 'Weekly Intelligence Summary' no. 26, 10 Jan. 1946, State Dept. Decimal File 1945–9, 740.00119 Control (Germany), RG 59, NA.

71 Seventh Army, Memo 'Military Operations in Germany Territory,' 10 Apr. 1945, WO 219/3513, PRO; and D. Lerner, SHAEF PWD 'Notes on a Trip through Occupied Germany,' 18 Apr. 1945, State Dept. Decimal Files 740.0011 EW, Micf. M982, Reel 217, NA. Special CIC squads were formed and sent to isolated villages in southern Germany reported as possible centres of clandestine resistance: Sixth Army Group Report 'Resistance Organizations (Germany),' IRR File XE 049 888 'Werewolf Activities Vol. I,' RG 319, NA.

72 SHAEF G-3 (Main) Memo 'German Guerrilla Warfare Tactics and Underground Activity,' 1 Nov. 1944, WO 219/1602, PRO.

73 On 11 Apr., SHAEF JIC advised that there was not enough unrest in the rear to justify stationing Allied combat forces away from the front: SHAEF JIC (45) 14 (JIC Draft) 'Security Problems Facing the Allies in Germany,' 11 Apr. 1945, WO 219/1659, PRO.

74 Eisenhower, *Crusade in Europe*, 398.

75 De Lattre, *Reconquérir*, 328–9; and Ministre de l'Information 'Articles et Documents,' 17 Sep. 1945, Nouvelle Série no. 274, 7P 125, SHAT.

76 Kenneth Strong, *Intelligence at the Top* (London 1968), 187–8; Stephen Ambrose, *Eisenhower and Berlin: The Decision to Halt at the Elbe* (New York 1967), 74–5; Henke, *Die amerikanische Besetzung Deutschlands*, 938–40; Jenkins, 'The Battle of the German National Redoubt – Planning Phase,' 3; 'Intelligence Bulletin' no. 28, 20 Nov. 1944, British Embassy/Washington, FO 115/3614, PRO; Ministère de la Guerre, EMSS 5ème Bureau 'La Situation Intérieure de l'Allemagne d'Après les Renseignements du 4 Dec. au 28 Dec.,' 29 Dec. 1944; État Major de l'Armée 2ème Bureau 'Le Reduit National,' 24 Apr. 1945, both in 7P 125, SHAT; Minott, *The Fortress That Never Was*, 93; OSS R & A no. 1934 'The Problem of the Nazi Underground,' 21 Aug. 1944; JIC 'German Plans for Underground Operations following Surrender,' JIC 208/M, 9 Aug. 1944, both in *OSS/State Department Intelligence and Research Reports*, Micf. Reel XIII; OSS R & A no. 1934.1 'The Clandestine Nazi Movement in Post-War Germany,' 13 Oct. 1944, in *OSS/State Department Intelligence and Research Reports*, Micf. Reel XIV; *Time*, 17 Jul. 1944, 17; OSS Report

from Switzerland, no. TB-192, 12 Aug. 1944, OSS 86424, RG 226, NA; OSS Report, 2 Sep. 1944, OSS L 45338, RG 226, NA; OSS Report from England no. 5BP-397, 5 Sep. 1944, OSS 91402, RG 226, NA; PID 'News Digest,' 5 Oct. 1944, no. 1570, Bramstedt Col. , BLPES; ECAD 'General Intelligence Bulletin,' no. 25, 12 Nov. 1944, WO 219/3761A, PRO; OSS Report from Paris no. FF-2182, 27 Dec. 1944, WO 219/1602, PRO; PWE 'German Propaganda and the German,' 8 Jan. 1945, FO 898/187, PRO; ECAD 'General Intelligence Bulletin' no. 48, 27 Feb. 1945, OSS 118572, RG 226, NA; U.S. Seventh Army G-2 'Information from an Allied Source in Switzerland,' 21 Feb. 1945, WO 219/1602, PRO; ECAD "General Intelligence Bulletin" no. 42, 11 Apr. 1945, WO 219/3760A, PRO; *FO Weekly Political Intelligence Summaries* 11, Summary 290, 25 Apr. 1945; and OSS Report from Switzerland no. B-2612, 25 Apr. 1945, OSS 125162, RG 226, NA.

77 Ralph Bennett, *Ultra in the West: The Normandy Campaign, 1944–45* (London 1979), 238; and Ultra Document BT 7004, 12 Mar. 1945, Ultra Document Collection, Reel 65. Ultra intelligence on the Werwolf was immediately reinforced by the interrogations of German POWs who had seen the memos circulated by the Bureau 'Prützmann' in February 1945, which called for Army volunteers to attend the Werwolf training course at 'Army School' II: Field Interrogation Unit no. 1 'PW Intelligence Bulletin' no. 1/47, 13 Mar. 1945, G-2 Intelligence Div. Captured Personnel and Material Branch Enemy POW Interrogation File (MIS-Y) 1943–5, RG 165, NA. See also Strong, *Intelligence at the Top*, 188.

78 Combined Intelligence Committee Memo no. 49 'Ability of the German Army in the West to Continue the War,' 15 Mar. 1945, Enclosure, *Records of the JCS, Part I, 1942–45: European Theatre*, Micf. Reel no. 10.

79 Jenkins, 'The Battle of the National Redoubt – Planning Phase,' 4; Minott, *The Fortress that Never Was*, 47–55, 68; SHAEF G-5 'Weekly Journal of Information' no. 9, 19 Apr. 1945, WO 219/3918, PRO; Omar Bradley, *A General's Life* (New York 1983), 418–20; Eisenhower, *Crusade in Europe*, 397–8; James Gavin, *On to Berlin* (New York 1981), 308, 313–15, 333–7; Henke, *Die amerikanische Besetzung Deutschlands*, 940–2, 944–5; Tony Sharp, *The Wartime Alliance and the Zonal Division of Germany* (Oxford 1975), 123; Stephen Ambrose, *Eisenhower, The Soldier* (London 1984), 391–2; Ambrose, *Eisenhower and Berlin*, 67, 77–80; Childs, 'The Far Right in Germany since 1945,' 291; Walter Bedell Smith, *Eisenhower's Six Great Decisions* (New York 1956), 182–3; Strong, *Intelligence at the Top*, 191; L.F. Ellis, *Victory in the West* (London 1968), 298–9, 302–4; MacDonald, *The Last Offensive* 340–1, 407–9; and *The New York Times*, 6 Apr. 1945.

80 For Hitler's decision, see Trevor-Roper, *The Last Days of Hitler*, 158–9; Fest, *Hitler*, 737–8; and Alan Bullock, *Hitler: A Study in Tyranny* (London 1964), 783.

81 Eisenhower, *Crusade in Europe*, 397; and Strong, *Intelligence at the Top*, 188.

82 S.M. Shtemenko, *The Soviet General Staff at War, 1941–1945* (Moscow 1970), 307;

Erickson, *The Road to Berlin*, 554; and *Pravda*, cited in *The Christian Science Monitor*, 5 Mar. 1945, Part II.

83 'Memorandum of Conference with Marshal Stalin, 15th January, 1945,' *David Irving, Papers Relating to the Allied High Command, 1943/45*, Reel no. 4.

84 Abt. FHO (IIb) 'Übersicht über das im Monat Oktober beim Referat IIb eingegangen Material,' 14 Nov. 1944 (Reel 497, frame 6485409); 'Auszug aus "Wichtigen Gefg.-Aussagen" – I/A vom 26.12.44' (Reel 488, frames 6474545–6474546), both in Records of OKH, Microfilm no. T-78, NA; and letter to the author from Lev Kopelev, 11 Jun. 1990. For a good lyrical evocation of the mood among advancing Soviet troops in East Prussia, see Alexander Solzhenitsyn, *Prussian Nights* (New York 1977).

85 Susan Brownmiller, *Against Our Will: Men, Women and Rape* (New York 1975), 33, 37–8; and Ruth Seifert, 'War and Rape: A Preliminary Analysis,' in *Mass Rape*, ed. Alexandria Stiglmayer (Lincoln, Neb. 1994), 59. See also Naimark, *The Russians in Germany*, 113–15.

86 Marion Gräfin Dönhoff, *Namen die keiner mehr nennt: Ostpreussen Menschen und Geschichte* (Düsseldorf 1962), 18–19.

87 H. Kober, untitled report, 7 Feb. 1951, Ost Dok. 2/189, BA; *Silesian Inferno*, 43; *The Tragedy of Silesia*, 190; *The Martyrdom and Heroism of the Women of East Germany*, 74; and Heeresgruppe Mitte Abt. Ic/AO 'Sowjetische Befehle über Verhalten der RA auf deutschen Boden,' 3 Feb. 1945, Microcopy T-78, Reel 488, frame 6474524, NA. For similar cases from the Soviet Zone proper, see Naimark, *The Russians in Germany*, 116.

88 Jahn, *Pommersche Passion*, 87; and Auswertestelle Ost (Heer) des OKH 'Auszug aus o. a. Meldungen,' 11 Apr. 1945, RH 2/2330, BMA. 'The Bolsheviks,' sneered one report, 'do not feel very secure.'

89 *The Age*, 1 May 1945.

90 Thorwald, *Defeat in the East*, 64–5; Horst Gerlach, 'The Final Years of Mennonites in East and West Prussia, 1943–1945,' *The Mennonite Quarterly Review*, 66/3 (Jul. 1992), 392; Wiskemann, *Germany's Eastern Neighbours*, 93; Pastor Weichert 'An den grossen und kleinen brennpunkten der Schlesischen Kirche vom 25.5.1943 bis 31.12.1946,' Ost Dok. 2/177, BA; and Karl Hielsacher, 'Das Kriegsende 1945 im Westteil des Warthelandes und im Osten der Neumark,' *Zeitschrift für Ostforschung* 34/2, (1985), 235.

91 Heeresgruppe Mitte Abt. Ic/AO 'Sowjetische Befehle über Verhalten der RA auf deutschen Boden,' 3 Feb. 1945, Microcopy no. T-78, Reel 488, frame 6474524, NA.

92 M. Gross 'Beglaubigte Abschrift im Auszuge,' 23 Nov. 1950, Ost Dok. 2/13, BA.

93 Jahn, *Pommersche Passion*, 65–7.

94 Jahnke, *Hitlers letztes Aufgebot*, 27.

95 Georg Gunter, *Letzter Lorbeer* (Darmstadt 1974), 353, and *Jugend unterm Schicksal*, 140.

96 E. Breuer 'J'accuse! (Ich klage an!),' Jul. 1948, Ost Dok. 2/279, BA. This source claims that it was later discovered (after the forced march) that a Ukrainian was actually resonsible for the killing.

97 *Dokumente der Menschlichkeit*, 149–50.

98 Kuby, *The Russians and Berlin*, 238; *Der Kampf um Berlin*, 285; and Tittman to the Secretary of State, 15 Oct. 1945, Enclosure, State Dept. Decimal File 1945–9, 740.00119 Control (Germany), RG 59, NA.

99 HQ Berlin Area 'Intelligence Summary' no. 1, 8 Jul. 1945, WO 205/1078, PRO; and MI-14 'Mitropa,' 29 Jul. 1945, FO 371/46967, PRO. For continuing Werwolf attacks in Berlin, see *The Stars and Stripes*, 13 Jun. 1945, and PID 'Germany: Weekly Background Notes' no. 2, 15 Jun. 1945, FO 371/46933, PRO.

100 PID 'Germany: Weekly Background Notes' no. 1, 8 Jun. 1945, FO 371/46933, PRO.

101 Dickens, *Lübeck Diary*, 86, and *The Washington Post*, 4 Jun. 1945.

102 Naimark, *The Russians in Germany*, 73–4, 84, 90–1, 102–3, 120–1.

103 Louis Weisner, Memo no. 119 'Conditions of Political Life in the Soviet Zone of Germany and in Berlin,' 18 Mar. 1946; OMGUS Director of Intelligence 'Special Intelligence Summary – Soviet Russia in Germany,' 8 Mar. 1947, both in State Dept. Decimal File 1945–9, 740.00119 Control (Germany), RG 59, NA; Gen. Konev 'Befehl an die Truppen der 1. Ukrainischen Front,' no. 004 (Germ. transl.), 26 Mar. 1945 (frames 6474428–6474430); Maljarof to the Military Justice Division (Germ. transl.), Forty-eighth Army, 23 Jan. 1945 (frames 6474499–6474500); Rodionov to the Political Office of the Regimental Commission (Germ. transl.), 25 Jan. 1945 (frames 6474471–6474472); Gen. Rokossovsky 'Befehl an die Truppen der 2. Weissruss. Front' no. 006 (Germ. transl.), 22 Jan. 1945 (frames 6474495–6474496); Shatilov to Chief of the Political Section of the 3rd Artillery Brigade (Germ. transl.), 12 Jan. 1945 (frames 6474537–6474539); 'Auszug aus "Feststellungen zur Feindlage (A/Ausw. III)" – Leist. III Ost für FAK no. 2012/45 geh. Lage vom 9.2.45' (frame 6474479), all in Records of OKH, Microform no. T-78, Reel 488, NA; *Pravda*, 14 Apr. 1945; and Naimark, *The Russians in Germany*, 79, 86, 88, 90, 92.

104 According to Soviet POWs, a Soviet Army daily order of 13 October 1944 instructed that occupied German territory be treated the same as 'liberated' territory, provided the civilian population offered no resistance. 'Analage zu VI Wi Wiesbaden, no. 708/45,' Records of OKH, Microform no. T-78, Reel 488, frame 6474435, NA. See also K. Rokossovsky, *A Soldier's Duty* (Moscow 1970), 288–9; and Naimark, *The Russians in Germany*, 76–7.

105 Arnold Sywottek, *Deutsche Volksdemokratie: Studien zur Politische Konzeption der KPD, 1935–1945* (Düsseldorf 1971), 186; and Naimark, *The Russians in*

Germany, 10, 18–19, 41–2, 251–2, 259, 275. see also Naimark, 184, and
Wolfgang Leonhard, *Child of the Revolution* (London 1957), 280–3.

106 *Silesian Inferno*, 181, 183; PID 'Weekly Background Notes' no. 1, 8 Jun. 1945, FO
371/46933, PRO; *The Times*, 2 Jun. and 5 Jun. 1945.

107 Leonhard, *Child of the Revolution*, 307–8, 319; *The Memoirs of Marshal Zhukov*
(New York 1971), 636; and Martin McCauley, 'East Germany,' in *Communist
Power in Europe, 1944–1949*, ed. Martin McCauley (London 1973), 61.

108 Leonhard, *Child of the Revolution*, 326–9; Naimark, *The Russians in Germany*, 26,
257–8; and R.C. Raack, 'Stalin Plans his Post-War Germany,' *The Journal of Contemporary History* 28/1 (1993), 58–61.

109 Fritz Löwenthal, *News from Soviet Germany* (London 1950), 228, 267; Naimark,
The Russians in Germany, 390–2; CCG(BE) 'Intelligence Division Summary'
no. 2, 15 Nov. 1947, FO 1005/1703, PRO; USFET 'Weekly Intelligence Summary'
no. 44, 16 May 1946; Murphy to the Sec. of State, 16 Aug. 1946; 'Summary of
Coordinating Committee Meeting of 29 Oct. 1946,' all in State Dept. Decimal
File 1945–9, 740.00119 Control (Germany), RG 59, NA; *The Washington Post*, 1
Sep. 1946; and *The Times*, 19 Aug. 1946. For a firsthand account, see Horst
Wiener, *Anklage: Werwolf – Die Gewalt der frühen Jahre oder Wie ich Stalins
Lager überlebte* (Reinbek bei Hamburg 1991).

110 Richard Holmes, *Firing Line* (London 1987), 387.

8: Consequences and Significance of the Werwolf

1 David Welch, *The Third Reich: Politics and Propaganda* (London 1993), 124; and
Lili Hahn, *White Flags of Surrender* (Washington 1974), 345–6.

2 *The Montreal Daily Star*, 6 Apr. 1945.

3 Speer, *Inside the Third Reich*, 440, 456–7; Fest, *Hitler*, 731; Steinert, *Capitulation
1945*, 136; Ultra Document BT 9227, 2 Apr. 1945, Ultra Document Collection,
Reel 68; *Der Kampf um Berlin*, 318; Galante and Silianoff, *Last Witnesses in the
Bunker*, 18; Koller, *Der letzte Monat*, 12; and Air Div. HQ, U.S. Forces in Austria
'Last Days in Hitler's Air Raid Shelter,' 8 Oct. 1945, *Covert Warfare* 14. The only
evidence suggesting that Hitler gave Himmler his original mandate to organize the
Werwolf comes from SA-General Fritz Marrenbach: CSDIC WEA BAOR 'Final
Report on SA Brigf. u. HDL Fritz Marrenbach,' FR 29, Appendix 'A,' ETO MIS-
Y-Sect. Final Interrogation Reports, 1945–9, RG 332, NA. According to Goebbels,
however, Hitler did approve of the dispatch of Vehme teams behind Allied lines in
western Germany, and he was also critical of the SS-Werwolf for not being active
enough, particularly in attempting to turn public opinion against the Anglo-Americans. Thus, Hitler was 'extraordinarily pleased' with Goebbels's work on the Werwolf – 'this is the way things must be done if people are not to become prey to

despair': *Final Entries*, 105, 277, 310. Hitler also said to Speer: 'When the Werwolf becomes active it may be as successful as the Army 'Wenck': Enemy Personnel Exploitation, Field Information Agency Technical CC(BE) 'Two Brief Discussions of German CW Policy with Albert Speer,' 12 Oct. 1945, OSS XL 22595, RG 226, NA.

4 032 Civilian Interrogation Camp, I Corps Dist. BAOR 'Boldt, Gerhard Friedrich Wilhelm,' 25 Jan. 1946, *Covert Warfare* 14.

5 Direction Générale des Études et Recherche 'Rapport sur les Organisations des Partisans en Allemagne,' 23 Apr. 1945, 7P 125, SHAT.

6 Peterson, *The American Occupation of Germany*, 341; Henke, *Die amerikanische Besetzung Deutschlands*, 820–1, 834, 840–2; and Kershaw, *Popular Opinion and Political Dissent in the Third Reich*, 294–5. See also Childs, 'The Far Right in Germany since 1945,' 292; CSDIC WEA BAOR 'Second Interim Report on SS Obergruf. Karl Michael Gutenberger,' IR 34, 1 Nov. 1945, ETO MIS-Y-Sect. CSDIC/WEA Interim Interrogation Reports 1945–6, RG 332, NA; DIC(MIS) 'Possibilities of Guerrilla Warfare in Germany as Seen by a Group of Seventeen German Generals,' 17 May 1945, OSS 130749, RG 226, NA; and Morris Janowitz and Edward Shils, 'Cohesion and Disintigration in the Wehrmacht in World War II,' *Military Conflict: Essays in the Institutional Analysis of War and Peace* (Beverly Hills 1975), 205–6.

7 Beck, *Under the Bombs*, 187.

8 Clifford Kirkpatrick, 'Reactions of Educated Germans to Defeat,' *American Journal of Sociology* 54 (1948/9), 39–42, 46–7; and USSBS 'The Effects of Strategic Bombing on German Morale' (May 1947), pt. I, 1, 12, 17–18, 21, 51–2, 62, 76–7, 97–9, *The United States Strategic Bombing Survey*, vol. 4. Contrary to all expectations, Allied forces reported that the inhabitants of towns which were heavily bombed actually tended to have a more cooperative attitude towards the occupiers than the inhabitants of towns which were undamaged: SHAEF G-5 'Political Intelligence Letter' no. 8, 28 May 1945, State Dept. Decimal Files 1945–9, 740.00119 Control (Germany), RG 59, NA.

9 See, for instance, Boldt, *Die Letzten Tage der Reichskanzlei*, 52; Ambrose, *Eisenhower and Berlin*, 73–4; ECAD 'General Intelligence Bulletin' no. 25, 12 Nov. 1944, WO 219/3761A, PRO; *The New York Times*, 8 Apr. 1945, Sect. IV; and Fayard, 'L'Allemagne sous la Croix de Lorraine,' 64–5.

10 DIC (MIS) 'Possibilities of Guerrilla Warfare as Seen by a Group of Seventeen German Generals,' 17 May 1945, OSS 130749, RG 226, NA; SHAEF JIC (45) 14 (JIC Draft) 'Security Problems Facing the Allies in Germany,' 11 Apr. 1945, WO 219/1659, PRO; and SHAEF G-5 'Weekly Intelligence Summary' no. 1, 22 Feb. 1945, WO 219/3918, PRO. See also, Heuss, *Aufzeichnungen*, 48; Henke, *Die amerikanische Besetzung Deutschlands*, 255; and Boldt, *Die Letzten Tage der Reichskanzlei*,

52. Kershaw notes that 'a very large number' of Germans were prepared to surrender by 1944, or perhaps even earlier, mainly in order to cut their losses and prevent further destruction: Kershaw, *Popular Opinion and Political Dissent in the Third Reich*, 383.

11 Hamburg Regional Intelligence Office 'Political Intelligence Summary' no. 7, 31 Jan. 1947; no. 8, 28 Feb. 1947, both in FO 371/64527, PRO; 'Monthly Report of the Military Governor, US Zone: Intelligence and Confidential Annexes' no. 6, 20 Jan. 1946, FO 371/55659, PRO; and State Dept. summary of NBC 'Our Foreign Policy' program – interview of John Hilldring and Howard Peterson, 17 May 1946, FO 371/55664, PRO.

12 PWE 'German Propaganda and the German,' 23 Apr. 1945, FO 898/187, PRO; SHAEF Report 'Observations Concerning Occupied Germany,' 5 May 1945, State Dept. Decimal Files 1945–9, 740.00119 Control (Germany), RG 59, NA; SHAEF PWD 'Consolidated Report on the Reaction of 18 Ps/W on the "Werewolf," ' 16 Apr. 1945, WO 219/1602, PRO; Direction Générale des Études et Recherches 'Bulletin de Renseignements – Allemagne: Wehrwolf,' 26 Jun. 1945, 7P 125, SHAT; CCG(BE) 'Intelligence Review' no. 12, Sep. 1946, FO 1005/1700, PRO; and Bornemann, *Die letzten tage in der Festung Harz*, 17–19.

13 Ultra Document KO 340, 13 Apr. 1945, Ultra Document Collection, Reel 70.

14 Intelligence Div., Office of Chief of Naval Operations, 'Intelligence Report,' 25 Jun. 1945, OSS XL 12705, RG 226, NA. One of the main aims of the 'Antifas' established in the spring of 1945 was the neutralization of the Werwolf: See, for instance, Luth Niethammer, 'Activität und Grenzen der Antifa-Ausschuss 1945: Das Bespiel Stuttgart,' *Vierteljahrshefte für Zeitgeschichte* 25/3 (1975), 307–8, 312. An anti-Nazi pamphlet circulated in Berlin in the spring of 1945 openly encouraged Berliners to exterminate Werwolf members: Intelligence Div., Office of Chief of Naval Operations 'Intelligence Report,' 25 Jun. 1945, OSS XL 12705, RG 226, NA.

15 Erikson, cited in Louise Hoffman, 'Allied Psychological Interpretations of Germans and Nazis During and After World War II,' in *Essays in European History* (Lanham 1989), 23.

16 For estimates that the 'hard core of resistance' comprised approximately 10 to 15 per cent of the German population and soldiery, *circa* 1944–7, see PWE 'German Propaganda and the German,' 9 Oct. 1944, FO 898/187, PRO; 'Weekly Summary of Psychological Warfare' no. 25, 19 Mar. 1945, FO 371/46894, PRO; OMGUS Information Control 'Weekly Review' no. 13, 1 Mar. 1947, State Department Decimal Files 1945–9, 740.00119 Control (Germany), RG 59, NA; Janowitz and Shils, 'Cohesion and Disintegration in the Wehrmacht in World War II,' 183; M.I. Gurfein and Morris Janowitz, 'Trends in Wehrmacht Morale,' *The Public Opinion Quarterly* 10/1 (Spring 1946), 82; and Henry Dicks, 'Personality Traits and National Socialist Ideology,' *Human Relations* 3/2 (Jun. 1950), 152. Dennis Bark and David Gress esti-

mate that perhaps 25 per cent of the German population remained Nazi in their sympathies in 1945: Dennis Bark and David Gress, *From Shadow to Substance* (London 1989), 45.

17 SHAEF PWD, Memo, 25 Sep. 1944, WO 219/1648A, PRO.
18 Roger Trinquier, *Modern Warfare* (New York 1964), 19.
19 Martha Gellhorn, 'Das Deutsche Volk,' in *Writers on World War II*, ed. Mordecai Richler (Toronto 1991), 646.
20 Sayward Farnum, *'The Five by Five': A History of the 55th Anti-Aircraft Artillery Automatic Weapons Battalion* (Boston 1946), 37.
21 *A History of the 90th Division in World War II* (US Army 1945), 78.
22 *The Manchester Guardian*, 2 Jun. 1945.
23 *The Montreal Daily Star*, 6 Apr. 1945.
24 *The Age* (Melbourne), 21 Mar. 1945.
25 Kirby, *1100 Miles with Monty*, 112, 169.
26 MI-14 'Mitropa' no. 13, 12 Jan. 1946, FO 371/55630, PRO. See also MI-14 'Mitropa' no. 9, 16 Nov. 1945, FO 371/46933, PRO; USFET G-2 'Weekly Intelligence Summary' no. 16, 1 Nov. 1945, State Dept. Decimal File 1945–9, 740.00119 Control (Germany), RG 59, NA; and *With the 102d Infantry Division through Germany*, 245.
27 USFET G-2 'Weekly Intelligence Summary' no. 32, 21 Feb. 1946, State Dept. Decimal File 1945–9, 740.00119 Control (Germany), RG 59, NA.
28 USFET G-2 'Weekly Intelligence Summary' no. 24, 27 Dec. 1945, State Dept. Decimal File 1945–9, 740.00119 Control (Germany), RG 59, NA.
29 Comments on jacket file C 8339, 15 Nov. 1945, FO 371/46935, PRO.
30 Norbert Frei, *National Socialist Rule in Germany: The Führer State, 1933–1945* (Oxford 1993), 147.
31 Bosch, *Der Neubeginn*, 24.
32 H.E. Balthin, Memo 'Attitude towards the German People,' 22 May 1945, WO 219/3513, PRO.

Appendix A

1 Struve, *Aufstieg und Herrschaft des Nationalsozialismus in einer industriellen Kleinstadt*, 491.
2 Hermann Neubacher, *Sonderauftrag Südost, 1940–1945* (Göttingen 1956), 29–30; Michael Balfour, 'Four Power Control in Germany,' in Michael Balfour and John Mair, *Four Power Control in Germany and Austria, 1945–1946* (New York 1972), 57; Charles Thayer, *Guerrilla* (London 1964), 162; and Görlitz, *Der Zweite Weltkrieg* vol. 2, 519, 544–5.
3 MacKsey, *The Partisans of Europe in World War II*, 248–9.

4 Carsten Kuther, *Räuber und Gauner in Deutschland* (Göttingen 1976); and T.C.W. Blanning, *The French Revolution in Germany* (Oxford 1983), 286–300. For the theory of 'social banditry,' see E.J. Hobsbawm, *Primitive Rebels* (Manchester 1959).

5 Fritz Kern, *Kingship and Law in the Middle Ages* (New York 1970), 85–92; Günther Franze, *Der deutsche Bauernkrieg* (Darmstadt 1977); Heiko Oberman, 'The Gospel of Social Unrest,' 39–51; Siegfried Hoyer, 'Arms and Military Organization in the German Peasant War,' 98–108; Horst Buszello, 'The Common Man's View of the State in the German Peasant's War,' 109–122, all in *The German Peasant War, 1525: New Viewpoints*, ed. Bob Scribner and Gerhard Benecke (London 1979); Perez Zagornin, *Rebels and Rulers, 1500–1660* (Cambridge 1982), vol. 1, 186–208; Peter Blickle, *The Revolution of 1525: The German Peasant's War from a New Perspective* (Baltimore 1981); Adolf Laube, 'Die Volksbewegung in Deutschland von 1470 bis 1517: Ursachen und Charakter,' in *Historische Zeitschrifte – Revolte und Revolution in Europa*, ed. Peter Blickle (Munich 1975), 84–98; Adolf Laube, 'Precursors of the Peasant War: Bundschuh and Armer Conrad – Movements at the Eve of the Reformation,' 49–53, and Heide Wunder, ' "Old Law" and "Divine Law" in the German Peasant War,' 56–60, both in *The German Peasant War of 1525*, ed. Jano Bak (London 1976).

6 Löns, *Der Wehrwolf*, ch.7

7 Stefan Sonderegger, 'Der Kampf an der Letzi,' *Revue Internationale d'Histoire Militaire* 65 (1988), 77–89.

8 Herbert Handel, *Der Gedanke der allgemeinen Wehrpflicht in der Wehrfassung des königreiches Preussen* (Frankfurt am Main 1962), 59–61; William O. Shanahan, *Prussian Military Reforms, 1786–1813* (New York 1945), 96, 108, 116–24, 152–3, 158–9, 185–215, 229; Dennis Showalter, 'The Prussian Landwehr and its Critics,' *Central European History* 4/1 (Mar. 1971), 5–12; Christoph Prignitz, *Vaterlandliebe und Freiheit* (Wiesbaden 1981), 105–11; Geoffrey Best, *War and Society in Revolutionar Europe* (London 1982); Rudolf Olden, *History of Liberty in Germany* (London 1946), 38–9, 43–4; Friedrich Meinecke, *The Age of German Liberation* (Berkeley 1977), 104–15; Walter Simon, *Failure of the Prussian Reform Movement* (New York), 161–70; Gerhard Ritter, *The Sword and the Scepter* (Coral Gables 1969), vol. 1, 93–126; Peter Paret, *York and the Era of Prussian Reform* (Princeton 1966), 120, 122, 134–5, 137–8, 155–7, 194–5; Andreas Dorpalen, 'The German Struggle against Napoleon,' *The Journal of Modern History* 64/4 (Dec. 1969), 494–503; 508–10; Roger Parkinson, *Clausewitz* (New York 1971), 135, 210–14, 227; Hans Kohn, *Prelude to the Nation States* (Princeton 1967), 220, 270, 280–3; Obermann, *Soldaten – Bürger – Militäristen*, 149; and Gordon Craig, *The Politics of the Prussian Army, 1640–1945* (Oxford 1955), 49, 53–4, 59–60.

9 Ernst von Salomon ed., *Das Buch vom deutschen Freikorpskämpfer* (Berlin 1938), 11–304, 417–42; Waite, *Vanguard of Nazism* 33–139, 190–1, 193, 227–38; Ernst von

Salomon, *The Outlaws* (Millwood 1983), 11–134, 215–27; Jones, Hitler's Heralds 47–97, 113–45, 221–2, 227–8; Craig, *The Politics of the Prussian Army, 1640–1945* (Oxford 1955), 355–61; Hunt Tooley, 'German Political Violence in the Border Plebiscite in Upper Silesià, 1919–1921,' *Central European History* 21/1 (1988), 69–72, 79–87, 95–7; F.L. Carsten, *The Reichswehr and Politics, 1918–1933* (Oxford 1966), 149–50; Harry Rosenthal, 'National Self-Determination: The Example of Upper Silesia,' *The Journal of Contemporary History* 7/3–4 (Jul.–Oct. 1972), 236–7; Patricia Gajda, *Postscript to Victory: British Policy in the German-Polish Borderlands, 1919–1925* (Washington 1982), 65, 68–71, 76–7, 86, 95–6, 127–9; Emil Julius Gumbel, *Vier Jahre Politischer Mord* (Heidelberg 1980), 129–30; Sir James Edmonds, *The Occupation of the Rhineland, 1918–1929* (London 1987), 232–9; von Heydebreck, *Wir Wehr-Wölfe*, 85–110; Richard Watt, *Bitter Glory: Poland and Its Fate, 1918–1939* (New York 1977), 158–9; Gregory Campbell, 'The Struggle for Upper Silesia, 1919–1921,' *The Journal of Modern History* 42/3 (Sep. 1970), 378; Howard Stern, 'The Organisation Consul,' *The Journal of Modern History* 35/1 (Mar. 1963), 23; Jean-Claude Fauez, *La Reich devant l'occupation franco-belge de la Ruhr* (Geneva 1969), 194–208; John Wheeler-Bennett, *The Nemesis of Power* (New York 1954), 104; Jay Baird, *To Die for Germany* (Bloomington 1990), 21–2; and *Jugend Contra Nationalsozialismus*, 189–91.

10 Baird, *To Die for Germany*, 25–40; Krausnik, *Anatomy of the SS State*, 327–8; William Sheridan Allen, *The Nazi Seizure of Power* (New York 1984), 211–12; *Das Buch vom deutschen Freikorpskämpfer*, 475–90; Fauez, *La Reich devant l'occupation franco-belge*, 200–2; Waite, *Vanguard of Nazism*, 235–8, 264; Wheeler-Bennett, *The Nemesis of Power*, 104; and Jones, *Hitler's Heralds*, 228.

11 Modris Eksteins, *Rites of Spring: The Great War and the Birth of the Modern Age* (Toronto 1989), 157.

12 For the cult of Nordic Man as part of nature, see Robert Pois, *National Socialism and the Religion of Nature* (London 1986), ch. 3; and Anna Bramwell, *Blood and Soil: Walther Darré and Hitler's Green Party* (Abbotsbrook 1985), 10–11.

13 Walser, *Die illegale NSDAP in Tirol und Voralberg*, 40–87, 80–104, 124–33, 144–5; Kurt Schuschnigg, *The Brutal Takeover* (London 1971), 48–9, 92–3, 112–15, 155–7, 168, 172; Ernst Rudiger Prince Starhemberg, *Between Hitler and Mussolini* (London 1942), 136–8, 152–72; Gottfried-Karl Kindermann, *Hitler's Defeat in Austria, 1933–1934* (Boulder 1988), 35, 91–131; Radomir Luza, *Austro-German Relations in the Anschluss Era* (Princeton 1975), 24–5, 40; Jurgen Gehl, *Austria, Germany, and the Anschluss, 1931–1938* (London 1963), 58, 62, 89–91, 97–100; Bruce Pauley, *Hitler and the Forgotten Nazis: A History of Austrian National Socialism* (Chapel Hill 1981), 105–7, 125–33; Vaclav Kral, 'Odsun Nemcov z Československá,' in *Nemecka Otazka a Československo (1938–1961)* (Brataslava 1962), 27–8; Martin Broszat, 'Das Sudetendeutsche Freikorps,' *Vierteljahrshefte für Zeitgeschichte* 9/1 (Jan.

1961), 30–49; Zdenêk Liška, 'Vznik tvz. Sudetoněmeckéno Freikorpsu a Jeho Akce na Ašsku v Září,' *Historia a Vojenství* 34/4 (1985), 56–68; Reitlinger, *The SS*, 117–18; Anthony Komjathy and Rebecca Stockwell, *German Minorities and the Third Reich* (New York 1980), 40–1, 93–6, 141–2, 159, 161, 178, 191, 199; *Das Buch vom Deutschen Freikorpskämpfer*, 338–42; MacAlister Brown, 'The Third Reich's Mobilization of the German Fifth Column in Eastern Europe,' *The Journal for Central European Affairs* 19/2 (Jul. 1959), 134; Vera Olivova, *The Doomed Democracy* (Montreal 1972), 240–3; Mader, *Hitlers Spionagegenerale sagen aus*, 13–14, 115–21, 154–7, 309, 315, 318–19, 346, 349, 399; Karol Marian Pospieszalski, *Sprawa 58,000 'Volksdeutschow'* (Posnan 1959), 47–52; Edmund Zarzycki, 'La Diversion Allemande le 3 Septembre 1939 à Bydgoszcz à la Lumiere des Actes du Tribunal Special Hitlerien de la Ville,' 279–94, and Tadeuz Jasowski, 'La Diversion Hitlerienne le 3 Septembre 1939 à Bydgoszcz,' 295–308, both in *Polish Western Affairs/La Pologne et les Affaires Occidentales* 22/2 (1981); Peter Aurich, *Der Deutsch-polnische September 1939: Eine Volksgruppe zwischen den Fronten* (Munich 1969), 10–11, 108–25; De Jong, *The German Fifth Column*, 43–5, 150–1, 153–6, 230, 232–3; Herbert Kriegsheim, *Getarnt, Getäuscht und Doch Getreu* (Berlin 1958), 293–5; Helmuth Spaeter, *Die Brandenburger: eine deutsche Kommandotruppe zbV800* (Munich 1978), 13–18; Wiskemann, *Germany's Eastern Neighbours*, 43–6; Paul Leverkeuhn, *German Military Intelligence* (London 1954), 45–6; Karol Marian Pospieszalski, 'O Znaczeniu Zamachu Bombowego w Tarnowie i Innych Prowokacjach Nazistowskich z Sierpnia i Września 1939 r. dla Polityki Okupacyjnej Trzeciej Rzeszy Wobec Polski,' *Przegląd Zachodni* 41/5–6, (1985), 97–109; and Włodzimierz Jastrzębski, 'Tzw. Bydgoska Krwawa Niedziela w Świetle Zachodnioniemieckiej Literatury Historycznej,' 39/5–6 (1983), 255–62.

14 A.N. Kichikhin, 'Sovetskie Nemtsy: Otkuda, Kuda i Pochemu' (Part II), *Voenno-Istoricheskii Zhurnal*, 9 (1990), 30–2; and D.M. Smirnov, *Zapiski Chekista* (Minsk 1972), 180–92.

15 Paul Wigand, *Das Femgericht Westfalens* (Aalen 1968); and F.R.H. Du Boulay, 'Law Enforcement in Medieval Germany,' *History* 63/209 (1978), 345–55.

16 Waite, *Vanguard of Nazism*, 212–27; Salomon, *The Outlaws*, 228–314; Wheeler-Bennett, *Nemesis of Power* 69, 93–4; Gumbel, *Vier Jahre Politischer Mord*, 64–78, 178, 182; and Jones, *Hitler's Heralds*, 192–210.

17 Best, *Humanity in Warfare*, 235–7.

18 'Kleinkrieg in eigenen Land,' RH 11 III/34, BMA. Note also the remarks made by Werwolf Radio on 4 Apr. 1945 – 'We hear that we are abused and derided and mud is slung at us ... Cowards say that the Germans are unsuited for the role of "werewolves." Is not the "werewolf" a German invention dating back to the Thirty Years War?': PWE 'German Propaganda and the German,' 9 Apr. 1945, FO 898/187, PRO.

19 USFET MIS Center 'Intermediate Interrogation Report (IIR) #18 – Krim. Rat. Stu-

baf. Ernst Wagner,' 30 Aug. 1945, IRR File XE 049 888 'Werewolf Activities Vol. I,' RG 319, NA.

20 Rose, *Werwolf*, 8; and Watt, 'Wehrwolf or Werwolf,' 884.

21 See, for instance, Kröner, 'Nahkampfbataillon "Werwolf",' 209–13.

22 ACA (BE) Intelligence Organisation 'Joint Fortnightly Intelligence Summary' no. 50, 24 Jan. 1948, FO 1007/303, PRO; and FORD 'Digest for Germany and Austria' no. 698, 17 Jan. 1948, FO 371/70791, PRO.

23 Borth, *Nicht zu Jung zum Sterben*, 55.

24 Peter Watson, *War on the Mind* (London 1978), 342–3.

25 *The Stars and Stripes*, 28 Sep. 1945.

26 *The Washington Post*, 1 Apr. 1945.

27 Col. Sheen, SHAEF G-2 to ACoS Sixth Army Group G-2, ACoS Twelfth Army Group G-2, BGS (I) Twenty-first Army Group, and ACoS ETOUSA G-2, 16 Apr. 1945, WO 219/1602, PRO. See also Minutes of the 3rd Meeting, Political Intelligence Committee, SHAEF JIC, 14 Apr. 1945, WO 219/1603, PRO.

28 R.F. Weigley, *History of the United States Army* (New York 1967), 161.

29 Humbert, *Notre Guerre* 357–8.

30 Vokes, *Vokes: My Story*, 194–5, and Foster, *Meeting of Generals*, 489.

31 SHAEF JIC 'Political Intelligence Report,' 7 May 1945, WO 219/1700, PRO; and *The New York Times*, 26 Apr. 1945.

32 Ziemke, *The US Army in the Occupation of Germany*, 184.

33 Goodsill to Heyman, 7 Jan. 1945, WO 219/3512, PRO.

34 Twelfth Army Group from Sands from Sibert sgnd. Bradley to SHAEF Main G-2 (CIB), 9 Apr. 1945; N.B.J. Huilsman, PWD SHAEF (Fwd) to SHAEF (Fwd), 28 Apr. 1945; G. Warden, Press Censors Guidance no. 57 (New Series) – ' "Werewolves" or German Underground,' 20 Jun. 1945, all in WO 219/1602, PRO; PWE Central Directive, 5 Apr. 1945; PWE Political Warfare Directive (European Theatre), 8 Jun. 1945, both in FO 371/46790, PRO; and SHAEF PRD, Press Censors Guidance no. 1 (New Series) – 'Level of Security after V-E Day,' 5 May 1945, State Dept. Decimal Files 1945–9, 862.911, RG 59, NA.

35 For the final termination of censorship in the European Theatre, see *The Stars and Stripes*, 6 Sep. and 7 Sep. 1945; and *The New York Times*, 7 Sep. 1945.

36 *The Washington Post*, 23 Jul. 1945.

37 Harold Zink, *The United States in Germany, 1944–1955* (Princeton 1957), 89–90.

38 Naimark, *The Russians in Germany*, 22.

39 Ibid. 104–5; Heinrich von Einsiedel, *The Shadow of Stalingrad* (London 1953), 170; ... *By Inni Mogli Żyč Spokojne*, 71, 203; Mashin to Alexeev, 1 Jul. 1945, *Pogranichnye Voiska SSSR Mai, 1945–1950*, 82; *Das Ende des zweiten Weltkrieges* (Berlin 1961), 42–3; Igor Vitukhin, ed., *Soviet Generals Recall World War II* (New York 1981), xiv; I.A. Kosikov, 'Diversanty "Tret'ego Reicha," ' *Novaia i Noveishaia Isto-*

ria 2 (Mar.–Apr. 1986), 225; Peter Gosztony, *Endkampf an der Donau* (Vienna 1969), 195; and Steinhardt to Secretary of State, 6 Dec. 1945, State Dept. Decimal Files 1945–9, 860.00, RG 59, NA.

40 American military police overran bands in Berlin masquerading as Soviet soldiers: *The Stars and Stripes*, 29 Nov. 1945.

41 Auerbach, 'Die Organisation des "Werwolf." '

42 Rose, *Werwolf.*

43 Watt, 'Wehrwolf or Werwolf,' 886.

44 Henke, *Die amerikanische Besetzung Deutschlands.*

45 V. Styrkul, *The SS Werewolves* (Lvov 1982), 37; Drška, *Československá Armáda v Národni a Demokratické Revoluci*, 62–4.

46 *Current Digest of the Soviet Press* 1/8 (22 Mar. 1949), 34. See also *Pravda*, 16 Apr. 1945.

47 Shtemenko, *The Last Six Months*, 409.

48 For the Soviet definition of a 'diversionist,' see *Soviet Partisans in World War Two*, 12.

49 Whiting, *Hitler's Werewolves*; and Lucas, *Kommando*, Part 4.

50 Watt, 'Wehrwolf or Werwolf,' 884.

51 Cookridge, *Gehlen.*

52 Hugonnet, 'La Préparation du "Maquis" allemand,' 59.

Bibliography

Unpublished Document Collections

Archives nationales, Paris
Rapports de le Commissariat de la République de Nancy et Strasbourg (F/1a/4024)
Rapports de la Préfecture de la Moselle (F/1cIII/1222)

British Library of Political and Economic Science, London
Bramstedt Collection˙

Bundesarchiv, Koblenz.
Deutschesnachrichtenbüro (R34)
Ost Dokumente
Parteikanzlei (NS 6)
Persönlicher Stab Reichsführer-SS (NS 19)
Reichsministerium für die besetzten Ostgebiete (R6)
Reichssicherheitshauptamt (R 58)
SS-Führungshauptamt (NS 34)

Bundesmilitärarchiv, Freiburg
Heeresgruppenkommandos (RH 19)
Oberkommandos des Heeres/Generalstab des Heeres (RH 2)
OKH/Allgemeines Heeresamt (RH 15)
OKW/Wehrmachtführungstab (RW 4)

Imperial War Museum, London
Office of U.S. Chief of Counsel for War Crimes (Interrogations)

National Archives, Washington, DC, and Suitland Maryland
Army Staff (RG 319)
History of the Counter Intelligence Corps (Baltimore: U.S. Army Intelligence Center, 1959), vols. 17, 18, 19, 20, 25, 26, 27, and 36.
Office of Military Government, United States (RG 260)
Office of Strategic Services (RG 226)
General Records of the Treasury, Office of the Secretary, General Correspondence, 1933–45 (RG 56)
State Department (RG 59)
U.S. Theatres of War, WWII (RG 332)
War Department (RG 165)
World War II Operations Reports (RG 407)

Public Archives of Canada, Ottawa
D Hist. Operational Orders and Instructions (581.009 D 103)

Public Records Office, Kew Gardens, London
Allied Commission, Austria, Library Material (FO 1007)
Allied Forces, HQ (WO 204)
Control Commission, Germany (FO 1005)
Control Commission, Germany HQ T-Force and Field Information Agency (FO 1031)
Embassy and Consular Archives, USA Correspondence (FO 115)
Foreign Office (FO 371)
Political Warfare Executive (FO 898)
Supreme Headquarters, Allied Expeditionary Force (photostats) (WO 219)
Twenty First Army Group (WO 205)
War Cabinet, Committees on Reconstruction (CAB 87)

Service Historique de l'Armée de Terre, Vincennes, Paris
Le Moral de la population civile et la résistance allemande (7P 125)

Document Collections on Microfilm

German Military Records. National Archives
   Records of OKH (Microcopy no. T-78)
   Records of OKW (Microcopy no. T-77)
   Records of the NSDAP (Microcopy no. T-81)
   Records of the Reich Leader of the SS and Chief of the German Police (Microcopy no. T-175)

Records of the Waffen-SS (Microcopy no. T-354)

Biographical Records (NSDAP, Reich Ministries, etc.) (Microcopy no. T-580)

Ultra Documents Collection. The Public Records Office. Reels 45, 50, 51, 59, 61, 62, 65, 67, 68, 69, 70, 71, 72, and 73.

Published Documents and Diaries

Covert Warfare: Intelligence, Counterintelligence and Military Deception during the World War II Era, ed. John Mendelsohn, 18 vols. New York 1989.

Dokumente zur Austreibung der Sudetendeutschen, ed. Wilhelm Turnwald. Munich *Dokumente der Menschlichkeit.* Kitzingen *c.* 1950.

Das Ende des zweiten Weltkrieges. Berlin 1961.

Falk, Lucy. *Ich bleib in Königsberg: Tagebuchblätter aus dunkeln Nachkriegsjahren.* Munich 1966.

Final Entries, 1945: The Diaries of Joseph Goebbels, ed. Hugh Trevor-Roper. New York 1978.

Foreign Office Weekly Political Intelligence Summaries, nos. 10, 11, and 12.

Geheimtagesbuch der deutschen Wehrmachtführung im zweite Weltkrieg, 1939–1945, 12 vols. Osnabrück 1984.

Granzow, Klaus. *Tagebuch eines Hitlerjungen: Kriegsjugend in Pommern.* Hamburg 1974.

Jugend Contra Nationalsozialismus, ed. Hans Ebeling and Dieter Hespers. Frechen 1968.

Jugend unterm Schicksal: Lebensbericht junger Deutscher, 1946–1949, ed. Kurt Hass. Hamburg 1950.

Justiz und NS-Verbrechen: Sammlung deutscher Strafurteile wegen nationalsozialistischer Tötungsverbrechen, 1945–1966, 22 vols. Amsterdam 1967–81.

De Lattre, Jean. *Reconquérir: Écrits, 1944–1945.* Paris 1985.

The Law of War: A Documentary History, ed. Leon Friedman. New York 1972.

Die Nationalsozialistische Zeit (1933–1945) in Neuss. Neuss 1988.

Pogranichnye Voiska SSSR Mai, 1945–1950. Moscow 1975.

Pogranichnye Voiska v Velikoi Otechestvennoi Voine, 1942–1945. Moscow 1976.

Reckitt, B.N. *Diary of Military Government in Germany, 1945.* Elms Court 1989.

Silesian Inferno: War Crimes of the Red Army on Its March into Silesia in 1945: A Collection of Documents, ed. Karl Friedrich Grau. Cologne 1970.

The Tragedy of Silesia, 1945–46, ed. Johannes Kaps. Munich 1952–3.

Trial of the Major War Criminals before the International Military Tribunal, vols. 14 and 17. Nuremberg 1948.

Die Verhinderte Alpenfestung Berchtesgaden 1945, ed. Hellmut Schöner. Berchtesgaden 1971.

Die Vertreibung der deutschen Bevölkerung aus der Gebieter ostlich der Oder Neisse, vol. 1, ed. Theodor Scheide Bonn 1956.
Vertreibung und Vertreibungsverbrechen, 1945–1948. Bonn 1989.
Werwolf: Winke für Jagdeinheiten. 1945; reprint Düsseldorf 1989.
World War II German Military Studies. nos. 2, 3, 18, 19, and 24. New York 1979.

Newspapers

The Age (Melbourne)
L'Aube (Paris)
The Christian Science Monitor
Combat (Paris)
The Daily Express
Le Figaro
The Globe and Mail (Toronto)
Izvestia
Journal de Genève
Libération (Paris)
The Manchester Guardian
Le Monde
The Montreal Daily Star

The New York Times
The News Chronicle
The Observer
Pravda
Rhein-Mainische Zeitung
The St Louis Post–Dispatch
The Stars and Stripes
Tägliche Rundschau
The Times (London)
Trud
Völkischer Beobachter (Berlin and Munich)
The Washington Post

Principal Books

Balfour, Michael. *Propaganda in War, 1939–1945.* London 1979.
Beck, Earl. *Under the Bombs: The German Home Front, 1942–1945.* Lexington 1986.
Birn, Ruth Bettina. *Die Höheren SS- und Polizeiführer.* Dusseldorf 1986.
Blond, Georges. *The Death of Hitler's Germany.* New York 1955.
Bornemann, Manfred. *Die letzten Tage in der Festung Harz.* Clausthal-Zellerfeld 1978.
Borth, Fred. *Nicht zu jung zum Sterben: Die 'Hitler-Jugend' im Kampf um Wien 1945.* Vienna 1988.
Bosch, Manfred. *Der Neubeggin. Aus der deutscher Nachkriegszeit Südbaden, 1945–1950.* Constance 1988.
Chuikov, Vasily. *The End of the Third Reich.* London 1967.
Cookridge, E.H. *Gehlen: Spy of the Century.* New York 1971.
Dahl, Walther. *Rammjäger: Das letzte Aufgebot.* Heusenstamm 1961.
Drška, Pavel. *Československá Armáda v Národní a Demokratické Revoluci, 1945–1948* Prague 1979.
Hallig, Christian. *Festung Alpen – Hitlers letzter Wahn.* Freiburg im Breisgau 1989.

Hasenclever, Walter. *Ihr Werdet Deutschland nicht wiederkennen.* N.p. 1975.

Haupt, Werner. *Das Ende im Westen.* Dorheim n.d.

Heitman, Jan. *Das Ende des Zweiten Weltkrieges in Hamburg.* Frankfurt am Main 1990.

Henke, Klaus-Dietmar. *Die amerikanische Besetzung Deutschlands.* Munich 1995.

Heydebreck, Peter von. *Wir Wehr-Wölfe: Erinnerungen eines Freikorps-Führers.* Leipzig 1931.

Höhne, Heinz, and Hermann Zolling. *The General Was a Spy.* New York 1972.

Holzträger, Hans. *Die Wehrertüchtigungslager der Hitler-Jugend, 1942–1945/Ein Dokumentarbericht.* Ippesheim 1991.

... *By Inni Mogli Żyć Spokojne: Z Dziejów Walk o Utrwalenie Władzy Ludowej na Dolnym Śląsku.* Wroclaw 1967.

Infield, Glenn. *Secrets of the SS.* New York 1982.

Jahn, Hans Edgar. *Pommersche Passion.* Preetz/Holstein 1964.

Jahnke, Karl Heinz. *Hitlers letztes Aufgebot: Deutsche Jugend im sechsten Kriegsjahr, 1944/45.* Essen 1993.

Kershaw, Ian. *Popular Opinion and Political Dissent in the Third Reich.* Oxford 1983.

Kissel, Hans. *Der deutsche Volkssturm, 1944/45: Eine territoriale Miliz im Rahmen der Landesverteidigung.* Frankfurt am Main 1962.

Konev, I. *Year of Victory.* Moscow 1969.

Kramp, Hans. *Rurfront, 1944/45.* Geilenkirchen 1981.

Kuby, Erich. *The Russians and Berlin, 1945.* London 1965.

Löns, Hermann. *Der Wehrwolf.* Stuttgart 1965.

Lucas, James. *Kommando: German Special Forces of World War Two.* New York 1985.

– *Last Days of the Reich.* London 1986.

Mammach, Klaus. *Der Volkssturm: Bestandteil des totalen Kriegseinsatz der deutschen Bevölkerung, 1944/45.* Berlin 1981.

Maschmann, Melita. *Account Rendered.* London 1964.

Minott, Rodney. *The Fortress That Never Was.* New York 1964.

Moczarski, Kazimierz. *Conversations with an Executioner.* Englewood Cliffs 1981.

Murawski, Erich. *Die Eroberung Pommerns durch die Rote Armee.* Boppard am Rhein 1969.

Naimark, Norman. *The Russians in Germany.* Cambridge, MA. 1995.

Rauchensteiner, Manfred. *Krieg in Österreich 1945.* Vienna 1970.

Rempel, Gerhard. *Hitler's Children: The Hitler Youth and the SS.* Chapel Hill 1989.

Riedel, Hermann. *Marbach: Eine Badische Dorf bei Villingen im Schwarzwald und ein französische Kompanie im Wirbel des Krieges Ende April 1945.* Villingen 1971.

Rose, Arno. *Werwolf, 1944–1945: Eine Dokumentation.* Stuttgart 1980.

Rusinek, Bernd-A. *Gesellschaft in der Katastrophe: Terror, Illegalität, Widerstand – Köln, 1944/45.* Essen 1989.

Sayer, Ian, and Douglas Botting. *America's Secret Army*. London 1989.

Schenk, Ernst-Günther. *Ich sah Berlin Sterben*. Herford 1970.

Schwarzwälder, Herbert. *Bremen und Nordwestdeutschland am Kriegsende 1945*, vol. 2. Bremen 1973.

Seidler, Franz. *"Deutscher Volkssturm": Das letzte Aufgebot, 1944/45*. Munich 1989.

Skorzeny, Otto. *La Guerre inconnue*. Paris 1975.

Steinart, Marlis. *Capitulation 1945: The Story of the Dönitz Regime*. London 1969.

Steinhoff, Johannes, Peter Pechel, and Dennis Showalter. *Voices from the Third Reich: An Oral History*. Washington 1989.

Strölin, Karl. *Stuttgart in Endstadium des Krieges*. Stuttgart 1950.

Struve, Walter. *Aufstieg und Herrschaft des Nationalsozialismus in einer industriellen Kleinstadt: Osterode am Harz, 1918–1945*. Essen 1992.

Tauber, Kurt. *The Eagle and the Swastika*. Middletown, CT 1967.

Trees, Wolfgang, and Charles Whiting. *Unternehmen Karnival: Der Werwolf-Mord an Aachens Oberbürgermeister Oppenhoff*. Aachen 1982.

Trevor-Roper, Hugh. *The Last Days of Hitler*. London 1950.

Tully, Andrew. *Berlin: The Story of a Battle*. Westport, CT 1977.

Weibel-Altmeyer, Heinz. *Alpenfestung: Ein Dokumentarbericht*. Vienna 1966.

Whiting, Charles. *Hitler's Werewolves: The Story of the Nazi Resistance Movement, 1944–45*. New York 1972.

Werner, Hermann. *Tübingen 1945: Eine Chronik*. Tübingen 1986.

Wiener, Horst. *Anklage: Werwolf – Die Gewalt der frühen Jahre oder Wie ich Stalins Lager überlebte*. Reinbeck bei Hamburg 1991.

Principal articles

Auerbach, Hellmuth. 'Die Organisation des "Werwolf."' *Gutachten des Instituts für Zeitgeschichte*. Munich 1958.

Baird, J.W. 'La Campaign de propagande nazie en 1945.' *Revue d'Historique de la Deuxieme Guerre Mondiale* 75 (Jul. 1969).

Bönisch, Georg. 'Alles Leer, oder zerstört: Köln 1945.' In *1945 – Deutschland in der Stunde Null*, ed. Wolfgang Malanowski. Hamburg 1985.

Childs, David. 'The Far Right in Germany since 1945,' in *The Far Right in Western and Eastern Europe*. London 1995.

Gołąbek, Czesław, and Ryszard Tryc. 'Z Genezy Powstania i Działalności Werwolfu na Polskich Ziemiach Zachodnich.' *Wojskowy Przegląd Historyczny* 8/2 (1963).

Hugonnet, Jean. 'La Preparation du "Maquis" allemand.' *Cahier Internationaux de la Resistance*. 3/6 (Jul. 1961).

James, Reuben. 'The Battle of the German National Redoubt – Operational Phase.' *Military Review*, 26/10 (Jan. 1947).

- 'The Battle of the German National Redoubt - Planning Phase.' *Military Review* 26/9 (Dec. 1946).

Kosikov, I.A. 'Diversanty "Tret'ego Reikha,"' *Novaia i Noveishaia Istorija*. 2 (Mar.– Apr. 1986).

Kröner, Rolf 'Nahkampfbataillon "Wehrwolf".' In *Tübingen 1945: Eine Chronik*, ed. Hermann Werner. Tübingen 1986.

Misztal, Jan. 'Działalność Propagandowa Podziemia Poniemieckiego na Śląsku Opol- skim w Latach, 1945–1949.' *Kwartalnik Historyczny* 85/1 (1978).

Müller, Franz. 'Die Besatzung des Bezirkes Gänserndorf durch die Rote Armee im April 1945.' *Unsere Heimat*. 55/3 (1984).

Ogmore, Lord. 'A Journey to Berlin, 1944–45 – Part I.' *Contemporary Review* 206/1188 (Jan. 1965), and 'Part II,' 206/1189 (Feb. 1965).

Paul, Wolfgang. 'Veränderungen aus dem Tagebuch 1945.' In *Das Jahr '45: Dichtung, Bericht, Protokoll deutscher Autoren*, ed. Hans Rauschning. Gütersloh 1970.

Rinser, Luise. 'Zwischen den Zeiten.' In *Das Jahr '45: Dichtung, Bericht, Protokoll deutscher Autoren*, ed. Hans Rauschning. Gütersloh 1970.

Schade, Gunter. 'Verluste Berliner Museum Güter während des zweiten Weltkrieges.' *Wissenschaftliche Zeitschrift der Humboldt Universität zu Berlin. Reihe Gesellschaftswissenschaften* 37/5 (1988).

Schneider, Rolf. 'Der Frieden begann mit Süssigkeit – Wernigerode/Harz 1945.' In *1945 – Deutschland in der Stunde Null*, ed. Wolfgang Malanowski. Hamburg 1985.

Scholz, Hans. 'Fortuna ist ihr Name.' In *Das Jahr '45: Dichtung, Bericht, Protokoll deutscher Autoren*, ed. Hans Rauschning. Gütersloh 1970.

Seewald, Peter. 'Gruss Gott, ihr seid frei.' In *1945 – Deutschland in der Stunde Null*, ed. Wolfgang Malanowski. Hamburg 1985.

Ueberschär, Gerd. '"Volksturm" und "Werwolf" – Das letzte Aufgebot in Baden.' In *Wer Zurückweicht Wird Erschossen!*, eds. Rolf-Dieter Müller, Gerd Ueberschär, Wolfram Wette. Freiburg 1985.

Watt, Roderick. 'Wehrwolf or Werwolf? Literature, Legend, or Lexical Error into Nazi Propaganda.' *Modern Language Review* 87/4 (Oct. 1992).

Zolling, Peter. '"Was machen wir am Tag nach unserem Sieg?": Freiburg 1945.' In *1945 – Deutschland in der Stunde Null*, ed. Wolfgang Malanowsky. Hamburg 1985.

Interviews

Lord Nöel Annon (Apr. 1986)
R. Jussenhofen (Dec. 1991)
John Weitz (Jul. 1993)

Correspondence

Joseph Dax (Feb. 1992)
Lev Kopelev (Jun. 1990)
Dr Karl Schikorski (Feb. 1992)

Illustration Sources and Credits

Every effort has been made to acquire permission to reproduce the illustrations in this book. Any errors or omissions brought to the publisher's attention will be corrected in future printings.

The Age (Melbourne): 'A Toothless Wonder,' from *The Age*, 18 April 1945

Army & Navy Publishing Co., Baton Rouge, LA, from the publication *42nd "Rainbow" Infantry Division: A Combat History of World War II*: civilian snipers captured in Würzburg by the U.S. 42nd Infantry Division

Associated Press: Werwolf stencil, 'the sign of the dark men,' from *Life*, 28 May 1945

The Illustrated London News Picture Library: U.S. 35th Division infantrymen sweep Saareguemines, ILN 23 December 1944 p708; Montgomery and liaison officers, ILN 5 May 1945 p491

Infantry Journal Press, Washington, DC, from the publication *The 89th Infantry Division, 1942–1945*: bodies of guerrillas killed by U.S. 89th Infantry Division

Opencountry Ltd.: Hitler and Himmler as Werewolves, from *Punch*, 11 April 1945

Public Records Office, London, England: graph showing incidents of sabotage and violence in British zone, FO 1005/1700; leaflet signed by National Committee chairman Vondras, FO 371/46901

Thornes Stanley Publishers Ltd: Werewolf Richard Jarczyk facing execution, from *Picture Post*, 12 May 1945 (Hulton Press)

TIME LIFE Syndication: remains of hotel and radio tower in Mount Brocken, from *Life*, 28 May 1945, William Vandivert/LIFE Magazine © Time Inc.

XII Corps History Association, from George Dyer's *XII Corps: Spearhead of Patton's Third Army*: U.S. anti-aircraft machine gunners outside Bad Kreuznach; U.S. halftrack near Rheinhards; fire in U.S. 4th Armoured Division fuel dump; suspected Werewolves being brought in for questioning in Lower Bavaria

U.S. 15th Army, from the publication *History of the Fifteenth United States Army, 21 August 1944 to 11 July 1945*: display of Werwolf equipment

Völkischer Beobachter: instructional diagram on firing a Panzerfaust, 17 February 1945 (no. 41, p. 2); cartoon of German children with U.S. soldiers, 19 January 1945 (no. 16, p. 2)

Werwolf: Winke für Jagdeinheiten (January 1945): Werwolf camouflage; cross-sectional view of bunker; training diagram for ambush

Index